Revenue Statistics in Latin America and the Caribbean 2021

Estadísticas tributarias en América Latina y el Caribe 2021

1990-2019

Please cite this publication as:
OECD et al. (2021), *Revenue Statistics in Latin America and the Caribbean 2021*, OECD Publishing, Paris, *https://doi.org/10.1787/96ce5287-en-es.*

Por favor, cite esta publicación de la siguiente manera:
OCDE et al. (2021), *Estadísticas tributarias en América Latina y el Caribe 2021*, OECD Publishing, Paris, *https://doi.org/10.1787/96ce5287-en-es.*

ISBN 978-92-64-36517-9 (print/impresa)
ISBN 978-92-64-34260-6 (pdf)

Revenue Statistics in Latin America and the Caribbean/*Estadísticas tributarias en América Latina y el Caribe*
ISSN 2410-4728 (print/impresa)
ISSN 2410-4736 (online/en línea)

Photo credits/Imágenes: Cover/Portada © some of the graphic elements in the main cover illustration were adapted from Freepik.com.

Corrigenda to publications may be found on line at: *www.oecd.org/about/publishing/corrigenda.htm.*
Las erratas de las publicaciones se encuentran en línea en: www.oecd.org/about/publishing/corrigenda.htm.

Foreword

Revenue Statistics in Latin America and the Caribbean 2021 *is a joint publication by the Organisation for Economic Co-operation and Development (OECD) Centre for Tax Policy and Administration, the OECD Development Centre, the United Nations Economic Commission for Latin America and the Caribbean (UN-ECLAC), the Inter-American Center of Tax Administrations (CIAT) and the Inter-American Development Bank (IDB), with the support of the European Union Regional Facility for Development in Transition for Latin America and the Caribbean. It presents detailed, internationally comparable data on tax revenues for 27 Latin American and Caribbean (LAC) economies, three of which are OECD members. On 15 May 2020, the OECD Council invited Costa Rica to become a member. At the time of preparation of this publication, the deposit of Costa Rica's instrument of accession to the OECD Convention was pending and therefore Costa Rica does not appear in the list of OECD members and is not included in the OECD averages reported.*

Revenue Statistics in Latin America and the Caribbean 2021 *is based on the well-established methodology of the OECD* Revenue Statistics *database, which is an essential reference source for OECD member countries. Comparisons are also made with the average tax indicators for OECD economies. In this publication, the term "taxes" is confined to compulsory, unrequited payments to general government. As outlined in the Interpretative Guide to Revenue Statistics, taxes are "unrequited" in the sense that benefits provided by government to taxpayers are not normally in proportion to their payments. The OECD methodology classifies a tax according to its base: income, profits and capital gains (classified under heading 1000); payroll (heading 3000); property (heading 4000); goods and services (heading 5000); and other taxes (heading 6000). Compulsory social security contributions paid to general government are treated as taxes and classified under heading 2000. Much greater detail on the tax concept, the classification of taxes and the accrual basis of reporting is set out in the Interpretative Guide in Annex A.*

Extending the OECD methodology to Latin American and Caribbean countries enables comparisons of tax systems on a consistent basis both across this region and with OECD countries. In a few cases, this methodology differs from the approach used by UN-ECLAC, CIAT and IDB; these differences are noted in the text and in the tables with a footnote.

The report provides an overview of the main taxation trends in Latin America and the Caribbean. It examines changes in both the level and the composition of taxation plus the attribution of tax collection by sub-level of government between 1990 and 2019. The report includes two special features: the first examines fiscal policy responses to the COVID-19 crisis in the LAC region and the second identifies trends in fiscal revenues from non-renewable natural resources for selected LAC countries in 2019 and 2020.

Presentación

La publicación Estadísticas tributarias en América Latina y el Caribe 2021 ha sido elaborada conjuntamente por el Centro de Política y Administración Tributaria de la Organización para la Cooperación y el Desarrollo Económicos (OCDE), el Centro de Desarrollo de la OCDE, la Comisión Económica de las Naciones Unidas para América Latina y el Caribe (NU-CEPAL), el Centro Interamericano de Administraciones Tributarias (CIAT) y el Banco Interamericano de Desarrollo (BID), con el apoyo del Fondo Regional para el Desarrollo en Transición para América Latina y el Caribe de la Unión Europea. Esta publicación presenta datos detallados y comparables a nivel internacional sobre los ingresos tributarios de 27 economías de América Latina y del Caribe (ALC), tres de las cuales son miembros de la OCDE. El 15 de mayo de 2020, el Consejo de la OCDE invitó a Costa Rica a convertirse en miembro de la organización. En el momento de preparar esta publicación, el depósito del instrumento de adhesión de Costa Rica a la Convención de la OCDE estaba pendiente y, por lo tanto, Costa Rica no aparece en la lista de miembros de la OCDE y no está incluida en los promedios de la OCDE reportados en esta publicación.

La publicación Estadísticas tributarias en América Latina y el Caribe 2021 se basa en la metodología bien establecida de la base de datos Estadísticas tributarias de la OCDE, que se ha convertido en una referencia esencial para los países miembros de la OCDE. Se presentan también comparaciones con los promedios de indicadores tributarios para las economías de la OCDE. En la presente publicación, el término "impuestos" se limita exclusivamente a los pagos obligatorios sin contraprestación efectuados al gobierno general. Tal y como lo indica la Guía de Interpretación de Revenue Statistics, los impuestos carecen de contraprestación en el sentido en que, normalmente, las prestaciones proporcionadas por el gobierno a los contribuyentes no guardan relación directa con los pagos realizados por estos. La metodología de la OCDE clasifica un impuesto de acuerdo con su base: renta, utilidades y ganancias del capital (categoría 1000); nómina (categoría 3000); propiedad (categoría 4000); bienes y servicios (categoría 5000); y otros impuestos (categoría 6000). Las contribuciones obligatorias a la seguridad social pagadas al gobierno general se tratan aquí como impuestos y se clasifican en la categoría 2000. Para mayor detalle sobre el concepto de impuesto, su clasificación y su registro según el criterio de devengo, véase la Guía de Interpretación que figura en el Anexo A.

Aplicar la metodología de la OCDE a América Latina y el Caribe permite la comparación de sistemas tributarios a partir de una base coherente en la región, entre los países de ALC, y con los países miembros de la OCDE. Sin embargo, en algunas ocasiones, esta metodología difiere de la empleada por la NU-CEPAL, el CIAT y el BID; en esos casos, las diferencias se han indicado en el texto y los cuadros, con una nota a pie de página.

El informe ofrece un panorama general de las principales tendencias en materia tributaria en América Latina y en el Caribe. Examina los cambios registrados entre 1990 y 2019 en el nivel y la composición de la tributación, así como en la atribución de la recaudación tributaria a los diversos subsectores de gobierno. El informe incluye dos capítulos especiales: el primero examina las respuestas de la política fiscal a la crisis del COVID-19 en ALC y el segundo identifica las tendencias de los ingresos fiscales procedentes de los recursos naturales no renovables para determinados países de ALC en 2019 y 2020.

Acknowledgements

Revenue Statistics in Latin America and the Caribbean 2021 was jointly produced by the Organisation for Economic Co-operation and Development (OECD) Centre for Tax Policy and Administration, the OECD Development Centre, the United Nations Economic Commission for Latin America and the Caribbean (UN-ECLAC), the Inter-American Center of Tax Administrations (CIAT) and the Inter-American Development Bank (IDB), with the support of the European Union Regional Facility for Development in Transition for Latin America and the Caribbean.

The staff from these organisations with responsibility for producing the publication were: Emmanuelle Modica of the OECD Centre for Tax Policy and Administration, under the supervision of the Director, Pascal Saint-Amans, the Deputy Director, Grace Perez-Navarro, the Head of the Tax Policy and Tax Statistics Division, David Bradbury, and the Head of the Tax Data and Statistical Analysis Unit, Michelle Harding; Jingjing Xia of the OECD Development Centre, under the supervision of the Director, Mario Pezzini, the Deputy-Director, Federico Bonaglia, the Head of the Latin America and the Caribbean Unit, Sebastian Nieto Parra, and the Co-ordinator of *Revenue Statistics* for the Development Centre, Alexander Pick; Michael Hanni of the Economic Development Division of UN-ECLAC, under the supervision of Director Daniel Titelman, and the Chief of the Fiscal Affairs Unit, Noel Pérez Benítez; Julio Alberto López from the CIAT Tax Studies and Research Directorate, under the supervision of Director Santiago Díaz de Sarralde; and Alberto Barreix, Principal Technical Leader in Fiscal Economics at the IDB under the supervision of Ubaldo González de Frutos, Lead Specialist, Public Finance. Jean-Baptiste Carpentier, Michael Hanni and Noel Pérez Benítez of UN-ECLAC authored the Special feature on fiscal policy responses to the COVID-19 crisis in Latin America; the OECD, including René Orozco from the OECD Development Centre, who contributed to the box on public debt and the COVID-19 crisis in the LAC region (Chapter 2). Michael Hanni authored the Special feature on fiscal revenues from non-renewable natural resources in Latin America and the Caribbean (Chapter 3).

The authors would like to thank other staff at the OECD Development Centre and the Centre for Tax Policy and Administration for their invaluable support in completing and improving the 2021 edition of this publication. Delphine Grandrieux, Elizabeth Nash and Anne Thomas from the OECD Development Centre's Communications and Publications team, and statistical editors from the OECD Publications and Communications Directorate, ensured the production of the publication, in both paper and electronic form. Michael Sharratt from the OECD Centre for Tax Policy and Administration provided invaluable assistance with the databases, website and other dissemination tools. Nicolas Miranda and Sofia Mora Restrepo, from the OECD Centre for Tax Policy and Administration and the OECD Development Centre respectively, provided precious help in checking the translation in Spanish.

Finally, the OECD Centre for Tax Policy and Administration and the OECD Development Centre would like to thank our colleagues working in national entities, with whom we have consulted regularly. In particular, we are grateful to Rosario López Palazzo and Marcelo Adrián

Calissano from the Ministry of Finance of Argentina; Jorge Richard Muñoz Nuñez of Costa Rica's Ministry of Finance; Fidelia Raulina Pérez Castillo from the Dominican Republic's Finance Ministry; Ruben Nehemías Ordoñez Gutiérrez, Luis Antonio Campos and Sara Guadalupe García de Reyes from the Ministry of Finance of El Salvador; David Fernando Pineda Pinto from the Revenue Administration Service and Kervin Andre Sánchez Valle and Neffy Noel Velásquez Sagastume from the Secretary of Finances in Honduras; Andrea Gregory from Jamaica's Tax Administration and Customs Agency; Emma Isaza from Panama's Economy and Finance Ministry; Diego Dominguez from Paraguay's Finance Ministry; and Óscar Núñez Del Arco Mendoza and Jorge Rivera Calderón from Peru's Ministry of Economy and Finance.

This document was produced with the financial assistance of the European Commission. The opinions expressed and arguments employed herein do not necessarily reflect the official views of OECD member countries or the European Union.

In Memoriam Juan Carlos Gómez Sabaini

Juan Carlos Gómez Sabaini, who passed away in March 2021, leaves an indelible mark on tax policy in Latin America and the Caribbean. Over the course of his career, he worked as a researcher, professor and policymaker in his native Argentina. He also served as an official at the Organization of American States and as a consultant for the Inter-American Development Bank, the International Monetary Fund and the Economic Commission of Latin America and the Caribbean, among others. Through all these roles, he not only made an incalculable contribution to enhancing tax policy across the region but also provided invaluable training to future generations of tax experts everywhere he worked, through whom his legacy will live on. He will be remembered for his commitment to social justice, his openness to points of view different from his own and the ceaseless encouragement he provided to those around him.

Agradecimientos

La publicación *Estadísticas tributarias en América Latina y el Caribe 2021* ha sido elaborada conjuntamente por el Centro de Política y Administración Tributaria de la Organización para la Cooperación y el Desarrollo Económicos (OCDE), el Centro de Desarrollo de la OCDE, la Comisión Económica de las Naciones Unidas para América Latina y el Caribe (NU-CEPAL), el Centro Interamericano de Administraciones Tributarias (CIAT) y el Banco Interamericano de Desarrollo (BID), con el apoyo del Fondo Regional para el Desarrollo en Transición para América Latina y el Caribe de la Unión Europea.

Las personas de estas organizaciones responsables de redactar la presente publicación han sido: Emmanuelle Modica del Centro de Política y Administración Tributaria de la OCDE, bajo la supervisión del Director, Pascal Saint-Amans, de la Sub-directora, Grace Perez-Navarro, del Jefe de la División de Políticas y Estadísticas Tributarias, David Bradbury, y de la Jefe de la Unidad de Análisis de Datos Tributarios y Estadísticas, Michelle Harding; Jingjing Xia del Centro de Desarrollo de la OCDE, bajo la supervisión del Director, Mario Pezzini, del Director adjunto, Federico Bonaglia, del Jefe de la Unidad de América Latina y el Caribe, Sebastián Nieto Parra, y del Coordinador de estadísticas tributarias para el Centro de Desarrollo, Alexander Pick; Michael Hanni de la División de Desarrollo Económico de la CEPAL, bajo la supervisión del Director, Daniel Titelman, y del Jefe de la Unidad de Asuntos Fiscales, Noel Pérez Benítez; Julio Alberto López de la Dirección de Estudios e Investigaciones Tributarias del CIAT, bajo la supervisión del Director, Santiago Díaz de Sarralde; y Alberto Barreix, Líder Técnico Principal en Economía Fiscal del BID bajo la supervisión del Especialista Fiscal Líder, Ubaldo González de Frutos. Jean-Baptiste Carpentier, Michael Hanni y Noel Pérez Benítez de la CEPAL son autores del capítulo especial sobre las respuestas de política fiscal a la crisis de COVID-19 en América Latina. La OCDE, incluido René Orozco del Centro de Desarrollo de la OCDE, quien contribuyó al recuadro sobre la deuda pública y la crisis del COVID-19 en ALC (Capítulo 2). Michael Hanni escribió el capítulo especial sobre ingresos fiscales de recursos naturales no renovables en América Latina y el Caribe (Capítulo 3).

Los autores desean agradecer a otras personas del Centro de Desarrollo y del Centro de Política y Administración Tributaria de la OCDE por su invaluable contribución a la mejora y finalización de la edición 2021 de esta publicación. Delphine Grandrieux, Elizabeth Nash y Anne Thomas, del equipo de Comunicaciones y Publicaciones del Centro de Desarrollo de la OCDE, y editores estadísticos del equipo de Publicaciones y Comunicaciones de la OCDE, aseguraron la producción de la publicación, tanto física como en formato electrónico. Michael Sharratt, del Centro de Política y Administración Tributaria de la OCDE, brindó una valiosa ayuda con las bases de datos, el sitio web y otras herramientas de difusión. Nicolas Miranda y Sofia Mora Restrepo, del Centro de Política y Administración Tributaria de la OCDE y del Centro de Desarrollo de la OCDE respectivamente, proporcionaron una ayuda preciosa para comprobar la traducción al español.

Por último, el Centro de Política y Administración Tributaria y el Centro de Desarrollo de la OCDE quisieran agradecer a nuestros colegas de entidades nacionales, a los que hemos consultado con frecuencia. En particular, damos gracias a Rosario López Palazzo y Marcelo Adrián Calissano, del Ministerio de Hacienda de Argentina; Jorge Richard Muñoz Núñez, del Ministerio de Hacienda de Costa Rica; Fidelia Raulina Pérez Castillo, del Ministerio de Hacienda de la República Dominicana; Rubén Nehemías Ordoñez Gutiérrez, Luis Antonio Campos y Sara Guadalupe García de Reyes del Ministerio de Hacienda de El Salvador; David Fernando Pineda Pinto, del Servicio de Administración de Rentas, y Kervin Andre Sánchez Valle y Neffy Noel Velásquez Sagastume, de la Secretaría de Finanzas de Honduras; Andrea Gregory, de la Administración de Impuestos y Aduanas de Jamaica; Emma Isaza, del Ministerio de Economía y Finanzas de Panamá; Diego Domínguez, del Ministerio de Hacienda de Paraguay; y Óscar Núñez Del Arco Mendoza y Jorge Rivera Calderón, del Ministerio de Economía y Finanzas de Perú.

Este documento fue producido con el apoyo financiero de la Comisión Europea. Las opiniones expresadas y los argumentos aquí empleados no reflejan necesariamente las opiniones oficiales de los países miembros de la OCDE o de la Unión Europea.

In Memoriam Juan Carlos Gómez Sabaini

Juan Carlos Gómez Sabaini, que falleció en marzo de 2021, deja una huella indeleble en la política tributaria de América Latina y el Caribe. A lo largo de su carrera, trabajó como investigador, profesor y formulador de políticas públicas en su Argentina natal. También se desempeñó como funcionario de la Organización de Estados Americanos y como consultor para el Banco Interamericano de Desarrollo, el Fondo Monetario Internacional y la Comisión Económica de América Latina y el Caribe, entre otros. A través de todos estos roles, no solo hizo una contribución incalculable para mejorar la política tributaria en la región, sino que también brindó una capacitación invaluable a las generaciones futuras de expertos tributarios en todos los lugares donde trabajó, a través de los cuales su legado perdurará. Será recordado por su compromiso con la justicia social, su apertura a puntos de vista diferentes al suyo y el incesante aliento que brindaba a quienes lo rodeaban.

Table of contents

Índice

LIST OF TABLES/LISTA DE CUADROS

Chapter 1/Capítulo 1
Tax revenue trends, 1990-2019/Tendencias tributarias, 1990-2019

Chapter 2/Capítulo 2
Special feature/Sección especial

Chapter 3/Capítulo 3
Special feature/Sección especial

Chapter 4/Capítulo 4

Tax levels and tax structures, 1990-2019/ Niveles impositivos y estructuras tributarias, 1990-2019

Chapter 5/Capítulo 5

**Country tables, 1990-2019 – Tax revenues/
Cuadros país, 1990-2019 – Ingresos tributarios**

Chapter 6/Capítulo 6

**Tax revenues by sub-sectors of general government/
Ingresos tributarios por subsectores de gobierno general**

LIST OF FIGURES/LISTA DE GRÁFICOS

Chapter 1/Capítulo 1

Tax revenue trends, 1990-2019/Tendencias tributarias, 1990-2019

Chapter 2/Capítulo 2

Special feature/Sección especial

Chapter 3/Capítulo 3

Special feature/Sección especial

Executive summary

Revenue Statistics in Latin America and the Caribbean 2021 provides internationally comparable data on tax levels and tax structures for 27 Latin American and Caribbean (LAC) countries: Antigua and Barbuda, Argentina, the Bahamas, Barbados, Belize, Bolivia, Brazil, Chile, Colombia, Costa Rica, Cuba, the Dominican Republic, Ecuador, El Salvador, Guatemala, Guyana, Honduras, Jamaica, Mexico, Nicaragua, Panama, Paraguay, Peru, Saint Lucia, Trinidad and Tobago, Uruguay and Venezuela.

In this publication, "taxes" are defined as compulsory, unrequited payments to general government. Compulsory social security contributions (SSCs) paid to general government are classified as taxes. More information on the tax classification is set out in the Interpretative Guide in Annex A.

Tax-to-GDP ratios in the LAC region in 2019

In 2019, the average tax-to-GDP ratio in the LAC region was 22.9%. The LAC average represents the unweighted average of 26 Latin American and Caribbean countries included in this publication, but excludes Venezuela due to data availability issues.

Across the LAC region, tax-to-GDP ratios ranged from 13.1% in Guatemala to 42.0% in Cuba in 2019, with all LAC countries other than Cuba recording ratios below the OECD average of 33.8%. Between 2018 and 2019, the average LAC tax-to-GDP ratio increased by 0.3 percentage points despite a slowdown in economic growth in the region in 2019 (0.1% GDP growth) and social unrest in several Latin American countries.

At a sub-regional level, the tax-to-GDP ratio of the Caribbean registered the largest increase between 2018 and 2019 compared to the other two sub-regions, at 0.8 percentage points, reaching 24.9% in 2019. A number of Caribbean countries have undertaken reforms that contributed to recent increases in the tax-to-GDP ratio, and the Caribbean economy grew more than the rest of the region in 2019 (0.7% compared to 0.1%). The average tax-to-GDP ratio in Central America and Mexico increased by 0.2 percentage points to 21.3% of GDP between 2018 and 2019, while the ratio in South America decreased by 0.1 percentage points to 22.9% of GDP.

Across the LAC region, 14 countries reported an increase in their tax-to-GDP ratio in 2019, while 12 countries recorded a decrease. The largest increases between 2018 and 2019 occurred in Nicaragua (2.7 percentage points), Belize (2.2 percentage points) and the Bahamas (2.1 percentage points). In Nicaragua, the increases followed revenue-raising measures in 2019 (mainly increases in income tax and social security contribution rates, as well as rates on imports of specific goods). The Bahamas recorded increases in value-added tax (VAT) revenues and property taxes as a result of tax reforms that increased the standard VAT rate and stamp duties. The only other increase of 1.0 percentage point or more between 2018 and 2019 occurred in Guyana. By contrast, there were no declines of more than 1.0 percentage point between 2018 and 2019. The largest declines were in Antigua and Barbuda (0.8 percentage points) and Panama (0.7 percentage points), in both cases due to a weaker economic environment as well as challenges in tax administration and collection in Antigua and Barbuda.

Evolution of tax-to-GDP ratios in the LAC region since 1990

Between 1990 and 2019, the average tax-to-GDP ratio in LAC countries rose by more than 7 percentage points, from 15.7% to 22.9%, bringing it closer to the OECD average: the difference against the OECD average tax-to-GDP ratio decreased from 15.4 percentage points in 1990 to 10.9 percentage points in 2019. The main drivers of the increase in the LAC region were value-added taxes and taxes on income and profits, which increased respectively by 3.8 and 3.0 percentage points.

On average, South America recorded the strongest growth between 1990 and 2019, with an increase of 9.2 percentage points. South America recorded a strong increase in its tax-to-GDP ratio during the 1990s and has been higher than the LAC average since 2000. Since 2015, South America's tax-to-GDP ratio has been declining towards the LAC average. Between 1990 and 2019, the Caribbean's average tax-to-GDP ratio was consistently higher than the LAC average. Over the same period, the average tax-to-GDP ratio of Central America and Mexico increased gradually but remained below the average for the LAC region.

Tax structures in the LAC region

In 2019, the LAC average tax mix was highly reliant on revenues from taxes on goods and services, which made up about half of total tax revenues (49.8%) compared with a third in the OECD (32.7% in 2018, the latest year available for the OECD). VAT revenues were the principal source of these revenues in the LAC region in 2019, on average accounting for 27.7% of total tax revenues.

The LAC region received 27.0% of tax revenues from taxes on income and profits in 2019. The LAC region is more reliant on revenues from corporate income tax (CIT) than OECD countries and significantly less reliant on personal income tax (PIT). In 2019, CIT and PIT revenues accounted for 15.8% and 9.2% of total tax revenues on average, compared with 10.0% and 23.5% in the OECD (2018 figures). Similarly, the average share of SSCs in total tax revenues was 17.1% in the LAC region, well below the OECD average of 25.7% (2018 figure).

Environmentally related tax revenues (ERTRs) amounted to 1.2% of GDP on average in 2019 in the 25 LAC countries for which data is available, below the OECD average of 2.1% (5.7% of total tax revenues in the LAC region compared to 6.4% in the OECD in 2019). Approximately two-thirds of ERTRs in the LAC region are derived from taxes on energy, most commonly excises on diesel and petrol (0.7% of GDP on average). Revenues from motor vehicle and transport service taxes represented most of the remainder.

Special feature: Fiscal policy responses to the COVID-19 crisis in the LAC region

The COVID-19 pandemic has triggered an economic crisis, increasing poverty, unemployment and inequality in many countries. The LAC region has been hit particularly hard by the pandemic and the resulting economic crisis. LAC countries rapidly adopted a wide range of fiscal and liquidity measures to support households and firms during the pandemic. Due to the crisis and the support measures provided by governments, tax revenues fell precipitously in the first half of 2020 but showed some signs of recovery by year's end. Active fiscal policies, supported by a fiscal sustainability framework to finance sustainable development, will play a key role addressing the region's development gaps (particularly in relation to social vulnerability and productive structure) and reducing entrenched inequalities. In addition to better management of public expenditures and co-ordination of public debt management, bolstering progressive taxation, under a well-defined sequence of policies, will be an essential means of achieving these goals and increasing fiscal sustainability.

Special feature: Trends in fiscal revenues from non-renewable natural resources

Despite declining oil prices and weak global economic growth, hydrocarbon-related revenues in the LAC region rose from 2.5% of GDP on average in 2018 to 2.7% in 2019, driven by one-off extraordinary receipts. Meanwhile, revenues from mining as a proportion of GDP fell very slightly to 0.37% on average in 2019 from 0.39% in 2018; this decline was driven by weak international prices for a range of industrial minerals and metals and lower production. Estimates for 2020 suggest that revenues from non-renewable natural resources will record a significant decline driven by a fall in prices provoked by the COVID-19 pandemic.

Resumen ejecutivo

Estadísticas tributarias en América Latina y el Caribe 2021 proporciona datos comparables a nivel internacional sobre niveles y estructuras tributarias para 27 países de América Latina y el Caribe (ALC): Antigua y Barbuda, Argentina, Bahamas, Barbados, Belice, Bolivia, Brasil, Chile, Colombia, Costa Rica, Cuba, República Dominicana, Ecuador, El Salvador, Guatemala, Guyana, Honduras, Jamaica, México, Nicaragua, Panamá, Paraguay, Perú, Santa Lucía, Trinidad y Tobago, Uruguay y Venezuela.

En esta publicación, los "impuestos" se definen como pagos obligatorios y no requeridos por las administraciones públicas. Las cotizaciones obligatorias a la seguridad social (CSS) pagadas a las administraciones públicas se clasifican como impuestos. En la Guía Interpretativa del Anexo A se ofrece más información sobre la clasificación tributaria.

Recaudación tributaria (% del PIB) en la región de ALC en 2019

En 2019, en la región de ALC el promedio de la proporción entre los impuestos y el PIB fue del 22.9%. El promedio de ALC representa el promedio no ponderado de 26 países de América Latina y el Caribe, incluidos en esta publicación, y excluye a Venezuela debido a problemas de disponibilidad de datos.

En toda la región de ALC, la proporción de recaudación tributaria y PIB osciló entre el 13.1% en Guatemala y el 42.0% en Cuba en 2019, y todos los países de ALC, salvo Cuba, registraron ratios por debajo del promedio de la OCDE que ascendió al 33.8%. Entre 2018 y 2019, el promedio entre la recaudación tributaria y el PIB de ALC aumentó en 0.3 puntos porcentuales a pesar de una desaceleración del crecimiento económico de la región en 2019 (0.1% de crecimiento del PIB) y un descontento social en varios países latinoamericanos.

A nivel subregional, la relación entre la recaudación tributaria y el PIB del Caribe registró el mayor aumento entre 2018 y 2019 en comparación con las otras dos subregiones, con 0.8 puntos porcentuales, alcanzando el 24.9% en 2019. Varios países del Caribe han emprendido reformas que contribuyeron a los recientes aumentos de la proporción de la recaudación tributaria con respecto al PIB, y el crecimiento del PIB del Caribe fue mayor que el resto de la región en 2019 (0.7% en comparación con 0.1 % de la región). La relación entre los impuestos y el PIB promedio en América Central y México aumentó en un 0.2% del PIB entre 2018 y 2019, llegando a 21.3% del PIB, mientras que esta relación en América del Sur disminuyó en 0.1 puntos porcentuales hasta el 22.9% del PIB.

En toda la región de ALC, 14 países registraron un aumento en la proporción entre la recaudación tributaria y el PIB en 2019, mientras que 12 países registraron una disminución. Los mayores incrementos entre 2018 y 2019 se produjeron en Nicaragua (2.7 puntos porcentuales), Belice (2.2 puntos porcentuales) y Bahamas (2.1 puntos porcentuales). En Nicaragua, los aumentos fueron el resultado de la mayor recaudación de ingresos en 2019 (principalmente aumentos en las tasas de impuestos sobre la renta y de cotizaciónes a la seguridad social, así como en las tasas de importación de bienes específicos). Las Bahamas registraron aumentos en los ingresos del impuesto sobre el valor añadido (IVA) y en los impuestos a la propiedad como resultado de reformas fiscales que aumentaron el tipo único de IVA y los derechos de timbre. El único otro aumento de 1.0 puntos porcentuales o superior entre 2018 y 2019 ocurrió en Guyana. Por el contrario, no hubo disminuciones de más de 1.0 puntos porcentuales entre 2018 y 2019. Los mayores descensos se registraron en Antigua y Barbuda (0.8 puntos porcentuales) y Panamá (0.7 puntos porcentuales); en ambos casos debido a un contexto económico más débil, así como a los desafíos relativos a la gestión y recaudación tributaria en Antigua y Barbuda.

Evolución de la recaudación tributaria con respecto al PIB de ALC desde 1990

Entre 1990 y 2019, la proporción entre la recaudación tributaria y el PIB promedio en los países de ALC aumentó más de 7 puntos porcentuales, de 15.7% a 22.9%, acercándose cada vez más a la media de la OCDE. La diferencia respecto a la relación entre la recaudación tributaria y el PIB promedio de la OCDE disminuyó de 15.4 puntos porcentuales en 1990 a 10.9 puntos porcentuales en 2019. Los principales impulsores del aumento en la región de ALC fueron los impuestos sobre el valor añadido y los impuestos sobre la renta y los beneficios, que aumentaron en 3.8 y 3.0 puntos porcentuales, respectivamente.

En promedio, América del Sur registró el mayor crecimiento entre 1990 y 2019, con un aumento de 9.2 puntos porcentuales. América del Sur registró un fuerte aumento en la proporción de la recaudación del impuesto y el PIB durante la década de los noventa y fue superior al promedio de ALC desde el año 2000. A partir del 2015, la relación entre la recaudación tributaria y el PIB de América del Sur ha venido disminuyendo hacia el promedio de ALC. Entre 1990 y 2019, la proporción entre la recaudación tributaria y el PIB promedio del Caribe fue consistentemente más alta que el promedio de ALC. En el mismo periodo, la proporción promedio de recaudación tributaria y el PIB de América Central y México ha aumentado gradualmente, pero se mantuvo por debajo del promedio de la región de ALC.

Estructuras tributarias en la región

En 2019, el promedio de impuestos de ALC se apoya en gran medida en los ingresos de impuestos sobre bienes y servicios, que representaron aproximadamente la mitad de los ingresos tributarios totales (49.8%) en comparación con un tercio en la OCDE (32.7% en 2018, el último año disponible para la OCDE). Los ingresos por IVA fueron la principal fuente de estos ingresos en la región de ALC en 2019, representando en promedio un 27.7% del total de ingresos tributarios.

La región de ALC recaudó el 27.0% de los ingresos tributarios de los impuestos sobre la renta y los beneficios en 2019. De todos los impuestos, la región de ALC depende más de los ingresos procedentes del impuesto de sociedades (IS), al contrario que los países de la OCDE y es significativamente menos dependiente del impuesto sobre la renta de las personas físicas (IRPF). En 2019, los ingresos del IS y el IRPF representaron un promedio de un 15.8% y un 9.2% del total de los ingresos tributarios, en comparación con el 10.0% y el 23.5% en la OCDE (cifras de 2018), respectivamente. De manera similar, la participación promedio de las cotizaciones a la seguridad social en los ingresos tributarios totales fue de 17.1% en la región de ALC, muy por debajo del promedio de la OCDE de 25.7% (cifra de 2018).

Los ingresos tributarios relacionados con el medio ambiente ascendieron a un promedio del 1.2% del PIB en 2019 en los 25 países de ALC para los que se dispone de datos, por debajo del promedio de la OCDE del 2.1%. (5.7% del total de los ingresos tributarios en la región de ALC frente al 6.4% en la OCDE en 2019). Aproximadamente dos tercios de los ingresos tributarios relacionados con el medio ambiente en la región de ALC se derivan de impuestos sobre la energía, más comúnmente impuestos especiales relacionados con el diésel y la gasolina (0.7% del PIB en promedio). Los ingresos procedentes de los impuestos sobre los vehículos de motor y los servicios de transporte representaron la mayor parte del resto.

Sección especial: Respuestas de la política fiscal a la crisis del COVID-19 en ALC

La pandemia del COVID-19 ha desencadenado una crisis económica que ha aumentado la pobreza, el desempleo y la desigualdad en muchos países. La región de ALC se ha visto especialmente afectada por la pandemia y la consiguiente crisis económica. Los países de ALC adoptaron rápidamente una amplia gama de medidas fiscales y de liquidez para apoyar a los hogares y las empresas durante la pandemia. Debido a la crisis y a las medidas de apoyo proporcionadas por los gobiernos, los ingresos tributarios cayeron de forma acusada en la primera mitad de 2020, pero mostraron algunas señales de recuperación hacia finales de año. Las políticas fiscales activas, acompañadas por un marco de sostenibilidad fiscal para financiar el desarrollo sostenible, desempeñarán un papel clave para abordar las brechas del desarrollo en la región (particularmente en relación con la vulnerabilidad social y la estructura productiva) y reducir las desigualdades arraigadas. Además de mejorar la gestión del gasto público y la coordinación de la gestión de la deuda pública, fortalecer la tributación progresiva, bajo una secuencia de políticas bien definida, será un medio esencial para lograr estos objetivos y aumentar la sostenibilidad fiscal.

Sección especial: Tendencias de los ingresos tributarios procedentes de recursos naturales no renovables

A pesar de la caída de los precios del petróleo y el débil crecimiento económico mundial, los ingresos promedio relacionados con los hidrocarburos en la región de ALC aumentaron del 2.5% del PIB en 2018 a un 2.7% en 2019, debido a ingresos puntuales extraordinarios. Mientras tanto, los ingresos procedentes de la minería como proporción del PIB disminuyeron muy ligeramente, a un promedio del 0.37% en 2019, frente al 0.39% en 2018; esta disminución se debió a la debilidad de los precios internacionales de una serie de minerales y metales industriales y a una menor producción. Las estimaciones para 2020 sugieren que los ingresos procedentes de recursos naturales no renovables registrarán una disminución significativa debido a una contracción de los precios provocada por la pandemia del COVID-19.

Chapter 1

Tax revenue trends, 1990-2019

Capítulo 1

Tendencias tributarias, 1990-2019

Chapter 1

Tax revenue trends, 1990-2019

Financing the development agenda of Latin America and the Caribbean (LAC) and its achievement of the Sustainable Development Goals (SDG) requires a step change in domestic resource mobilisation. The current COVID-19 crisis has further deepened the need for LAC countries to strengthen the collection of tax revenues to address structural weaknesses in their fiscal, social protection and health systems. The region was already challenged by widespread social unrest and subdued growth when the COVID-19 crisis began. While countries were quick to implement health and fiscal measures in response to the crisis to support the most vulnerable households and firms, their efforts were hindered by high levels of informality, underdeveloped social protection systems and limited fiscal space (see Chapter 2). Once the region has emerged from the COVID pandemic, under a well-defined sequence of policies, fiscal policies will need to be reformed and tax systems strengthened to support the economic recovery for all and to ensure a sustainable and fair fiscal position over the medium to long term.

Fiscal policy has an important role to play in catalysing inclusive economic growth in the region once the COVID-19 crisis has passed. In the long term, higher levels of revenue generation will also be crucial to address urgent demands from citizens across the region to improve equity via the provision of public goods, mitigating high levels of vulnerability, particularly in the labour market, and implementing comprehensive social protection systems. Improving the structure of the taxation system is important to promote entrepreneurship and enhance redistribution. Taxes can also influence behaviour, for example in incentivising a move away from dependency on fossil fuels in the context of the climate crisis.

Revenue Statistics in Latin America and the Caribbean is an integral part of the European Union Regional Facility for Development in Transition for LAC, an EU-led initiative, jointly implemented with the OECD and its Development Centre and ECLAC. Now in its tenth edition, it provides internationally comparable data on tax revenues in 27 countries in the region both as a basis for in-depth policy analysis and as a common starting point for knowledge sharing and capacity development. This first chapter discusses the evolution of several key tax indicators since 1990, including the tax-to-GDP ratio, the tax mix and the share of tax revenue generation by different levels of government. It also analyses the effectiveness of value-added taxes (VAT, a major source of tax revenues in the region) and revenues from environmental related taxes. This chapter highlights recent developments in selected countries' tax systems and complements this analysis with case studies on particular topics. Chapters 5 and 6 provide a detailed country-by-country breakdown of tax revenues.

Tax-to-GDP ratios

Tax to-GDP ratios in 2019

The tax-to-GDP ratio measures tax revenues (including social security contributions paid to the general government) as a proportion of gross domestic product (GDP). The LAC average represents the unweighted average of 26 of the countries included in this publication and excludes Venezuela due to lack of data.

The average tax-to-GDP ratio in the LAC region was 22.9% in 2019 (Figure 1.1). Levels varied widely across the region, ranging from 13.1% in Guatemala to 42.0% in Cuba. With the exception of Cuba, all LAC countries recorded a tax-to-GDP ratio below the OECD average[1] of 33.8%.

The highest tax-to-GDP ratios in the LAC region were registered by Cuba (42.0%), Barbados and Brazil (both 33.1%). The countries with the lowest tax-to-GDP ratios were Guatemala (13.1%), the Dominican Republic (13.5%) and Paraguay (13.9%).

Figure 1.1. **Tax-to-GDP ratios in the LAC region, 2019**

Total tax revenues as percentage of GDP

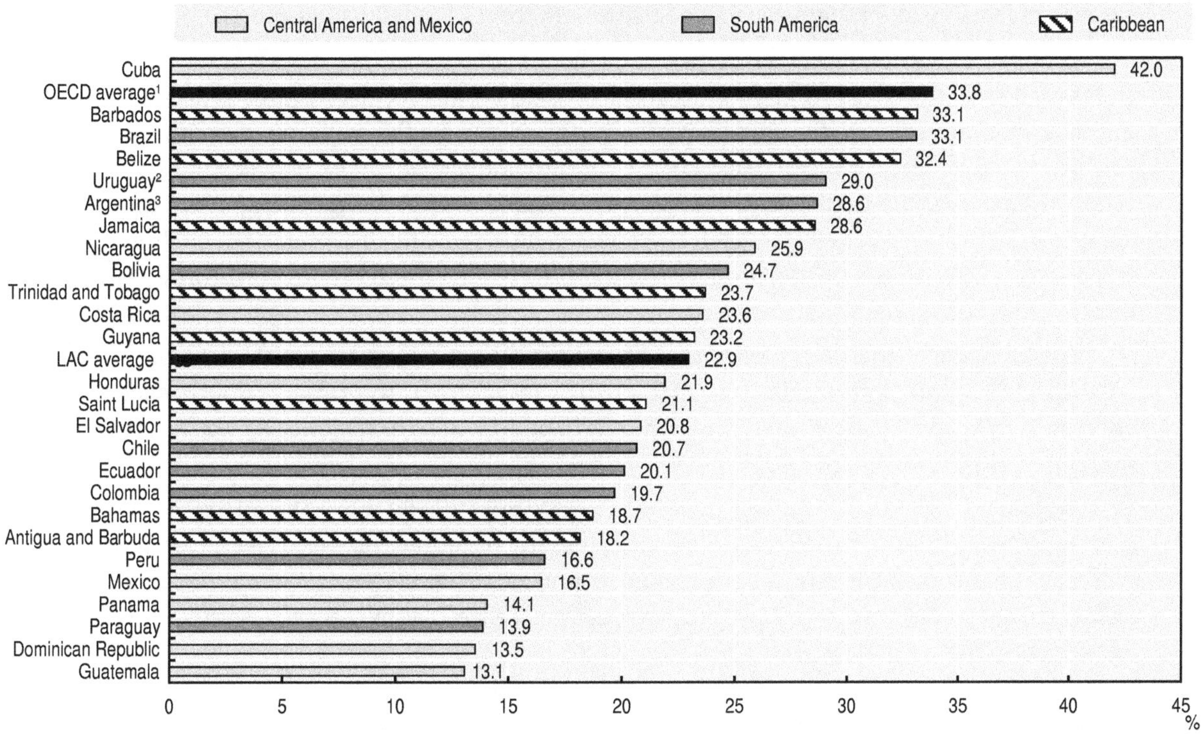

Note: The classification of countries into different sub-regions follows ECLAC's classification and is based on the spoken language of countries. The "Caribbean" includes the English-speaking countries and Guyana, while "Central America and Mexico" covers Spanish-speaking countries including Dominican Republic and Cuba.

The figures exclude local government revenues for Antigua and Barbuda, Argentina (but include provincial revenues), the Bahamas, Barbados, Cuba (except for 2002-12), the Dominican Republic, Saint Lucia, Trinidad and Tobago, and Venezuela as the data are not available.

1. Represents the unweighted average of the 37 OECD member countries. Chile, Colombia and Mexico are also part of the OECD (37). For Mexico, data on state and local government revenues are not available for 2019. They are estimated to calculate the total tax-to-GDP ratio.
2. The tax-to-GDP ratio does not take into account the recent rebasing of GDP in Uruguay. Preliminary estimates of the rebased GDP indicate that the tax-to-GDP ratio in Uruguay would be about 2.3 percentage points lower on average for the 2016-2019 period.
3. The tax-to-GDP may be under-estimated as it excludes certain types of social security contributions for which data are not readily available.
4. Represents the group of 26 Latin American and Caribbean countries included in this publication and excludes Venezuela due to data availability issues.

Source: OECD et al. (2021[1]), Table 4.1.

StatLink https://doi.org/10.1787/888934233872

There were important differences in tax levels between Central America and Mexico, South America and the Caribbean.[2] Countries in Central America and Mexico typically had lower tax-to-GDP ratios, with an average of 21.3% in 2019, whereas countries in the Caribbean had higher tax-to-GDP ratios and an average of 24.9%. While the tax-to-GDP ratios of South American countries varied widely, they averaged 22.9% in 2019, the same as the LAC average.

In 2019, the average LAC tax-to-GDP ratio was 0.3 percentage points higher than in 2018, This increase occurred in a context of continuing sluggish economic growth across the region since 2014 (average real growth amounted to 0.3% over the 2014-2019 period). The region experienced a two-year recession in 2015 and 2016 followed by two years of growth driven by improvements in domestic demand (ECLAC, 2019[2]) as well as steady increases in commodity prices (OECD/CAF/UN ECLAC, 2018[3]). However, 2019 was characterised by social unrest and weak economic growth in several Latin American countries. While real GDP growth amounted to 1.1% in 2018, it dropped to 0.1% in 2019 (ECLAC, 2021[4]) and is estimated to have fallen dramatically in 2020 due to the COVID-19 pandemic (OECD, 2020[5]).

Changes in tax-to-GDP ratios between 2018 and 2019 varied greatly across the region, influenced by differences in economic growth patterns across sub-regions. The increase in the Caribbean was the largest, at 0.8 percentage points for the second consecutive year. The increases in the Caribbean's tax-to-GDP ratio took place against a backdrop of positive economic growth. The Caribbean's economy rebounded in 2018 from the impact of natural disasters the previous year (ECLAC, 2019[2]) but growth slowed in 2019 due partly to droughts in Belize and Jamaica (CDB, 2020[6]). A number of Caribbean countries have undertaken reforms that contributed to the increase in the sub-region's tax-to-GDP ratio for both years.

The increase in the average tax-to-GDP ratio in Central America and Mexico between 2018 and 2019 was more modest, at 0.2% of GDP. In contrast, the ratio in South America decreased by 0.1 percentage points over the same period. In both regions, economic growth weakened in 2019 (ECLAC, 2021[4]).

Across the region as a whole, 14 countries reported an increase in their tax-to-GDP ratio in 2019 while the remaining countries recorded a decrease. The three largest increases in tax-to-GDP ratios between 2018 and 2019 exceeded 2.0 percentage points and occurred in Nicaragua (2.7 percentage points), Belize (2.2 percentage points) and the Bahamas (2.1 percentage points).

In Nicaragua, the increases in tax revenues between 2018 and 2019 occurred across all categories and ranged from 0.5 percentage points in revenues from VAT to 0.9 percentage points in revenues from taxes on income and profits (all from corporate income tax [CIT]). In 2019, the government implemented measures to increase tax revenues and to strengthen the solvency of the Social Security Institute (INSS) in response to significant declines in tax revenues in 2018 and the reduction in external financing due to social unrest.

- The increase in revenues from taxes on income and profits followed the approval of the Tax Harmonisation Law that increased income tax rates for large taxpayers and medium-sized companies over a certain income threshold. The government increased rates of the alternative minimum tax (AMT) and introduced AMT anti-avoidance rules. In addition, withholding tax rates were raised on income for non-resident individuals (Orbitax, 2019[7]).
- Social security contributions recorded an increase of 0.7 percentage points in 2019. Nicaragua amended the General Regulations of the Social Security Act to strengthen the solvency of the pension and health system. The changes mainly included higher contribution rates in different schemes. For example, the rate for Disability, Old Age, Death and Occupational Hazards was raised from 10% to between 12.5% and 13.5% for employers (depending on the number of workers) while the rate increased from 4% to 4.75% for employees (Orbitax, 2019[7]).

- Revenues from VAT and other taxes on goods and services increased by 0.5 and 0.6 percentage points respectively between 2018 and 2019. Higher tax rates on imports for different goods (e.g. beverages) contributed to these increases (CentralAmericaData, 2020[8]).

Figure 1.2. **Annual changes in tax-to-GDP ratios in the LAC region in 2018 and 2019**

Percentage points of GDP

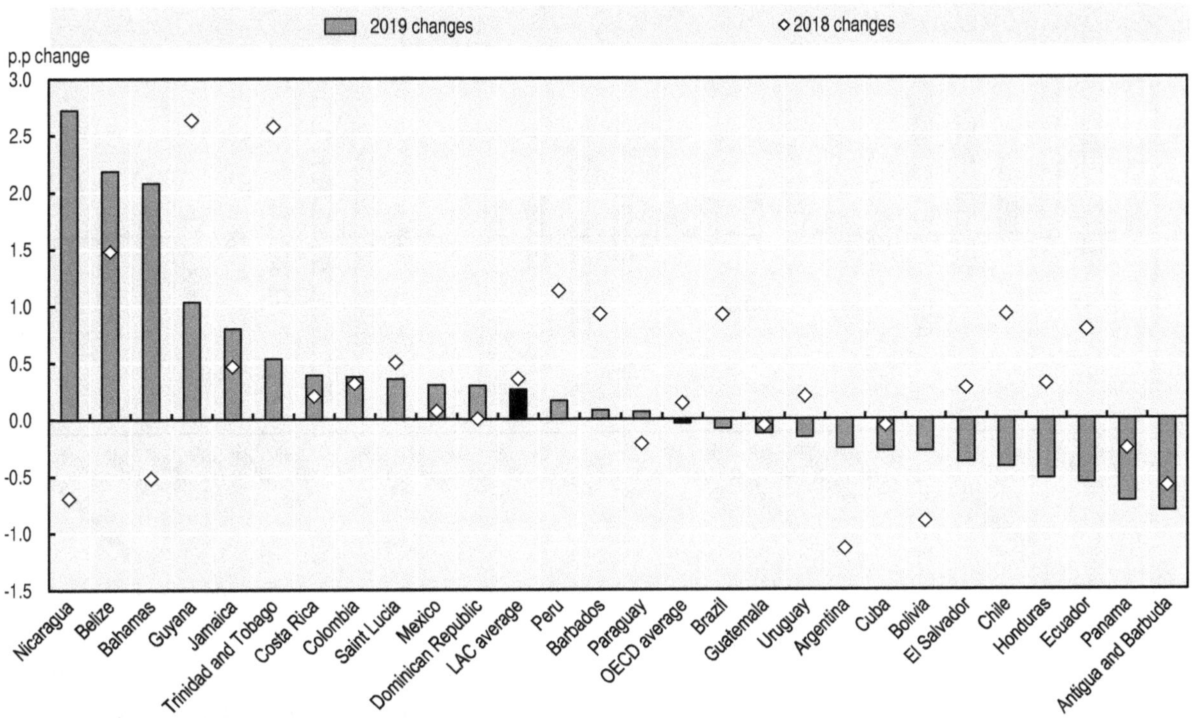

Note: The LAC average represents the unweighted average of 26 LAC countries included in this publication and excludes Venezuela due to data availability issues. The OECD average represents the unweighted average of the 37 OECD member countries. Chile, Colombia and Mexico are also part of the OECD (37).

Source: Authors' calculations based on OECD et al. (2021[1]), Table 4.1.

StatLink https://doi.org/10.1787/888934233891

Belize recorded increases in all main categories of tax revenue as a proportion of GDP in 2019. The overall increase in the tax-to-GDP ratio resulted from tax revenues increasing by 5% between 2018 and 2019 while nominal GDP decreased by 2% over the same period. The economy experienced three quarters of deceleration in 2019, caused largely by a drought affecting the primary and secondary sectors of the economy. Belize also recorded a slowdown in the key tourism sector in 2019 after years of strong growth (Barrow, 2020[9]).

The overall increase in tax revenues in the Bahamas was mainly driven by increases in VAT revenues (of 1.4 percentage points) and revenues from property taxes (0.7 percentage points, shown in Figure 1.3 under the heading "other taxes"). These increases were mainly the result of tax reforms intended to reduce the budget deficit to 1.8% of GDP in Fiscal Year (FY) 2018/19, from 5.5% in FY2016/17 and 3.4% of GDP in FY2017/18. The reforms included an increase of the standard VAT rate from 7.5% to 12% in July 2018 as well as an increase in stamp duties.

Figure 1.3. **Changes in tax-to-GDP ratios in LAC countries by main tax heading between 2018 and 2019**

Percentage points of GDP

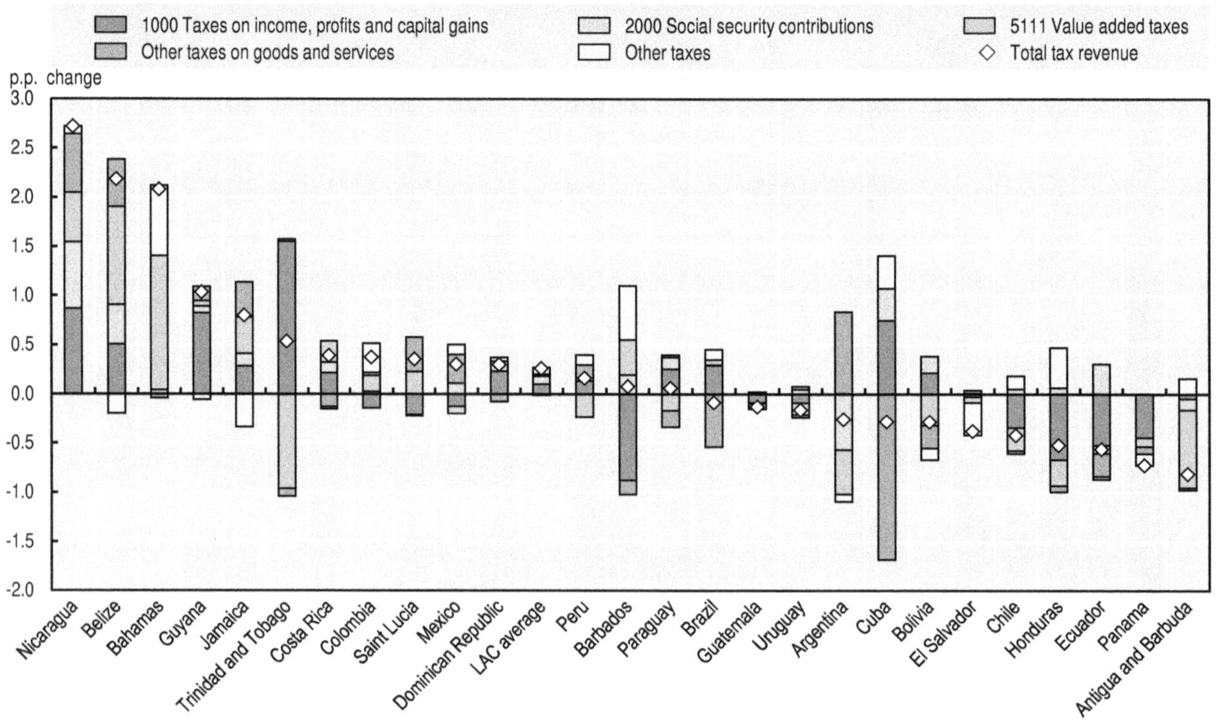

Note: The LAC average represents the unweighted average of 26 LAC countries included in this publication and excludes Venezuela due to data availability issues.

Source: Authors' calculations based on OECD et al. (2021[1]), Chapter 4.

StatLink https://doi.org/10.1787/888934233910

Antigua and Barbuda, Ecuador and Panama recorded the largest decreases between 2018 and 2019, each of more than 0.5 percentage points. In 2019, Antigua and Barbuda experienced the largest decline, of 0.8 percentage points, principally due to a drop in VAT revenues, which fell by the same amount. The economic environment and challenges in tax administration and tax collection in Antigua and Barbuda contributed to the overall decrease in the tax-to-GDP ratio in 2019. Antigua and Barbuda's economy decelerated in 2019 after a strong performance in 2018 (real GDP growth in 2019 was 3.4%, about half its rate in 2018). IDB (2019[10]) explains that "taxes on income and profits, and domestic goods and services fell below the budget target during the review period, highlighting key challenges the authorities faced concerning tax collection and administration".

Panama recorded the second-largest fall across countries in 2019 (of 0.7 percentage points) due to decreases across all tax categories, reflecting the economic situation in the country. Meanwhile, Ecuador recorded a decline of 0.6 percentage points in 2019, causing its tax-to-GDP ratio to revert to its pre-2018 level. The year 2018 was a year of exceptional tax collection for Ecuador, whose tax ratio increased by 0.8 percentage points from the previous year.

Figure 1.3 shows other significant increases between 2018 and 2019 in certain tax revenue categories in countries that implemented tax reforms. For example:

- The tax-to-GDP ratio in Trinidad and Tobago increased by 0.5 percentage points between 2018 and 2019 as the authorities implemented a three-month tax amnesty in June 2019 that brought exceptional revenues from taxes on income and profits, which increased by 1.6 percentage points between 2018 and 2019 (ECLAC, 2020[11]).

- Argentina saw decreases in revenues from all tax categories between 2018 and 2019 except for revenues from taxes on goods and services other than VAT, which increased by 0.8 percentage points. The increase was entirely due to the increase in revenues from export taxes by 1.1 percentage points over the same period following the introduction of temporary export duties on services in September 2018. In December 2019, authorities raised export tax rates for goods that had a zero rate (EY, 2019[12]; ITR, 2020[13]).
- Barbados registered increases in VAT revenues and taxes on property (shown under heading "other taxes" in Figure 1.3) of 0.4 and 0.5 percentage points respectively between 2018 and 2019. Barbados has increased the VAT rates for hotel accommodation from 7.5% to 10% and expanded the VAT base in certain sectors (such as the tourism sector) by eliminating exemptions and preferential rates (IMF, 2019[14]). The authorities also increased property tax rates to render the property tax system more progressive. In contrast, revenues from taxes on income and profits declined by 0.9 percentage points between 2018 and 2019 following legislative changes relating to personal income tax (PIT) and CIT. The most important reform concerned CIT: In January 2019, Barbados reformed its CIT system, following the OECD's assessment (through its Base Erosion and Profit Shifting [BEPS] initiative) that it had harmful preferential regimes for non-resident companies (OECD, 2020[15]). As a result of the reform, CIT rates for domestic and non-resident companies were aligned, with the domestic rate being reduced from 25% to between 1% to 5.5% depending on the level of profits, and CIT rates for non-resident companies (that had previously ranged between 0.25% and 2.5%) being increased to the same levels as for domestic companies. The second important reform concerned PIT, for which the rates were gradually reduced, starting with the top PIT rate (IMF, 2019[14]).

Evolution of tax-to-GDP ratios since 2000

Enhancing domestic resource mobilisation, particularly through increased tax revenues, is critical for LAC's sustainable development, as reflected in the Development in Transition agenda for the recovery post-COVID-19 (see Box 1.1). The average tax-to-GDP ratio in LAC countries has risen since 1990 (Figure 1.4), increasing by more than 7 percentage points overall, from 15.7% in 1990 to 22.9% in 2019. This trend contrasts with that of OECD countries, where the average tax-to-GDP ratio has been relatively stable since 1990 (although at a higher level than the LAC average); the OECD tax-to-GDP ratio reached 33.8% in 2019, 2.7 percentage points above its level in 1990. The difference between the LAC and OECD average tax-to-GDP ratio in 2019 was at 10.9 percentage points.

Figure 1.5 shows the evolution of the average tax-to-GDP ratio for the three LAC sub-regions since 1990. While all three sub-regions have shown an upward trend in tax levels between 1990 and 2019, their evolution shows notable differences:

- On average, the Caribbean recorded the lowest growth over the period, of 5.6 percentage points. The Caribbean's average tax-to-GDP ratio was consistently higher than the LAC average. The difference has widened since 2017 due to the relatively sharp increase in the tax-to-GDP ratio of the Caribbean.
- In contrast, the increase in the average tax-to-GDP ratio for Central America and Mexico has been more gradual. Throughout this period, the average tax-to-GDP ratio of Central America and Mexico remained below the average for the LAC region. The average tax-to-GDP ratio for Central America and Mexico has been steady at 21.1% since 2016 before increasing slightly in 2019.

- South America recorded a strong increase in its tax-to-GDP ratio during the 1990s and exceeded the LAC average in 2004. Since 2015, South America's tax-to-GDP ratio has been declining towards the LAC average; the two converged in 2019.

Box 1.1. *Revenue Statistics in Latin America and the Caribbean* and Development in Transition approach

This edition of *Revenue Statistics in Latin America and the Caribbean* is the third to be produced with the support of the European Union (EU) Regional Facility for Development in Transition for Latin America and the Caribbean (LAC). This facility results from a joint work led by the EU, the Organisation for Economic Co-operation and Development (OECD) and its Development Centre, and the Economic Commission for Latin America and the Caribbean (ECLAC).

The pandemic hit LAC countries at a time when the region already faced deep structural challenges. The COVID-19 crisis posed new challenges to the structural development traps already highlighted in the "Development in Transition" (OECD et al., 2019[16]). The four traps of low productivity, social vulnerability, institutional weaknesses and environmental sustainability exacerbate the socio-economic consequences of the crisis and reduce countries' ability to design and implement medium and long-term responses. The COVID-19 crisis underscored the need to adopt a multi-dimensional approach to development to overcome the interlinked challenges posed by the development traps. Moreover, the pandemic has shed light on the pressing need to redefine national policies by building consensus across citizens, regional integration and international co-operation, as part of the region's economic and social recovery that includes all countries regardless of their development level (OECD et al., 2020[17]).

In this context, the recovery must be seen as an opportunity to transform the development strategy of the region, with inclusiveness, resilience and sustainability. Fiscal policy is essential to build capacities, address development traps and ensure an inclusive and sustainable revovery (OECD et al., 2020[17]). *Revenue Statistics in Latin America and the Caribbean* represents an invaluable resource for governments as they look to strengthen fiscal policy. By providing harmonised and detailed tax data across the region, it allows for in-depth tax-policy analysis, identifying not only how the level of tax revenues varies by country but also which instruments generate these revenues, reflecting the fact that *how* tax revenues are collected can be as important as *how much* is collected. *Revenue Statistics in Latin America and the Caribbean* also represents a common starting point for knowledge-sharing and capacity development between countries, as well as with the broader international community.

Reflecting the critical relationship between effective taxation and effective public spending to promote inclusive and sustainable development, the Development in Transition Facility brings *Revenue Statistics in Latin America and the Caribbean* together with the work of ECLAC and OECD on public expenditure, and social spending in particular. The objective of this project is to provide unprecedented insights and invaluable tools for the development of fiscal policy in the region, which are particularly relevant and needed in the context of the COVID-19 crisis.

Tax-to-GDP ratios in LAC countries increased in the early 1990s after a decade of macroeconomic instability. During the 1980s, many countries ran large fiscal imbalances and some resorted to alternative ways of financing expenditure (borrowing or printing money). This caused rapid inflation across the region, which eroded the real value of tax revenues. Reforms in the 1990s focused on price stability, trade liberalisation and fiscal discipline. Most LAC governments reduced spending and implemented policies aimed at increasing tax revenues; budget management and fiscal balances improved considerably. Policy makers implemented reforms to tax policy and administration to reinforce tax systems against inflationary episodes by shortening collection lags and indexing tax liabilities (ECLAC, 2018[18]).

Figure 1.4. **Tax-to-GDP ratios, LAC and OECD averages, 1990-2019**

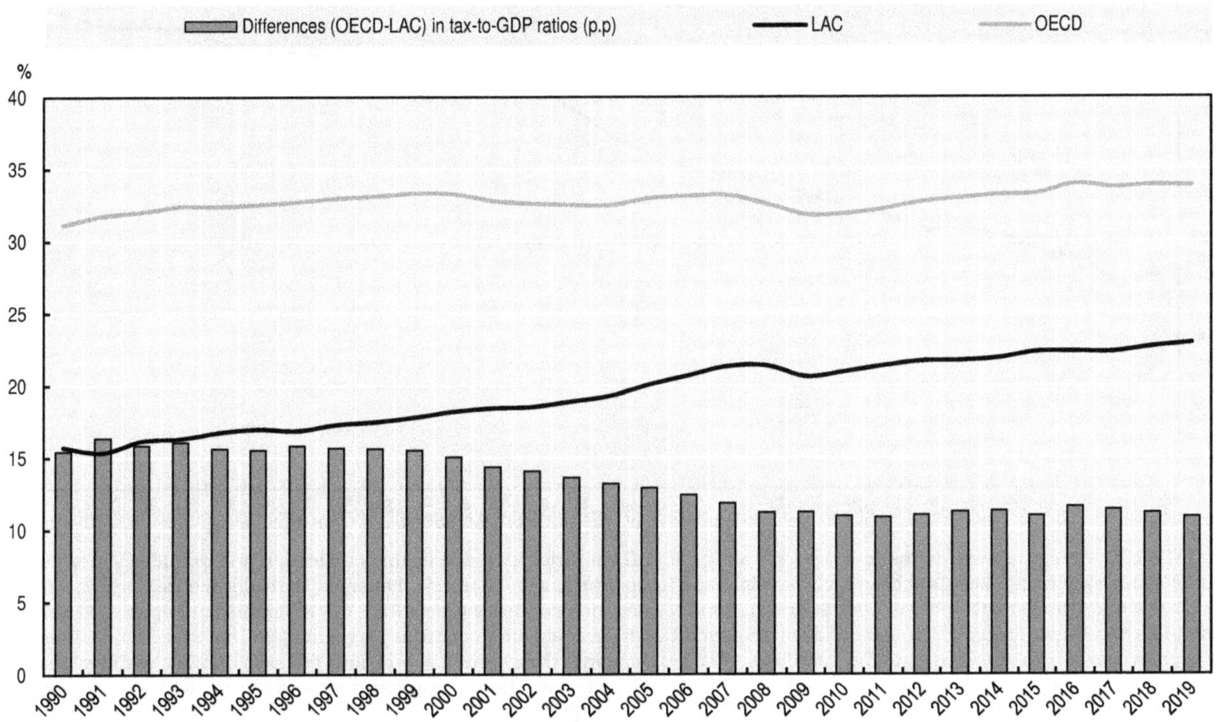

Note: The LAC average represents the unweighted average of 26 LAC countries included in this publication and excludes Venezuela due to data availability issues. The OECD average represents the unweighted average of the 37 OECD member countries. Chile, Colombia and Mexico are also part of the OECD (37).

Source: Authors' calculations based on OECD et al. (2021[1]), "Revenue Statistics in Latin America: Comparative tables", *OECD Tax Statistics* (database), *http://dx.doi.org/ 10.1787/data-00641-en*.

StatLink *https://doi.org/10.1787/888934233929*

The introduction of VAT has been the most significant tax reform in LAC of the past three decades. By the early 1990s, almost all countries were implementing a VAT system and subsequent reforms aimed to increase its rate, to widen the tax base and to improve collections. Several countries have moved towards single-rate VAT schemes (ECLAC, 2018[18]).

LAC countries have undertaken significant efforts to modernise tax administration over the last two decades. New information technology systems have been implemented, tax collection systems became more efficient and staff have gained in expertise (IDB, 2013[19]). Tax reforms included the introduction or development of simplified regimes for small taxpayers, the taxation of property based on presumed incomes and the expansion of taxation to labour and capital income, including dividends. Reforms have also included the establishment of minimum taxes, taxes on financial transactions and gradual reductions in the real income level taxed at the top marginal rate (ECLAC, 2013[20]; ECLAC, 2018[18]).

Figure 1.5. **Average tax-to-GDP ratios, LAC and sub-regions, 1990-2019**

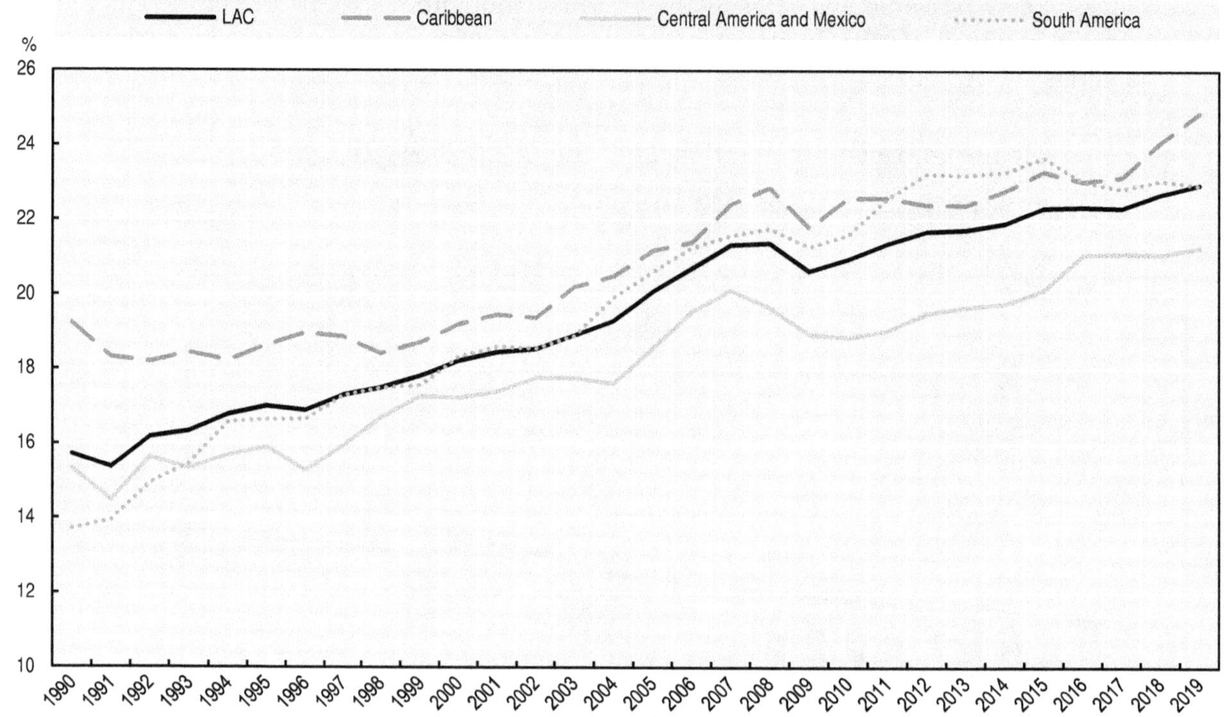

Note: The LAC average represents the unweighted average of LAC countries included in this publication and excludes Venezuela due to data availability issues. The Caribbean includes eight countries (Antigua and Barbuda, Bahamas, Barbados, Belize, Guyana, Jamaica, Saint Lucia and Trinidad and Tobago), Central America and Mexico nine countries (Costa Rica, Cuba, Dominican Republic, El Salvador, Guatemala, Honduras, Mexico, Nicaragua and Panama) and South America nine countries (Argentina, Bolivia, Brazil, Chile, Colombia, Ecuador, Paraguay, Peru and Uruguay). The classification of countries into the different sub-regions follows ECLAC's classification and is based on the spoken language of countries. The Caribbean includes the English-speaking countries and Guyana while Central America and Mexico covers Spanish-speaking countries including Dominican Republic and Cuba.

Source: Authors' calculations based on OECD et al. (2021[1]), "Revenue Statistics in Latin America: Comparative tables", *OECD Tax Statistics* (database), *http://dx.doi.org/ 10.1787/data-00641-en*.

StatLink *https://doi.org/10.1787/888934233948*

The increase in the average tax-to-GDP ratio in the LAC region since 1990 has largely been driven by increases in revenues from income taxes and VAT, which increased by 3.0 and 3.8 percentage points respectively between 1990 and 2019. In 2019, revenues from VAT amounted to 6.0% of GDP while revenues from taxes on income and profits were equivalent to 6.2% of GDP (Figure 1.6). Between 1990 and 2019, revenues from other taxes on goods and services (e.g. excises, customs and import duties) in LAC decreased as a percentage of GDP. This decline was associated with trade liberalisation, as a result of which LAC countries changed the way they taxed imported and exported goods as well as specific goods and services. These changes included a reduction of import tariffs, narrowing the base of products and services subject to excises, and the elimination of taxes on exports. One important exception is Argentina, where taxes on exports were re-established in 2002, partly abolished in 2015, and reintroduced in September 2018.

Four distinct phases in the evolution of tax revenues can be distinguished:

- Between 1990 and 2002, VAT contributed more to the increase in tax revenues than taxes on income and profits (1.9% of GDP versus 1.0%). Over that period, five countries introduced VAT (Barbados, Belize, El Salvador, Jamaica and Paraguay).

- Between 2002 and 2008, the opposite is observed: revenue from taxes on income and profits contributed more than VAT revenues to the increase in the average tax-to-GDP ratio (the increases amounted to 1.7% and 1.3% of GDP respectively). The increase in income taxes is partly explained by the commodity boom after 2003, which drove up CIT revenue from the natural resources sector (ECLAC, 2014[21]; Barreix, Benítez and Pecho, 2017[22]). In several countries, it was also a result of policies that reduced tax incentives in free-trade zones, the introduction of minimum taxes for corporations, reforms in international taxation and agreements between countries to fight tax evasion.
- VAT and revenues from income taxes declined strongly during the global financial crisis. During the subsequent recovery, VAT revenues grew quickly to reach 5.9% of GDP in 2016. During this period, two more Caribbean countries introduced VAT (Saint Lucia in 2012 and the Bahamas in 2015). Commodity prices declined steadily and then sharply in 2015.
- From 2016, commodity prices recovered and income tax revenues rebounded. Between 2017 and 2018, revenues from income taxes recorded their highest increase since 2011, at 0.3 percentage points on average due to strong profits in the mining and oil and gas extraction sectors. In 2019, the increase in income tax revenues (driven by CIT revenue) was more modest at 0.1 percentage points.

Figure 1.6. **Revenue from selected taxes in the LAC region, 1990-2019**

Percentage of GDP

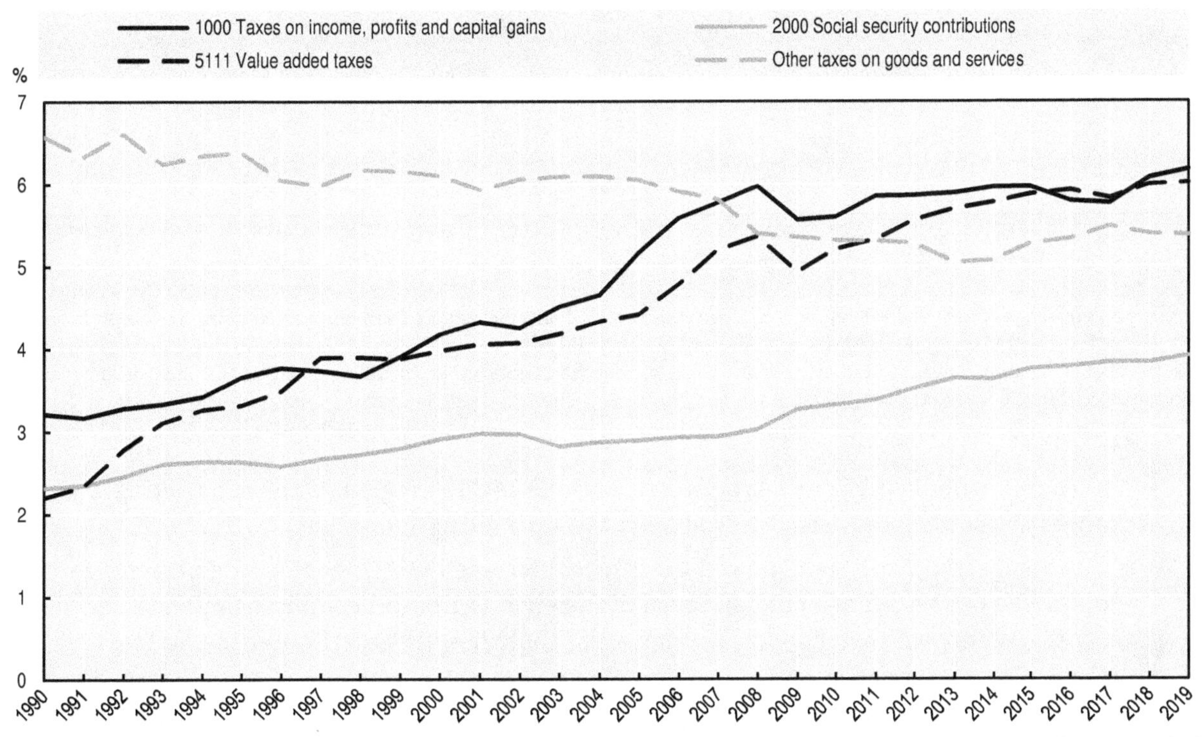

Note: The LAC average represents the unweighted average of 26 LAC countries included in this publication and excludes Venezuela due to data availability issues.

Source: Authors' calculations based on OECD et al. (2021[1]), "Revenue Statistics in Latin America: Comparative tables", *OECD Tax Statistics* (database), *http://dx.doi.org/ 10.1787/data-00641-en.*

StatLink https://doi.org/10.1787/888934233967

Figure 1.7 shows the evolution of CIT and PIT since 2005. In 2019, the LAC averages for CIT and PIT revenues stood at 3.6% and 2.2% of GDP respectively. Over this period, CIT revenues as a percentage of GDP have been more volatile than revenues from PIT, which have steadily increased on average across the region.

Figure 1.7. **Revenue from taxes on income and profits, CIT and PIT in the LAC region, 2005-19**

Percentage of GDP

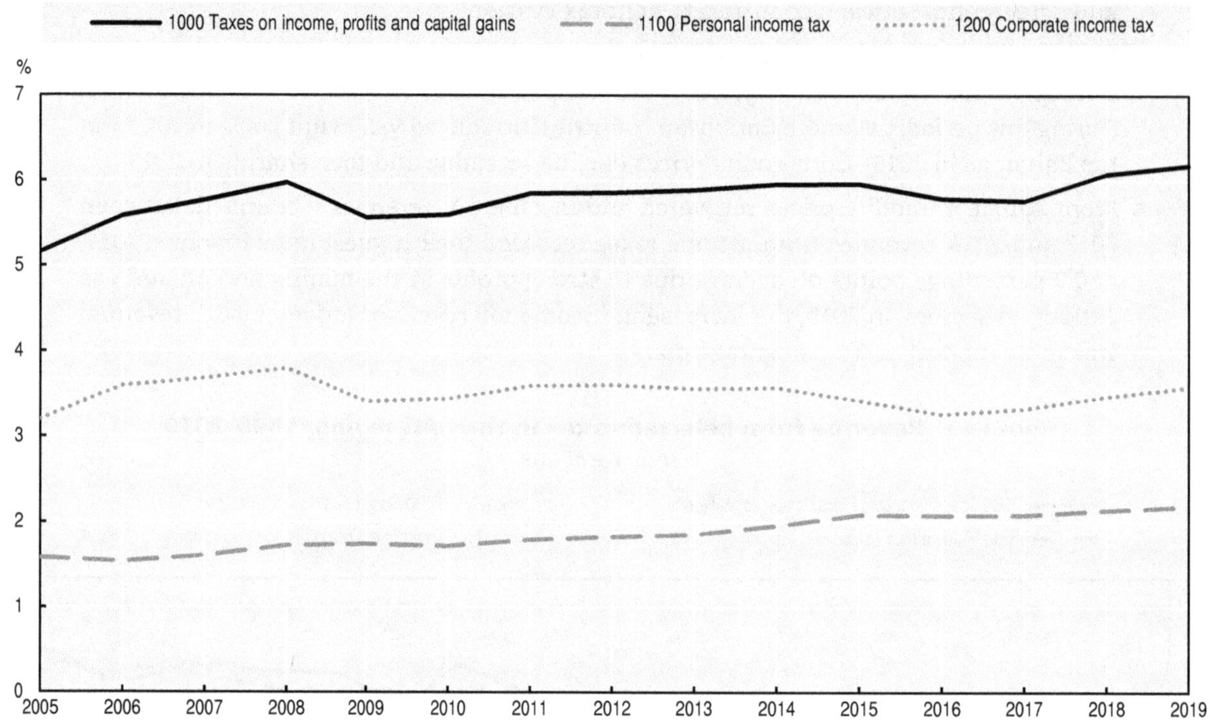

Note: Average CIT and PIT as a percentage of GDP should be interpreted with caution as Ecuador and Venezuela are excluded from the calculation. The LAC average excludes Venezuela due to data availability issues. Ecuador is excluded from the LAC average for CIT revenue as a percentage of GDP and PIT revenue as a percentage of GDP as more than a third of its revenue from taxes on income and profits cannot be allocated to either CIT revenue (1200) or PIT revenue (1100).

Source: OECD et al. (2021[1]), "Revenue Statistics in Latin America and the Caribbean: Comparative tables", *OECD Tax Statistics* (database), *http://dx.doi.org/10.1787/data-00641-en.*

StatLink *https://doi.org/10.1787/888934233986*

There are notable differences between the three LAC sub-regions when considering the changes in the main tax categories between 1990 and 2019 (Figure 1.8).

- On average, the Caribbean showed the largest increase in VAT revenue as a percentage of GDP (of 6.1 percentage points). Seven of the eight Caribbean countries implemented[3] a VAT system over the period, later than most countries in Central America and Mexico and in South America.
- In Central America and Mexico and in South America, the largest increases between 1990 and 2019 were from taxes on income and profits (3.9% and 3.7% of GDP), followed by VAT (2.8% and 3.2% of GDP respectively). Revenues from taxes on income and profits (and indirectly from VAT) were influenced by large increases in mineral and oil prices between 2003 and 2010.

Figure 1.8. **Changes in revenue from selected taxes for LAC and sub-region averages, between 1990 and 2019**

Percentage points

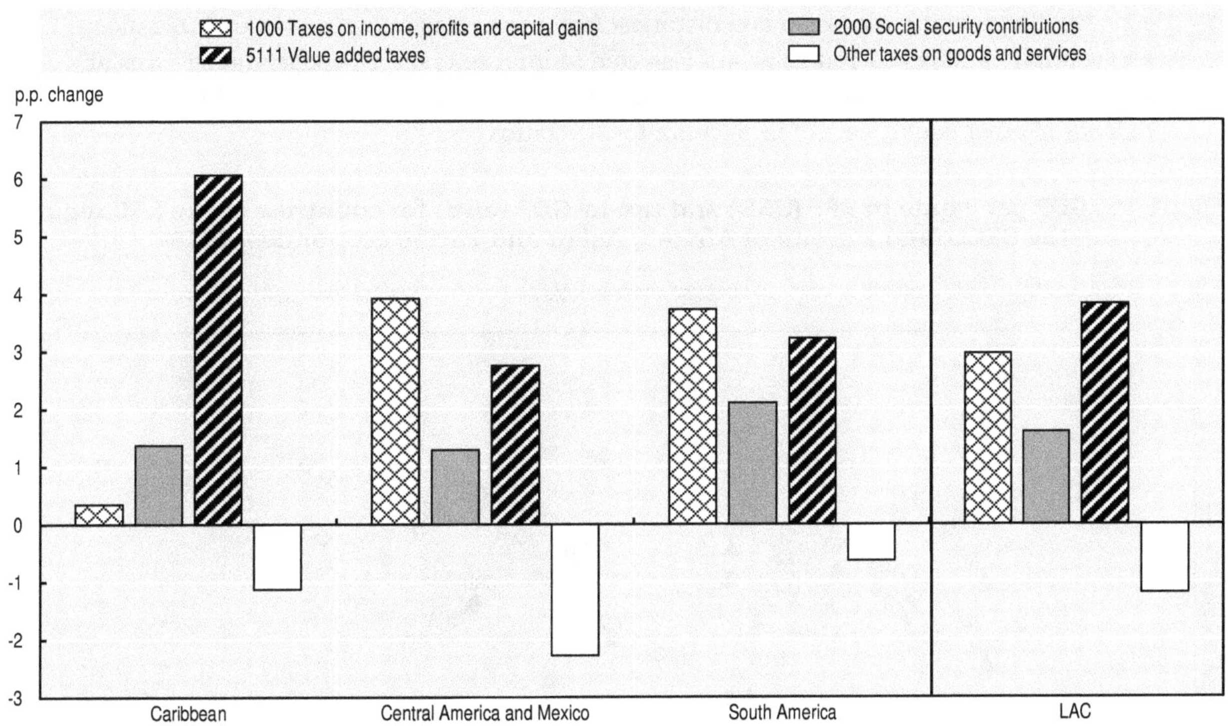

Note: The LAC average represents the unweighted average of 26 LAC countries included in this publication and excludes Venezuela due to data availability issues. The Caribbean includes eight countries (Antigua and Barbuda, Bahamas, Barbados, Belize, Guyana, Jamaica, Trinidad and Tobago, and Saint Lucia), Central America and Mexico includes nine countries (Costa Rica, Cuba, Dominican Republic, El Salvador, Guatemala, Honduras, Mexico, Nicaragua and Panama) and South America includes nine countries (Argentina, Bolivia, Brazil, Chile, Colombia, Ecuador, Paraguay, Peru and Uruguay). The classification of countries into the different sub-regions follows ECLAC's classification and is based on the spoken language of countries. The Caribbean includes the English-speaking countries and Guyana while Central America and Mexico cover Spanish-speaking countries, including Dominican Republic and Cuba.

Source: Authors' calculations based on OECD et al. (2021[1]), Chapter 4.

StatLink https://doi.org/10.1787/888934234005

Factors influencing tax-to-GDP ratios

Differences between the LAC and OECD average tax-to-GDP ratios are consistent with the tendency for countries at higher income levels to have higher tax-to-GDP ratios. The data implies a positive correlation between GDP per capita (a measure of the level of income of a country) and tax-to-GDP ratios (Figure 1.9). In general, OECD countries have higher average incomes than LAC countries and collect higher tax revenues as a proportion of GDP. Argentina, Barbados, Brazil, and Uruguay show similar tax-to-GDP ratios and levels of income to some OECD countries. Empirical analysis suggests that stronger tax collection, accompanied by better institutions, education and skills, and economic diversification allowed many OECD countries to evade the middle income trap, in contrast to LAC (Melguizo et al., 2017[23]).

Tax-to-GDP ratios are influenced by a range of economic and structural factors. GDP per capita, openness to trade, the extent of the informal economy, natural resource endowments and the importance of agriculture in the economy are all factors that can influence tax-to-GDP ratios. Socio-demographic determinants are also important, such as the level of education or the level of female participation in the labour force. The power of tax administrations, levels of corruption and tax morale (the willingness of people to pay taxes) are also strongly linked to the level of tax revenues (OECD, 2014[26]; OECD, 2019[25]). The tax-to-GDP ratio also reflects political choices regarding the role of the government and its size. Finally, geographic location and historical factors can also influence tax-to-GDP ratios: for example, landlocked countries are less able to impose taxes on goods and services at a port of entry than coastal countries. In addition, international factors, including the tax policies of other countries, can impact tax-to-GDP ratios.

Figure 1.9. **GDP per capita in PPP (USD) and tax-to-GDP ratios for countries in the LAC region, the OECD, and a group of African, Asian and Pacific economies, 2018**

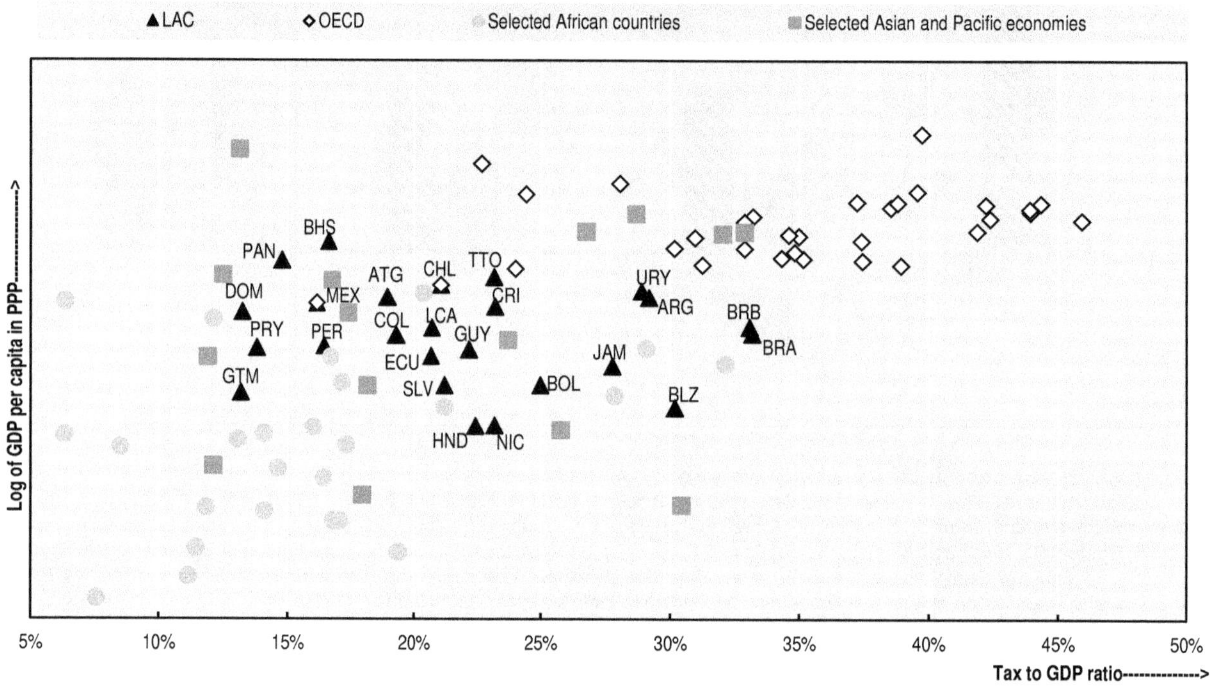

Note: The year of comparison is 2018 as the 2019 data for the tax-to-GDP ratios are not available for the selected African, Asian and Pacific economies. Cuba and Venezuela are not included in this figure due to data availability issues. The purchasing-power-parity (PPP) between two countries is the rate at which the currency of one country needs to be converted into that of a second country to ensure that a given amount of the first country's currency will purchase the same volume of goods and services in the second country as it does in the first. The implied PPP conversion rate is expressed as national currency per current international dollar. An international dollar has the same purchasing power as the U.S. dollar has in the United States. An international dollar is a hypothetical currency that is used as a means of translating and comparing costs from one country to the other using a common reference point, the US dollar (USD).

Source: IMF (2020[24]) for figures of GDP per capita. Tax-to-GDP ratios are sourced from the *Global Revenue Statistics Database* (*http://www.oecd.org/tax/tax-policy/global-revenue-statistics-database.htm*).

StatLink https://doi.org/10.1787/888934234024

The extent of state participation in financing social security is another important factor behind disparate tax ratios in the LAC region. From the 1980s onwards, many LAC countries privatised healthcare and pensions to greater or lesser degrees. Chile, El Salvador and Mexico, for example, have shifted their public pension programme to a mostly private, fully funded pension system. In Colombia and Peru, private and public programmes compete and employees opt for one of them (OECD et al., 2015[27]; OECD/IDB/The World Bank, 2014[28]). On the other hand, Argentina, Brazil and Uruguay follow a model where public and private systems are complementary. In these countries, substantial reforms were undertaken to extend coverage of social security systems to those previously excluded. This has also been instrumental in the increase of tax revenues (ECLAC, 2014[21]).

Informality constrains tax collection in LAC by significantly reducing the taxable base. The COVID-19 crisis is likely to increase informal employment, which already accounts for close to 60% of workers in Latin America (OECD, 2020[5]). Despite rapid and effective government measures in several LAC coutries since the second quarter 2020 to support the most vulnerable families, the social impact of the pandemic is particularly difficult for about 40% of workers – and their families – who are not protected by any safety net. This situation affects even more the 61% of vulnerable informal workers who are not part of a household covered by a major social assistance programme, either direct transfers from the largest transfer programmes or non-contributory pensions (OECD, 2020[5]).

The LAC region loses significant amounts of tax revenues due to tax evasion and aggressive tax planning. Foregone revenues due to tax non-compliance in LAC is estimated at 6.1% of GDP in 2018 mainly in income tax (3.8% of GDP) and VAT (2.3% of GDP) (ECLAC, 2020[11]). Many countries in the region have implemented measures to address tax evasion, including strengthening the capacity of tax administrations and implementing voluntary compliance programmes.

Tax structures

The tax structure (defined as the share of major tax types in total tax revenue) depicts the composition of tax revenues by different tax types. It is an important indicator for understanding the economic and social effects of tax systems in the LAC region.

Evolution of tax structures

Taxes on goods and services provided the largest share of total tax revenues in the LAC region in 2019, representing half of total taxation on average. Between 1990 and 2019, the average LAC tax mix shifted towards VAT, taxes on income and profits and social security contributions and away from other taxes on goods and services.

- The share of VAT revenues in total tax revenues reached 27.7% in 2019, corresponding to an increase of 12.3 percentage points since 1990. The revenue share of other taxes on goods and services (including excise, customs and import duties) declined by 20.2 percentage points over the same period (Figure 1.10).
- The share of revenues from taxes on incomes and profits grew by 7.4 percentage points (from 19.7% to 27.0% of total tax revenues) between 1990 and 2019.
- The share of social security contributions in total tax revenues has increased by 3.2 percentage points from 1990, reaching 17.1% in 2019. Two major (and opposing) factors have influenced the trajectory of social security contributions in the region. While rising personal incomes have led to higher collections, this was counter-balanced by the full or partial privatisation of social security that occurred in many countries, principally between the mid-1990s and 2010 (OECD et al., 2015[27]).

The share of PIT revenues grew from 7.7% of total tax revenues in 2005 to 9.2% in 2019, in part due to increases in personal incomes across the region. However, the average share of PIT revenue remains low in LAC countries despite some countries implementing reforms to expand their tax base. After the global financial crisis, several countries established flat rates on capital income that had previously been exempt and implemented progressive rates on labour income (ECLAC, 2014[21]). However, there are relatively few taxpayers, given the concentration of income earners at low-income levels: in 2013, only 10% of the population in Latin America were registered taxpayers (IDB, 2013[19]).

Figure 1.10. **Average tax structure in the LAC region, 1990 and 2019**

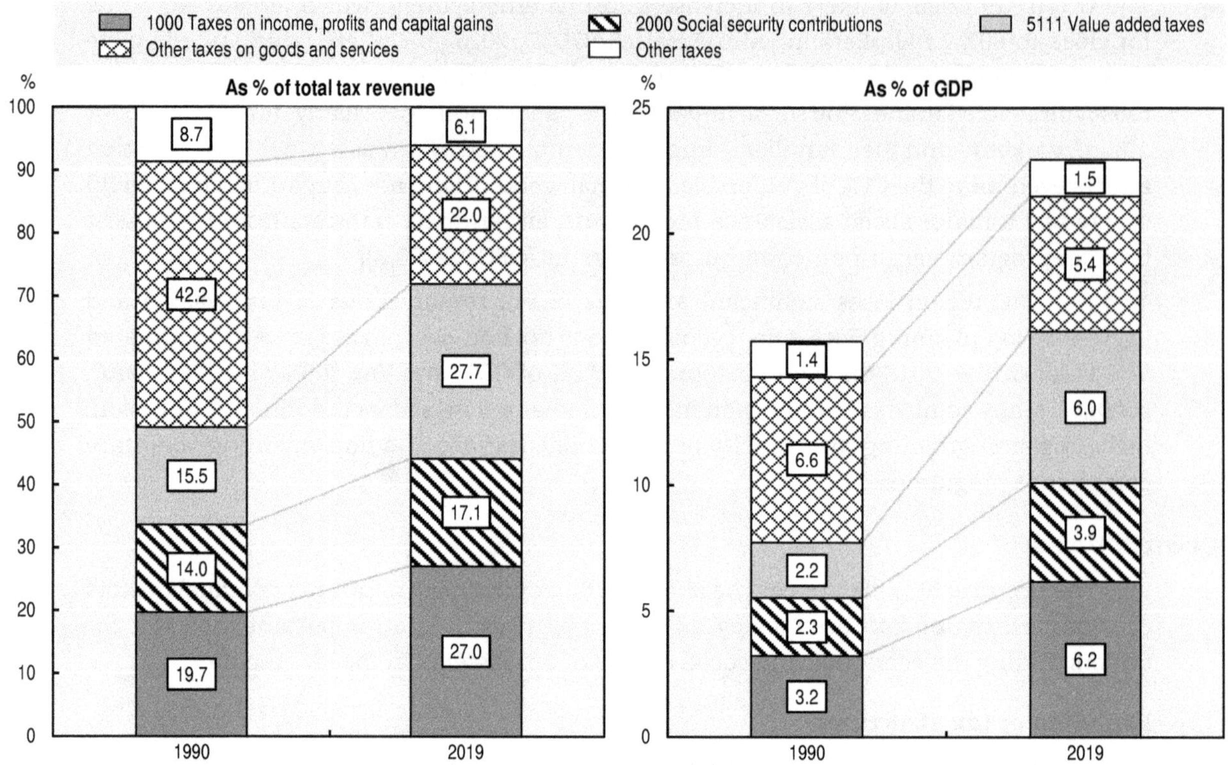

Note: The LAC average represents the unweighted average of 26 LAC countries included in this publication and excludes Venezuela due to data availability issues.

Source: Authors' calculations based on OECD et al. (2021[1]), Chapter 4.

StatLink https://doi.org/10.1787/888934234043

Several other factors continue to limit PIT revenues, including a small tax base that is comprised primarily of wages (since tax privileges are often granted to returns on capital) and high levels of evasion (Barreix, Benítez and Pecho, 2017[22]; ECLAC, 2014[21]). ECLAC (2020[11]) states that the evasion rates for PIT are high in selected LAC countries that conducted tax evasion studies, ranging from 18.7% in Mexico (2016 figure, equivalent to tax revenue losses of 0.8% of GDP) to 69.9% in Guatemala (2006 figure, equivalent to tax revenue losses of 0.5% of GDP). Evasion is more common among the self-employed than employees. A study for Mexico that disaggregated the evasion rate for different groups concluded that the tax revenue losses as percentage of GDP are nearly five times higher for individuals with business activities than for wage earners (ECLAC, 2020[11]).

The share of CIT revenues in total tax revenues has increased by 0.8 percentage points since 2005, reaching 15.8% in 2019. CIT evasion is also a significant issue in the LAC region, with higher evasion rates than PIT. Given that the CIT revenue share is nearly double than the PIT share, the losses in tax revenues are far from negligible. ECLAC (2020[11]) states that "evasion rates for corporate income tax range from 19.9% in Mexico to almost 80% in Guatemala". Because of high evasion rates, tax revenue losses are estimated to be more than 4% of GDP in the Dominican Republic, Guatemala, Peru and Panama.

Figure 1.11. **Average tax structure in the LAC region, 2005 and 2019**

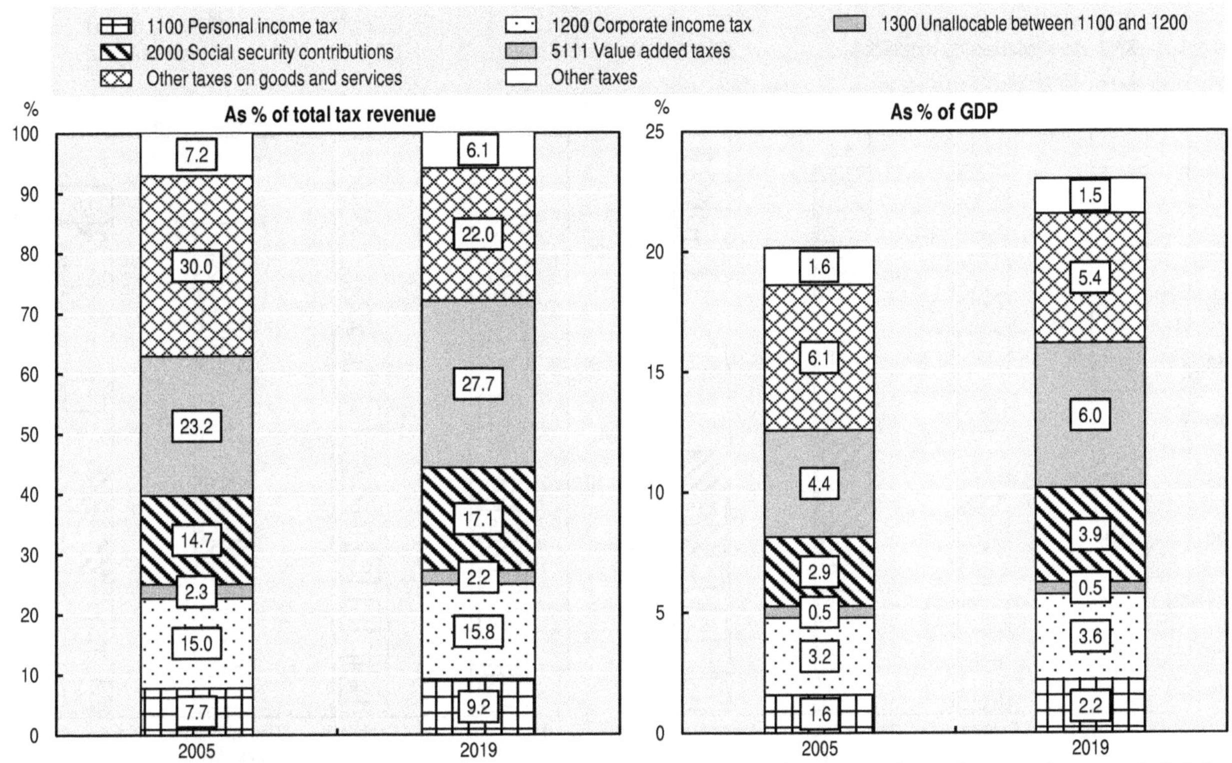

Note: Average CIT and PIT as a percentage of GDP should be interpreted with caution as Ecuador and Venezuela are excluded from the calculation. The LAC average excludes Venezuela due to data availability issues. Ecuador is excluded from the LAC average for CIT revenue as a percentage of GDP and PIT revenue as a percentage of GDP as more than a third of its revenue from taxes on income and profits cannot be allocated to either CIT revenue (1200) or PIT revenue (1100).

Source: Authors' calculations based on OECD et al. (2021[1]), "Revenue Statistics in Latin America: Comparative tables", *OECD Tax Statistics* (database), *http://dx.doi.org/ 10.1787/data-00641-en.*

StatLink https://doi.org/10.1787/888934234062

In 2019, there were notable differences in average tax structure across the sub-regions (Figure 1.12). The largest share of revenue in the Caribbean was derived from taxes on goods and services other than VAT, which on average represented 29.3% of total tax revenues. These taxes contributed 17.2% of total tax revenues in South America and 20.4% in Central America and Mexico. In contrast, South America had the highest share of VAT revenue in 2019 at 30.5% on average, compared with 27.9% in the Caribbean and 24.8% in Central America and Mexico. Social security contributions were lowest in the Caribbean in 2019, at 11.5% of total tax revenues on average. This was slightly above half of the average for the other sub-regions (19.3% in Central America and Mexico, and 20.0% in South America). All three sub-regions generated higher revenues from CIT than from PIT.

Average tax structure in LAC and the OECD

The average tax mix in the LAC region exhibits low revenues from income taxes and social security contributions relative to the OECD average (Figure 1.13). In particular, LAC countries rely heavily on taxes on goods and services, which make up more than half of tax revenues on average, compared with around one-third in OECD economies on average. However, as a percentage of GDP, revenues from taxes on goods and services in the LAC and OECD regions were similar in 2018, at 11.4% and 10.9% respectively.[4]

Figure 1.12. **Average tax structure in the LAC region and sub-regions, 2019**

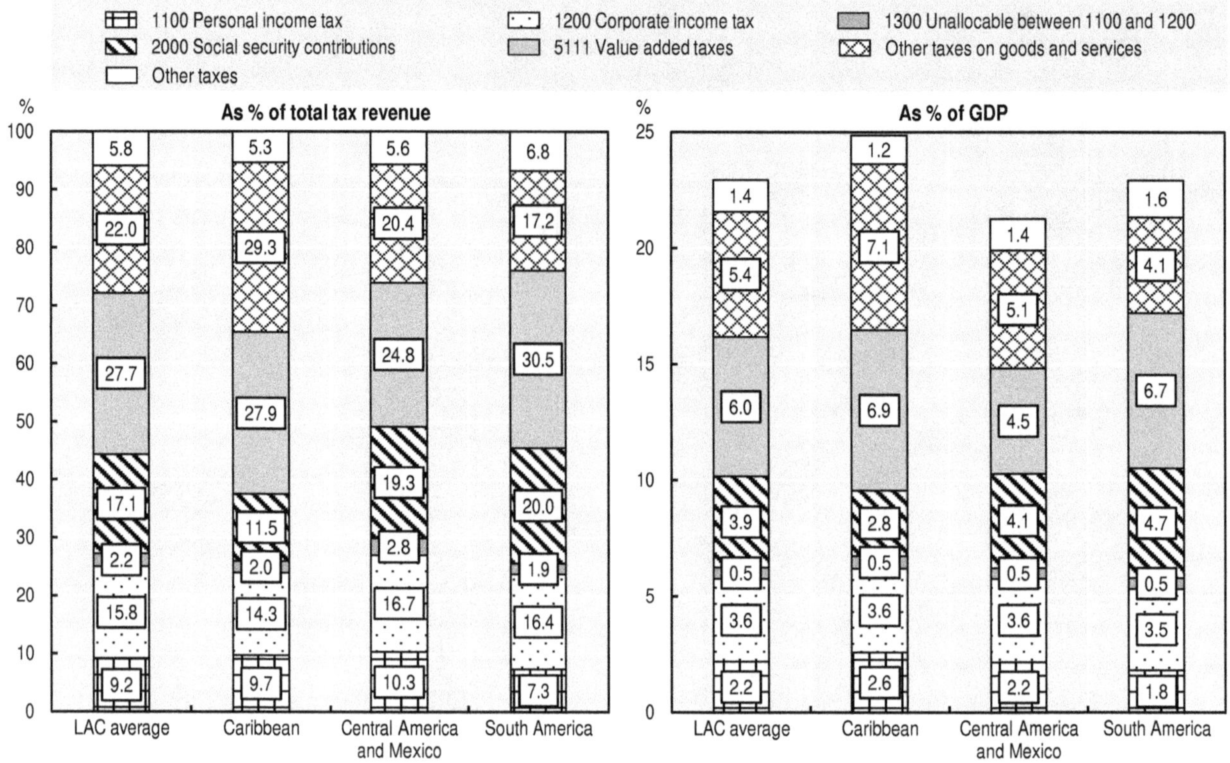

Note: Average CIT and PIT as a percentage of GDP for LAC should be interpreted with caution as Ecuador and Venezuela are excluded from the calculation. The LAC average excludes Venezuela due to data availability issues. Ecuador is excluded from the LAC average for CIT revenue as a percentage of GDP and PIT revenue as a percentage of GDP as more than a third of its revenue from taxes on income and profits cannot be allocated to CIT (1200) or PIT (1100). The Caribbean includes eight countries (Antigua and Barbuda, Bahamas, Barbados, Belize, Guyana, Jamaica, Trinidad and Tobago, and Saint Lucia), Central America and Mexico includes nine countries (Costa Rica, Cuba, Dominican Republic, El Salvador, Guatemala, Honduras, Mexico, Nicaragua and Panama) and South America includes nine countries (Argentina, Bolivia, Brazil, Chile, Colombia, Ecuador, Paraguay, Peru and Uruguay). The classification of countries into the different sub-regions follows ECLAC's classification and is based on the spoken language of countries. The Caribbean includes English-speaking countries and Guyana while Central America and Mexico covers Spanish-speaking countries including Dominican Republic and Cuba.

Source: Authors' calculations based on OECD et al. (2021[1]), "Revenue Statistics in Latin America: Comparative tables", *OECD Tax Statistics* (database), *http://dx.doi.org/ 10.1787/data-00641-en.*

StatLink https://doi.org/10.1787/888934234081

By contrast, the combined share of taxes on income and profits and social security contributions was much lower in the LAC region than in the OECD (43.9% versus 60.0% in 2018, on average). As a percentage of GDP, the sum of these two categories amounted to 10.0% in the LAC region, less than half the average OECD level (20.5%). The tendency towards private provision of social security in many LAC countries explains some of this difference.

On average, CIT generated 15.5% of total tax revenue in the LAC region in 2018 compared to 10.0% in the OECD area (respectively 3.5% and 3.1% of GDP) (Figure 1.13). The most striking difference between the regions relates to revenues from PIT, which contributed 23.5% of total tax revenues, on average, in the OECD in 2018, and 9.1% of total tax revenues in the LAC region. PIT revenues were 2.1% of GDP in the LAC region on average, compared to 8.1% for the OECD.

Taxes on immovable property and payroll (contained within the category "other taxes") are a less important source of revenue for the LAC region on average than in the OECD, although there are challenges with data availability for property taxes.

Figure 1.13. **Average tax structure in the LAC and OECD regions, 2018**

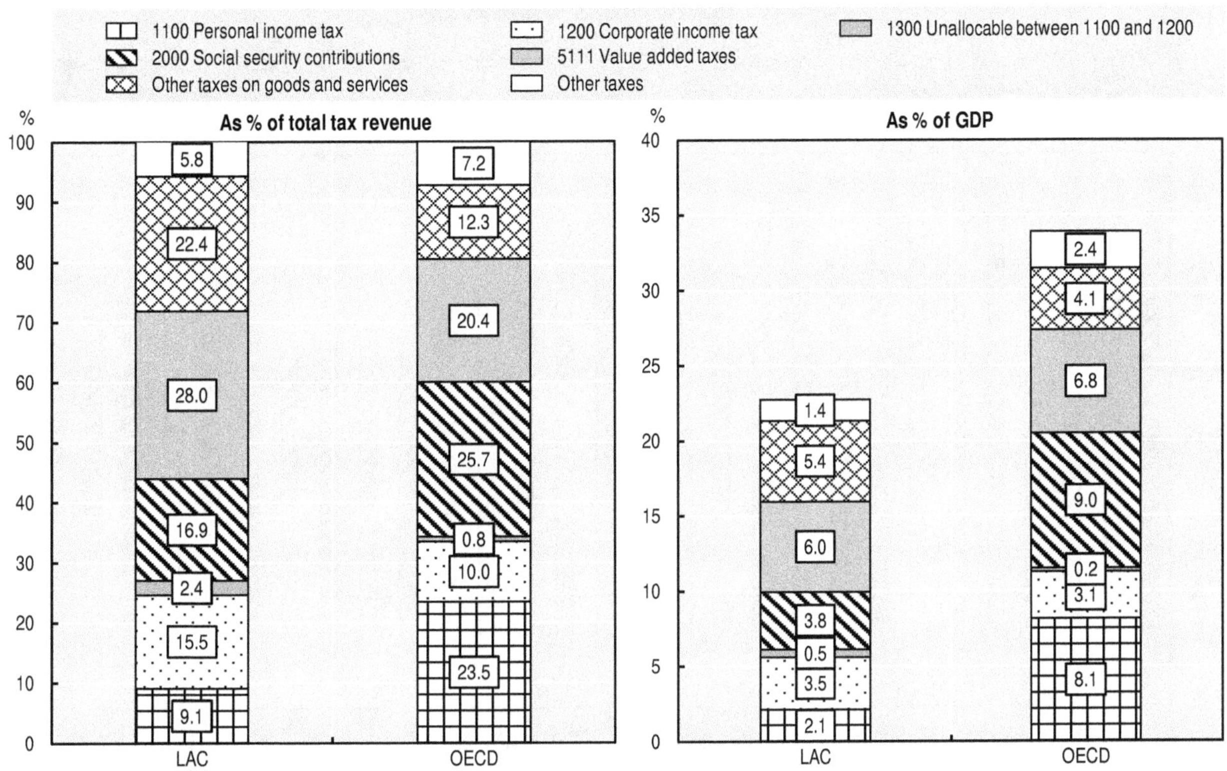

Note: The year of comparison is 2018 as the 2019 data for the OECD average are not available. The average CIT and PIT as a percentage of GDP for LAC should be interpreted with caution as Ecuador and Venezuela are excluded from the calculation. The LAC average excludes Venezuela due to data availability issues. Ecuador is excluded from the LAC average for CIT revenue as a percentage of GDP and PIT revenue as a percentage of GDP as more than a third of its revenue from taxes on income and profits cannot be allocated to CIT (1200) or PIT (1100). The OECD average represents the unweighted average of the 37 OECD member countries. Chile, Colombia and Mexico are also part of the OECD (37).

Source: Authors' calculations based on OECD et al. (2021[1]), "Revenue Statistics in Latin America: Comparative tables", *OECD Tax Statistics* (database), *http://dx.doi.org/10.1787/data-00641-en*.

StatLink *https://doi.org/10.1787/888934234100*

Figure 1.14 examines the evolution of the differences as a percentage of GDP in the main tax categories between the LAC and OECD regions between 1990 and 2018. The tax-to-GDP ratio for the LAC region was 15.4 percentage points lower than the OECD average in 1990. The difference between the two regions fell to 11.2 percentage points in 2018. The increases in revenues in taxes on income and profits and VAT as well as decreases in other goods and services taxes in the LAC region over the same period contributed to the reduction in the difference in average tax-to-GDP ratios between the LAC and OECD. However, there was an increase in the difference between the LAC and OECD averages for social security contributions between 1990 and 2018 as the OECD average increased more than the LAC average over the same period.

These trends have affected the convergence of tax structures between the regions. Figure 1.15 shows the D-index[5] between 2005 and 2018, which indicates the convergence between the LAC average tax structure and the OECD average. It is calculated as the sum of the absolute differences between the share of each tax category in the LAC average and its share in the OECD average tax mix at a more granular level (breaking down income tax revenues by PIT and CIT revenues). A figure of 0 indicates perfect similarity, whereas 200 indicates complete dissimilarity.

Figure 1.14. **Differences in tax-to-GDP ratios between LAC and OECD by main tax heading, 1990-2018**

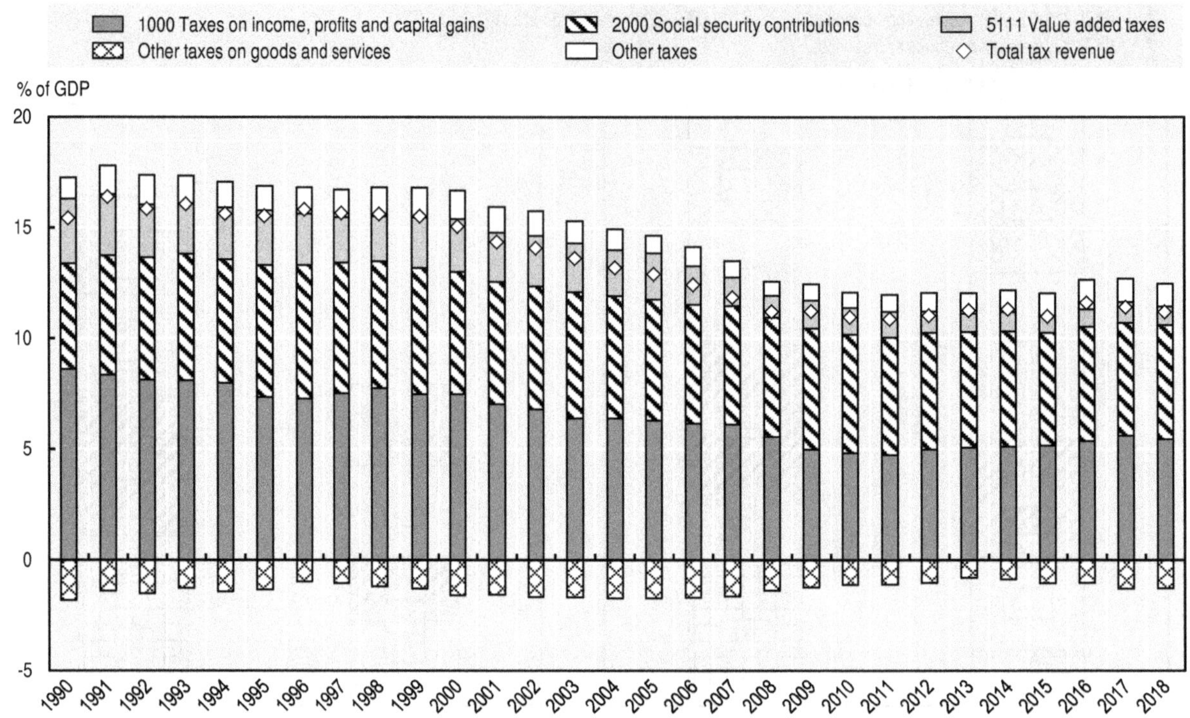

Note: Data cover 1990-2018 as the 2019 data for the OECD average are not available. The LAC average represents the group of 26 Latin American and Caribbean countries in the publication and excludes Venezuela due to data availability issues. The OECD average represents the unweighted average of the 37 OECD member countries. Chile, Colombia and Mexico are also part of the OECD (37).

Source: Authors' calculations based on OECD et al. (2021[1]), "Revenue Statistics in Latin America: Comparative tables", *OECD Tax Statistics* (database), *http://dx.doi.org/ 10.1787/data-00641-en.*

StatLink *https://doi.org/10.1787/888934234119*

Three distinct phases in the evolution of the convergence between the LAC and OECD tax structure can be distinguished:

- Between 2005 and 2007, the LAC tax structure increasingly diverged from the OECD tax structure.
- Between 2008 and 2017, the LAC tax structure converged steadily towards the OECD tax structure. LAC's share of revenue from PIT increased towards the OECD average between 2008 and 2017 (from 8.0% of total tax revenues to 9.2% in 2017 compared to 23.4% in the OECD), while the share of revenue from other taxes on goods and services decreased towards the OECD average over the same period (from 24.4% of total tax revenues to 23.1% compared to 12.6% in the OECD). In contrast, the VAT shares in the LAC region and in the OECD have grown more dissimilar over the period. LAC's share increased from 26.6% of total tax revenues in 2008 to 27.6% in 2017, while the OECD average rose more slowly, from 19.9% to 20.4% over the same period.
- The LAC tax structure diverged from the OECD's between 2017 and 2018 (the latest year available for the OECD average). This can be explained by different factors:
  - In 2018, PIT and social security contributions decreased in the LAC region (both by 0.1 percentage points) while both categories increased as a share of total tax revenues in the OECD. Moreover, the amount of income tax revenues unallocable between PIT and CIT in the LAC region increased in 2018.

- Average VAT revenues as percentage of total tax revenues in the LAC region increased by 0.4 percentage points to 28.0%, thereby moving further from the OECD average of 20.4%.

Figure 1.15. **Distance between the LAC and OECD average tax structure (D index), 2005-18**

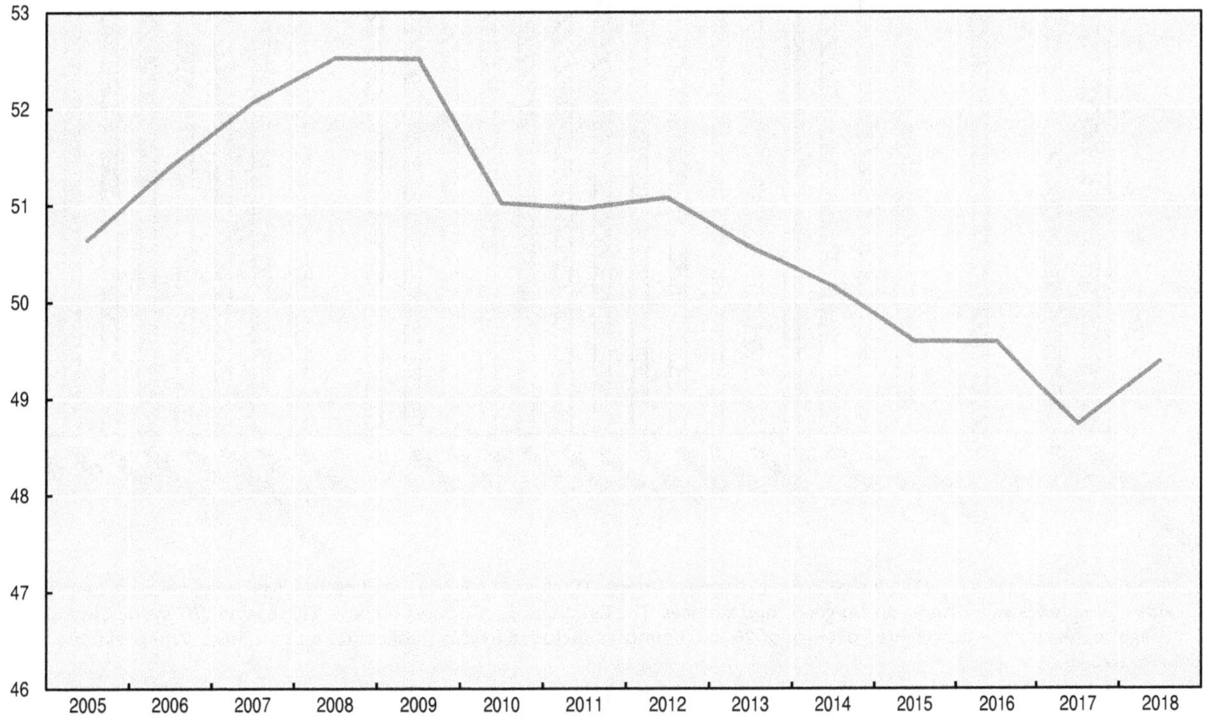

Note: The D-index is calculated as the sum of the absolute differences between the share of each tax category in the LAC average and its share in the OECD average tax mix. A figure of 0 indicates perfect similarity, whereas 200 indicates complete dissimilarity. The LAC average represents the unweighted average of 26 LAC countries included in this publication and excludes Venezuela due to data availability issues. The OECD average represents the unweighted average of the 37 OECD member countries. Chile, Colombia and Mexico are also part of the OECD (37).

Source: Authors' calculations based on OECD et al. (2021[1]), "Revenue Statistics in Latin America: Comparative tables", *OECD Tax Statistics* (database), *http://dx.doi.org/ 10.1787/data-00641-en.*

StatLink *https://doi.org/10.1787/888934234138*

Tax structures in LAC countries

Taxes on goods and services are the main source of revenue for all LAC countries except Mexico, Panama and Trinidad and Tobago. For Mexico and Trinidad and Tobago, revenue from taxes on income and profits accounted for the largest share, whereas social security contributions were the most important source of tax revenue for Panama (Figure 1.16).

In most of the countries in which revenue from taxes on goods and services are the main source of revenues, VAT revenues contributed a larger share than taxes on goods and services other than VAT, such as excises and import duties. Fifteen countries recorded higher tax revenues from VAT revenues, ranging from 22.5% of total tax revenues in Nicaragua to 39.9% in Chile, In contrast, eight countries (including five from the Caribbean) received a larger share of revenue from taxes on goods and services other than VAT. This group also includes Argentina, which sourced 27.3% of total tax revenues from revenue from taxes on goods and services other than VAT: export taxes represented just under a quarter of this category and were equivalent to 1.9% of GDP, compared to less than 0.1% of GDP in the LAC region on average.

Figure 1.16. **Tax structures in LAC countries, 2019**

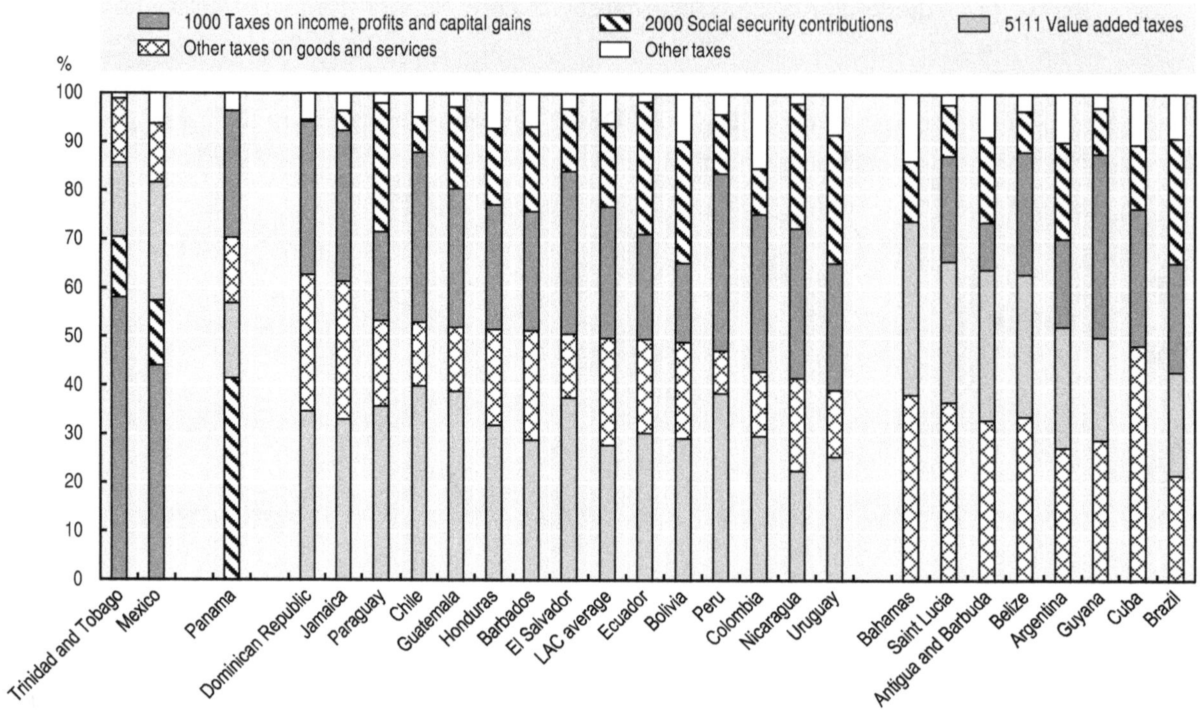

Note: Countries are grouped by the main share of tax revenues among 1000 taxes on income and profits, 2000 social security contributions, 5111 value added taxes and other taxes on goods and services. The Bahamas does not tax income. There is no VAT system in Cuba. The LAC average represents the unweighted average of 26 LAC countries included in this publication and excludes Venezuela due to data availability issues.

Source: Authors' calculations based on OECD et al. (2021[1]), Chapter 4.

StatLink https://doi.org/10.1787/888934234157

In 2019, social security contributions ranged from 0.4% of total tax revenues in the Dominican Republic to 41.5% in Panama. The level of these revenues reflects choices on how to finance social security: in countries with public or mixed social security schemes (including Argentina, Brazil, Costa Rica, Panama, Paraguay and Uruguay), social security contributions accounted for over 20% of total tax revenues.

The D-index was also used to analyse the convergence of tax structures in each LAC country with the LAC average. In 2019, the D-index was the lowest for Barbados (5.1) and Honduras (10.1), indicating that these countries are most similar to the LAC average structure, and the highest for Trinidad and Tobago, Cuba and the Bahamas (all three have a D-index over 60), indicating that these countries have the most dissimilar structures in the region.

Figure 1.17 shows the tax structure of the LAC average in comparison with LAC countries by increasing level of dissimilarity. The dissimilarity to the LAC average tax structure is explained by the absence of an income tax system in the Bahamas, by the absence of VAT and the high share of other taxes on goods and services (principally the sales tax) in Cuba and by the high share of income tax in Trinidad and Tobago.

The five Caribbean countries whose tax structures showed the greatest convergence to the LAC average between 2000 and 2019 were Antigua and Barbuda, the Bahamas, Belize, Guyana and Saint Lucia. This is explained by the introduction of VAT in those countries during the period. In 2019, VAT revenues in these countries ranged from 21.0% of total tax revenues in Guyana to 35.7% in the Bahamas. Between 2000 and 2019, tax structures have also become more similar across the LAC region as many countries have increased the share of revenues from VAT, PIT and social security contributions while decreasing the share of revenues from other taxes on goods and services.

Figure 1.17. **Tax structures in LAC countries by increasing level of dissimilarity with the LAC average, 2019**

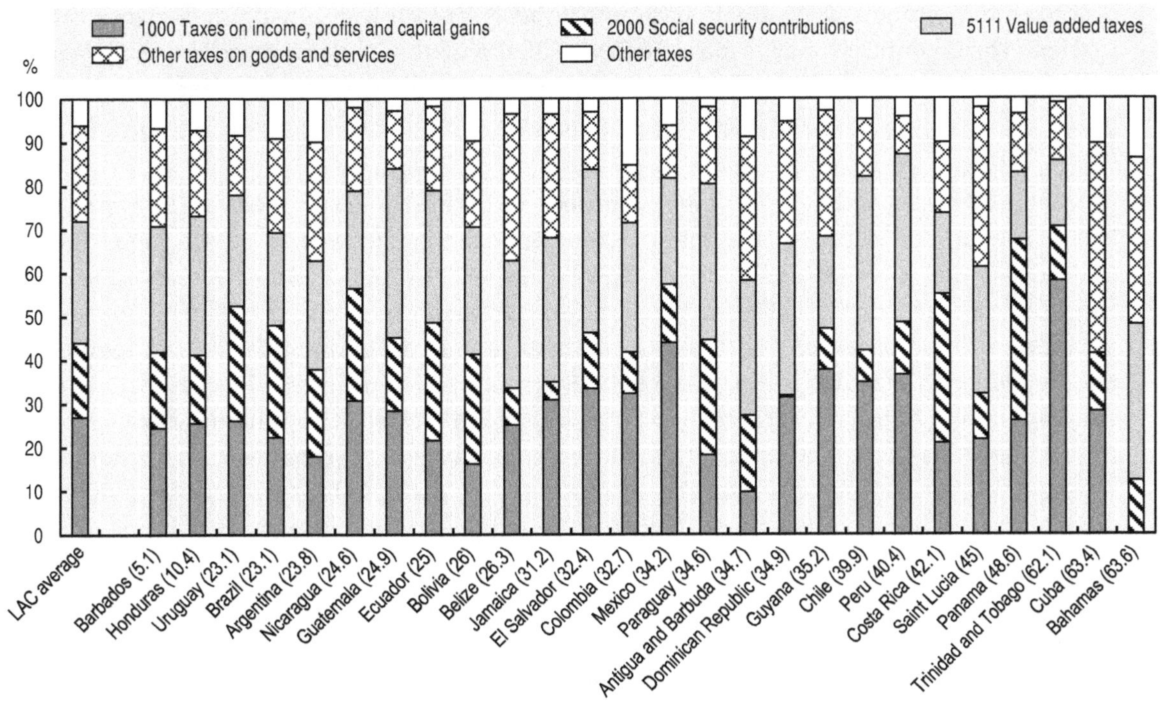

Note: The Bahamas does not tax income. There is no VAT system in Cuba. The LAC average represents the unweighted average of 26 LAC countries included in this publication and excludes Venezuela due to data availability issues. The D-index shown in brackets next to the country names show the D-index for each country. The D-index is calculated as the sum of the absolute differences between the share of each tax category in every LAC country and its share in the LAC average tax mix. A figure of 0 indicates perfect similarity, whereas 200 indicates complete dissimilarity. The LAC average represents the unweighted average of 26 LAC countries included in this publication and excludes Venezuela due to data availability issues

Source: Authors' calculations based on OECD et al. ($2021_{[1]}$), Chapter 4.

StatLink https://doi.org/10.1787/888934234176

VAT revenue ratio

This section discusses the VAT revenue ratio (VRR) in LAC countries in 2019. The VRR "measures the difference between the VAT revenue actually collected and what would theoretically be raised if VAT was applied at the standard rate to the entire potential tax base in a "pure" VAT regime and all revenue was collected" (OECD, $2020_{[29]}$). The VRR is the ratio of the actual VAT revenues to the product of final consumption (net of VAT revenues) and the standard VAT rate. The calculation is shown below.

$$\frac{\text{VAT revenues}}{(\text{final consumption expenditure} - \text{VAT revenues}).\text{standard VAT rate}}$$

This indicator provides a sense of VAT revenue loss related to exemptions and reduced rates, fraud, evasion and tax planning as well as weaknesses in tax administrations. However, this indicator needs to be interpreted with reference to the underlying characteristics of the VAT system in each country, as a higher VRR could result from cascading effects (for example when exemption occurs early in the supply chain) or from a failure to refund VAT input credits. Other factors may also influence the ratio upwards or downwards, for example when the place of taxation rules for international trade diverge from the destination principle or when the tax on inbound digital supplies is not collected. It is also important to note that the interpretation of the VRR is also more difficult for countries relying significantly on tourism. These countries may record a high VRR due to methodological reasons: purchases by non-residents may not be included in final consumption expenditure (the denominator) whereas the VAT on these purchases is included in the overall VAT revenues (the numerator) (Keen, 2013[30]).

Table 1.1 presents the VRR for LAC countries and for the three sub-regions. The highest VRR is seen in the Bahamas, and many other Caribbean countries also have a high VRR. Countries in this sub-region only introduced VAT in the 2000s, much later than countries in the other sub-regions. Their VRR partly reflect a commitment to international good practice, including a broad-based VAT with a low standard rate, a limited number of exemptions and no reduced rates. This is the case for the Bahamas, which introduced VAT in 2015 at a standard rate at 7.5% (later increased to 12.0% in July 2018). While the Bahamas had one of the highest VRRs in the LAC region, this may be in part because it receives a high share of revenue from tourism compared to other countries: receipts from international tourism as a percentage of total exports were 77% in 2018, compared to an average of 8% in the LAC region as a whole (World Bank, 2021[31]).

By contrast, the lowest VRRs were seen in the Dominican Republic, Guyana and Mexico (both below 0.35). Several factors contribute to the low VRR in Mexico, including the scope of VAT exemptions, the application of a domestic zero rate to numerous goods and services, as well as low compliance (OECD, 2020[29]; OECD, 2018[32]). However, Mexico implemented a VAT reform in January 2014 including the replacement of some reduced and zero rates with the standard rate and the introduction of improved processes. The VRR in Mexico increased from 0.28 in 2013 to 0.32 in 2014. The VRR may further increase as a result of the broadening of the VAT base for digital services in line with OECD recommendations (KPMG, 2019[33]), effective from June 2020.

A number of factors may contribute to the low VRR in the Dominican Republic. The design of VAT in the country is one factor: the Dominican Republic includes numerous VAT exemptions and suffer from low compliance (Schlotterbeck, 2017[34]). VAT evasion is another important factor for the low VRR. ECLAC (2020[11]) calculates that VAT evasion in the Dominican Republic is among the highest in the LAC region at 43.8% (2017 figure) against an average of 30% in a sample of 12 LAC countries.

VAT evasion remains an important challenge in the LAC region. ECLAC (2020[11]) examined various studies on VAT evasion in 12 countries and observed that VAT non-compliance rates in the region ranged from 14.8% in Uruguay to 45.3% in Panama in 2016. Guatemala, the Dominican Republic and Panama recorded the highest increases (by 30% of more) in their VAT evasion rate since 2009.

Table 1.1. **VRR and VAT rates in LAC countries by region, 2019**

	VRR	VAT rate (%)
Central America and Mexico	**0.47**	**13.6**
Costa Rica	0.45	13.0
Dominican Republic	0.35	18.0
El Salvador	0.66	13.0
Guatemala	0.46	12.0
Honduras	0.54	15.0
Mexico	0.33	16.0
Nicaragua	0.47	15.0
Panama	0.51	7.0
South America	**0.57**	**16.8**
Argentina	0.46	21.0
Bolivia	0.70	13.0
Chile	0.63	19.0
Colombia	0.39	19.0
Ecuador	0.74	12.0
Paraguay	0.71	10.0
Peru	0.50	18.0
Uruguay	0.45	22.0
Caribbean	**0.64**	**14.4**
Antigua and Barbuda	0.63	15.0
Bahamas	0.82	12.0
Barbados	0.68	17.5
Belize	0.99	12.5
Guyana	0.28	14.0
Jamaica	0.71	16.5
Saint Lucia	0.64	15.0
Trinidad and Tobago	0.35	12.5
LAC average	**0.56**	**14.9**
OECD average (2018)	**0.56**	**19.3**

Note: Brazil, Cuba and Venezuela are excluded. Brazil operates a multiple-rate system with tax levied at different rates for each sub-national level. Cuba did not operate a VAT system in 2019. Venezuela tax revenue data are not available in 2019.
Source: VAT rates are sourced from the CIAT, Trading Economics and Deloitte websites, the final expenditure consumption figures from the United Nations Statistics Division website and VAT revenues from the country tables in OECD et al. (2021[1]), Chapter 5. OECD (2020[29]) for the OECD figures.

StatLink https://doi.org/10.1787/888934234632

Environmental tax revenues

Through the Paris Agreement of 2016, countries have committed to decarbonise their economies by mid-century, implying a shift away from fossil fuels as a source of energy. Environmentally related taxes, and price-based policy instruments more generally, play an increasingly significant role in many countries. By incorporating a price signal into consumer decisions, these taxes give effect to the polluter-pays principle and encourage businesses and households to consider the environmental costs of their behaviour.

An environmentally related tax is a tax whose base is a physical unit (or a proxy of a physical unit) of something that has a proven, specific harmful impact on the environment regardless of whether the tax is intended to change behaviours or is levied for another purpose (OECD, 2005[35]).

A detailed examination of country-specific taxes[6] for 25 LAC countries in this report demonstrates that, on average, revenue from environmentally related taxes amounted to 1.2%[7] of GDP in 2019, a lower level than the OECD average of 2.1% of GDP (estimated 2019 figure) (OECD, 2021[36]). However as a percentage of total tax revenues, environmentally related tax revenues (ERTR) were at similar levels in the LAC region and the OECD [5.7% and 6.4% (estimated) in 2019 respectively] (OECD, 2021[36]).

In 2019, revenues from energy taxes (most commonly from diesel and petrol) generated the highest share of total environmentally related tax revenue in the LAC region. Revenues from energy products amounted to 0.7% of GDP on average in 2019 and represented around 65% of environmentally related tax revenue. Revenues from motor vehicle and transport services tax revenue amounted to 0.4% of GDP and represented most of the remainder (35%) of environmentally related tax revenue. Revenues from tax levied on other environmentally related bases were negligible. Environmentally related tax revenues for the OECD were higher than the LAC region across the different bases, notably for energy and transport related taxes (OECD, 2021[36]). The OECD averages for energy and transport related tax revenues in 2019 amounted to 1.5% and 0.5% of GDP respectively.

There were notable differences in the composition of environmentally related tax revenues across the sub-regions in 2019, on average (Figure 1.18). While energy-related tax revenues represented the highest share of environmentally related tax revenues in Central America and Mexico and South America in 2019, in the Caribbean the largest share of environmentally related tax revenues was derived from transport taxes. Transport-related taxes in Central America and Mexico and in South America were at 0.3% of GDP in both sub-regions, approximately half the amount in the Caribbean. Transport-related tax revenues for most Caribbean countries were mainly sourced from travel or departure taxes, an important source of revenues for countries reliant on tourism.

Figure 1.18. **Environmentally related tax revenue for the OECD, LAC and sub-region averages by main tax base, 2019**

Percentage of GDP

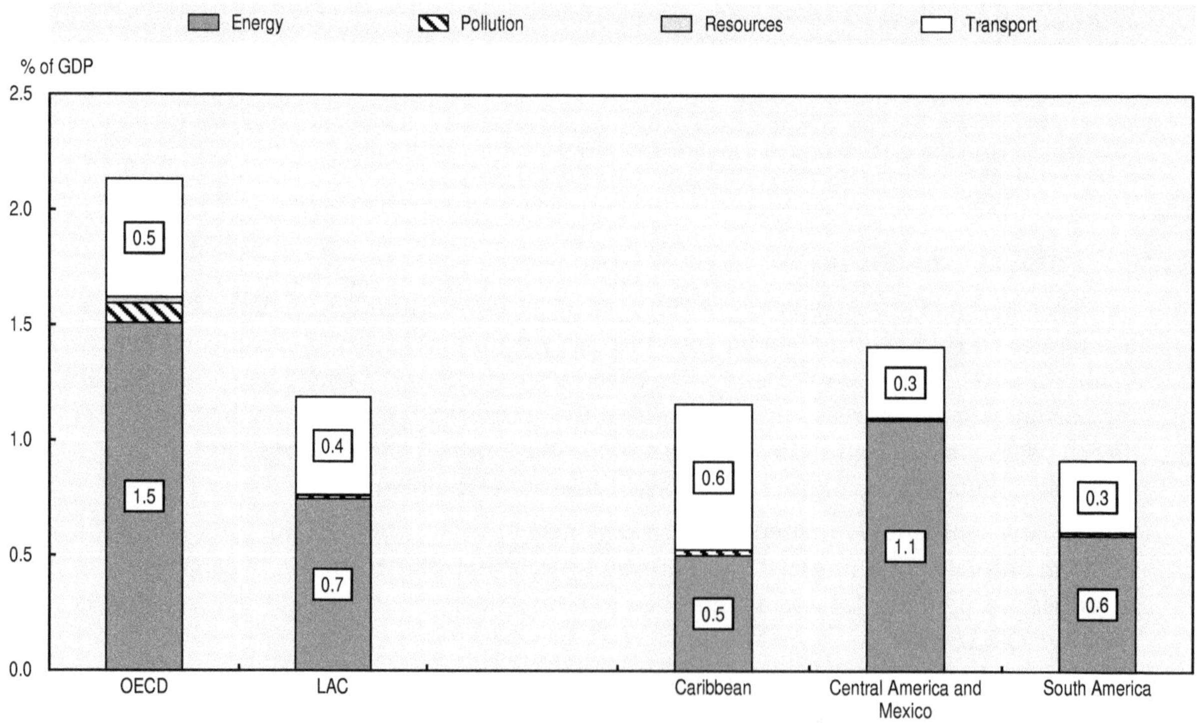

Note: The LAC average represents the unweighted average of 25 LAC countries included in this publication and excludes Cuba and Venezuela due to data availability issues. The OECD average represents the unweighted average of the 37 OECD member countries. Chile, Colombia and Mexico are also part of the OECD (37).

Source: PINE database for Chile and Mexico, and authors' calculations for other countries based on OECD et al. (2021[1]), Chapter 5.

StatLink https://doi.org/10.1787/888934234195

Environmentally related tax revenue in 2019 ranged from 0.1% of GDP in Belize to 4.0% in Guyana (Figure 1.19). In Guyana, the tax on the import of petroleum products alone represented 2.7% of GDP in 2019.

Figure 1.19. **Environmentally related tax revenue in LAC countries by main tax base, 2019**

Percentage of GDP

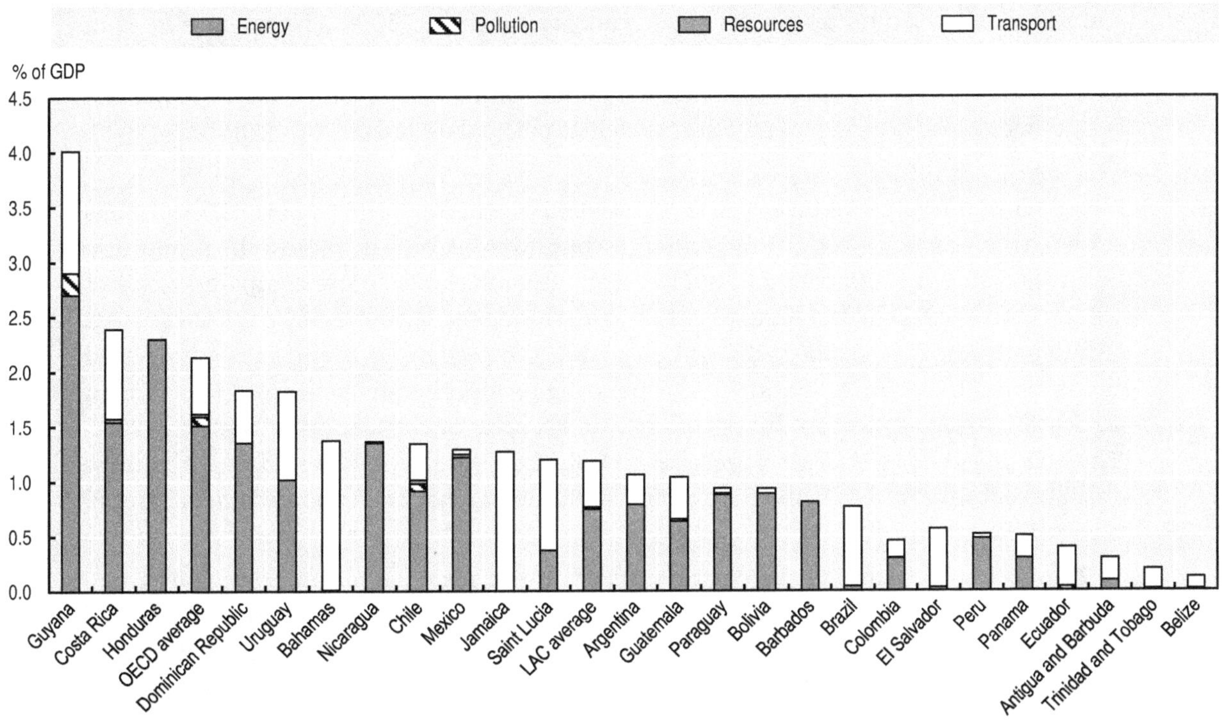

Note: The LAC average represents the unweighted average of 25 LAC countries included in this publication and excludes Cuba and Venezuela due to data availability issues. The figure does not include Jamaica's revenues from the special consumption tax on petroleum products (estimated to be more than 2.0% of GDP in 2018) (OECD, 2021[37]) as the data are not available. The OECD average represents the unweighted average of the 37 OECD member countries. Chile, Colombia and Mexico are also part of the OECD (37).

Source: PINE database for Chile and Mexico, and authors' calculations for other countries based on OECD et al. (2021[1]), Chapter 5.

StatLink https://doi.org/10.1787/888934234214

In 2019, taxes on energy were predominantly raised from excises. By contrast, revenues from motor vehicles and transport-services taxes were sourced from three different types of taxes according to the OECD classification set out in the Interpretative Guide: around half came from taxes on use and ownership of vehicles, a quarter came from taxes on specific services (mainly travel or departure tax) and another quarter from excises on vehicles.

LAC countries have been slow to implement environmentally related taxes. Although they have introduced fuel taxes (mainly for revenue collection rather than environmental purposes), many countries also provide subsidies for energy products (Lorenzo, 2016[38]) in order to mitigate the impact of high and volatile petroleum prices, control inflation, boost competitiveness and protect the poorest sections of the population. Energy subsidies can put a strain on national budgets. However, energy tax revenues were greater than the cost of subsidies for 5 of the 6 LAC countries included in the a recent OECD report (OECD, 2021[37]) (Costa Rica, Dominican Republic, Guatemala, Jamaica and Uruguay, with the exception being Ecuador), representing on average a net positive impact on public finances in these six countries (roughly 0.6% of GDP in 2018 on average).

Beyond taxes on fuel and the registration or use of vehicles, environmental taxes are still underdeveloped across the LAC region. However, a few LAC countries have introduced significant green tax reforms, including Chile, Mexico and Colombia.

- In Chile, a major tax reform including new environmentally related taxes was approved in 2014 (OECD/UN ECLAC, 2016[39]). This included a tax on purchases of motor vehicles, which was introduced in 2015 based on energy efficiency and emissions of vehicles. Chile introduced a carbon tax as part of new green taxes (Law 20.780) that came into force in 2017. A uniform rate of USD 5 per tonne of CO_2 applies to CO_2 emissions for facilities of which the total thermal power capacity of boilers and turbines is at least 50 MWt. The green taxes are also levied on pollutants such as particulate matter, NO_X, and SO_2 (OECD, 2019[40]).
- Mexico introduced a carbon tax in 2014, applied on the sale and import of fossil fuels (except for natural gas) according to their carbon content. This increased the proportion of emissions that was taxed, although prices remain relatively low compared to other OECD countries and do not reflect the full costs associated with the carbon in these fuels (Arlinghaus and Van Dender, 2017[41]). However, the carbon tax significantly increased tax revenues between 2014 and 2015, generating revenues equivalent to 1.2% of GDP in 2015 (OECD, 2021[36]). Mexico further increased tax rates on different fossils fuels in 2016. The IEPS (*Impuesto Especial sobre Producción y Servicios*) – Mexico's excise tax to automotive gasoline, automotive diesel and their biofuel equivalents – has been updated and increased on a regular basis.
- In 2016, Colombia introduced a carbon tax and an excise tax on plastic bags. The carbon tax is levied on fossil fuels according to the amount of carbon produced by fossil fuel combustion at the price of USD 5 per tonne. Revenues are allocated to a special fund to address specific environmental issues, including coastal erosion, conservation of water sources and ecosystem protection (Monge, 2018[42]).

Effective Carbon Rates (OECD, 2021 forthcoming[43]) provides an overview of carbon prices for all energy-related emissions in 44 OECD and G20 countries including Argentina, Brazil, Chile and Mexico. *Taxing Energy Use* (OECD, 2019[40]) contains detailed information on tax rates, energy use and the base they apply to for the same set of countries.

Taxes by level of government

In LAC countries, tax revenues are collected predominantly by central or federal entities; sub-national public spending is financed through transfers from upper to lower levels of government to a greater extent than is the case in OECD countries. Where sub-national data for LAC countries is available, it indicates that tax revenues collected by central government accounted for more than two-thirds of the total collected in general, whereas the corresponding figure for OECD countries was about 60% (2018 figure). Brazil is a notable exception: central government tax revenue amounted to 43.5% of tax collected in 2019[8] (Table 1.2).

There are two statistical issues to consider when comparing the attribution of revenues for LAC countries with that of OECD members. First, revenues of both groups have been attributed to different levels of government according to guidelines set out in the 2008 System of National Accounts (SNA).[9] The second issue is that some LAC countries lack tax revenue statistics at sub-national level.

For the 19 LAC countries for which sub-national data is available (2018 data are used for Mexico), the share of sub-national tax revenues in total tax revenue was below 9.0%

in 2019 except in Argentina, Brazil and Colombia. In Brazil, states and municipalities collect about 31% of total tax revenues, indicating a significant degree of decentralisation of tax collection. A large part of the VAT (ICMS – *imposto sobre operações relativas à circulação de mercadorias e prestação de serviços de transporte interestadual e intermunicipal e de comunicação*) is collected at the state level. Sub-national tax revenue in Argentina and Colombia account for more than 15% of total tax revenue. Argentina has a significant collection at state level, which is explained in part by the provincial sales tax (*impuesto sobre los ingresos brutos*).

Table 1.2. **Attribution of tax revenue to sub-sectors of general government in LAC countries[1]**

Percentage of total tax revenue

	Central government			State or regional government			Local government			Social security funds		
	1995	2000	2019	1995	2000	2019	1995	2000	2019	1995	2000	2019
Federal countries												
Argentina	59.0	66.4	63.1	17.5	17.8	16.9	..	..	..	23.4	15.8	19.9
Brazil	44.8	47.9	43.5	26.5	25.0	24.6	3.7	3.4	6.2	25.0	23.7	25.7
Mexico[3]	73.9	78.3	80.9	2.8	2.7	4.0	1.5	1.0	1.6	21.8	18.0	13.4
Venezuela[4]	94.6	94.6	..	..	..	..	..	..	..	5.4	5.4	..
Regional countries												
Colombia[5]	63.2	68.7	73.0	5.5	5.6	5.0	8.6	9.4	12.5	22.7	16.3	9.5
Unitary countries												
Antigua and Barbuda[2]	100.0	100.0	82.4				..	..	..	..	..	17.6
Bahamas[2]	89.1	88.1	87.6				..	..	..	10.9	11.9	12.4
Barbados	85.6	84.4	82.5				..	..	..	14.4	15.6	17.5
Belize	93.2	93.5	91.1				0.5	0.7	0.5	6.3	5.8	8.4
Bolivia	94.3	75.6	70.3				5.7	5.5	4.6	..	18.9	25.1
Chile	89.9	87.8	85.7				6.5	7.9	8.2	3.6	4.4	6.1
Costa Rica	65.5	63.3	57.8				1.6	1.9	3.0	33.0	34.8	39.2
Cuba[6]	..	..	..	..	..	..	..	..	..	11.3	10.4	13.2
Dominican Republic	99.3	99.0	99.6				..	..	..	0.7	1.0	0.4
Ecuador[2]	70.5	87.7	70.2				4.0	1.6	2.6	25.5	10.7	27.1
El Salvador	80.9	80.5	85.2				..	..	1.9	19.1	19.5	12.8
Guatemala	83.3	83.6	82.3				0.7	0.9	0.9	16.1	15.5	16.8
Guyana	92.6	88.6	90.5				..	..	0.0	7.4	11.4	9.5
Honduras	86.1	85.3	80.5				4.4	5.2	3.9	9.5	9.4	15.6
Jamaica	100.0	99.3	94.4				..	0.7	1.5	..	..	4.1
Nicaragua	80.4	72.5	68.3				4.6	9.5	6.0	15.0	18.0	25.7
Panama	67.2	59.6	56.9				..	2.2	1.6	32.8	38.2	41.5
Paraguay	92.0	74.4	70.9				..	..	2.7	8.0	25.6	26.4
Peru	88.7	86.5	85.3				..	1.6	2.7	11.3	11.9	12.1
Saint Lucia[2]	100.0	90.0	89.5				..	..	..	..	10.0	10.5
Trinidad and Tobago[2]	96.8	93.6	87.6				..	..	..	3.2	6.4	12.4
Uruguay	61.7	63.6	67.9				8.8	8.9	5.7	29.5	27.5	26.4

1. The figures exclude local government revenues for Antigua and Barbuda, Argentina (but include provincial revenues), the Bahamas, Barbados, Cuba, the Dominican Republic, Saint Lucia, Trinidad and Tobago and Venezuela as the data are not available. Local government revenue data have been available since 1991 for Nicaragua, since 1994 for Bolivia, since 1995 for Guatemala, since 1998 for Jamaica, since 1999 for Panama, since 2000 for Peru, since 2002 for El Salvador and Guyana, since 2006 for Paraguay and since 1990 for all other countries.
2. The data include the following estimations: Antigua and Barbuda (social security contributions for 2019), Bahamas (social security contributions for 2018 and 2019), Ecuador (local tax revenues for 2019), Saint Lucia (social security contributions for 2018 and 2019) and Trinidad and Tobago (social security contributions for 2019). See the corresponding country tables for more information.
3. Data for 2018 are used as Mexico's state and local tax revenues for 2019 are not available.
4. Some tax revenue data between 2014 and 2017 and all data for 2018 and 2019 are not available. The breakdown by sub-sectors of general government is not available for those years.
5. Colombia is constitutionally a unitary country with high autonomy of its territorial entities.
6. Data for sub-sectors of general government in Cuba are only available between 2002 and 2012.

Source: OECD et al. (2021[1]), Table 4.11.

StatLink https://doi.org/10.1787/888934234651

These figures reflect the fact that sub-national governments in LAC countries tend to have a relatively narrow range of taxes under their jurisdiction. The taxes most frequently assigned to sub-national entities are property taxes, motor-vehicle licenses, taxes on specific services and municipal fees. The revenue-generation potential of these instruments is relatively limited compared with the tax bases under central jurisdiction, such as VAT and income taxes. The COVID-19 crisis highlights pending structural reforms to improve the collection and the sources of revenues at the sub-national level. These include improvements in the information and statistics regarding the revenues of these taxes, the administrative capacity to collect at the local level, the effective co-ordination with national authorities, and the need to promote sustainable and stable sources of tax revenues at the sub-national level) (Nieto-Parra and Orozco, 2020[44]).

In 2019, the entire subnational tax revenue in Belize, Guatemala and Jamaica, and more than 50% of tax revenue collected at the sub-national level in Peru, Uruguay, Ecuador and Paraguay, was sourced from property taxes (Figure 1.20). All other countries rely principally on revenues from taxes on goods and services. Mexico is the only country that also collected revenue from different tax bases. In 2018 (latest available data for Mexico assumed unchanged for 2019), 43% of sub-national tax revenue in Mexico came from payroll taxes. In OECD countries, sub-national entities tend to have much broader potential tax bases. A substantial proportion of revenue collection by sub-national governments in OECD countries is through income taxes and profits (representing more than a third of the total collected at sub-national level on average).

Figure 1.20. **Tax mix of sub-national tax revenue in LAC countries, 2019**

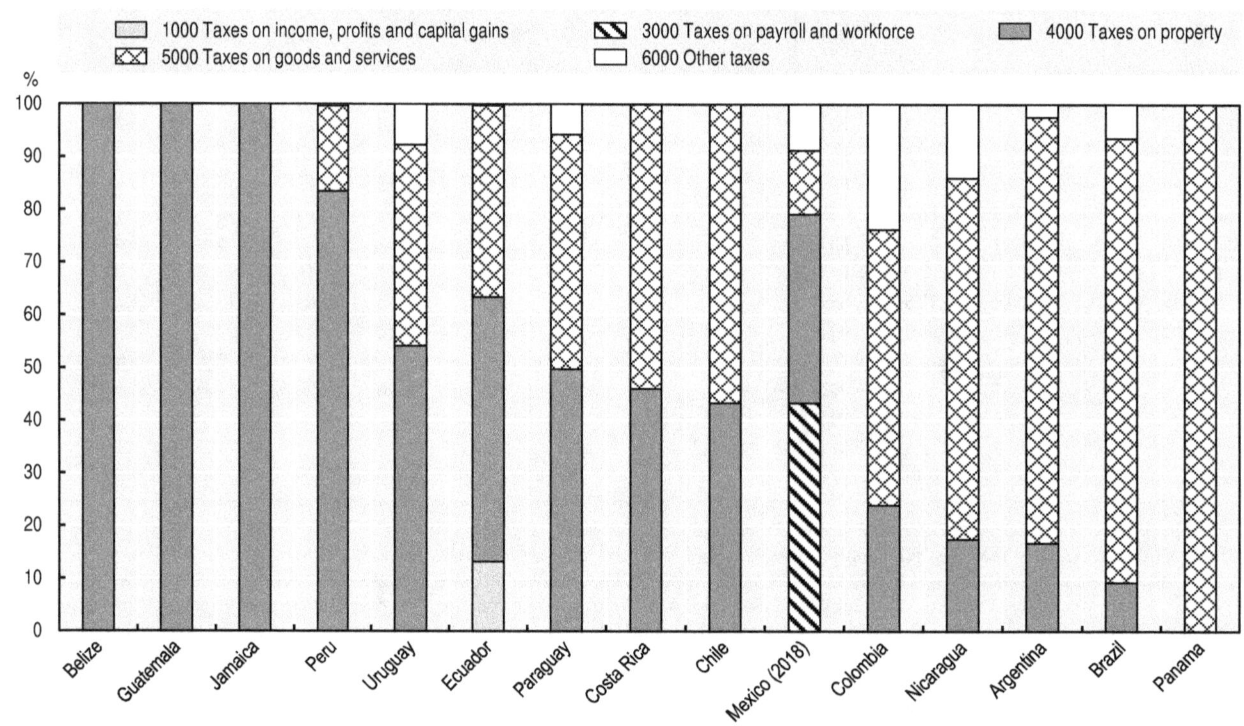

Note: 2018 data for Mexico. The figures for Antigua and Barbuda, Bahamas, Barbados, Bolivia, Cuba, Dominican Republic, El Salvador, Guyana, Honduras, Saint Lucia, Trinidad and Tobago and Venezuela are excluded as either the sub-national tax revenue data or the breakdown of sub-national tax revenue data by the main type of tax category are not available. The figures exclude local government revenues for Argentina (but include provincial revenues).

Source: Authors' calculations based on OECD et al. (2021[1]), Chapter 6.

StatLink https://doi.org/10.1787/888934234233

Low tax revenues at the sub-national level in LAC countries may result from a lack of administrative and technical capacity, in particular regarding property taxes. Property taxes – a common source of sub-national revenue – require sophisticated systems and information and the collection of this revenue is expensive. In addition, appropriate property registers are lacking in many countries; where they exist, they are rarely updated (Canavire-Bacarreza, Martínez-Vázquez and Sepúlveda, 2012[45]; OECD et al., 2019[46]). As a result, tax authorities have minimal access to accurate valuations of lands and buildings and real estate registries are often reluctant to share this information. Property tax also suffers from a high level of informality: buildings are constructed without permits, properties are not registered and reported prices of some real estate transactions are falsified. As property tax is one of the most controversial taxes with citizens and has high political costs, local politicians are often unwilling to invest the appropriate resources to levy this revenue.

Notes

1. The figure is provisional and has been calculated by applying the unweighted average percentage change for 2019 in the 35 countries providing data for that year to the overall average tax-to-GDP ratio in 2018.
2. The Caribbean average includes eight countries (Antigua and Barbuda, the Bahamas, Barbados, Belize, Guyana, Jamaica, Saint Lucia and Trinidad and Tobago), Central America and Mexico, nine countries (Costa Rica, Cuba, Dominican Republic, El Salvador, Guatemala, Honduras, Mexico, Nicaragua and Panama), and South America, nine countries (Argentina, Bolivia, Brazil, Chile, Colombia, Ecuador, Paraguay, Peru and Uruguay).
3. VAT was introduced in 1991 for Jamaica, 1997 for Barbados, 2006 for Belize (the General Sales Tax), 2007 for Guyana and Antigua and Barbuda, 2012 for Saint Lucia and 2015 for the Bahamas.
4. The year of comparison is 2018 as the 2019 data for the OECD average are not available.
5. The D-index was used in *Revenue Statistics 2018* to analyse the convergence of tax structures in OECD countries between 1995 and 2016 (OECD, 2018[47]).
6. Although environmentally related tax revenues are not separately identified in the standard OECD classification of tax revenues, they can be identified through the detailed list of specific taxes included for most countries within this overarching classification. It is on this basis that they are included in the OECD Policy Instruments for the Environment (PINE) database (OECD, 2021[36]). In 2019, the OECD started the collection of Environmentally Related Tax Revenue accounts in line with the System of Environmental and Economic Accounting and ERTR accounts are disaggregated by industries and households (OECD, 2021[48]).
7. Unweighted average of 37 OECD countries.
8. The year of comparison is 2018 as the 2019 data for Mexico are not available.
9. This means that revenues are generally attributed to the level of government that exercises the authority to impose the tax or has the final discretion to set and vary the tax rate. This has implications for situations where one level of government collects tax revenues and transfers them in whole or in part to other levels. Regional examples of this type of mechanism are the Co-participation Law in Argentina, federal participations in Mexico (mandated in the Fiscal Co-ordination Law) and participation funds in Brazil (defined in Article 159 of the Constitution).

References

Arlinghaus, J. and K. van Dender (2017), “The environmental tax and subsidy reform in Mexico”, *OECD Taxation Working Papers*, No. 31, OECD Publishing, Paris, *https://dx.doi.org/10.1787/a9204f40-en.* [41]

Barreix, A., J. Benítez and M. Pecho (2017), “Revisiting personal income tax in Latin America: Evolution and impact”, *OECD Development Centre Working Papers*, No. 338, OECD Publishing, Paris, *https://dx.doi.org/10.1787/16d42b4a-en.* [22]

Barrow, D. (2020), *Budget Speech for Fiscal Year 2020/2021*, Government of Belize, *http://caribbeanelections.com/eDocs/budget/bz_budget/bz_budget_2020.pdf.* [9]

Canavire-Bacarreza, G., J. Martínez-Vázquez and C. Sepúlveda (2012), *Sub-national Revenue Mobilization in Peru, IDB Working Paper Series No. 299*, IDB, *https://publications.iadb.org/en/sub-national-revenue-mobilization-peru.* [45]

CDB (2020), *Fact Sheet - 2019 Caribbean Economic Review and 2020 Outlook*, Caribbean Development Bank, *https://issuu.com/caribank/docs/cdb_fact_sheet_2019_economic_review_and_2020_outlo.* [6]

CentralAmericaData (2020), *Tax Reform in Nicaragua*, *https://webmail.centralamericadata.com/en/search?q1=content_en_le:%22tax+reform%22&q2=mattersInCountry_es_le:%22Nicaragua%22.* [8]

ECLAC (2021), *Preliminary Overview of the Economies of Latin America and the Caribbean 2020*, Economic Commission for Latin America and the Caribbean, Santiago, *https://www.cepal.org/en/publications/type/preliminary-overview-economies-latin-america-and-caribbean.* [4]

ECLAC (2020), *Fiscal Panorama of Latin America and the Caribbean 2020: Fiscal policy amid the crisis arising from the coronavirus disease (COVID-19) pandemic*, Economic Commission for Latin America and the Caribbean, *https://repositorio.cepal.org/handle/11362/45731.* [11]

ECLAC (2019), *Preliminary Overview of the Economies of Latin America and the Caribbean, 2018*, (LC/PUB.2019/1-P), Santiago, *https://repositorio.cepal.org/bitstream/handle/11362/44327/135/S1801218_en.pdf.* [2]

ECLAC (2018), *The Fiscal Panorama of Latin America and the Caribbean*, United Nations, *https://www.cepal.org/en/publications/43406-fiscal-panorama-latin-america-and-caribbean-2018-public-policy-challenges.* [18]

ECLAC (2014), *Tax policy in Latin America: Assessment and guidelines for a second generation of reforms*, United Nations, *https://repositorio.cepal.org/handle/11362/36806.* [21]

ECLAC (2013), *Fiscal Panorama of Latin America and the Caribbean: tax reform and renewal of the fiscal covenant*, United Nations, *https://www.cepal.org/en/publications/3101-fiscal-panorama-latin-america-and-caribbean-2013-tax-reform-and-renewal-fiscal.* [20]

EY (2019), *Argentina establishes temporary duties on export of services*, Ernst & Young, *https://www.ey.com/en_gl/tax-alerts/argentina-establishes-temporary-duties-on-export-of-services.* [12]

IDB (2019), *Building Opportunities to Grow in a Challenging-World*, *http://dx.doi.org/10.18235/0001633.* [10]

IDB (2013), *More than revenues, Taxation as a development tool*, Inter-American Development Bank. [19]

IMF (2020), *World Economic Outlook Database (October)*, International Monetary Fund, Washington, D.C., *https://www.imf.org/en/Publications/WEO/weo-database/2020/October.* [24]

IMF (2019), *Barbados: 2019 Article IV Consultation*, International Monetary Fund, Washington, D.C., *https://www.imf.org/en/Publications/CR/Issues/2019/12/18/Barbados-2019-Article-IV-Consultation-Second-Review-Under-the-Extended-Arrangement-Request-48886.* [14]

ITR (2020), *Argentina: Argentina introduces major tax reform*, International Tax Review, *https://www.internationaltaxreview.com/article/b1k41n6smqd3jy/argentina-argentina-introduces-major-tax-reform.* [13]

Keen, M. (2013), *The anatomy of VAT, WP/13/111*, IMF, *https://www.imf.org/en/Publications/WP/Issues/2016/12/31/The-Anatomy-of-the-VAT-40543.* [30]

KPMG (2019), *Mexico: Tax reform 2020, VAT on services provided from digital platforms*, *https://home.kpmg/us/en/home/insights/2019/11/tnf-mexico-tax-reform-2020-vat-services-digital-platforms.html.* [33]

Lorenzo, F. (2016), *Inventario de instrumentos fiscales verdes en América Latina*, CEPAL, *https://agua.org.mx/biblioteca/inventario-instrumentos-fiscales-verdes-en-america-latina-experiencias-efectos-alcances/.* [38]

Melguizo, A. et al. (2017), *No sympathy for the devil! Policy priorities to overcome the middle-income trap in Latin America, OECD Development Centre Working Papers, No. 340*, OECD Publishing, Paris, *http://dx.doi.org/10.1787/26b78724-en.* [23]

Monge, C. (2018), *Colombia Puts a Tax on Carbon*, *https://www.conservationfinancenetwork.org/2018/11/27/colombia-puts-tax-on-carbon.* [42]

Nieto-Parra, S. and R. Orozco (2020), *Potencializar los impuestos subnacionales en América Latina y el Caribe en tiempos del Covid-19 in Los desafíos de las finanzas intergubernamentales ante el Covid-19*, AIFIL - Asociación Iberoamericana de Financiación, *https://www.aifil-jifl.org/wp-content/uploads/2020/11/AIFIL-2.11.pdf.* [44]

OECD (2021), *Environmental policy: Environmentally related tax revenue accounts, OECD Environment Statistics (database)*, *https://stats.oecd.org/Index.aspx?DataSetCode=ERTR_ACC.* [48]

OECD (2021), *PINE database*, OECD Publishing, Paris, *http://www.oecd.org/environment/tools-evaluation/environmentaltaxation.htm.* [36]

OECD (2021), *Taxing Energy Use for Sustainable Development*, OECD Publishing, Paris, *https://www.oecd.org/tax/tax-policy/taxing-energy-use-for-sustainable-development.htm*. [37]

OECD (2020), "COVID-19 in Latin America and the Caribbean: Regional socio-economic implications and policy priorities", *OECD Policy Responses to Coronavirus (COVID-19)*, *https://www.oecd.org/coronavirus/policy-responses/covid-19-in-latin-america-and-the-caribbean-regional-socio-economic-implications-and-policy-priorities-93a64fde/*. [5]

OECD (2020), *Harmful Tax Practices: peer review results on preferential regimes.*, OECD Publishing, Paris, *https://www.oecd.org/tax/beps/harmful-tax-practices-peer-review-results-on-preferential-regimes.pdf*. [15]

OECD (2020), *Consumption Tax Trends 2020: VAT/GST and Excise Rates, Trends and Policy Issues*, OECD Publishing, Paris, *https://doi.org/10.1787/152def2d-en*. [29]

OECD (2019), *Tax Morale: What Drives People and Businesses to Pay Tax?*, OECD Publishing, Paris, *https://doi.org/10.1787/f3d8ea10-en*. [25]

OECD (2019), *Taxing Energy Use 2019: Using Taxes for Climate Action*, OECD Publishing, Paris, *https://doi.org/10.1787/058ca239-en*. [40]

OECD (2018), *Consumption Tax Trends 2018: VAT/GST and Excise Rates, Trends and Policy Issues*, OECD Publishing, Paris, *https://doi.org/10.1787/ctt-2018-en*. [32]

OECD (2018), *Revenue Statistics 2018*, OECD Publishing, Paris, *https://doi.org/10.1787/rev_stats-2018-en*. [47]

OECD (2014), *Development Co-operation Report 2014: Mobilising Resources for Sustainable Development*, OECD Publishing, Paris, *https://dx.doi.org/10.1787/dcr-2014-en*. [26]

OECD (2005), *Glossary of statistical terms*, *https://stats.oecd.org/glossary/detail.asp?ID=6437*. [35]

OECD (2021 forthcoming), *Effective Carbon Rates 2021: Pricing Carbon Emissions through Taxes and Emissions Trading*, OECD Publishing, Paris, *https://doi.org/10.1787/0e8e24f5-en*. [43]

OECD et al. (2021), *Revenue Statistics in Latin America and the Caribbean 2021*, OECD Publishing, Paris, *https://doi.org/10.1787/96ce5287-en-es*. [1]

OECD et al. (2019), *Revenue Statistics in Latin America and the Caribbean*, OECD Publishing, Paris, *https://doi.org/10.1787/25666b8d-en-es*. [46]

OECD/CAF/UN ECLAC (2018), *Latin American Economic Outlook 2018: Rethinking Institutions for Development*, OECD Publishing, Paris, *https://dx.doi.org/10.1787/leo-2018-en*. [3]

OECD et al. (2015), *Revenue Statistics in Latin America and the Caribbean 2015*, OECD Publishing, Paris, *https://dx.doi.org/10.1787/rev_lat-2015-en-fr*. [27]

OECD et al. (2019), *Latin American Economic Outlook 2019: Development in Transition*, OECD Publishing, Paris, *https://doi.org/10.1787/g2g9ff18-en*. [16]

OECD et al. (2020), *Latin American Economic Outlook 2020: Digital Transformation for Building Back Better*, OECD Publishing, Paris, *https://doi.org/10.1787/e6e864fb-en*. [17]

OECD/IDB/The World Bank (2014), *Pensions at a Glance: Latin America and the Caribbean*, OECD Publishing, Paris, *https://dx.doi.org/10.1787/pension_glance-2014-en*. [28]

OECD/UN ECLAC (2016), *OECD Environmental Performance Reviews: Chile 2016*, OECD Environmental Performance Reviews, OECD Publishing, Paris, *https://dx.doi.org/10.1787/9789264252615-en*. [39]

Orbitax (2019), *Nicaragua 2019 Tax Reform Measures*, *https://www.orbitax.com/news/archive.php/Nicaragua-2019-Tax-Reform-Meas-37133*. [7]

Schlotterbeck, S. (2017), *Tax Administration Reforms in the Caribbean, "Challenges, Achievements, and Next Steps"*. [34]

World Bank (2021), *International tourism, receipts (% of total exports)*, *https://data.worldbank.org/indicator/ST.INT.RCPT.XP.ZS*. [31]

Capítulo 1

Tendencias tributarias, 1990-2019

El financiamiento de la agenda de desarrollo de América Latina y el Caribe y el logro de los Objetivos de Desarrollo Sostenible (ODS) exigen cambios significativos en la movilización de los recursos nacionales. La actual crisis del COVID-19 ha intensificado aún más la necesidad de los países de América Latina y el Caribe de incrementar la recaudación tributaria para hacer frente a las debilidades estructurales de sus sistemas fiscales, de protección social y de salud. La región ya se enfrentaba al reto de un amplio malestar social y un crecimiento débil cuando se inició la crisis del COVID-19. A pesar de que los países reaccionaron rápidamente mediante la puesta en práctica de medidas sanitarias y fiscales, en respuesta a la crisis, para apoyar a los hogares y empresas más vulnerables, sus esfuerzos se vieron obstaculizados por altos niveles de informalidad, sistemas de protección social poco desarrollados y un espacio tributario limitado (véase el capítulo 2). Una vez que la región salga de la pandemia del COVID, será necesario, bajo una secuencia de políticas bien definida, reformar las políticas tributarias y fortalecer los sistemas fiscales para apoyar la recuperación económica inclusiva y garantizar una posición fiscal sostenible y justa a mediano y largo plazo.

Una vez que la crisis del COVID-19 quede en el pasado, la política fiscal debe desempeñar un papel importante como catalizador inclusivo que estimule el crecimiento económico en la región. A largo plazo, niveles más altos de ingresos también serán un aspecto crucial para hacer frente a las necesidades urgentes de los ciudadanos en toda la región y mejorar la equidad a través del suministro de bienes públicos, con el objetivo de reducir los altos niveles de vulnerabilidad, en particular en el mercado laboral, y mejorar los sistemas de protección social. La mejora de la estructura tributaria también es importante para fomentar el espíritu empresarial e impulsar la redistribución. Los impuestos también pueden incidir en el comportamiento de las personas; por ejemplo, pueden reducir la dependencia de los combustibles fósiles en el contexto del cambio climático.

Este informe, *Estadísticas tributarias en América Latina y el Caribe*, forma parte de la Facilidad Regional de la Unión Europea para el Desarrollo en Transición para ALC, una iniciativa liderada por la UE, implementada conjuntamente con la OCDE y su Centro de Desarrollo y la CEPAL. Esta es su décima edición y proporciona datos internacionales comparables sobre los ingresos tributarios de 27 países de la región, datos que pueden servir de base para análisis de políticas en profundidad o que pueden ser un punto de partida para intercambiar información y crear capacidad. En este primer capítulo se analiza la evolución desde 1990 de varios indicadores tributarios clave; entre ellos, la proporción entre la recaudación tributaria y el PIB, la combinación de impuestos y la generación de ingresos tributarios por parte de los distintos niveles de la Administración. También se analiza la eficacia de los impuestos sobre el valor agregado (el IVA, una de las principales fuentes de ingresos tributarios de la región) y los ingresos procedentes de los impuestos ambientales. En el presente capítulo se destacan asimismo las novedades en los sistemas tributarios de países seleccionados y se complementa el análisis con estudios de casos sobre temas precisos. Para un desglose de los ingresos tributarios detallado por países, pueden consultar los capítulos 5 y 6.

La recaudación tributaria como proporción del PIB

La recaudación tributaria como proporción del PIB en 2019

La recaudación tributaria como proporción del PIB mide los ingresos tributarios (incluidas las cotizaciones a la Seguridad Social pagadas a la Administración central) como proporción del producto interno bruto (PIB). En el promedio de América Latina y el Caribe se incluye el promedio no ponderado de los 26 países de la región incluidos en esta publicación, excepto a Venezuela por problemas de disponibilidad de datos.

En 2019, en promedio la recaudación tributaria en América Latina y el Caribe se situó en 22.9% del PIB (Gráfico 1.1). En la región se registraron variaciones considerables: desde el 13.1% del PIB en Guatemala al 42.0% de Cuba. A excepción de Cuba, todos los países de América Latina y el Caribe presentaron una recaudación tributaria inferior al promedio de la OCDE[1], que se situó en 33.8% del PIB.

Gráfico 1.1. **Recaudación tributaria en América Latina y el Caribe, 2019**

Total de ingresos tributarios como porcentaje del PIB

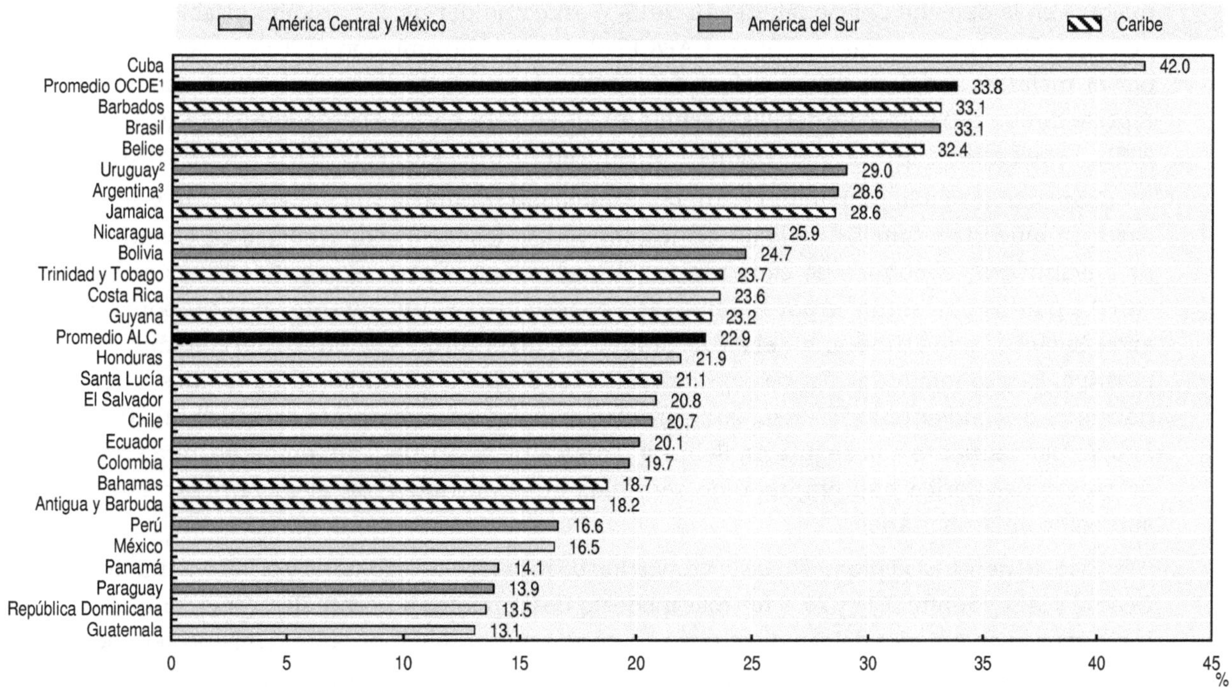

Nota: La clasificación de países en distintas subregiones sigue la clasificación de CEPAL y se basa en la lengua oficial de los países. El Caribe incluye a los países de habla inglesa de la región y Guyana, y América Central y México abarca los países de habla hispana, incluyendo República Dominicana y Cuba.

Las cifras no tienen en cuenta los ingresos de la Administración local de Antigua y Barbuda, Argentina (sí se incluyen los ingresos de las provincias) y las Bahamas, Barbados, la República Dominicana, Cuba (exceptuando 2002-2012), la República Dominicana, Santa Lucía, Trinidad y Tobago, y Venezuela, puesto que los datos no se encuentran disponibles.

1. El promedio de la OCDE es el promedio no ponderado de los 37 países miembros de la OCDE. Chile, Colombia y México también forman parte del grupo de la OCDE (37). Para México, los datos sobre los ingresos de la administración estatal y local no están disponibles para 2019. Se realiza una estimación para calcular la proporción entre la recaudación tributaria y el PIB.
2. La proporción entre la recaudación tributaria y el PIB no toma en cuenta el establecimiento de una nueva base del PIB en Uruguay. Las estimaciones preliminares de la nueva base del PIB indican que la proporción entre la recaudación tributaria y el PIB en Uruguay sería de alrededor de 2.3 puntos porcentuales inferior a la media del período 2016-2019.
3. La proporción entre la recaudación tributaria y el PIB se puede subestimar ya que excluye determinados tipos de contribuciones a la seguridad social, para los cuales no existen datos fácilmente disponibles.
4. Representa el grupo de 26 países de América Latina y el Caribe incluidos en esta publicación y excluye a Venezuela debido a problemas de disponibilidad de datos.

Fuente: OCDE et al. (2021[1]), Cuadro 4.1.

StatLink https://doi.org/10.1787/888934234252

El porcentaje más alto de este indicador se registró en Cuba (42.0%), y en Barbados y Brasil (33.1% en ambos casos). Los países con la menor recaudación tributaria como porcentaje del PIB fueron Guatemala (13.1%), República Dominicana (13.5%) y Paraguay (13.9%).

Se han detectado diferencias importantes en el nivel de tributación entre Centroamérica y México, América del Sur y el Caribe[2]. Los países de Centroamérica y México, en general, presentaron una proporción entre la recaudación tributaria y el PIB más baja, con un promedio de 21.3% en 2019, mientras que en los países del Caribe el porcentaje era más alto, con un promedio de 24.9%. Aunque entre los países de América del Sur se detectan variaciones importantes, su promedio fue del 22.9% en 2019, igual que el promedio de América Latina y el Caribe.

En 2019, el promedio de la proporción entre la recaudación tributaria y el PIB en América Latina y el Caribe superó en 0.3 puntos porcentuales la cifra de 2018. Este incremento se produjo en un contexto de débil situación económica en la región desde 2014 (el promedio del crecimiento real en ALC ascendió a un 0.3% durante el período 2014-2019). La región experimentó una recesión de dos años en 2015 y 2016, seguida por dos años de crecimiento impulsado por mejoras en la demanda nacional (CEPAL, 2019[2]) así como por un incremento estable en los precios de los productos básicos (OCDE/CAF/CEPAL, 2018[3]). Sin embargo, el 2019 se caracterizó por el malestar social en varios países de América Latina y débil crecimiento económico. A pesar de que el crecimiento del PIB ascendió a 1.1% en 2018, en 2019 descendió a 0.1% (CEPAL, 2021[4]) y se estima que descienda dramáticamente en 2020 debido al COVID-19 (OCDE, 2020[5]).

Los cambios en la proporción entre la recaudación tributaria y el PIB entre 2018 y 2019 variaron mucho en función de las regiones, influenciados por las diferencias en el patrón de crecimiento económico de cada región. El mayor incremento se registró en el Caribe, con 0.8 puntos porcentuales por segundo año consecutivo. El incremento en la proporción entre la recaudación tributaria y el PIB se produjo en un entorno económico del crecimiento positivo. La economía del Caribe repuntó en 2018, después del impacto de los desastres naturales del año anterior (CEPAL, 2019[2]) aunque dicho crecimiento se ralentizó en 2019, debido parcialmente a la sequía en Belice y Jamaica (BDC, 2020[6]). Sin embargo, una serie de países del Caribe han emprendido reformas que contribuyeron al incremento en la subregión en ambos años.

El incremento en el promedio de la proporción de recaudación tributaria y el PIB en América Central y México entre 2018 y 2019 fue más modesto, de 0.2 puntos porcentuales. Por el contrario, la proporción en América del Sur disminuyó 0.1 puntos porcentuales durante el mismo período. En ambas regiones, el crecimiento económico se debilitó en 2019 (CEPAL, 2021[4]).

En toda la región, 14 países registraron un incremento en la proporción de recaudación tributaria y el PIB en 2019, mientras que el resto de países registraron una disminución. Los tres mayores incrementos en la proporción entre la recaudación tributaria y el PIB entre 2018 y 2019 excedieron los 2.0 puntos porcentuales, y se produjeron en Nicaragua (2.7 puntos porcentuales), Belice (2.2 puntos porcentuales) y las Bahamas (2.1 puntos porcentuales).

En Nicaragua, los incrementos en los ingresos tributarios entre 2018 y 2019 se produjeron en todas las categorías y fueron desde los 0.5 puntos porcentuales procedentes de ingresos de IVA hasta 0.9 puntos porcentuales de impuestos sobre la renta y beneficios (todos procedentes del impuesto de sociedades [IS]). En 2019, el gobierno puso en práctica medidas para incrementar los ingresos tributarios e incrementar los ingresos del Instituto de la Seguridad Social (INSS), en respuesta a la disminución significativa en los ingresos tributarios en 2018 y la reducción de la financiación externa debido al malestar social.

- El aumento de los ingresos por el impuesto sobre la renta de sociedades se debió a la aprobación de la Ley de Armonización de Impuestos, por la que se incrementaron las tasas impositivas para los grandes contribuyentes y medianas empresas por encima de un determinado umbral de ingresos. El gobierno incrementó las tasas del impuesto mínimo alternativo e introdujo normas para evitar la evasión de este tipo de impuesto. Asimismo, también aumentaron las tasas de las retenciones fiscales sobre los ingresos para personas no residentes (Orbitax, 2019[7]).
- Las cotizaciones a la Seguridad Social registraron un repunte de 0.7 puntos porcentuales en 2019. Nicaragua modificó el Reglamento General de la Ley de Seguridad Social para fortalecer la solvencia del sistema de pensiones y salud. Los cambios se refirieron principalmente a tasas más altas para las contribuciones en distintos planes. Por ejemplo, la tasa correspondiente a la incapacidad, pensiones de jubilación, fallecimiento y riesgos laborales se incrementó de un 10% a entre un 12.5% y un 13.5% para los empleadores (dependiendo del número de empleados), mientras que para los empleados pasó de un 4% a un 4.75% (Orbitax, 2019[7]).
- Los ingresos procedentes del IVA y otros impuestos sobre bienes y servicios aumentaron 0.5 puntos porcentuales y 0.6 puntos porcentuales, respectivamente, entre 2018 y 2019. Unos tipos tributarios más altos sobre las importaciones de determinados bienes (p. ej. bebidas) contribuyeron a estos incrementos (CentralAmericaData, 2020[8]).

Gráfico 1.2. **Variación anual de la recaudación tributaria en América Latina y el Caribe en 2018 y 2019**

Puntos porcentuales del PIB

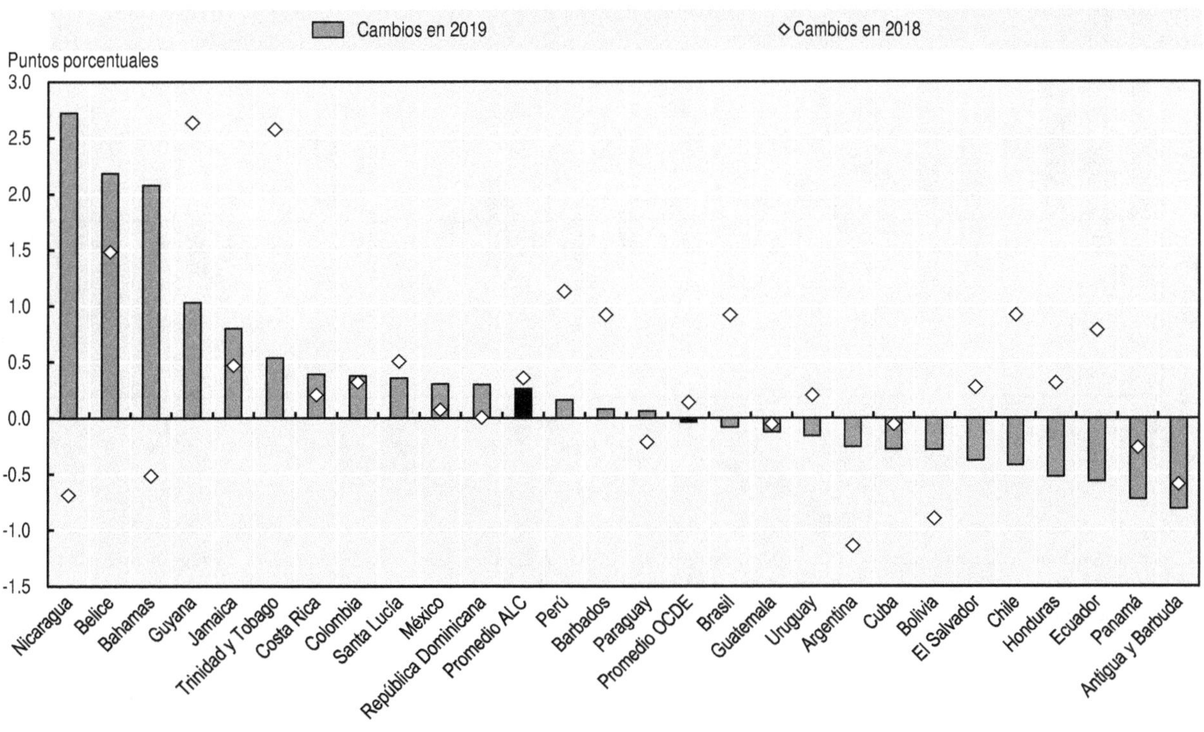

Nota: El promedio de América Latina y el Caribe representa el promedio no ponderado de 26 países de la región incluidos en esta publicación y excluye a Venezuela, debido a problemas de disponibilidad de datos. El promedio de la OCDE representa el promedio no ponderado de los 37 países miembros de la OCDE. Chile, Colombia y México también forman parte del grupo OCDE (37).

Fuente: Cálculos propios basados en OCDE et al. (2021[1]), Cuadro 4.1.

StatLink https://doi.org/10.1787/888934234271

Belice registró incrementos en todas las categorías principales de ingresos tributarios como una proporción del PIB en 2019. El aumento global en la proporción entre la recaudación tributaria y el PIB resultó en un aumento del 5% en los ingresos tributarios entre 2018 y 2019, mientras que el PIB nominal disminuyó en un 2%. La economía de Belice experimentó tres trimestres de desaceleración en 2019, en gran parte causada por una sequía que afectó a los sectores primario y secundario de la economía. Belice también registró una desaceleración en el sector turístico clave en 2019, después de años de fuerte crecimiento (Barrow, 2020[9]).

El aumento global de los ingresos tributarios en Bahamas fue impulsado principalmente por el aumento de los ingresos del IVA (1.4 puntos porcentuales) e ingresos por impuestos sobre la propiedad (0.7 puntos porcentuales, que se muestran en el Gráfico 1.3 bajo el epígrafe "otros impuestos"). Estos aumentos fueron principalmente el resultado de las reformas fiscales destinadas a reducir el déficit presupuestario al 1.8% del PIB en el ejercicio fiscal 2018/19, del 5.5% en ejercicio fiscal 2016/17 y del 3.4% del PIB en el ejercicio fiscal 2017/18. Las reformas incluyen un aumento de la tasa única del IVA de 7.5% a 12% en julio de 2018, así como un aumento de los derechos de timbre.

Gráfico 1.3. **Variaciones en la proporción de la recaudación tributaria y el PIB en América Latina y el Caribe en función de las partidas tributarias entre 2018 y 2019**

Puntos porcentuales de PIB

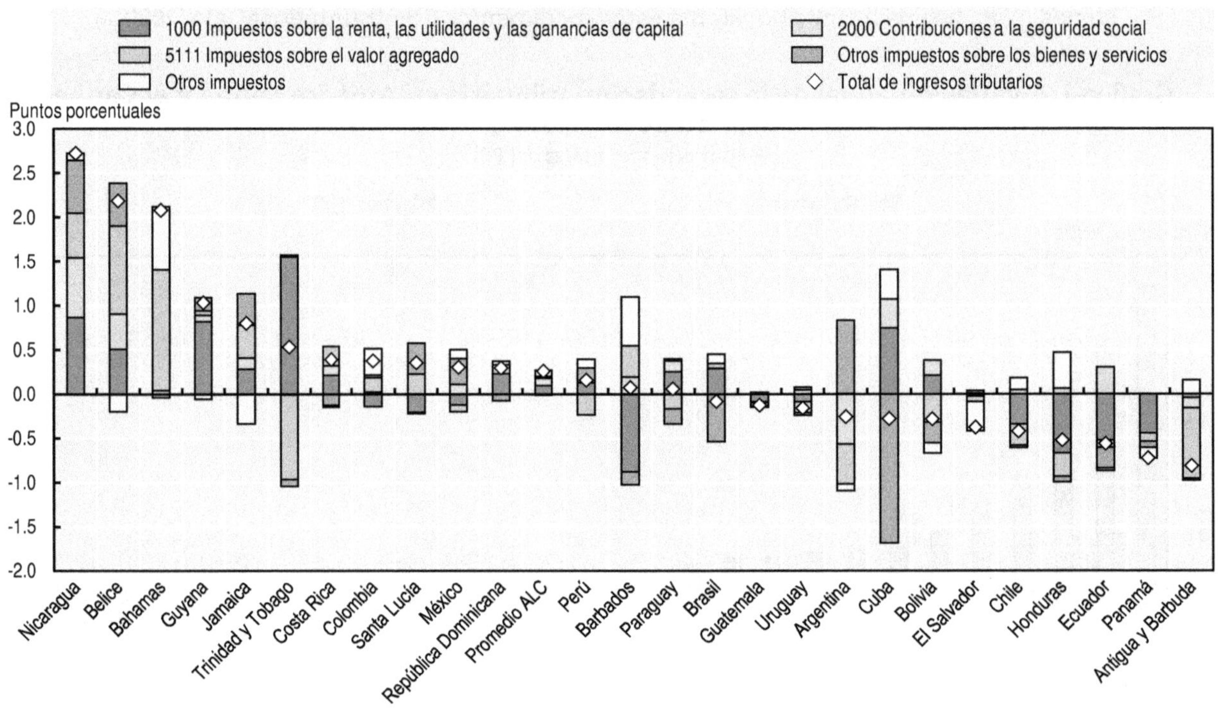

Nota: El promedio de América Latina y el Caribe representa el promedio no ponderado de 26 países de la región incluidos en esta publicación y excluye a Venezuela, debido a problemas de disponibilidad de datos.

Fuente: Cálculos propios basados en OCDE et al. (2021[1]), Capítulo 4.

StatLink https://doi.org/10.1787/888934234290

Antigua y Barbuda, Ecuador y Panamá registraron las caídas más pronunciadas entre 2018 y 2019, de más de 0.5 puntos porcentuales. Antigua y Barbuda experimentó la mayor caída, 0.8 puntos porcentuales, principalmente debido a un descenso de los ingresos provenientes del IVA, que disminuyeron en la misma proporción. El entorno económico y los retos relativos a la agencia tributaria y la recaudación tributaria en Antigua y Barbuda contribuyeron a la disminución global de la proporción entre la recaudación tributaria y el PIB en 2019. La economía de Antigua y Barbuda se desaceleró en 2019 después de un fuerte rendimiento en 2018 (el crecimiento real del PIB en 2019 fue del 3.4%, aproximadamente la mitad de la tasa registrada en 2018). Los impuestos sobre la renta y bienes, los servicios y bienes nacionales cayeron por debajo del objetivo presupuestario durante el período objeto de revisión, siendo necesario destacar principales retos a los que se enfrentan las autoridades en relación con la recaudación y gestión de impuestos (BID, 2019[10]).

Panamá registró la segunda mayor caída de estos países en 2019 (0.7 puntos porcentuales) debido a la disminución en todas las categorías de impuestos, lo que refleja la situación económica en el país. Mientras tanto, Ecuador registró una disminución de 0.6 puntos porcentuales en 2019, causando la reversión de la proporción entre la recaudación tributaria y el PIB a niveles anteriores a 2018. El 2018 fue un año excepcional de recaudación de impuestos para Ecuador, cuya proporción tributaria aumentó en 0.8 puntos porcentuales desde el año anterior.

El Gráfico 1.3 muestra otros aumentos significativos entre 2018 y 2019 en algunas categorías de ingresos tributarios en los países que implementaron reformas fiscales. Por ejemplo:

- La proporción entre recaudación tributaria y PIB en Trinidad y Tobago aumentó en 0.5 puntos porcentuales entre 2018 y 2019, ya que las autoridades llevaron a cabo una amnistía fiscal de tres meses en junio de 2019, lo que tuvo como consecuencia la obtención de ingresos excepcionales procedentes de impuestos sobre la renta y beneficios, que aumentaron 1.6 puntos porcentuales entre 2018 y 2019 (CEPAL, 2020[11]).
- Argentina experimentó pérdidas en sus ingresos en relación con todas las categorías de impuestos entre 2018 y 2019, excepto en aquellos procedentes de impuestos sobre bienes y servicios distintos del IVA, que aumentaron en 0.8 puntos porcentuales. El incremento se debió exclusivamente al aumento de los ingresos resultado de la recaudación de impuestos a la exportación en 1.1 puntos porcentuales, en comparación con el mismo período, tras la introducción de los derechos de exportación temporales sobre servicios, en septiembre de 2018. En diciembre de 2019, las autoridades aumentaron la tasa del impuesto a la exportación de bienes, que tenían una tasa de cero, para aumentar los ingresos tributarios (EY, 2019[12]; ITR, 2020[13]).
- Barbados registró incrementos en los ingresos procedentes del IVA y de los impuestos sobre la propiedad (que se muestran bajo el epígrafe "otros Impuestos" en el Gráfico 1.3) de 0.4 y 0.5 puntos porcentuales, respectivamente, entre 2018 y 2019. Barbados ha incrementado las tasas de IVA de alojamiento en hoteles de 7.5% a 10% y ampliado la base del IVA en determinados sectores (como el turístico) mediante la eliminación de exenciones y tasas preferenciales (FMI, 2019[14]). Las autoridades también aumentaron las tasas de impuestos de bienes inmuebles para hacer que el sistema de impuestos sobre la propiedad sea más progresivo. Por el contrario, los ingresos procedentes de los impuestos sobre la renta y los beneficios disminuyeron en 0.9 puntos porcentuales entre 2018 y 2019 tras los cambios legislativos relativos al impuesto sobre la renta de las personas físicas (IRPF) y el Impuesto de Sociedades (IS). La reforma más importante fue la relativa al IS: en enero de 2019, Barbados reformó su sistema de IS, tras la evaluación de la OCDE (a través de su iniciativa de Erosión de la Base y Traslado de Beneficios [BEPS por sus siglas en inglés]) de que tenía regímenes preferenciales perjudiciales para las empresas no residentes (OCDE, 2020[15]). La reforma supuso la equiparación de los tipos del impuesto de sociedades para las empresas nacionales y no residentes, reduciendo el tipo nacional del 25% a entre el 1% y el 5.5%, dependiendo del nivel de beneficios, y aumentando los tipos del impuesto de

sociedades para las empresas no residentes (que anteriormente oscilaban entre el 0.25% y el 2.5%) hasta los mismos niveles que para las empresas nacionales. La segunda reforma importante se refirió al IRPF, en relación con el cual se redujeron gradualmente las tasas, empezando con la tasa de los impuestos sobre las rentas más altas (FMI, 2019[14]).

Evolución de la proporción entre la recaudación tributaria y el PIB desde el 2000

La mejora en la movilización de los recursos nacionales, en particular mediante el aumento de los ingresos tributarios, es fundamental para el desarrollo sostenible de ALC, tal y como se refleja en la agenda de Desarrollo en Transición para la recuperación posterior a la COVID-19 (Recuadro 1.1). El promedio de la proporción entre la recaudación tributaria y el PIB en los países de América Latina y el Caribe ha aumentado desde 1990 (Gráfico 1.4), en más de 7 puntos porcentuales en general, del 15.7% en 1990 al 22.9% en 2019. Esta tendencia contrasta con la de los países de la OCDE, donde el promedio entre la recaudación tributaria y el PIB ha sido relativamente estable desde 1990 (aunque en un nivel superior al promedio de América Latina y el Caribe); la proporción entre la recaudación tributaria y el PIB de la OCDE alcanzó el 33.8% en 2019, 2.7 puntos porcentuales por encima de su nivel de 1990. La diferencia del promedio entre la recaudación tributaria y el PIB entre América Latina y el Caribe y la OCDE en 2019 fue de 10.9 puntos porcentuales.

Recuadro 1.1. ***Estadísticas tributarias en América Latina y el Caribe y el enfoque de Desarrollo en Transición***

Esta edición de *Estadísticas tributarias en América Latina y el Caribe* es la tercera que se realiza con el apoyo de la Facilidad Regional de la Unión Europea (UE) para el Desarrollo en Transición para América Latina y el Caribe (ALC). Esta facilidad es el resultado de un trabajo conjunto dirigido por la UE, la Organización para la Cooperación y el Desarrollo Económicos (OCDE) y su Centro de Desarrollo y la Comisión Económica para América Latina y el Caribe (CEPAL).

Los países de ALC se han visto golpeados por la pandemia en un momento en el que la región ya se enfrentaba a profundos desafíos estructurales. La crisis del COVID-19 plantea nuevos retos a las trampas ya existentes a las que se enfrenta el desarrollo estructural ya señaladas en el enfoque de "Desarrollo en Transición" (OCDE et al., 2019[16]). Las cuatro trampas de baja productividad, vulnerabilidad social, debilidad institucional y sostenibilidad medioambiental agravan las consecuencias socioeconómicas de la crisis y reducen la capacidad de los países de diseñar e implementar respuestas a medio y largo plazo. La crisis del COVID-19 puso de manifiesto la necesidad de adoptar un enfoque multidimensional del desarrollo, con el objeto de superar los desafíos interrelacionados que plantean las trampas de desarrollo. Por otra parte, la pandemia ha puesto el foco en la necesidad de redefinir las políticas nacionales mediante el establecimiento de un consenso entre los ciudadanos, la integración regional y la cooperación internacional, como parte de la recuperación económica y social de la región que incluye a todos los países, independientemente de su nivel de desarrollo (OCDE et al., 2020[17]).

En este contexto, la recuperación se debe considerar una oportunidad para transformar la estrategia de desarrollo de la región, enfocada hacia la inclusión, la resiliencia y la sostenibilidad. La política fiscal es esencial para construir capacidades, hacer frente a las trampas de desarrollo y garantizar una recuperación inclusiva y sostenible (OCDE et al., 2020[17]). Las *Estadísticas Tributarias en América Latina y el Caribe* representan un recurso valioso para los gobiernos, ya que buscan fortalecer la política fiscal. Al proporcionar los datos fiscales armonizados y detallados de toda la región, se permite el análisis de la política tributaria en profundidad y la identificación, no sólo el nivel de ingresos tributarios según el país, sino también qué instrumentos generan estos ingresos, lo que refleja que la forma de recaudar los impuestos puede ser tan importante como la cantidad recaudada. Las *Estadísticas Tributarias en América Latina y el Caribe* también representa un punto de partida común para el intercambio de conocimientos y el desarrollo de capacidades entre los países, así como con la comunidad internacional en general.

Recuadro 1.1. ***Estadísticas tributarias en América Latina y el Caribe* y el enfoque de Desarrollo en Transición** *(cont.)*

Debido a la relación estrecha entre la tributación efectiva y el gasto público eficaz para promover el desarrollo inclusivo y sostenible, la Facilidad de Desarrollo en Transición une las *Estadísticas Tributarias en América Latina y el Caribe* con el trabajo de la OCDE y la CEPAL sobre el gasto público y el gasto social en particular. El objetivo es proporcionar una visión totalmente nueva y una herramienta muy útil para el desarrollo de la política fiscal en la región, particularmente necesaria en el contexto de la crisis del COVID-19.

Gráfico 1.4. **Evolución de la recaudación tributaria, América Latina y el Caribe y OCDE, 1990-2019**

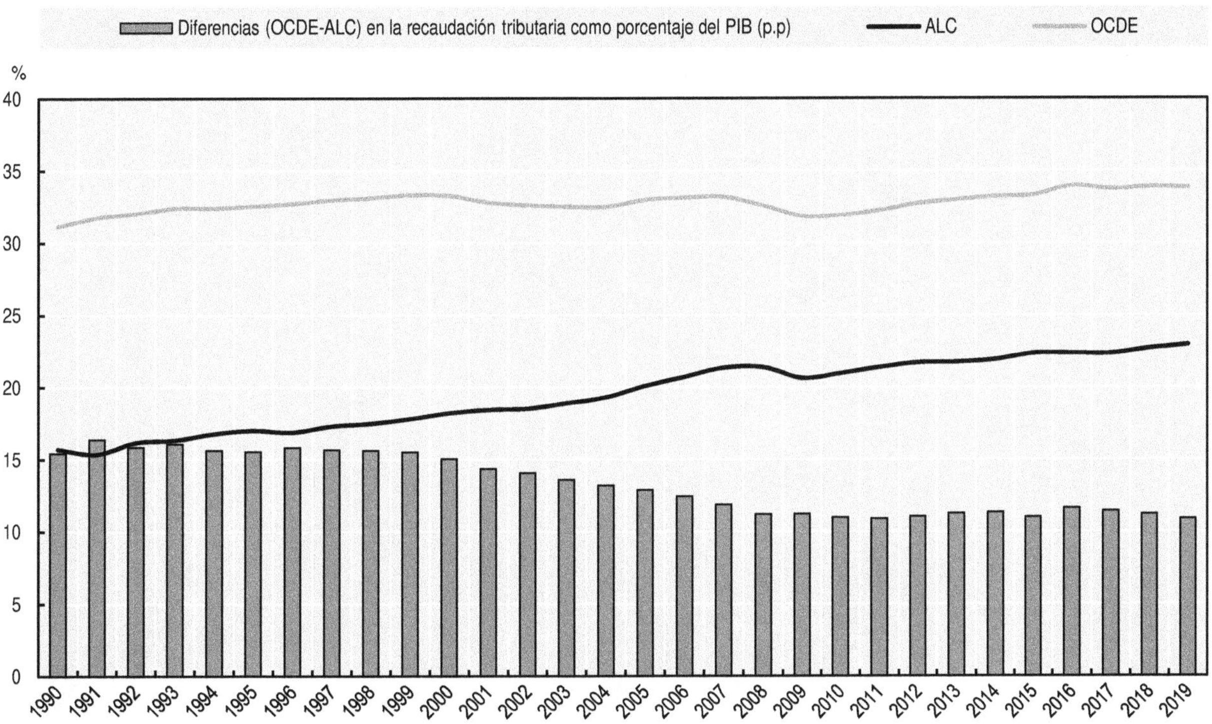

Nota: El promedio de América Latina y el Caribe representa el promedio no ponderado de 26 países de la región incluidos en esta publicación y excluye a Venezuela, debido a problemas de disponibilidad de datos. El promedio de la OCDE representa el promedio no ponderado de los 37 países miembros de la OCDE. Chile, Colombia y México también forman parte del grupo OCDE (37).

Fuente: Los cálculos de los autores se basan en OCDE et al (2021[1]), "Revenue Statistics in Latin America: Comparative tables", *OECD Tax Statistics* (database), *http://dx.doi.org/ 10.1787/data-00641-en.*

StatLink https://doi.org/10.1787/888934234309

El Gráfico 1.5 muestra la evolución del promedio de la proporción entre la recaudación tributaria y el PIB para las tres subregiones de América Latina y el Caribe desde 1990. Si bien las tres subregiones han mostrado una tendencia al alza en los niveles impositivos entre 1990 y 2019, su evolución presenta notables diferencias:

- En promedio, el Caribe registró el crecimiento más bajo en el período, de 5.6 puntos porcentuales. La relación del promedio de la proporción entre la recaudación tributaria y el PIB fue consistentemente superior que el promedio de América Latina y el Caribe. La diferencia se ha ampliado desde 2017 debido al aumento relativamente pronunciado de la relación entre la recaudación tributaria y el PIB en el Caribe.

- En contraste, el aumento en el promedio de la proporción entre la recaudación tributaria y el PIB para Centroamérica y México ha sido más gradual. A lo largo de este período, se mantuvo por debajo del promedio de la región de América Latina y el Caribe. La tasa promedio de la proporción entre la recaudación tributaria y el PIB para Centroamérica y México se ha mantenido estable en 21.1% desde 2016, antes de aumentar ligeramente en 2019.
- América del Sur registró un fuerte aumento en su proporción entre impuestos y PIB durante la década de 1990 y superó el promedio de América Latina y el Caribe en 2004. Desde 2015, la proporción entre impuestos y PIB de América del Sur ha ido disminuyendo hacia el promedio de América Latina y el Caribe; los dos convergieron en 2019.

Gráfico 1.5. **Evolución de la recaudación tributaria, América Latina y el Caribe y subregiones, 1990-2019**

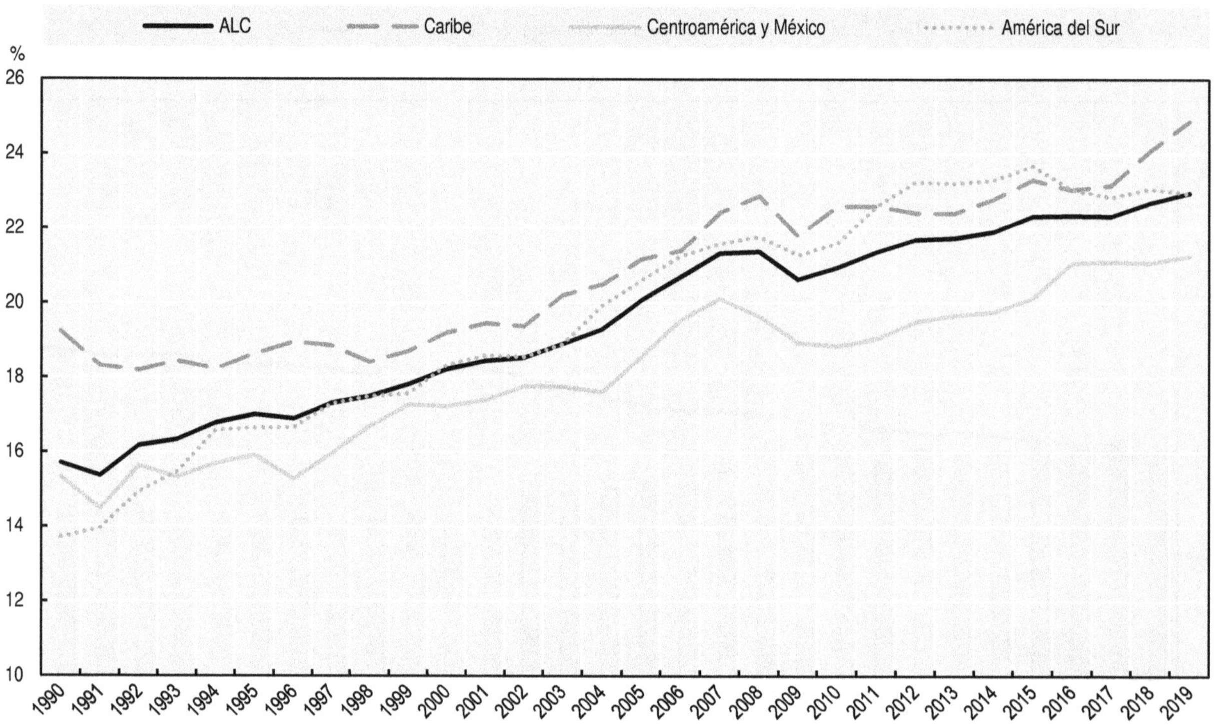

Nota: El promedio de América Latina y el Caribe representa el promedio no ponderado de 26 países de la región incluidos en esta publicación y excluye a Venezuela, debido a problemas de disponibilidad de datos. El Caribe incluye ocho países (Antigua y Barbuda, Bahamas, Barbados, Belice, Guyana, Jamaica, Santa Lucía y Trinidad y Tobago), América Central y México nueve países (Costa Rica, Cuba, República Dominicana, El Salvador, Guatemala, Honduras, México, Nicaragua y Panamá) y América del Sur nueve países (Argentina, Bolivia, Brasil, Chile, Colombia, Ecuador, Paraguay, Perú y Uruguay). La clasificación de los países en las diferentes subregiones sigue la clasificación de CEPAL y se basa en el idioma oficial de los países. El Caribe incluye a los países de habla inglesa de la región y Guyana y Centroamérica y México abarca los países de habla hispana, incluyendo República Dominicana y Cuba.

Fuente: Los cálculos de los autores se basan en OCDE et al. (2021[1]), "Revenue Statistics in Latin America: Comparative tables", *OECD Tax Statistics* (database), *http://dx.doi.org/ 10.1787/data-00641-en.*

StatLink https://doi.org/10.1787/888934234328

La proporción entre la recaudación tributaria y el PIB en los países de América Latina y el Caribe aumentó a principio de los años noventa, tras una década de inestabilidad macroeconómica. Durante la década de los ochenta, muchos países presentaron grandes desequilibrios fiscales y algunos recurrieron a formas alternativas de financiamiento de los gastos (pedir prestado o imprimir dinero). Esto causó una inflación rápida en toda la región, lo que erosionó el valor real de los ingresos tributarios. Las reformas en los noventa se centraron en la estabilidad de precios, la liberalización del comercio y la disciplina fiscal. La mayoría de los gobiernos de América Latina y el Caribe redujeron el gasto y pusieron en práctica políticas destinadas a aumentar los ingresos tributarios; la gestión presupuestaria y las balanzas fiscales mejoraron considerablemente. Los actores políticos implementaron reformas de la política tributaria y la gestión para reforzar los sistemas tributarios contra episodios inflacionistas, acortando los desfases de recaudación e indexando pasivos fiscales (CEPAL, 2018[18]).

La introducción del IVA ha sido la reforma tributaria más importante en América Latina y el Caribe de las últimas tres décadas. A principios de los años noventa, casi todos los países aplicaban un sistema de IVA y las reformas tenían como objetivo aumentar su tasa, ampliar la base imponible y mejorar la recaudación. Varios países han pasado a sistemas de IVA de tipo único (CEPAL, 2018[18]).

Los países de América Latina y el Caribe han realizado importantes esfuerzos para modernizar la gestión tributaria en las últimas dos décadas. Se han implementado nuevos sistemas de información tecnológica, los sistemas de recaudación de impuestos han pasado a ser más eficientes y la plantilla ha obtenido conocimientos técnicos (BID, 2013[19]). Las reformas fiscales incluyeron la introducción o desarrollo de regímenes simplificados para los pequeños contribuyentes, la tributación de propiedades basada en los presuntos ingresos y la expansión de la tributación a los ingresos laborales y de capital, incluyendo dividendos. Las reformas también han incluido el establecimiento de impuestos mínimos, impuestos sobre transacciones financieras y reducciones graduales del nivel real de ingresos gravados en la máxima tasa marginal (CEPAL, 2013[20]; CEPAL, 2018[18]).

Gráfico 1.6. **Evolución de la recaudación tributaria por tipos de impuestos seleccionados en la región de América Latina y el Caribe, 1990-2019**

Porcentaje del PIB

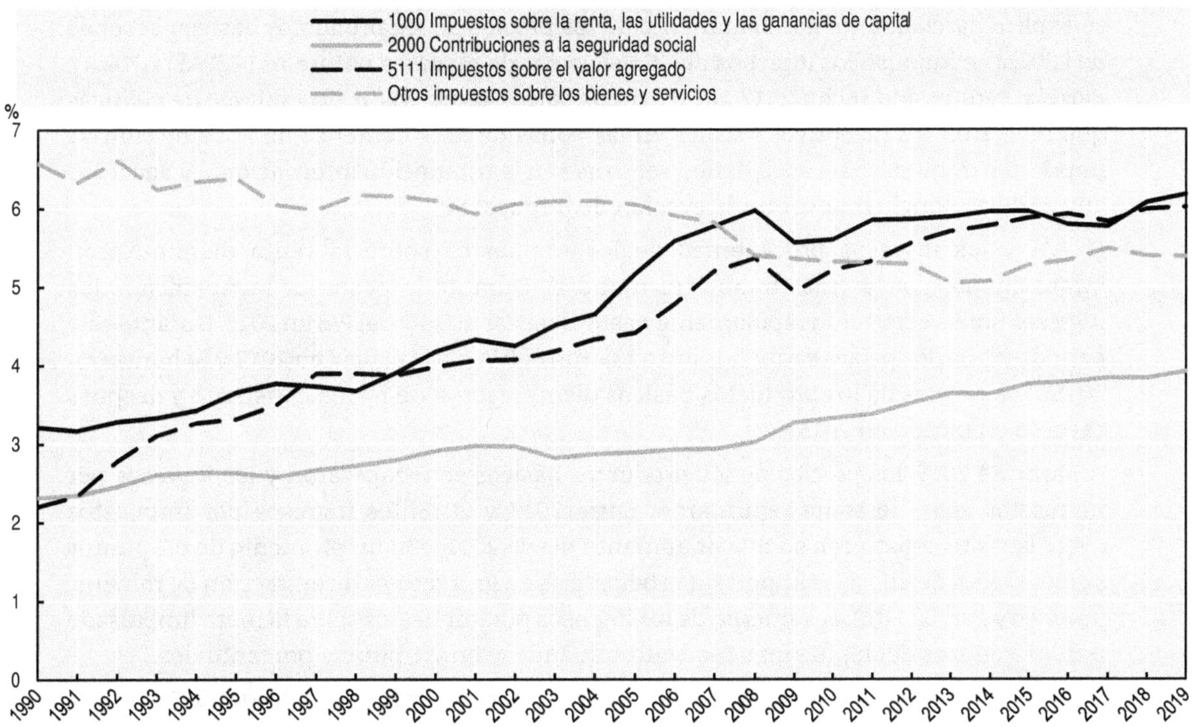

Nota: El promedio de América Latina y el Caribe representa el promedio no ponderado de 26 países de la región incluidos en esta publicación y excluye a Venezuela, debido a problemas de disponibilidad de datos.

Fuente: Cálculos propios a partir OCDE et al. (2021[1]), "Revenue Statistics in Latin America: Comparative tables", *OECD Tax Statistics* (database), *http://dx.doi.org/ 10.1787/data-00641-en.*

StatLink https://doi.org/10.1787/888934234347

El aumento del promedio de la proporción entre recaudación tributaria y el PIB en América Latina y el Caribe desde 1990 se ha visto impulsado en gran medida por los ingresos del impuesto sobre la renta y el IVA, que aumentaron un 3.0 y 3.8 puntos porcentuales, respectivamente, entre 1990 y 2019. En 2019, los ingresos procedentes del IVA ascendieron al 6.0% del PIB, mientras que los ingresos procedentes de los impuestos sobre la renta y los beneficios fueron de un 6.2% del PIB (Gráfico 1.6). Entre 1990 y 2019, los ingresos procedentes de otros impuestos sobre bienes y servicios (p. ej. impuestos especiales, aduanas y aranceles de importación) en América Latina y el Caribe disminuyeron como porcentaje del PIB. Esta disminución se asoció con la liberalización del comercio, y como resultado de ello los países de América Latina y el Caribe cambiaron la forma de gravar los bienes importados y exportados, así como bienes y servicios específicos. Estos cambios incluyeron una reducción de los aranceles a la importación, la reducción de la base de productos y servicios sujetos a impuestos especiales, y la eliminación de los aranceles a las exportaciones. Una importante excepción es Argentina, donde se restablecieron los impuestos a las exportaciones en 2002, se abolieron en 2015 y se reintrodujeron en septiembre de 2018.

Se pueden distinguir cuatro fases distintas en la evolución de los ingresos tributarios:

- Entre 1990 y 2002, el IVA contribuyó más al aumento de los ingresos tributarios que los impuestos sobre la renta y los beneficios (1.9% del PIB frente al 1.0%). Durante ese período, cinco países introdujeron el IVA (Barbados, Belice, El Salvador, Jamaica y Paraguay).
- Entre 2002 y 2008, se observó lo contrario: los ingresos procedentes del impuesto sobre la renta y los beneficios contribuyeron más que los ingresos del IVA al incremento en el promedio de la proporción entre la recaudación tributaria y PIB (el incremento ascendió a 1.7% y un 1.3% del PIB, respectivamente). El incremento en los impuestos sobre la renta se explica parcialmente por el aumento de los precios de los productos básicos después de 2003, que impulsó los ingresos del IS del sector de recursos naturales (CEPAL, 2014[21]; Barreix, Benítez and Pecho, 2017[22]). En varios países, también fue el resultado de políticas que redujeron los incentivos fiscales en las zonas de libre comercio, la introducción de impuestos mínimos para sociedades, reformas en la tributación internacional y acuerdos entre países para luchar contra la evasión de impuestos.
- El IVA y los ingresos procedentes de los impuestos sobre la renta disminuyeron intensamente por la crisis financiera mundial. Durante la posterior recuperación, los ingresos por IVA crecieron rápidamente hasta alcanzar el 5.9% del PIB en 2016. Durante este período, otros dos países caribeños introdujeron el IVA (Santa Lucía en 2012 y Bahamas en 2015). Los precios de los productos básicos disminuyeron de forma constante y después cayeron en picado en 2015.
- A partir de 2016, los precios de los productos básicos se recuperaron y los ingresos por impuestos sobre la renta repuntaron. Entre 2017 y 2018, los ingresos por impuestos sobre la renta registraron su mayor aumento desde 2011, con un promedio de 0.3 puntos porcentuales, debido a los importantes beneficios en los sectores de extracción de minería, petróleo y gas. En 2019, el aumento de los ingresos por impuestos sobre la renta (impulsado por los ingresos del IS) fue más modesto, situándose en 0.1 puntos porcentuales.

El Gráfico 1.7 muestra la evolución del IS y el impuesto sobre la renta desde 2005. En 2019, los promedios de América Latina y el Caribe relativos a ingresos del IS y el impuesto de la renta de personas físicas se estableció en 3.6% y 2.2%, respectivamente, del PIB. Durante este período, los ingresos del IS como porcentaje del PIB han sido más volátiles que los ingresos del impuesto sobre la renta de personas físicas, cuyo promedio ha aumentado constantemente en toda la región.

Gráfico 1.7. **Recaudación del impuesto sobre la renta y los beneficios sobre sociedades y personas físicas, América Latina y el Caribe, 2005-19**

Porcentaje del PIB

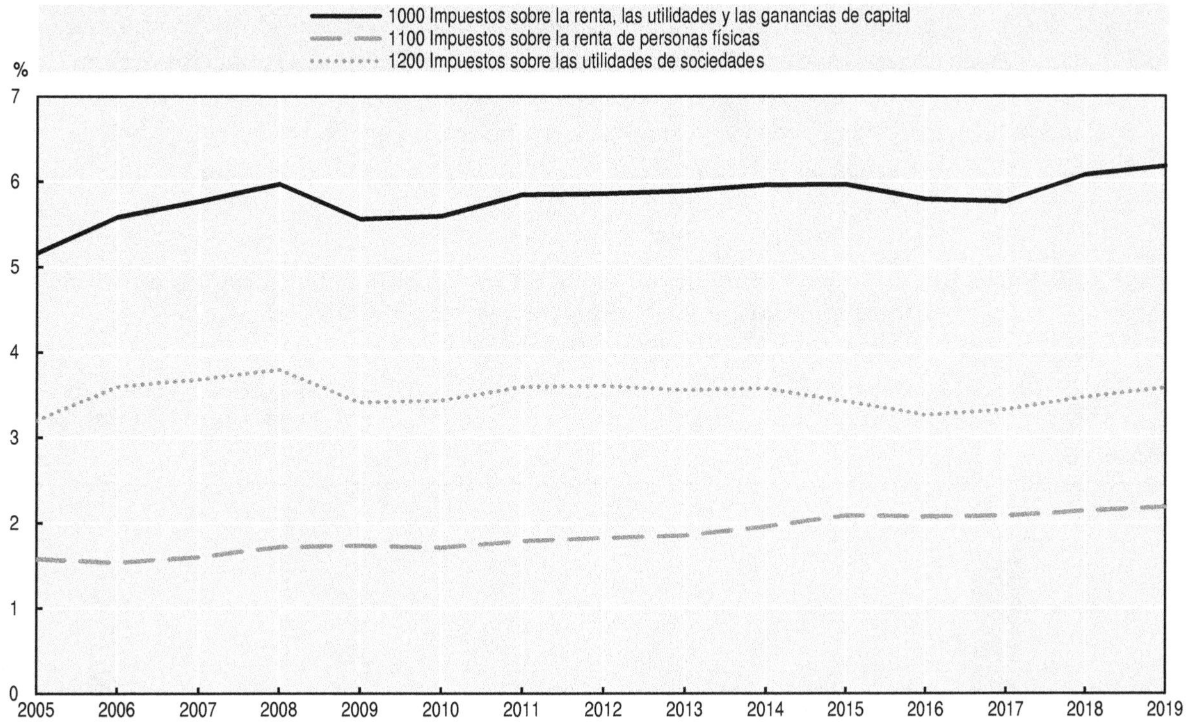

Nota: Los promedios del IS y el IRPF, como porcentaje del PIB, deben interpretarse con precaución, ya que Ecuador y Venezuela se excluyen del cálculo. El promedio de América Latina y el Caribe excluye a Venezuela debido a problemas de disponibilidad de datos. Ecuador está excluido del promedio de América Latina y el Caribe en relación con los ingresos del IS como porcentaje del PIB y los ingresos del IRPF como porcentaje del PIB ya que más de un tercio de sus ingresos procedentes de impuestos sobre la renta y beneficios no se puede asignar a los ingresos del IS (1200) o a ingresos del IRPF (1100).

Fuente: OCDE et al. (2021[1]), "Revenue Statistics in Latin America and the Caribbean: Comparative tables", *OECD Tax Statistics* (database), *http://dx.doi.org/10.1787/data-00641-en.*

StatLink https://doi.org/10.1787/888934234366

Hay diferencias notables entre las tres subregiones de América Latina y el Caribe, al tomar en consideración los cambios en las principales categorías fiscales entre 1990 y 2019 (Gráfico 1.8).

- En promedio, el Caribe registró el mayor incremento en los ingresos por IVA como porcentaje del PIB (6.1 puntos porcentuales). Siete de los ocho países del Caribe implementaron[3] un sistema de IVA durante el período, más tarde que la mayoría de los países de Centroamérica, México y en América del Sur.
- En Centroamérica y México, y en América del Sur, los mayores aumentos entre 1990 y 2019 procedieron de impuestos sobre la renta y beneficios (3.9% y 3.7% del PIB), seguidos del IVA (2.8% y 3.2% del PIB, respectivamente). Entre 2003 y 2010, los ingresos procedentes de los impuestos sobre la renta y los beneficios (e indirectamente del IVA) se vieron influidos por los importantes incrementos de los precios de los minerales y el petróleo.

Factores que influyen en la proporción de la recaudación tributaria y el PIB

Las diferencias en la proporción entre la recaudación tributaria y el PIB en América Latina y el Caribe y la OCDE van en línea con la tendencia de los países con niveles de ingresos más altos de contar con una mayor proporción entre la recaudación tributaria y el PIB. Los datos implican una correlación positiva entre el PIB per cápita (una medida del nivel de ingresos de un país) y la proporción de la recaudación tributaria y el PIB (Gráfico 1.9). En general, los países de la OCDE tienen un promedio más alto de ingresos que los países de América Latina y el Caribe y recaudan mayores ingresos tributarios como proporción del PIB. Argentina, Barbados, Brasil y Uruguay muestran una proporción entre la recaudación tributaria y el PIB y niveles de ingresos similares a los de algunos países de la OCDE. El análisis empírico sugiere que una recaudación tributaria más intensa, acompañada de unas instituciones mejores, educación y habilidades y diversificación económica permitió a muchos países de la OCDE evitar "la trampa de la renta media", en contraste con América Latina y el Caribe (Melguizo et al., 2017[23]).

Gráfico 1.8. **Variación de la recaudación por tipos de impuestos seleccionados en América Latina y el Caribe y subregiones, entre 1990 y 2019**

Puntos porcentuales

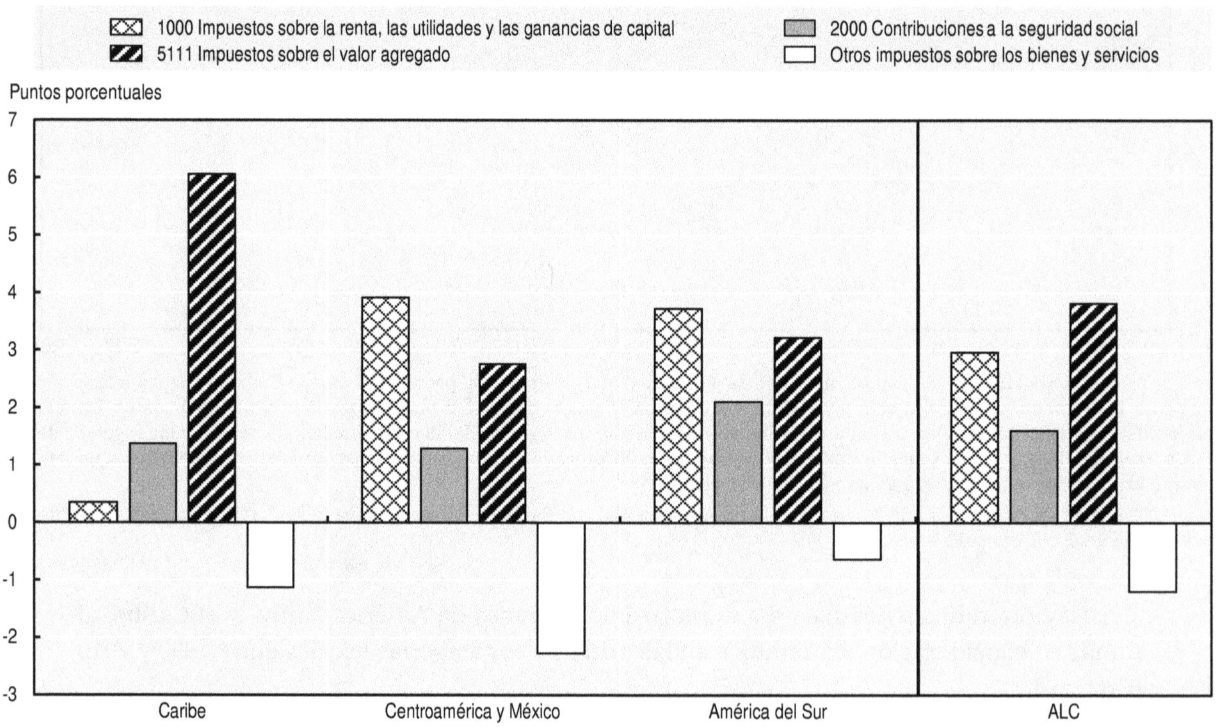

Nota: El promedio de América Latina y el Caribe representa el promedio no ponderado de 26 países de la región incluidos en esta publicación y excluye a Venezuela, debido a problemas de disponibilidad de datos. El Caribe incluye ocho países (Antigua y Barbuda, Bahamas, Barbados, Belice, Guyana, Jamaica, Trinidad y Tobago, y Santa Lucía), América Central y México nueve países (Costa Rica, Cuba, República Dominicana, El Salvador, Guatemala, Honduras, México, Nicaragua y Panamá) y América del Sur nueve países (Argentina, Bolivia, Brasil, Chile, Colombia, Ecuador, Paraguay, Perú y Uruguay). La clasificación de los países en las diferentes subregiones sigue la clasificación de CEPAL y se basa en el lenguaje oficial de los países. El Caribe incluye a los países de habla inglesa de la región y Guyana, y Centroamérica y México abarca los países de habla hispana, incluyendo República Dominicana y Cuba.

Fuente: Los cálculos de los autores se basan en OCDE et al. (2021[1]), Capítulo 4.

StatLink https://doi.org/10.1787/888934234385

La proporción entre recaudación tributaria y el PIB está influida por una serie de factores económicos y estructurales. El PIB per cápita, la apertura al comercio, la extensión de la economía informal, la dotación de recursos naturales y la importancia de la agricultura en la economía son factores que pueden influir en la proporción entre la recaudación tributaria y el PIB. Los factores sociodemográficos también son determinantes; por ejemplo el nivel de educación o el nivel de participación femenina en la mano de obra. El poder de las agencias tributarias, los niveles de corrupción y la moral tributaria (la disposición de las personas a pagar impuestos están también fuertemente ligados al nivel de ingresos tributarios (OCDE, 2019[25]; OCDE, 2014[26]). La proporción de la recaudación tributaria y el PIB también refleja las opciones políticas con respecto al papel del gobierno y su tamaño. Por último, la ubicación geográfica y los factores históricos también pueden influir; por ejemplo, los países sin litoral tienen menos capacidad de imponer impuestos sobre bienes y servicios en un puerto de entrada que los países costeros. Además, los factores internacionales, incluyendo las políticas fiscales de otros países, pueden afectar a la proporción entre los impuestos y el PIB.

Gráfico 1.9. **PIB per cápita en PPA (USD) y recaudación tributaria como porcentaje del PIB en América Latina y el Caribe, la OCDE y un grupo de países de África, Asia y el Pacífico, 2018**

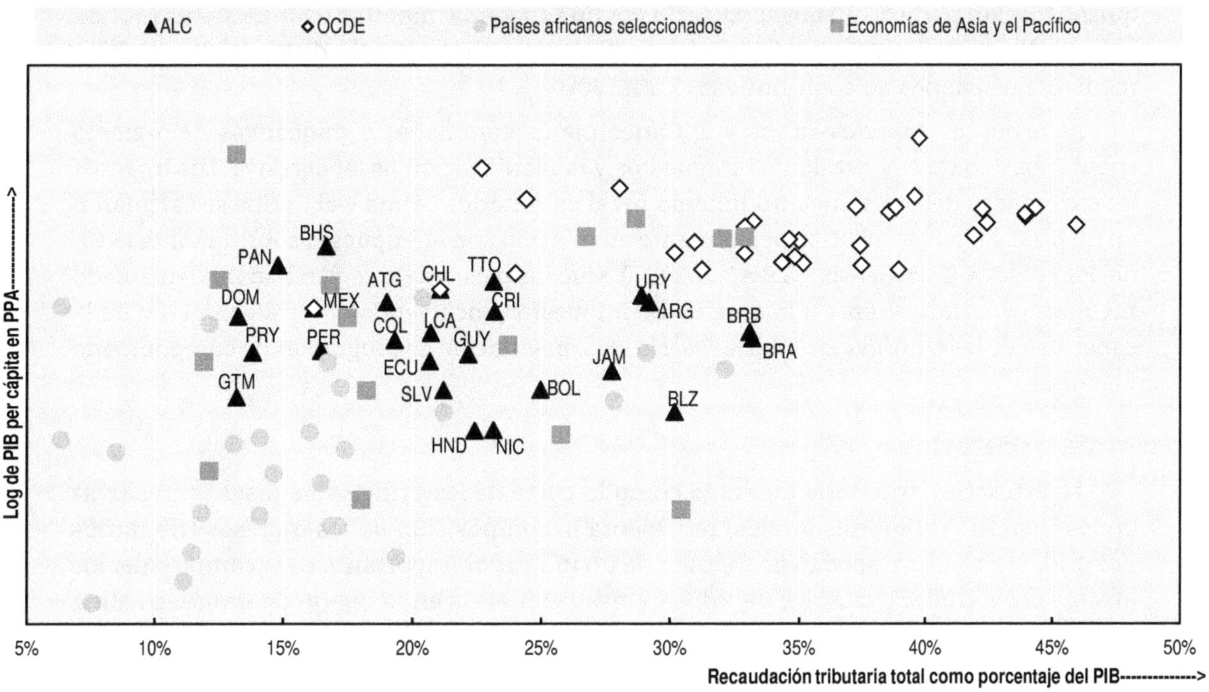

Nota: El año de comparación es 2018, dado que los datos relativos a la proporción entre la recaudación tributaria y el PIB en 2019 no están disponibles para las economías de África, Asia y el Pacífico seleccionadas. Cuba y Venezuela no están incluidas en esta figura, debido a problemas de disponibilidad de datos. La paridad del poder adquisitivo (PPA) entre dos países es el tipo a la que la moneda de un país deber ser convertida a la moneda de otro para garantizar que con una determinada cantidad de moneda del primer país se pueda adquirir el mismo volumen de bienes y servicios en el segundo país. La tasa de conversión PPA implícita se expresa como moneda nacional por dólar internacional corriente. Un dólar internacional tiene el mismo poder adquisitivo que el dólar estadounidense en los Estados Unidos. El dólar internacional es una moneda hipotética que se utiliza como medio de conversión y comparación de costos de un país a otro, utilizando un punto de referencia común, el dólar estadounidense (USD).

Fuente: FMI (2020[24]) para las cifras del PIB per cápita. La fuente de la proporción entre la recaudación tributaria y PIB es la *Global Revenue Statistics Database* (*http://www.oecd.org/tax/tax-policy/global-revenue-statistics-database.htm*).

StatLink https://doi.org/10.1787/888934234404

El grado de participación del Estado en la financiación de la seguridad social es otro factor importante relativo a los coeficientes tributarios dispares en la región de América Latina y el Caribe. Desde los ochenta, muchos países de América Latina y el Caribe privatizaron la salud y las pensiones en mayor o menor medida. Chile, El Salvador y México, por ejemplo, han cambiado de un sistema pensiones público a un sistema de pensiones en su mayor parte financiado de forma privada. En Colombia y Perú, los programas públicos y privados conviven y los empleados pueden optar por uno de ellos (OCDE et al., 2015[27]; OCDE/BID/Banco Mundial, 2014[28]). Por otro lado, Argentina, Brasil y Uruguay siguen un modelo en el que los sistemas públicos y privados son complementarios. En estos países, se llevaron a cabo reformas sustanciales para ampliar la cobertura de los sistemas de seguridad social a los excluidos. Esto también ha sido fundamental para el aumento de los ingresos tributarios (CEPAL, 2014[21]).

La informalidad limita la recaudación tributaria en ALC, reduciendo significativamente la base imponible. Es probable que la crisis del COVID-19 incremente el empleo informal, que ya representa cerca del 60% de los empleados en América Latina (OCDE, 2020[5]). A pesar de que los gobiernos de determinados países de esta región han tomado medidas rápidas y eficaces desde el segundo trimestre de 2020 para apoyar a las familias más vulnerables, el impacto social de la pandemia está siendo especialmente fuerte para cerca del 40% de los trabajadores – y sus familias – que no están protegidos por ninguna red de seguridad. Esta situación afecta de forma aún más dura al 61% de los trabajadores informales y vulnerables que no forman parte de un hogar cubierto por un programa importante de asistencia social, bien mediante transferencias directas de los programas importantes de transferencia, bien mediante pensiones no contributivas (OCDE, 2020[5]).

La región de América Latina y el Caribe pierde cantidades significativas de ingresos tributarios debido a la evasión de impuestos y la planificación fiscal agresiva. Los ingresos no recaudados debido al incumplimiento fiscal en América Latina y el Caribe se calcularon en un 6.1% del PIB en 2018, principalmente en relación con el impuesto sobre la renta (3.8% del PIB) y el IVA (2.3% del PIB) (CEPAL, 2020[11]). Muchos países de la región han implementado medidas para hacer frente a la evasión de impuestos, incluyendo el fortalecimiento de la capacidad de las autoridades tributarias y la implementación de programas de cumplimiento voluntario.

Estructuras tributarias

La estructura tributaria (definida como la parte de las principales tasas impositivas en los ingresos tributarios totales) representa la composición de los ingresos tributarios por diferentes tasas impositivas. Se trata de un indicador importante para comprender los efectos económicos y sociales de los sistemas tributarios en la región de América Latina y el Caribe.

Evolución de las estructuras tributarias

Los impuestos sobre bienes y servicios supusieron la mayor parte de los ingresos tributarios totales en la región de América Latina y el Caribe en 2019, representando en promedio la mitad de la tributación total. Entre 1990 y 2019, el promedio de ingresos tributarios de América Latina y el Caribe procedió principalmente del IVA, el impuesto sobre la renta y los beneficios y las cotizaciones a la seguridad social, y no de otros impuestos sobre bienes y servicios.

- La participación de los ingresos por IVA en los ingresos tributarios totales alcanzó el 27.7% en 2019, lo que equivale a un aumento de 12.3 puntos porcentuales desde 1990. La participación de los ingresos por otros impuestos sobre bienes y servicios (incluidos los impuestos especiales, derechos aduaneros y de importación) disminuyó en 20.2 puntos porcentuales en comparación con el mismo período (Gráfico 1.10).
- Entre 1990 y 2019, la proporción de los ingresos procedentes de los impuestos sobre la renta y los beneficios creció en 7.4 puntos porcentuales (del 19.7% al 27.0% de los ingresos tributarios totales).
- El porcentaje de cotizaciones a la Seguridad Social en los ingresos tributarios totales ha subido 3.2 puntos porcentuales en comparación con 1990, y alcanzó el 17.1%

en 2019. Dos factores principales (y opuestos) han influido en la trayectoria de las contribuciones a la seguridad social en la región. A pesar de que el incremento de los ingresos personales ha llevado a una recaudación más elevada, esto se ha visto contrarrestado por la privatización completa o parcial de la seguridad social, que se ha llevado a cabo en muchos países principalmente entre la mitad de los noventa y 2010 (OCDE et al., 2015[27]).

Gráfico 1.10. **Estructura tributaria promedio en América Latina y el Caribe, 1990 y 2019**

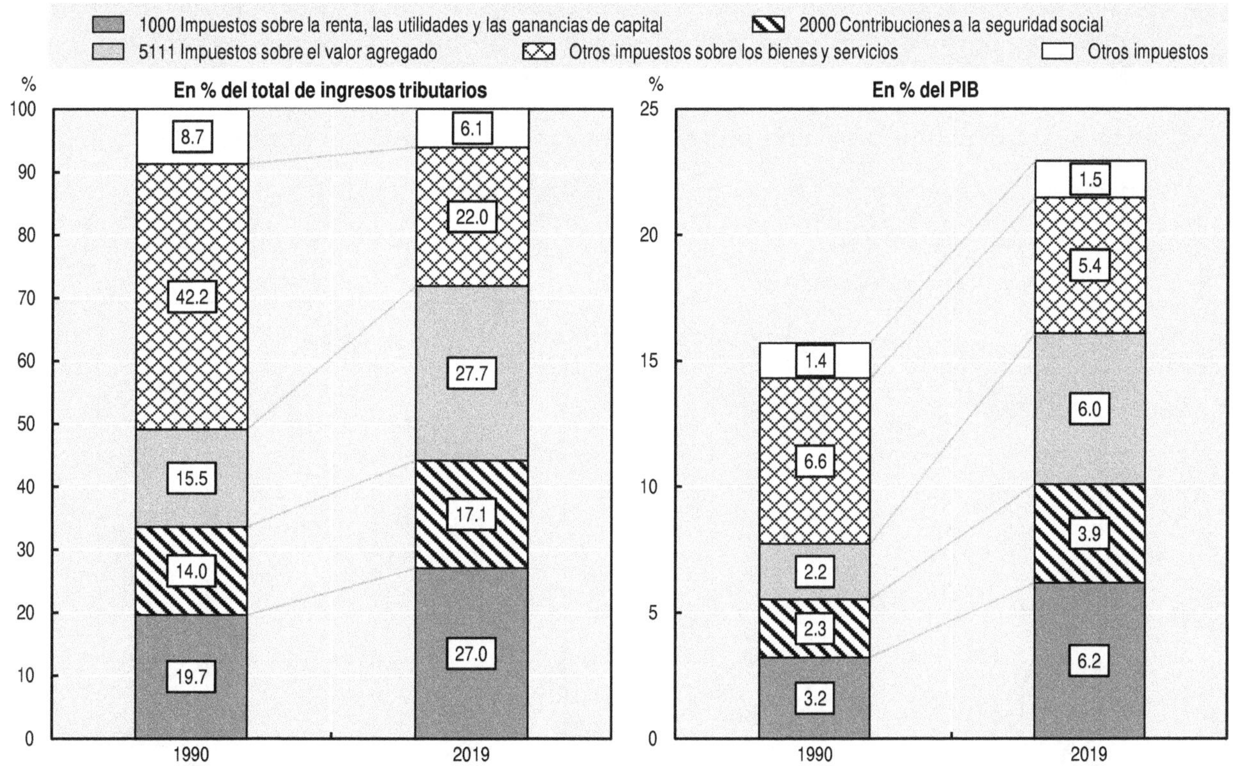

Nota: El promedio de América Latina y el Caribe representa el promedio no ponderado de 26 países de la región incluidos en esta publicación y excluye a Venezuela, debido a problemas de disponibilidad de datos.

Fuente: Los cálculos de los autores se basan en OCDE et al. (2021[1]), Capítulo 4.

StatLink https://doi.org/10.1787/888934234423

La parte de los ingresos procedentes del IRPF creció hasta un 7.7% de los ingresos tributarios totales en 2005 y hasta un 9.2% en 2019, en parte debido al aumento de los ingresos por impuesto sobre la renta en toda la región. Sin embargo, la parte proporcional de los ingresos procedentes del IRPF siguen siendo bajos en América Latina y el Caribe, a pesar de que algunos países han puesto en práctica reformas para ampliar su base impositiva. Tras la crisis financiera global, varios países establecieron tasas planas sobre los ingresos de capital que antes habían estado exentos e implantaron tasas progresivas sobre las rentas del trabajo (CEPAL, 2014[21]). Sin embargo, hay relativamente pocos contribuyentes, dada la concentración de generadores de ingresos con bajos niveles de ingresos: en 2013, únicamente estaban registrados como contribuyentes el 10% de la población de América Latina (BID, 2013[19]).

Otros factores siguen limitando los ingresos por IRPF, incluyendo una pequeña base tributaria compuesta principalmente por salarios (dado que los privilegios fiscales a menudo se otorgan a los rendimientos del capital) y existen altos niveles de evasión (Barreix, Benítez y Pecho, 2017[22]; CEPAL, 2014[21]). CEPAL (2020[11]) afirma que las tasas de evasión relativas al IRPF son altas en determinados países de América Latina y el Caribe, en los que se han realizado estudios sobre evasión fiscal, que van desde 18.7% en México (cifra de 2016, equivalente a pérdidas de ingresos tributarios de un 0.8% del PIB) al 69.9% en Guatemala (cifra de 2006, equivalente a unas pérdidas de ingresos tributarios del 0.5% del PIB). La evasión es más común entre los trabajadores por cuenta propia que entre los empleados. Un estudio relativo a México, en el que se realizaba un desglose de la tasa de evasión para diferentes grupos, llegaba a la conclusión de que las pérdidas de ingresos tributarios como porcentaje del PIB eran cerca de cinco veces más altos para las personas físicas que desarrollaban actividades comerciales que para los asalariados (CEPAL, 2020[11]).

Gráfico 1.11. **Estructura tributaria promedio en América Latina y el Caribe, 2005 y 2019**

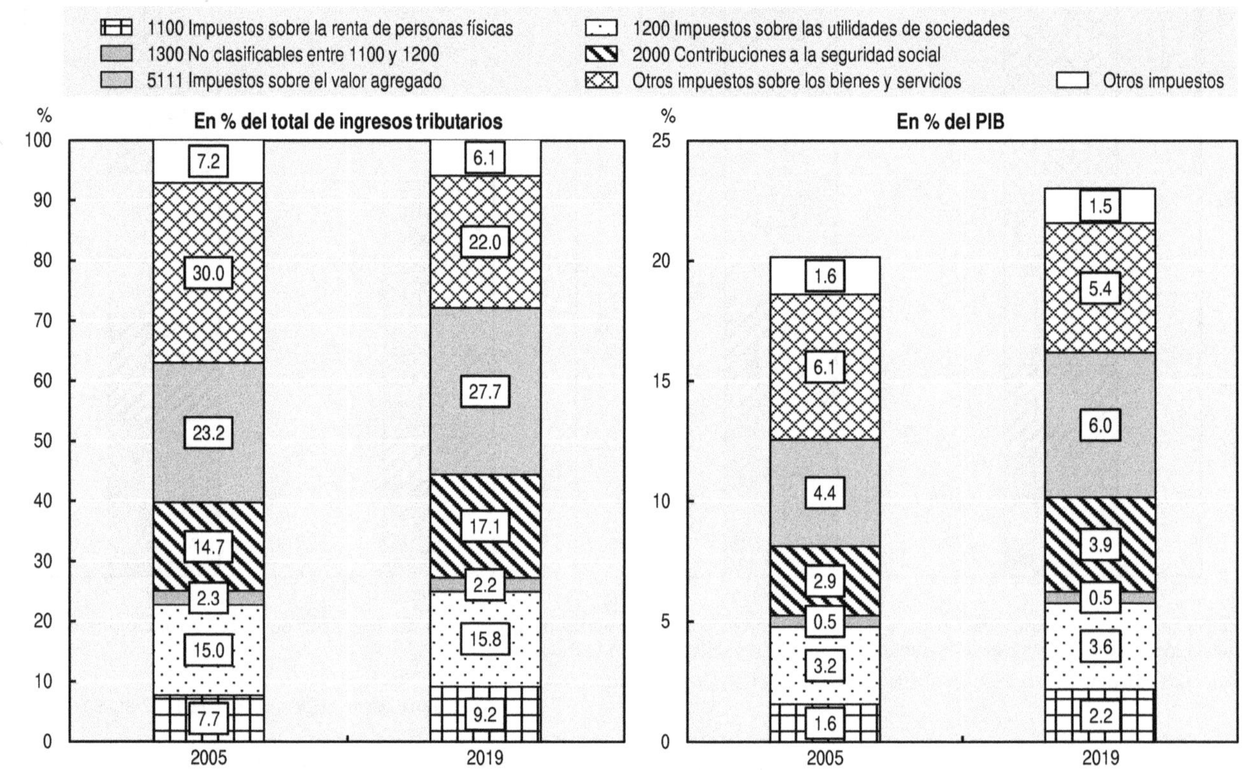

Nota: El promedio del IS y el IRPF, como porcentaje del PIB, deben interpretarse con precaución, ya que Ecuador y Venezuela se excluyen del cálculo. El promedio de América Latina y el Caribe excluye a Venezuela debido a problemas de disponibilidad de datos. Ecuador está excluido del promedio de América Latina y el Caribe en relación con los IS como porcentaje del PIB y los ingresos del IRPF como porcentaje del PIB, dado que más de un tercio de sus ingresos procedentes de impuestos sobre la renta y beneficios no se puede asignar a los ingresos del IS (1200) o ingresos del IRPF (1100).

Fuente: Los cálculos de los autores se basan en OCDE et al. (2021[1]), "Revenue Statistics in Latin America: Comparative tables", *OECD Tax Statistics* (database), *http://dx.doi.org/ 10.1787/data-00641-en.*

StatLink *https://doi.org/10.1787/888934234442*

La participación de los ingresos procedentes del IS en ingresos tributarios totales aumentó 0.8 puntos porcentuales desde 2005 y alcanzó un 15.8% en 2019. La evasión del IS también es un tema importante en la región de América Latina y el Caribe, con tasas de evasión más altas que las del IRPF. Dado que la cuota de los ingresos procedente del IS prácticamente dobla la cuota del IRPF, las pérdidas de ingresos tributarios están lejos de ser insignificantes. CEPAL (2020[11]) afirma que "las tasas de evasión relativas al impuesto de sociedad van de un 19.9% en México a casi un 80% en Guatemala". Debido a las altas tasas de evasión, se estima que las pérdidas de ingresos tributarios son superiores al 4.0% del PIB en la República Dominicana, Guatemala, Perú y Panamá.

En 2019, en general existieron diferencias notables en la estructura tributaria en todas las subregiones (Gráfico 1.12). La mayor parte de los ingresos en el Caribe se derivaron de impuestos sobre bienes y servicios distintos del IVA, que en promedio representaban el 29.3% de los ingresos tributarios totales. Estos impuestos contribuyeron al 17.2% de los ingresos tributarios totales en América del Sur y al 20.4% en Centroamérica y México. Por su parte, América del Sur tuvo la mayor participación en los ingresos por IVA en 2019, con un promedio de un 30.5%, en comparación con un 27.9% en el Caribe y un 24.8% en Centroamérica y México. Las cotizaciones a la seguridad social fueron las más bajas en el Caribe en 2019, con un promedio de un 11.5% de los ingresos tributarios totales. Esto fue ligeramente superior a la mitad del promedio del resto de subregiones (19.3% en Centroamérica y México, y 20.0% en América del Sur). Por último, las tres subregiones generaron mayores ingresos por el IS que por el IRPF.

Gráfico 1.12. **Estructura tributaria promedio en América Latina y subregiones, 2019**

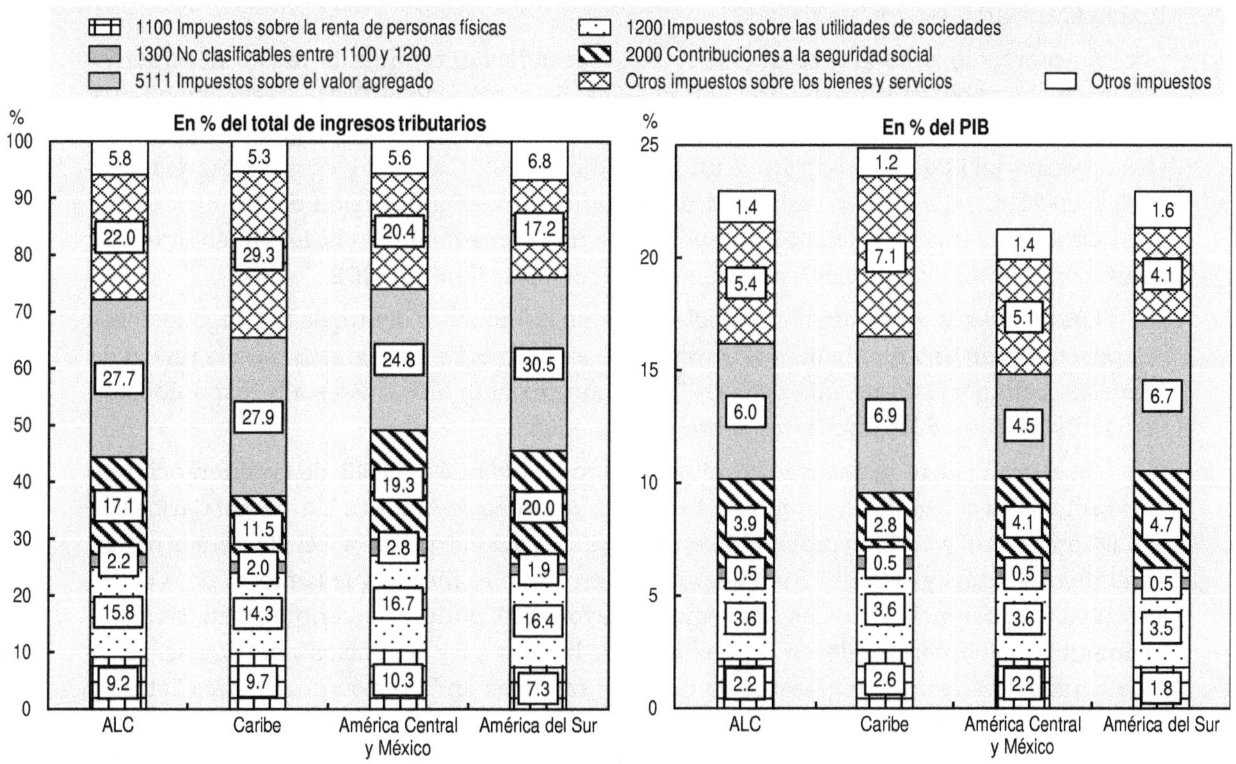

Nota: El promedio del IS y el IRPF, como porcentaje del PIB, de América Latina y el Caribe deben interpretarse con precaución, ya que Ecuador y Venezuela se excluyen del cálculo. El promedio de América Latina y el Caribe excluye a Venezuela debido a problemas de disponibilidad de datos. Ecuador está excluido del promedio de América Latina y el Caribe en relación con los ingresos del IS como porcentaje del PIB y los ingresos del IRPF como porcentaje del PIB, dado que más de un tercio de sus ingresos procedentes de impuestos sobre la renta y beneficios no se puede asignar a los ingresos del IS (1200) o ingresos del IRPF (1100). El Caribe incluye ocho países (Antigua y Barbuda, Bahamas, Barbados, Belice, Guyana, Jamaica, Trinidad y Tobago, y Santa Lucía), América Central y México nueve países (Costa Rica, Cuba, República Dominicana, El Salvador, Guatemala, Honduras, México, Nicaragua y Panamá) y América del Sur nueve países (Argentina, Bolivia, Brasil, Chile, Colombia, Ecuador, Paraguay, Perú y Uruguay). La clasificación de los países en las diferentes subregiones sigue la clasificación de CEPAL y se basa en el idioma oficial de los países. El Caribe incluye a los países de habla inglesa de la región y Guyana, y Centroamérica y México abarca los países de habla hispana, incluyendo República Dominicana y Cuba.

Fuente: Los cálculos de los autores se basan en OCDE et al. (2021[1]), "Revenue Statistics in Latin America: Comparative tables", *OECD Tax Statistics* (database), *http://dx.doi.org/ 10.1787/data-00641-en.*

StatLink https://doi.org/10.1787/888934234461

Estructura tributaria promedio en la región de América Latina y el Caribe y la OCDE

El promedio de ingresos impositivos en la región de América Latina y el Caribe muestra bajos ingresos de impuestos sobre la renta y las contribuciones a la Seguridad Social en comparación con el promedio de la OCDE (Gráfico 1.13). En particular, los países de América Latina y el Caribe dependen en gran medida de los impuestos sobre bienes y servicios, que en promedio representan más de la mitad de los ingresos tributarios, en comparación con el promedio de alrededor de un tercio en las economías de la OCDE. Sin embargo, como porcentaje del PIB, los ingresos por impuestos sobre bienes y servicios en las regiones de América Latina y el Caribe y de la OCDE fueron similares en 2018, situados en 11.4% y 10.9%, respectivamente[4].

Por el contrario, la participación combinada de los impuestos sobre la renta, los beneficios y las cotizaciones a la seguridad social fue mucho menor en la región de América Latina y Caribe que en la OCDE (un promedio del 43.9% frente al 60.0% en 2018). Como porcentaje del PIB, la suma de estas dos categorías representaron un 10.0% en la región América Latina y el Caribe, menos de la mitad del promedio del nivel de la OCDE (20.5%). La tendencia a las prestaciones privadas de la seguridad social en muchos países de la región explica, en parte, esta diferencia.

En promedio, el IS generó un 15.5% de la recaudación total en la región de América Latina y el Caribe, en comparación con el 10.0% en el área de la OCDE (respectivamente 3.5% y 3.1% del PIB) (Gráfico 1.13). La diferencia más notable entre las regiones se refiere a los ingresos del IRPF, que contribuyó un promedio del 23.5% a los ingresos tributarios de la OCDE en 2018, y del 9.1% de los ingresos tributarios totales en la región de América Latina y el Caribe. Los ingresos del IRPF ascendieron a un promedio del 2.1% del PIB en la región de América Latina y el Caribe, en comparación con el 8.1% de la OCDE.

Los impuestos sobre bienes inmuebles y nóminas (incluidos dentro de la categoría "otros impuestos") son una fuente menos importante, en promedio, de ingresos para la región de América Latina y el Caribe que en la OCDE, aunque existen dificultades a la disponibilidad de datos relativos a los impuestos sobre la propiedad.

En el Gráfico 1.14 se analiza la evolución, como porcentaje del PIB, de las diferencias en las principales categorías de impuestos entre las regiones de América Latina y el Caribe y la OCDE entre 1990 y 2018. La proporción entre la recaudación tributaria y el PIB para la región de América Latina y el Caribe fue 15.4 puntos porcentuales menor que la media de la OCDE en 1990. La diferencia entre las dos regiones cayó a 11.2 puntos porcentuales en 2018. Los aumentos en los ingresos de los impuestos sobre la renta y los beneficios y del IVA, así como la disminución de otros impuestos de bienes y servicios en la región de América Latina y el Caribe durante dicho período contribuyó a la reducción de la diferencia en el promedio de la proporción entre la recaudación tributaria y el PIB entre América Latina y el Caribe y la OCDE. Sin embargo, se produjo un incremento en la diferencia entre los promedios de América Latina y el Caribe y la OCDE en relación con las cotizaciones a la seguridad social entre 1990 y 2018, dado que el promedio de la OCDE aumentó más que el promedio de América Latina y el Caribe durante el mismo período.

Estas tendencias han afectado a la convergencia de las estructuras tributarias entre las regiones. El Gráfico 1.15 muestra el índice-D[5] entre 2005 y 2018, que muestra la convergencia de la estructura tributaria promedio de América Latina y el Caribe con el promedio de la OCDE. Se calcula como la suma de las diferencias absolutas entre la proporción de cada categoría tributaria en el promedio de América Latina y el Caribe y su proporción en el promedio de los ingresos tributarios de la OCDE a un nivel más granular (desglosando los ingresos derivados del impuesto sobre la renta procedente del IRPF y el IS). Una cifra de 0 indica paridad perfecta, mientras que 200 indica una disparidad absoluta.

Gráfico 1.13. **Estructura tributaria promedio en América Latina y el Caribe y la OCDE, 2018**

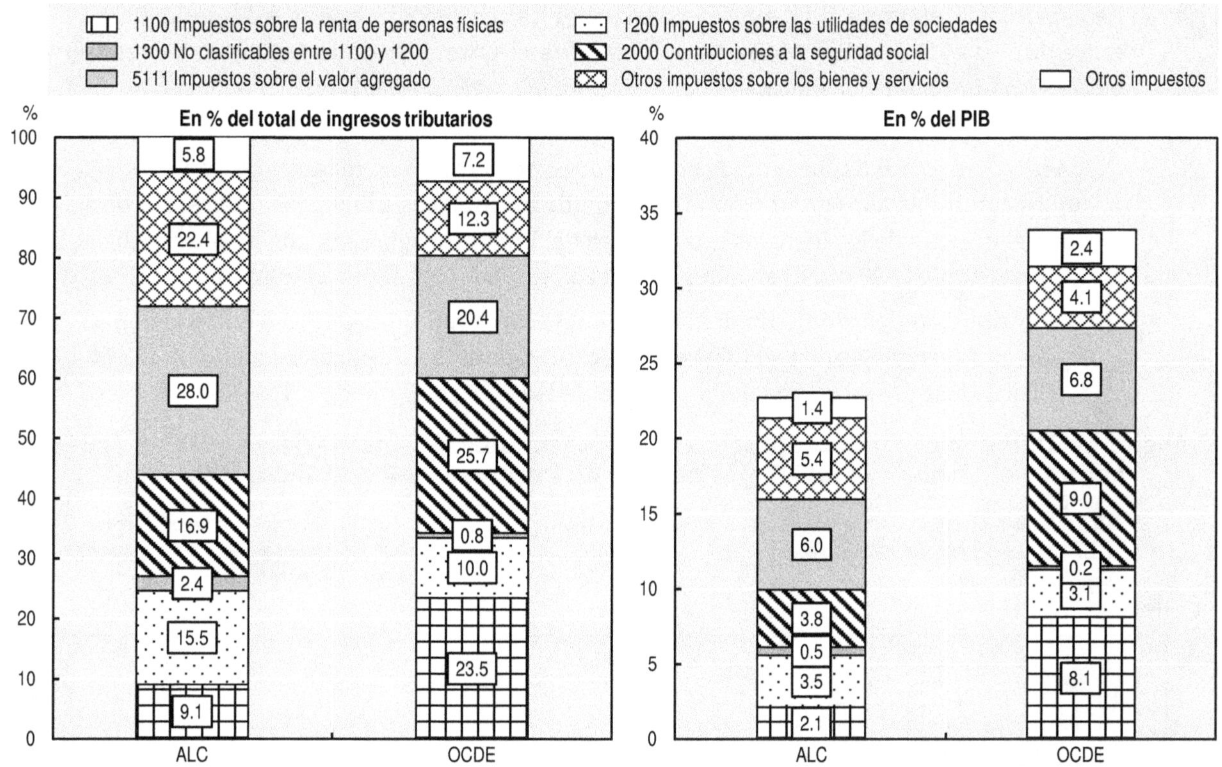

Nota: El año de comparación es 2018, dado que los datos de 2019 para el promedio de la OCDE no están disponibles. El promedio del IS y el IRPF, como porcentaje del PIB de América Latina y el Caribe, deben interpretarse con precaución, ya que Ecuador y Venezuela se excluyen del cálculo. El promedio de América Latina y el Caribe excluye a Venezuela debido a problemas de disponibilidad de datos. Ecuador está excluido del promedio de América Latina y el Caribe en relación con los ingresos del IS y del IRPF como porcentaje del PIB, dado que más de un tercio de sus ingresos procedentes de impuestos sobre la renta y beneficios no se puede asignar a los ingresos del IS (1200) o ingresos del IRPF (1100). El promedio de la OCDE representa el promedio no ponderado de los 37 países miembros de la OCDE. Chile, Colombia y México también forman parte del grupo OCDE (37).

Fuente: Los cálculos de los autores se basan en OCDE et al. (2021[1]), "Revenue Statistics in Latin America: Comparative tables", *OECD Tax Statistics* (database), *http://dx.doi.org/10.1787/data-00641-en.*

StatLink *https://doi.org/10.1787/888934234480*

Se pueden distinguir tres fases distintas en la evolución de la convergencia de la estructura tributaria de América Latina y el Caribe y la OCDE:

- Entre 2005 y 2007, la estructura tributaria de América Latina y el Caribe comenzó a ser cada vez más divergente de la estructura tributaria de la OCDE.
- Entre 2008 y 2017, la estructura tributaria de América Latina y el Caribe se desplazó de forma constante hacia la estructura tributaria de la OCDE. La participación de los ingresos procedentes del IRPF se incrementaron en América Latina y el Caribe acercándose al promedio de la OCDE entre 2008 y 2017 (de un 8.0% de los ingresos tributarios totales a un 9.2% en 2017, en comparación con el 23.4% de la OCDE), mientras que la parte de ingresos de otros impuestos sobre bienes y servicios se redujo hacia el promedio de la

OCDE durante el mismo período (del 24.4% de los ingresos tributarios totales al 23.1% en comparación con el 12.6% de la OCDE). Por el contrario, el nivel de ingresos por IVA en la región de América Latina y el Caribe y la OCDE creció de forma más dispar durante el período. La participación de América Latina y el Caribe aumentó del 26.6% de los ingresos tributarios totales en 2008 a un 27.6% en 2017, mientras que la media de la OCDE aumentó más lentamente, del 19.9% al 20.4% durante el mismo período.

- La estructura tributaria de América Latina y el Caribe fue divergente a la de la OCDE entre 2017 y 2018 (el último año disponible para el promedio de la OCDE). Esto puede explicarse por diferentes factores:
  - En 2018, el IRPF y las cotizaciones a la seguridad social disminuyeron en la región de América Latina y el Caribe (ambos en 0.1 puntos porcentuales); mientras que en la OCDE ambas categorías aumentaron su proporción de los ingresos tributarios totales. Por otra parte, el importe de los ingresos procedentes del impuesto sobre la renta no susceptibles de asignación al IRPF o al IS en la región de América Latina y el Caribe aumentó en 2018.
  - La contribución del promedio del IVA al porcentaje total de ingresos tributarios en la región de América Latina y el Caribe aumentó 0.4 puntos porcentuales hasta un 28.0%, desplazándose así más lejos del promedio de la OCDE, que fue de un 20.4%.

Gráfico 1.14. **Diferencias en la proporción entre la recaudación tributaria y el PIB en América Latina y el Caribe y la OCDE por partida de impuesto seleccionado, 1990-2018**

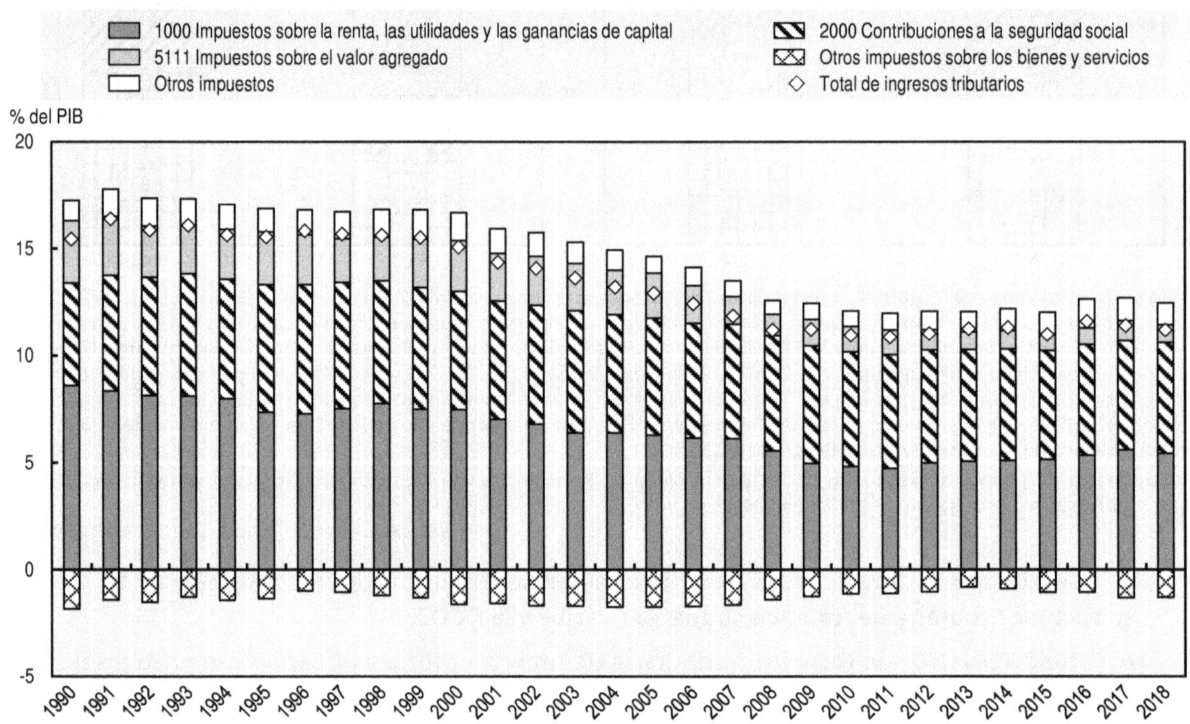

Nota: Los datos cubren el período 1990-2018, dado que los datos de 2019 para el promedio de la OCDE no están disponibles. El promedio de América Latina y el Caribe representa el grupo de 26 países de la región incluidos en esta publicación y excluye a Venezuela, debido a problemas de disponibilidad de datos. El promedio de la OCDE representa el promedio no ponderado de los 37 países miembros de la OCDE. Chile, Colombia y México también forman parte del grupo OCDE (37).

Fuente: Los cálculos de los autores se basan en OCDE et al. (2021[1]), "Revenue Statistics in Latin America: Comparative tables", *OECD Tax Statistics* (database), *http://dx.doi.org/ 10.1787/data-00641-en.*

StatLink https://doi.org/10.1787/888934234499

Gráfico 1.15. **Distancia con respecto a la estructura tributaria promedio de América Latina y el Caribe y la OCDE (índice-D), 2005-18**

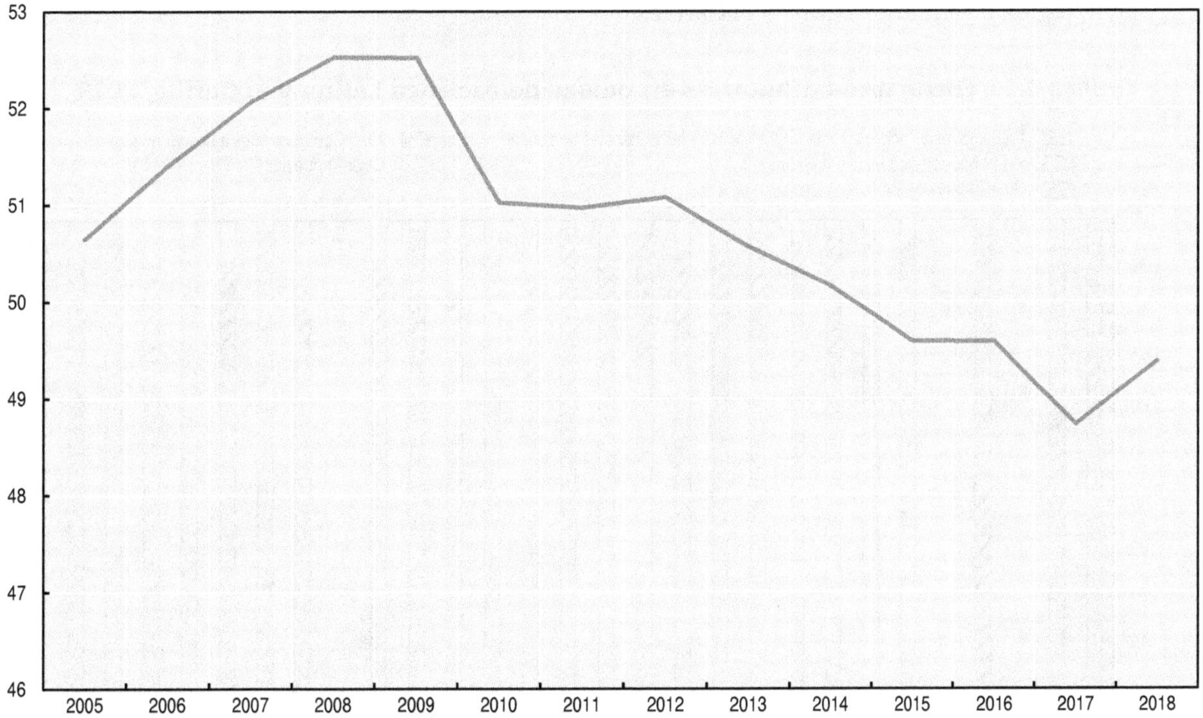

Nota: El índice-D se calcula como la suma de las diferencias absolutas entre la proporción de cada categoría tributaria en el promedio de América Latina y el Caribe y su proporción en el promedio de los ingresos tributarios de la OCDE. Una cifra de 0 indica paridad perfecta, mientras que 200 indica una disparidad absoluta. El promedio de América Latina y el Caribe representa el promedio no ponderado de 26 países de la región incluidos en esta publicación y excluye Venezuela, debido a problemas de disponibilidad de datos. El promedio de la OCDE representa el promedio no ponderado de los 37 países miembros de la OCDE. Chile, Colombia y México también forman parte del grupo OCDE (37).

Fuente: Los cálculos de los autores se basan en OCDE et al. (2021[1]), "Revenue Statistics in Latin America: Comparative tables", *OECD Tax Statistics* (database), *http://dx.doi.org/ 10.1787/data-00641-en.*

StatLink *https://doi.org/10.1787/888934234518*

Estructura tributaria en los países de América Latina y el Caribe

Los impuestos sobre bienes y servicios son la principal fuente de ingresos para todos los países de la región, excepto México, Panamá y Trinidad y Tobago. Para México y Trinidad y Tobago, los ingresos por impuestos sobre la renta y los beneficios representaron la mayor proporción, mientras que los ingresos de las cargas sociales fue la fuente más importante de ingresos tributarios para Panamá (Gráfico 1.16).

En la mayoría de los países en los que los ingresos procedentes de los impuestos sobre bienes y servicios son la principal fuente de ingresos, los ingresos por IVA aportaron una mayor proporción que los impuestos sobre bienes y servicios distintos del IVA, tales como los impuestos específicos y derechos de importación. Quince países registraron mayores ingresos tributarios procedentes de la recaudación del IVA, que fueron desde el 22.5% de los ingresos tributarios totales en Nicaragua hasta el 39.9% en Chile; por el contrario, ocho países (incluyendo cinco del Caribe) registraron una mayor proporción de los ingresos procedentes de los impuestos sobre bienes y servicios distintos al IVA. Este grupo también incluye a Argentina, que obtiene un 27.3% de los ingresos tributarios totales de los ingresos procedentes de los impuestos sobre bienes y servicios distintos al IVA: los impuestos de exportación representaron poco menos de una cuarta parte de esta categoría y constituyeron el equivalente al 1.9% del PIB, en comparación con un promedio de menos de 0.1% del PIB en la región de América Latina y el Caribe.

Gráfico 1.16. **Estructuras tributarias en países de América Latina y el Caribe, 2019**

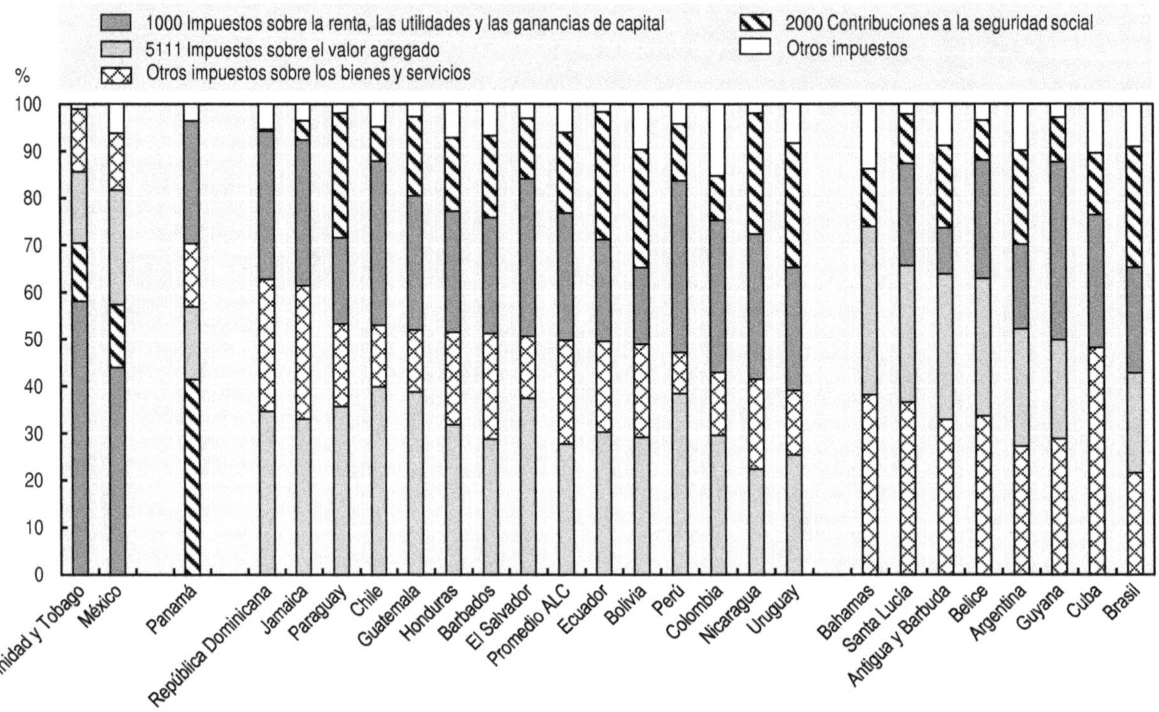

Nota: Los países están agrupados en función de la proporción principal de los ingresos tributarios por la parte principal de los ingresos tributarios entre 1000 impuestos sobre la renta y beneficios, 2000 de cotizaciones a la seguridad social, 5111 impuestos sobre el valor añadido y otros impuestos sobre bienes y servicios. Las Bahamas no aplica impuesto sobre la renta. No existe un sistema de IVA en Cuba. El promedio de América Latina y el Caribe representa el promedio no ponderado de 26 países de la región incluidos en esta publicación y excluye a Venezuela, debido a problemas de disponibilidad de datos.

Fuente: Los cálculos de los autores se basan en OCDE et al. (2021[1]), Capítulo 4.

StatLink https://doi.org/10.1787/888934234537

En 2019, las cotizaciones a la seguridad social variaron desde el 0.4% de los ingresos tributarios totales en la República Dominicana hasta un 41.5% en Panamá. El nivel de estos ingresos refleja las opciones sobre la forma de financiar la seguridad social: en los países con regímenes públicos o mixtos de seguridad social (incluyendo Argentina, Brasil, Costa Rica, Panamá, Paraguay y Uruguay), las cotizaciones a la seguridad social representan más del 20% del total de los ingresos de impuestos.

El índice-D también se utilizó para analizar la convergencia de las estructuras tributarias en cada país de América Latina y el Caribe con el promedio de América Latina y el Caribe. En 2019, el índice-D registró el nivel más bajo en Barbados (5.1) y Honduras (10.1), lo que indica que estos países guardan una mayor similitud con la estructura media, y el nivel más alto fue para Trinidad y Tobago, Cuba y las Bahamas (los tres tienen un índice-D superior a 60), lo que indica que estos países tienen las estructuras más dispares a las de la mayoría de los países de la región (Gráfico 1.17).

El Gráfico 1.17 muestra el promedio de la estructura de impuestos de América Latina y el Caribe en comparación con la de los países de América Latina y el Caribe mediante el aumento del nivel de disparidad. La disparidad del promedio de la estructura tributaria de América Latina y el Caribe se explica por la ausencia de un sistema de impuestos sobre la renta en las Bahamas, por la ausencia de la aplicación del IVA y la alta proporción de otros impuestos sobre bienes y servicios (principalmente el impuesto sobre las ventas) en Cuba y por la alta proporción del impuesto sobre la renta en Trinidad y Tobago.

Los cinco países del Caribe, cuyas estructuras tributarias mostraron la mayor convergencia con el promedio de América Latina y el Caribe entre 2000 y 2019 fueron Antigua y Barbuda, Bahamas, Belice, Guyana y Santa Lucía. Esto se explica por la introducción del IVA en esos países. En 2019, los ingresos por IVA representaron el 21.0% de los ingresos tributarios totales en Guyana y el 35.7% en las Bahamas. Entre 2000 y 2019, las estructuras tributarias también se volvieron más similares en toda la región de América Latina y el Caribe, ya que muchos países incrementaron sus proporciones de IVA, IRPF y cotizaciones a la Seguridad Social, a la vez que disminuyeron la proporción de los ingresos procedentes de otros impuestos sobre bienes y servicios.

Gráfico 1.17. **Estructuras tributarias en los países de ALC mediante el aumento del nivel de disparidad con el promedio ALC, 2019**

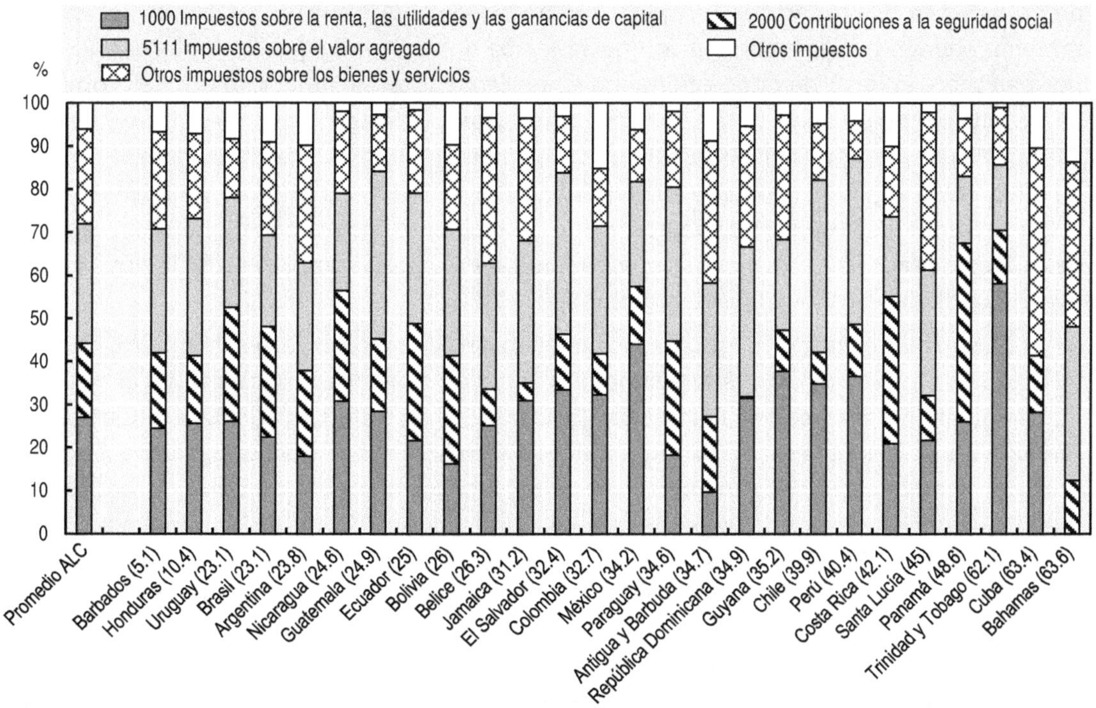

Nota: Las Bahamas no aplica impuesto sobre la renta. No existe un sistema de IVA en Cuba. El promedio de América Latina y el Caribe representa el promedio no ponderado de 26 países de la región incluidos en esta publicación y excluye a Venezuela, debido a problemas de disponibilidad de datos. El índice-D mostrado entre paréntesis junto a los nombres de los países refleja el índice-D de cada país. El índice-D se calcula como la suma de las diferencias absolutas entre la proporción de cada categoría tributaria en cada país de América Latina y el Caribe y su proporción en el promedio de los ingresos tributarios de América Latina y el Caribe. Una cifra de 0 indica paridad perfecta, mientras que 200 indica una disparidad absoluta. El promedio de América Latina y el Caribe representa el promedio no ponderado de 26 países de la región incluidos en esta publicación y excluye a Venezuela, debido a problemas de disponibilidad de datos.

Fuente: Los cálculos de los autores se basan en OCDE et al. (2021[1]), Capítulo 4.

StatLink https://doi.org/10.1787/888934234556

Ratio de recaudación de IVA

En esta sección se analiza el ratio de recaudación de IVA en los países de América Latina y el Caribe en 2019. El ratio de recaudación de IVA "mide la diferencia entre la recaudación observada efectiva del IVA y la recaudación teórica del IVA si se aplicara un tipo único a toda la base potencial impositiva en un régimen de IVA "puro" y se recaudaran todos los ingresos" (OCDE, 2020[29]). El ratio de recaudación de IVA es el ratio de los ingresos efectivos procedentes del IVA con respecto al producto o consumo final (neto de los ingresos del IVA) y el tipo único del IVA. Los cálculos se muestran a continuación.

$$\frac{\text{Ingresos del IVA}}{(\text{gastos de consumo final} - \text{ingresos de IVA}).\text{tipo de IVA único}}$$

Este indicador da una idea de los ingresos por IVA que se pierden a causa de las exenciones y los tipos reducidos, el fraude, la evasión y la planificación tributaria, así como por las deficiencias de las agencias tributarias. Sin embargo, este indicador debe interpretarse teniendo en cuenta las características subyacentes del sistema del IVA de cada país, ya que un ratio de recaudación de IVA elevado podría ser el resultado de efectos en cascada (por ejemplo, cuando la exención se produce en las primeras etapas de la cadena de suministro) o porque no se ha conseguido recuperar un crédito por IVA soportado. Otros factores que también pueden influir en la relación hacia arriba o hacia abajo: por ejemplo, cuando las normas sobre el lugar de imposición para el comercio internacional difieren del principio de destino o cuando no se recauda el impuesto sobre los suministros digitales entrantes. También es importante señalar que la interpretación del ratio es más difícil para los países que dependen significativamente del turismo. Estos países pueden tener un ratio elevado por razones metodológicas: las compras de los no residentes no pueden incluirse en el gasto de consumo final (el denominador) mientras que el IVA de esas compras sí se incluye en los ingresos globales del IVA (el numerador) (Keen, 2013[30]).

El Cuadro 1.1 presenta el ratio de recaudación del IVA para los países de América Latina y el Caribe y para las distintas subregiones. El mayor ratio de recaudación del IVA se registró en las Bahamas y muchos otros países del Caribe tienen también un ratio de recaudación de IVA alto. Los países de la región introdujeron el IVA en la década de dos mil, mucho después que los países del resto de subregiones. Esto refleja en parte un compromiso con las buenas prácticas internacionales, incluyendo una base amplia de IVA con un tipo único bajo, un número limitado de exenciones y sin tipo reducido. Este es el caso de las Bahamas, que introdujo el IVA en 2015, con un tipo único del 7.5% (que más tarde incrementó al 12.0% en julio de 2018). Las Bahamas registró uno de los niveles más altos del ratio de recaudación de IVA en la región de América Latina y el Caribe. Esto puede ser en parte porque recibe una alta proporción de ingresos del turismo en comparación con otros países: los ingresos del turismo internacional como un porcentaje de las exportaciones totales ascendieron al 77% en 2018, en comparación con un promedio del 8% en la región de América Latina y el Caribe (Banco Mundial, 2021[31]).

Por el contrario, los ratios de recaudación del IVA más bajos se registraron en la República Dominicana, Guyana y México (todos por debajo de 0.35). Varios factores contribuyen al bajo ratio de recaudación de IVA en México, incluyendo el alcance de la exención del IVA, la aplicación de una tasa interna de cero a numerosos bienes y servicios, así como un bajo cumplimiento (OCDE, 2020[29]; OCDE, 2018[32]). Sin embargo, México implementó una reforma del IVA en enero de 2014 que incluyó la sustitución de algunas tasas reducidas y cero con un tipo único y la introducción de procesos mejorados. El ratio de recaudación de IVA en México aumentó de 0.28 en 2013 a 0.32 en 2014. El ratio de recaudación IVA puede aumentar aún más como resultado de la ampliación de la base de IVA para los servicios digitales en línea con las recomendaciones de la OCDE (KPMG, 2019[33]), en vigor desde junio de 2020.

Cuadro 1.1. **Ratio de recaudación del IVA en los países de América Latina y el Caribe por regiones, 2019**

	Ratio de recaudación del IVA	Tipo del IVA (%)
América Central y México	**0.47**	**13.6**
Costa Rica	0.45	13.0
República Dominicana	0.35	18.0
El Salvador	0.66	13.0
Guatemala	0.46	12.0
Honduras	0.54	15.0
México	0.33	16.0
Nicaragua	0.47	15.0
Panamá	0.51	7.0
América del Sur	**0.57**	**16.8**
Argentina	0.46	21.0
Bolivia	0.70	13.0
Chile	0.63	19.0
Colombia	0.39	19.0
Ecuador	0.74	12.0
Paraguay	0.71	10.0
Perú	0.50	18.0
Uruguay	0.45	22.0
Caribe	**0.64**	**14.4**
Antigua y Barbuda	0.63	15.0
Bahamas	0.82	12.0
Barbados	0.68	17.5
Belice	0.99	12.5
Guyana	0.28	14.0
Jamaica	0.71	16.5
Santa Lucía	0.64	15.0
Trinidad y Tobago	0.35	12.5
Promedio América Latina y el Caribe	**0.56**	**14.9**
Promedio OCDE	**0.56**	**19.3**

Nota: Brasil, Cuba y Venezuela están excluidos. Brasil opera un sistema de múltiples tasas, y los impuestos se aplican con diferentes tasas en cada nivel subnacional. Cuba no aplicó ningún sistema de IVA en 2019. Los datos de ingresos tributarios de Venezuela no estaban disponibles en 2019.

Fuente: Los tipos de IVA se han obtenido de los sitios web de CIAT, Trading Economics y Deloitte; las cifras de consumo del gasto final de la página web División de Estadística de Naciones Unidas y los ingresos procedentes del IVA de los cuadros de países de la OCDE et al. (2021[1]), Capítulo 5 OCDE (2020[29]) para las cifras de la OCDE.

StatLink https://doi.org/10.1787/888934234670

Una serie de factores pueden contribuir al bajo ratio de recaudación del IVA en la República Dominicana. Uno de los factores es el diseño del IVA: la República Dominicana cuenta con numerosas exenciones del IVA y sufre un bajo nivel de cumplimiento (Schlotterbeck, 2017[34]). La evasión del IVA es otro factor importante para el bajo ratio de recaudación. CEPAL (2020[11]) calcula que la evasión del IVA en la República Dominicana se encuentra entre las más altas de la región de América Latina y el Caribe, que se sitúa en un 43.8% (cifra de 2017) frente a un promedio del 30% en una muestra de 12 países de América Latina y el Caribe.

La evasión del IVA sigue siendo un reto importante en la región de América Latina y el Caribe. CEPAL (2020[11]) ha examinado varios estudios sobre la evasión del IVA en 12 países y observó que las tasas de incumplimiento del pago del IVA en la región variaron de 14.8% en Uruguay a 45.3% en Panamá en el 2016. Guatemala, República Dominicana y Panamá registraron los mayores aumentos (de un 30% o más) en la tasa de evasión del IVA desde el año 2009.

Ingresos por impuestos relacionados con el medio ambiente

A raíz del Acuerdo de París de 2016, los países se han comprometido a reducir las emisiones de carbono de sus economías para mediados de siglo, lo que implica una sustitución de los combustibles fósiles como fuente de energía. Los impuestos ambientales, y los instrumentos de política basados, de forma más general, en los precios, han ido ganando protagonismo en muchos países. Mediante la incorporación de una señal de precio en las decisiones de los consumidores, estos impuestos implementan el principio de "quien contamina paga" y llevan a empresas y hogares a plantearse el costo ambiental de sus acciones.

Un impuesto ambiental es un impuesto cuya base es una unidad física (o un equivalente de una unidad física) de algo que tiene un probado y específico impacto nocivo sobre el medio ambiente, independientemente de si el impuesto está destinado a cambiar las conductas o se aplica para otro objetivo (OCDE, 2005[35]).

Un examen detallado de los impuestos específicos de cada país[6] para los 25 países de la región objeto de este informe demuestra que el promedio de los ingresos por impuestos relacionados con el medio ambiente ascendió a 1.2%[7] del PIB en 2019, un nivel más bajo que la media de la OCDE de 2.1% del PIB (cifra estimada de 2019) (OCDE, 2021[36]). Sin embargo, como porcentaje de los ingresos tributarios totales, los ingresos por impuestos relacionados con el medio ambiente se situaron en niveles similares en la región de ALC y la OCDE [5.7% y 6.4% (estimado) en 2019, respectivamente] (OCDE, 2021[36]).

En 2019, los ingresos provenientes de la imposición energética (más comúnmente, sobre el diésel y la gasolina) generaron la mayor proporción de los ingresos tributarios relacionados con el medio ambiente en la región de América Latina y el Caribe. Los ingresos procedentes de productos relacionados con la energía ascendieron al 0.7% del PIB en promedio en 2019 y representaron en torno al 65% de los ingresos tributarios relacionados con el medio ambiente. La recaudación por impuestos sobre los vehículos motorizados y servicios de transporte ascendió al 0.4% del PIB y representa la mayor parte del resto (35%) de los ingresos tributarios relacionados con el medio ambiente. Los ingresos procedentes de impuestos aplicados a otras bases relacionadas con el medio ambiente fueron poco significativos. Los ingresos tributarios relacionados con el medio ambiente para la OCDE fueron superiores a los de la región de América Latina y el Caribe en las diferentes bases, especialmente para los impuestos relacionados con la energía y el transporte (OCDE, 2021[36]). Los promedios de la OCDE de ingresos tributarios relacionados con la energía y el transporte en 2019 ascendieron a 1.5% y 0.5% del PIB, respectivamente (OCDE, 2021[36]).

En 2019, en general existieron diferencias notables en composición de los ingresos tributarios relacionados con el medio ambiente entre las subregiones (Gráfico 1.18). A pesar de que los ingresos tributarios relacionados con la energía representaron la mayor proporción de los ingresos tributarios relacionados con el medio ambiente en Centroamérica y México y América del Sur en 2019, en el Caribe la mayor parte de los ingresos tributarios relacionados con el medio ambiente procedieron de los impuestos al transporte. Los impuestos relacionados con el transporte en Centroamérica y México y en América del Sur se situaron en el 0.3% del PIB en ambas subregiones, aproximadamente la mitad de dicha cantidad en el Caribe. Los ingresos tributarios relacionados con el transporte para la mayoría de los países del Caribe se obtuvieron principalmente de impuestos de viaje o salida, una importante fuente de ingresos para los países que dependen del turismo.

Gráfico 1.18. **Ingresos tributarios relacionados con el medio ambiente en la OCDE, América Latina y el Caribe y las subregiones por base imponible principal, 2019**

Porcentaje del PIB

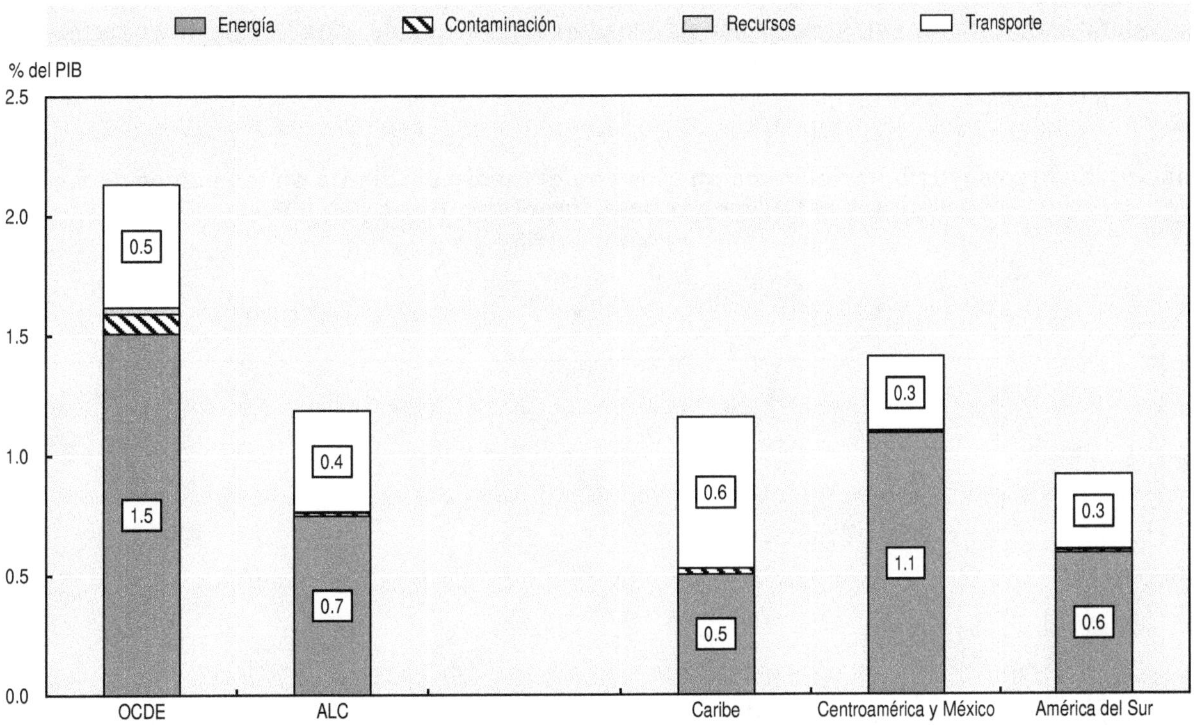

Nota: El promedio de América Latina y el Caribe representa el promedio no ponderado de 25 países de América Latina y el Caribe incluidos en esta publicación y excluye a Cuba y Venezuela debido a problemas de disponibilidad de datos. El promedio de la OCDE representa el promedio no ponderado de los 37 países miembros de la OCDE. Chile, Colombia y México también forman parte del grupo OCDE (37).

Fuente: Base de datos *PINE* para Chile y México, y cálculos para otros países propios a partir de OCDE et al. ($2021_{[1]}$), Capítulo 5.

StatLink https://doi.org/10.1787/888934234575

Los ingresos tributarios relacionados con el medio ambiente en 2019 oscilaron entre el 0.1% del PIB en Belice y el 4.0% en Guyana (Gráfico 1.19). En Guyana, el impuesto sobre la importación de productos petrolíferos representó por sí solo el 2.7% del PIB en 2019.

En 2019, los impuestos sobre la energía se recaudaron sobre todo mediante impuestos especiales. Por el contrario, los ingresos procedentes de los impuestos sobre vehículos de motor y servicios de transporte procedían de tres tipos diferentes de impuestos según la clasificación de la OCDE establecida en la Guía Interpretativa: alrededor de la mitad procedían de impuestos sobre el uso y la propiedad de vehículos, una cuarta parte procedía de impuestos sobre servicios específicos (principalmente impuestos sobre viajes o salidas) y otra cuarta parte de los impuestos especiales sobre los vehículos.

Los países de América Latina y el Caribe han sido lentos en aplicar impuestos relacionados con el medio ambiente. A pesar de que se han introducido impuestos sobre el combustible (principalmente por la recaudación de ingresos más que para fines medioambientales), muchos países también proporcionan subsidios para los productos energéticos (Lorenzo, 2016[37]) con el objeto de mitigar el impacto de los altos y volátiles precios del petróleo, control de la inflación, impulso de la competitividad y la protección de los sectores más pobres de la población. Los subsidios a la energía pueden suponer una carga para los presupuestos nacionales, sin embargo, los ingresos por impuestos a la energía fueron mayores que el costo de los subsidios para 5 de los 6 países de ALC incluidos en el reciente informe de la OCDE (OCDE, 2021[38]) (Costa Rica, República Dominicana, Guatemala, Jamaica y Uruguay, con la excepción de Ecuador), representando en promedio un impacto positivo neto en las finanzas públicas de estos seis países (aproximadamente el 0.6% del PIB en 2018 en promedio).

Gráfico 1.19. **Ingresos tributarios relacionados con el medio ambiente en los países de América Latina y el Caribe por base imponible principal, 2019**

Porcentaje del PIB

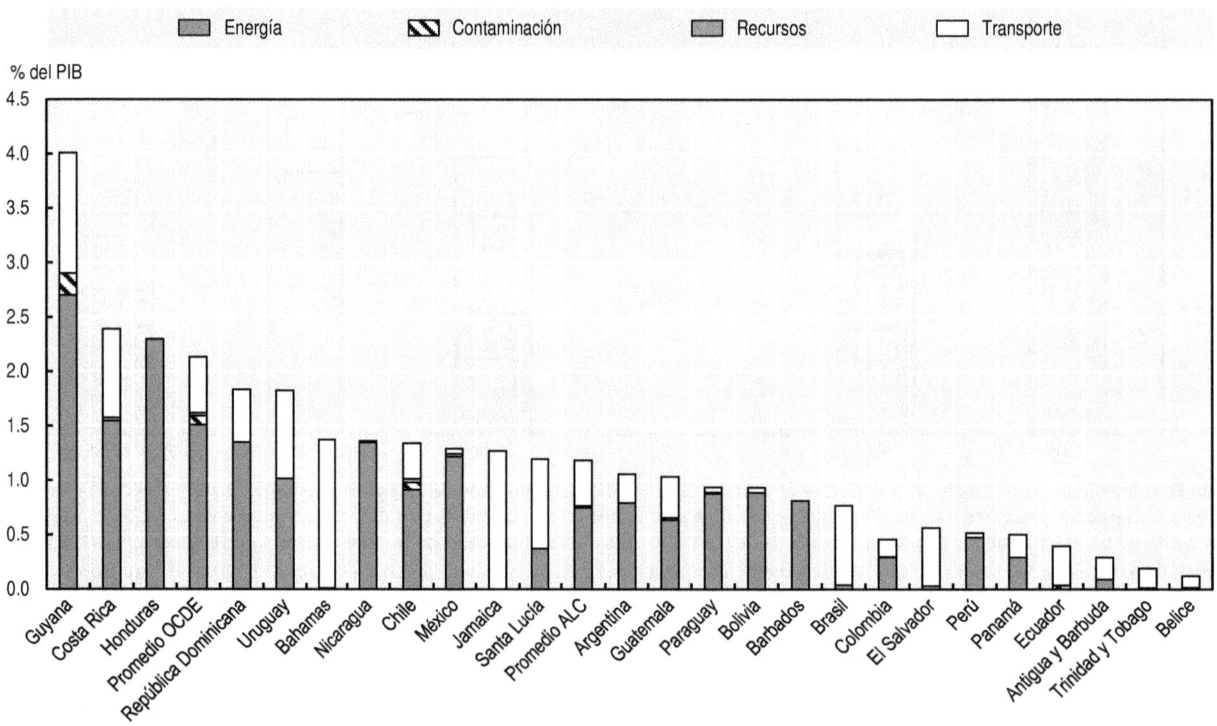

Nota: El promedio de América Latina y el Caribe representa el promedio no ponderado de 25 países de América Latina y el Caribe incluidos en esta publicación y excluye a Cuba y Venezuela debido a problemas de disponibilidad de datos. La cifra no incluye los ingresos de Jamaica procedentes del impuesto especial sobre el consumo de productos petrolíferos (estimados en torno al 2.0% del PIB en 2018) (OCDE, 2021[37]) ya que los datos no están disponibles. El promedio de la OCDE representa el promedio no ponderado de los 37 países miembros de la OCDE. Chile, Colombia y México también forman parte del grupo OCDE (37).

Fuente: Base de datos *PINE* para Chile y México, y los cálculos de los autores para otros países basado en OCDE et al. (2021[1]), Capítulo 5.

StatLink https://doi.org/10.1787/888934234594

Más allá de los impuestos sobre el combustible y la matriculación o uso de vehículos, los impuestos ambientales siguen estando poco desarrollados en toda la región de América Latina y el Caribe. Sin embargo, algunos países de América Latina y el Caribe han introducido importantes reformas fiscales ambientales, incluyendo Chile, México y Colombia:

- En Chile, se aprobó una importante reforma tributaria que incluye nuevos impuestos relacionados con el medio ambiente en 2014 (OCDE/CEPAL, 2016[39]). Esto incluyó un impuesto sobre las compras de vehículos a motor, que se introdujo en 2015 sobre la base de la eficiencia energética y las emisiones de los vehículos. Chile introdujo un impuesto al carbono como parte de los nuevos impuestos verdes (Ley 20.780) que entraron en vigor en 2017. Se aplica una tasa uniforme de 5 USD por tonelada de CO_2 a las emisiones de CO_2 de las instalaciones cuya capacidad total de energía térmica de calderas y turbinas sea de al menos 50 MWt. Los impuestos verdes también se aplican a contaminantes como el material particulado, el NO_X y el SO_2 (OCDE, 2019[40]).
- México introdujo un impuesto sobre el carbono en 2014, aplicado a la venta e importación de combustibles fósiles (excepto el gas natural), de acuerdo con su contenido de carbono. Esto incrementó la proporción de emisiones gravadas, aunque los precios siguen siendo relativamente bajos en comparación con otros países de la OCDE y no reflejan los costos totales asociados con el carbono en estos combustibles (Arlinghaus y Van Dender, 2017[41]). Sin embargo, el impuesto sobre el carbono incrementó significativamente los ingresos tributarios entre 2014 y 2015, generando ingresos equivalentes al 1.2% del PIB en 2015 (OCDE, 2021[36]). México aumentó aún más las tasas impositivas sobre los diferentes combustibles fósiles en 2016. El IEPS (Impuesto Especial Sobre Producción y Servicios) – impuesto al consumo a la gasolina de automoción, gasóleo de automoción y sus equivalentes de biocombustibles en México – se ha actualizado y aumentado de forma periódica.
- En 2016, Colombia introdujo un impuesto sobre el carbono y un impuesto especial sobre las bolsas de plástico. El impuesto sobre el carbono se aplica a los combustibles fósiles de acuerdo con la cantidad de carbono producida por la combustión de combustibles fósiles al precio de 5 dólares USA por tonelada. Los ingresos se asignan a un fondo especial para abordar asuntos ambientales específicos, incluyendo la erosión costera, las fuentes de conservación de agua y la protección del ecosistema (Monge, 2018[42]).

El documento *Effective Carbon Rates* (OCDE, 2021 próximamente[43]) ofrece una descripción general de los precios del carbono en todas las emisiones relacionadas con la energía en 44 países de la OCDE y del G-20 (entre otros, Argentina, Brasil, Chile y México). El documento *Taxing Energy Use* (OCDE, 2019[40]) contiene información detallada sobre tasas tributarias, utilización de energía y la base aplicada al mismo conjunto de países.

Impuestos por nivel de gobierno

En los países de América Latina y el Caribe, los ingresos tributarios se recaudan sobre todo a través de la Administración central o las agencias federales; el gasto público de los gobiernos subnacionales se financia a través de transferencias de niveles superiores a niveles inferiores de gobierno en mayor medida que en los países de la OCDE. Cuando se dispone de datos subnacionales de los países de América Latina y el Caribe, estos indican que los ingresos tributarios recaudados por el gobierno central representaron más de dos tercios del total recaudado en general, mientras que la cifra correspondiente para los países de la OCDE fue de aproximadamente el 60% (cifra de 2018). Brasil es una excepción notable: los ingresos tributarios del gobierno central ascendieron al 43.5% de los impuestos recaudados en 2019[8] (Cuadro 1.2).

Cuadro 1.2. **Atribución de ingresos tributarios a subsectores de la administración general en los países de América Latina y el Caribe[1]**

Porcentaje del total de los ingresos tributarios

	Gobierno central			Gobierno estatal o regional			Administraciones locales			Fondos de seguridad social		
	1995	2000	2019	1995	2000	2019	1995	2000	2019	1995	2000	2019
Países federales												
Argentina	59.0	66.4	63.1	17.5	17.8	16.9	..	..	..	23.4	15.8	19.9
Brasil	44.8	47.9	43.5	26.5	25.0	24.6	3.7	3.4	6.2	25.0	23.7	25.7
Mexico[3]	73.9	78.3	80.9	2.8	2.7	4.0	1.5	1.0	1.6	21.8	18.0	13.4
Venezuela[4]	94.6	94.6	..	..	..	..	..	..	..	5.4	5.4	..
Países regionales												
Colombia[5]	63.2	68.7	73.0	5.5	5.6	5.0	8.6	9.4	12.5	22.7	16.3	9.5
Países unitarios												
Antigua y Barbuda[2]	100.0	100.0	82.4				..	..	..	..	..	17.6
Bahamas[2]	89.1	88.1	87.6				..	..	..	10.9	11.9	12.4
Barbados	85.6	84.4	82.5				..	..	..	14.4	15.6	17.5
Belice	93.2	93.5	91.1				0.5	0.7	0.5	6.3	5.8	8.4
Bolivia	94.3	75.6	70.3				5.7	5.5	4.6	..	18.9	25.1
Chile	89.9	87.8	85.7				6.5	7.9	8.2	3.6	4.4	6.1
Costa Rica	65.5	63.3	57.8				1.6	1.9	3.0	33.0	34.8	39.2
Cuba[6]	..	..	..	..	..	..	..	..	..	11.3	10.4	13.2
República Dominicana	99.3	99.0	99.6				..	..	..	0.7	1.0	0.4
Ecuador[2]	70.5	87.7	70.2				4.0	1.6	2.6	25.5	10.7	27.1
El Salvador	80.9	80.5	85.2				..	..	1.9	19.1	19.5	12.8
Guatemala	83.3	83.6	82.3				0.7	0.9	0.9	16.1	15.5	16.8
Guyana	92.6	88.6	90.5				..	..	0.0	7.4	11.4	9.5
Honduras	86.1	85.3	80.5				4.4	5.2	3.9	9.5	9.4	15.6
Jamaica	100.0	99.3	94.4				..	0.7	1.5	..	..	4.1
Nicaragua	80.4	72.5	68.3				4.6	9.5	6.0	15.0	18.0	25.7
Panamá	67.2	59.6	56.9				..	2.2	1.6	32.8	38.2	41.5
Paraguay	92.0	74.4	70.9				..	..	2.7	8.0	25.6	26.4
Perú	88.7	86.5	85.3				..	1.6	2.7	11.3	11.9	12.1
Santa Lucía[2]	100.0	90.0	89.5				..	..	..	..	10.0	10.5
Trinidad y Tobago[2]	96.8	93.6	87.6				..	..	..	3.2	6.4	12.4
Uruguay	61.7	63.6	67.9				8.8	8.9	5.7	29.5	27.5	26.4

1. Las cifras excluyen los ingresos del gobierno local para Antigua y Barbuda, Argentina (pero incluyen ingresos provinciales), Bahamas, Barbados, Cuba, República Dominicana, Santa Lucía, Trinidad y Tobago y Venezuela, ya que los datos no están disponibles. Los datos de ingresos del gobierno local están disponibles desde 1991 para Nicaragua, desde 1994 para Bolivia, desde 1995 para Guatemala, desde 1998 para Jamaica, desde 1999 para Panamá, desde 2000 para Perú, desde 2002 para El Salvador y Guyana, desde 2006 para Paraguay y desde 1990 para el resto de países.
2. Los datos incluyen las siguientes estimaciones: Antigua y Barbuda (cotizaciones a la seguridad social de 2019), Bahamas (cotizaciones a la seguridad social de 2018 y 2019), Ecuador (ingresos locales de impuestos de 2019), Santa Lucía (cotizaciones a la seguridad social de 2018 y 2019) y Trinidad y Tobago (cotizaciones a la seguridad social de 2019). Consulte los cuadros correspondientes a cada país para obtener más información.
3. Se utilizan los datos de 2018 ya que los ingresos tributarios estatales y locales de México no estaban disponibles en 2019.
4. No están disponibles algunos datos de ingresos tributarios entre 2014 y 2017 y todos los datos de 2018 y 2019. El desglose por subsectores del gobierno central no está disponible para esos años.
5. Colombia es constitucionalmente un país unitario con alta autonomía de sus entidades territoriales.
6. Los datos de los subsectores del gobierno central en Cuba sólo están disponibles entre 2002 y 2012.

Fuente: OCDE et al. ($2021_{[1]}$), Cuadro 4.11.

StatLink https://doi.org/10.1787/888934234689

Hay dos cuestiones estadísticas que deben tenerse en cuenta al comparar la atribución de recaudación de ingresos para los países de América Latina y el Caribe y los países miembros de la OCDE. En primer lugar, los ingresos de ambos grupos se han atribuido a diferentes niveles de gobierno de acuerdo con las guías del Sistema de Cuentas Nacionales (SCN) de 2008[9]. La segunda cuestión es que algunos países de América Latina y el Caribe carecen de estadísticas de ingresos tributarios a nivel subnacional.

En el caso de los 19 países de América Latina y el Caribe respecto a los que están disponibles datos subnacionales (se utilizan datos de 2018 en México), la proporción de ingresos tributarios subnacionales en los ingresos tributarios totales estuvo por debajo del 9.0% en 2019, excepto en Argentina, Brasil y Colombia. En Brasil, los estados y municipios recaudan alrededor del 31% de los ingresos tributarios totales, lo que indica un grado significativo de descentralización de la recaudación tributaria. Gran parte del IVA (ICMS – *imposto sobre operações relativas à circulação de mercadorias e prestação de servição de transporte interestadual e intermunicipal e de comunicação*) se recauda a nivel estatal. Los ingresos tributarios subnacionales en Argentina y Colombia representan más del 15% de los ingresos tributarios totales. Argentina tiene una recaudación significativa a nivel estatal, lo cual se explica en parte por el impuesto provincial sobre las ventas *(impuestos sobre los ingresos brutos)*.

Estas cifras reflejan el hecho de que los gobiernos subnacionales de los países de América Latina y el Caribe tienden a tener una gama relativamente estrecha de impuestos bajo su jurisdicción. Los impuestos más frecuentemente asignados a las entidades subnacionales son los impuestos sobre la propiedad, las licencias de vehículos de motor, los impuestos sobre servicios específicos y las tasas municipales. El potencial de generación de ingresos de estos instrumentos es relativamente limitado en comparación con las bases imponibles bajo jurisdicción central, como el IVA y los impuestos sobre la renta. La crisis del COVID-19 ha puesto de manifiesto la existencia de reformas estructurales pendientes para mejorar la recaudación y las fuentes de ingresos a nivel subnacional. Estas incluyen mejoras en la información y estadísticas sobre los ingresos de estos impuestos, la capacidad administrativa de recaudar a nivel local, la coordinación efectiva con las autoridades nacionales y la necesidad de promover fuentes sostenibles y estables de ingresos tributarios a nivel subnacional (Nieto-Parra y Orozco, 2020[44]).

En 2019, todos los ingresos tributarios subnacionales en Belice, Guatemala y Jamaica, y más del 50% de los ingresos tributarios recaudados a nivel subnacional en Perú, Uruguay, Ecuador y Paraguay, se obtuvieron de impuestos sobre la propiedad (Gráfico 1.20). Todos los demás países dependen principalmente de los ingresos procedentes de impuestos sobre bienes y servicios. México es el único país que también recaudó ingresos de diferentes bases impositivas. En 2018 (últimos datos disponibles para México asimilados sin cambios para 2019), el 43% de los ingresos tributarios subnacionales en México procedieron de impuestos sobre nóminas. En los países de la OCDE, las entidades subnacionales tienden a tener bases impositivas potenciales mucho más amplias. Una proporción sustancial de la recaudación de ingresos por parte de los gobiernos subnacionales de los países de la OCDE es a través de impuestos sobre la renta y beneficios (lo que representa un promedio de más de un tercio del total recaudado a nivel subnacional).

Los bajos ingresos tributarios a nivel subnacional en los países de América Latina y el Caribe también pueden ser el resultado de la falta de capacidad administrativa y técnica, en particular en lo que respecta a los impuestos sobre la propiedad. Los impuestos sobre la propiedad – una fuente común de ingresos subnacionales – requieren sistemas e información sofisticados y la recaudación de estos ingresos es costosa. Asimismo, muchos países no cuentan con registros de la propiedad adecuados. En los países donde existen muy pocas veces se procede a su actualización (Canavire-Bacarreza, Martínez-Vázquez y Sepúlveda, 2012[45]; OCDE et al., 2019[46]). Como resultado, las autoridades tributarias tienen un acceso mínimo a valoraciones precisas de tierras y edificios y los registros inmobiliarios a menudo son reacios a compartir esta información. El impuesto sobre la propiedad también sufre un alto nivel de informalidad: los edificios se construyen sin permisos, las propiedades no están registradas y los precios de algunas transacciones inmobiliarias están falsificados. Como el impuesto sobre la propiedad es uno de los impuestos más controvertidos para los ciudadanos y tiene un alto costo político, los políticos locales a menudo no están dispuestos a dedicar los recursos apropiados para cobrar estos ingresos.

Gráfico 1.20. **Distribución impositiva de los ingresos tributarios subnacionales en los países de América Latina y el Caribe, 2019**

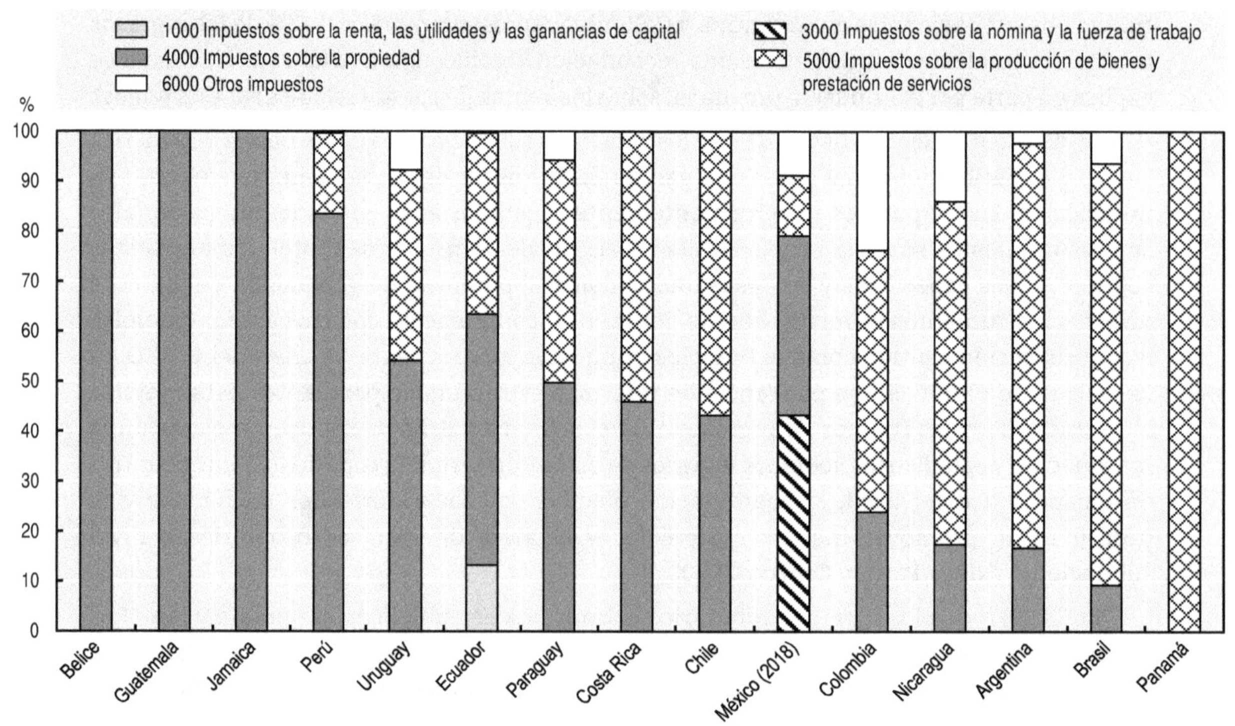

Nota: Datos de 2018 para México. Las cifras de Antigua y Barbuda, Bahamas, Barbados, Bolivia, Cuba, República Dominicana, El Salvador, Guyana, Honduras, Santa Lucía, Trinidad y Tobago y Venezuela están excluidas, bien como datos de ingresos tributarios subnacionales, bien como consecuencia de la falta de disponibilidad de ingresos tributarios subnacionales o del desglose de ingresos tributarios subnacionales por principales tipos de categorías de impuestos. Las cifras excluyen los ingresos del gobierno local de Argentina (pero incluyen los ingresos provinciales).

Fuente: Los cálculos de los autores se basan en OCDE et al. (2021[1]), Capítulo 6.

StatLink *https://doi.org/10.1787/888934234613*

Notas

1. Calculado mediante la aplicación del cambio porcentual promedio no ponderado para 2019 en los 35 países que proporcionan datos para ese año al promedio de la recaudación tributaria sobre el PIB en 2018.
2. El promedio del Caribe incluye ocho países (Antigua y Barbuda, Bahamas, Barbados, Belice, Guyana, Jamaica, Santa Lucía y Trinidad y Tobago), Centroamérica y México, nueve países (Costa Rica, Cuba, República Dominicana, El Salvador, Guatemala, Honduras, México, Nicaragua y Panamá), y América del Sur, nueve países (Argentina, Bolivia, Brasil, Chile, Colombia, Ecuador, Paraguay, Perú y Uruguay).
3. El IVA se introdujo en 1991 en Jamaica, 1997 en Barbados, 2006 en Belice (el impuesto general sobre las ventas), 2007 en Guyana y Antigua y Barbuda, 2012 en Santa Lucía y 2015 en las Bahamas.
4. El año de comparación es 2018, dado que los datos de 2019 para el promedio de la OCDE no están disponibles.
5. El índice-D se utilizó en el informe de *Estadísticas Tributarias 2018* para analizar la convergencia de las estructuras tributarias en los países de la OCDE entre 1995 y 2016 (OCDE, 2018[47]).
6. Si bien los ingresos tributarios relacionados con el medio ambiente no pueden identificarse en la clasificación general de impuestos de la OCDE, sí se detallan en la lista de impuestos específicos incluidos, para la mayor parte de los países, dentro de la clasificación general. Es sobre esta base que se incluyen en la base de datos de la OCDE de Instrumentos de Políticas para el Medio Ambiente (Policy Instruments for the Environment, PINE) (OCDE, 2021[36]). En 2019, la OCDE comenzó la recopilación de las cuentas de ingresos tributarios relacionados con el medio ambiente en línea con el Sistema de Contabilidad Ambiental y Económica y las cuentas están desagregadas por industrias y hogares (OCDE, 2021[50]).
7. Promedio no ponderado de 37 países de la OCDE.
8. El año de comparación es 2018 ya que los datos de 2019 para México no están disponibles.
9. Esto significa que los ingresos se atribuyen generalmente al nivel de gobierno que ejerce la autoridad para imponer el impuesto o tiene la discreción final para variar la tasa de impuestos. Esto tiene implicaciones para situaciones en las que un nivel de gobierno recauda ingresos tributarios y los transfiere total o parcialmente a otros niveles. Los ejemplos regionales de este tipo de mecanismo son la Ley de Coparticipación en Argentina, las participaciones federales en México (establecida en la Ley de Coordinación Fiscal) y los fondos de participación en Brasil (definidos en el Artículo 159 de la Constitución).

Referencias

Arlinghaus, J. y K. van Dender (2017), "The environmental tax and subsidy reform in Mexico", *OECD Taxation Working Papers*, No. 31, Publicaciones de la OCDE, París, *https://dx.doi.org/10.1787/a9204f40-en.* [41]

Banco Mundial (2021), *Turismo internacional, recibos (% del total de exportaciones)*, *https://datos.bancomundial.org/indicador/ST.INT.RCPT.XP.ZS.* [31]

Barreix, A., J. Benítez y M. Pecho (2017), "Revisiting personal income tax in Latin America: Evolution and impact", *OECD Development Centre Working Papers*, No. 338, OCDE, *https://doi.org/10.1787/16d42b4a-en.* [22]

Barrow, D. (2020), *Budget Speech for Fiscal Year 2020/2021*, Government of Belize, *http://caribbeanelections.com/eDocs/budget/bz_budget/bz_budget_2020.pdf.* [9]

BDC (2020), *Fact Sheet - 2019 Caribbean Economic Review and 2020 Outlook*, Banco de Desarrollo del Caribe, *https://issuu.com/caribank/docs/cdb_fact_sheet_2019_economic_review_and_2020_outlo.* [6]

BID (2019), *Informe macroeconomico de America Latina y el Caribe 2019 Construir oportunidades para crecer en un mundo desafiante*, *http://dx.doi.org/10.18235/0001633.* [10]

BID (2013), *More than revenues, Taxation as a development tool*, Banco Interamericano de Desarrollo. [19]

Canavire-Bacarreza, G., J. Martínez-Vázquez y C. Sepúlveda (2012), *Sub-national Revenue Mobilization in Peru, IDB Working Paper Series No. 299*, BID, *https://publications.iadb.org/en/sub-national-revenue-mobilization-peru.* [45]

CentralAmericaData (2020), *Tax Reform in Nicaragua*, *https://webmail.centralamericadata.com/en/search?q1=content_en_le:%22tax+reform%22&q2=mattersInCountry_es_le:%22Nicaragua%22.* [8]

CEPAL (2021), *Balance Preliminar de las Economías de América Latina y el Caribe, 2020*, Comisión Económica para América Latina y el Caribe, Santiago, *https://www.cepal.org/es/publicaciones/46501-balance-preliminar-economias-america-latina-caribe-2020*. [4]

CEPAL (2020), *Fiscal Panorama of Latin America and the Caribbean 2020: Fiscal policy amid the crisis arising from the coronavirus disease (COVID-19) pandemic*, Comisión Económica para América Latina y el Caribe, *https://repositorio.cepal.org/handle/11362/45731*. [11]

CEPAL (2019), *Balance Preliminar de las Economías de América Latina y el Caribe, 2018*, (LC/PUB.2019/1-P), Santiago, *https://www.cepal.org/es/publicaciones/bp*. [2]

CEPAL (2018), *Panorama Fiscal de América Latina y el Caribe 2018: los desafíos de las políticas públicas en el marco de la Agenda 2030*, Naciones Unidas, *http://repositorio.cepal.org/bitstream/handle/11362/43405/7/S1800082_es.pdf*. [18]

CEPAL (2014), *Tax policy in Latin America: Assessment and guidelines for a second generation of reforms*, Naciones Unidas, *https://repositorio.cepal.org/handle/11362/36806*. [21]

CEPAL (2013), *Fiscal Panorama of Latin America and the Caribbean: Tax reform and renewal of the fiscal covenant*, Naciones Unidas, *https://www.cepal.org/en/publications/3101-fiscal-panorama-latin-america-and-caribbean-2013-tax-reform-and-renewal-fiscal*. [20]

EY (2019), *Argentina establishes temporary duties on export of services*, Ernst & Young, *https://www.ey.com/en_gl/tax-alerts/argentina-establishes-temporary-duties-on-export-of-services*. [12]

FMI (2020), *World Economic Outlook Database (Octubre)*, Fondo Monetario Internacional, Washington, D.C., *https://www.imf.org/en/Publications/WEO/weo-database/2020/October*. [24]

FMI (2019), *Barbados: 2019 Article IV Consultation*, Fondo Monetario Internacional, *https://www.imf.org/en/Publications/CR/Issues/2019/12/18/Barbados-2019-Article-IV-Consultation-Second-Review-Under-the-Extended-Arrangement-Request-48886*. [14]

ITR (2020), *Argentina: Argentina introduces major tax reform*, International Tax Review, *https://www.internationaltaxreview.com/article/b1k41n6smqd3jy/argentina-argentina-introduces-major-tax-reform*. [13]

Keen, M. (2013), *The anatomy of VAT*, WP/13/111, FMI, *https://www.imf.org/en/Publications/WP/Issues/2016/12/31/The-Anatomy-of-the-VAT-40543*. [30]

KPMG (2019), *Mexico: Tax reform 2020, VAT on services provided from digital platforms*, *https://home.kpmg/us/en/home/insights/2019/11/tnf-mexico-tax-reform-2020-vat-services-digital-platforms.html*. [33]

Lorenzo, F. (2016), *Inventario de instrumentos fiscales verdes en América Latina*, CEPAL, *https://agua.org.mx/biblioteca/inventario-instrumentos-fiscales-verdes-en-america-latina-experiencias-efectos-alcances/*. [38]

Melguizo, Á. et al. (2017), "No sympathy for the devil! Policy priorities to overcome the middle-income trap in Latin America", *OECD Development Centre Working Papers*, No. 340, OCDE, *https://dx.doi.org/10.1787/26b78724-en*. [23]

Monge, C. (2018), *Colombia Puts a Tax on Carbon*, *https://www.conservationfinancenetwork.org/2018/11/27/colombia-puts-tax-on-carbon*. [42]

Nieto-Parra, S. y R. Orozco (2020), *Potencializar los impuestos subnacionales en América Latina y el Caribe en tiempos del Covid-19 in Los desafíos de las finanzas intergubernamentales ante el Covid-19*, AIFIL - Asociación Iberoamericana de Financiación, *https://www.aifil-jifl.org/wp-content/uploads/2020/11/AIFIL-2.11.pdf*. [44]

OCDE (2021 próximamente), *Effective Carbon Rates 2021: Pricing Carbon Emissions through Taxes and Emissions Trading*, Publicaciones de la OCDE, París, *https://doi.org/10.1787/0e8e24f5-en*. [43]

OCDE (2021), *Environmental policy: Environmentally related tax revenue accounts, OECD Environment Statistics (database)*, *https://stats.oecd.org/Index.aspx?DataSetCode=ERTR_ACC*. [48]

OCDE (2021), *PINE database*, Publicaciones de la OCDE, París, *http://www.oecd.org/environment/tools-evaluation/environmentaltaxation.htm*. [36]

OCDE (2021), *Taxing Energy Use for Sustainable Development*, Publicaciones de la OCDE, París, *https://www.oecd.org/tax/tax-policy/taxing-energy-use-for-sustainable-development.htm*. [37]

OCDE (2020), "COVID-19 in Latin America and the Caribbean: Regional socio-economic implications and policy priorities", *OECD Policy Responses to Coronavirus (COVID-19)*, *https://www.oecd.org/coronavirus/policy-responses/covid-19-in-latin-america-and-the-caribbean-regional-socio-economic-implications-and-policy-priorities-93a64fde/*. [5]

OCDE (2020), *Harmful Tax Practices: peer review results on preferential regimes.*, Publicaciones de la OCDE, París, *https://www.oecd.org/tax/beps/harmful-tax-practices-peer-review-results-on-preferential-regimes.pdf*. [15]

OCDE (2020), *Consumption Tax Trends 2020: VAT/GST and Excise Rates, Trends and Policy Issues*, Publicaciones de la OCDE, París, *https://doi.org/10.1787/152def2d-en*. [29]

OCDE (2019), *Tax Morale: What Drives People and Businesses to Pay Tax?*, Publicaciones de la OCDE, París, *https://doi.org/10.1787/f3d8ea10-en*. [25]

OCDE (2019), *Taxing Energy Use 2019: Using Taxes for Climate Action*, OCDE, *https://doi.org/10.1787/058ca239-en*. [40]

OCDE (2018), *Consumption Tax Trends 2018: VAT/GST and Excise Rates, Trends and Policy Issues*, Publicaciones de la OCDE, París, *https://doi.org/10.1787/ctt-2018-en*. [32]

OCDE (2018), *Revenue Statistics 2018*, Publicaciones de la OCDE, París, *https://doi.org/10.1787/rev_stats-2018-en*. [47]

OCDE (2014), *Development Co-operation Report 2014: Mobilising Resources for Sustainable Development*, Publicaciones de la OCDE, París, *https://dx.doi.org/10.1787/dcr-2014-en*. [26]

OCDE (2005), *Glossary of statistical terms*, *https://stats.oecd.org/glossary/detail.asp?ID=6437*. [35]

OCDE/BID/Banco Mundial (2014), *Un Panorama de las Pensiones en America Latina y el Caribe*, Publicaciones de la OCDE, París, *https://doi.org/10.1787/9789264233195-es*. [28]

OCDE/CAF/CEPAL (2018), *Perspectivas económicas de América Latina 2018: Repensando las instituciones para el desarrollo*, Publicaciones de la OCDE, París, *https://doi.org/10.1787/leo-2018-es*. [3]

OCDE/CEPAL (2016), *OECD Environmental Performance Reviews: Chile 2016*, OECD Environmental Performance Reviews, Publicaciones de la OCDE, París, *https://dx.doi.org/10.1787/9789264252615-en*. [39]

OCDE et al. (2021), *Estadísticas tributarias en América Latina y el Caribe 2021*, Publicaciones de la OCDE, París, *https://doi.org/10.1787/96ce5287-en-es*. [1]

OCDE et al. (2019), *Perspectivas económicas de América Latina*, Publicaciones de la OCDE, París, *https://doi.org/10.1787/g2g9ff1a-es*. [16]

OCDE et al. (2015), *Estadísticas tributarias en América Latina y el Caribe 2015*, Publicaciones de la OCDE, París, *https://dx.doi.org/10.1787/rev_lat-2015-en-fr*. [27]

OCDE et al. (2020), *Perspectivas económicas de América Latina*, OECD Publishing, Paris, *https://doi.org/10.1787/f2fdced2-es*. [17]

OCDE et al. (2019), *Estadísticas tributarias en América Latina y el Caribe*, Publicaciones de la OCDE, París, *https://dx.doi.org/10.1787/25666b8d-en-es*. [46]

Orbitax (2019), *Nicaragua 2019 Tax Reform Measures*, *https://www.orbitax.com/news/archive.php/Nicaragua-2019-Tax-Reform-Meas-37133*. [7]

Schlotterbeck, S. (2017), *Tax Administration Reforms in the Caribbean, "Challenges, Achievements, and Next Steps"*. [34]

Chapter 2

SPECIAL FEATURE

Fiscal policy responses to the COVID-19 crisis in Latin America

Capítulo 2

SECCIÓN ESPECIAL

Respuestas de política fiscal a la crisis del COVID-19 en América Latina

Chapter 2

SPECIAL FEATURE

Fiscal policy responses to the COVID-19 crisis in Latin America

Principal findings

Tax policy was used widely and rapidly in LAC as an instrument to offset the impact of the COVID-19 crisis on families and firms. Most countries took prompt action to reduce the cost of medical supplies through modifications of import duties and the value-added tax (VAT), including zero-rating and exemptions. Support for families and firms largely centred on tax deferrals and the creation of programmes to ease the liquidation of tax liabilities as opposed to the outright write-off of tax liabilities.

Tax revenues fell precipitously in the first half of the year, while showing some signs of recovery by year's end. Tax receipts for the region's two principal taxes, the VAT and the income tax, contracted sharply in the first half of the year as a result of the fall in economic activity and the extension of tax relief as part of COVID-19 policy packages. In the second half of the year the fall in tax revenues began to gradually revert as countries eased public health measures and taxpayers liquidated liabilities that had been deferred earlier in the year.

LAC countries rapidly adopted a wide range of expenditure and liquidity support measures to support families and firms. Public expenditure served as the central pillar of the fiscal response to the crisis in LAC. This included the expansion of existing social support programmes or created emergency subsidies to support household incomes and wellbeing. Countries also sought to limit the impact of the crisis on firms' cash-flow through subsidies to cover payroll and operation expenses. Below-the-line support in the form of concessional lending as well as State-backed credit guarantees also played an important role in supporting firms.

Fiscal policy became exceptionally expansionary in 2020. Central government primary expenditure – which excludes interest payments – registered significant year-on-year growth, exceeding 20% in real terms in some cases. This increase was driven by greater current transfers, principally due to the rapid expansion in subsidies and current transfers associated with the fiscal response to the crisis. Rising spending and falling public revenues led to a significant erosion of the region's fiscal balances and provoked a sharp increase in central government gross public debt levels.

The impact of the COVID-19 crisis on public debt calls for globally co-ordinated efforts on debt management. To face the fiscal needs brought about by the pandemic, debt issuance by LAC countries on international markets increased considerably thanks to their increased access to international financial markets and by emergency lending by international financial institutions. If liquidity conditions change in the context of limited fiscal space, this could affect debt sustainability in some emerging economies. This underlines the need for globally co-ordinated debt management with an array of different policy actions available and with specific solutions for each country.

Building back better and achieving the Sustainable Development Goals in LAC will require active fiscal policies supported by a fiscal sustainability framework. The crisis has laid bare the weaknesses of LAC's existing development model. Entrenched inequalities and the accumulation of structural development gaps – social inclusion, productive structure, among others – over time severely hampered the region's ability to face the pandemic and its fallout. Shifting LAC's development path will require a concerted effort by the public sector. Active fiscal policies, supported by a fiscal sustainability framework, will need to play a key role. Under a well-defined sequence of policies, bolstering revenues, especially tax revenues, stands out as a key challenge for making these policies sustainable. It is time for the region to take strides in implementing structural tax reforms with the aim of financing sustainable development.

Fiscal policy proved to be a potent tool to tackle the crisis in the region

The COVID-19 pandemic has triggered the worst economic crisis in Latin America and the Caribbean for 120 years, causing significant short- and medium-term reductions in growth and increases in inequality, poverty and unemployment (ECLAC, 2021[1]). Necessary public health measures to protect human life precipitated a decline in GDP through two channels: on the supply side, the sudden interruption of supply chains associated with the closure of a large part of the companies that carry out activities identified as non-essential. On the demand side, layoffs or partial unemployment strongly impacted household income, thereby reducing consumption.

The crisis has had an asymmetrical impact on the region's societies. It has been regressive in nature, deepening existing inequalities in a region that is already the most unequal in the world. This has been reflected in a sharp increase in vulnerability indexes for social groups such as youth, women, immigrants, senior citizens, among others. The pre-existing digital divide in the region had a deleterious impact on education, as schools transitioned to online modalities (OECD et al., 2020[2]; ECLAC, 2020[3]). In the labour market, informal and independent workers have been disproportionately impacted as they often have little or no link to existing social security systems and might be less able to work from home (OECD, 2020[4]; ECLAC/ILO, 2020[5]).

Latin America has been one of the regions most impacted by COVID-19 in the world. While many countries adopted strict public health measures, the pandemic still spread through the region. The region's public health systems, which have suffered from chronic underinvestment, were quickly overwhelmed by the rising incidence of coronavirus patients. The outsized role of the informal economy also limited the effectiveness of restriction of movement measures as informal workers rely on daily earnings for their survival.

Faced with this situation, countries across the region took prompt action, adopting ambitious packages of fiscal policy measures to bolster public healthcare systems, support households – particularly the most vulnerable – and protect productive capacity in order to facilitate the economic recovery post-pandemic (ECLAC, 2020[6]; OECD, 2020[4]). In pursuit of these objectives, countries mobilised unprecedented resources – 4.3% of GDP on average in Latin America – through tax relief, budget reallocations and additional expenditure, as well as liquidity instruments supported by governments (concessional lending) (ECLAC, 2020[6]). Additionally, several countries have created or strengthened state credit guarantee programmes to provide additional liquidity to firms, particularly SMEs, with limited access to the formal banking system.

All these policy responses came at a cost, and the region's fiscal position has deteriorated. The upswing in public spending and plummeting public revenues have created historically deep deficits and rising public debt levels, particularly from external sources including international financial markets and multilateral lending institutions. Nevertheless, active fiscal policies will be key for the recovery effort and in building back better societies in the post-pandemic world. Thus, austerity is not an option.

Maintaining active fiscal policies will be crucial to boost economic growth and achieve the transformative economic and social change that the region needs to meet the Sustainable Development Goals (SDGs). These policies will need to address the region's existing structural development gaps, while building universal social protection systems and improving the quality of public goods and services.

The region faces the challenge of maintaining an active fiscal policy approach within a fiscal sustainability framework. This will require the development of strategies aimed at strengthening revenues and improving the quality of expenditure.

Tax policy measures were widely and rapidly adopted as part of the response to the crisis

While public spending represented the principal pillar of LAC's fiscal response to the COVID-19 pandemic, tax policy was also used as a strategic tool to mitigate the economic impacts of the crisis. Compared with programmes that involved budgetary reallocations and additional spending, tax relief measures were enacted promptly, as they were mostly adopted by decree. Despite their importance – temporarily foregone revenues due to these measures was significant, in some cases equivalent to more than 1% of GDP[1] – tax relief measures were based principally on tax deferrals that shifted the collection of tax receipts as opposed to outright reductions in tax liabilities (ECLAC, 2021[7]; 2020[6]). In general, these measures were targeted at the health sector or provided temporary liquidity to households and firms. The effectiveness of tax relief was hampered, however, by the region's outsized informal sector and the limited participation of individuals and SMEs in the tax and social security systems.

Given the scale of the pandemic and the generally under-developed health systems in the region, countries rapidly enacted measures to reduce the cost of crucial medical goods (Table 2.1). In many countries this took the form of temporary exemptions or zero-ratings of medical supplies to respond to the COVID-19 pandemic (alcohol, laboratory items, gloves, disinfectant, equipment and other health supplies), reflecting the dependence on external suppliers. These measures were accompanied in some cases, such as in Colombia, by the exemption of medical goods from VAT. Countries also sought to incentivise direct donations to health systems by providing temporary deductions for personal and corporate income taxes (PIT/CIT).

Tax relief measures for households and self-employed workers were implemented to compensate for lost wages and to support consumption. The most common of these tax measures were deferrals, suspensions of advance payments and the creation of favourable tax payment facilities – such as instalment plans with no interest or penalties – for VAT and PIT. Several countries – including Chile, Colombia, Peru, and Trinidad and Tobago – also implemented accelerated PIT refunds to provide further support. Households were also supported in some countries – such as Argentina, Colombia, Costa Rica, Dominica, Guyana, Honduras and St Vincent and the Grenadines – by VAT exemptions on essential medical supplies, products from the basic basket of consumption goods and services such as electricity. In Colombia, an innovative VAT refund scheme targeted one million families living in poverty, extending five payments of COP 75 000 during the year. Tax relief measures for families had a relatively limited impact in the region, reflecting the reduced universe of households incorporated in existing PIT systems. Additionally, these measures were general in nature, without providing additional benefits to particularly impacted populations such as women (Box 2.1).

Table 2.1. **COVID-19 related tax relief measures in Latin America and the Caribbean**

Instrument	Addressing the health crisis	Provision of liquidity to households and businesses							
		Deferral and payment facilities				Accelerated refunds	Preferential treatment		
		Households	Businesses				Households	Businesses	
			All	Specific sector	SMEs			All	SMEs
Income tax	Bolivia (Plurinational State of) Guyana	Argentina Belize Brazil Dominican Republic El Salvador Guatemala Guyana Panama Paraguay Peru Saint Lucia Saint Vincent and the Grenadines	Argentina Belize Brazil Bolivia (Plurinational State of) Chile Colombia Costa Rica Dominican Republic El Salvador Grenada Guatemala Guyana Honduras Panama Paraguay Peru Saint Lucia	Colombia Dominican Republic Ecuador El Salvador Honduras	Chile Panama Peru Paraguay	Belize Chile Peru Trinidad and Tobago	Venezuela (Bolivarian Republic of)	Bolivia (Plurinational State of) Chile Honduras Saint Kitts and Nevis Saint Lucia	Bolivia (Plurinational State of) Honduras Panama
Social or parastatal contributions			Argentina Brazil Barbados Colombia Uruguay	Argentina Colombia	Argentina Uruguay			Argentina Brazil	
Goods and services tax	Argentina Bolivia (Plurinational State of) Brazil Colombia Ecuador El Salvador Guatemala Guyana Honduras Jamaica Panama Paraguay Peru Saint Kitts and Nevis Saint Vincent and the Grenadines Venezuela (Bolivarian Republic of)		Brazil Chile Colombia Costa Rica Dominican Republic Ecuador Honduras Paraguay Uruguay	Colombia Ecuador Saint Vincent and the Grenadines	Chile	Belize Peru Trinidad and Tobago	Dominica Guyana Saint Vincent and the Grenadines	Colombia Costa Rica Dominica	Bolivia (Plurinational State of) Colombia
Other taxes		Chile	Brazil Chile Colombia Grenada Guatemala Guyana		Brazil Colombia		Brazil Chile	Brazil Chile Colombia	

Source: Economic Commission for Latin America and the Caribbean (ECLAC), on the basis of Fiscal Panorama of Latin America and the Caribbean 2020 (LC/PUB.2020/6-P), Santiago, 2020.

StatLink https://doi.org/10.1787/888934234784

Box 2.1. **Incorporating a gender perspective in tax policy responses**

Women are at the core of the fight against the COVID-19 crisis: they make up the vast majority of healthcare workers and shoulder much of the childcare and home schooling burden during lockdowns. While tax policy measures play a crucial role in supporting individuals and businesses, the gender impact of taxation must also be considered in responding to the crisis.

Although tax provisions that explicitly disadvantage women relative to men are rare, tax can, in practice, exhibit an implicit bias that exacerbates gender inequalities, particularly in times of crises. This is due to tax systems interacting with underlying socioeconomic gender differences between men and women, such as differences in income levels, consumption patterns, entrepreneurship and wealth.

Under income taxes, for example, although men and women are typically taxed under the same rules, their different wage levels and labour force participation mean that the tax system can have differing effects. Women are typically more responsive to changes in wages than men in their decisions to participate in the labour market and are more likely to work part-time. The progressivity of the tax system is therefore an important factor in women's labour market participation, particularly if the withdrawal of dependent spouse or child benefits increases the effective tax rates on second earners – who are disproportionally female – entering the labour force.

Consumption taxes also directly affect the distribution of income between men and women within households, due to gendered differences in consumption patterns. They may also indirectly contribute to another implicit bias, as consumption taxes on services such as cleaning and childcare make it more attractive to produce these services at home rather than buying them on the market, especially for low-income households. This can decrease the second-earner labour supply.

COVID-19 amplifies these dynamics by increasing women's unpaid work burdens and by destabilising the labour market. Widespread closure of schools and childcare facilities and other confinement measures have increased the time that parents have to spend on childcare and home schooling as well as on routine housework, much of which is undertaken by women, and which can increase the risk of second-earner women leaving the workforce.

There are also gender differences in employment patterns between men and women. In LAC countries, women are more likely to be self-employed, and to work in domestic service and sectors with lower wages and precarious conditions (36% of women employment against 28.4% of male employment in 2017 on average in the Latin America region). In addition, 78% of employed women on average in Latin America are concentrated in the most affected sectors by COVID-19 (e.g. social services, restaurant and hotels, transportation) (ECLAC, $2020_{[8]}$). These workers are among the most vulnerable during the current crisis, facing higher risks of job or income loss, and they are often not covered by social insurance due to the non-standard or informal nature of some of these jobs. In the LAC region, women's non-agricultural informality rate in LAC stood at 52%, compared to 47% for men (OECD, $2020_{[9]}$).

To address the complex interactions of tax and gender in the post COVID world, governments will need to consider options to redesign key taxes to avoid exacerbating existing gender differences, or use tax or other instruments to compensate for differences in income levels as part of their long-term response to the crisis. To ensure that the tax system does not inadvertently reinforce gender biases in society, governments need to include the impact of taxes on gender as a key policy dimension in their tax policy framework. Improving data on the impact of COVID-19 on women in the region will be crucial to understand these impacts.

Source: Adapted based on Harding et al. ($2020_{[10]}$).

As in the case of households, tax relief for firms also consisted principally of temporary measures to bolster cash flow, especially in the early months of the crisis, through deferrals and suspension of advance payments of VAT and CIT. VAT relief, in particular, played an important role in the region, especially for micro, small and medium-sized companies

(MSMEs). In several cases, tax relief was targeted at MSMEs or sectors particularly impacted by the crisis, such as construction, tourism and personal services. Countries also extended relief to firms by modifications to social contribution schemes, such as the Programa de Asistencia de Emergencia al Trabajo y la Producción (ATP) in Argentina, which introduced a reduction of up to 95% in the payment of employer contributions to the Integrated Social Security System. In Brazil, payments to the Unemployment Insurance Fund (FGTS) were suspended and contributions to the Sistema S system, which finances technical and vocational education, were reduced by 50% for April, May and June.

The combination of the severe contraction in economic activity, with its concomitant decline in private consumption and income, and COVID-19 tax relief caused a significant decline in public revenues in Latin America. VAT receipts, one of the principal sources of tax revenues in the region, plummeted between March and May as the pandemic evolved and countries established strict quarantine measures (Figure 2.1). May was especially grave in many countries of the region, with year-on-year declines in real terms of 40% or more of VAT receipts in Chile, Costa Rica, Ecuador and Honduras. Income tax revenues also registered significant declines in the first months of the year, principally due to the extension of tax relief measures, as the liquidation of 2019 tax liabilities were deferred and advance tax payments were suspended.

Figure 2.1. **VAT receipts in Latin America, January-December 2020**

Year-on-year real variation in percentage

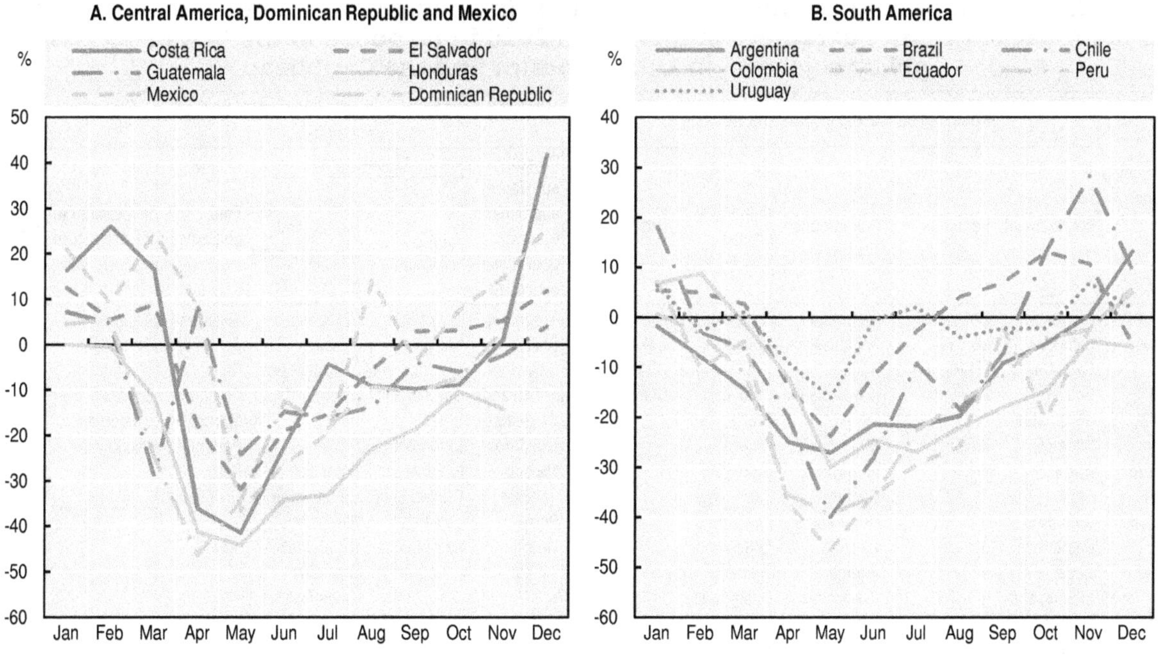

Note: Data for Brazil corresponds to receipts of the Tax on Commerce and Services (Imposto sobre Circulaçao de Mercadorias e Serviços, ICMS), a state-level tax.

Source: Economic Commission for Latin America and the Caribbean (ECLAC), on the basis of Fiscal Panorama of Latin America and the Caribbean 2021.

StatLink https://doi.org/10.1787/888934234708

The slow rebound in economic activity experienced in the middle of 2020 as public health measures were eased and the retirement of certain COVID-19 related tax deferrals allowed for a progressive deceleration in the year-on-year declines in tax revenues. This was especially evident in the case of VAT receipts, which improved throughout the second half of the year. By the fourth quarter, VAT receipts in some countries approached or exceeded their level of the previous year, nevertheless for the year they declined sharply (ECLAC, 2021[7]).

However, COVID-19 tax relief was repeatedly rolled over in several countries, potentially shifting VAT revenues to 2021. Based on the reports of the tax administrations of 18 countries across the LAC region, the Inter-American Center of Tax Administrations (CIAT)[2] calculates that total tax revenues declined by 11.2% in 2020 from the previous year. The largest declines were in excises (down 13.7% year-on-year), followed by income taxes (-9.9%), and VAT (-9.2%). Other unclassified tax revenues declined by 14.2%.

Expenditure measures accounted for the bulk of the response to the crisis

Public spending policies in Latin America and the Caribbean in 2020 channelled significant additional resources to strengthen public health systems, support families and protect productive capacity (Table 2.2). These efforts were especially important in the region as existing development gaps leave significant swathes of the population and firms, mainly informal SMEs, exceptionally vulnerable to economic downturns. As highlighted in ECLAC (2020[11]), the bulk of COVID-19 measures related to budgetary reassignments and additional spending in the form of current transfers to channel resources directly to households and small enterprises. These spending policies were accompanied by additional measures that are not strictly public outlays in the current period – such as below-the-line transactions including the extension of credit at favourable conditions and state-backed credit guarantees – but that create contingent liabilities for public expenditure in future periods.

Table 2.2. **Spending instruments (above-the-line), financing instruments (below-the-line) and state-backed credit guarantees employed in 2020 in response to the COVID-19 crisis, by policy objective, in Latin America and the Caribbean**

	Protecting household income and well-being					Protecting productive capacity and ensuring private sector liquidity				Supporting economic activity	
							Lines of credit				
Strengthening the health system	Employment	Pensions	Consumption	Vulnerable groups	Other	Payroll subsidies and benefits to cover operational expenses	Total	Micro-, small- and medium-sized enterprises	State guarantees	Investment in infrastructure	Housing
Bahamas Barbados Brazil Chile Colombia Ecuador El Salvador Grenada Guatemala Haiti Honduras Mexico Panama Paraguay Peru Saint Kitts and Nevis Saint Vincent and the Grenadines Suriname Trinidad and Tobago	Argentina Bahamas Barbados Bolivia (Plurinational State of) Brazil Chile Colombia Costa Rica Cuba El Salvador Grenada Haiti Jamaica Mexico Paraguay Dominican Republic Saint Lucia Trinidad and Tobago Uruguay	Argentina Bolivia (Plurinational State of) Brazil Mexico	Argentina Bahamas Bolivia (Plurinational State of) Chile El Salvador Guatemala Honduras Panama Paraguay Dominican Republic Uruguay	Argentina Bolivia (Plurinational State of) Brazil Chile Colombia Costa Rica Ecuador El Salvador Grenada Guatemala Haiti Honduras Jamaica Mexico Panama Paraguay Uruguay	Argentina Bolivia (Plurinational State of)	Argentina Chile Colombia El Salvador Guatemala Honduras Mexico Panama Peru Uruguay	Argentina Bolivia (Plurinational State of) Brazil Colombia El Salvador Guatemala Jamaica Saint Lucia	Bahamas Bolivia (Plurinational State of) Brazil Chile Ecuador El Salvador Grenada Guatemala Honduras Jamaica Mexico Panama Paraguay Peru Trinidad and Tobago Uruguay	Argentina Bahamas Chile Colombia Mexico Paraguay Peru Uruguay	Argentina Barbados El Salvador Grenada Guatemala Mexico	Antigua and Barbuda Argentina Grenada Guatemala Mexico

Note: The data include budget reallocations, additional expenditure, concessional lending and State-backed credit guarantees.

Source: Economic Commission for Latin America and the Caribbean (ECLAC), on the basis of Fiscal Panorama of Latin America and the Caribbean 2020 (LC/PUB.2020/6-P), Santiago, 2020.

StatLink https://doi.org/10.1787/888934234803

Most countries in the region adopted measures to strengthen the capacity of their health systems (Table 2.2). In most cases, this consisted of budgetary reallocations and additional spending to finance the acquisition of medical supplies, expand health infrastructure, and hire additional personnel. In the large federal countries of the region – such as Argentina and Brazil – transfer programmes of considerable size were adopted to support sub-national governments that in many cases are the principal providers of public services such as healthcare. Similar programmes were implemented in Bolivia, Chile, Peru and the Dominican Republic through special funds to support municipalities.

Supporting household income, and therefore private consumption, represented the principal axis of expenditure policy in the region. Measures included the design of new programmes – or the strengthening of existing programmes – of targeted transfers to unemployed informal workers and vulnerable social groups (ECLAC, 2020[6]; OECD, 2020[4]). Examples of newly created transfers include the *Ingreso Familiar de Emergencia* in Argentina, the *Benefício Emergencial de Preservação do Emprego e da Renda* in Brazil (the single largest programme in the region at BRL 321 billion or USD 62 billion), the *Ingreso Familiar de Emergencia* in Chile *Ingreso Solidario* in Colombia, the *Family Subsidy* in El Salvador, and the expansion of *Bono Familiar Universal* in Peru (ECLAC, 2020[6]; OECD et al., 2020[2]). Transfers were also directed to formal sector workers, including benefits to cover temporary loss of income – for example, the *Programa de Asistencia de Emergencia al Trabajo y la Producción* in Argentina – and to fill gaps in the existing social protection framework, such as the *Subsidio al Empleo Formal* in Paraguay, where there is no established unemployment insurance system.

Countries also implemented measures to increase the coverage and the value of benefits provided by existing social protection programmes, including unemployment insurance (for example in Chile, Ecuador, Mexico and Uruguay, among others) and social security benefits such as pensions (for example, in Argentina, Colombia, Guatemala, Mexico and Paraguay, among others). In-kind support was also provided to households in several countries, where governments provided food packages directly to low-income households. This was accompanied in some cases with subsidies to cover the cost of basic household services (electricity, gas and water).

Productive capacity protection measures were largely aimed at providing subsidies and financing to ensure that companies had sufficient cashflow during the year in a context of intense demand and supply shocks. In terms of public expenditure, countries such as Chile, Colombia, Peru and Uruguay established employment protection schemes by providing payroll subsidies to companies that chose to participate and met specific requirements. For example, Colombia established the *Programa de Apoyo al Empleo Formal* to provide a monthly subsidy, equivalent to 40% of the minimum wage, to assist with payroll costs for firms that could prove they suffered a 20% decline in revenues between February and March 2020. Similar programmes were established in El Salvador and Honduras that focused on MSMEs. In Guatemala, Mexico and Panama, business subsidies were established to offset operation expenses related to the purchase of supplies needed in the agricultural sector. Some countries, such as Argentina and Peru, implemented productivity support programmes by financing research and development (R&D) projects, promoting digitisation and promoting entrepreneurship.

The use of below-the-lines measures, such as the provision of special lines of credit and the capitalisation of state-owned financial institutions, allowed countries to ensure that firms had access to necessary liquidity, especially those with already limited access such as MSMEs. For example, the *Reactívate Ecuador* programme provided credit to MSMEs at a preferential rate (5%) with terms of 36 months and a six-month grace period. Concessional loans were also provided by several countries – such as Bolivia, Brazil and Paraguay – as part of employment retention schemes to help cover payroll costs. While less widespread, state-backed credit programmes were used with success to bolster liquidity in the financial system. In some cases, this was implemented as the expansion of existing schemes, such as financing programmes of BNDES in Brazil and a large capital injection in the *Fondo de Garantía de Pequeños Empresarios* in Chile. In Peru, a new programme was established as part of the *Reactiva Perú*, where Treasury-guaranteed credits were supported by a contribution by the Central Bank. In Colombia, Bancoldex launched new credit lines to respond to the COVID-19 crisis under the programme *Colombia Responde* to support more than 38 000 firms, of which more than 90% are microenterprises.

As a result of these support measures, fiscal policy was highly expansionary in many countries in LAC during 2020 (ECLAC, 2021[7]). This contrasted sharply with the relatively modest growth of public spending in recent years, during which countries adopted fiscal consolidation policies to control a rise in public debt. Central government primary expenditure rose by double-digits rates in some countries during the year, in some cases reaching more than 20% in real terms compared to 2019 (Figure 2.2). This dynamic was driven by a significant increase in subsidies and current transfers as a result of the COVID-19 related expenditure measures adopted during the year (ECLAC, 2021[7]; 2021[1]). However, the experience of the region was not uniform: fiscal policy remained contractionary in a few countries, mostly reflecting their capacity to expand fiscal space, derived from existing elevated fiscal deficits or public debt. Some countries were able to tap global and domestic financial markets, international financial institutions and, in some cases, central banks to finance their response.

Figure 2.2. **Central government primary expenditure in 15 Latin American countries, 2019-20**

Year-on-year real variation in percentage

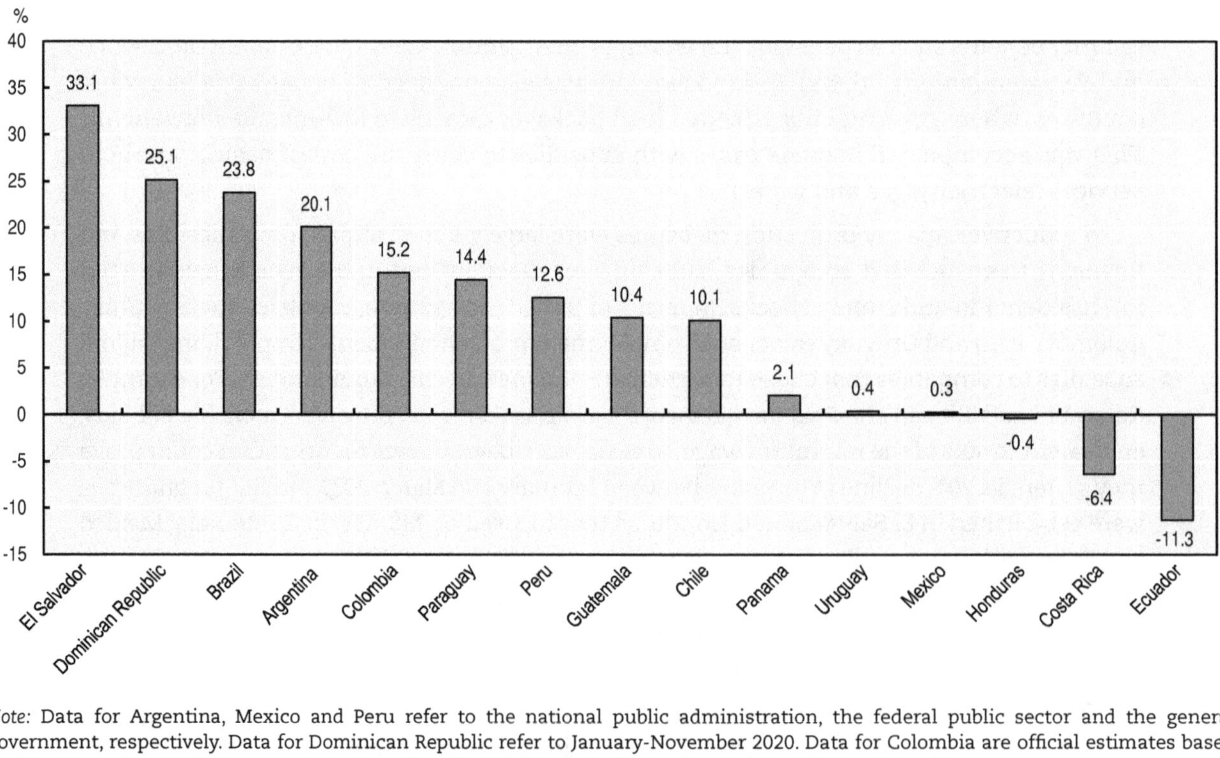

Note: Data for Argentina, Mexico and Peru refer to the national public administration, the federal public sector and the general government, respectively. Data for Dominican Republic refer to January-November 2020. Data for Colombia are official estimates based on Plan Financiero 2021: Documento de Actualización, Ministerio de Hacienda y Crédito Público, Colombia.

Source: Economic Commission for Latin America and the Caribbean (ECLAC), on the basis of Fiscal Panorama of Latin America and the Caribbean 2021.

StatLink https://doi.org/10.1787/888934234727

The road ahead: Fiscal policy in LAC to achieve sustainable development

The COVID-19 pandemic has laid bare the weaknesses of LAC's existing development model. The crisis has had an asymmetric impact on society, amplifying the entrenched inequalities – of income, wealth, gender, ethnicity, and age, among others – that characterise the region. At the same time, the crisis has highlighted the structural gaps that LAC countries have accumulated over time in several aspects including their social protection systems, productive structures, education, digital infrastructure and regional integration. Building back better in the region will be a significant undertaking that will require a transition to a new model of development that contemplates transformative economic and social changes.

Prior to the crisis, LAC countries already experienced rising and widespread social discontent. Weak public health, education and pension systems not only reinforce inequality, but they also undercut economic development. Low-quality public goods leave countries in a low-level equilibrium trap, with a sub-optimal level of investment in human capital limiting sustainable development. Public investment in sustainable infrastructure has declined in relative terms during the past decade, as fiscal consolidation efforts intensified. Realising the catalytic role of public investment, which can crowd-in private investment, countries should consider means of channelling financing flows to investment projects and establishing fiscal frameworks that protect capital expenditures from undue cuts.

In this context, active fiscal policies will play a key role in transitioning the region's development path to achieve the SDGs (ECLAC, 2021[7]; 2020[11]). During the post-pandemic period, governments should seek to address entrenched inequality by improving the quality of public goods and services and promoting universal social protection systems. Public health systems were quickly overwhelmed by the crisis, providing limited relief as the pandemic has spread. At the same time, the region's generally underdeveloped social protection systems – social assistance, unemployment insurance, pension schemes – required countries to take extraordinary measures to support individuals. Pension systems, that are already coming under significant strain as the region's population ages, require innovative policy developments to increase coverage and improve their fiscal sustainability (Arenas de Mesa, 2019[12]). Monetary transfer programmes, such as a basic income for targeted people in poverty, should also be examined as a means of achieving the goal of ending poverty and reducing inequality. These efforts need to be complemented with concrete steps to improve the efficiency and effectiveness of public spending.

Similarly, in the short run, given the increasing limited fiscal space and the urgent need to finance the complex challenges linked to the COVID-19 crisis, global co-ordination of public debt management should be a priority so as not to compromise the recovery over medium and long run (Box 2.2). The fall in tax revenues, coupled with the implementation of expenditure and liquidity support measures to face the COVID-19 crisis, put additional pressure in the LAC region with already limited fiscal space. Before the crisis, fiscal space in the majority of countries was limited, with budget deficits as the norm in most countries in the region. Similarly, debt levels were on the rise in almost all countries since 2014. Public debt-to-tax ratios, a proxy indicator of countries' financial capacity to pay the public debt, increased in most countries, leaving them in a weaker position to face the COVID-19 crisis than they were in 2007, before the global financial crisis (OECD et al., 2020[2]; Nieto-Parra and Orozco, 2020[13]).

Box 2.2. **Public debt and the COVID-19 crisis: paying for the crisis**

The magnitude of the fiscal response to the crisis in the region, which led to an in increase public outlays in a context of falling revenues, led to a substantial increase in public debt levels. Central government gross public debt in 2020 reached an average of 55.7% of GDP, an increase of 10.2 percentages points of GDP over the 2019 average of 45.6% of GDP (ECLAC, $2021_{[7]}$). The composition of this increase reflected the financing opportunities open to the region's countries. Sovereign debt issuance in international markets rose significantly (45% in the first 10 months of the year), as some countries were able to tap international markets, often favourable terms, to cover their increased 2020 financing needs, and in some cases pre-finance 2021 budgets (ECLAC, $2021_{[1]}$). Emergency financing from international financial institutions also played an important role, extending upwards of US 47.8 billion in new credit and the redirection of existing credit lines, in support of those countries with little or no access to international financial markets (ECLAC, $2021_{[7]}$).

Nevertheless, financial conditions may change rapidly in the medium term if monetary policy normalises in advanced economies, which could affect debt sustainability in some emerging economies with limited fiscal space. If this is the case, issuer or creditor inaction can lead to debt defaults and debt crises, adding to an already complicated scenario. This underlines the need for a globally co-ordinated debt management (OECD et al., $2020_{[2]}$; Nieto-Parra and Orozco, $2020_{[13]}$).

There is no single solution to public debt management in the region: countries differ in terms of their initial fiscal conditions, type of foreign creditors and capacity to tap into capital markets (OECD et al., $2020_{[2]}$). There are several policy actions in response to the COVID-19 crisis to be considered, depending on public debt levels and financial conditions across LAC countries:

- Official support should prioritise economies that have little or no access to capital markets.
- Countries with strong public finances going into the crisis must retain access to capital markets where risk premia remain low and through which they can raise funds needed to respond to the crisis, thanks to their abundant liquidity.
- Another group of countries might have access to capital markets but face high debt costs due to a deterioration in perceptions of debt sustainability. The deterioration includes current and potential downgrades in credit ratings or expectations of low future economic growth and public revenues. There are several policy options, including debt standstills or moratorium, debt relief, creation of a special vehicle to finance the crisis or pay the debt, and greater use of Special Drawing Rights. All require international co-operation, involving multilateral banks, public creditors or private creditors (Nieto-Parra and Orozco, $2020_{[13]}$); (Bolton, P et al., $2020_{[14]}$).
- Debt-to-COVID or debt-to-SDG swaps could be implemented, through which debtor countries channel planned debt service payments into national COVID-19 mitigation measures or SDG and environmental investments (UN/DESA, $2020_{[15]}$). Similarly, debt for climate and nature swaps could benefit lender and debtor governments, as well as private creditors, while avoiding potential debt crises and addressing climate change and biodiversity loss (Steele and Patel, $2020_{[16]}$).
- Social and environmental sustainability linked-bonds would link sustainable foreign financing with SDG commitments. This would allow countries to raise financial resources to respond to the COVID-19 crisis while also committing to the achievement of national climate and biodiversity sustainable goals (Caputo Silva and Stewart, $2021_{[17]}$). Mexico has recently become the first country in LAC to issue a bond linked to the fulfilment of the SDGs (ECLAC, $2021_{[1]}$).
- Future debt instruments that include 'insurance-like' clauses while rearranging pay-outs to creditors conditioned on the debtor country's economic performance would provide countries some relief in difficult economic situations, repaying creditors as the country´s outlook improves (Breuer and Cohen, $2020_{[18]}$).
- Recent experiences in Argentina and Ecuador of debt restructuring shows the importance of including Collective Action Clauses in sovereign bond contracts.

Building the fiscal sustainability framework required to support active fiscal policies aimed at achieving transformative economic and social change in the region is predicated on improving revenue generation in the medium-term to finance permanent expenditures aimed at closing structural development gaps. The analysis of the challenges and opportunities to strengthening the region's tax systems – bolstering direct taxation, addressing opportunities for improving indirect taxation and identifying new areas for tax policy development – is predicated on the availability of high-quality, comparable statistics. In that regard, the annual *Revenue Statistics in Latin America* report is a unique resource in the region, providing detailed, comparable and historical data. It also serves as an important complement to the analysis of fiscal measures in other policy domains, such as public spending for development.

There are multiple avenues open to the region, particularly in the area of tax policy, to strengthen revenue generation and reduce inequalities. There is an urgent need to reduce tax evasion and avoidance, which cost Latin America USD 325 billion in 2018 – equivalent to 6.1% of GDP – in lost PIT, CIT and VAT receipts (ECLAC, 2020[11]). Countries in the region have made strides in address this challenge but there remain significant tax compliance gaps for corporate and personal income taxes. Costly tax expenditures – which averaged 3.7% of GDP in Latin America between 2015 and 2019 – should be reviewed to ensure they are achieving their objectives and, if found not, be redirected to incentivise investment in the Sustainable Development Goals (ECLAC, 2020[11]).

At the level of individual instruments, there is also significant space for improvement (IADB, 2020[19]; ECLAC, 2021[1]; ECLAC, 2019[20]; ECLAC, 2021[7]). PIT, the principal factor behind the tax gap between the region and the OECD (see Chapter 1 of this report), is weak, limiting not only potential revenues but also the redistributive power of the tax system. This is compounded by the underdeveloped taxation of immovable property and wealth. There are numerous options for improving indirect taxation, including measures to improve the efficiency of the VAT by reducing the number and scope of exemptions and reduced rates while addressing its regressive impact by using VAT receipts to provide support to low-income households through cash transfers (also known as personalized-VAT). Experiences with such reforms in Argentina, Bolivia, Colombia, Ecuador and Uruguay are instructive for the region (Rasteletti, 2021[21]). In addition, corrective taxes, such as environmental taxes or taxes related to public health objectives, can play a key role in shaping the incentives of economic actors in favour of the SDGs. Finally, another key issue for the region's tax systems is the need to comprehensively tackle the challenges posed by the digital economy (OECD et al., 2020[2]).

This is the moment to start a concerted move towards a fundamental restructuring of tax systems to generate the revenues necessary to finance sustainable development and to strengthen the redistributive power of tax policy. These efforts in LAC benefit from partnerships with international and regional organisations and with forums such as the Inclusive Framework on Base Erosion and Profit Shifting. Similarly, support of domestic resource mobilisation in LAC – as part of SDG 17.1 – by bilateral and multilateral donors could significantly bolster the region's efforts to achieve the SDGs.

Notes

1. An estimated 1.4% of GDP in Chile (DIPRES, 2020[22]) and a similar amount in Peru (1.5% of GDP) (MEF Peru, 2020[23]).
2. The figures are sourced from (CIAT, 2021[24]).

References

Arenas de Mesa, A. (2019), *Los sistemas de pensiones en la encrucijada: desafíos para la sostenibilidad en América Latina*, United Nations Economic Commission for Latin America and the Caribbean, Santiago, *https://www.cepal.org/es/publicaciones/44851-sistemas-pensiones-la-encrucijada-desafios-la-sostenibilidad-america-latina.* [12]

Bolton, P et al. (2020), *Born Out of Necessity: A Debt Standstill for COVID-19, Center for Economic Policy Research; Policy Insight No. 103 (2020), Duke Law School Public Law & Legal Theory Series No. 2020-23, https://ssrn.com/abstract=3586785.* [14]

Breuer, P. and C. Cohen (2020), *Time is Ripe for Innovation in the World of Sovereign Debt Restructuring*, International Monetary Fund, Washington, D.C., *https://blogs.imf.org/2020/11/19/time-is-ripe-for-innovation-in-the-world-of-sovereign-debt-restructuring/.* [18]

Caputo Silva, A. and F. Stewart (2021), *My word is my bond: Linking sovereign debt with national sustainability commitments*, World Bank, Washington, D.C., *https://blogs.worldbank.org/climatechange/my-word-my-bond-linking-sovereign-debt-national-sustainability-commitments.* [17]

CIAT (2021), Revenue Report Covid-19 (RRC), Balance of 2020, CIAT. [24]

DIPRES (2020), *Informe de Ejecución del Gobierno Central Tercer Trimestre 2020*, The Budget Office of Chile. [22]

ECLAC (2021), *Fiscal Panorama of Latin America and the Caribbean 2021*, United Nations Economic Commission for Latin America and the Caribbean, Santiago. [7]

ECLAC (2021), *Preliminary Overview of the Economies of Latin America and the Caribbean 2020*, United Nations Economic Commission for Latin America and the Caribbean, Santiago, *https://www.cepal.org/en/publications/46504-preliminary-overview-economies-latin-america-and-caribbean-2020.* [1]

ECLAC (2020), *Economic Survey of Latin America and the Caribbean 2020*, United Nations Economic Commission for Latin America and the Caribbean, Santiago, *https://www.cepal.org/en/publications/46071-economic-survey-latin-america-and-caribbean-2020-main-conditioning-factors-fiscal.* [11]

ECLAC (2020), *Fiscal Panorama of Latin America and the Caribbean 2020*, United Nations Economic Commission for Latin America and the Caribbean, Santiago, *https://www.cepal.org/en/publications/45731-fiscal-panorama-latin-america-and-caribbean-2020-fiscal-policy-amid-crisis.* [6]

ECLAC (2020), *Latin America and the Caribbean and the COVID-19 pandemic: Economic and social effects and the impact on women's lives*, United Nations Economic Commission for Latin America and the Caribbean, Santiago, *https://www.cepal.org/sites/default/files/presentations/latin_america_and_the_caribbean_and_the_covid-19_pandemic_economic_and_social_effects_andthe_impact_on_womens_lives_0.pdf.* [8]

ECLAC (2020), *Universalizing access to digital technologies to address the consequences of COVID-19*, United Nations Economic Commission for Latin America and the Caribbean, Santiago, *https://www.cepal.org/en/publications/45939-universalizing-access-digital-technologies-address-consequences-covid-19.* [3]

ECLAC (2019), *Fiscal Panorama of Latin America and the Caribbean 2019*, United Nations Economic Commission for Latin America and the Caribbean, Santiago, *https://www.cepal.org/en/publications/44517-fiscal-panorama-latin-america-and-caribbean-2019-tax-policies-resource.* [20]

ECLAC/ILO (2020), *Work in times of pandemic: The challenges of the coronavirus disease (COVID-19)*, United Nations Economic Commission for Latin America and the Caribbean and International Labour Organization, *https://www.cepal.org/en/presentations/work-times-pandemic-challenges-coronavirus-disease-covid-19.* [5]

Harding, M. et al. (2020), *In Tax, Gender Blind is not Gender Neutral: why tax policy responses to COVID-19 must consider women*, OECD Publishing, Paris, *https://oecdecoscope.blog/2020/06/01/in-tax-gender-blind-is-not-gender-neutral-why-tax-policy-responses-to-covid-19-must-consider-women/.* [10]

IADB (2020), *Ideas para una mejor tributación en la post-crisis del COVID-19*, Inter-American Development Bank, Washington, D.C., *https://blogs.iadb.org/gestion-fiscal/es/ideas-para-una-mejor-tributacion-post-crisis-coronavirus/.* [19]

MEF Peru (2020), *Reporte Fiscal Trimestral: Seguimiento de las Reglas Macrofiscales, Segundo Trimestre 2020*, Ministry of Economy and Finance of Peru, *https://www.mef.gob.pe/contenidos/pol_econ/Reporte_Fiscal/Informe_Trimestral_de_Reglas_Fiscales_II_Trim2020.pdf.* [23]

Nieto-Parra, S. and R. Orozco (2020), *Public debt and COVID-19. Paying for the crisis in Latin America and the Caribbean*, Le Grand Continent, *https://legrandcontinent.eu/fr/2020/07/22/public-debt-and-covid-19-paying-for-the-crisis-in-latin-america-and-the-caribbean/.* [13]

OECD (2020), *COVID-19 in Latin America and the Caribbean: Regional socio-economic implications and policy priorities*, OECD Publishing, Paris, *http://www.oecd.org/coronavirus/policy-responses/covid-19-in-latin-america-and-the-caribbean-regional-socio-economic-implications-and-policy-priorities-93a64fde/*. [4]

OECD (2020), *SIGI 2020 Regional Report for Latin America and the Caribbean*, OECD Publishing, Paris, *https://doi.org/10.1787/cb7d45d1-en*. [9]

OECD et al. (2020), *Latin American Economic Outlook 2020: Digital Transformation for Building Back Better*, OECD Publishing, Paris, *https://doi.org/10.1787/e6e864fb-en*. [2]

Rasteletti, A. (2021), *IVA personalizado: Experiencia de 5 países y su importancia estratégica para la política y la administración tributaria*, Inter-American Development Bank, Washington, D.C., *https://blogs.iadb.org/gestion-fiscal/es/iva-personalizado-experiencia-latinoamericana-y-su-importancia-para-las-administraciones-tributarias/*. [21]

Steele, P. and S. Patel (2020), *Tackling the triple crisis: Using debt swaps to address debt, climate and nature loss post-COVID-19*, International Institute for Environment and Development, *https://pubs.iied.org/sites/default/files/pdfs/migrate/16674IIED.pdf*. [16]

UN/DESA (2020), *COVID-19 and sovereign debt*, United Nations Department of Economic and Social Affairs, New York, *https://www.un.org/development/desa/dpad/publication/un-desa-policy-brief-72-covid-19-and-sovereign-debt/*. [15]

Capítulo 2

SECCIÓN ESPECIAL
Respuestas de política fiscal a la crisis del COVID-19 en América Latina

Principales hallazgos

La política tributaria se utilizó amplia y rápidamente en América Latina y el Caribe como un instrumento para contrarrestar el impacto de la crisis del COVID-19 en las familias y empresas. La mayoría de los países tomaron medidas para reducir el costo de los suministros médicos mediante modificaciones de los gravámenes de importación y el impuesto al valor agregado (IVA), incluidas la tasa cero y las exenciones. El apoyo a las familias y empresas se centró en gran medida en los aplazamientos de impuestos y la creación de programas para facilitar la liquidación de obligaciones tributarias en lugar de la cancelación total de dichas obligaciones.

Los ingresos tributarios cayeron vertiginosamente en el primer semestre del año, aunque mostraron algunos signos de recuperación a finales de año. La recaudación tributaria de los dos principales impuestos de la región, el IVA y el impuesto sobre la renta, se contrajo drásticamente en el primer semestre del año como resultado de la caída de la actividad económica y la extensión de la desgravación fiscal como parte de los paquetes de políticas COVID-19. En la segunda mitad del año, la caída de los ingresos fiscales comenzó a revertirse gradualmente a medida que los países flexibilizaron las medidas de salud pública y los contribuyentes liquidaron pasivos que habían sido aplazados a principios de año.

Los países de América Latina y el Caribe adoptaron rápidamente una amplia gama de medidas de gasto y liquidez para apoyar a las familias y empresas. El gasto público sirvió como pilar central de la respuesta fiscal a la crisis en América Latina y el Caribe. Esto incluyó la expansión de los programas de apoyo social existentes o la creación de subsidios de emergencia para apoyar los ingresos y el bienestar de los hogares más vulnerables. Los países también buscaron limitar el impacto de la crisis en el flujo de caja de las empresas mediante subsidios para cubrir los gastos de nómina y operación. El apoyo por debajo de la línea en forma de préstamos en condiciones favorables, así como garantías de crédito respaldadas por el Estado, también desempeñaron un papel importante en el apoyo a las empresas.

La política fiscal se volvió excepcionalmente expansiva en 2020. El gasto primario del gobierno central, que excluye los pagos de intereses, registró un crecimiento interanual significativo, superior al 20% en términos reales en algunos casos. Este incremento fue impulsado por mayores transferencias corrientes, principalmente por la rápida expansión de los subsidios y transferencias asociadas a la respuesta fiscal a la crisis. El aumento del gasto y la caída de los ingresos públicos provocaron una erosión significativa de los saldos fiscales de la región y provocaron un fuerte aumento de los niveles de deuda pública bruta del gobierno central.

El impacto de la crisis de COVID-19 en la deuda pública requiere esfuerzos coordinados a nivel global en la gestión de la deuda. Para hacer frente a las presiones fiscales provocadas por la pandemia, los países de la región aumentaron la emisión de deuda en mercados financieros internacionales y accedieron a financiamiento de emergencia de las instituciones financieras internacionales. En el actual contexto de limitado espacio fiscal, una restricción en las condiciones de liquidez podría afectar la sostenibilidad de la deuda de algunas economías emergentes. Esto subraya la necesidad de una coordinación a escala mundial de la gestión de la deuda, aprovechando las distintas acciones de política disponibles y con soluciones específicas para cada país.

Reconstruir mejor y lograr los Objetivos de Desarrollo Sostenible en América Latina y el Caribe requerirá políticas fiscales activas respaldadas por un marco de sostenibilidad fiscal. La crisis ha puesto al descubierto las debilidades del modelo de desarrollo existente en América Latina y el Caribe. Las arraigadas desigualdades y la acumulación de brechas estructurales de desarrollo (inclusión social, estructura productiva, entre otras) a lo largo del tiempo obstaculizaron gravemente la capacidad de la región para hacer frente a la pandemia y sus consecuencias. Cambiar el camino del desarrollo de América Latina y el Caribe requerirá un esfuerzo concertado del sector público. Las políticas fiscales activas, respaldadas por un marco de sostenibilidad fiscal,

Principales hallazgos *(cont.)*

deberán desempeñar un papel clave en este proceso. Un desafío para hacer que estas políticas sean sostenibles radica en fortalecer los ingresos públicos, especialmente los ingresos fiscales, bajo una secuencia de políticas bien definidas. Es hora de que la región dé pasos para diseñar reformas fiscales estructurales con el objetivo de financiar el desarrollo sostenible.

La política fiscal demostró ser una herramienta potente para abordar la crisis en la región

La pandemia COVID-19 ha desencadenado la peor crisis económica en América Latina y el Caribe en 120 años, lo que ha provocado importantes reducciones en el crecimiento a corto y mediano plazo y aumentos en la desigualdad, la pobreza y el desempleo (CEPAL, 2021[1]). Las necesarias medidas de salud pública para proteger la vida humana precipitaron una caída del PIB a través de dos canales: por el lado de la oferta, la brusca interrupción de las cadenas de suministro, asociada al cierre de gran parte de las empresas que realizan actividades identificadas como no esenciales. Por el lado de la demanda, los despidos o el desempleo parcial impactaron fuertemente en los ingresos de los hogares, reduciendo así el consumo.

La crisis ha tenido un impacto asimétrico en las sociedades de la región. Ha sido de carácter regresivo, profundizando las desigualdades existentes en una región que ya es la más desigual del mundo. Esto se ha reflejado en un fuerte aumento de los índices de vulnerabilidad de grupos sociales como jóvenes, mujeres, inmigrantes, adultos mayores, entre otros. La brecha digital preexistente en la región tuvo un impacto perjudicial en la educación, ya que las escuelas pasaron a modalidades en línea (OCDE et al., 2020[2]; CEPAL, 2020[3]). En el mercado laboral, los trabajadores informales e independientes se han visto afectados de manera desproporcionada, ya que a menudo tienen poco o ningún vínculo con los sistemas de seguridad social existentes y podrían tener menor capacidad para trabajar desde casa (OCDE, 2020[4]; CEPAL/OIT, 2020[5]).

América Latina ha sido una de las regiones más afectadas por el COVID-19 en el mundo. Si bien muchos países adoptaron estrictas medidas de salud pública, la pandemia se propagó por la región. Los sistemas de salud pública de la región, que han sufrido una subinversión crónica, se vieron rápidamente abrumados por la creciente incidencia de pacientes con coronavirus. El enorme papel de la economía informal también limitó la eficacia de las medidas de restricción de movimiento, ya que los trabajadores informales dependen de los ingresos diarios para sobrevivir.

Ante esta situación, los países de la región impulsaron ambiciosos paquetes de medidas de política fiscal para fortalecer los sistemas públicos de salud, apoyar a los hogares, particularmente a los más vulnerables, y proteger la capacidad productiva para facilitar la recuperación económica en la pospandemia (CEPAL, 2020[6]; OCDE, 2020[4]). Los países hicieron esfuerzos fiscales sin precedentes que en promedio representaron – 4.3% del PIB en América Latina – a través de alivio tributario, reasignaciones presupuestarias y gastos adicionales, así como instrumentos de liquidez respaldados por los gobiernos (préstamos concesionales) (CEPAL, 2020[6]). Además, varios países han creado o fortalecido programas estatales de garantía crediticia para brindar liquidez adicional a las empresas, en particular a las pymes, con acceso limitado al sistema bancario formal.

Todas estas respuestas de políticas tuvieron un costo y la situación fiscal de la región se ha deteriorado. El repunte del gasto público y la caída de los ingresos públicos han resultado en elevados déficits fiscales en términos históricos y niveles crecientes de deuda pública, en particular de fuentes externas, incluidos los mercados financieros internacionales y las instituciones crediticias multilaterales. No obstante, las políticas fiscales activas serán clave para el esfuerzo de recuperación y para reconstruir mejores sociedades en el mundo de la pospandemia. Por tanto, la austeridad fiscal no es una opción de política para la región.

Mantener políticas fiscales activas será crucial para impulsar el crecimiento económico y lograr el cambio económico y social transformador que la región necesita para cumplir con éxito los Objetivos de Desarrollo Sostenible (ODS). Estas políticas deberán abordar las brechas estructurales de desarrollo existentes en la región, al mismo tiempo que contribuyan a la construcción de sistemas de protección social universales y se mejora la calidad de los bienes y servicios públicos.

La región enfrenta el desafío de mantener un enfoque de política fiscal activo dentro de un marco de sostenibilidad fiscal. Esto requerirá del desarrollo de estrategias destinadas a fortalecer los ingresos y mejorar la calidad del gasto.

Las medidas de política tributaria se adoptaron amplia y rápidamente como parte de la respuesta a la crisis

Si bien el gasto público representó el pilar principal de la respuesta fiscal de América Latina y el Caribe a la pandemia de COVID-19, la política tributaria también se utilizó como una herramienta estratégica para mitigar los impactos económicos de la crisis. En comparación con las medidas que implicaban reasignaciones presupuestarias y gastos adicionales, las medidas de alivio se promulgaron con prontitud, ya que en su mayoría fueron adoptadas por decretos. A pesar de su importancia (los ingresos no percibidos temporalmente debido a estas medidas fueron significativos, en algunos casos representando más del 1% del PIB[1]), las medidas de desgravación fiscal se basaron principalmente en postergaciones y facilidades de pago que desplazaron la recaudación de ingresos tributarios en lugar de reducciones directas de las obligaciones fiscales (CEPAL, 2021[7]; 2020[6]). En general, estas medidas estaban dirigidas al sector de la salud o proporcionaron liquidez temporal a hogares y empresas. Sin embargo, la eficacia de la desgravación fiscal se vio obstaculizada por la amplitud del sector informal de la economía en la región y la participación limitada de las personas y las PYMES en los sistemas tributarios y de seguridad social.

Dada la escala de la pandemia y las limitaciones de los sistemas de salud en la región, los países promulgaron rápidamente medidas para reducir el costo de los insumos médicos cruciales (Cuadro 2.1). En muchos países, esto tomó la forma de exenciones temporales o una tasa cero para suministros médicos con el objeto de responder a la pandemia de COVID-19 (alcohol, artículos de laboratorio, guantes, desinfectantes, equipos y otros suministros de salud), lo que refleja la dependencia de proveedores externos. Estas medidas fueron acompañadas en algunos casos, como en Colombia, de la exención del IVA a los productos médicos. Los países también buscaron incentivar las donaciones directas a los sistemas de salud proporcionando deducciones temporales de los impuestos sobre la renta de personas físicas y sociedades (IRPF y IRS).

Adicionalmente, se implementaron medidas de alivio tributario para los hogares y los trabajadores autónomos para compensar los salarios perdidos y apoyar el consumo. Las medidas más comunes fueron los aplazamientos, las suspensiones de anticipos y las facilidades para el pago de impuestos, como planes de pago a plazos sin intereses ni penalizaciones del IVA y el IRPF. Varios países, incluidos Chile, Colombia, Perú y Trinidad y Tobago, también implementaron devoluciones aceleradas del IRPF para brindar mayor apoyo. Los hogares también recibieron apoyo en algunos países, como Argentina, Colombia, Costa Rica, Dominica, Guyana, Honduras y San Vicente y las Granadinas, mediante exenciones del IVA sobre suministros y productos médicos esenciales de la canasta básica de bienes y servicios de consumo como la electricidad.

En Colombia, un innovador esquema de devolución del IVA se dirigió a un millón de familias en situación de pobreza, a través de cinco pagos de COP 75 000 durante el año. Las medidas de alivio tributario para las familias tuvieron un impacto relativamente limitado en la región, lo que refleja el reducido universo de hogares incorporados en los sistemas IRPF. Además, estas medidas fueron de naturaleza general, sin brindar beneficios adicionales a las poblaciones particularmente afectadas, como las mujeres (Recuadro 2.1).

Cuadro 2.1. **Medidas de desgravación tributaria relacionadas con COVID-19 en América Latina y el Caribe**

Instrumento	Abordando la crisis sanitaria	Provisión de liquidez a hogares y empresas							
		Facilidades de aplazamiento y pago				Reembolsos acelerados	Tratamiento preferencial		
		Hogares	Empresas				Hogares	Empresas	
			Todos	Sector específico	PYMES			Todos	PYMES
Impuesto sobre la renta	Bolivia (Estado Plurinacional de) Guyana	Argentina Belice Brasil República Dominicana El Salvador Guatemala Guyana Panamá Paraguay Perú Santa Lucía San Vincente y las Granadinas	Argentina Belice Brasil Bolivia (Estado Plurinacional de) Chile Colombia Costa Rica República Dominicana El Salvador Granada Guatemala Guyana Honduras Panamá Paraguay Perú Santa Lucía	Colombia República Dominicana Ecuador El Salvador Honduras	Chile Panamá Perú Paraguay	Belice Chile Perú Trinidad y Tobago	Venezuela (República Bolivariana de)	Bolivia (Estado Plurinacional de) Chile Honduras Saint Kitts y Nevis Santa Lucía	Bolivia (Estado Plurinacional de) Honduras Panamá
Contribuciones sociales o paraestatales			Argentina Brasil Barbados Colombia Uruguay	Argentina Colombia	Argentina Uruguay			Argentina Brasil	
Impuesto sobre bienes y servicios	Argentina Bolivia (Estado Plurinacional de) Brasil Colombia Ecuador El Salvador Guatemala Guyana Honduras Jamaica Panamá Paraguay Perú Saint Kitts y Nevis San Vincente y las Granadinas Venezuela (República Bolivariana de)		Brasil Chile Colombia Costa Rica República Dominicana Ecuador Honduras Paraguay Uruguay	Colombia Ecuador San Vincente y las Granadinas	Chile	Belice Perú Trinidad y Tobago	Dominica Guyana San Vincente y las Granadinas	Colombia Costa Rica Dominica	Bolivia (Estado Plurinacional de) Colombia
Otros impuestos		Chile	Brasil Chile Colombia Granada Guatemala Guyana		Brasil Colombia		Brasil Chile	Brasil Chile Colombia	

Fuente: Comisión Económica para América Latina y el Caribe (CEPAL), sobre la base de Panorama Fiscal de América Latina y el Caribe 2020 (LC/PUB.2020/6-P), Santiago, 2020.

StatLink https://doi.org/10.1787/888934234822

Recuadro 2.1. **Incorporación de una perspectiva de género en las respuestas de política tributaria**

Las mujeres están en el centro de la lucha contra la crisis de COVID-19: constituyen la gran mayoría de los trabajadores de la salud y asumen gran parte de la carga del cuidado infantil y la educación en el hogar durante los encierros. Si bien las medidas de política tributaria juegan un papel importante en el apoyo a las personas y las empresas, el impacto de género de los impuestos también debe tenerse en cuenta al responder a la crisis.

Aunque las disposiciones fiscales que explícitamente ponen en desventaja a las mujeres en relación con los hombres son poco comunes, los impuestos pueden, en la práctica, mostrar un sesgo implícito que exacerba las desigualdades de género, especialmente en tiempos de crisis. Esto se debe a que los sistemas tributarios interactúan con las diferencias socioeconómicas de género subyacentes entre hombres y mujeres, como las diferencias en los niveles de ingresos, los patrones de consumo, el espíritu empresarial y la riqueza.

En el caso de los impuestos sobre la renta, por ejemplo, aunque los hombres y las mujeres suelen estar sujetos a las mismas reglas, sus diferentes niveles salariales y participación en la fuerza laboral significan que el sistema tributario puede tener efectos diferentes. Las mujeres suelen ser más sensibles a los cambios en los salarios que los hombres en sus decisiones de participar en el mercado laboral y es más probable que trabajen a tiempo parcial. Por lo tanto, la progresividad del sistema tributario es un factor importante en la participación de la mujer en el mercado laboral, en particular si el retiro de las prestaciones por cónyuge o hijo a cargo aumenta las tasas impositivas efectivas sobre los segundos ingresos – que son mayormente mujeres – que ingresan a la fuerza laboral.

Los impuestos al consumo también afectan directamente la distribución del ingreso entre hombres y mujeres dentro de los hogares, debido a las diferencias de género en los patrones de consumo. También pueden contribuir indirectamente a otro sesgo implícito, ya que los impuestos al consumo de servicios como la limpieza y el cuidado de los hijos hacen que sea más atractivo producir estos servicios en el hogar que comprarlos en el mercado, especialmente para los hogares de bajos ingresos. Esto puede disminuir la oferta laboral de la segunda fuente de ingresos.

El COVID-19 amplifica esta dinámica aumentando la carga de trabajo no remunerado de las mujeres y desestabilizando el mercado laboral. El cierre generalizado de escuelas y guarderías y otras medidas de confinamiento han aumentado el tiempo que hay que dedicar al cuidado de los hijos y a la educación en el hogar, así como a las tareas domésticas de rutina, muchas de las cuales son realizadas por mujeres, y que pueden aumentar el riesgo de que las mujeres que sean la segunda fuente de ingresos del hogar abandonen la fuerza laboral.

También existen diferencias de género en los patrones de empleo entre hombres y mujeres. En los países de América Latina y el Caribe, las mujeres tienen más probabilidades de trabajar por cuenta propia y de trabajar en el servicio doméstico y en sectores con salarios más bajos y condiciones precarias (36% del empleo de mujeres contra 28.4% del empleo de hombres en 2017 en promedio en la región de América Latina). Además, el 78% de las mujeres ocupadas en promedio en América Latina se concentra en los sectores más afectados por el COVID-19 (por ejemplo, servicios sociales, restaurantes y hoteles, transporte) (CEPAL, 2020[8]). Este grupo laboral se encuentran entre los más vulnerables durante la crisis actual, enfrentan mayores riesgos de pérdida de empleo o ingresos, y a menudo no están cubiertos por la seguridad social debido a la naturaleza no estándar o informal de algunos de estos trabajos. En la región de América Latina y el Caribe, la tasa de informalidad no agrícola de las mujeres se situó en 52%, en comparación con el 47% de los hombres (OCDE, 2020[9]).

Para abordar las complejas interacciones de impuestos y género en el mundo post-COVID-19, los gobiernos deberán considerar opciones para rediseñar impuestos clave para evitar exacerbar las diferencias de género existentes, o utilizar impuestos u otros instrumentos para compensar las diferencias en los niveles de ingresos como parte de su respuesta a largo plazo de la crisis. Para garantizar que el sistema tributario no refuerce inadvertidamente los sesgos de género en la sociedad, los gobiernos deben incluir el impacto de los impuestos sobre el género como una dimensión clave de la política tributaria. Mejorar los datos sobre el impacto del COVID-19 en las mujeres de la región será fundamental para comprender estos impactos.

Fuente: Adaptado de Harding et al. (2020[10]).

Al igual que en el caso de los hogares, el alivio tributario para las empresas también consistió principalmente de medidas temporales para potenciar el flujo de caja, especialmente en los primeros meses de la crisis, mediante aplazamientos y suspensión de anticipos del IVA y del impuesto sobre sociedades (ISR). La desgravación del IVA, en particular, jugó un papel importante en la región, especialmente para las micro, pequeñas y medianas empresas (MIPYMES). En varios casos, el alivio tributario se dirigió a las MIPYMES o sectores particularmente afectados por la crisis, como la construcción, el turismo y los servicios personales. Los países también extendieron el alivio a las empresas mediante modificaciones a los esquemas de contribución social, como el Programa de Asistencia de Emergencia al Trabajo y la Producción (ATP) en Argentina, que introdujo una reducción de hasta el 95% en el pago de las cotizaciones de los empleadores al Sistema Integrado de Seguridad Social. En Brasil, se suspendieron los pagos al Fondo del Seguro de Desempleo (FGTS) y se redujeron en un 50% los aportes al Sistema S, que financia la educación técnica y profesional, durante abril, mayo y junio.

La combinación de la severa contracción de la actividad económica, con su concomitante declive en el consumo y los ingresos privados, y las medidas de alivio tributario provocaron una importante disminución de los ingresos públicos en América Latina. Los ingresos por IVA, una de las principales fuentes de ingresos fiscales en la región, se desplomaron entre marzo y mayo a medida que evolucionó la pandemia y los países establecieron estrictas medidas de cuarentena (Gráfico 2.1). El mes de mayo fue especialmente complejo en muchos países de la región, con caídas interanuales en términos reales del 40% o más en la recaudación del IVA en Chile, Costa Rica, Ecuador y Honduras. Los ingresos por impuestos a la renta también registraron caídas importantes en los primeros meses del año, principalmente por la extensión de medidas como el diferimiento de la liquidación de los pasivos fiscales de 2019 y la suspensión de los pagos anticipados de impuestos.

Gráfico 2.1. **Ingresos por IVA, enero-diciembre de 2020**

Variación interanual real en porcentaje

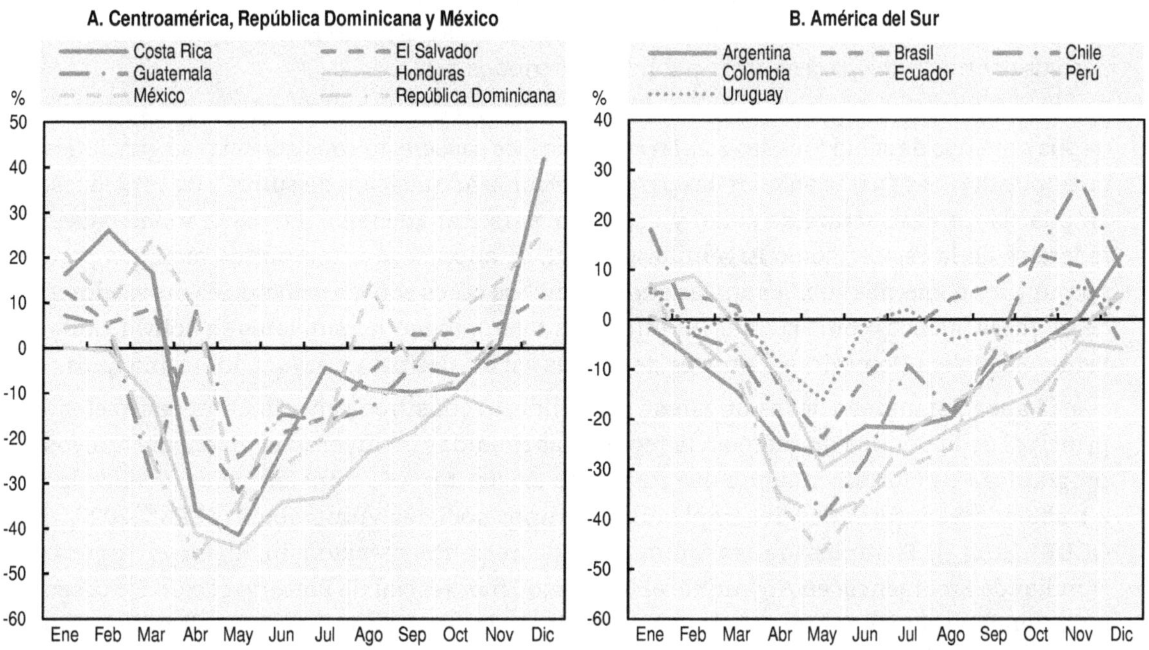

Nota: Los datos de Brasil corresponden a los ingresos del Impuesto sobre Comercio y Servicios (Imposto sobre Circulaçao de Mercadorias e Serviços, ICMS), un impuesto a nivel estatal.

Fuente: Comisión Económica para América Latina y el Caribe (CEPAL), sobre la base de Panorama Fiscal de América Latina y el Caribe 2021.

StatLink https://doi.org/10.1787/888934234746

El lento repunte de la actividad económica experimentado a mediados de 2020 cuando se suavizaron las medidas de salud pública y el retiro de ciertos aplazamientos de impuestos relacionados con las medidas de alivio tributario permitió una desaceleración progresiva en las caídas interanuales de los ingresos tributarios. Esto fue especialmente evidente en el caso de los ingresos por IVA, que mejoraron a lo largo de la segunda mitad del año. Para el cuarto trimestre, los ingresos por IVA en algunos países se acercaron o superaron su nivel del año anterior, sin embargo, para el agregado del año disminuyeron (CEPAL, 2021[7]). No obstante, algunas medidas de alivio tributario se renovaron repetidamente en varios países, lo que potencialmente trasladó ingresos del IVA a 2021. Basándose en los informes de las administraciones tributarias de 18 países de la región de ALC, el Centro Interamericano de Administraciones Tributarias (CIAT)[2] calcula que los ingresos tributarios totales disminuyeron en un 11.2% en 2020 con respecto al año anterior. Las mayores caídas se observan en los impuestos selectivos al consumo (13.7% interanual), seguidos de los impuestos sobre la renta (-9.9%), y el IVA (-9.2%). Los demás ingresos tributarios no clasificados disminuyeron un 14.2%.

Las medidas de gasto representaron la mayor parte de la respuesta a la crisis

Las políticas de gasto público en América Latina y el Caribe en 2020 canalizaron importantes recursos adicionales para fortalecer los sistemas de salud pública, apoyar a las familias y proteger la capacidad productiva (Cuadro 2.2). Estos esfuerzos fueron especialmente importantes en la región, ya que las brechas de desarrollo existentes dejan a sectores importantes de la población y las empresas, principalmente PYMES informales, excepcionalmente vulnerables a las recesiones económicas. Como se destaca en CEPAL (2020[11]), la mayor parte de las medidas de gasto para enfrentar la emergencia comprendieron reasignaciones presupuestarias y gasto adicional en forma de transferencias corrientes para canalizar recursos directamente a los hogares y las pequeñas empresas. Estas políticas fueron acompañadas de medidas adicionales que no son estrictamente gastos públicos en el período actual, como transacciones por debajo de la línea – incluidos crédito en condiciones favorables y garantías crediticias respaldadas por el Estado – pero que crean pasivos contingentes para el gasto público en períodos futuros.

La mayoría de los países de la región adoptaron medidas para fortalecer la capacidad de sus sistemas de salud (Cuadro 2.2). En casi todos los casos, esto consistió en reasignaciones presupuestarias y gastos adicionales para financiar la adquisición de suministros médicos, ampliar la infraestructura de salud y contratar personal adicional. En los grandes países federales de la región, como Argentina y Brasil, se adoptaron importantes medidas para apoyar a los gobiernos subnacionales que en muchos casos son los principales proveedores de servicios públicos como la salud. Se implementaron programas similares en Bolivia, Chile, Perú y República Dominicana a través de fondos especiales para apoyar a los municipios.

El apoyo al ingreso de los hogares y, por ende, al consumo privado, representó el eje principal de la política de gasto en la región. Las medidas incluyeron el diseño de nuevos programas – o el fortalecimiento de programas existentes – de transferencias focalizadas a trabajadores informales desempleados y grupos sociales vulnerables (CEPAL, 2020[6]; OCDE, 2020[4]). Ejemplos de transferencias de reciente creación incluyen el Ingreso Familiar de Emergencia en Argentina, el Benefício Emergencial de Preservação do Emprego e da Renda en Brasil (el programa más grande de la región con BRL 321 mil millones o USD 62 mil millones), el Ingreso Familiar de Emergencia en Chile, el Ingreso Solidario en Colombia, el Subsidio Familiar en El Salvador y la expansión del Bono Familiar Universal en Perú (CEPAL, 2020[6]; OCDE et al., 2020[2]). Las transferencias también se dirigieron a los trabajadores del sector formal, incluidos los beneficios para cubrir la pérdida temporal de ingresos, por ejemplo, el Programa de Asistencia de Emergencia al Trabajo y la Producción en Argentina, y para llenar vacíos en el marco de protección social existente, como el Subsidio al Empleo Formal en Paraguay, donde no existe un sistema de seguro de desempleo establecido.

Cuadro 2.2. **Instrumentos de gasto (por encima de la línea), instrumentos de financiamiento (por debajo de la línea) y garantías de crédito respaldadas por el Estado empleadas en 2020 en respuesta a la crisis del COVID-19, por objetivo de política, en América Latina y el Caribe**

Protección de los ingresos y el bienestar de los hogares						Protección de la capacidad productiva y garantizar la liquidez del sector privado				Apoyo a la actividad económica	
						Subsidios y beneficios de nómina para cubrir gastos operativos	Líneas de crédito				
Fortalecimiento del sistema de salud	Empleo	Pensiones	Consumo	Grupos vulnerables	Otros		Total	Micro, pequeñas y medianas empresas	Garantías estatales	Inversión en infraestructura	Viviendas
Bahamas Barbados Brasil Chile Colombia Ecuador El Salvador Granada Guatemala Haití Honduras México Panamá Paraguay Perú Saint Kitts y Nevis San Vincente y las Granadinas Surinam Trinidad y Tobago	Argentina Bahamas Barbados Bolivia (Plurinational State of) Brasil Chile Colombia Costa Rica Cuba El Salvador Granada Haiti Jamaica México Paraguay República Dominicana Santa Lucía Trinidad y Tobago Uruguay	Argentina Bolivia (Estado Plurinacional de) Brasil México	Argentina Bahamas Bolivia (Estado Plurinacional de) Chile El Salvador Guatemala Honduras Panamá Paraguay República Dominicana Uruguay	Argentina Bolivia (Estado Plurinacional de f) Brasil Chile Colombia Costa Rica Ecuador El Salvador Granada Guatemala Haiti Honduras Jamaica México Panamá Paraguay Uruguay	Argentina Bolivia (Estado Plurinacional de)	Argentina Chile Colombia El Salvador Guatemala Honduras México Panamá Perú Uruguay	Argentina Bolivia (Estado Plurinacional de) Brasil Colombia El Salvador Guatemala Jamaica Santa Lucía	Bahamas Bolivia (Estado Plurinacional de) Brasil Chile Ecuador El Salvador Granada Guatemala Honduras Jamaica México Panamá Paraguay Perú Trinidad y Tobago Uruguay	Argentina Bahamas Chile Colombia México Paraguay Perú Uruguay	Argentina Barbados El Salvador Granada Guatemala México	Antigua y Barbuda Argentina Granada Guatemala México

Nota: Los datos incluyen reasignaciones presupuestarias, gastos adicionales, préstamos en condiciones favorables y garantías de crédito respaldadas por el Estado.

Fuente: Comisión Económica para América Latina y el Caribe (CEPAL), sobre la base de Panorama Fiscal de América Latina y el Caribe 2020 (LC/PUB.2020/6-P), Santiago, 2020.

StatLink https://doi.org/10.1787/888934234841

Los países también implementaron medidas para aumentar la cobertura y el valor de los beneficios que brindan los programas de protección social existentes, incluido el seguro de desempleo (por ejemplo, en Chile, Ecuador, México y Uruguay, entre otros) y los beneficios de seguridad social como las pensiones (por ejemplo, en Argentina, Colombia, Guatemala, México y Paraguay, entre otros). También se brindó apoyo en especie a los hogares de varios países, donde los gobiernos proporcionaron paquetes de alimentos directamente a los hogares de bajos ingresos. Esto fue acompañado en algunos casos con subsidios para cubrir el costo de los servicios básicos del hogar (luz, gas y agua).

Las medidas de protección de la capacidad productiva estuvieron orientadas en gran medida a otorgar subsidios y financiamiento para facilitar a las empresas flujo de caja durante el año, en un contexto de intensos choques de oferta y demanda. En términos de gasto público, países como Chile, Colombia, Perú y Uruguay establecieron esquemas de protección laboral al otorgar subsidios a la nómina a las empresas que optaron por participar y cumplían con requisitos específicos. Por ejemplo, Colombia estableció el Programa de Apoyo al Empleo Formal para proporcionar un subsidio mensual, equivalente al 40% del salario mínimo, para ayudar con los costos de nómina de empresas que pudieran demostrar que sufrieron una disminución del 20% en los ingresos entre febrero y marzo de 2020. Se establecieron programas similares en El Salvador y Honduras que se enfocaron en las MIPYMES. En Guatemala, México y Panamá se establecieron subsidios comerciales para compensar los gastos de operación relacionados con la compra de insumos necesarios en el sector agrícola. Algunos países, como Argentina y Perú, implementaron programas de apoyo a la productividad, financiyo proyectos de investigación y desarrollo (I + D), promoviendo la digitalización y fomentando el espíritu empresarial.

El uso de medidas por debajo de las líneas, como la provisión de líneas especiales de crédito y la capitalización de instituciones financieras estatales, permitió a los países garantizar que las empresas tuvieran acceso a la liquidez necesaria, especialmente aquellas con acceso ya limitado, como las MIPYMES. Por ejemplo, el programa Reactívate Ecuador otorgó crédito a las MIPYMES a una tasa preferencial (5%) con plazos de 36 meses y un período de gracia de seis meses. Varios países, como Bolivia, Brasil y Paraguay, también otorgaron préstamos en condiciones favorables como parte de planes de retención de empleo para ayudar a cubrir los costos de nómina. Aunque menos generalizados, los programas de crédito respaldados por el Estado se utilizaron con éxito para reforzar la liquidez del sistema financiero. En algunos casos, esto se implementó como la expansión de esquemas existentes, como los programas de financiamiento del BNDES en Brasil y una gran inyección de capital en el Fondo de Garantía de Pequeños Empresarios en Chile. En Perú, se estableció un nuevo programa como parte del Reactiva Perú, donde los créditos garantizados por el Tesoro fueron respaldados por un aporte del Banco Central. En Colombia, Bancoldex lanzó nuevas líneas de crédito para responder a la crisis del COVID-19 en el marco del Programa Colombia Responde para apoyar a más de 38 000 empresas de las cuales más del 90% son microempresas.

Como resultado de estas medidas de apoyo, la política fiscal fue altamente expansiva en muchos países de América Latina y el Caribe durante 2020 (CEPAL, 2021[7]). Esto contrasta fuertemente con el crecimiento relativamente modesto del gasto público en los últimos años, durante los cuales los países adoptaron políticas de consolidación fiscal para controlar el aumento de la deuda pública. El gasto primario del gobierno central aumentó a tasas de dos dígitos en algunos países durante el año, llegando en algunos casos a más del 20% en términos reales en comparación con 2019 (Gráfico 2.2). Esta dinámica fue impulsada por un aumento significativo de los subsidios y transferencias corrientes como resultado de las medidas de gasto relacionadas con el COVID-19 adoptadas durante el año (CEPAL, 2021[7]; 2021[1]). Sin embargo, la experiencia de la región no fue uniforme: la política fiscal siguió siendo contractiva en unos pocos países, reflejando principalmente su capacidad para expandir el espacio fiscal, a consecuencia de elevados déficits fiscales o altos niveles de deuda pública previos a la crisis. Algunos países pudieron aprovechar el acceso a los mercados financieros nacionales e internacionales, las instituciones financieras internacionales y, en algunos casos, los bancos centrales para financiar su respuesta ante la pandemia.

Gráfico 2.2. **Gasto primario del gobierno central en 15 países de América Latina, 2019-20**

Variación real interanual en porcentaje

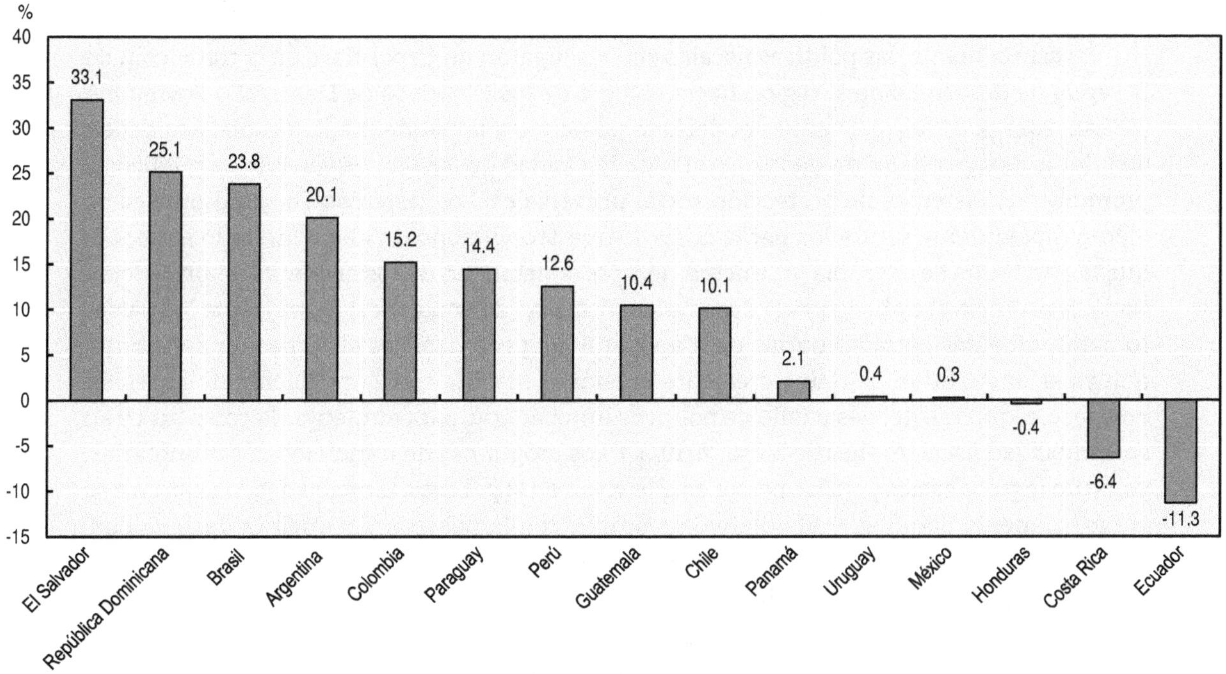

Nota: Los datos de Argentina, México y Perú se refieren a la administración pública nacional, el sector público federal y el gobierno general, respectivamente. Los datos de la República Dominicana se refieren a enero-noviembre de 2020. Los datos de Colombia son estimaciones oficiales basadas en Plan Financiero 2021: Documento de Actualización, Ministerio de Hacienda y Crédito Público, Colombia.

Fuente: Comisión Económica para América Latina y el Caribe (CEPAL), sobre la base de Panorama Fiscal de América Latina y el Caribe 2021.

StatLink https://doi.org/10.1787/888934234765

El camino hacia delante: La política fiscal en América Latina y el Caribe para alcanzar el desarrollo sostenible

La pandemia de COVID-19 ha puesto al descubierto las debilidades del modelo de desarrollo existente en América Latina y el Caribe. La crisis ha tenido un impacto asimétrico en la sociedad, amplificó las arraigadas desigualdades – de ingresos, riqueza, género, etnia y edad, entre otras – que caracterizan a la región. Al mismo tiempo, la crisis ha puesto de relieve las brechas estructurales que los países han acumulado a lo largo del tiempo en varios aspectos, incluidos sus sistemas de protección social, estructuras productivas, educación, infraestructura digital e integración regional. Reconstruir mejor en la región será una tarea importante que requerirá una transición hacia un nuevo modelo de desarrollo que contemple cambios económicos y sociales transformadores.

Antes de la crisis, los países de la región ya experimentaban descontentos sociales crecientes. Los débiles sistemas de salud pública, educación y pensiones no solo refuerzan la desigualdad, sino que también socavan el desarrollo económico. Los servicios públicos de baja calidad dejan a los países en una trampa de equilibrio de bajo nivel, con un nivel subóptimo de inversión en capital humano que limita el desarrollo sostenible. La inversión pública en infraestructura sostenible ha disminuido en términos relativos durante la última década, a medida que se intensificaron los esfuerzos de consolidación fiscal. Ante el papel catalizador de la inversión pública, y su efecto de atracción de la inversión privada, los países deberían considerar medios para canalizar flujos de financiamiento hacia proyectos de inversión y establecer marcos fiscales que protejan los gastos de capital de recortes indebidos.

En este contexto, las políticas fiscales activas jugarán un papel clave en la transición de la senda de desarrollo de la región hacia el logro de los Objetivos de Desarrollo Sostenible (CEPAL, 2021[7]; 2020[11]). Durante el período posterior a la pandemia, los gobiernos deben abordar la desigualdad arraigada, mejorando la calidad de los bienes y servicios públicos y promoviendo sistemas de protección social universales. Los sistemas de salud pública se vieron rápidamente saturados por la crisis, lo que proporcionó un alivio limitado a medida que la pandemia se extendía. Al mismo tiempo, la debilidad de los sistemas de protección social (asistencia social, seguro de desempleo, sistemas de pensiones) requirió que los países tomaran medidas extraordinarias para apoyar a las personas. Los sistemas de pensiones, que ya se encuentran bajo una creciente presión a medida que la población de la región envejece, requieren del desarrollo de políticas innovadoras para aumentar la cobertura y su sostenibilidad fiscal (Arenas de Mesa, 2019[12]). Los programas de transferencias monetarias, como un ingreso básico para las personas que viven en la pobreza, también deben examinarse como un medio para lograr el objetivo de acabar con la pobreza y reducir la desigualdad. Estos esfuerzos deben complementarse con medidas concretas para mejorar la eficiencia, eficacia y equidad del gasto público.

Asimismo, en el corto plazo, dado el cada vez más limitado espacio fiscal y la urgente necesidad de financiar los complejos desafíos vinculados a la crisis del COVID-19, la coordinación global de la gestión de la deuda pública debe ser una prioridad para no comprometer el mediano y largo plazo (Recuadro 2.2). La caída de los ingresos tributarios en América Latina, sumada a la implementación de medidas de apoyo al gasto y la liquidez para enfrentar la crisis del COVID-19, ejerció una presión adicional en el reducido espacio fiscal y una dinámica creciente de la deuda pública. Antes de la crisis, el espacio fiscal en la mayoría de los países ya era limitado y los déficits presupuestarios eran la norma en la mayoría de los países de la región. De manera similar, los niveles de deuda aumentaron en casi todos los países desde 2014. La relación deuda pública / impuestos, un indicador proxy de la capacidad financiera de los países para pagar la deuda pública, aumentó en la mayoría de los países, dejándolos en una posición más débil para enfrentar la crisis del COVID-19 que en 2007, previo a la crisis financiera global (OCDE et al., 2020[2]; Nieto-Parra and Orozco, 2020[13]).

La construcción de un marco de sostenibilidad fiscal necesario para respaldar las políticas fiscales activas destinadas a lograr un cambio económico y social transformador en la región, requiere de fortalecer la generación de ingresos en el mediano plazo para financiar gastos permanentes destinados a cerrar las brechas de desarrollo estructural. El análisis de los desafíos y oportunidades para fortalecer los sistemas tributarios de la región – reforzar la tributación directa, abordar oportunidades para mejorar la tributación indirecta e identificar nuevas áreas para el desarrollo de políticas tributarias – requiere de la disponibilidad de estadísticas comparables de alta calidad. En ese sentido, las *Estadísticas tributarias en América Latina y el Caribe* es un recurso único en la región, que proporciona datos detallados, comparables e históricos. También sirve como un complemento importante para el análisis de las medidas fiscales en otros campos de políticas, como el gasto público para el desarrollo.

Recuadro 2.2. **La deuda pública y la crisis del COVID-19: financiando la crisis**

La magnitud de la respuesta fiscal ante la crisis en la región, que provocó un aumento del gasto público, en un contexto de caída de los ingresos, derivó en un incremento sustancial de los niveles de deuda pública. La deuda pública bruta de los gobiernos centrales en 2020 alcanzó un promedio de 55.7% del PIB, un aumento de 10.2 puntos porcentuales del PIB sobre el promedio de 2019 de 45.6% del PIB (CEPAL, 2021[7]). La composición de este aumento reflejó las oportunidades de financiamiento disponibles para los países de la región. La emisión de deuda soberana en los mercados internacionales aumentó significativamente (45% en los primeros diez meses del año), reflejando el acceso de algunos países a los mercados internacionales, a menudo en condiciones favorables, para cubrir sus crecientes necesidades de financiamiento para 2020 y, en algunos casos, prefinanciar los Presupuestos de 2021 (CEPAL, 2021[1]). El financiamiento de emergencia de las instituciones financieras internacionales también jugó un papel importante, extendiendo más de USD 47.8 mil millones en nuevos créditos y la reorientación de las líneas de crédito existentes, en apoyo de aquellos países con limitado acceso a los mercados financieros internacionales (CEPAL, 2021[7]).

No obstante, las condiciones financieras podrían cambiar rápidamente en el mediano plazo si la política monetaria se normaliza en las economías avanzadas, lo que podría afectar la sostenibilidad de la deuda en algunas economías emergentes con espacio fiscal limitado. Si este es el caso, la inacción del emisor o acreedor puede conducir a incumplimientos de deuda y a una crisis de deuda, lo que se sumaría a un escenario ya complicado. Esto subraya la necesidad de una gestión de la deuda coordinada a nivel mundial (OCDE et al., 2020[2]; Nieto-Parra y Orozco, 2020[13]).

No existe una solución única para la gestión de la deuda pública en la región: los países varían en términos de sus condiciones fiscales iniciales, tipo de acreedores externos y capacidad para acceder a los mercados de capitales (OCDE et al., 2020[2]). Hay varias acciones de política en respuesta a la crisis del COVID-19 que se deben considerar, dependiendo de los niveles de deuda pública y las condiciones financieras en los países de América Latina y el Caribe:

- El apoyo oficial debe priorizar las economías que tienen poco o nulo acceso a los mercados de capitales.
- Los países que previo a la crisis contaban con finanzas públicas más sólidas deberían mantener el acceso a los mercados de capitales, donde las primas de riesgo siguen siendo relativamente bajas y a través de las cuales pueden recaudar los fondos necesarios para responder a la crisis, gracias a su abundante liquidez.
- Otro grupo de países puede tener acceso a los mercados de capitales pero enfrenta altos costos de financiamiento debido a un deterioro en las percepciones de sostenibilidad de la deuda. El deterioro podría explicarse por reducciones actuales o potenciales en las calificaciones crediticias o expectativas de bajo crecimiento económico e ingresos fiscales futuros. Hay varias opciones de política, que incluyen la suspensión o moratoria de la deuda, el alivio de la deuda, la creación de un vehículo especial para financiar la crisis o pagar la deuda y un mayor uso de los derechos especiales de giro. Todos requieren cooperación internacional, involucrando a bancos multilaterales, acreedores públicos o acreedores privados (Nieto-Parra y Orozco, 2020[13]), (Bolton, P et al., 2020[14])
- Se podrían implementar canjes de deuda a COVID o deuda a Objetivos de Desarrollo Sostenible (ODS), a través de los cuales los países deudores canalizarían los pagos del servicio de la deuda planificados hacia medidas nacionales de mitigación del COVID-19 o inversiones ambientales y de ODS (ONU/DESA, 2020[15]). De manera similar, los canjes de deuda por cambio climático y naturaleza podrían beneficiar a los gobiernos prestamistas y deudores, así como a los acreedores privados, al tiempo que evitan posibles crisis de deuda y abordan el cambio climático y la pérdida de biodiversidad (Steele y Patel, 2020[16]).
- Los bonos vinculados a la sostenibilidad social y ambiental vincularían el financiamiento externo sostenible con los compromisos de los ODS. Esto permitiría a los países disponer de recursos financieros para responder a la crisis del COVID-19 y al mismo tiempo comprometerse con el logro de los objetivos nacionales de sostenibilidad climática y de biodiversidad (Caputo Silva y Stewart, 2021[17]). México se ha convertido recientemente en el primer país de la región en emitir un bono vinculado al cumplimiento de los ODS (CEPAL, 2021[1]).

Recuadro 2.2. **La deuda pública y la crisis del COVID-19: financiando la crisis** *(cont.)*

- Los instrumentos futuros de deuda que incluyan cláusulas 'similares a las de un seguro' mientras reorganizan los pagos a los acreedores condicionados al desempeño económico del país deudor proporcionarían a los países cierto alivio en situaciones económicas difíciles, reembolsando a los acreedores a medida que mejoran las perspectivas del país (Breuer y Cohen, 2020[18]).
- Experiencias recientes en Argentina y Ecuador de reestructuración de deuda muestran la importancia de incluir Cláusulas de Acción Colectiva en los contratos de bonos soberanos.

Existen múltiples posibilidades en la región, particularmente en el área de política tributaria, para fortalecer la generación de ingresos y reducir las desigualdades. Existe una necesidad urgente de reducir la evasión y elusión fiscal, que representó USD 325 mil millones en 2018 – equivalente al 6.1% del PIB – en ingresos perdidos de IRPF, IRS e IVA (CEPAL, 2020[11]). Los países de la región han avanzado mucho en abordar este desafío, pero siguen existiendo importantes brechas en el cumplimiento tributario de los impuestos sobre la renta de personas y sociedades. Los costosos gastos tributarios, que promediaron el 3.7% del PIB en América Latina entre 2015 y 2019, deben revisarse para asegurarse que están logrando sus objetivos y, si no es así, reorientarse para incentivar la inversión en los Objetivos de Desarrollo Sostenible (CEPAL, 2020[11]).

A nivel de instrumentos individuales, también hay un importante espacio de mejora (BID, 2020[19]; CEPAL, 2021[1]; CEPAL, 2019[20]; CEPAL, 2021[7]). El IRPF, el principal factor detrás de la brecha tributaria entre la región y la OCDE (ver Capítulo 1 de este informe), es débil, lo que limita no solo los ingresos potenciales sino también el poder redistributivo del sistema tributario. Esto se ve agravado por la baja tributación de los bienes inmuebles y la riqueza. Existen numerosas opciones para mejorar la tributación indirecta, incluidas medidas para mejorar la eficiencia del IVA mediante la reducción del número y el alcance de las exenciones y las tasas reducidas, al tiempo que se aborda su impacto regresivo mediante el uso de los ingresos del IVA para brindar apoyo a los hogares de bajos ingresos mediante transferencias de efectivo (también conocido como IVA personalizado). Las experiencias con tales reformas en Argentina, Bolivia, Colombia, Ecuador y Uruguay son instructivas para la región (Rasteletti, 2021[21]). Además, los impuestos correctivos, al igual que los impuestos ambientales y aquellos relacionados con los objetivos de salud pública, pueden desempeñar un papel clave en la configuración de los incentivos de los actores económicos a favor de los ODS. Finalmente, otro tema clave para los sistemas tributarios de la región es la necesidad de abordar de manera integral los desafíos que plantea la economía digital (OCDE et al., 2020[2]).

Este es el momento de iniciar acciones concertadas hacia una reestructuración profunda de los sistemas tributarios para generar los ingresos necesarios para financiar el desarrollo sostenible y fortalecer el poder redistributivo de la política tributaria. Estos esfuerzos en ALC deben beneficiarse y potenciarse a través de alianzas con organizaciones internacionales y regionales, y con foros como el Marco Inclusivo sobre BEPS. De manera similar, el apoyo a la movilización de recursos internos en la región – como parte del ODS 17.1 – por parte de donantes bilaterales y multilaterales podría impulsar significativamente los esfuerzos de la región para lograr los ODS.

Notas

1. Se estima un 1.4% del PIB en Chile (DIPRES, 2020[22]) y aproximadamente una cantidad similar en Perú (1.5% del PIB) (MEF Perú, 2020[23]).
2. Los datos proceden de (CIAT, 2021[24]).

Referencias

Arenas de Mesa, A. (2019), *Los sistemas de pensiones en la encrucijada: desafíos para la sostenibilidad en América Latina*, Comisión Económica para América Latina y el Caribe, Santiago, *https://www.cepal.org/es/publicaciones/44851-sistemas-pensiones-la-encrucijada-desafios-la-sostenibilidad-america-latina*. [12]

BID (2020), *Ideas para una mejor tributación en la post-crisis del COVID-19*, Banco Interamericano de Desarrollo, Washington, D.C., *https://blogs.iadb.org/gestion-fiscal/es/ideas-para-una-mejor-tributacion-post-crisis-coronavirus/*. [19]

Bolton, P et al. (2020), *Born Out of Necessity: A Debt Standstill for COVID-19, Center for Economic Policy Research; Policy Insight No. 103 (2020), Duke Law School Public Law & Legal Theory Series No. 2020-23*, *https://ssrn.com/abstract=3586785*. [14]

Breuer, P. y C. Cohen (2020), *Time is Ripe for Innovation in the World of Sovereign Debt Restructuring*, Fondo Monetario Internacional, Washington, D.C., *https://blogs.imf.org/2020/11/19/time-is-ripe-for-innovation-in-the-world-of-sovereign-debt-restructuring/*. [18]

Caputo Silva, A. y F. Stewart (2021), *My word is my bond: Linking sovereign debt with national sustainability commitments*, Banco Mundial, Washington, D.C., *https://blogs.worldbank.org/climatechange/my-word-my-bond-linking-sovereign-debt-national-sustainability-commitments*. [17]

CEPAL (2021), *Balance Preliminar de las Economías de América Latina y el Caribe 2020*, Comisión Económica para América Latina y el Caribe, Santiago, *https://www.cepal.org/es/publicaciones/46501-balance-preliminar-economias-america-latina-caribe-2020*. [1]

CEPAL (2021), *Panorama Fiscal de América Latina y el Caribe 2021*, Comisión Económica para América Latina y el Caribe, Santiago. [7]

CEPAL (2020), *América Latina y el Caribe ante la pandemia del COVID-19: Efectos económicos y sociales e impacto en la vida de las mujeres*, Comisión Económica para América Latina y el Caribe, Santiago, *https://www.cepal.org/sites/default/files/presentations/latin_america_and_the_caribbean_and_the_covid-19_pandemic_economic_and_social_effects_andthe_impact_on_womens_lives_0.pdf*. [8]

CEPAL (2020), *Estudio Económico de América Latina y el Caribe 2020*, Comisión Económica para América Latina y el Caribe, Santiago, *https://www.cepal.org/es/publicaciones/46070-estudio-economico-america-latina-caribe-2020-principales-condicionantes*. [11]

CEPAL (2020), *Panorama Fiscal de América Latina y el Caribe 2020*, Comisión Económica para América Latina y el Caribe, Santiago, *https://www.cepal.org/es/publicaciones/45730-panorama-fiscal-america-latina-caribe-2020-la-politica-fiscal-la-crisis-derivada*. [6]

CEPAL (2020), *Universalizar el acceso a las tecnologías digitales para enfrentar los efectos del COVID-19*, Comisión Económica para América Latina y el Caribe, Santiago, *https://www.cepal.org/es/publicaciones/45938-universalizar-acceso-tecnologias-digitales-enfrentar-efectos-covid-19*. [3]

CEPAL (2019), *Panorama Fiscal de América Latina y el Caribe 2019*, Comisión Económica para América Latina y el Caribe, Santiago, *https://www.cepal.org/es/publicaciones/44516-panorama-fiscal-america-latina-caribe-2019-politicas-tributarias-la-movilizacion*. [20]

CEPAL/OIT (2020), *El trabajo en tiempos de pandemia: Desafíos frente a la enfermedad por coronavirus (COVID-19)*, Comisión Económica para América Latina y el Caribe y Organización Internacional del Trabajo, *https://www.cepal.org/sites/default/files/presentation/files/ppt_version_final_oit-cepal-_covid-19_-_21-05-20.pdf*. [5]

CIAT (2021), Revenue Report Covid-19 (RRC), Balance of 2020, CIAT. [24]

DIPRES (2020), *Informe de Ejecución del Gobierno Central Tercer Trimestre 2020*, Dirección de Presupuestos de Chile. [22]

Harding, M. et al. (2020), *In Tax, Gender Blind is not Gender Neutral: why tax policy responses to COVID-19 must consider women*, Publicaciones de la OCDE, París, *https://oecdecoscope.blog/2020/06/01/in-tax-gender-blind-is-not-gender-neutral-why-tax-policy-responses-to-covid-19-must-consider-women/*. [10]

MEF Perú (2020), *Reporte Fiscal Trimestral: Seguimiento de las Reglas Macrofiscales, Segundo Trimestre 2020*, Ministerio de Economía y Finanzas del Perú, *https://www.mef.gob.pe/contenidos/pol_econ/Reporte_Fiscal/Informe_Trimestral_de_Reglas_Fiscales_II_Trim2020.pdf.* [23]

Nieto-Parra, S. y R. Orozco (2020), *Public debt and COVID-19. Paying for the crisis in Latin America and the Caribbean*, Le Grand Continent, *https://legrandcontinent.eu/fr/2020/07/22/public-debt-and-covid-19-paying-for-the-crisis-in-latin-america-and-the-caribbean/.* [13]

OCDE (2020), *COVID-19 in Latin America and the Caribbean: Regional socio-economic implications and policy priorities*, Publicaciones de la OCDE, París, *http://www.oecd.org/coronavirus/policy-responses/covid-19-in-latin-america-and-the-caribbean-regional-socio-economic-implications-and-policy-priorities-93a64fde/.* [4]

OCDE (2020), *SIGI 2020 Regional Report for Latin America and the Caribbean*, Publicaciones de la OCDE, París, *https://doi.org/10.1787/cb7d45d1-en.* [9]

OCDE et al. (2020), *Perspectivas económicas de América Latina 2020: Transformación digital para una mejor reconstrucción*, Publicaciones de la OCDE, París, *https://doi.org/10.1787/f2fdced2-es.* [2]

ONU/DESA (2020), *COVID-19 and sovereign debt*, Departamento de Asuntos Económicos y Sociales de Naciones Unidas, Nueva York, *https://www.un.org/development/desa/dpad/publication/un-desa-policy-brief-72-covid-19-and-sovereign-debt/.* [15]

Rasteletti, A. (2021), *IVA personalizado: Experiencia de 5 países y su importancia estratégica para la política y la administración tributaria*, Banco Interamericano de Desarrollo, Washington, D.C., *https://blogs.iadb.org/gestion-fiscal/es/iva-personalizado-experiencia-latinoamericana-y-su-importancia-para-las-administraciones-tributarias/.* [21]

Steele, P. y S. Patel (2020), *Tackling the triple crisis: Using debt swaps to address debt, climate and nature loss post-COVID-19*, International Institute for Environment and Development, *https://pubs.iied.org/sites/default/files/pdfs/migrate/16674IIED.pdf.* [16]

Chapter 3

SPECIAL FEATURE

Fiscal revenues from non-renewable natural resources in Latin America and the Caribbean

Capítulo 3

SECCIÓN ESPECIAL

Ingresos fiscales provenientes de recursos naturales no renovables en América Latina y el Caribe

Chapter 3

SPECIAL FEATURE

Fiscal revenues from non-renewable natural resources in Latin America and the Caribbean

This special feature was prepared by Michael Hanni, Economic Affairs Officer, Fiscal Affairs Unit, Economic Development Division, Economic Commission for Latin America and the Caribbean (ECLAC).

Principal findings

Trends in fiscal revenues from non-renewable natural resources in 2019

Oil and gas revenues in Latin America and the Caribbean (LAC) rose in 2019 despite unfavourable global market conditions. The increase in hydrocarbon revenues, which reached 2.7% of GDP on average compared to 2.5% of GDP in 2018, was largely the result of extraordinary receipts. Signing bonuses for new oil and gas concessions generated excess revenues equivalent to 1% of GDP in Brazil. In Trinidad and Tobago, payments under a tax amnesty programme and receipts deriving from a negotiated settlement with a large producer resulted in a one-time increase equivalent to 1.6% of GDP. Property rents, however, fell during the year in line with international prices, as regional production was largely flat.

Weak international prices for a range of industrial minerals and metals and lower production led to a decline in LAC's mining revenues in 2019. The year-on-year variation relative to GDP was marginal: average revenues fell to 0.37% of GDP from 0.39% of GDP in 2018. Similarly, aggregate revenues in US dollar terms edged down slightly (-3.9%), although the scale of the fall was reduced due to a sharp increase in Brazil (+75.1%). Excluding Brazil, overall revenues declined 17.3% in US dollar terms, with significant contractions registered in Chile, Colombia, Guatemala, Jamaica, Mexico and Peru.

The impact of the COVID-19 pandemic on revenues from extractive activities

The COVID-19 pandemic has provoked one of the greatest social and economic crises in modern times. It has also created significant turmoil in commodity markets. Oil markets have been especially impacted, with plunging demand, especially in advanced economies, leading to a sharp decline in crude oil spot prices. In contrast, international prices for minerals and metals recovered quickly after an initial decline, on the back of accelerating industrial production in China. High-frequency data for a sample of countries suggests that there is likely to be a significant decline in fiscal revenues from non-renewable natural resources at the regional level for the year compared to 2019.

Hydrocarbon revenues rise in LAC, boosted by one-off extraordinary revenues

Global oil markets stabilised to some extent in 2019 following volatility in the fourth quarter of 2018 related to significant over-supply. In December 2018, the members of OPEC and allied oil-producing countries – most notably the Russian Federation – committed to reducing their overall output volume by a combined 1.2 million barrels per day (0.8 million for OPEC members) for the first half of 2019. The accord was largely successful and overall world liquid fuels production slowed markedly in the first quarter of 2019 (Figure 3.1). Crude oil spot prices rallied as the market moved to greater equilibrium during the first months of the year. Nevertheless, prices again trended lower in May on the back of weakening macroeconomic fundamentals, rising trade tensions between China and the United States and a build-up of crude oil stockpiles in the United States. In response, OPEC and allied exporters agreed in July to extend crude oil production cuts until 2020. These trends notwithstanding, oil consumption jumped in the second half of the year, largely bolstered by record crude oil imports in China as several new mega-refineries came online. Despite the up-tick registered in the fourth quarter, annual average crude oil spot prices fell for the year, with Brent down 10% (from USD 71.1 per barrel to USD 64.0) and Western Texas Intermediate (WTI) declining by 12% (from USD 64.8 per barrel to USD 57.0).

Figure 3.1. **World liquid fuels production and consumption balance and international spot prices for crude oil, 2018-19**

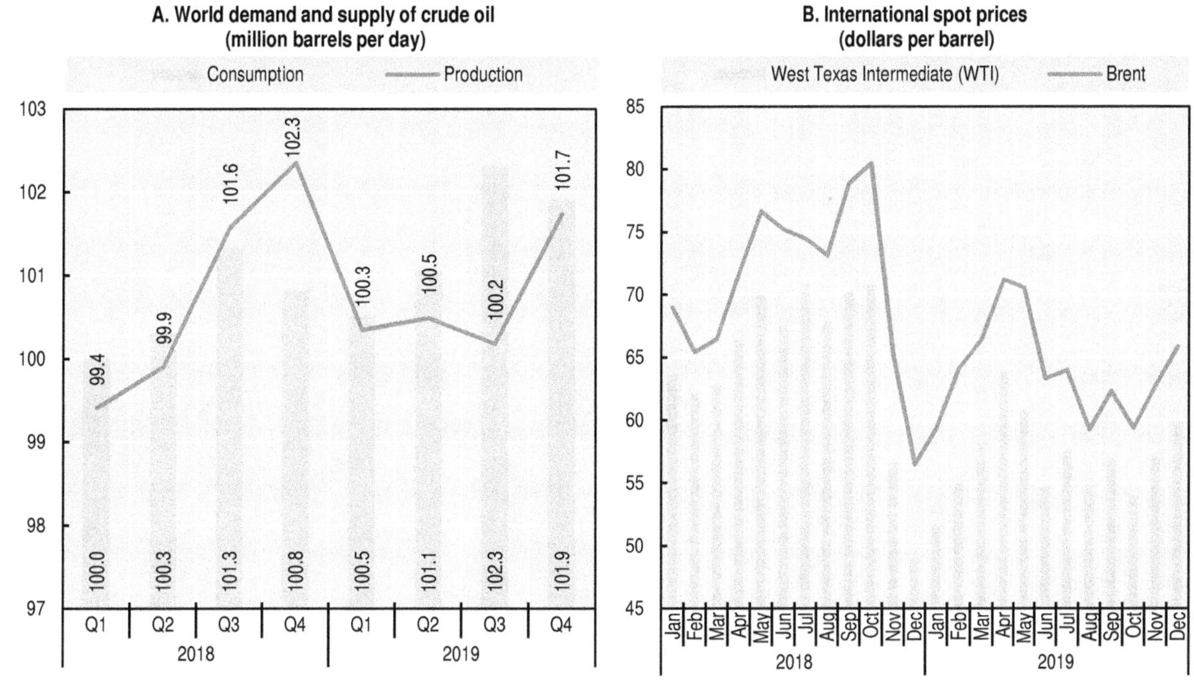

Source: Economic Commission for Latin America and the Caribbean (ECLAC), on the basis of EIA (2020[1]) and World Bank Commodity Price Data (The Pink Sheet), World Bank.

StatLink https://doi.org/10.1787/888934234860

Production levels of hydrocarbons in LAC declined in 2019, although with significantly different trends at the country level (Table 3.1). Overall crude oil output fell substantially, contracting by 4.9% due largely to the 37.7% plunge in production in the Bolivarian Republic of Venezuela. While output rose slightly excluding the latter country, this reflected a rebound in production in Brazil and to a smaller extent in Argentina, Colombia and Ecuador, while crude oil production in Mexico fell sharply. Natural gas production also registered a decline due to falling output in the Bolivarian Republic of Venezuela, Mexico and the Plurinational State of Bolivia. Nevertheless, these declines were attenuated to some extent by increases in Argentina (where output reached its highest level since 2009), Brazil, Peru, and Trinidad and Tobago.

Hydrocarbon revenues in the LAC region increased in 2019 despite the prevailing international context, characterised by falling crude oil spot prices, and regional production trends (Table 3.2). Overall hydrocarbon revenues in LAC reached USD 79.8 billion in 2019, up 10.4% from 2018. In relative terms, this result was relatively modest, equivalent to 2.7% of GDP on average compared to 2.5% of GDP in 2018. Although greater production and currency depreciations softened the impact of lower international prices in some countries, this rise in revenues was largely due to extraordinary receipts. Brazil and Trinidad and Tobago registered one-off oil revenues during the year equivalent to 1.0% of GDP and 1.6% of GDP, respectively.[1] Excluding these transactions, hydrocarbon revenues contracted by 14.8% in US dollar (USD) terms. This correlates with the trajectory of revenues from royalties and production levies tied to the commercial value of production, which fell by 12.6% in USD terms in line with international prices and regional production dynamics. However, results at the country level were varied, reflecting strong heterogeneity in production, export and regulatory dynamics over the year.

Table 3.1. **Crude oil and natural gas production in Latin America and the Caribbean and selected country groupings, 2018-19**

Selected country groupings and countries	Crude oil (thousand barrels daily)			Natural gas (billion cubic metres)		
	2018	2019	2019-2018 (% change)	2018	2019	2019-2018 (% change)
Latin America and the Caribbean	**8 012**	**7 632**	**-4.7**	**199**	**196**	**-1.4**
excluding Venezuela	6 502	6 619	1.8	174	176	0.8
Argentina	489	509	3.9	41	43	5.7
Bolivia	..	..	..	19	17	-10.7
Brazil	2 587	2 788	7.8	22	24	9.5
Colombia	865	886	2.4	10	10	3.1
Ecuador	517	531	2.6	0	0	..
Guatemala	9	10	4.1	..	..	..
Mexico	1 813	1 678	-7.4	33	31	-6.8
Peru	49	53	8.4	12	13	0.7
Trinidad and Tobago	64	59	-7.3	35	36	2.1
Venezuela	1 510	1 013	-32.9	25	21	-17.1
Other LAC	115	113	-1.3	1	1	2.0
Total World	**75 822**	**75 263**	**-0.7**	**3 946**	**4 093**	**3.7**
OPEC	31 238	29 375	-6.0	..	..	..
Saudi Arabia	10 317	9 808	-4.9	..	..	..
Non-OPEC	44 584	45 887	2.9	..	..	..
Russian Federation	10 527	10 625	0.9	..	..	..
United States	10 991	12 232	11.3	..	..	..

Source: Economic Commission for Latin America and the Caribbean (ECLAC) on the basis of OPEC (2020[2]).

StatLink https://doi.org/10.1787/888934235012

Oil and gas revenues in ***Argentina*** contracted in 2019, although the year-on-year variation in relative terms was marginal (down 0.01% of GDP). Revenues from the corporate income tax (CIT) and royalties registered sharp contractions (-19.1% and -15.9% in USD terms, respectively), which exceeded the decline in international crude oil spot prices and was at odds with the increase in oil and gas production. This was largely due to the issuance of Decree No. 566/2019 of 15 August, which imposed price controls on petroleum products for a period of 90 days. The decree established that all deliveries of crude oil to the domestic market had to be invoiced at the price that had been agreed to between producers and refiners as of 9 August, applying a fixed ARS-USD exchange rate and Brent reference price to the transaction. Subsequent decrees modified the exchange rate used to calculate payments, but domestic crude oil prices nevertheless continued to lag international benchmarks.

Lower natural gas output and falling prices produced a significant decrease in hydrocarbon revenues in the ***Plurinational State of Bolivia***. Overall oil and natural gas revenues reached 3.8% of GDP in 2019, down from 4.6% of GDP in the previous year, as a result of falling non-tax revenues from the Direct Tax on Hydrocarbons (a royalty) and other State participation in the commercial value of production. Maturing natural gas fields and limited investment have led to a steady decline in output, which in 2019 reached its lowest level since 2011, 21.2% below the high attained in 2014 (Table 3.1; OPEC (2020[2])). Increased production of natural gas in Argentina and Brazil continues to put pressure on Bolivian hydrocarbon revenues and exports (BCB, 2020[4]).

Table 3.2. **General government fiscal revenues from oil and gas exploration and production in nine LAC countries, by type of revenue, 2018-19**

Percentage of GDP unless otherwise specified

Type of revenue	Period	Region / country									
		LAC	Argentina	Bolivia (Plurinational State of)	Brazil	Colombia	Ecuador	Guatemala	Mexico	Peru	Trinidad and Tobago
Total revenues	2018	**2.5**	0.5	4.6	1.2	1.8	7.6	0.1	2.3	0.7	3.9
	2019	**2.7**	0.5	3.8	1.9	2.4	7.2	0.0	1.8	0.5	6.5
	2019-2018 (p.p. of GDP)	**0.2**	0.0	-0.8	0.7	0.5	-0.4	0.0	-0.5	-0.2	2.5
	2019-2018 (% change in NC)	..	43.3	-15.4	67.6	39.7	-4.8	-31.8	-20.0	-22.6	67.2
	2019-2018 (% change in USD)	**10.4**	-16.4	-15.4	56.0	25.9	-4.8	-33.4	-20.1	-23.8	67.6
Tax revenues	2018	**0.4**	0.1	0.3	0.1	0.7	0.0	0.0	0.0	0.2	1.8
	2019	**0.5**	0.1	0.2	0.1	0.6	0.0	0.0	0.0	0.1	3.1
	2019-2018 (p.p. of GDP)	**0.1**	0.0	0.0	0.0	-0.2	0.0	0.0	0.0	0.0	1.3
Non-tax revenues	2018	**2.2**	0.4	4.3	1.1	1.1	7.6	0.1	2.3	0.5	2.2
	2019	**2.3**	0.4	3.6	1.8	1.8	7.2	0.0	1.8	0.4	3.4
	2019-2018 (p.p. of GDP)	**0.1**	0.0	-0.7	0.7	0.7	-0.4	0.0	-0.5	-0.1	1.2
of which: royalties and production levies	2018	**2.1**	0.4	4.3	0.8	0.7	7.6	0.1	2.3	0.5	2.2
	2019	**1.9**	0.4	3.6	0.8	0.7	7.2	0.0	1.8	0.4	2.2
	2019-2018 (p.p. of GDP)	**-0.2**	0.0	-0.7	0.0	0.0	-0.4	0.0	-0.5	-0.1	0.0
	2019-2018 (% change in USD)	**-12.6**	-15.9	-15.7	-1.8	-4.5	-4.8	-45.5	-20.4	-24.9	3.7

Note: Data for Mexico correspond to federal government oil revenue and they exclude own revenues of Pemex, the State-owned oil and gas producer. Data for Ecuador correspond to oil revenues of the non-financial public sector. The revenue-to-GDP ratio for Latin America and the Caribbean (LAC) corresponds to a simple average of the countries included in the sample. Figures may not sum due to rounding.

Source: Economic Commission for Latin America and the Caribbean (ECLAC), based on data from CEPALSTAT (2020[3]).

StatLink https://doi.org/10.1787/888934235031

Hydrocarbon revenues surged in ***Brazil*** in 2019 on the back of extraordinary one-time receipts. Overall fiscal revenues from crude oil and natural gas rose to 1.9% of GDP from 1.2% of GDP in 2018, an increase of 56% in USD terms. In April 2019, the federal government and Petrobras concluded a multi-year negotiation on contractual terms for the "pré sal" area within the framework of the initial oil-for-shares swap deal struck in 2010 (Petrobras, 2020[5]). The agreement allowed the federal government to auction production-sharing contracts for the remainder of the oil reserves – above and beyond that which had previously been allotted to Petrobras – in the off-shore area in November 2019. The auction resulted in R$ 69.96 billion of signing bonuses (equivalent to 1.0% of GDP). However, revenues from royalties and other government participations in the commercial value of production fell slightly (-1.8% in USD terms) as rising output was offset by falling prices.

In ***Colombia***, oil and gas revenues jumped in 2019 due to an exceptionally large dividend payment by EcoPetrol – the State-owned producer – to the national government. At COP 11.42 billion, equivalent to USD 3.5 billion or 1.1% of GDP, the dividend was well above the previous year's payment of 0.3% of GDP. As a result, overall hydrocarbon revenues reached 2.4% of GDP in 2019, up from 1.8% of GDP in 2018. Nevertheless, revenues from other instruments registered declines. Tax revenues in the form of CIT receipts fell, reflecting the impact of lower prices on profit margins and the high base of comparison with the previous year when EcoPetrol reported strong profits. Property rents from royalties were largely unchanged relative to GDP, but they fell in US dollar terms as a modest increase in production was offset by lower prices.

Hydrocarbon revenues in ***Ecuador*** registered a marginal decline in 2019 (-4.8% in USD terms) as higher production and exports by State-owned Petroamazonas (+4.4% and +9.9%, in millions of barrels, respectively) largely offset the decline in prices (BCE, 2020$_{[6]}$). The country's oil sector was impacted by social unrest caused by the promulgation of Decree 883 of 11 October that eliminated fuel subsidies. Although this decree was later revoked by Decree 894 of 14 October work stoppages across the countries continued during the month.

Oil revenues in ***Guatemala*** fell sharply in 2019, down 33.4% in USD terms and from 0.07% of GDP in 2018 to 0.05% of GDP, despite rising output. Non-tax revenues from the State's participation in the production of hydrocarbons fell sharply (-58.8% in USD terms) reflecting the high base of comparison with the previous year when these revenues registered an increase much greater than was budgeted (MINFIN, 2019$_{[7]}$).

A confluence of factors precipitated a decline in federal government oil revenues in ***Mexico***, including international price dynamics, slumping production and policy measures.[2] Overall hydrocarbon revenues of the federal government fell from 2.3% of GDP in 2018 to 1.8% of GDP, as property rents from oil exploration and production activities declined. Revenues of the Profit-Sharing Duty (Derecho por la Utilidad Compartida) paid by Petroleos Mexicanos, which make up the bulk of non-tax oil revenues, contracted as a result of the application of a government decree in May 2019 that allowed the company to make greater deductions for investments (PEMEX, 2020$_{[8]}$; FMPED, 2020$_{[9]}$). Likewise, beginning in January 2019, the rate used to calculate the Profit-Sharing Duty declined to 65%, from 66.25% in 2018, in line with the changes in the oil and gas fiscal framework established in the Hydrocarbons Revenue Law of 2014.

Oil and gas revenues in ***Peru*** declined to 0.5% of GDP in 2019 from 0.7% of GDP in 2018, principally due to flagging external demand. Revenues from royalties fell by 24.9% in USD terms, or from 0.5% of GDP in 2018 to 0.4% of GDP, despite increased output of crude oil. The decline in royalties was largely due to the lower value of exports of crude oil and natural gas, which serves as the basis for the calculation of certain property rent payments. In particular, liquified natural gas exports registered a sharp contraction as the value of sales to Spain, a key trade partner, fell from USD 333.9 million in 2018 to just USD 35.6 million in 2019 (-89%).[3] Weaker sales also translated into a decline in profit margins and, in turn, tax revenues.

Hydrocarbon revenues in ***Trinidad and Tobago*** were up sharply in 2019, rising from 3.9% of GDP in 2018 to 6.5% of GDP, boosted by extraordinary tax and non-tax receipts. A three-month tax amnesty that allowed taxpayers to liquidate outstanding liabilities free of penalties and interest resulted in higher than anticipated tax revenues. Oil companies alone made payments worth TTD 750 million (0.5% of GDP) under the programme. These receipts and stronger revenues from income taxes reflecting higher profits obtained in the previous fiscal year pushed oil and gas tax revenues up from 1.8% of GDP in 2018 to 3.1% of GDP. Non-tax revenues also rose markedly, from 2.2% of GDP in 2018 to 3.4% of GDP, due to an initial TTD 1.9 billion payment during FY2018/19, equivalent to 1.2% of GDP, by Shell Trinidad and Tobago Limited – a subsidiary of Royal Dutch Shell – to the government as a result of an agreement to address outstanding tax issues.

Mining revenues in LAC declined, with significant heterogeneity at the country level

The weakening macroeconomic fundamentals that characterised the year, worsened by rising trade tensions, served to reinforce the decline in international spot prices for a range of industrial minerals and metals that began in mid-2018 (Figure 3.2). Prices for iron ore, however, rose sharply as a result of record steel production in China and production disruptions caused by the tragic Corrego do Feijão mine disaster in Brazil and Cyclone Veronica in Australia (IMF, 2019[10]). Nickel prices also increased in the second half of the year as Indonesia – the world's largest exporter – announced a complete ban on exports of raw nickel to begin in 2020 (World Bank, 2019[11]). These factors notwithstanding, price dynamics reflected to some extent changes in market sentiment as underlying demand remained relatively stable. For example, although global copper consumption was essentially flat in 2019 compared to 2018 (-0.4%), demand for lead, zinc and nickel all rose.[4]

Figure 3.2. **International spot prices for selected minerals and metals, Q1 2018-Q4 2019**

Quarterly growth over the previous year

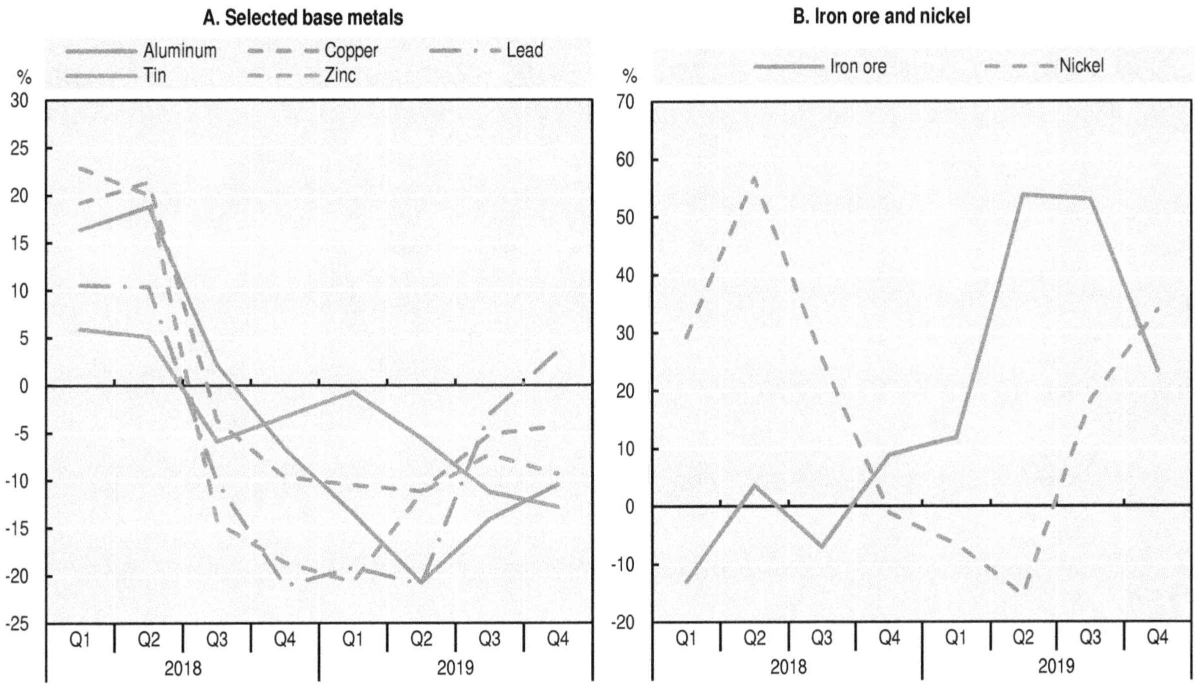

Source: Economic Commission for Latin America and the Caribbean (ECLAC), on the basis of World Bank Commodity Price Data (The Pink Sheet), World Bank.

StatLink https://doi.org/10.1787/888934234879

The impact of falling prices on mining revenues in LAC was further reinforced by lower mining output in several countries (Table 3.3). This trend was influenced in part by ongoing social conflicts (such as at the Las Bambas mine in Peru operated by Minerals and Metals Group), strikes and work stoppages (as was the case with the strike by workers at Codelco's Chuquicamata mine in Chile), and environmental damage (most notably the Corrego do Feijão mine disaster in Brazil). At a more structural level, mining output in the region continues to be tempered by the progressive decline in ore grades as existing large-scale mines mature.[5] This phenomenon requires ever greater ore extraction to maintain metals and minerals output levels. The associated higher production costs and the need for costly investments to improve productivity and exploit less accessible reserves, ceteris paribus, can impact profitability and in turn tax receipts. This is especially relevant as CIT and other profit-based instruments are the primary mechanism in the region for capturing the economic rents arising from mining (OECD et al., 2020[12]; Hanni et al., 2018[13]).

Table 3.3. **International prices and production of metals and minerals in selected LAC countries, 2018-19**

Metals and minerals	Year and percent change	Price (US dollars) and %	Production by country in thousands of metric tons unless otherwise specified								
			Argentina	Bolivia	Brazil	Chile	Colombia	Dominican Republic	Jamaica	Mexico	Peru
Copper	2018	6529.8		5.2	750.6	5831.6				473.6	2437.0
	2019	6010.1		4.5	363.3	5787.4				486.9	2455.4
	% change	-8.0		-14.1	-51.6	-0.8				2.8	0.8
Zinc	2018	2922.4		519.6						381.5	1474.4
	2019	2550.4		528.1						325.3	1404.4
	% change	-12.7		1.6						-14.7	-4.7
Lead	2018	2240.4		112.0						131.8	289.1
	2019	1996.5		88.0						149.1	308.1
	% change	-10.9		-21.5						13.1	6.6
Tin	2018	20145.2		17.3	19.3						18.6
	2019	18661.2		17.1	14.9						19.9
	% change	-7.4		-0.7	-23.1						6.7
Nickel	2018	13114.1			67.7		43.0				
	2019	13913.9			55.7		40.6				
	% change	6.1			-17.7		-5.8				
Iron	2018	69.8			317502.4	8942.6	575.5			7085.4	9533.9
	2019	93.8			255272.6	8427.2	665.2			7140.9	10120.0
	% change	34.5			-19.6	-5.8	15.6			0.8	6.1
Coal	2018	107.0					86255.2			8151.8	
	2019	77.9					84342.8			6616.9	
	% change	-27.2					-2.2			-18.8	
Bauxite / alumina	2018	2108.5			19437.8				10058.2		
	2019	1794.5			15248.5				9022.3		
	% change	-14.9			-21.6				-10.3		
Gold (metric tons)	2018	1269.2	59.8	6.2	85.4	37.1	35.6	32.3		91.2	140.2
	2019	1392.5	59.8	5.5	75.2	38.5	36.7	31.9		73.5	128.4
	% change	9.7	0.0	-11.6	-11.9	3.7	3.1	-1.2		-19.5	-8.4
Silver (metric tons)	2018	15.7	545.5	1191.6		1370.2	16.0	169.8		3694.0	4160.2
	2019	16.2	715.3	1153.1		1309.3	11.7	108.7		3498.5	3860.3
	% change	3.2	31.1	-3.2		-4.4	-26.9	-36.0		-5.3	-7.2

Source: Economic Commission for Latin America and the Caribbean (ECLAC), on the basis of World Bank Commodity Price Data (The Pink Sheet), World Bank; Instituto Nacional de Estadísticas del Estado Plurinacional de Bolivia, estadísticas mineras; Agência Nacional de Mineração do Brasil, Anuário Mineral Brasileiro: Principais Substâncias Metálicas; Comisión Chilena de Cobre (Cochilco), Anuario de Estadísticas del Cobre y Otros Minerales 2000-2019; Agencia Nacional de Minería de Colombia, Sistema de Información Minero Colombiano; Jamaica Bauxite Institute, Local Bauxite/Alumina; Monthly Statistical Bulletin; Instituto Nacional de Estadística y Geografía de México, Estadística Mensual de la Industria Minerometalúrgica and Ministerio de Energía y Minas del Perú, Reporte de la producción minera anual.

StatLink https://doi.org/10.1787/888934235050

Despite these overall trends, mining revenues in LAC registered a modest decline in 2019. For the year these revenues reached USD 12.7 billion, down 3.9% from USD 13.2 billion in 2018 (Table 3.4). However, this result was due in large part to the exceptional increase in mining revenues in Brazil (+75.1% in USD terms). Excluding Brazil, overall revenues in LAC fell 17.3%. Mining revenues as a share of GDP registered a slight decline between years, with a marginal increase in tax revenues offset by a greater decline in non-tax revenues. Results at the country level, however, varied significantly.

Table 3.4. General government fiscal revenues from mining in nine LAC countries, by type of revenue, 2018-19

Percentage of GDP unless otherwise specified

Type of revenue	Period	Region / country											
		LAC	Argentina	Bolivia (Plurinational State of)	Brazil	Chile	Colombia	Dominican Republic	Ecuador	Guatemala	Jamaica	Mexico	Peru
Total revenues	2018	**0.39**	0.04	0.85	0.10	1.40	0.45	0.21	0.08	0.01	0.04	0.23	0.90
	2019	**0.37**	0.04	1.11	0.18	1.31	0.32	0.22	0.08	0.01	0.04	0.18	0.62
	2019-2018 (p.p. of GDP)	**-0.02**	0.01	0.27	0.08	-0.10	-0.13	0.02	0.00	0.00	-0.01	-0.05	-0.28
	2019-2018 (% change in NC)	..	70.6	33.3	88.2	-3.3	-24.5	16.5	-0.7	-24.9	-12.9	-18.3	-28.7
	2019-2018 (% change in USD)	**-3.9**	-0.5	33.3	75.1	-11.8	-32.0	12.4	-0.7	-26.6	-15.8	-18.3	-29.8
Tax revenues	2018	**0.23**	0.03	0.37	0.05	0.82	0.19	0.15	0.03	0.01	0.00	0.20	0.72
	2019	**0.24**	0.03	0.64	0.11	0.98	0.10	0.17	0.03	0.01	0.00	0.15	0.42
	2019-2018 (p.p. of GDP)	**0.01**	0.00	0.27	0.06	0.16	-0.09	0.02	0.00	0.00	0.00	-0.04	-0.30
Non-tax revenues	2018	**0.16**	0.01	0.48	0.05	0.58	0.26	0.05	0.05	0.00	0.04	0.03	0.19
	2019	**0.13**	0.01	0.48	0.07	0.32	0.21	0.05	0.05	0.00	0.04	0.03	0.20
	2019-2018 (p.p. of GDP)	**-0.03**	0.00	0.00	0.02	-0.26	-0.05	0.00	0.00	0.00	-0.01	0.00	0.01
of which: royalties and production levies	2018	**0.14**	0.01	0.48	0.05	0.38	0.26	0.05	0.03	0.00	0.04	0.03	0.18
	2019	**0.13**	0.01	0.48	0.07	0.32	0.21	0.05	0.03	0.00	0.04	0.03	0.20
	2019-2018 (p.p. of GDP)	**-0.01**	0.00	0.00	0.02	-0.06	-0.05	0.00	0.00	0.00	-0.01	0.00	0.02
	2019-2018 (% change in USD)	**-1.4**	28.1	0.9	33.3	-19.2	-20.0	-1.1	-4.1	-49.8	-15.8	-7.0	11.3

Note: The revenue-to-GDP ratio for Latin America and the Caribbean (LAC) corresponds to a simple average of the countries included in the sample. Figures may not sum due to rounding.

Source: Economic Commission for Latin America and the Caribbean (ECLAC), based on data from CEPALSTAT (2020[3]).

StatLink https://doi.org/10.1787/888934235069

Fiscal revenues from mining rose significantly in the ***Plurinational State of Bolivia*** despite falling output volumes and weak international prices. During the year, production at the San Cristóbal mine – one of the largest in the country – was impacted by a month-long strike in August 2019 as well as scheduled maintenance in October (BCB, 2020[4]). Nevertheless, overall mining fiscal revenues rose from 0.85% of GDP in 2018 to 1.11% of GDP in 2019 on the back of buoyant tax revenues bolstered by strong 2018 fiscal year financial results and a large advance payment on 2020 taxes made at the end of 2019 (BCB, 2019[14]; MSC, 2020[15]). Tax revenues were also likely boosted by a general tax amnesty, established by Law #1105 Regularization of Taxes at the Central Level of the State (Regularización de Tributos del Nivel Central del Estado), that was enacted during the year.

During 2019, the mining sector in ***Brazil*** was marked by a tailings dam failure at the Corrego do Feijão mine operated by Vale S.A. in Brumadinho that occurred on 25 January. The resulting mudflow inundated local communities and farms, leading to the death of 270 individuals and significant damage to the local eco-system. Despite lower production because of the disaster, the jump in iron ore prices globally resulted in a significant increase in mining revenues, which rose to 0.18% of GDP from 0.10% of GDP in 2018, a 75.1% increase in USD terms. CIT payments by Vale more than doubled, despite recording a financial loss for the year, as financial provisions for the Brumadinho disaster could not be deducted from the calculation of taxable income until they are effectively incurred (Vale, 2020[16]). Royalty payments from the Compensation for Exploitation of Mineral Resources (Compensação

Financeira pela Exploração de Recursos Minerais) and the Rate for Controlling, Monitoring and Supervision of Exploration and Mining Activities of Mineral Resources (Taxa de Fiscalização de Recursos Minerários) of the State of Minas Gerias reached a record level, rising 33.3% in USD terms.

Fiscal revenues from mining in ***Chile*** declined in 2019 as a result of lower copper output and falling international prices. During the year, total revenues dropped to 1.31% of GDP compared to 1.40% of GDP in 2018. Nevertheless, this overall trend belies a more complex dynamic at the level of individual fiscal instruments. Non-tax revenues contracted sharply as dividend payments by Codelco, the State-owned copper producer, fell to nil. In 2018, the company made excess payments that were subsequently deducted from those that were due for 2019 (DIPRES, 2019[17]). Tax revenues, in contrast, rose as the liquidation of prior year tax liabilities of private producers strengthened due in part to the final increase in the CIT rate as established in the 2014 tax reform.[6]

The collapse in international prices for coal provoked a sharp decrease in mining revenues in ***Colombia***. Lower tax and non-tax receipts contributed to the decline in overall revenues, which reached 0.32% of GDP compared to 0.45% of GDP in 2018. CIT payments of companies operating in the coal sector, who accounted for 79% of mining CIT receipts in 2018, more than halved (-58%) as profits were impacted by lower prices. Likewise, non-tax revenues from royalties associated with coal production registered a significant decline, in line with coal prices, although this was offset in part by higher receipts from gold production.

Robust gold prices buoyed mining revenues in the ***Dominican Republic*** in 2019, which rose to 0.22% of GDP from 0.21% of GDP in 2018, or an increase of 12.4% in USD terms. While gold production contracted slightly, the near 10% increase in the annual average price more than compensated, bolstering profitability and CIT receipts. During the year, the government proposed new legislation for regulating the mining sector – National Mining Law (Ley de Minería) – that would establish a minimum State participation in mining rents among other modifications.

In ***Ecuador***, revenues from mining contracted marginally (-0.7% in USD terms) in 2019 due to lower property rents. Royalty payments have exhibited significant swings in the preceding years as operators of new mines liquidate advance payments as part of their agreements with the government. Excluding these advance payments, revenues from royalties rose 23.9% in USD terms, reflecting higher production and the favourable increase in the price of gold. Several large-scale mining operations commenced production during the year. The Mirador open-pit copper and gold mine, owned by a consortium of companies led by Tongling Nonferrous Metals Group (China), commenced production in June. This was followed in November, when the Fruta del Norte mine, operated by Lundin Gold (Canada), began production with exports of gold commencing by year's end.

Mining revenues continued to fall in ***Guatemala***, as the country grappled with social conflicts associated with the sector. Several of the country's largest mines remain closed. A consultative process with local communities, being held within the framework of ILO-Convention 169, is ongoing.

In ***Jamaica***, mining revenues from bauxite and alumina showed little dynamism, continuing the trend observed in recent years. While total revenues were essentially unchanged relative to GDP, they contracted 15.8% in USD terms as receipts of the bauxite levy fell to nil.

Fiscal revenues from mining in ***Mexico*** contracted in 2019, as lower precious metals output and falling prices for industrial metals reduced the profitability of the sector. During the year several mines, such as Peñasquito gold and silver mine in Zacatecas operated by Newmont-Goldcorp, were temporarily shuttered as a result of protests (Camimex, 2020[18]). These price and production dynamics served to reduce CIT receipts, which in turn left total revenues at 0.18% of GDP, down from 0.23% of GDP in 2018.

Mining revenues in ***Peru*** contracted significantly during the year as falling prices offset production gains for some of the country's key export goods. Total fiscal revenues from mining fell to 0.62% of GDP from 0.9% of GDP in 2018, led by a 0.3 percentage point decline in tax receipts from the sector. CIT receipts weakened as a result of lower profits caused by social conflicts, environmental issues and reduced production.[7] Rising non-tax revenues offset this decline in part, although this increase was due largely to extraordinary receipts. During the year, mining companies liquidated a significant amount of accumulated royalty liabilities from previous periods (MEF Peru, 2020[19]). These receipts accounted for 12% of royalty revenue in 2019 and in their absence revenues from this instrument would have registered no change compared to 2018 as a percentage of GDP.

The outbreak of the COVID-19 pandemic and the resulting economic paralysis has strongly impacted the region's non-renewable natural resources related revenues

The COVID-19 pandemic has created an unprecedented human, social and economic crisis that has enveloped the entire world. Public health measures to prevent the spread of the virus and protect human life have resulted in the paralysation of economic activity, rising unemployment and increasing poverty in many countries. In LAC, the crisis is forecast to result in a 7.7% contraction of GDP in 2020, the largest decline in the last century (ECLAC, 2021[20]). Governments in LAC have responded to the crisis by implementing ambitious packages of fiscal and financial measures – including tax relief, public spending and liquidity measures – to bolster public health systems, support families and limit damage to productive capacity (ECLAC, 2020[21]).

This context notwithstanding, the impact of the crisis on international commodity markets has been mixed. During the first half of the year, spot prices fell sharply as economic activity and private consumption collapsed (Figure 3.3). Nevertheless, the prices of many minerals and metals rebounded and exceed their pre-pandemic levels by year's end, largely due to accelerating industrial output and investment in China and supply disruptions for some minerals and metals caused by the pandemic (World Bank, 2020[22]). Oil markets, however, were turbulent after experiencing a sharp drop in spot prices in March and April. In April, OPEC and non-OPEC partners agreed to a large-scale cut in production – 9.7 million barrels per day – during May and June, which would be slowly tapered over time. Nevertheless, the price of crude oil was slow to rebound, reflecting in part continued weakness in demand, particularly among advanced economies.

Fiscal revenues from non-renewable natural resources in LAC largely moved with global market conditions in 2020 (Figure 3.4). In the first half of the year oil and gas revenues in Ecuador and Mexico, essentially property rents tied to the commercial value of production, tumbled as a result of the decline in spot prices and lower production levels. In Mexico, hydrocarbons output slowed between May and July in line with commitments made under the OPEC+ agreement in April, although the country declined to extend these reductions beyond June (PEMEX, 2020[8]). Additionally, receipts from the Profit-Sharing Duty – the largest single generator of oil and gas revenues – fell as the levy rate declined from 65% to 58% as stipulated as part of the Hydrocarbons Revenue Law of 2014. Oil production in Ecuador also contracted sharply in the first half of the year – by 60% year-on-year in April and 37% in May – due in part to the rupture of hydrocarbons transport infrastructure in April (BCE, 2020[23]; MEF Ecuador, 2020[24]).[8] By mid-year the rate of decline in oil and gas revenues was attenuated by an increase in prices, but revenues for the year were sharply lower, down 38% in real terms in Ecuador and 56% in Mexico.

Figure 3.3. **International spot prices for crude oil and selected minerals and metals, 2020**

Index = 100 based on US dollars at current prices

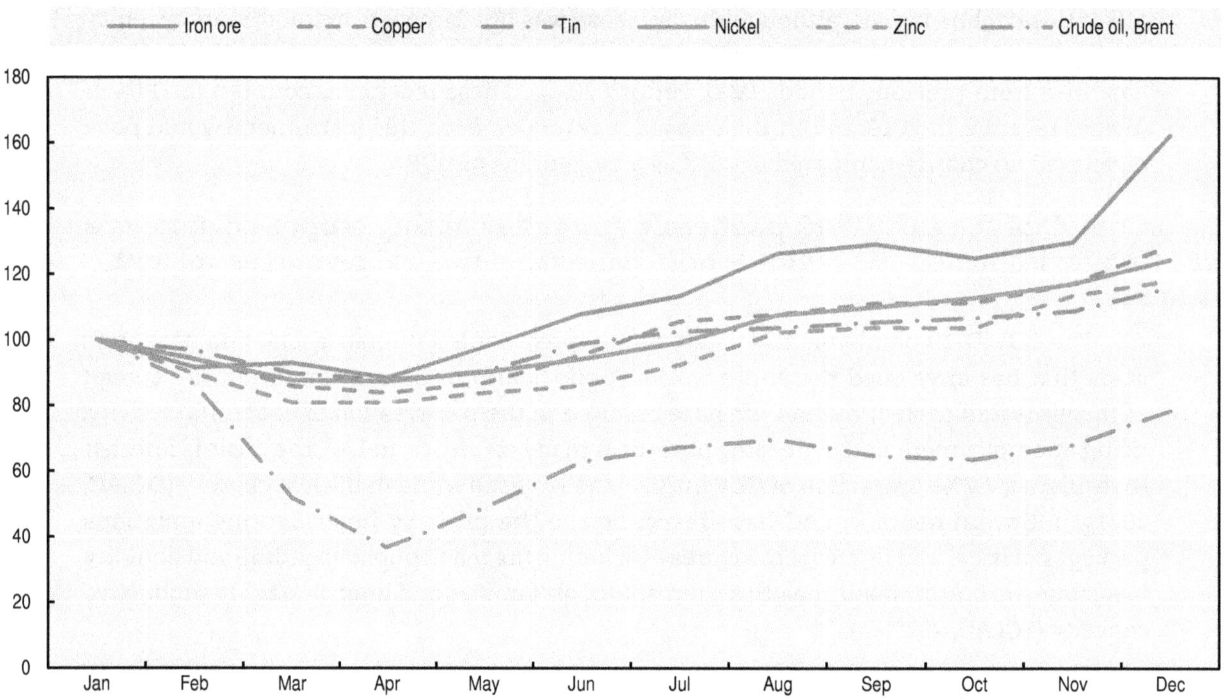

Source: Economic Commission for Latin America and the Caribbean (ECLAC), on the basis of World Bank Commodity Price Data (The Pink Sheet), World Bank.

StatLink https://doi.org/10.1787/888934234898

Mining revenues also contracted sharply in the first half of the year. Tax revenues, in particular CIT receipts, declined due to falling prices, lower estimated tax payments and COVID-19 related tax relief measures such as tax deferrals. As a result, overall mining revenues in Chile and Peru fell between April and July, reflecting the important role the CIT plays in capturing the economic rents generated by the sector. However, in contrast to the tepid recovery of crude oil prices, the dynamism of minerals and metals prices in the second half of year supported a rebound in revenues. The fourth quarter was especially strong in Chile, although this was due in part to a USD 200 million advance payment of 2021 dividends by the State-owned producer Codelco (DIPRES, 2020[25]). In Peru, despite registering a more modest increase in the last three months of the year, due to weak CIT receipts, non-tax revenues from royalties rose sharply (+20% year-on-year in real terms). Nevertheless, taken as a whole mining revenues declined markedly in 2020 in real terms, by 21.6% in Peru and 12.5% in Chile.

Figure 3.4. **General government fiscal revenues from non-renewable natural resources in selected Latin American countries, by commodity, 2020**

Year-on-year real variation in percentage

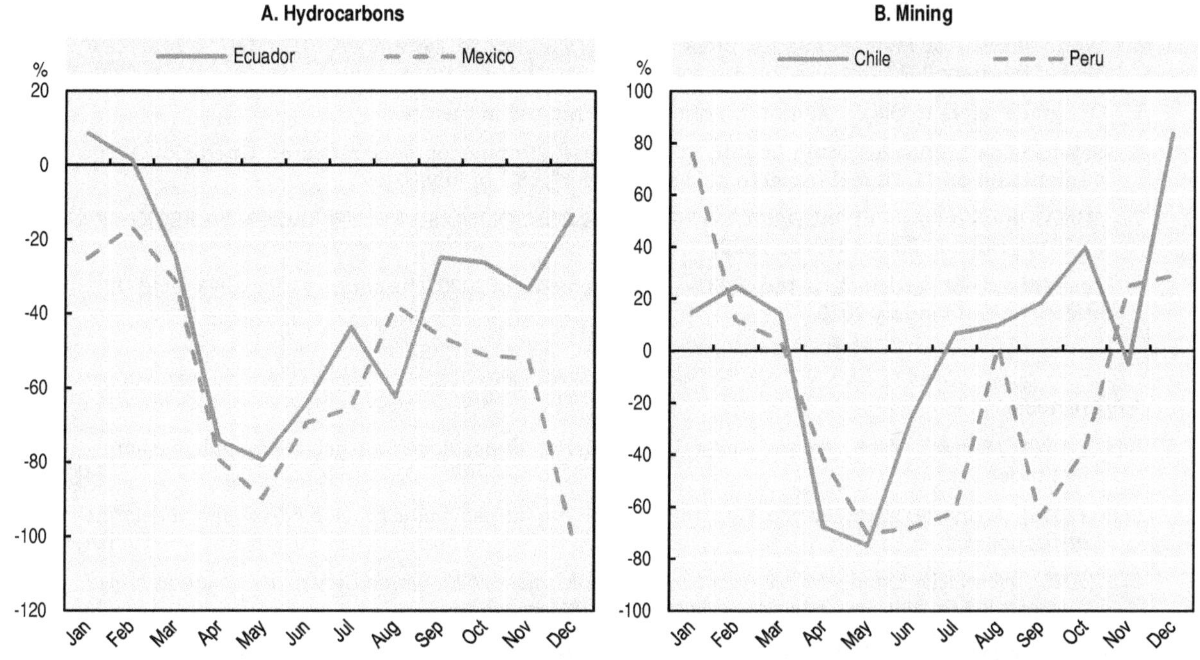

Source: Economic Commission for Latin America and the Caribbean (ECLAC), on the basis of official figures.

StatLink https://doi.org/10.1787/888934234917

Projecting fiscal revenues from non-renewable natural resources for Latin America and the Caribbean in this environment is fraught with peril. The evolution of the pandemic at the global level and in the region remains uncertain. An up-tick in cases could precipitate another round of closures that would impact economic activity, putting downward pressure on demand for commodities. Geopolitical and trade tensions remain high and could upset market conditions, particularly in the global oil market. Tax relief measures, whose effect is difficult to model, could shift revenues from 2020 to 2021. Likewise, the expected financial losses of companies operating in the sector could sharply reduce revenues and, in some cases, may result in tax refunds if pre-payments exceed final tax liabilities. Based on results in Ecuador and Mexico, oil revenues in LAC on average are likely to have ended 2020 well below their 2019 levels. Similarly, mining revenues are likely to have contracted, as revealed by final data in Chile and Peru, as a result of falling CIT receipts and lower production despite the quick rebound in international prices.

Notes

1. The importance of these extraordinary revenues on overall public revenues cannot be overstated. In Brazil, total revenues of the federal government rose from 21.6% of GDP in 2018 to 22.5% of GDP in 2019, an increase of 0.9 percentage points of GDP. Excluding the receipts from oil and gas concession signing bonuses (1.0% of GDP) would have left federal government revenues essentially flat, with consequences for the overall and primary balances. Likewise, in Trinidad and Tobago central government total revenues rose from 27.2% of GDP in 2018 to 28.8% of GDP in 2019, an increase of 1.6 percentage points of GDP, largely on the back of extraordinary oil revenues (1.7% of GDP) that offset declines in other sources.

2. Statistics in ECLAC's Fiscal Revenues from Non-Renewable Natural Resources in Latin America and the Caribbean database for Mexico have been updated to refer solely to federal government oil and gas revenues.
3. UN Comtrade Database.
4. World Bureau of Metal Statistics press release, "January to December 2019 Metals Balances", 19th of February 2020.
5. Ore grade refers to the concentration of metal or mineral in the ore.
6. Servicios de Impuestos Internos (SII) press release, "Impuestos declarados en Operación Renta aumentaron un 16,2% real respecto del año anterior", 18th of July 2019.
7. SUNAT press release "RECAUDACIÓN TRIBUTARIA CONSOLIDÓ SU RECUPERACIÓN Y CRECIÓ 3,7% EL 2019", Nota de Prensa N° 003-2020.
8. Ecuador did not participate in the OPEC+ production cuts of 2020. The country officially exited OPEC effective 1st of January 2020.

References

BCB (2020), *Memoria 2019*, Banco Central de Bolivia, *https://www.bcb.gob.bo/?q=pub_memorias-institucionales.* [4]

BCB (2019), *Memoria 2018*, Banco Central de Bolivia, *https://www.bcb.gob.bo/?q=pub_memorias-institucionales.* [14]

BCE (2020), *Información Estadística Mensual No. 2026 – Diciembre 2020*, Banco Central de Ecuador, *https://contenido.bce.fin.ec/home1/estadisticas/bolmensual/IEMensual.jsp.* [23]

BCE (2020), *Reporte del Sector Petrolero, IV Trimestre de 2019*, Banco Central de Ecuador, *https://contenido.bce.fin.ec/documentos/Estadisticas/Hidrocarburos/ASP201906.pdf.* [6]

Camimex (2020), *Informe Anual 2020*, Cámara Minera de México, *https://camimex.org.mx/application/files/4416/0204/8995/02_info_2020.pdf.* [18]

DIPRES (2020), *Informe de Ejecución del Gobierno Central Cuarto Trimestre 2020*, Dirección de Presupuestos, Ministerio de Hacienda, Chile, *http://bibliotecadigital.dipres.gob.cl/handle/11626/17632.* [25]

DIPRES (2019), *Informe de Ejecución del Gobierno Central Cuarto Trimestre 2019*, Dirección de Presupuestos, Ministerio de Hacienda, Chile, *https://www.dipres.gob.cl/598/articles-187247_doc_pdf_Presentacion_IT.pdf.* [17]

ECLAC (2021), *Preliminary Overview of the Economies of Latin America and the Caribbean 2020*, United Nations Economic Commission for Latin America and the Caribbean, *https://www.cepal.org/en/publications/46504-preliminary-overview-economies-latin-america-and-caribbean-2020.* [20]

ECLAC (2020), *"Fiscal revenues from non-renewable natural resources", CEPALSTAT (database)*, United Nations Economic Commission for Latin America and the Caribbean, *https://estadisticas.cepal.org/cepalstat/web_cepalstat/estadisticasIndicadores.asp?idioma=i.* [3]

ECLAC (2020), *Fiscal Panorama of Latin America and the Caribbean 2020*, United Nations Economic Commission for Latin America and the Caribbean, *https://www.cepal.org/en/publications/45731-fiscal-panorama-latin-america-and-caribbean-2020-fiscal-policy-amid-crisis.* [21]

EIA (2020), *Short-Term Energy Outlook, October 2020*, United States Energy Information Administration, *https://www.eia.gov/outlooks/steo/data.php?type=figures.* [1]

FMPED (2020), *Informe anual 2019*, Fondo Mexicano del Petróleo para la Estabilización y el Desarrollo, *https://www.fmped.org.mx/transparencia/%7BE2BBCC11-A6A2-F5FF-25D7-F1E291954902%7D.pdf.* [9]

Hanni, M., J. Jimenez and I. Ruelas (2018), *Ciclo de precios y regímenes fiscales vinculados con los recursos naturales no renovables en América Latina y el Caribe*, Serie de Macroeconomía del Desarrollo, United Nations Economic Commission for Latin America and the Caribbean, *https://www.cepal.org/es/publicaciones/44239-ciclo-precios-regimenes-fiscales-vinculados-recursos-naturales-renovables.* [13]

IMF (2019), *World Economic Outlook, October 2019: Global Manufacturing Downturn, Rising Trade Barriers*, International Monetary Fund, Washington, D.C., *https://www.imf.org/en/Publications/WEO/Issues/2019/10/01/world-economic-outlook-october-2019.* [10]

MEF Ecuador (2020), *Informe Semestral de Ejecución, Presupuesto General del Estado, Enero-Junio 2020*, Ministry of Economy and Finance of Ecuador, *https://www.finanzas.gob.ec/wp-content/uploads/downloads/2020/09/28092020-Informe-semestral-ejecucion-2020-CNv6-RL.pdf.* [24]

MEF Peru (2020), *Marco Macroeconómico Multianual 2020-2023*, Ministry of Economy and Finance of Peru, *https://www.mef.gob.pe/contenidos/pol_econ/marco_macro/MMM_2020_2023.pdf.* [19]

MINFIN (2019), *Liquidación del Presupuesto, General de Ingresos y Egresos del Estado y Cierre Contable, Ejercicio fiscal Enero – Diciembre 2018*, Ministry of Finance of Guatemala, *https://www.minfin.gob.gt/images/archivos/liquidacion/2018/enero_diciembre2018.pdf.* [7]

MSC (2020), *Reporte de Sostenibilidad 2019*, Minera San Cristobal, *https://www.minerasancristobal.com/v3/es/wp-content/uploads/2020/09/Reporte_de_Sostenibilidad_2019_MSC.pdf.* [15]

OECD et al. (2020), *Revenue Statistics in Latin America and the Caribbean 2020*, OECD Publishing, Paris, *https://dx.doi.org/10.1787/68739b9b-en-es.* [12]

OPEC (2020), *Annual Statistical Bulletin 2020*, Organization of the Petroleum Exporting Countries, *https://www.opec.org/opec_web/en/publications/202.htm.* [2]

PEMEX (2020), *Annual Report submitted to the United States Securities and Exchange Commission (20-F)*, Petróleos Mexicanos, *https://www.pemex.com/en/investors/regulatory-filings/Paginas/sec-filings.aspx.* [8]

Petrobras (2020), *Annual Report and Form 20-F*, Petróleo Brasileiro S.A., *https://www.investidorpetrobras.com.br/en/results-and-notices/annual-reports/.* [5]

Vale (2020), *Relatório de Transparência Fiscal 2019*, Vale S.A., *http://www.vale.com/esg/pt/Documents/Relat%C3%B3rio%20de%20Transpar%C3%AAncia%20Fiscal%202019_pt%201.pdf.* [16]

World Bank (2020), *Commodity Markets Outlook, October 2020*, World Bank, Washington, D.C., *https://openknowledge.worldbank.org/handle/10986/34621.* [22]

World Bank (2019), *Commodity Markets Outlook, October 2019*, World Bank, Washington, D.C., *https://openknowledge.worldbank.org/handle/10986/32633.* [11]

Capítulo 3

SECCIÓN ESPECIAL

Ingresos fiscales provenientes de recursos naturales no renovables en América Latina y el Caribe

Esta sección especial fue preparada por Michael Hanni, Oficial de Asuntos Económicos, Unidad de Asuntos Fiscales, División de Desarrollo Económico, Comisión Económica para América Latina y el Caribe (CEPAL).

Principales hallazgos

Tendencias de los ingresos fiscales provenientes de recursos naturales no renovables en 2019

Los ingresos fiscales provenientes de la exploración y producción de petróleo y gas en América Latina y el Caribe (ALC) aumentaron en 2019 a pesar de las desfavorables condiciones del mercado global. El aumento de los ingresos por hidrocarburos, que alcanzaron el 2.7% del PIB en promedio en comparación con el 2.5% del PIB en 2018, se debió en gran parte a los ingresos extraordinarios. Las bonificaciones de firma para nuevas concesiones de petróleo y gas generaron un exceso de ingresos equivalente al 1% del PIB en Brasil. En Trinidad y Tobago, los pagos en virtud de un programa de amnistía fiscal y los ingresos derivados de un acuerdo negociado con un gran productor dieron como resultado un aumento único equivalente al 1.6% del PIB. Sin embargo, las rentas de la propiedad cayeron durante el año en línea con los precios internacionales, ya que la producción regional se mantuvo en gran medida plana.

Los bajos precios internacionales para una variedad de minerales y metales industriales y la menor producción llevaron a una disminución de los ingresos mineros de ALC durante 2019. La variación interanual en relación con el PIB fue marginal: los ingresos promedio cayeron a 0.37% del PIB desde un 0.39% durante 2018. Del mismo modo, los ingresos agregados en dólares estadounidenses disminuyeron levemente (-3.9%), aunque la magnitud de la caída se redujo debido a un fuerte aumento en Brasil (+75.1%). Excluyendo Brasil, los ingresos totales disminuyeron un 17.3% en términos de dólares estadounidenses, con importantes contracciones registradas en Chile, Colombia, Guatemala, Jamaica, México y Perú.

El impacto de la pandemia COVID-19 en los ingresos provenientes de actividades extractivas

La pandemia COVID-19 ha provocado una de las mayores crisis sociales y económicas de los tiempos modernos. También ha creado una gran agitación en los mercados de productos básicos. Los mercados petroleros se han visto especialmente afectados con la disminución significativa de la demanda, principalmente en las economías avanzadas, lo que ha provocado una fuerte caída de los precios spot del crudo. Por el contrario, los precios internacionales de los minerales y metales se recuperaron rápidamente después de una caída inicial, gracias a la aceleración de la producción industrial en China. Los datos de alta frecuencia para una muestra de países sugieren que es probable que haya una disminución significativa en los ingresos fiscales de los recursos naturales no renovables a nivel regional para el año en relación con 2019.

Aumentan los ingresos provenientes de hidrocarburos en América Latina, impulsados por ingresos extraordinarios

Los mercados mundiales de petróleo se estabilizaron hasta cierto punto durante 2019, tras la volatilidad observada en el cuarto trimestre de 2018 relacionada con un exceso de oferta significativa. En diciembre de 2018, los miembros de la OPEP y los países productores de petróleo aliados, sobre todo la Federación de Rusia, se comprometieron a reducir su volumen total de producción en 1.2 millones de barriles diarios combinados (0.8 millones para los miembros de la OPEP) durante el primer semestre de 2019. En general el acuerdo fue exitoso y la producción mundial de combustibles líquidos se desaceleró notablemente en el primer trimestre de 2019 (Gráfico 3.1). Los precios spot del petróleo crudo se recuperaron a medida que el mercado se movió hacia un mayor equilibrio durante los primeros meses del año. No obstante, los precios volvieron a mostrar una tendencia a la baja en mayo debido al debilitamiento de los fundamentos macroeconómicos, el aumento de las tensiones comerciales entre China y Estados Unidos y la acumulación de reservas de crudo en Estados Unidos. En respuesta, la OPEP y los exportadores aliados acordaron en julio extender los recortes de producción de petróleo crudo hasta 2020. A pesar de estas tendencias, el consumo de petróleo se disparó en la segunda mitad del año, impulsado en gran medida por las importaciones récord de petróleo crudo en China, como resultado de la entrada en funcionamiento de nuevas megarrefinerías. A pesar del repunte registrado en el cuarto trimestre, los precios spot del petróleo crudo en promedio presentaron una caída durante el año, el Brent cayó un 10% (de USD 71.1 por barril a USD 64.0) y el Western Texas Intermediate (WTI) disminuyó en un 12% (desde USD 64.8 por barril a USD 57.0).

Gráfico 3.1. **Balanza mundial de producción y consumo de combustibles líquidos y precios spot internacionales del petróleo crudo, 2018-19**

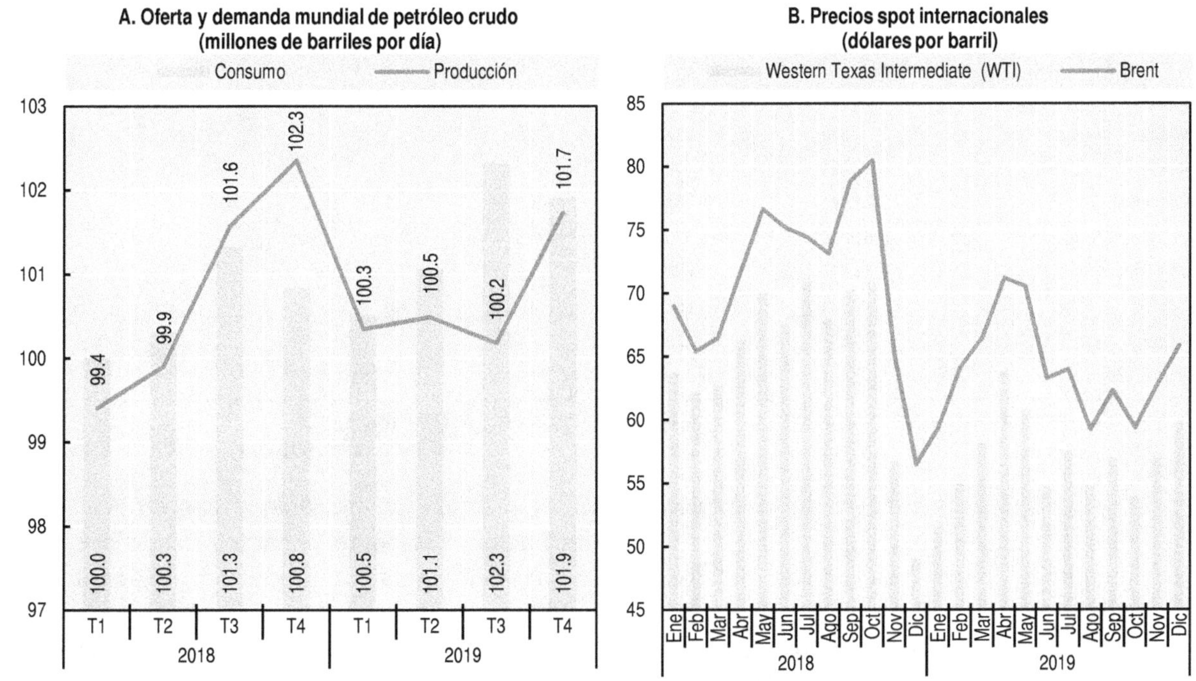

Fuente: Comisión Económica para América Latina y el Caribe (CEPAL), sobre la base de EIA (2020[1]) y Datos de Precios de Materias Primas del Banco Mundial (The Pink Sheet), Banco Mundial.

StatLink https://doi.org/10.1787/888934234936

Los niveles de producción de hidrocarburos en ALC variaron significativamente a nivel de país en 2019 (Cuadro 3.1). La producción total de petróleo crudo se redujo sustancialmente, contrayéndose en un 4.9% debido en gran parte a la caída del 37.7% de la producción en la República Bolivariana de Venezuela. Aunque la producción aumenta ligeramente al excluir a Venezuela, principalmente por el repunte de la producción en Brasil y, en menor medida, en Argentina, Colombia y Ecuador, mientras que la producción de petróleo crudo en México se redujo significativamente. La producción total de gas natural también registró una disminución debido a la caída de la producción en la República Bolivariana de Venezuela, México y el Estado Plurinacional de Bolivia. Sin embargo, estas caídas fueron atenuadas en cierta medida por aumentos en Argentina (donde la producción alcanzó su nivel más alto desde 2009), Brasil, Perú y Trinidad y Tobago.

Cuadro 3.1. **Producción de petróleo crudo y gas natural en América Latina y el Caribe y grupos de países seleccionados, 2018-19**

Grupos de países seleccionados	Petróleo crudo (miles de barriles diarios)			Gas natural (miles de millones de metros cúbicos)		
	2018	2019	2019-2018 (variación %)	2018	2019	2019-2018 (variación %)
América Latina y el Caribe	**8 012**	**7 632**	**-4.7**	**199**	**196**	**-1.4**
excluyendo a Venezuela	6 502	6 619	1.8	174	176	0.8
Argentina	489	509	3.9	41	43	5.7
Bolivia	..	..	..	19	17	-10.7
Brasil	2 587	2 788	7.8	22	24	9.5
Colombia	865	886	2.4	10	10	3.1
Ecuador	517	531	2.6	0	0	..
Guatemala	9	10	4.1	..	..	..
México	1 813	1 678	-7.4	33	31	-6.8
Perú	49	53	8.4	12	13	0.7
Trinidad y Tobago	64	59	-7.3	35	36	2.1
Venezuela	1 510	1 013	-32.9	25	21	-17.1
Otros	115	113	-1.3	1	1	2.0
Total mundial	**75 822**	**75 263**	**-0.7**	**3 946**	**4 093**	**3.7**
OPEP	31 238	29 375	-6.0	..	..	..
Arabia Saudita	10 317	9 808	-4.9	..	..	..
No-OPEP	44 584	45 887	2.9	..	..	..
Federación Rusa	10 527	10 625	0.9	..	..	..
Estados Unidos	10 991	12 232	11.3	..	..	..

Fuente: Comisión Económica para América Latina y el Caribe (CEPAL) sobre la base de OPEP (2020[2]).

StatLink https://doi.org/10.1787/888934235088

Los ingresos fiscales de la exploración y producción de petróleo y gas en ALC aumentaron en 2019 a pesar del contexto internacional imperante, caracterizado por la caída de los precios spot del petróleo crudo y las tendencias de producción regional (Cuadro 3.2). Los ingresos totales provenientes de hidrocarburos en la región alcanzaron USD 79.8 mil millones en 2019, un 10.4% más que en 2018. En términos relativos, este resultado fue relativamente modesto, equivalente al 2.7% del PIB en promedio en comparación con el 2.5% del PIB en 2018. Si bien la mayor producción y las depreciaciones monetarias lograron suavizar el impacto de los menores precios internacionales en algunos países, el aumento de los ingresos se debió en gran parte a los ingresos extraordinarios. Brasil y Trinidad y Tobago registraron ingresos petroleros extraordinarios durante el año equivalentes al 1.0% del PIB y al 1.6% del PIB, respectivamente[1]. Excluyendo estas transacciones, los ingresos por hidrocarburos se contrajeron un 14.8% en términos de dólares estadounidenses (USD). Esto se correlaciona con la trayectoria de los ingresos por regalías y gravámenes a la producción ligados al valor comercial de la producción, los cuales cayeron 12.6% en términos de USD en línea con los precios internacionales y la dinámica productiva regional. Sin embargo, los resultados a nivel de país fueron variados, reflejando una fuerte heterogeneidad en la producción, las exportaciones y la dinámica regulatoria durante el año.

Cuadro 3.2. **Ingresos fiscales de las administraciones públicas procedentes de la exploración y producción de petróleo y gas en nueve países de ALC, por tipo de ingresos, 2018-19**

Porcentaje del PIB, a menos que se especifique lo contrario

Tipos de ingresos	Período	Región / país									
		ALC	Argentina	Bolivia (Estado Plurinacional de)	Brasil	Colombia	Ecuador	Guatemala	México	Perú	Trinidad y Tobago
Ingresos totales	2018	**2.5**	0.5	4.6	1.2	1.8	7.6	0.1	2.3	0.7	3.9
	2019	**2.7**	0.5	3.8	1.9	2.4	7.2	0.0	1.8	0.5	6.5
	2019-2018 (p.p. del PIB)	**0.2**	0.0	-0.8	0.7	0.5	-0.4	0.0	-0.5	-0.2	2.5
	2019-2018 (variación en MN %)	..	43.3	-15.4	67.6	39.7	-4.8	-31.8	-20.0	-22.6	67.2
	2019-2018 (variación en USD %)	**10.4**	-16.4	-15.4	56.0	25.9	-4.8	-33.4	-20.1	-23.8	67.6
Ingresos tributarios	2018	**0.4**	0.1	0.3	0.1	0.7	0.0	0.0	0.0	0.2	1.8
	2019	**0.5**	0.1	0.2	0.1	0.6	0.0	0.0	0.0	0.1	3.1
	2019-2018 (p.p. del PIB)	**0.1**	0.0	0.0	0.0	-0.2	0.0	0.0	0.0	0.0	1.3
Ingresos no tributarios	2018	**2.2**	0.4	4.3	1.1	1.1	7.6	0.1	2.3	0.5	2.2
	2019	**2.3**	0.4	3.6	1.8	1.8	7.2	0.0	1.8	0.4	3.4
	2019-2018 (p.p. del PIB)	**0.1**	0.0	-0.7	0.7	0.7	-0.4	0.0	-0.5	-0.1	1.2
de los cuales: regalías y gravámenes a la producción	2018	**2.1**	0.4	4.3	0.8	0.7	7.6	0.1	2.3	0.5	2.2
	2019	**1.9**	0.4	3.6	0.8	0.7	7.2	0.0	1.8	0.4	2.2
	2019-2018 (p.p. del PIB)	**-0.2**	0.0	-0.7	0.0	0.0	-0.4	0.0	-0.5	-0.1	0.0
	2019-2018 (variación en USD %)	**-12.6**	-15.9	-15.7	-1.8	-4.5	-4.8	-45.5	-20.4	-24.9	3.7

Nota: Los datos de México corresponden a los ingresos petroleros del gobierno federal y excluyen los ingresos propios de Pemex, el productor estatal de petróleo y gas. Los datos de Ecuador corresponden a los ingresos petroleros del sector público no financiero. La relación ingresos/PIB para América Latina y el Caribe (ALC) corresponde a una media simple de los países incluidos en la muestra. Las cifras pueden no sumar debido al redondeo.

Fuente: Comisión Económica para América Latina y el Caribe (CEPAL), sobre la base de datos de CEPALSTAT (2020[3]).

StatLink https://doi.org/10.1787/888934235107

Los ingresos por petróleo y gas en ***Argentina*** se contrajeron en 2019, aunque la variación interanual en términos relativos fue marginal (0.01% menos del PIB). Los ingresos por el impuesto sobre la renta corporativa (ISR) y regalías registraron fuertes contracciones (-19.1% y -15.9% en términos de USD, respectivamente), que superaron la caída de los precios spot internacionales del crudo y los aumentos de la producción del petróleo y gas. Esto se debió en gran parte a la emisión del Decreto N° 566/2019 de 15 de agosto, que impuso controles de precios a los productos petrolíferos por un período de 90 días. El decreto estableció que todas las entregas de crudo al mercado interno debían facturarse al precio acordado entre productores y refinerías a partir del 9 de agosto, aplicando a la transacción un tipo de cambio fijo ARS-USD y precio de referencia Brent. Posteriormente, diversos decretos modificaron el tipo de cambio utilizado para calcular los pagos, pero los precios internos del petróleo crudo continuaron estando por debajo de los índices de referencia internacionales.

La menor producción de gas natural y la caída de los precios produjeron una disminución significativa de los ingresos por hidrocarburos en el ***Estado Plurinacional de Bolivia***. Los ingresos totales de petróleo y gas natural alcanzaron el 3.8% del PIB en 2019, frente al 4.6% del PIB del año anterior, como resultado de la caída de los ingresos no tributarios del Impuesto Directo a los Hidrocarburos (una regalía) y otras participaciones del Estado en el valor comercial de la producción. La maduración de los campos de gas natural y la inversión limitada han llevado a una disminución progresiva de la producción, que en 2019 alcanzó su nivel más bajo desde 2011, un 21.2% por debajo del máximo alcanzado en 2014 (Cuadro 3.1; OPEP (2020[2])). Al mismo tiempo, el aumento de la producción de gas natural en Argentina y Brasil continúa ejerciendo presión sobre los ingresos y las exportaciones de hidrocarburos de Bolivia (BCB, 2020[4]).

Los ingresos por hidrocarburos aumentaron en ***Brasil*** en 2019 gracias a los ingresos extraordinarios. Los ingresos fiscales del petróleo crudo y el gas natural aumentaron al 1.9% del PIB desde el 1.2% del PIB en 2018, un aumento del 56% en términos de USD. En abril de 2019, el gobierno federal y Petrobras concluyeron una negociación plurianual sobre los términos contractuales para el área "pre-sal" en el marco del acuerdo inicial de canje de petróleo por acciones alcanzado en 2010 (Petrobras, 2020[5]). El acuerdo permitió al gobierno federal subastar contratos de producción compartida por el resto de las reservas de petróleo, más allá de lo que previamente había sido asignado a Petrobras, en el área *off-shore* en noviembre de 2019. La subasta resultó en R$ 69.96 mil millones de bonificaciones a la firma (equivalente al 1.0% del PIB). Sin embargo, los ingresos por regalías y otras participaciones gubernamentales en el valor comercial de la producción disminuyeron levemente (-1.8% en términos de USD), dado que el aumento de la producción se vio compensado por la caída de los precios.

En ***Colombia***, los ingresos por petróleo y gas aumentaron en 2019 principalmente por el pago de dividendos excepcionalmente grandes por parte de EcoPetrol, empresa de propiedad estatal, al gobierno nacional. A COP $ 11.42 mil millones, equivalente a USD 3.5 mil millones o 1.1% del PIB, el dividendo estuvo muy por encima del pago del año anterior del 0.3% del PIB. Como resultado, los ingresos totales de hidrocarburos alcanzaron el 2.4% del PIB en 2019, frente al 1.8% en 2018. No obstante, los ingresos de otros instrumentos registraron descensos. Los ingresos tributarios en forma del ISR se redujeron, lo que refleja el impacto de los precios más bajos en los márgenes de utilidad y la alta base de comparación con el año anterior cuando EcoPetrol reportó fuertes ganancias. Las rentas de la propiedad derivadas de las regalías se mantuvieron prácticamente sin cambios en relación con el PIB, pero cayeron en términos de dólares estadounidenses, ya que la caída en precios se vio compensada por un modesto aumento en la producción.

Los ingresos por hidrocarburos en ***Ecuador*** registraron una caída marginal en 2019 (-4.8% en términos de USD) debido a que la mayor producción y exportaciones de Petroamazonas, de propiedad estatal (+ 4.4% y + 9.9%, en millones de barriles, respectivamente) compensaron en gran medida la caída de los precios (BCE, 2020[6]). El sector petrolero del país se vio afectado por las tensiones sociales provocadas por la promulgación del Decreto 883 del 11 de octubre, que eliminó los subsidios a los combustibles. Aunque este decreto fue posteriormente revocado por el Decreto 894 del 14 de octubre, los paros laborales continuaron durante todo el mes.

Los ingresos petroleros en ***Guatemala*** cayeron significativamente en 2019, un 33.4% en términos de USD y de 0.07% del PIB en 2018 a 0.05% del PIB, a pesar del aumento de la producción. Los ingresos no tributarios por la participación del Estado en la producción de hidrocarburos cayeron fuertemente (-58.8% en términos de USD) reflejando la alta base de comparación con el año anterior cuando estos ingresos registraron un incremento mucho mayor al presupuestado (MINFIN, 2019[7]).

Una confluencia de factores precipitó una disminución de los ingresos petroleros del gobierno federal en ***México***, incluida la dinámica de los precios internacionales, la caída de la producción y las medidas de política[2]. Los ingresos generales de hidrocarburos del gobierno federal cayeron del 2.3% del PIB en 2018 al 1.8% del PIB, ya que las rentas de las propiedades de las actividades de exploración y producción de petróleo disminuyeron. Los ingresos del Derecho por la Utilidad Compartida pagados por Petróleos Mexicanos, que constituyen el grueso de los ingresos petroleros no tributarios, contrajeron como resultado de la aplicación de un decreto gubernamental en mayo de 2019 que permitió a la empresa realizar mayores deducciones por inversiones (PEMEX, 2020$_{[8]}$; FMPED, 2020$_{[9]}$). Asimismo, a partir de enero de 2019, la tasa utilizada para calcular la Tasa de Reparto de Utilidades se redujo a 65%, desde 66.25% en 2018, en línea con los cambios en el marco fiscal de petróleo y gas establecidos en la Ley de Ingresos sobre Hidrocarburos de 2014.

Los ingresos por petróleo y gas en ***Perú*** se redujeron al 0.5% del PIB en 2019 desde el 0.7% en 2018, principalmente debido al debilitamiento de la demanda externa. Los ingresos por regalías cayeron un 24.9% en términos de USD, o del 0.5% del PIB en 2018 al 0.4% del PIB, a pesar del aumento de la producción de petróleo crudo. La disminución de las regalías se debió en gran parte al menor valor de las exportaciones de petróleo crudo y gas natural, que sirve de base para el cálculo de ciertos pagos de alquiler de propiedades. En particular, las exportaciones de gas natural licuado registraron una fuerte contracción ya que el valor de las ventas a España, un socio comercial clave, cayó de USD 333.9 millones en 2018 a USD 35.6 millones en 2019 (-89%)[3]. Las ventas más débiles también se tradujeron en una disminución de los márgenes de beneficio y, a su vez, en los ingresos tributarios.

Los ingresos por hidrocarburos en ***Trinidad y Tobago*** aumentaron drásticamente en 2019, pasando del 3.9% del PIB en 2018 al 6.5% del PIB, impulsados por ingresos extraordinarios tributarios y no tributarios. Una amnistía tributaria de tres meses que permitió a los contribuyentes liquidar pasivos pendientes sin multas e intereses resultó en ingresos tributarios superiores a los previstos. Solo las empresas petroleras realizaron pagos por un valor de TT $ 750 millones (0.5% del PIB) en el marco del programa. Estos ingresos y los mayores ingresos por el ISR que reflejan las mayores ganancias obtenidas en el año fiscal anterior hicieron que los ingresos tributarios provenientes del petróleo y gas natural aumentaran del 1.8% del PIB en 2018 al 3.1% del PIB. Los ingresos no tributarios también aumentaron notablemente, del 2.2% del PIB en 2018 al 3.4% del PIB, debido a un pago inicial de TT $ 1.9 mil millones durante el año fiscal 2018/19, equivalente al 1.2% del PIB, por Shell Trinidad and Tobago Limited –una subsidiaria de Royal Dutch Shell– al gobierno como resultado de un acuerdo para abordar cuestiones tributarias pendientes.

Los ingresos de la minería en América Latina y el Caribe disminuyeron, con una heterogeneidad significativa a nivel de países

El debilitamiento de los fundamentos macroeconómicos que caracterizaron el año, agravado por el aumento de las tensiones comerciales, sirvió para reforzar la caída de los precios spot internacionales de una variedad de minerales y metales industriales que comenzó a mediados de 2018 (Gráfico 3.2). Sin embargo, los precios del mineral de hierro aumentaron bruscamente como resultado de la producción récord de acero en China y las interrupciones de la producción causadas por el trágico desastre de la mina Corrego do Feijão en Brasil y el ciclón Verónica en Australia (FMI, 2019$_{[10]}$). Los precios del níquel también aumentaron en la segunda mitad del año cuando Indonesia, el mayor exportador del mundo, anunció una prohibición completa de las exportaciones de níquel a partir de

2020 (Banco Mundial, 2019[11]). A pesar de estos factores, la dinámica de los precios reflejó en cierta medida cambios en el sentimiento del mercado, ya que la demanda subyacente se mantuvo relativamente estable. Por ejemplo, aunque el consumo mundial de cobre permaneció prácticamente sin cambios en 2019 en comparación con 2018 (-0.4%), la demanda de plomo, zinc y níquel aumentó[4].

Gráfico 3.2. **Precios spot internacionales para minerales y metales seleccionados, T1 2018-T4 2019**

Crecimiento trimestral respecto al año anterior

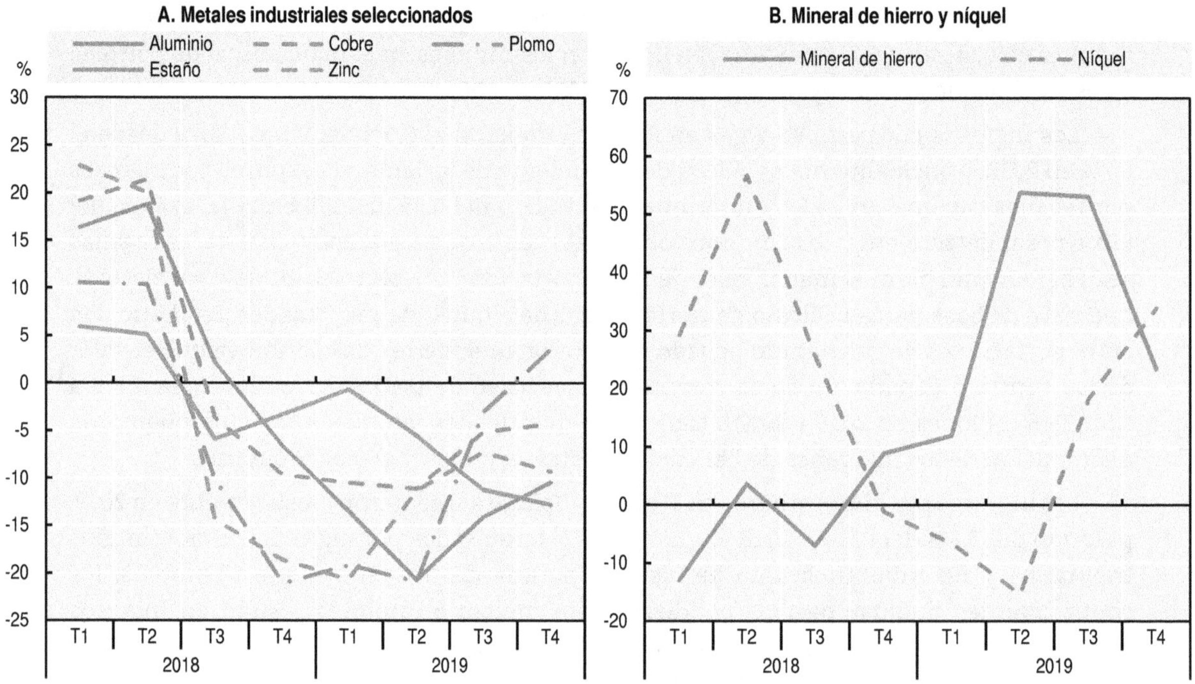

Fuente: Comisión Económica para América Latina y el Caribe (CEPAL), sobre la base de Datos de Precios de Materias Primas del Banco Mundial (The Pink Sheet), Banco Mundial.

StatLink https://doi.org/10.1787/888934234955

El impacto de la caída de los precios en los ingresos de la minería en ALC se vio reforzado por la menor producción minera en varios países (Cuadro 3.3). Esta tendencia fue influenciada en parte por los conflictos sociales en curso (como la mina Las Bambas en Perú operada por Minerals and Metals Group), huelgas y paros laborales (como fue el caso de la huelga de los trabajadores en la mina Chuquicamata de Codelco en Chile), y daño ambiental (más notablemente el desastre de la mina Corrego do Feijão en Brasil). A un nivel más estructural, la producción minera en la región continúa siendo atenuada por la disminución progresiva de las leyes del mineral a medida que maduran las minas a gran escala existentes[5]. Este fenómeno requiere una extracción de mineral cada vez mayor para mantener los niveles de producción de metales y minerales. Los mayores costos de producción asociados y la necesidad de inversiones costosas para mejorar la productividad y explotar reservas menos accesibles, *ceteris paribus*, pueden afectar la rentabilidad y, a su vez, los ingresos tributarios. Esto es especialmente relevante dado que el ISR y otros instrumentos que gravan utilidades son el mecanismo principal en la región para capturar las rentas económicas derivadas de la minería (OCDE et al., 2020[12]; Hanni et al., 2018[13]).

Cuadro 3.3. **Precios internacionales y producción de metales y minerales en países seleccionados de ALC, 2018-19**

Metales y minerales	Año y variación porcentual	Precio (USD) y %	Producción por país en miles de toneladas métricas a menos que se especifique lo contrario								
			Argentina	Bolivia	Brasil	Chile	Colombia	República Dominicana	Jamaica	México	Perú
Cobre	2018	6529.8		5.2	750.6	5831.6				473.6	2437.0
	2019	6010.1		4.5	363.3	5787.4				486.9	2455.4
	variación %	-8.0		-14.1	-51.6	-0.8				2.8	0.8
Zinc	2018	2922.4		519.6						381.5	1474.4
	2019	2550.4		528.1						325.3	1404.4
	variación %	-12.7		1.6						-14.7	-4.7
Plomo	2018	2240.4		112.0						131.8	289.1
	2019	1996.5		88.0						149.1	308.1
	variación %	-10.9		-21.5						13.1	6.6
Estaño	2018	20145.2		17.3	19.3						18.6
	2019	18661.2		17.1	14.9						19.9
	variación %	-7.4		-0.7	-23.1						6.7
Níquel	2018	13114.1			67.7		43.0				
	2019	13913.9			55.7		40.6				
	variación %	6.1			-17.7		-5.8				
Hierro	2018	69.8			317502.4	8942.6	575.5			7085.4	9533.9
	2019	93.8			255272.6	8427.2	665.2			7140.9	10120.0
	variación %	34.5			-19.6	-5.8	15.6			0.8	6.1
Cobre	2018	107.0					86255.2			8151.8	
	2019	77.9					84342.8			6616.9	
	variación %	-27.2					-2.2			-18.8	
Bauxita / alúmina	2018	2108.5			19437.8				10058.2		
	2019	1794.5			15248.5				9022.3		
	variación %	-14.9			-21.6				-10.3		
Oro (ton. métricas)	2018	1269.2	59.8	6.2	85.4	37.1	35.6	32.3		91.2	140.2
	2019	1392.5	59.8	5.5	75.2	38.5	36.7	31.9		73.5	128.4
	variación %	9.7	0.0	-11.6	-11.9	3.7	3.1	-1.2		-19.5	-8.4
Plata (ton. métricas)	2018	15.7	545.5	1191.6		1370.2	16.0	169.8		3694.0	4160.2
	2019	16.2	715.3	1153.1		1309.3	11.7	108.7		3498.5	3860.3
	variación %	3.2	31.1	-3.2		-4.4	-26.9	-36.0		-5.3	-7.2

Fuente: Comisión Económica para América Latina y el Caribe (CEPAL), sobre la base de Datos de Precios de Materias Primas del Banco Mundial (The Pink Sheet), Banco Mundial; Instituto Nacional de Estadísticas del Estado Plurinacional de Bolivia, estadísticas mineras; Agência Nacional de Mineração do Brasil, Anuário Mineral Brasileiro: Principais Substâncias Metálicas; Comisión Chilena de Cobre (Cochilco), Anuario de Estadísticas del Cobre y Otros Minerales 2000-2019; Agencia Nacional de Minería de Colombia, Sistema de Información Minero Colombiano; Instituto de Bauxita de Jamaica, Boletín Estadístico Mensual Local de Bauxita / Alúmina; Instituto Nacional de Estadística y Geografía de México, Estadística Mensual de la Industria Minerometalúrgica y Ministerio de Energía y Minas del Perú, Reporte de la producción minera anual.

StatLink https://doi.org/10.1787/888934235126

A pesar de estas tendencias generales, los ingresos de la minería en ALC registraron una modesta disminución en 2019. Para el año, estos ingresos alcanzaron los USD 12.7 mil millones, un 3.9% menos que los USD 13.2 mil millones en 2018 (Cuadro 3.4). Sin embargo, este resultado se debió en gran parte al aumento excepcional de los ingresos mineros en Brasil (+ 75.1% en términos de USD). Excluyendo Brasil, los ingresos totales en la región cayeron un 17.3%. Los ingresos de la minería como porcentaje del PIB registraron una ligera disminución entre años, con un aumento marginal en los ingresos tributarios que fue compensado por una mayor disminución en los ingresos no tributarios. Sin embargo, los resultados a nivel de país variaron significativamente.

Los ingresos fiscales de la minería aumentaron significativamente en el ***Estado Plurinacional de Bolivia*** a pesar de la caída de los volúmenes de producción y los bajos precios internacionales. Durante el año, la producción en la mina San Cristóbal, una de las más grandes del país, se vio afectada por una huelga de un mes durante agosto, así como por el mantenimiento programado realizado en octubre (BCB, 2020[4]). No obstante, los ingresos fiscales totales de la minería aumentaron del 0.85% del PIB en 2018 al 1.11% del PIB gracias a los ingresos tributarios impulsados por los sólidos resultados financieros del año fiscal 2018 y a un gran pago por anticipado de los impuestos de 2020 efectuados a finales de 2019 (BCB, 2019[14]; MSC, 2020[15]). Los ingresos tributarios también se vieron impulsados por una amnistía fiscal general, establecida por la Ley # 1105 de Regularización de Tributos del Nivel Central del Estado, que se promulgó durante el año.

Cuadro 3.4. **Ingresos fiscales del gobierno general procedentes de la minería en nueve países de ALC, por tipo de ingresos, 2018-19**

Porcentaje del PIB, salvo que se especifique lo contrario

Tipos de ingresos	Período	Región / país											
		ALC	Argentina	Bolivia (Estado Plurinacional de)	Brasil	Chile	Colombia	República Dominicana	Ecuador	Guatemala	Jamaica	México	Perú
Ingresos totales	2018	**0.39**	0.04	0.85	0.10	1.40	0.45	0.21	0.08	0.01	0.04	0.23	0.90
	2019	**0.37**	0.04	1.11	0.18	1.31	0.32	0.22	0.08	0.01	0.04	0.18	0.62
	2019-2018 (p.p. del PIB)	**-0.02**	0.01	0.27	0.08	-0.10	-0.13	0.02	0.00	0.00	-0.01	-0.05	-0.28
	2019-2018 (variación en MN %)	..	70.6	33.3	88.2	-3.3	-24.5	16.5	-0.7	-24.9	-12.9	-18.3	-28.7
	2019-2018 (variación en USD %)	**-3.9**	-0.5	33.3	75.1	-11.8	-32.0	12.4	-0.7	-26.6	-15.8	-18.3	-29.8
Ingresos tributarios	2018	**0.23**	0.03	0.37	0.05	0.82	0.19	0.15	0.03	0.01	0.00	0.20	0.72
	2019	**0.24**	0.03	0.64	0.11	0.98	0.10	0.17	0.03	0.01	0.00	0.15	0.42
	2019-2018 (p.p. del PIB)	**0.01**	0.00	0.27	0.06	0.16	-0.09	0.02	0.00	0.00	0.00	-0.04	-0.30
Ingresos no tributarios	2018	**0.16**	0.01	0.48	0.05	0.58	0.26	0.05	0.05	0.00	0.04	0.03	0.19
	2019	**0.13**	0.01	0.48	0.07	0.32	0.21	0.05	0.05	0.00	0.04	0.03	0.20
	2019-2018 (p.p. del PIB)	**-0.03**	0.00	0.00	0.02	-0.26	-0.05	0.00	0.00	0.00	-0.01	0.00	0.01
de los cuales: regalías y gravámenes a la producción	2018	**0.14**	0.01	0.48	0.05	0.38	0.26	0.05	0.03	0.00	0.04	0.03	0.18
	2019	**0.13**	0.01	0.48	0.07	0.32	0.21	0.05	0.03	0.00	0.04	0.03	0.20
	2019-2018 (p.p. del PIB)	**-0.01**	0.00	0.00	0.02	-0.06	-0.05	0.00	0.00	0.00	-0.01	0.00	0.02
	2019-2018 (variación en USD %)	**-1.4**	28.1	0.9	33.3	-19.2	-20.0	-1.1	-4.1	-49.8	-15.8	-7.0	11.3

Nota: La relación ingresos/PIB de América Latina y el Caribe (ALC) corresponde a una media simple de los países incluidos en la muestra. Las cifras pueden no sumar debido al redondeo.

Fuente: Comisión Económica para América Latina y el Caribe (CEPAL), sobre la base de datos de CEPALSTAT (2020[3]).

StatLink https://doi.org/10.1787/888934235145

Durante 2019, el sector minero en ***Brasil*** estuvo marcado por una falla en la presa de relaves en la mina Corrego do Feijão, operada por Vale S.A. en Brumadinho, que ocurrió el 25 de enero. El flujo de lodo resultante inundó comunidades y granjas locales, y provocó la muerte de 270 personas y daños importantes al ecosistema local. A pesar de la menor producción debido al desastre, el salto en los precios del mineral de hierro a nivel mundial resultó en un aumento significativo en los ingresos de la minería, que aumentaron al 0.18% del PIB desde el 0.10% del PIB en 2018, un aumento del 75.1% en términos de USD. Los pagos del ISR de Vale se duplicaron con creces, a pesar de registrar una pérdida financiera para el año, ya que las provisiones financieras para el desastre de Brumadinho no pudieron deducirse del cálculo de la renta imponible hasta que se incurra efectivamente (Vale, 2020[16]). Pagos de regalías de la Compensación por Explotación de Recursos Minerales

(Compensação Financeira pela Exploração de Recursos Minerais) y la Tasa de Control, Monitoreo y Supervisión de las Actividades de Exploración y Minería de Recursos Minerales (Taxa de Fiscalização de Recursos Minerários) del Estado de Minas Gerais alcanzó un nivel récord, al aumentar un 33.3% en términos de USD.

Los ingresos fiscales de la minería en ***Chile*** disminuyeron en 2019 como resultado de una menor producción de cobre y la caída de los precios internacionales. Durante el año, los ingresos totales cayeron al 1.31% del PIB en comparación con el 1.40% del PIB en 2018. No obstante, esta tendencia general oculta una dinámica más compleja a nivel de los instrumentos fiscales individuales. Los ingresos no tributarios se contrajeron drásticamente debido a que los pagos de dividendos de Codelco, el productor de cobre estatal, cayeron a cero. En 2018, la empresa realizó pagos en exceso que posteriormente fueron descontados de los adeudados para 2019 (DIPRES, 2019[17]). Los ingresos tributarios, por el contrario, aumentaron a medida que se fortaleció la liquidación de las obligaciones tributarias de los productores privados del año anterior, debido en parte al aumento final en la tasa del ISR según lo establecido en la reforma tributaria de 2014[6].

El colapso de los precios internacionales del carbón provocó una fuerte disminución de los ingresos de la minería en ***Colombia***. Los menores ingresos tributarios y no tributarios contribuyeron a la disminución de los ingresos totales, que alcanzaron el 0.32% del PIB en comparación con el 0.45% del PIB en 2018. Los pagos del ISR de las empresas que operan en el sector del carbón, que representaron el 79% de los ingresos del ISR de la minería en 2018, se redujeron a más de la mitad (-58%) ya que las ganancias se vieron afectadas por precios más bajos. Asimismo, los ingresos no tributarios por regalías asociadas a la producción de carbón registraron una caída significativa, en línea con los precios del carbón, aunque esto fue compensado en parte por mayores ingresos por la producción de oro.

Los sólidos precios del oro impulsaron los ingresos de la minería en la ***República Dominicana*** en 2019, aumentando al 0.22% del PIB desde el 0.21% del PIB en 2018, o un incremento del 12.4% en términos de USD. Si bien la producción de oro se contrajo levemente, el aumento de cerca del 10% en el precio promedio anual compensó esta caída con creces, reforzando la rentabilidad y los ingresos por concepto del ISR. Durante el año, el gobierno propuso una nueva legislación para regular el sector minero – Ley de Minería Nacional – que establecería una participación mínima del Estado en las rentas mineras, entre otras modificaciones.

En ***Ecuador***, los ingresos de la minería se contrajeron marginalmente (-0.7% en términos de USD) en 2019 debido a menores rentas de la propiedad. Los pagos de regalías han exhibido cambios significativos en los años anteriores a medida que los operadores de nuevas minas liquidan los pagos anticipados como parte de sus acuerdos con el gobierno. Excluyendo estos anticipos, los ingresos por regalías aumentaron un 23.9% en términos de USD, reflejando una mayor producción y el favorable incremento del precio del oro. Varias operaciones mineras a gran escala comenzaron a producir durante el año. La mina de oro y cobre a cielo abierto Mirador, propiedad de un consorcio de empresas liderado por Tongling Nonferrous Metals Group (China), comenzó la producción en junio. A esto le siguió en noviembre la mina Fruta del Norte, operada por Lundin Gold (Canadá), iniciando la producción con exportaciones de oro que comenzaron a fines de año.

Los ingresos de la minería continuaron cayendo en ***Guatemala***, mientras el país lidiaba con conflictos sociales asociados con el sector. Varias de las minas más grandes del país permanecen cerradas. Se está llevando a cabo un proceso de consulta con las comunidades locales en el marco del Convenio 169 de la OIT.

En *Jamaica*, los ingresos de la minería de bauxita y alúmina mostraron poco dinamismo, continuando la tendencia observada en los últimos años. Si bien los ingresos totales se mantuvieron esencialmente sin cambios en relación con el PIB, se contrajeron un 15.8% en términos de USD, ya que los ingresos por el gravamen de bauxita cayeron a cero.

Los ingresos fiscales de la minería en *México* se contrajeron en 2019, ya que la menor producción de metales preciosos y la caída de los precios de los metales industriales redujeron la rentabilidad del sector. Durante el año, varias minas, como la mina de oro y plata Peñasquito en Zacatecas operada por Newmont-Goldcorp, fueron cerradas temporalmente como resultado de las protestas (Camimex, 2020[18]). Esta dinámica de precios y producción sirvió para reducir los ingresos por concepto del ISR, lo que fue reflejado en los ingresos totales que alcanzaron un 0.18% del PIB, frente al 0.23% del PIB en 2018.

Los ingresos de la minería en *Perú* se contrajeron significativamente durante el año, ya que la caída de los precios compensó las ganancias de producción de algunos de los principales bienes de exportación del país. Los ingresos fiscales totales de la minería cayeron al 0.62% del PIB desde el 0.9% del PIB en 2018, impulsados por una disminución de 0.3 puntos porcentuales en los ingresos tributarios del sector. Los ingresos por el ISR se debilitaron como resultado de menores ganancias causadas por conflictos sociales, problemas ambientales y reducción de la producción[7]. El aumento de los ingresos no tributarios compensó en parte esta disminución, aunque este incremento se debió en gran medida a unos ingresos extraordinarios. Durante el año, las empresas mineras liquidaron una cantidad significativa de pasivos por regalías acumuladas de períodos anteriores (MEF Perú, 2020[19]). Estos ingresos representaron el 12% de los ingresos por regalías en 2019 y, en su ausencia, los ingresos de este instrumento no hubieran registrado cambios en comparación con 2018 relativo al producto.

El estallido de la pandemia COVID-19 y la paralización económica resultante ha tenido un fuerte impacto en los ingresos fiscales provenientes de los recursos naturales no renovables de la región

La pandemia de COVID-19 ha creado una crisis humana, social y económica sin precedentes que ha afectado al mundo entero. Las medidas de salud pública para prevenir la propagación del virus y proteger la vida humana han tenido como resultado la paralización de la actividad económica, el aumento del desempleo y la pobreza en muchos países. En ALC, se prevé que la crisis provoque una contracción del PIB del 7.7% en 2020, la mayor caída del último siglo (CEPAL, 2021[20]). Los gobiernos de ALC han respondido a la crisis mediante la implementación de ambiciosos paquetes de medidas fiscales y financieras, que incluyen desgravaciones fiscales, gasto público y medidas de liquidez, para fortalecer los sistemas de salud pública, apoyar a las familias y limitar el daño a la capacidad productiva (CEPAL, 2020[21]).

A pesar de este contexto, el impacto de la crisis en los mercados internacionales de materias primas ha sido mixto. Durante la primera mitad del año, los precios spot cayeron abruptamente debido al colapso de la actividad económica y el consumo privado (Gráfico 3.3). No obstante, los precios de varios minerales y metales se recuperaron y superaron sus niveles prepandémicos para fines de año, en gran parte debido a la aceleración de la producción industrial y la inversión en China y las interrupciones del suministro de algunos minerales y metales causadas por la pandemia (Banco Mundial, 2020[22]). Los mercados del petróleo, sin embargo, estuvieron turbulentos después de experimentar una fuerte caída en los precios spot en marzo y abril. En abril, los socios de la OPEP y los productores aliados acordaron un recorte a gran escala de la producción (9.7 millones de barriles por día) durante mayo y junio, que se iría reduciendo progresivamente con el tiempo. No obstante, el precio del petróleo crudo se recuperó lentamente, reflejando en parte la continua debilidad de la demanda, especialmente entre las economías avanzadas.

Gráfico 3.3. **Precios spot internacionales del petróleo crudo y minerales y metales seleccionados, 2020**

Índice = 100 basado en dólares estadounidenses a precios corrientes

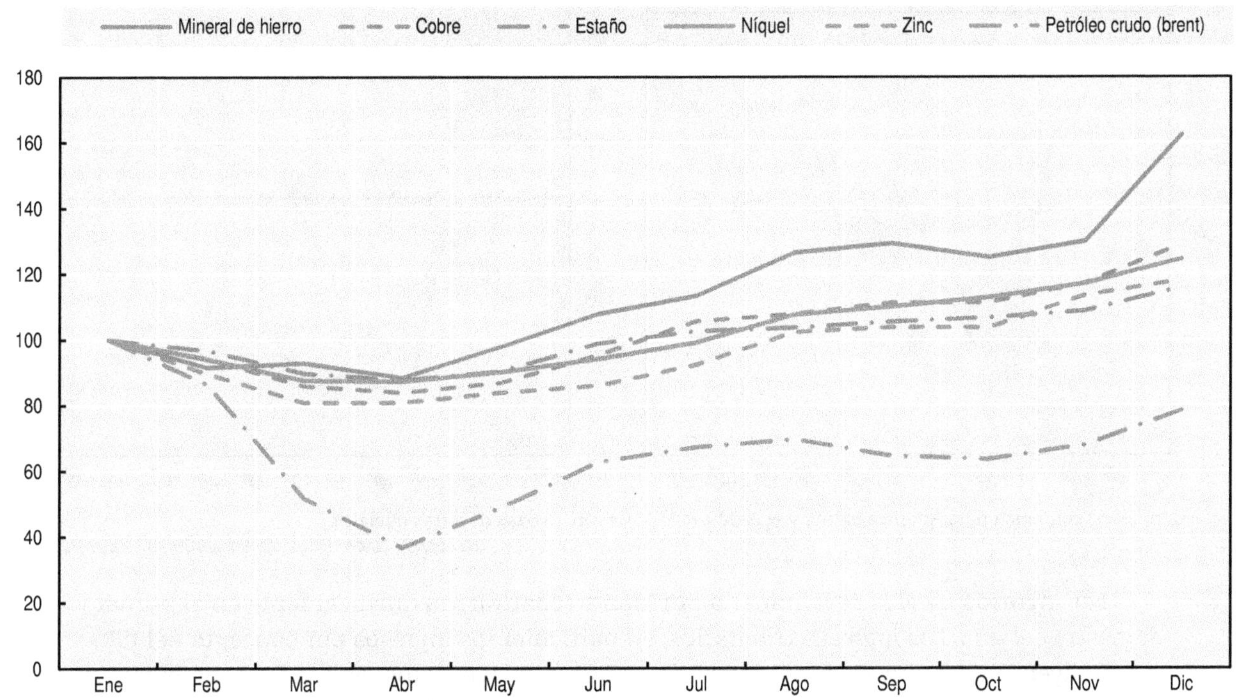

Fuente: Comisión Económica para América Latina y el Caribe (CEPAL), sobre la base de Datos de Precios de Materias Primas del Banco Mundial (The Pink Sheet), Banco Mundial.

StatLink https://doi.org/10.1787/888934234974

Los ingresos fiscales de los recursos naturales no renovables en ALC se movieron en gran medida con las condiciones del mercado global en 2020 (Gráfico 3.4). En la primera mitad del año, los ingresos por petróleo y gas en Ecuador y México, esencialmente rentas de propiedad ligadas al valor comercial de la producción, disminuyeron como resultado de la caída de los precios spot y los menores niveles de producción. En México, la producción de hidrocarburos se desaceleró entre mayo y julio en línea con los compromisos asumidos en el acuerdo OPEP + durante abril, aunque el país se negó a extender estas reducciones más allá de junio (PEMEX, 2020[8]). Además, los ingresos por el Derecho por la Utilidad Compartida, el mayor generador de ingresos por petróleo y gas, cayeron debido a la disminución de la tasa del gravamen del 65% al 58%, según lo estipulado en la Ley de Ingresos de Hidrocarburos de 2014. La producción de petróleo en Ecuador también se contrajo drásticamente en la primera mitad del año, un 60% interanual en abril y un 37% en mayo, debido en parte a la ruptura de la infraestructura de transporte de hidrocarburos en abril (BCE, 2020[23]; MEF Ecuador, 2020[24])[8]. A mediados de año, la tasa de disminución de los ingresos por petróleo y gas se vio atenuada por un aumento de los precios, pero por el año los ingresos cayeron marcadamente, un 38% en términos reales en Ecuador y un 56% en México.

Gráfico 3.4. **Ingresos fiscales de las administraciones públicas procedentes de recursos naturales no renovables en determinados países de América Latina, por productos básicos, 2020**

Variación interanual en porcentaje

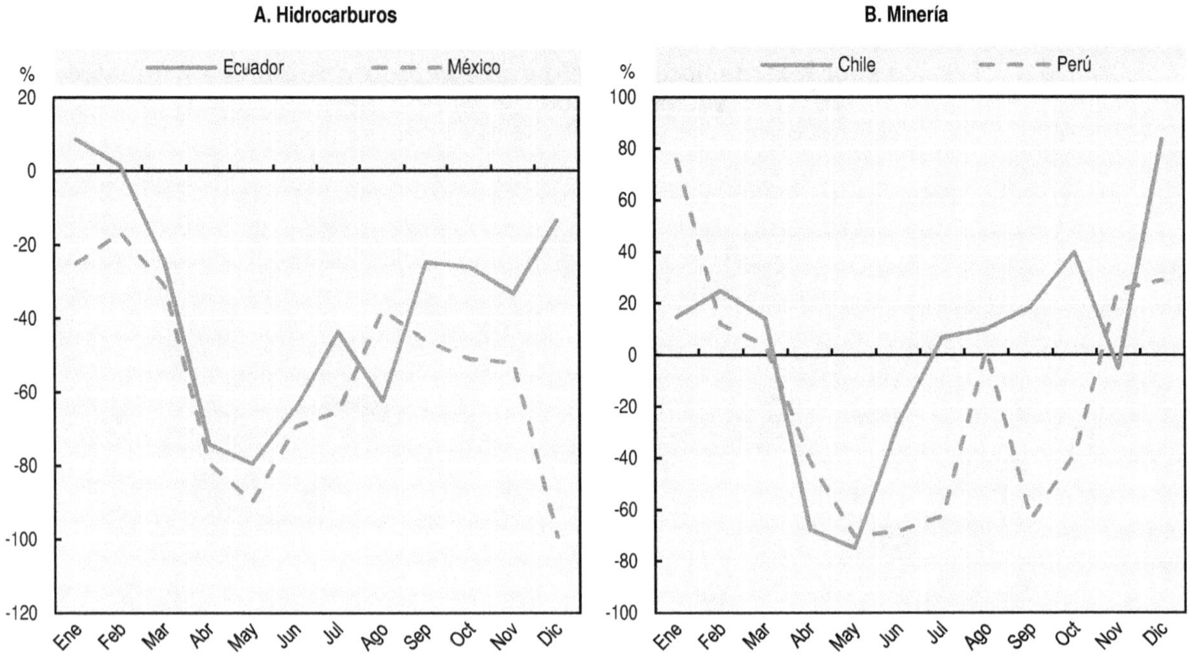

Fuente: Comisión Económica para América Latina y el Caribe (CEPAL), sobre la base de cifras oficiales.

StatLink https://doi.org/10.1787/888934234993

Los ingresos fiscales de la minería también se contrajeron drásticamente en el primer semestre del año. Los ingresos tributarios, en particular los ingresos por concepto del ISR, disminuyeron debido a la caída de precios, pagos de impuestos estimados más bajos y medidas de alivio tributario relacionadas con la pandemia COVID-19, como la postergación de pagos. Como resultado, los ingresos totales de la minería en Chile y Perú cayeron entre abril y julio, lo que refleja el importante papel que juega el ISR en la captura de las rentas económicas generadas por el sector. Sin embargo, en contraste con la tibia recuperación de los precios del crudo, el dinamismo de los precios de los minerales y metales en la segunda mitad del año apoyó un repunte de los ingresos mineros. El cuarto trimestre fue especialmente fuerte en Chile, aunque esto se debió en parte a un anticipo de USD 200 millones de dividendos de 2021 por parte de la productora estatal Codelco (DIPRES, 2020[25]). En Perú, a pesar de registrar un incremento más modesto en los últimos tres meses del año, debido a la debilidad de los ingresos tributarios, los ingresos no tributarios por regalías aumentaron fuertemente (+20% interanual en términos reales). No obstante, tomados en conjunto, los ingresos mineros se redujeron notablemente en 2020 en términos reales, un 21.6% en Perú y un 12.5% en Chile.

Proyectar los ingresos fiscales de fin de año provenientes de recursos naturales no renovables para ALC en este entorno está plagado de peligros. La evolución de la pandemia a nivel mundial y en la región sigue siendo incierta. Un repunte en los casos podría precipitar otra ronda de cierres que afectarían la actividad económica, ejerciendo presión a la baja sobre la demanda de materias primas. Las tensiones geopolíticas y comerciales siguen siendo elevadas y podrían alterar las condiciones del mercado, especialmente en el mercado mundial del petróleo. Las medidas de alivio tributario, cuyo efecto es difícil de modelar, podrían trasladar ciertos ingresos de 2020 a 2021. Asimismo, las pérdidas financieras esperadas de las empresas que operan en el sector podrían reducir significativamente los ingresos y, en algunos casos, pueden resultar en devoluciones de impuestos si los pagos anticipados exceden las obligaciones tributarias finales. Según los resultados de Ecuador y México, es probable que los ingresos petroleros en ALC en promedio terminen el año muy por debajo de sus niveles de 2019. De manera similar, es probable que los ingresos de la minería se contraigan, como revelan los datos finales en Chile y Perú, como resultado de la caída de los ingresos por concepto del ISR y la menor producción a pesar del rápido repunte de los precios internacionales.

Notas

1. La importancia de estos ingresos extraordinarios en los ingresos públicos totales no puede subestimarse. En Brasil, los ingresos totales del gobierno federal aumentaron del 21.6% del PIB en 2018 al 22.5% del PIB en 2019, un aumento de 0.9 puntos porcentuales del PIB. Excluir los ingresos por bonificaciones de firma de concesiones de petróleo y gas (1,0% del PIB) habría dejado los ingresos del gobierno federal prácticamente sin cambios, con consecuencias para los saldos general y primario. Asimismo, en Trinidad y Tobago, los ingresos totales del gobierno central aumentaron del 27.2% del PIB en 2018 al 28.8% del PIB en 2019, un aumento de 1.6 puntos porcentuales del PIB, principalmente gracias a los ingresos extraordinarios del petróleo (1.7% del PIB) que lograron compensar las disminuciones en otras fuentes.
2. Las estadísticas de la base de datos de la CEPAL sobre ingresos fiscales provenientes de recursos naturales no renovables en América Latina y el Caribe para México se actualizaron para referirse únicamente a los ingresos por petróleo y gas natural del gobierno federal.
3. Base de datos Comtrade de la ONU.
4. Comunicado de prensa de la World Bureau of Metal Statistics, "January to December 2019 Metals Balances", 19 de febrero de 2020.
5. La ley del mineral se refiere a la concentración de metal o mineral en el mismo.
6. Comunicado de prensa del Servicios de Impuestos Internos (SII) "Impuestos declarados en Operación Renta aumentaron un 16.2% real respecto del año anterior", 18 de julio de 2019.
7. Comunicado de Prensa de la SUNAT "Recaudación tributaria consolidó su recuperación y creció 3.7% el 2019", Nota de Prensa N ° 003-2020.
8. Ecuador no participó en los recortes de producción de la OPEP + de 2020. El país se retiró oficialmente de la OPEP a partir del 1 de enero de 2020.

Referencias

Banco Mundial (2020), *Commodity Markets Outlook, October 2020*, Banco Mundial, Washington, D.C., *https://openknowledge.worldbank.org/handle/10986/34621.* [22]

Banco Mundial (2019), *Commodity Markets Outlook, October 2019*, Banco Mundial, Washington, D.C., *https://openknowledge.worldbank.org/handle/10986/32633.* [11]

BCB (2020), *Memoria 2019*, Banco Central de Bolivia, *https://www.bcb.gob.bo/?q=pub_memorias-institucionales.* [4]

BCB (2019), *Memoria 2018*, Banco Central de Bolivia, *https://www.bcb.gob.bo/?q=pub_memorias-institucionales.* [14]

BCE (2020), *Información Estadística Mensual No. 2026 – Diciembre 2020*, Banco Central de Ecuador, *https://contenido.bce.fin.ec/home1/estadisticas/bolmensual/IEMensual.jsp.* [23]

BCE (2020), *Reporte del Sector Petrolero, IV Trimestre de 2019*, Banco Central de Ecuador, *https://contenido.bce.fin.ec/documentos/Estadisticas/Hidrocarburos/ASP201906.pdf.* [6]

Camimex (2020), *Informe Anual 2020*, Cámara Minera de México, *https://camimex.org.mx/application/files/4416/0204/8995/02_info_2020.pdf.* [18]

CEPAL (2021), *Balance Preliminar de las Economías de América Latina y el Caribe 2020*, Comisión Económica para América Latina y el Caribe, *https://www.cepal.org/es/publicaciones/46501-balance-preliminar-economias-america-latina-caribe-2020.* [20]

CEPAL (2020), *"Ingresos fiscales provenientes de recursos naturales no renovables"*, CEPALSTAT *(bases de datos)*, Comisión Económica para América Latina y el Caribe, *https://estadisticas.cepal.org/cepalstat/web_cepalstat/estadisticasIndicadores.asp?idioma=e.* [3]

CEPAL (2020), *Panorama Fiscal de América Latina y el Caribe 2020*, Comisión Económica para América Latina y el Caribe, *https://www.cepal.org/es/publicaciones/45730-panorama-fiscal-america-latina-caribe-2020-la-politica-fiscal-la-crisis-derivada.* [21]

DIPRES (2020), *Informe de Ejecución del Gobierno Central Cuarto Trimestre 2020*, Dirección de Presupuestos, Ministerio de Hacienda, Chile, *http://bibliotecadigital.dipres.gob.cl/handle/11626/17632.* [25]

DIPRES (2019), *Informe de Ejecución del Gobierno Central Cuarto Trimestre 2019*, Dirección de Presupuestos, Ministerio de Hacienda, Chile, *https://www.dipres.gob.cl/598/articles-187247_doc_pdf_Presentacion_IT.pdf.* [17]

EIA (2020), *Short-Term Energy Outlook, October 2020*, United States Energy Information Administration, *https://www.eia.gov/outlooks/steo/data.php?type=figures.* [1]

FMI (2019), *Informes de Perspectivas de la Economía Mundial, octubre de 2019*, Fondo Monetario Internacional, Washington, D.C., *https://www.imf.org/es/Publications/WEO/Issues/2019/10/01/world-economic-outlook-october-2019.* [10]

FMPED (2020), *Informe anual 2019*, Fondo Mexicano del Petróleo para la Estabilización y el Desarrollo, *https://www.fmped.org.mx/transparencia/%7BE2BBCC11-A6A2-F5FF-25D7-F1E291954902%7D.pdf.* [9]

Hanni, M., J. Jimenez y I. Ruelas (2018), *Ciclo de precios y regímenes fiscales vinculados con los recursos naturales no renovables en América Latina y el Caribe*, Serie de Macroeconomía del Desarrollo, Comisión Económica para América Latina y el Caribe, *https://www.cepal.org/es/publicaciones/44239-ciclo-precios-regimenes-fiscales-vinculados-recursos-naturales-renovables.* [13]

MEF Ecuador (2020), *Informe Semestral de Ejecución, Presupuesto General del Estado, Enero-Junio 2020*, Ministerio de Economía y Finanzas del Ecuador, *https://www.finanzas.gob.ec/wp-content/uploads/downloads/2020/09/28092020-Informe-semestral-ejecucion-2020-CNv6-RL.pdf.* [24]

MEF Perú (2020), *Marco Macroeconómico Multianual 2020-2023*, Ministerio de Economía y Finanzas del Perú, *https://www.mef.gob.pe/contenidos/pol_econ/marco_macro/MMM_2020_2023.pdf.* [19]

MINFIN (2019), *Liquidación del Presupuesto General de Ingresos y Egresos del Estado y Cierre Contable, Ejercicio fiscal Enero – Diciembre 2018*, Ministerio de Finanzas Públicas de Guatemala, *https://www.minfin.gob.gt/images/archivos/liquidacion/2018/enero_diciembre2018.pdf.* [7]

MSC (2020), *Reporte de Sostenibilidad 2019*, Minera San Cristóbal, *https://www.minerasancristobal.com/v3/es/wp-content/uploads/2020/09/Reporte_de_Sostenibilidad_2019_MSC.pdf.* [15]

OCDE et al. (2020), *Estadísticas tributarias en América Latina y el Caribe 2020*, Publicaciones de la OCDE, París, *https://doi.org/10.1787/68739b9b-en-es.* [12]

OPEP (2020), *Annual Statistical Bulletin 2020*, Organization of the Petroleum Exporting Countries, *https://www.opec.org/opec_web/en/publications/202.htm.* [2]

PEMEX (2020), *Annual Report submitted to the United States Securities and Exchange Commission (20-F)*, Petróleos Mexicanos, *https://www.pemex.com/en/investors/regulatory-filings/Paginas/sec-filings.aspx.* [8]

Petrobras (2020), *Annual Report and Form 20-F*, Petróleo Brasileiro S.A., *https://www.investidorpetrobras.com.br/en/results-and-notices/annual-reports/.* [5]

Vale (2020), *Relatório de Transparência Fiscal 2019*, Vale S.A., *http://www.vale.com/esg/pt/Documents/Relat%C3%B3rio%20de%20Transpar%C3%AAncia%20Fiscal%202019_pt%201.pdf.* [16]

Chapter 4

Tax levels and tax structures, 1990-2019

Capítulo 4

Niveles impositivos y estructuras tributarias, 1990-2019

Chapter 4 / Capítulo 4

4.1. Comparative tables, 1990-2019

In all of the following tables a (..) indicates not available. The main series in this volume cover the years 1990 to 2019.

Figures referring to 1991-99, 2001-06, 2008-09 and 2011-13 in Tables 4.1 to 4.2 and Tables 4.15 to 4.17, figures relating to 1991-99, 2001-09 and 2011-17 in Tables 4.5 to 4.10 and figures relating to 1990-94, 1996-99 and 2001-18 in Tables 4.11 to 4.13 have been omitted because of lack of space. Complete series are, however, available on line at *www.latameconomy.org* and in the database OECD (2021), "Revenue Statistics in Latin America: Comparative tables", *OECD Tax Statistics*, *http://dx.doi.org/10.1787/data-00641-en*.

4.2. Cuadros comparativos, 1990-2019

En todos los cuadros siguientes, (..) indica dato indisponible. Las principales series de datos de esta sección cubren el periodo que va de 1990 a 2019.

Las cifras relativas a 1991-99, 2001-06, 2008-09 y a 2011-13 en Cuadros 4.1 hasta 4.2 y Cuadros 4.15 hasta 4.17 y las cifras relativas a 1991-99, 2001-09 y 2011-17 en Cuadros 4.5 hasta 4.10 y las cifras relativas a 1990-94, 1996-99 y 2001-18 en Cuadros 4.11 hasta 4.13 se han omitido por falta de espacio. Sin embargo, las series completas están disponibles en línea en *www.latameconomy.org* y en la base de datos OCDE (2021), "Revenue Statistics in Latin America: Comparative tables", *OECD Tax Statistics*, *http://dx.doi.org/10.1787/data-00641-en*.

Table 4.1. **Total tax revenue as % of GDP, 1990-2019**
Cuadro 4.1. **Total de ingresos tributarios en % del PIB, 1990-2019**

	1990	2000	2007	2010	2014	2015	2016	2017	2018	2019
Antigua and Barbuda / Antigua y Barbuda[1]	..	11.9	21.6	21.3	19.9	20.4	19.6	19.6	19.0	18.2
Argentina[2]	13.3	19.2	26.4	29.1	31.1	31.5	30.7	30.0	28.9	28.6
Bahamas[1]	9.7	12.2	13.1	12.7	13.7	15.4	16.5	17.2	16.7	18.7
Barbados	25.3	30.9	30.0	30.0	28.9	29.6	31.2	32.1	33.1	33.1
Belize / Belice	21.6	19.1	25.7	26.9	27.9	27.5	28.3	28.7	30.2	32.4
Bolivia	6.5	20.1	22.2	22.9	27.9	29.5	27.9	25.9	25.0	24.7
Brazil / Brasil	27.8	29.4	33.6	32.4	31.8	32.0	32.2	32.3	33.2	33.1
Chile	16.9	18.8	22.7	19.6	19.6	20.4	20.1	20.2	21.1	20.7
Colombia	11.3	15.7	19.3	18.1	19.6	19.9	19.1	19.0	19.3	19.7
Costa Rica	22.5	21.1	23.1	22.1	22.6	22.9	23.5	23.0	23.2	23.6
Cuba	31.9	37.2	44.0	37.2	37.1	38.1	41.1	42.4	42.3	42.0
Dominican Republic / República Dominicana	8.3	12.3	15.0	12.4	13.5	13.0	13.1	13.2	13.2	13.5
Ecuador[1]	7.1	11.6	15.1	16.0	19.2	21.3	19.9	19.9	20.7	20.1
El Salvador	11.3	14.2	18.8	18.7	19.8	19.9	20.5	20.9	21.2	20.8
Guatemala	7.6	11.7	14.0	12.5	13.2	12.8	13.2	13.2	13.2	13.1
Guyana	15.2	15.7	15.6	16.0	17.8	18.1	18.4	19.5	22.2	23.2
Honduras	12.4	17.2	19.8	18.2	20.4	21.0	22.7	22.1	22.4	21.9
Jamaica	20.3	22.2	24.8	24.9	24.8	25.8	26.5	27.3	27.8	28.6
Mexico / México[3]	12.1	11.5	12.0	12.8	13.7	15.9	16.6	16.1	16.2	16.5
Nicaragua	..	14.3	18.8	19.3	21.8	22.3	23.3	23.8	23.2	25.9
Panama / Panamá	16.6	15.5	15.5	16.4	15.7	15.1	15.5	15.1	14.8	14.1
Paraguay	8.5	11.6	10.8	12.1	13.9	13.7	13.4	14.0	13.8	13.9
Peru / Perú	12.0	15.2	18.5	17.8	19.2	17.4	16.2	15.3	16.5	16.6
Saint Lucia / Santa Lucía[1]	..	19.6	20.9	20.3	20.5	21.2	21.3	20.2	20.7	21.1
Trinidad and Tobago / Trinidad y Tobago[1]	23.3	21.9	27.8	28.7	28.8	28.4	22.4	20.6	23.2	23.7
Uruguay[4]	20.0	23.2	25.7	26.3	27.4	27.4	27.8	29.0	29.2	29.0
Venezuela[5]	21.2	13.5	17.0	11.8	..	..	..	..	..	..
Unweighted average / Promedio no ponderado										
LAC / ALC[6]	**15.7**	**18.2**	**21.3**	**20.9**	**21.9**	**22.3**	**22.4**	**22.3**	**22.7**	**22.9**
OECD / OCDE[7]	**31.1**	**33.3**	**33.2**	**31.9**	**33.2**	**33.3**	**34.0**	**33.7**	**33.9**	**33.8**

.. Not available

Note: The figures exclude local government revenues for Antigua and Barbuda, Argentina (but include provincial revenues), the Bahamas, Barbados, Cuba (except for 2002-2012), the Dominican Republic, Saint Lucia, Trinidad and Tobago and Venezuela as the data are not available. Local government revenue data have been available since 1991 for Nicaragua, since 1994 for Bolivia, since 1995 for Guatemala, since 1998 for Jamaica, since 1999 for Panama, since 2000 for Peru, since 2002 for El Salvador and Guyana, since 2006 for Paraguay and since 1990 for all other countries.

1. The data include the following estimations: Antigua and Barbuda (social security contributions for 2019), Bahamas (social security contributions for 2018 and 2019), Ecuador (local tax revenues for 2019), Saint Lucia (social security contributions for 2018 and 2019) and Trinidad and Tobago (social security contributions for 2019). See the corresponding country tables for more information.
2. The tax-to-GDP may be under-estimated as it excludes certain types of social security contributions for which data are not readily available.
3. Data on state and local government revenues are not available. They are estimated in order to calculate the total tax-to-GDP ratio for 2019.
4. The tax-to-GDP ratio does not take into account the recent rebasing of GDP in Uruguay. Preliminary estimates of the rebased GDP indicate that the tax-to-GDP ratio in Uruguay would be about 2.3 percentage points lower on average for the 2016-2019 period.
5. Some tax revenue data are not available between 2014 and 2017 and therefore total figures have not been included. Data for 2018 and 2019 are not available.
6. Represents the group of 26 Latin American and Caribbean countries included in this publication and excludes Venezuela due to data availability issues. Chile, Colombia and Mexico are also part of the OECD (37) group.
7. Calculated by applying the unweighted average percentage change for 2019 in the 35 countries providing data for that year to the overall average tax to GDP ratio in 2018.

.. Non disponible

Nota: Las cifras excluyen los ingresos subnacionales para Antigua y Barbuda, Argentina (pero se incluyen los ingresos de las provincias), Las Bahamas, Barbados, Cuba (excepto 2002-2012), República Dominicana, Santa Lucía, Trinidad y Tobago y Venezuela, dado que los datos no están disponibles. Los datos de ingresos subnacionales están disponibles desde 1991 para Nicaragua, desde 1994 para Bolivia, desde 1995 para Guatemala, desde 1998 para Jamaica, desde 1999 para Panamá, desde 2000 para Perú, desde 2002 para El Salvador y Guyana, desde 2006 para Paraguay y desde 1990 para todos los demás países.

1. Los datos incluyen las siguientes estimaciones: Antigua y Barbuda (contribuciones a la seguridad social para 2019), Bahamas (contribuciones a la seguridad social para 2018 y 2019), Ecuador (ingresos tributarios locales para 2019), Santa Lucía (contribuciones a la seguridad social para 2018 y 2019) y Trinidad y Tobago (contribuciones a la seguridad social para 2019). Consulte las tablas de países correspondientes para obtener más información.

Table 4.1. **Total tax revenue as % of GDP, 1990-2019** *(cont.)*
Cuadro 4.1. **Total de ingresos tributarios en % del PIB, 1990-2019** *(cont.)*

2. La relación entre impuestos y PIB puede estar subestimada, ya que excluye ciertos tipos de contribuciones a la seguridad social para los que no hay datos disponibles.
3. No se dispone de datos sobre los ingresos de las administraciones estatales y locales. Se estiman para calcular la relación total entre impuestos y PIB para 2019.
4. El ratio impuestos/PIB no tiene en cuenta la reciente reevaluación del PIB en Uruguay. Las estimaciones preliminares del PIB rebasado indican que la relación entre impuestos y PIB en Uruguay sería aproximadamente 2,3 puntos porcentuales más baja en promedio para el período 2016-2019.
5. Algunos datos de ingresos tributarios no están disponibles entre 2014 y 2017 y, por lo tanto, no se han incluido las cifras totales. Los datos para 2018 y 2019 no están disponibles.
6. Representa al grupo de 26 países de América Latina y el Caribe incluidos en esta publicación y excluye a Venezuela debido a problemas de disponibilidad de datos. Chile, Colombia y México también forman parte del grupo OCDE (37).
7. Calculado mediante la aplicación del cambio porcentual promedio no ponderado para 2019 en los 35 países que proporcionan datos para ese año al promedio del recaudación tributario sobre PIB en 2018.

StatLink https://doi.org/10.1787/888934235164

Table 4.2. **Total tax revenue in millions of USD at market exchange rates, 1990-2019**
Cuadro 4.2. **Total de ingresos tributarios en millones de US dólares a tipos de cambio de mercado, 1990-2019**

	1990	2000	2007	2010	2014	2015	2016	2017	2018	2019
Antigua and Barbuda / Antigua y Barbuda[1]	..	99	283	244	248	272	281	287	305	302
Argentina	20 952	61 084	75 919	123 456	175 413	202 079	170 714	193 442	149 495	127 318
Bahamas[1]	505	965	1 360	1 277	1 490	1 761	1 940	2 118	2 126	2 509
Barbados	513	946	1 412	1 368	1 357	1 406	1 521	1 609	1 692	1 679
Belize / Belice	89	159	326	370	464	473	503	527	565	595
Bolivia	317	1 689	2 940	4 527	9 258	9 805	9 547	9 777	10 136	10 173
Brazil / Brasil	133 077	192 661	468 987	715 679	779 998	576 176	578 290	665 542	625 649	608 722
Chile	5 829	14 645	39 427	42 814	51 101	49 734	50 417	55 852	62 866	58 319
Colombia	5 136	14 655	39 791	51 858	74 509	58 412	53 960	59 206	64 384	63 715
Costa Rica	1 286	3 177	6 246	8 416	11 901	13 102	13 983	14 024	14 535	15 162
Cuba	6 870	11 367	25 787	23 949	29 940	33 182	37 597	41 021	42 307	43 504
Dominican Republic / República Dominicana	664	2 986	6 614	6 670	9 087	9 260	9 905	10 603	11 340	12 056
Ecuador[1]	1 078	2 125	7 698	11 133	19 577	21 146	19 883	20 745	22 238	21 608
El Salvador	543	1 669	3 192	3 447	4 478	4 659	4 963	5 230	5 539	5 629
Guatemala	573	2 129	4 782	5 153	7 650	7 944	8 734	9 481	9 643	10 018
Guyana	104	234	425	549	733	774	825	927	1 061	1 200
Honduras	515	1 219	2 426	2 867	4 024	4 415	4 927	5 117	5 350	5 459
Jamaica	1 027	1 998	3 192	3 286	3 433	3 647	3 744	4 026	4 338	4 514
Mexico / México	36 267	81 139	126 471	135 822	180 123	186 360	179 131	186 354	197 351	195 492
Nicaragua	..	733	1 399	1 693	2 586	2 846	3 092	3 288	3 025	3 244
Panama / Panamá	948	1 942	3 298	4 815	7 832	8 193	9 004	9 366	9 631	9 394
Paraguay	494	1 029	1 921	3 287	5 579	4 967	4 844	5 469	5 575	5 289
Peru / Perú	3 389	7 674	18 919	26 478	38 800	33 337	31 414	32 822	37 067	38 343
Saint Lucia / Santa Lucía[1]	..	178	283	307	363	387	404	407	431	437
Trinidad and Tobago / Trinidad y Tobago[1]	1 158	1 746	5 893	6 261	7 948	7 339	5 188	4 617	5 449	5 694
Uruguay	2 051	5 307	6 026	10 614	15 703	14 574	14 650	17 258	17 464	16 457
Venezuela[2]	10 259	12 758	39 055	38 220	..	..	..	..	..	..

.. Not available

Note: The figures exclude local government revenues for Antigua and Barbuda, Argentina (but include provincial revenues), the Bahamas, Barbados, Cuba (except for 2002-2012), the Dominican Republic, Saint Lucia, Trinidad and Tobago and Venezuela as the data are not available. Local government revenue data have been available since 1991 for Nicaragua, since 1994 for Bolivia, since 1995 for Guatemala, since 1998 for Jamaica, since 1999 for Panama, since 2000 for Peru, since 2002 for El Salvador and Guyana, since 2006 for Paraguay and since 1990 for all other countries.

1. The data include the following estimations: Antigua and Barbuda (social security contributions for 2019), Bahamas (social security contributions for 2018 and 2019), Ecuador (local tax revenues for 2019), Saint Lucia (social security contributions for 2018 and 2019) and Trinidad and Tobago (social security contributions for 2019). See the corresponding country tables for more information.
2. Some tax revenue data are not available between 2014 and 2017 and therefore total figures have not been included. Data for 2018 and 2019 are not available.

.. Non disponible

Nota: Las cifras excluyen los ingresos subnacionales para Antigua y Barbuda, Argentina (pero se incluyen los ingresos de las provincias), Las Bahamas, Barbados, Cuba (excepto 2002-2012), República Dominicana, Santa Lucía, Trinidad y Tobago y Venezuela, dado que los datos no están disponibles. Los datos de ingresos subnacionales están disponibles desde 1991 para Nicaragua, desde 1994 para Bolivia, desde 1995 para Guatemala, desde 1998 para Jamaica, desde 1999 para Panamá, desde 2000 para Perú, desde 2002 para El Salvador y Guyana, desde 2006 para Paraguay y desde 1990 para todos los demás países.

1. Los datos incluyen las siguientes estimaciones: Antigua y Barbuda (contribuciones a la seguridad social para 2019), Bahamas (contribuciones a la seguridad social para 2018 y 2019), Ecuador (ingresos tributarios locales para 2019), Santa Lucía (contribuciones a la seguridad social para 2018 y 2019) y Trinidad y Tobago (contribuciones a la seguridad social para 2019). Consulte las tablas de países correspondientes para obtener más información.
2. Algunos datos de ingresos tributarios no están disponibles entre 2014 y 2017 y, por lo tanto, no se han incluido las cifras totales. Los datos para 2018 y 2019 no están disponibles.

StatLink https://doi.org/10.1787/888934235183

Table 4.3. **Tax revenue of main headings as % of GDP, 2019**
Cuadro 4.3. **Ingresos tributarios en las principales partidas en % del PIB, 2019**

	1000 Income & profits / Ingresos y utilidades	2000 Social security / Seguridad social	3000 Payroll / Nómina	4000 Property / Propiedad	5000 Goods and services / Bienes y servicios	6000 Others / Otros
Antigua and Barbuda / Antigua y Barbuda[1]	1.8	3.2	0.0	1.6	11.6	0.0
Argentina	5.1	5.7	0.0	2.6	15.0	0.2
Bahamas[1]	0.0	2.3	0.0	2.6	13.8	0.0
Barbados	8.1	5.8	0.0	2.2	17.0	0.0
Belize / Belice	8.2	2.7	0.0	1.1	20.4	0.0
Bolivia	4.0	6.2	0.0	0.2	12.1	2.2
Brazil / Brasil	7.4	8.5	0.6	1.5	14.2	0.9
Chile	7.2	1.5	0.0	1.1	11.0	-0.1
Colombia	6.4	1.9	0.3	1.8	8.5	0.9
Costa Rica	4.9	8.1	1.4	0.4	8.2	0.5
Cuba	11.8	5.5	1.4	0.0	20.3	3.0
Dominican Republic / República Dominicana	4.3	0.1	0.1	0.6	8.5	0.0
Ecuador[1]	4.3	5.5	0.0	0.3	10.0	0.0
El Salvador	7.0	2.7	0.1	0.2	10.5	0.3
Guatemala	3.7	2.2	0.2	0.2	6.8	0.0
Guyana	8.8	2.2	0.0	0.5	11.6	0.2
Honduras	5.6	3.4	0.2	0.6	11.3	0.8
Jamaica	8.8	1.2	0.0	0.9	17.5	0.1
Mexico / México[2]	7.0	2.3	0.4	0.3	6.1	0.2
Nicaragua	8.0	6.7	0.0	0.3	10.8	0.2
Panama / Panamá	3.7	5.8	0.2	0.3	4.1	0.0
Paraguay	2.5	3.7	0.0	0.2	7.4	0.1
Peru / Perú	6.1	2.0	0.0	0.4	7.8	0.3
Saint Lucia / Santa Lucía[1]	4.6	2.2	0.0	0.5	13.8	0.0
Trinidad and Tobago / Trinidad y Tobago[1]	13.8	2.9	0.0	0.2	6.7	0.0
Uruguay	7.6	7.7	0.0	2.2	11.4	0.2
Venezuela[3]	..	..	..	..	..	..
Unweighted average / Promedio no ponderado						
LAC / ALC[4]	**6.2**	**3.9**	**0.2**	**0.9**	**11.4**	**0.4**
OECD / OCDE[5]	**11.5**	**9.0**	**0.4**	**1.9**	**10.9**	**0.1**

.. Not available

Note: The figures exclude local government revenues for Antigua and Barbuda, Argentina (but include provincial revenues), the Bahamas, Barbados, Cuba (except for 2002-2012), the Dominican Republic, Saint Lucia, Trinidad and Tobago and Venezuela as the data are not available. Local government revenue data have been available since 1991 for Nicaragua, since 1994 for Bolivia, since 1995 for Guatemala, since 1998 for Jamaica, since 1999 for Panama, since 2000 for Peru, since 2002 for El Salvador and Guyana, since 2006 for Paraguay and since 1990 for all other countries.

1. The data include the following estimations: Antigua and Barbuda (social security contributions for 2019), Bahamas (social security contributions for 2018 and 2019), Ecuador (local tax revenues for 2019), Saint Lucia (social security contributions for 2018 and 2019) and Trinidad and Tobago (social security contributions for 2019). See the corresponding country tables for more information.
2. Data for 2018 are used for 3000 and 4000 (local and state government data). Other data have been updated to 2019. Federal government data are used for 1000, 5000 and 6000.
3. Data for 2018 and 2019 are not available.
4. Represents the group of 26 Latin American and Caribbean countries included in this publication and excludes Venezuela due to data availability issues. Chile, Colombia and Mexico are also part of the OECD (37) group.
5. Represents the unweighted average for OECD member countries. Data for 2018 are used as data for 2019 were not available at the time of publication.

.. Non disponible

Nota: Las cifras excluyen los ingresos subnacionales para Antigua y Barbuda, Argentina (pero se incluyen los ingresos de las provincias), Las Bahamas, Barbados, Cuba (excepto 2002-2012), República Dominicana, Santa Lucía, Trinidad y Tobago y Venezuela, dado que los datos no están disponibles. Los datos de ingresos subnacionales están disponibles desde 1991 para Nicaragua, desde 1994 para Bolivia, desde 1995 para Guatemala, desde 1998 para Jamaica, desde 1999 para Panamá, desde 2000 para Perú, desde 2002 para El Salvador y Guyana, desde 2006 para Paraguay y desde 1990 para todos los demás países.

1. Los datos incluyen las siguientes estimaciones: Antigua y Barbuda (contribuciones a la seguridad social para 2019), Bahamas (contribuciones a la seguridad social para 2018 y 2019), Ecuador (ingresos tributarios locales para 2019), Santa Lucía (contribuciones a la seguridad social para 2018 y 2019) y Trinidad y Tobago (contribuciones a la seguridad social para 2019). Consulte las tablas de países correspondientes para obtener más información.
2. Los datos de 2018 se utilizan para 3000 y 4000 (datos del gobierno local y estatal). Los otros datos se han actualizado para 2019. Los datos del gobierno federal se utilizan para 1000, 5000 y 6000.
3. Los datos para 2018 y 2019 no están disponibles.
4. Representa al grupo de 26 países de América Latina y el Caribe incluidos en esta publicación y excluye a Venezuela debido a problemas de disponibilidad de datos. Chile, Colombia y México también forman parte del grupo OCDE (37).
5. Representa el promedio no ponderado de los países miembros de la OCDE. Se utilizan los datos de 2018 porque los datos de 2019 no estaban disponibles en el momento de la publicación.

StatLink https://doi.org/10.1787/888934235202

Table 4.4. **Tax revenue of main headings as % of total tax revenue, 2019**
Cuadro 4.4. **Ingresos tributarios en las principales partidas en % del total de ingresos tributarios, 2019**

	1000 Income & profits / Ingresos y utilidades	2000 Social security / Seguridad social	3000 Payroll / Nómina	4000 Property / Propiedad	5000 Goods and services / Bienes y servicios	6000 Others / Otros
Antigua and Barbuda / Antigua y Barbuda[1]	9.7	17.6	0.0	8.8	63.9	0.0
Argentina	18.0	20.0	0.0	9.1	52.2	0.7
Bahamas[1]	0.0	12.4	0.0	13.7	73.9	0.0
Barbados	24.5	17.5	0.0	6.7	51.3	0.0
Belize / Belice	25.2	8.4	0.0	3.5	62.9	0.0
Bolivia	16.3	25.1	0.0	0.7	49.0	8.9
Brazil / Brasil	22.4	25.7	1.8	4.6	42.8	2.7
Chile	34.8	7.3	0.0	5.4	53.1	-0.6
Colombia	32.3	9.5	1.7	9.1	42.9	4.4
Costa Rica	20.9	34.2	5.9	1.9	34.8	2.3
Cuba	28.2	13.2	3.3	0.0	48.3	7.1
Dominican Republic / República Dominicana	31.4	0.4	0.6	4.8	62.8	0.0
Ecuador[1]	21.6	27.1	0.0	1.6	49.6	0.1
El Salvador	33.5	12.8	0.7	0.8	50.6	1.6
Guatemala	28.4	16.8	1.2	1.5	52.0	0.0
Guyana	37.8	9.5	0.0	2.0	49.9	0.9
Honduras	25.6	15.6	0.7	2.5	51.6	3.9
Jamaica	30.9	4.1	0.0	3.2	61.5	0.4
Mexico / México[2]	44.0	13.4	2.5	2.0	36.4	1.7
Nicaragua	30.8	25.7	0.0	1.1	41.6	0.8
Panama / Panamá	26.0	41.5	1.5	1.8	28.9	0.3
Paraguay	18.2	26.4	0.0	1.3	53.4	0.6
Peru / Perú	36.5	12.1	0.1	2.4	47.2	1.7
Saint Lucia / Santa Lucía[1]	21.7	10.5	0.0	2.1	65.7	0.0
Trinidad and Tobago / Trinidad y Tobago[1]	58.1	12.4	0.0	1.1	28.5	0.0
Uruguay	26.1	26.4	0.0	7.7	39.1	0.6
Venezuela[3]	..	..	..	..	..	..
Unweighted average / Promedio no ponderado						
LAC / ALC[4]	**27.0**	**17.1**	**0.8**	**3.8**	**49.8**	**1.5**
OECD / OCDE[5]	**34.3**	**25.7**	**1.2**	**5.6**	**32.7**	**0.5**

.. Not available

Note: The figures exclude local government revenues for Antigua and Barbuda, Argentina (but include provincial revenues), the Bahamas, Barbados, Cuba (except for 2002-2012), the Dominican Republic, Saint Lucia, Trinidad and Tobago and Venezuela as the data are not available. Local government revenue data have been available since 1991 for Nicaragua, since 1994 for Bolivia, since 1995 for Guatemala, since 1998 for Jamaica, since 1999 for Panama, since 2000 for Peru, since 2002 for El Salvador and Guyana, since 2006 for Paraguay and since 1990 for all other countries.

1. The data include the following estimations: Antigua and Barbuda (social security contributions for 2019), Bahamas (social security contributions for 2018 and 2019), Ecuador (local tax revenues for 2019), Saint Lucia (social security contributions for 2018 and 2019) and Trinidad and Tobago (social security contributions for 2019). See the corresponding country tables for more information.
2. Data for 2018 are used for 3000 and 4000 (local and state government data). Other data have been updated to 2019. Federal government data are used for 1000, 5000 and 6000.
3. Data for 2018 and 2019 are not available.
4. Represents the group of 26 Latin American and Caribbean countries included in this publication and excludes Venezuela due to data availability issues. Chile, Colombia and Mexico are also part of the OECD (37) group.
5. Represents the unweighted average for OECD member countries. Data for 2018 are used as data for 2019 were not available at the time of publication.

.. Non disponible

Nota: Las cifras excluyen los ingresos subnacionales para Antigua y Barbuda, Argentina (pero se incluyen los ingresos de las provincias), Las Bahamas, Barbados, Cuba (excepto 2002-2012), República Dominicana, Santa Lucía, Trinidad y Tobago y Venezuela, dado que los datos no están disponibles. Los datos de ingresos subnacionales están disponibles desde 1991 para Nicaragua, desde 1994 para Bolivia, desde 1995 para Guatemala, desde 1998 para Jamaica, desde 1999 para Panamá, desde 2000 para Perú, desde 2002 para El Salvador y Guyana, desde 2006 para Paraguay y desde 1990 para todos los demás países.

1. Los datos incluyen las siguientes estimaciones: Antigua y Barbuda (contribuciones a la seguridad social para 2019), Bahamas (contribuciones a la seguridad social para 2018 y 2019), Ecuador (ingresos tributarios locales para 2019), Santa Lucía (contribuciones a la seguridad social para 2018 y 2019) y Trinidad y Tobago (contribuciones a la seguridad social para 2019). Consulte las tablas de países correspondientes para obtener más información.
2. Los datos de 2018 se utilizan para 3000 y 4000 (datos del gobierno local y estatal). Los otros datos se han actualizado para 2019. Los datos del gobierno federal se utilizan para 1000, 5000 y 6000.
3. Los datos para 2018 y 2019 no están disponibles.
4. Representa al grupo de 26 países de América Latina y el Caribe incluidos en esta publicación y excluye a Venezuela debido a problemas de disponibilidad de datos. Chile, Colombia y México también forman parte del grupo OCDE (37).
5. Representa el promedio no ponderado de los países miembros de la OCDE. Se utilizan los datos de 2018 porque los datos de 2019 no estaban disponibles en el momento de la publicación.

StatLink https://doi.org/10.1787/888934235221

Table 4.5. **Taxes on income and profits (1000) as % of GDP and as % of total tax revenue**
Cuadro 4.5. **Impuestos sobre la renta y las utilidades (1000) en % del PIB y del total de ingresos tributarios**

	% of GDP / % del PIB					% of total tax revenue / % del total de ingresos tributarios				
	1990	2000	2010	2018	2019	1990	2000	2010	2018	2019
Antigua and Barbuda / Antigua y Barbuda	..	1.7	3.0	1.8	1.8	..	14.0	14.0	9.5	9.7
Argentina	0.7	3.6	4.7	5.1	5.1	5.3	18.5	16.2	17.8	18.0
Bahamas	0.0	0.0	0.0	0.0	0.0	0.0	0.0	0.0	0.0	0.0
Barbados	6.1	9.8	8.4	9.0	8.1	24.3	31.7	28.0	27.2	24.5
Belize / Belice	4.5	4.6	9.0	7.6	8.2	20.9	23.9	33.6	25.3	25.2
Bolivia	0.4	2.3	4.6	3.8	4.0	6.7	11.6	20.0	15.2	16.3
Brazil / Brasil	5.1	5.7	6.7	7.1	7.4	18.3	19.5	20.5	21.5	22.4
Chile	3.9	4.4	7.5	7.5	7.2	23.2	23.3	38.1	35.8	34.8
Colombia	3.4	3.6	4.8	6.5	6.4	29.9	23.2	26.6	33.7	32.3
Costa Rica	2.3	2.8	3.8	4.7	4.9	10.0	13.2	17.1	20.4	20.9
Cuba	0.1	6.0	5.6	11.1	11.8	0.2	16.1	15.0	26.2	28.2
Dominican Republic / República Dominicana	2.2	2.7	2.7	4.0	4.3	26.0	22.3	21.9	30.4	31.4
Ecuador	0.9	1.5	3.4	4.9	4.3	12.9	12.6	21.2	23.6	21.6
El Salvador	2.0	3.6	5.4	7.0	7.0	17.6	25.7	28.9	32.8	33.5
Guatemala	1.5	2.3	3.1	3.8	3.7	19.7	19.9	24.8	28.8	28.4
Guyana	5.1	5.9	5.7	7.9	8.8	33.5	37.8	35.4	35.8	37.8
Honduras	2.5	2.7	4.4	6.3	5.6	20.3	15.9	24.3	28.0	25.6
Jamaica	10.3	9.9	10.3	8.5	8.8	50.9	44.8	41.3	30.8	30.9
Mexico / México[1]	4.1	4.1	5.1	7.1	7.0	34.0	36.0	39.8	44.0	44.0
Nicaragua	..	1.8	4.5	7.1	8.0	..	12.3	23.1	30.7	30.8
Panama / Panamá	3.8	3.9	4.5	4.1	3.7	22.9	25.0	27.4	27.7	26.0
Paraguay	1.0	1.5	1.6	2.3	2.5	12.1	13.1	13.4	16.5	18.2
Peru / Perú	0.7	2.9	6.5	5.9	6.1	5.8	19.0	36.5	36.1	36.5
Saint Lucia / Santa Lucía	..	5.6	5.5	4.8	4.6	..	28.6	27.1	23.1	21.7
Trinidad and Tobago / Trinidad y Tobago	12.3	12.4	19.6	12.2	13.8	52.7	56.8	68.5	52.7	58.1
Uruguay	0.9	3.2	5.3	7.7	7.6	4.7	13.6	20.0	26.3	26.1
Venezuela[2]	17.7	5.8	3.6	..	..	83.7	43.2	30.7	..	..
Unweighted average / Promedio no ponderado										
LAC / ALC[3]	**3.2**	**4.2**	**5.6**	**6.1**	**6.2**	**19.7**	**22.2**	**26.3**	**26.9**	**27.0**
OECD / OCDE[4]	**11.8**	**11.7**	**10.4**	**11.5**	..	**37.2**	**34.5**	**32.6**	**34.3**	..

.. Not available

Note: The figures exclude local government revenues for Antigua and Barbuda, Argentina (but include provincial revenues), the Bahamas, Barbados, Cuba (except for 2002-2012), the Dominican Republic, Saint Lucia, Trinidad and Tobago and Venezuela as the data are not available. Local government revenue data have been available since 1991 for Nicaragua, since 1994 for Bolivia, since 1995 for Guatemala, since 1998 for Jamaica, since 1999 for Panama, since 2000 for Peru, since 2002 for El Salvador and Guyana, since 2006 for Paraguay and since 1990 for all other countries.

1. For the figures as % of total tax revenue in 2019, data for 2018 are used as the state and local government revenue data for 2019 are not available.
2. Some tax revenue data between 2014 and 2017 are not available. In those years data as % of total tax revenue cannot be calculated. All data for 2018 and 2019 are not available.
3. Represents the group of 26 Latin American and Caribbean countries included in this publication and excludes Venezuela due to data availability issues. Chile, Colombia and Mexico are also part of the OECD (37) group.
4. Represents the unweighted average for OECD member countries.

.. Non disponible

Nota: Las cifras excluyen los ingresos subnacionales para Antigua y Barbuda, Argentina (pero se incluyen los ingresos de las provincias), Las Bahamas, Barbados, Cuba (excepto 2002-2012), República Dominicana, Santa Lucía, Trinidad y Tobago y Venezuela, dado que los datos no están disponibles. Los datos de ingresos subnacionales están disponibles desde 1991 para Nicaragua, desde 1994 para Bolivia, desde 1995 para Guatemala, desde 1998 para Jamaica, desde 1999 para Panamá, desde 2000 para Perú, desde 2002 para El Salvador y Guyana, desde 2006 para Paraguay y desde 1990 para todos los demás países.

1. Para los ingresos como porcentaje de los ingresos tributarios totales en 2019, se utilizan los datos de 2018 porque los datos de ingresos de los gobiernos estatales y locales no están disponibles para 2019.
2. Algunos datos de ingresos tributarios entre 2014 y 2017 no están disponibles. Para esos años, no se pueden calcular los ingresos como porcentaje de los ingresos tributarios totales. No están disponibles todos los datos de 2018 y 2019.
3. Representa al grupo de 26 países de América Latina y el Caribe incluidos en esta publicación y excluye a Venezuela debido a problemas de disponibilidad de datos. Chile, Colombia y México también forman parte del grupo OCDE (37).
4. Representa el promedio no ponderado para los países miembros de la OCDE.

StatLink https://doi.org/10.1787/888934235240

Table 4.6. **Social security contributions (2000) as % of GDP and as % of total tax revenue**
Cuadro 4.6. **Contribuciones a la seguridad social (2000) en % del PIB y del total de ingresos tributarios**

	% of GDP / % del PIB					% of total tax revenue / % del total de ingresos tributarios				
	1990	2000	2010	2018	2019	1990	2000	2010	2018	2019
Antigua and Barbuda / Antigua y Barbuda[1]	..	..	2.7	3.3	3.2	..	..	12.6	17.4	17.6
Argentina	3.4	3.0	6.2	6.3	5.7	25.3	15.8	21.2	21.7	20.0
Bahamas[1]	1.3	1.5	1.7	2.3	2.3	13.2	11.9	13.1	13.6	12.4
Barbados	3.3	4.8	6.2	5.6	5.8	13.1	15.6	20.6	16.9	17.5
Belize / Belice	1.2	1.1	2.2	2.3	2.7	5.7	5.8	8.2	7.7	8.4
Bolivia	0.0	3.8	3.8	6.0	6.2	0.0	18.9	16.7	24.1	25.1
Brazil / Brasil	6.8	7.0	8.1	8.5	8.5	24.3	23.7	25.1	25.6	25.7
Chile	1.5	1.4	1.3	1.5	1.5	9.0	7.3	6.8	6.9	7.3
Colombia	0.9	2.6	2.1	1.8	1.9	7.9	16.3	11.7	9.6	9.5
Costa Rica	6.5	6.4	7.3	8.0	8.1	28.9	30.4	33.1	34.3	34.2
Cuba	3.5	3.9	4.6	5.2	5.5	11.0	10.4	12.4	12.3	13.2
Dominican Republic / República Dominicana	0.1	0.1	0.1	0.1	0.1	0.8	1.0	0.8	0.4	0.4
Ecuador	1.6	1.2	3.7	5.2	5.5	22.5	10.7	22.8	24.9	27.1
El Salvador	2.2	2.8	2.5	2.7	2.7	19.2	19.5	13.6	12.7	12.8
Guatemala	1.3	1.8	1.9	2.2	2.2	17.0	15.5	15.2	16.7	16.8
Guyana	0.6	1.8	1.4	2.1	2.2	3.7	11.4	9.0	9.6	9.5
Honduras	1.0	1.6	2.9	3.4	3.4	8.5	9.4	15.9	15.0	15.6
Jamaica	..	..	0.7	1.0	1.2	..	..	2.9	3.7	4.1
Mexico / México[2]	2.0	2.1	2.1	2.2	2.3	16.8	18.0	16.2	13.4	13.4
Nicaragua	..	2.6	4.3	6.0	6.7	..	18.0	22.4	25.8	25.7
Panama / Panamá	5.7	5.9	5.6	5.8	5.8	34.2	38.2	34.0	39.4	41.5
Paraguay	0.4	3.0	2.8	3.5	3.7	4.8	25.6	22.7	25.7	26.4
Peru / Perú	0.9	1.8	1.9	2.0	2.0	7.8	11.9	10.6	12.2	12.1
Saint Lucia / Santa Lucía[1]	..	2.0	2.3	2.2	2.2	..	10.0	11.1	10.7	10.5
Trinidad and Tobago / Trinidad y Tobago[1]	0.9	1.4	1.9	2.9	2.9	3.7	6.4	6.7	12.7	12.4
Uruguay[3]	6.0	6.4	6.2	7.6	7.7	29.9	27.5	23.4	26.1	26.4
Venezuela[4]	1.0	0.7	1.0	..	..	4.9	5.4	8.1	..	..
Unweighted average / Promedio no ponderado										
LAC / ALC[5]	**2.3**	**2.9**	**3.3**	**3.8**	**3.9**	**14.0**	**15.8**	**15.7**	**16.9**	**17.1**
OECD / OCDE[6]	**7.1**	**8.4**	**8.7**	**9.0**	..	**21.5**	**24.8**	**26.4**	**25.7**	..

.. Not available

Note: The figures exclude local government revenues for Antigua and Barbuda, Argentina (but include provincial revenues), the Bahamas, Barbados, Cuba (except for 2002-2012), the Dominican Republic, Saint Lucia, Trinidad and Tobago and Venezuela as the data are not available. Local government revenue data have been available since 1991 for Nicaragua, since 1994 for Bolivia, since 1995 for Guatemala, since 1998 for Jamaica, since 1999 for Panama, since 2000 for Peru, since 2002 for El Salvador and Guyana, since 2006 for Paraguay and since 1990 for all other countries.

1. The social security contributions data are estimated in the following countries: Antigua and Barbuda (2019), Bahamas (2018 and 2019), Saint Lucia (2018 and 2019) and Trinidad and Tobago (2019).
2. For the figures as % of total tax revenue in 2019, data for 2018 are used as the state and local government revenue data for 2019 are not available.
3. Figures for 1990-98 are estimated by the Direction General of Taxes as the methodology they use to calculate social security contributions was not employed until 1999.
4. Some tax revenue data between 2014 and 2017 are not available. In those years data as % of total tax revenue cannot be calculated. All data for 2018 and 2019 are not available.
5. Represents the group of 26 Latin American and Caribbean countries included in this publication and excludes Venezuela due to data availability issues. Chile, Colombia and Mexico are also part of the OECD (37) group.
6. Represents the unweighted average for OECD member countries.

.. Non disponible

Nota: Las cifras excluyen los ingresos subnacionales para Antigua y Barbuda, Argentina (pero se incluyen los ingresos de las provincias), Las Bahamas, Barbados, Cuba (excepto 2002-2012), República Dominicana, Santa Lucía, Trinidad y Tobago y Venezuela, dado que los datos no están disponibles. Los datos de ingresos subnacionales están disponibles desde 1991 para Nicaragua, desde 1994 para Bolivia, desde 1995 para Guatemala, desde 1998 para Jamaica, desde 1999 para Panamá, desde 2000 para Perú, desde 2002 para El Salvador y Guyana, desde 2006 para Paraguay y desde 1990 para todos los demás países.

1. Los datos de las cotizaciones a la seguridad social se estiman en los siguientes países: Antigua y Barbuda (2019), Bahamas (2018 y 2019), Santa Lucía (2018 y 2019) y Trinidad y Tobago (2019).

Table 4.6. **Social security contributions (2000) as % of GDP and as % of total tax revenue** *(cont.)*
Cuadro 4.6. **Contribuciones a la seguridad social (2000) en % del PIB y del total de ingresos tributarios** *(cont.)*

2. Para los ingresos como porcentaje de los ingresos tributarios totales en 2019, se utilizan los datos de 2018 porque los datos de ingresos de los gobiernos estatales y locales no están disponibles para 2019.
3. Las cifras de 1990-98 son estimaciones de la Dirección General de Impuestos dado que el empleo de la metodología actual utilizada para calcular las contribuciones a la seguridad social tuvo lugar en 1999.
4. Algunos datos de ingresos tributarios entre 2014 y 2017 no están disponibles. Para esos años, no se pueden calcular los ingresos como porcentaje de los ingresos tributarios totales. No están disponibles todos los datos de 2018 y 2019.
5. Representa al grupo de 26 países de América Latina y el Caribe incluidos en esta publicación y excluye a Venezuela debido a problemas de disponibilidad de datos. Chile, Colombia y México también forman parte del grupo OCDE (37).
6. Representa el promedio no ponderado para los países miembros de la OCDE.

StatLink https://doi.org/10.1787/888934235259

Table 4.7. **Taxes on payroll (3000) as % of GDP and as % of total tax revenue**
Cuadro 4.7. **Impuestos sobre la nómina (3000) en % del PIB y del total ingresos tributarios**

	% of GDP / % del PIB					% of total tax revenue / % del total de ingresos tributarios				
	1990	2000	2010	2018	2019	1990	2000	2010	2018	2019
Antigua and Barbuda / Antigua y Barbuda	..	0.0	0.0	0.0	0.0	..	0.0	0.0	0.0	0.0
Argentina	0.0	0.0	0.0	0.0	0.0	0.0	0.0	0.0	0.0	0.0
Bahamas	0.0	0.0	0.0	0.0	0.0	0.0	0.0	0.0	0.0	0.0
Barbados	0.0	0.0	0.0	0.0	0.0	0.0	0.0	0.0	0.0	0.0
Belize / Belice	0.0	0.0	0.0	0.0	0.0	0.0	0.0	0.0	0.0	0.0
Bolivia	0.0	0.0	0.0	0.0	0.0	0.0	0.0	0.0	0.0	0.0
Brazil / Brasil	0.4	0.5	0.5	0.6	0.6	1.6	1.5	1.7	1.8	1.8
Chile	0.0	0.0	0.0	0.0	0.0	0.0	0.0	0.0	0.0	0.0
Colombia	0.0	0.7	0.7	0.4	0.3	0.0	4.2	4.1	1.8	1.7
Costa Rica	1.4	1.3	1.3	1.4	1.4	6.4	6.3	5.9	6.0	5.9
Cuba	0.0	3.2	6.9	1.3	1.4	0.0	8.5	18.4	3.0	3.3
Dominican Republic / República Dominicana	0.0	0.0	0.1	0.1	0.1	0.0	0.0	0.6	0.6	0.6
Ecuador	0.0	0.0	0.0	0.0	0.0	0.0	0.0	0.0	0.0	0.0
El Salvador	0.0	0.0	0.1	0.1	0.1	0.0	0.0	0.6	0.7	0.7
Guatemala	0.0	0.0	0.1	0.2	0.2	0.0	0.0	1.1	1.2	1.2
Guyana	0.0	0.0	0.0	0.0	0.0	0.0	0.0	0.0	0.0	0.0
Honduras	0.0	0.0	0.2	0.2	0.2	0.0	0.0	0.9	0.8	0.7
Jamaica	0.0	0.0	0.0	0.0	0.0	0.0	0.0	0.0	0.0	0.0
Mexico / México[1]	0.2	0.2	0.3	0.4	0.4	1.8	1.5	2.2	2.5	2.5
Nicaragua	..	0.0	0.0	0.0	0.0	..	0.0	0.0	0.0	0.0
Panama / Panamá	0.0	0.3	0.2	0.2	0.2	0.0	1.9	1.2	1.3	1.5
Paraguay	0.0	0.0	0.0	0.0	0.0	0.0	0.0	0.0	0.0	0.0
Peru / Perú	0.0	0.7	0.0	0.0	0.0	0.0	4.4	0.1	0.1	0.1
Saint Lucia / Santa Lucía	..	0.0	0.0	0.0	0.0	..	0.0	0.0	0.0	0.0
Trinidad and Tobago / Trinidad y Tobago	0.0	0.0	0.0	0.0	0.0	0.0	0.0	0.0	0.0	0.0
Uruguay	0.0	0.0	0.0	0.0	0.0	0.0	0.0	0.0	0.0	0.0
Venezuela[2]	0.0	0.0	0.0	..	..	0.0	0.0	0.0	..	..
Unweighted average / Promedio no ponderado										
LAC / ALC[3]	**0.1**	**0.3**	**0.4**	**0.2**	**0.2**	**0.4**	**1.1**	**1.4**	**0.8**	**0.8**
OECD / OCDE[4]	**0.3**	**0.4**	**0.3**	**0.4**	..	**1.0**	**1.0**	**1.0**	**1.2**	..

.. Not available

Note: The figures exclude local government revenues for Antigua and Barbuda, Argentina (but include provincial revenues), the Bahamas, Barbados, Cuba (except for 2002-2012), the Dominican Republic, Saint Lucia, Trinidad and Tobago and Venezuela as the data are not available. Local government revenue data have been available since 1991 for Nicaragua, since 1994 for Bolivia, since 1995 for Guatemala, since 1998 for Jamaica, since 1999 for Panama, since 2000 for Peru, since 2002 for El Salvador and Guyana, since 2006 for Paraguay and since 1990 for all other countries.

1. For the figures in 2019, data for 2018 are used as the data for 2019 are not available.
2. Some tax revenue data between 2014 and 2017 are not available. In those years data as % of total tax revenue cannot be calculated. All data for 2018 and 2019 are not available.
3. Represents the group of 26 Latin American and Caribbean countries included in this publication and excludes Venezuela due to data availability issues. Chile, Colombia and Mexico are also part of the OECD (37) group.
4. Represents the unweighted average for OECD member countries.

.. Non disponible

Nota: Las cifras excluyen los ingresos subnacionales para Antigua y Barbuda, Argentina (pero se incluyen los ingresos de las provincias), Las Bahamas, Barbados, Cuba (excepto 2002-2012), República Dominicana, Santa Lucía, Trinidad y Tobago y Venezuela, dado que los datos no están disponibles. Los datos de ingresos subnacionales están disponibles desde 1991 para Nicaragua, desde 1994 para Bolivia, desde 1995 para Guatemala, desde 1998 para Jamaica, desde 1999 para Panamá, desde 2000 para Perú, desde 2002 para El Salvador y Guyana, desde 2006 para Paraguay y desde 1990 para todos los demás países.

1. Para los datos de 2019 se utilizan los datos de 2018, ya que los de 2019 no están disponibles.
2. Algunos datos de ingresos tributarios entre 2014 y 2017 no están disponibles. Para esos años, no se pueden calcular los ingresos como porcentaje de los ingresos tributarios totales. No están disponibles todos los datos de 2018 y 2019.
3. Representa al grupo de 26 países de América Latina y el Caribe incluidos en esta publicación y excluye a Venezuela debido a problemas de disponibilidad de datos. Chile, Colombia y México también forman parte del grupo OCDE (37).
4. Representa el promedio no ponderado para los países miembros de la OCDE.

StatLink https://doi.org/10.1787/888934235278

Table 4.8. **Taxes on property (4000) as % of GDP and as % of total tax revenue**
Cuadro 4.8. **Impuestos sobre la propiedad (4000) en % del PIB y del total de ingresos tributarios**

	% of GDP / % del PIB					% of total tax revenue / % del total de ingresos tributarios				
	1990	2000	2010	2018	2019	1990	2000	2010	2018	2019
Antigua and Barbuda / Antigua y Barbuda	..	0.6	1.6	1.4	1.6	..	4.9	7.5	7.6	8.8
Argentina	1.5	1.2	2.6	2.7	2.6	11.4	6.3	9.0	9.3	9.1
Bahamas	1.1	2.6	2.7	1.9	2.6	11.2	21.6	21.1	11.2	13.7
Barbados	3.6	1.8	1.4	1.7	2.2	14.4	5.7	4.8	5.1	6.7
Belize / Belice	4.2	0.8	0.8	1.3	1.1	19.2	4.2	3.1	4.4	3.5
Bolivia	0.0	0.0	0.3	0.2	0.2	0.1	0.0	1.2	0.8	0.7
Brazil / Brasil	1.6	2.0	1.4	1.5	1.5	5.9	6.7	4.2	4.4	4.6
Chile	1.0	1.3	0.8	1.1	1.1	6.2	7.0	4.1	5.2	5.4
Colombia	0.2	1.0	1.6	1.5	1.8	2.2	6.6	8.7	8.0	9.1
Costa Rica	0.3	0.2	0.3	0.4	0.4	1.3	0.9	1.5	1.8	1.9
Cuba	0.0	0.0	0.0	0.0	0.0	0.0	0.0	0.0	0.0	0.0
Dominican Republic / República Dominicana	0.1	0.2	0.7	0.6	0.6	1.2	1.4	5.4	4.6	4.8
Ecuador	0.1	0.1	0.2	0.3	0.3	1.5	0.8	1.4	1.7	1.6
El Salvador	0.5	0.1	0.1	0.5	0.2	4.8	0.7	0.6	2.2	0.8
Guatemala	0.4	0.2	0.4	0.2	0.2	5.8	2.1	2.9	1.9	1.5
Guyana	0.2	0.3	0.3	0.5	0.5	1.0	1.6	1.8	2.2	2.0
Honduras	0.1	0.3	0.3	0.6	0.6	0.7	1.5	1.8	2.5	2.5
Jamaica	2.5	1.1	0.9	1.2	0.9	12.5	4.9	3.5	4.4	3.2
Mexico / México[1]	0.2	0.2	0.3	0.3	0.3	1.9	1.8	2.3	2.0	2.0
Nicaragua	..	0.0	0.2	0.2	0.3	..	0.1	1.2	1.0	1.1
Panama / Panamá	0.6	0.3	0.5	0.4	0.3	3.4	2.2	2.9	2.5	1.8
Paraguay	0.2	0.2	0.2	0.2	0.2	2.8	2.0	1.8	1.3	1.3
Peru / Perú	1.6	0.2	0.5	0.4	0.4	13.6	1.2	3.0	2.2	2.4
Saint Lucia / Santa Lucía	..	0.4	0.5	0.5	0.5	..	2.2	2.3	2.3	2.1
Trinidad and Tobago / Trinidad y Tobago	0.4	0.3	0.1	0.2	0.2	1.8	1.6	0.5	1.0	1.1
Uruguay	1.8	2.0	2.3	2.2	2.2	8.9	8.6	8.9	7.6	7.7
Venezuela[2]	0.1	0.5	0.0	..	..	0.3	3.7	0.2	..	..
Unweighted average / Promedio no ponderado										
LAC / ALC[3]	**1.0**	**0.7**	**0.8**	**0.8**	**0.9**	**5.7**	**3.7**	**4.0**	**3.7**	**3.8**
OECD / OCDE[4]	**1.7**	**1.7**	**1.7**	**1.9**	..	**5.6**	**5.5**	**5.5**	**5.6**	..

.. Not available

Note: The figures exclude local government revenues for Antigua and Barbuda, Argentina (but include provincial revenues), the Bahamas, Barbados, Cuba (except for 2002-2012), the Dominican Republic, Saint Lucia, Trinidad and Tobago and Venezuela as the data are not available. Local government revenue data have been available since 1991 for Nicaragua, since 1994 for Bolivia, since 1995 for Guatemala, since 1998 for Jamaica, since 1999 for Panama, since 2000 for Peru, since 2002 for El Salvador and Guyana, since 2006 for Paraguay and since 1990 for all other countries.

1. For the figures in 2019, data for 2018 are used as the data for 2019 are not available.
2. Some tax revenue data between 2014 and 2017 are not available. In those years data as % of total tax revenue cannot be calculated. All data for 2018 and 2019 are not available.
3. Represents the group of 26 Latin American and Caribbean countries included in this publication and excludes Venezuela due to data availability issues. Chile, Colombia and Mexico are also part of the OECD (37) group.
4. Represents the unweighted average for OECD member countries.

.. Non disponible

Nota: Las cifras excluyen los ingresos subnacionales para Antigua y Barbuda, Argentina (pero se incluyen los ingresos de las provincias), Las Bahamas, Barbados, Cuba (excepto 2002-2012), República Dominicana, Santa Lucía, Trinidad y Tobago y Venezuela, dado que los datos no están disponibles. Los datos de ingresos subnacionales están disponibles desde 1991 para Nicaragua, desde 1994 para Bolivia, desde 1995 para Guatemala, desde 1998 para Jamaica, desde 1999 para Panamá, desde 2000 para Perú, desde 2002 para El Salvador y Guyana, desde 2006 para Paraguay y desde 1990 para todos los demás países.

1. Para los datos de 2019 se utilizan los datos de 2018, ya que los de 2019 no están disponibles.
2. Algunos datos de ingresos tributarios entre 2014 y 2017 no están disponibles. Para esos años, no se pueden calcular los ingresos como porcentaje de los ingresos tributarios totales. No están disponibles todos los datos de 2018 y 2019.
3. Representa al grupo de 26 países de América Latina y el Caribe incluidos en esta publicación y excluye a Venezuela debido a problemas de disponibilidad de datos. Chile, Colombia y México también forman parte del grupo OCDE (37).
4. Representa el promedio no ponderado para los países miembros de la OCDE.

StatLink https://doi.org/10.1787/888934235297

Table 4.9. **Taxes on goods and services (5000) as % of GDP and as % of total tax revenue**

Cuadro 4.9. **Impuestos sobre bienes y servicios (5000) en % del PIB y del total de ingresos tributarios**

	% of GDP / % del PIB					% of total tax revenue / % del total de ingresos tributarios				
	1990	2000	2010	2018	2019	1990	2000	2010	2018	2019
Antigua and Barbuda / Antigua y Barbuda	..	9.7	14.0	12.4	11.6	..	81.1	65.9	65.5	63.9
Argentina	7.3	10.9	15.2	14.6	15.0	55.2	56.5	52.4	50.4	52.2
Bahamas	7.4	7.9	7.8	12.5	13.8	76.4	64.3	61.1	75.2	73.9
Barbados	12.2	14.5	14.0	16.8	17.0	48.2	47.0	46.6	50.8	51.3
Belize / Belice	11.7	12.7	14.8	18.9	20.4	54.1	66.1	55.2	62.6	62.9
Bolivia	5.9	12.8	12.9	12.7	12.1	90.2	63.6	56.4	50.6	49.0
Brazil / Brasil	13.5	14.1	14.9	14.7	14.2	48.7	48.0	45.9	44.2	42.8
Chile	10.6	12.0	10.0	11.2	11.0	62.9	63.8	51.2	53.3	53.1
Colombia	6.1	7.3	8.2	8.3	8.5	53.8	46.3	45.1	42.8	42.9
Costa Rica	10.2	9.9	8.9	8.1	8.2	45.5	46.7	40.3	35.0	34.8
Cuba	27.7	22.0	19.1	22.0	20.3	86.9	59.2	51.3	51.9	48.3
Dominican Republic / República Dominicana	5.8	9.1	8.8	8.5	8.5	69.5	74.2	71.4	64.0	62.8
Ecuador	4.5	8.8	8.7	10.3	10.0	63.0	75.7	54.5	49.7	49.6
El Salvador	5.4	7.7	10.2	10.6	10.5	47.7	54.1	54.5	49.9	50.6
Guatemala	4.4	7.3	7.0	6.8	6.8	57.5	62.4	56.0	51.4	52.0
Guyana	6.4	7.6	8.5	11.4	11.6	42.0	48.6	53.0	51.4	49.9
Honduras	8.2	11.7	9.7	11.6	11.3	66.2	68.0	53.1	51.8	51.6
Jamaica	7.4	11.1	13.0	16.8	17.5	36.4	50.1	52.1	60.6	61.5
Mexico / México[1]	5.3	4.8	4.9	5.9	6.1	44.0	41.7	38.0	36.4	36.4
Nicaragua	..	8.6	10.1	9.7	10.8	..	60.0	52.4	41.7	41.6
Panama / Panamá	6.1	4.9	5.5	4.2	4.1	36.8	31.3	33.7	28.6	28.9
Paraguay	6.1	6.7	7.3	7.7	7.4	72.1	58.0	60.5	56.0	53.4
Peru / Perú	8.5	9.2	8.6	7.9	7.8	71.4	60.8	48.6	48.1	47.2
Saint Lucia / Santa Lucía	..	11.6	12.1	13.3	13.8	..	59.1	59.5	64.0	65.7
Trinidad and Tobago / Trinidad y Tobago	9.7	7.7	7.0	7.8	6.7	41.7	35.2	24.3	33.6	28.5
Uruguay	11.3	11.6	12.4	11.5	11.4	56.6	50.1	47.1	39.4	39.1
Venezuela[2]	2.4	6.4	7.2	..	..	11.1	47.7	61.1	..	..
Unweighted average / Promedio no ponderado										
LAC / ALC[3]	**8.8**	**10.1**	**10.5**	**11.4**	**11.4**	**57.7**	**56.6**	**51.2**	**50.3**	**49.8**
OECD / OCDE[4]	**9.9**	**10.8**	**10.6**	**10.9**	..	**33.2**	**33.6**	**33.8**	**32.7**	..

.. Not available

Note: The figures exclude local government revenues for Antigua and Barbuda, Argentina (but include provincial revenues), the Bahamas, Barbados, Cuba (except for 2002-2012), the Dominican Republic, Saint Lucia, Trinidad and Tobago and Venezuela as the data are not available. Local government revenue data have been available since 1991 for Nicaragua, since 1994 for Bolivia, since 1995 for Guatemala, since 1998 for Jamaica, since 1999 for Panama, since 2000 for Peru, since 2002 for El Salvador and Guyana, since 2006 for Paraguay and since 1990 for all other countries.

1. In 2019, federal government data are used for the figure as % of GDP. For the figure as % of total tax revenue in 2019, data for 2018 are used as the state and local government revenue data for 2018 are not available.
2. Some tax revenue data between 2014 and 2017 are not available. In those years data as % of total tax revenue cannot be calculated. All data for 2018 and 2019 are not available.
3. Represents the group of 26 Latin American and Caribbean countries included in this publication and excludes Venezuela due to data availability issues. Chile, Colombia and Mexico are also part of the OECD (37) group.
4. Represents the unweighted average for OECD member countries.

.. Non disponible

Nota: Las cifras excluyen los ingresos subnacionales para Antigua y Barbuda, Argentina (pero se incluyen los ingresos de las provincias), Las Bahamas, Barbados, Cuba (excepto 2002-2012), República Dominicana, Santa Lucía, Trinidad y Tobago y Venezuela, dado que los datos no están disponibles. Los datos de ingresos subnacionales están disponibles desde 1991 para Nicaragua, desde 1994 para Bolivia, desde 1995 para Guatemala, desde 1998 para Jamaica, desde 1999 para Panamá, desde 2000 para Perú, desde 2002 para El Salvador y Guyana, desde 2006 para Paraguay y desde 1990 para todos los demás países.

1. Para 2019, se utilizan los datos del gobierno federal para la cifra como porcentaje del PIB. Para la cifra como porcentaje de los ingresos tributarios totales, los datos de 2018 se utilizan ya que los datos de ingresos del gobierno estatal y local para 2019 no están disponibles.
2. Algunos datos de ingresos tributarios entre 2014 y 2017 no están disponibles. Para esos años, no se pueden calcular los ingresos como porcentaje de los ingresos tributarios totales. No están disponibles todos los datos de 2018 y 2019.
3. Representa al grupo de 26 países de América Latina y el Caribe incluidos en esta publicación y excluye a Venezuela debido a problemas de disponibilidad de datos. Chile, Colombia y México también forman parte del grupo OCDE (37).
4. Representa el promedio no ponderado para los países miembros de la OCDE.

StatLink https://doi.org/10.1787/888934235316

Table 4.10. **Value added taxes (5111) as % of GDP and as % of total tax revenue**
Cuadro 4.10. **Impuesto al valor agregado (5111) en % del PIB y del total de ingresos tributarios**

	% of GDP / % del PIB					% of total tax revenue / % del total de ingresos tributarios				
	1990	2000	2010	2018	2019	1990	2000	2010	2018	2019
Antigua and Barbuda / Antigua y Barbuda	..	..	5.8	6.4	5.6	..	..	27.2	33.8	31.0
Argentina	2.1	6.0	7.0	7.6	7.1	15.6	31.1	24.1	26.3	24.9
Bahamas	0.0	0.0	0.0	5.3	6.7	0.0	0.0	0.0	32.0	35.7
Barbados	0.0	8.0	8.4	9.2	9.5	0.0	26.0	28.1	27.8	28.8
Belize / Belice	0.0	0.0	7.2	8.5	9.5	0.0	0.0	26.9	28.1	29.2
Bolivia	2.8	5.7	7.4	7.5	7.2	43.0	28.2	32.5	30.2	29.2
Brazil / Brasil	8.0	6.9	6.9	7.0	7.0	28.7	23.3	21.3	21.0	21.2
Chile	6.3	7.9	7.5	8.5	8.2	37.4	41.8	38.5	40.2	39.9
Colombia	2.6	4.3	5.3	5.7	5.8	22.6	27.6	29.3	29.4	29.6
Costa Rica	4.1	4.8	4.6	4.1	4.4	18.1	22.8	21.0	17.8	18.5
Cuba	0.0	0.0	0.0	0.0	0.0	0.0	0.0	0.0	0.0	0.0
Dominican Republic / República Dominicana	1.3	2.5	4.1	4.6	4.7	15.1	20.5	33.1	34.7	34.7
Ecuador	2.0	5.0	5.4	6.2	6.1	28.0	43.5	33.8	29.8	30.3
El Salvador	0.0	6.1	7.8	7.9	7.8	0.0	42.8	41.6	37.1	37.5
Guatemala	2.3	4.4	5.1	5.0	5.1	29.7	37.9	40.9	38.2	38.8
Guyana	0.0	0.0	3.9	4.8	4.9	0.0	0.0	24.2	21.8	21.1
Honduras	2.0	4.8	5.4	7.2	7.0	16.2	28.1	29.4	32.3	31.8
Jamaica	0.8	5.7	7.1	9.1	9.4	3.8	25.5	28.7	32.7	33.0
Mexico / México[1]	3.2	2.8	3.8	3.9	3.9	26.1	24.7	29.4	24.3	24.3
Nicaragua	..	4.5	5.5	5.3	5.8	..	31.5	28.6	22.9	22.5
Panama / Panamá	1.4	0.6	2.6	2.3	2.2	8.5	3.6	15.9	15.3	15.5
Paraguay	0.0	3.7	4.6	5.1	5.0	0.0	32.1	38.3	37.1	35.7
Peru / Perú	2.1	5.5	6.9	6.6	6.4	17.1	36.0	38.9	40.2	38.5
Saint Lucia / Santa Lucía	..	0.0	0.0	5.9	6.1	..	0.0	0.0	28.4	29.0
Trinidad and Tobago / Trinidad y Tobago	4.4	3.8	4.4	4.6	3.6	18.8	17.3	15.2	19.7	15.2
Uruguay	5.5	6.5	8.7	7.5	7.4	27.5	28.0	32.8	25.7	25.4
Venezuela[2]	0.0	4.1	5.5	..	..	0.0	30.2	46.7	..	..
Unweighted average / Promedio no ponderado										
LAC / ALC[3]	**2.2**	**4.0**	**5.2**	**6.0**	**6.0**	**15.5**	**22.9**	**26.1**	**28.0**	**27.7**
OECD / OCDE[4]	**5.1**	**6.3**	**6.4**	**6.8**	..	**16.9**	**19.6**	**20.5**	**20.4**	..

.. Not available

Note: The figures exclude local government revenues for Antigua and Barbuda, Argentina (but include provincial revenues), the Bahamas, Barbados, Cuba (except for 2002-2012), the Dominican Republic, Saint Lucia, Trinidad and Tobago and Venezuela as the data are not available. Local government revenue data have been available since 1991 for Nicaragua, since 1994 for Bolivia, since 1995 for Guatemala, since 1998 for Jamaica, since 1999 for Panama, since 2000 for Peru, since 2002 for El Salvador and Guyana, since 2006 for Paraguay and since 1990 for all other countries.

1. For the figures as % of total tax revenue in 2019, data for 2018 are used as the state and local government revenue data for 2019 are not available.
2. Some tax revenue data between 2014 and 2017 are not available. In those years data as % of total tax revenue cannot be calculated. All data for 2018 and 2019 are not available.
3. Represents the group of 26 Latin American and Caribbean countries included in this publication and excludes Venezuela due to data availability issues. Chile, Colombia and Mexico are also part of the OECD (37) group.
4. Represents the unweighted average for OECD member countries.

.. Non disponible

Nota: Las cifras excluyen los ingresos subnacionales para Antigua y Barbuda, Argentina (pero se incluyen los ingresos de las provincias), Las Bahamas, Barbados, Cuba (excepto 2002-2012), República Dominicana, Santa Lucía, Trinidad y Tobago y Venezuela, dado que los datos no están disponibles. Los datos de ingresos subnacionales están disponibles desde 1991 para Nicaragua, desde 1994 para Bolivia, desde 1995 para Guatemala, desde 1998 para Jamaica, desde 1999 para Panamá, desde 2000 para Perú, desde 2002 para El Salvador y Guyana, desde 2006 para Paraguay y desde 1990 para todos los demás países.

1. Para los ingresos como porcentaje de los ingresos tributarios totales en 2019, se utilizan los datos de 2018 porque los datos de ingresos de los gobiernos estatales y locales no están disponibles para 2019.
2. Algunos datos de ingresos tributarios entre 2014 y 2017 no están disponibles. Para esos años, no se pueden calcular los ingresos como porcentaje de los ingresos tributarios totales. No están disponibles todos los datos de 2018 y 2019.
3. Representa al grupo de 26 países de América Latina y el Caribe incluidos en esta publicación y excluye a Venezuela debido a problemas de disponibilidad de datos. Chile, Colombia y México también forman parte del grupo OCDE (37).
4. Representa el promedio no ponderado para los países miembros de la OCDE.

StatLink https://doi.org/10.1787/888934235335

Table 4.11. **Tax revenues of sub-sectors of general government as % of total tax revenue**
Cuadro 4.11. **Ingresos tributarios por subsector del gobierno general, en % del total de ingresos tributarios**

	Central government / Gobierno central			State or Regional government / Gobierno estatal o regional			Local government / Gobierno local			Social Security Funds / Fondos de seguridad social		
	1995	2000	2019	1995	2000	2019	1995	2000	2019	1995	2000	2019
Federal countries / Países federales												
Argentina	59.0	66.4	63.1	17.5	17.8	16.9	..	..	..	23.4	15.8	20.0
Brazil / Brasil	44.8	47.9	43.5	26.5	25.0	24.6	3.7	3.4	6.2	25.0	23.7	25.7
Mexico / México[1]	73.9	78.3	80.9	2.8	2.7	4.0	1.5	1.0	1.6	21.8	18.0	13.4
Venezuela[2]	94.6	94.6	..	..	..	..	..	..	..	5.4	5.4	..
Regional country / País régional												
Colombia	63.2	68.7	73.0	5.5	5.6	5.0	8.6	9.4	12.5	22.7	16.3	9.5
Unitary countries / Países unitarios												
Antigua and Barbuda / Antigua y Barbuda[3]	100.0	100.0	82.4	..	..	..	..	..	..	..	..	17.6
Bahamas[3]	89.1	88.1	87.6	..	..	..	..	..	..	10.9	11.9	12.4
Barbados	85.6	84.4	82.5	..	..	..	..	..	..	14.4	15.6	17.5
Belize / Belice	93.2	93.5	91.1	..	..	..	0.5	0.7	0.5	6.3	5.8	8.4
Bolivia	94.3	75.6	70.3	..	..	..	5.7	5.5	4.6	..	18.9	25.1
Chile	89.9	87.8	85.7	..	..	..	6.5	7.9	8.2	3.6	4.4	6.1
Costa Rica	65.5	63.3	57.8	..	..	..	1.6	1.9	3.0	33.0	34.8	39.2
Cuba	..	..	..	..	..	..	..	..	..	11.3	10.4	13.2
Dominican Republic / República Dominicana	99.3	99.0	99.6	..	..	..	..	..	..	0.7	1.0	0.4
Ecuador[3]	70.5	87.7	70.2	..	..	..	4.0	1.6	2.6	25.5	10.7	27.1
El Salvador	80.9	80.5	85.2	..	..	..	..	..	1.9	19.1	19.5	12.8
Guatemala	83.3	83.6	82.3	..	..	..	0.7	0.9	0.9	16.1	15.5	16.8
Guyana	92.6	88.6	90.5	..	..	..	..	..	0.0	7.4	11.4	9.5
Honduras	86.1	85.3	80.5	..	..	..	4.4	5.2	3.9	9.5	9.4	15.6
Jamaica	100.0	99.3	94.4	..	..	..	..	0.7	1.5	..	..	4.1
Nicaragua	80.4	72.5	68.3	..	..	..	4.6	9.5	6.0	15.0	18.0	25.7
Panama / Panamá	67.2	59.6	56.9	..	..	..	..	2.2	1.6	32.8	38.2	41.5
Paraguay	92.0	74.4	70.9	..	..	..	..	..	2.7	8.0	25.6	26.4
Peru / Perú	88.7	86.5	85.3	..	..	..	..	1.6	2.7	11.3	11.9	12.1
Saint Lucia / Santa Lucía[3]	100.0	90.0	89.5	..	..	..	..	..	..	..	10.0	10.5
Trinidad and Tobago / Trinidad y Tobago[3]	96.8	93.6	87.6	..	..	..	..	..	..	3.2	6.4	12.4
Uruguay	61.7	63.6	67.9	..	..	..	8.8	8.9	5.7	29.5	27.5	26.4

.. Not available

Note: The figures exclude local government revenues for Antigua and Barbuda, Argentina (but include provincial revenues), the Bahamas, Barbados, Cuba (except for 2002-2012), the Dominican Republic, Saint Lucia, Trinidad and Tobago and Venezuela as the data are not available. Local government revenue data have been available since 1991 for Nicaragua, since 1994 for Bolivia, since 1995 for Guatemala, since 1998 for Jamaica, since 1999 for Panama, since 2000 for Peru, since 2002 for El Salvador and Guyana, since 2006 for Paraguay and since 1990 for all other countries.

1. For the figures in 2019, data for 2018 are used as the state and local government revenue data for 2019 are not available.
2. Some tax revenue data between 2014 and 2017, and all data for 2018 and 2019 are not available. The breakdown by sub-sectors of general government is not available for those years.
3. The data include the following estimations: Antigua and Barbuda (social security contributions for 2019), Bahamas (social security contributions for 2018 and 2019), Ecuador (local tax revenues for 2019), Saint Lucia (social security contributions for 2018 and 2019) and Trinidad and Tobago (social security contributions for 2019). See the corresponding country tables for more information.

.. Non disponible

Nota: Las cifras excluyen los ingresos subnacionales para Antigua y Barbuda, Argentina (pero se incluyen los ingresos de las provincias), Las Bahamas, Barbados, Cuba (excepto 2002-2012), República Dominicana, Santa Lucía, Trinidad y Tobago y Venezuela, dado que los datos no están disponibles. Los datos de ingresos subnacionales están disponibles desde 1991 para Nicaragua, desde 1994 para Bolivia, desde 1995 para Guatemala, desde 1998 para Jamaica, desde 1999 para Panamá, desde 2000 para Perú, desde 2002 para El Salvador y Guyana, desde 2006 para Paraguay y desde 1990 para todos los demás países.

1. Para las cifras de 2019, se utilizan los datos de 2018, ya que no están disponibles los datos de ingresos de las administraciones estatales y locales para 2019.
2. Algunos datos de ingresos tributarios entre 2014 y 2017, y todos los datos de 2018 y 2019 no están disponibles. El desglose por subsectores del gobierno general no está disponible para esos años.
3. Los datos incluyen las siguientes estimaciones: Antigua y Barbuda (contribuciones a la seguridad social para 2019), Bahamas (contribuciones a la seguridad social para 2018 y 2019), Ecuador (ingresos tributarios locales para 2019), Santa Lucía (contribuciones a la seguridad social para 2018 y 2019) y Trinidad y Tobago (contribuciones a la seguridad social para 2019). Consulte las tablas de países correspondientes para obtener más información.

StatLink https://doi.org/10.1787/888934235354

Table 4.12. **Main central government taxes as % of total tax revenues of central government, 2019**

Cuadro 4.12. **Impuestos principales del gobierno central en % del total de ingresos tributarios del gobierno central, 2019**

	1000 Income & profits / Ingresos y utilidades	2000 Social security / Seguridad social[1]	3000 Payroll / Nómina	4000 Property / Propiedad	5000 Goods and services / Bienes y servicios	6000 Others / Otros
Federal countries / Países federales						
Argentina	28.5	0.0	0.0	10.0	61.0	0.5
Brazil / Brasil	51.5	0.0	4.1	4.1	38.8	1.6
Mexico / México	54.4	0.0	0.0	0.0	44.1	1.5
Venezuela	..	..	..	..	..	..
Regional country / País régional						
Colombia	44.2	0.0	2.4	6.7	46.3	0.4
Unitary countries / Países unitarios						
Antigua and Barbuda / Antigua y Barbuda	11.8	0.0	0.0	10.7	77.5	0.0
Bahamas	0.0	0.0	0.0	15.7	84.3	0.0
Barbados	29.7	0.0	0.0	8.2	62.2	0.0
Belize / Belice	27.6	0.0	0.0	3.3	69.1	0.0
Bolivia	23.1	0.0	0.0	1.1	69.7	6.1
Chile	40.7	1.4	0.0	2.2	56.5	-0.7
Costa Rica	36.2	1.5	0.0	0.9	57.4	3.9
Cuba	..	..	..	..	..	..
Dominican Republic / República Dominicana	31.6	0.0	0.6	4.8	63.0	0.0
Ecuador	30.3	0.0	0.0	0.4	69.2	0.1
El Salvador	39.3	0.0	0.8	0.8	59.1	0.0
Guatemala	34.5	0.0	1.5	0.8	63.2	0.0
Guyana	41.7	0.0	0.0	2.2	55.2	0.9
Honduras	31.8	0.0	0.9	3.2	64.1	0.0
Jamaica	32.8	0.0	0.0	1.8	65.1	0.4
Nicaragua	45.1	0.0	0.0	0.1	54.8	0.0
Panama / Panamá	45.7	0.0	2.6	3.2	47.9	0.6
Paraguay	25.8	0.0	0.0	0.0	73.6	0.6
Peru / Perú	42.9	0.0	0.1	0.2	54.8	2.0
Saint Lucia / Santa Lucía	24.2	0.0	0.0	2.4	73.4	0.0
Trinidad and Tobago / Trinidad y Tobago	66.3	0.0	0.0	1.2	32.5	0.0
Uruguay	38.5	0.0	0.0	6.8	54.4	0.3

.. Not available

Note: Excluding social security contributions collected by social security funds.

1. These comprise compulsory social security contributions collected by central government.

.. Non disponible

Nota: Se excluyen las contribuciones a la seguridad social recaudadas por los fondos de la seguridad social.

1. Estos comprenden contribuciones obligatorias a la seguridad social recaudadas por el gobierno central.

StatLink https://doi.org/10.1787/888934235373

Table 4.13. **Main state government taxes as % of total tax revenues of state government, 2019**
Cuadro 4.13. **Impuestos principales del gobierno estatal en % del total de ingresos tributarios del gobierno estatal, 2019**

	1000 Income & profits / Ingresos y utilidades	2000 Social security / Seguridad social	3000 Payroll / Nómina	4000 Property / Propiedad	5000 Goods and services / Bienes y servicios	6000 Others / Otros
Federal countries / Países federales						
Argentina	0.0	0.0	0.0	16.7	80.8	2.4
Brazil / Brasil	0.0	0.0	0.0	1.5	94.1	4.4
Mexico / México[1]	0.0	0.0	60.7	18.7	15.8	4.8
Venezuela	..	..	..	..	..	..
Regional country / País régional						
Colombia	0.0	0.0	0.0	0.0	71.5	28.5
Unitary countries / Países unitarios						
Antigua and Barbuda / Antigua y Barbuda	..	..	..	..	..	..
Bahamas	..	..	..	..	..	..
Barbados	..	..	..	..	..	..
Belize / Belice	..	..	..	..	..	..
Bolivia	..	..	..	..	..	..
Chile	..	..	..	..	..	..
Costa Rica	..	..	..	..	..	..
Cuba	..	..	..	..	..	..
Dominican Republic / República Dominicana	..	..	..	..	..	..
Ecuador	..	..	..	..	..	..
El Salvador	..	..	..	..	..	..
Guatemala	..	..	..	..	..	..
Guyana	..	..	..	..	..	..
Honduras	..	..	..	..	..	..
Jamaica	..	..	..	..	..	..
Nicaragua	..	..	..	..	..	..
Panama / Panamá	..	..	..	..	..	..
Paraguay	..	..	..	..	..	..
Peru / Perú	..	..	..	..	..	..
Saint Lucia / Santa Lucía	..	..	..	..	..	..
Trinidad and Tobago / Trinidad y Tobago	..	..	..	..	..	..
Uruguay	..	..	..	..	..	..

.. Not available

1. Data for 2018 are used as the state and local government revenue data for 2019 are not available.

.. Non disponible

1. Se utilizan los datos de 2018 ya que no están disponibles los datos de ingresos de las administraciones estatales y locales para 2019.

StatLink https://doi.org/10.1787/888934235392

Table 4.14. Main local government taxes as % of total tax revenues of local government, 2019
Cuadro 4.14. Impuestos principales del gobierno local en % del total de ingresos tributarios del gobierno local, 2019

	1000 Income & profits / Ingresos y utilidades	2000 Social security / Seguridad social	3000 Payroll / Nómina	4000 Property / Propiedad	5000 Goods and services / Bienes y servicios	6000 Others / Otros
Federal countries / Países federales						
Argentina	..	..	..	..	..	..
Brazil / Brasil	0.0	0.0	0.0	39.9	45.6	14.5
Mexico / México[1]	0.0	0.0	0.0	78.5	2.8	18.7
Venezuela	..	..	..	..	..	..
Regional country / País régional						
Colombia	0.0	0.0	0.0	33.5	44.7	21.8
Unitary countries / Países unitarios						
Antigua and Barbuda / Antigua y Barbuda	..	..	..	..	..	..
Bahamas	..	..	..	..	..	..
Barbados	..	..	..	..	..	..
Belize / Belice	0.0	0.0	0.0	100.0	0.0	0.0
Bolivia	0.0	0.0	0.0	0.0	0.0	100.0
Chile	0.0	0.0	0.0	43.3	56.7	0.0
Costa Rica	0.0	0.0	0.0	46.0	54.0	0.0
Cuba	..	..	..	..	..	..
Dominican Republic / República Dominicana	..	..	..	..	..	..
Ecuador	13.2	0.0	0.0	50.2	36.3	0.3
El Salvador	0.0	0.0	0.0	6.0	12.0	81.9
Guatemala	0.0	0.0	0.0	100.0	0.0	0.0
Guyana	0.0	0.0	0.0	0.0	0.0	100.0
Honduras	0.0	0.0	0.0	0.0	0.0	100.0
Jamaica	0.0	0.0	0.0	100.0	0.0	0.0
Nicaragua	0.0	0.0	0.0	17.5	68.5	14.0
Panama / Panamá	0.0	0.0	0.0	0.0	100.0	0.0
Paraguay	0.0	0.0	0.0	49.7	44.5	5.8
Peru / Perú	0.0	0.0	0.0	83.4	16.2	0.4
Saint Lucia / Santa Lucía	..	..	..	..	..	..
Trinidad and Tobago / Trinidad y Tobago	..	..	..	..	..	..
Uruguay	0.0	0.0	0.0	54.1	38.1	7.8

.. Not available

1. Data for 2018 are used as the state and local government revenue data for 2019 are not available.

.. Non disponible

1. Se utilizan los datos de 2018 ya que no están disponibles los datos de ingresos de las administraciones estatales y locales para 2019.

StatLink https://doi.org/10.1787/888934235411

Table 4.15. **Gross domestic product for tax reporting years at market prices, in millions of national currency**

Cuadro 4.15. **Producto interno bruto para los años fiscales a precios de mercado, en millones de moneda local**

		1990	2000	2007	2010	2014	2015	2016	2017	2018	2019
Antigua and Barbuda / Antigua y Barbuda	XCD	1 241	2 241	3 541	3 101	3 374	3 609	3 879	3 964	4 334	4 487
Argentina	ARS	77 060	317 759	896 980	1 661 721	4 579 086	5 954 511	8 228 160	10 660 228	14 542 722	21 447 250
Bahamas	BSD	5 218	7 880	10 393	10 039	10 840	11 411	11 795	12 341	12 767	13 394
Barbados	BBD	4 059	6 116	9 403	9 124	9 402	9 488	9 734	10 011	10 235	10 129
Belize / Belice	BZD	824	1 664	2 543	2 754	3 326	3 448	3 550	3 673	3 742	3 675
Bolivia	BOB	15 443	51 928	103 009	137 876	228 004	228 031	234 533	259 185	278 388	282 587
Brazil / Brasil	BRL	12	1 199 092	2 720 263	3 885 847	5 778 953	5 995 787	6 269 328	6 583 319	6 889 176	7 256 926
Chile	CLP	10 522 684	42 005 194	90 702 903	111 508 611	148 599 454	159 553 348	169 537 388	179 756 126	191 265 952	198 440 707
Colombia	COP	22 731 433	195 108 574	428 506 000	544 060 000	762 903 000	804 692 000	863 782 000	920 471 000	985 931 000	1 062 342 500
Costa Rica	CRC	523 319	4 627 051	13 889 053	19 802 011	28 001 328	30 171 919	32 056 288	34 343 647	35 966 118	37 558 144
Cuba	CUP	19 645	30 565	58 604	64 328	80 656	87 133	91 370	96 851	100 023	103 539
Dominican Republic / República Dominicana	DOP	77 344	393 303	1 458 417	1 983 202	2 925 665	3 205 655	3 487 293	3 802 656	4 235 847	4 562 235
Ecuador	USD	15 232	18 319	51 008	69 555	101 726	99 290	99 938	104 296	107 562	107 436
El Salvador	USD	4 818	11 785	17 012	18 448	22 593	23 438	24 191	24 979	26 117	27 023
Guatemala	GTQ	33 613	140 702	261 760	333 093	447 326	476 023	502 002	526 200	549 790	590 417
Guyana	GYD	34 523	273 054	552 603	699 064	852 153	883 787	925 677	980 498	994 472	1 078 729
Honduras	HNL	17 141	106 654	233 567	299 286	414 633	460 405	495 922	543 403	574 243	615 051
Jamaica	JMD	38 145	395 009	885 632	1 152 781	1 541 903	1 659 677	1 760 976	1 895 025	2 025 039	2 110 433
Mexico / México	MXN	843 623	6 693 683	11 504 076	13 366 377	17 473 842	18 551 459	20 118 101	21 911 894	23 491 507	24 239 132
Nicaragua	NIO	519	64 812	136 950	187 053	308 403	347 707	380 261	414 279	412 207	414 714
Panama / Panamá	PAB	5 723	12 502	21 296	29 440	49 921	54 092	57 908	62 219	65 128	66 801
Paraguay	PYG	7 147 738	30 874 088	89 866 049	128 989 495	179 721 609	188 230 723	204 447 278	219 188 417	231 489 278	238 054 148
Peru / Perú	PEN	5 322	175 862	319 693	420 738	574 302	609 365	656 161	698 310	740 420	769 963
Saint Lucia / Santa Lucía	XCD	1 559	2 446	3 654	4 075	4 775	4 921	5 127	5 443	5 616	5 596
Trinidad and Tobago / Trinidad y Tobago	TTD	21 105	50 098	133 468	138 557	176 665	164 125	151 422	151 430	158 992	162 385
Uruguay[1]	UYU	12 010	276 152	549 470	808 079	1 330 508	1 455 848	1 589 195	1 707 109	1 831 132	1 975 921
Venezuela	VES	0	1	5	10	30	80	281	2 009	1 057 236	137 482 062

1. The figures do not take into account the recent rebasing of GDP in Uruguay.

Source: OECD National Accounts data for Chile, Colombia and Mexico, the World Economic Outlook (IMF) for Barbados, Belize, and Trinidad & Tobago, and official National Accounts data for Antigua and Barbuda, Bolivia, Brazil, Ecuador, Paraguay and Peru. For Argentina, Bahamas, Costa Rica, Dominican Republic, El Salvador, Guatemala, Guyana, Honduras, Jamaica, Nicaragua, Panama, Uruguay and Venezuela, official national sources were used where available, together with data from the IMF. For Cuba, figures between 1996 and 2018 come from Oficina Nacional de Estadística e Información (ONEI), while data before 1996 and also in 2019 come from ECLAC/CEPAL. For Saint Lucia, GDP data are compiled based on most reliable information from national sources, IMF and ECLAC/CEPAL. For Bahamas, Barbados, Belize, Saint Lucia and Trinidad and Tobago, GDP figures are reported on a fiscal year basis. For Jamaica, GDP reported for 1990-2003 are reported on a fiscal year basis, while for other years, they are reported on a calendar year basis.

1. Las cifras no tienen en cuenta la reciente revisión del PIB en Uruguay.

Fuente: Datos de las Cuentas Nacionales de la OCDE para Chile, Colombia y México, Perspectivas de la economía mundial (FMI) para Barbados, Belice y Trinidad y Tobago, y datos de cuentas nacionales para Antigua y Barbuda, Bolivia, Brasil, Ecuador, Paraguay y Perú. Para Argentina, Bahamas, Costa Rica, República Dominicana, El Salvador, Guatemala, Guyana, Honduras, Jamaica, Nicaragua, Panamá, Uruguay y Venezuela, se utilizan fuentes nacionales oficiales donde los datos están disponibles, junto con los datos del FMI. Para Cuba, las cifras entre 1996 y 2018 provienen de la Oficina Nacional de Estadística e Información, mientras que los datos anteriores a 1996 y también en 2019 proceden de la CEPAL. En el caso de Santa Lucía, los datos del PIB se elaboran a partir de la información más fiable de las fuentes nacionales, el FMI y la CEPAL. Para Bahamas, Barbados, Belice, Santa Lucía y Trinidad y Tobago, las cifras del PIB se informan sobre la base del año fiscal. Para Jamaica, el PIB reportado para 1990-2003 se presenta sobre una base de año fiscal, mientras que para otros años, se presenta sobre una base de año calendario.

StatLink https://doi.org/10.1787/888934235430

Table 4.16. **Gross domestic product for tax reporting years at market prices, in millions of USD**
Cuadro 4.16. **Producto interno bruto para los años fiscales a precios de mercado, en millones de US dólares**

	1990	2000	2007	2010	2014	2015	2016	2017	2018	2019
Antigua and Barbuda / Antigua y Barbuda	459	830	1 311	1 149	1 250	1 337	1 437	1 468	1 605	1 662
Argentina	158 024	317 759	287 921	424 729	563 614	642 464	556 774	643 861	517 244	444 458
Bahamas	5 218	7 880	10 393	10 039	10 840	11 411	11 795	12 341	12 767	13 394
Barbados	2 030	3 058	4 702	4 562	4 701	4 744	4 867	5 006	5 118	5 065
Belize / Belice	412	832	1 272	1 377	1 663	1 724	1 775	1 837	1 871	1 838
Bolivia	4 868	8 385	13 216	19 786	33 237	33 241	34 189	37 782	40 581	41 193
Brazil / Brasil	478 052	655 453	1 397 114	2 208 704	2 456 054	1 800 046	1 796 622	2 062 842	1 885 470	1 839 077
Chile	34 512	77 847	173 606	218 538	260 542	243 919	250 440	277 045	298 258	282 318
Colombia	45 258	93 447	206 182	286 563	381 112	293 482	282 825	311 884	333 569	323 803
Costa Rica	5 716	15 029	26 997	38 028	52 637	57 095	59 537	61 015	62 682	64 304
Cuba	21 541	30 565	58 604	64 328	80 656	87 133	91 370	96 851	100 023	103 539
Dominican Republic / República Dominicana	7 995	24 306	44 067	53 921	67 264	71 254	75 777	80 082	85 630	89 032
Ecuador	15 232	18 319	51 008	69 555	101 726	99 290	99 938	104 296	107 562	107 436
El Salvador	4 818	11 785	17 012	18 448	22 593	23 438	24 191	24 979	26 117	27 023
Guatemala	7 493	18 124	34 108	41 326	57 835	62 180	66 034	71 583	73 121	76 694
Guyana	685	1 497	2 732	3 432	4 128	4 280	4 483	4 748	4 788	5 174
Honduras	4 169	7 104	12 275	15 730	19 757	20 980	21 718	23 136	23 857	24 921
Jamaica	5 058	8 997	12 881	13 193	13 864	14 154	14 107	14 756	15 631	15 808
Mexico / México	299 944	707 910	1 052 697	1 057 801	1 314 569	1 170 567	1 077 906	1 157 735	1 220 697	1 258 285
Nicaragua	519	5 109	7 423	8 759	11 880	12 757	13 286	13 786	13 064	12 535
Panama / Panamá	5 723	12 502	21 296	29 440	49 921	54 092	57 908	62 219	65 128	66 801
Paraguay	5 812	8 856	17 856	27 108	40 277	36 164	36 054	39 009	40 385	38 145
Peru / Perú	28 326	50 414	102 187	148 931	202 308	191 316	194 384	214 148	225 249	230 738
Saint Lucia / Santa Lucía	577	906	1 353	1 509	1 768	1 822	1 899	2 016	2 080	2 073
Trinidad and Tobago / Trinidad y Tobago	4 966	7 986	21 199	21 841	27 581	25 869	23 115	22 436	23 532	24 035
Uruguay[1]	10 270	22 832	23 461	40 285	57 236	53 275	52 687	59 530	59 828	56 686
Venezuela	48 391	94 665	229 896	323 200	206 042	325 122	279 160	143 834	98 400	63 960

1. The figures do not take into account the recent rebasing of GDP in Uruguay.

Source: The figures are derived by dividing the GDP data in Table 4.15 by the exchange rate in Table 4.17.

1. Las cifras no tienen en cuenta la reciente revisión del PIB en Uruguay.

Fuente: Las cifras se obtienen de la división de los datos del PIB en el Cuadro 4.15 por el tipo de cambio en el Cuadro 4.17.

StatLink https://doi.org/10.1787/888934235449

Table 4.17. **Exchange rates used, national currency per US dollar at market exchange rates**
Cuadro 4.17. **Tasas de cambio utilizadas, moneda local por US dólares a precios de mercado**

		1990	2000	2007	2010	2014	2015	2016	2017	2018	2019
Antigua and Barbuda / Antigua y Barbuda	XCD	2.700	2.700	2.700	2.700	2.700	2.700	2.700	2.700	2.700	2.700
Argentina	ARS	0.488	1.000	3.115	3.912	8.125	9.268	14.778	16.557	28.116	48.255
Bahamas	BSD	1.000	1.000	1.000	1.000	1.000	1.000	1.000	1.000	1.000	1.000
Barbados	BBD	2.000	2.000	2.000	2.000	2.000	2.000	2.000	2.000	2.000	2.000
Belize / Belice	BZD	2.000	2.000	2.000	2.000	2.000	2.000	2.000	2.000	2.000	2.000
Bolivia	BOB	3.172	6.193	7.794	6.968	6.860	6.860	6.860	6.860	6.860	6.860
Brazil / Brasil	BRL	0.000	1.829	1.947	1.759	2.353	3.331	3.490	3.191	3.654	3.946
Chile	CLP	304.903	539.588	522.464	510.249	570.348	654.124	676.958	648.834	641.277	702.897
Colombia	COP	502.259	2 087.904	2 078.292	1 898.570	2 001.781	2 741.881	3 054.122	2 951.327	2 955.704	3 280.832
Costa Rica	CRC	91.553	307.871	514.460	520.724	531.972	528.449	538.428	562.873	573.788	584.076
Cuba	CUP	0.912	1.000	1.000	1.000	1.000	1.000	1.000	1.000	1.000	1.000
Dominican Republic / República Dominicana	DOP	9.674	16.181	33.095	36.780	43.495	44.989	46.020	47.485	49.467	51.243
Ecuador	USD	1.000	1.000	1.000	1.000	1.000	1.000	1.000	1.000	1.000	1.000
El Salvador	USD	1.000	1.000	1.000	1.000	1.000	1.000	1.000	1.000	1.000	1.000
Guatemala	GTQ	4.486	7.763	7.674	8.060	7.735	7.656	7.602	7.351	7.519	7.698
Guyana	GYD	50.399	182.401	202.239	203.670	206.432	206.492	206.486	206.508	207.701	208.490
Honduras	HNL	4.112	15.013	19.028	19.026	20.987	21.945	22.835	23.487	24.070	24.680
Jamaica	JMD	7.541	43.907	68.755	87.378	111.213	117.257	124.828	128.427	129.555	133.504
Mexico / México	MXN	2.813	9.456	10.928	12.636	13.292	15.848	18.664	18.927	19.244	19.264
Nicaragua	NIO	1.000	12.686	18.449	21.356	25.960	27.256	28.621	30.051	31.553	33.084
Panama / Panamá	PAB	1.000	1.000	1.000	1.000	1.000	1.000	1.000	1.000	1.000	1.000
Paraguay	PYG	1 229.845	3 486.234	5 032.821	4 758.355	4 462.140	5 204.920	5 670.585	5 618.919	5 732.061	6 240.701
Peru / Perú	PEN	0.188	3.488	3.129	2.825	2.839	3.185	3.376	3.261	3.287	3.337
Saint Lucia / Santa Lucía	XCD	2.700	2.700	2.700	2.700	2.700	2.700	2.700	2.700	2.700	2.700
Trinidad and Tobago / Trinidad y Tobago	TTD	4.250	6.273	6.296	6.344	6.405	6.344	6.551	6.749	6.756	6.756
Uruguay	UYU	1.169	12.095	23.421	20.059	23.246	27.327	30.163	28.676	30.607	34.857
Venezuela	VES	0.000	0.000	0.000	0.000	0.000	0.000	0.001	0.014	10.744	2 149.501

Note: Annual average market exchange rates.
Source: World Economic Outlook (IMF), October 2020.
Nota: Se utilizan tasas de cambio de promedio anual de mercados.
Fuente: Perspectivas de la economía mundial (FMI), octubre de 2020.

StatLink https://doi.org/10.1787/888934235468

Chapter 5

Country tables, 1990-2019 – Tax revenues

Capítulo 5

Cuadros país, 1990-2019 – Ingresos tributarios

Table 5.1. **Antigua and Barbuda / Antigua y Barbuda**

Details of tax revenue / Ingresos tributarios detallados

Million XCD

	1990	2000	2007	2010	2014	2015	2016	2017	2018	2019
Total tax revenue	..	**268**	**763**	**660**	**671**	**735**	**760**	**776**	**823**	**816**
1000 Taxes on income, profits and capital gains	..	**38**	**100**	**92**	**73**	**89**	**76**	**74**	**78**	**79**
1100 Taxes Of individuals	..	0	50	33	37	37	26	2	0	1
1110 On income and profits	..	0	50	33	37	37	26	2	0	1
1120 On capital gains	..	..	..	..	..	..	..	..	..	..
1200 Corporate	..	37	50	59	36	52	50	72	78	79
1210 On profits	..	37	50	59	36	52	50	72	78	79
1220 On capital gains of corporates	..	..	..	..	..	..	..	..	..	..
1300 Unallocable between 1100 and 1200	..	0	0	0	0	0	0	0	0	0
2000 Social security contributions (SSC)	..	..	**78**	**83**	**100**	**113**	**119**	**140**	**143**	**143**
2100 Employees SSC	..	..	..	..	..	..	..	..	..	..
2110 On a payroll basis	..	..	..	..	..	..	..	..	..	..
2120 On an income tax basis	..	..	..	..	..	..	..	..	..	..
2200 Employers	..	..	..	..	..	..	..	..	..	..
2210 On a payroll	..	..	..	..	..	..	..	..	..	..
2220 On an income tax basis	..	..	..	..	..	..	..	..	..	..
2300 Self-employed or non-employed	..	..	..	..	..	..	..	..	..	..
2310 On a payroll basis	..	..	..	..	..	..	..	..	..	..
2320 On an income tax basis	..	..	..	..	..	..	..	..	..	..
2400 Unallocable between 2100, 2200 and 2300	..	..	78	83	100	113	119	140	143	143
2410 On a payroll basis	..	..	78	83	100	113	119	140	143	143
2420 On an income tax basis	..	..	0	0	0	0	0	0	0	0
3000 Taxes on payroll and workforce	..	**0**	**0**	**0**	**0**	**0**	**0**	**0**	**0**	**0**
4000 Taxes on property	..	**13**	**55**	**49**	**52**	**52**	**60**	**70**	**62**	**72**
4100 Recurrent taxes on immovable property	..	0	9	18	22	18	18	20	21	29
4110 Households	..	..	9	18	22	18	18	20	21	29
Property tax	..	..	9	18	21	18	17	19	20	24
Land tax	..	..	0	0	1	0	1	2	1	2
Non-Citizens Undeveloped Land Tax	..	..	0	0	0	0	0	0	0	3
4120 Others	..	..	0	0	0	0	0	0	0	0
4200 Recurrent taxes on net wealth	..	0	0	0	0	0	0	0	0	0
4210 Individual	..	..	..	..	..	..	..	..	..	..
4220 Corporate	..	..	..	..	..	..	..	..	..	..
4300 Estate, inheritance and gift taxes	..	0	0	0	0	0	0	0	0	0
4310 Estate and inheritance taxes	..	..	..	..	..	..	..	..	..	..
4320 Gift taxes	..	..	..	..	..	..	..	..	..	..
4400 Taxes on financial and capital transactions	..	13	46	32	31	34	42	50	41	43
Stamp duties	..	13	45	31	31	34	42	50	41	43
Other taxes on transactions	..	0	1	0	0	0	0	0	0	0
4500 Non-recurrent taxes	..	0	0	0	0	0	0	0	0	0
4510 On net wealth	..	..	..	..	..	..	..	..	..	..
4520 Other non-recurrent taxes	..	..	..	..	..	..	..	..	..	..
4600 Other recurrent taxes on property	..	0	0	0	0	0	0	0	0	0
5000 Taxes on goods and services	..	**217**	**530**	**435**	**446**	**481**	**506**	**492**	**539**	**521**
5100 Taxes on production, sale, transfer, etc	..	217	512	429	443	478	503	489	535	517
5110 General taxes	..	0	202	179	305	307	325	312	362	333
5111 Value added taxes	..	..	202	179	229	232	251	237	278	253
5112 Sales tax	..	..	0	0	76	75	74	75	84	80
5113 Other	..	..	0	0	0	0	0	0	0	0
5120 Taxes on specific goods and services	..	217	310	250	138	171	178	177	173	185
5121 Excises	..	72	66	34	45	69	81	68	56	67
Consumption duties	..	72	58	31	40	64	78	64	53	64
Environmental tax	..	0	8	3	5	5	4	3	3	3
5122 Profits of fiscal monopolies	..	0	0	0	0	0	0	0	0	0
5123 Customs and import duties	..	83	187	96	80	88	84	93	101	102
Import duties	..	57	93	79	79	82	82	88	97	98
Throughput Levy on Fuel Products	..	0	0	12	1	5	2	5	4	4
Other customs charges	..	26	94	5	0	0	0	0	0	0
5124 Taxes on exports	..	0	0	0	0	0	0	0	0	0
5125 Taxes on investment goods	..	0	0	0	0	0	0	0	0	0
5126 Taxes on specific services	..	53	57	54	13	14	13	17	16	15
Travel tax	..	4	7	4	6	6	5	6	7	7
Insurance levy	..	0	4	4	4	4	4	7	5	5
Money transfer levy	..	0	1	1	2	2	2	2	2	1
Other taxes on hospitality, transport and telecommunication services	..	49	44	44	1	2	1	2	2	2
5127 Other taxes on internat. trade and transactions	..	9	0	66	0	0	0	0	0	0
5128 Other taxes	..	0	0	0	0	0	0	0	0	0

Table 5.1. **Antigua and Barbuda / Antigua y Barbuda** *(cont.)*

Details of tax revenue / Ingresos tributarios detallados

Million XCD

	1990	2000	2007	2010	2014	2015	2016	2017	2018	2019
5130 Unallocable between 5110 and 5120	..	0	0	0	0	0	0	0	0	0
5200 Taxes on use of goods and perform activities	..	0	17	6	3	3	3	3	3	4
5210 Recurrent taxes	..	..	17	6	3	3	3	3	3	4
5211 Paid by households: motor vehicles	..	..	0	0	0	0	0	0	0	0
5212 Paid by others: motor vehicles	..	..	15	3	1	2	2	2	2	2
5213 Paid in respect of other goods	..	..	2	2	2	1	1	1	1	2
5220 Non-recurrent taxes	..	..	0	0	0	0	0	0	0	0
5300 Unallocable between 5100 and 5200	..	0	1	0	0	0	0	0	0	0
6000 Other taxes	**..**	**0**	**0**	**0**	**0**	**0**	**0**	**0**	**0**	**0**
6100 Paid solely by business	..	..	..	..	..	..	..	..	..	..
6200 Other	..	..	..	..	..	..	..	..	..	..

.. Not available

Note: Year ending 31st December.

The data are on a cash basis.

The figures do not include local tax revenues because data are not available.

Heading 2000: Social security contributions for 2019 are estimated.

Heading 5112: The Revenue Recovery Charge, levied on all goods imported into or manufactured in Antigua and Barbuda, is classified under this heading according to the OECD classification described in the Interpretative Guide.

Heading 5121: The environmental tax, levied on specific goods imported into or manufactured in Antigua and Barbuda, is classified under this heading according to the OECD classification described in the Interpretative Guide.

Source: Ministry of Finance; Corporate Governance and Social Security Board.

StatLink https://doi.org/10.1787/888934235487

Table 5.2. **Argentina**

Details of tax revenue / Ingresos tributarios detallados

Million ARS

	1990	2000	2007	2010	2014	2015	2016	2017	2018	2019
Total tax revenue	**10 217**	**61 084**	**236 516**	**483 014**	**1 425 148**	**1 872 915**	**2 522 854**	**3 202 762**	**4 203 177**	**6 143 732**
1000 Taxes on income, profits and capital gains	**542**	**11 303**	**44 226**	**78 427**	**269 809**	**384 536**	**436 927**	**559 755**	**746 994**	**1 102 982**
1100 Of individuals	141	3 937	12 777	23 980	125 503	188 218	174 483	236 284	296 224	434 464
1110 On income and profits	130	3 854	12 715	23 858	125 067	187 663	173 721	234 117	293 344	430 726
1120 On capital gains	11	82	62	122	436	555	762	2 167	2 880	3 739
1200 Corporate	357	6 575	29 145	50 664	132 178	185 725	236 286	297 111	401 683	591 961
1210 On profits	357	6 575	29 145	50 664	132 178	185 725	236 286	297 111	401 683	591 961
Corporate income taxes	198	5 956	27 837	49 012	129 881	183 207	233 028	294 546	399 623	589 240
Tax on assets	160	19	9	4	6	4	12	5	5	5
Tax on assumed minimum income	0	600	1 299	1 648	2 291	2 513	3 246	2 560	2 055	2 716
1220 On capital gains of corporates	..	..	..	..	..	..	..	..	..	..
1300 Unallocable between 1100 and 1200	43	792	2 304	3 783	12 128	10 593	26 159	26 360	49 086	76 556
Non resident taxpayers	11	792	2 304	3 783	12 128	10 593	26 159	26 360	49 086	76 556
Other	33	0	0	0	0	0	0	0	0	0
2000 Social security contributions	**2 583**	**9 670**	**36 612**	**102 460**	**307 656**	**415 410**	**556 067**	**733 527**	**913 427**	**1 225 673**
2100 Employees	..	2 486	7 052	37 990	121 276	163 590	219 446	288 985	361 756	475 772
2110 On a payroll basis	..	2 486	7 052	37 990	121 276	163 590	219 446	288 985	361 756	475 772
2120 On an income tax basis	..	0	0	0	0	0	0	0	0	0
2200 Employers	..	6 069	23 939	54 713	174 965	235 610	314 628	413 212	514 144	704 555
2210 On a payroll basis	..	6 069	23 939	54 713	174 965	235 610	314 628	413 212	514 144	704 555
2220 On an income tax basis	..	0	0	0	0	0	0	0	0	0
2300 Self-employed or non-employed	98	1 115	5 620	9 757	11 416	16 210	21 994	31 330	37 527	45 346
2310 On a payroll basis	98	1 115	5 620	9 757	11 416	16 210	21 994	31 330	37 527	45 346
2320 On an income tax basis	0	0	0	0	0	0	0	0	0	0
2400 Unallocable between 2100, 2200 and 2300	2 485	0	0	0	0	0	0	0	0	0
2410 On a payroll basis	2 485	..	..	..	..	..	..	..	..	..
2420 On an income tax basis	0	..	..	..	..	..	..	..	..	..
3000 Taxes on payroll and workforce	**0**	**0**	**0**	**0**	**0**	**0**	**0**	**0**	**0**	**0**
4000 Taxes on property	**1 164**	**3 867**	**23 978**	**43 538**	**128 941**	**166 182**	**224 193**	**303 382**	**389 044**	**561 734**
4100 Recurrent taxes on immovable property	419	1 809	3 025	5 035	17 429	21 738	32 770	44 236	59 589	88 405
4110 Households	0	0	0	0	0	0	0	0	0	0
4120 Others	419	1 809	3 025	5 035	17 429	21 738	32 770	44 236	59 589	88 405
4200 Recurrent taxes on net wealth	246	1 084	2 557	5 248	14 575	18 538	19 976	22 786	15 296	32 383
4210 Individual	3	1 024	2 492	5 147	14 356	18 210	19 541	22 165	14 517	31 184
Personal assets	0	1 024	2 492	5 147	14 356	18 210	19 541	22 165	14 517	31 184
Recurrent taxes on net wealth	3	0	0	0	0	0	0	0	0	0
4220 Corporate	242	60	65	101	220	327	435	621	778	1 199
4300 Estate, inheritance and gift taxes	0	0	0	0	0	0	0	0	0	0
4310 Estate and inheritance taxes	..	..	..	..	..	..	..	..	..	..
4320 Gift taxes	..	..	..	..	..	..	..	..	..	..
4400 Taxes on financial and capital transactions	459	904	18 390	33 252	96 937	125 906	171 447	236 360	314 159	440 946
Immovable property transfers	0	54	382	539	912	1 256	2 052	4 091	5 935	5 575
Movable property transfers	44	0	0	0	0	0	0	0	0	0
Bank accounts' credits and debits	205	0	15 065	26 885	76 740	97 480	131 669	172 838	234 300	349 559
Stamp taxes	211	850	2 942	5 829	19 285	27 170	37 726	59 431	73 924	85 812
4500 Non-recurrent taxes	40	70	6	3	0	0	0	0	0	0
4510 On net wealth	0	0	0	0	..	..	..	..	..	..
4520 Other non-recurrent taxes	40	70	6	3	..	..	..	..	..	..
4600 Other recurrent taxes on property	0	0	0	0	0	0	0	0	0	0
5000 Taxes on goods and services	**5 636**	**34 539**	**128 329**	**253 092**	**705 461**	**889 323**	**1 176 337**	**1 531 220**	**2 120 215**	**3 208 294**
5100 Taxes on production, sale, transfer, etc	5 462	34 288	128 321	252 550	704 671	881 120	1 167 379	1 520 300	2 113 174	3 180 080
5110 General taxes	2 384	25 123	86 803	167 534	515 878	671 297	901 584	1 188 317	1 671 483	2 316 719
5111 Value added taxes	1 594	19 009	62 669	116 386	331 203	433 076	583 217	765 336	1 104 580	1 532 597
5112 Sales tax	0	0	0	0	0	0	0	0	0	0
5113 Other	791	6 114	24 134	51 148	184 675	238 221	318 367	422 981	566 903	784 122
5120 Taxes on specific goods and services	3 077	9 166	41 517	85 016	188 793	209 822	265 795	331 983	441 691	863 362
5121 Excises	1 866	5 850	13 164	26 208	69 977	92 349	129 790	182 818	205 182	282 964
Alcoholic beverages	25	36	95	238	673	985	1 163	1 591	2 147	2 558
Non alcoholic beverages	25	90	312	501	1 586	2 168	2 477	3 136	3 627	4 006
Beers	0	50	149	212	879	1 384	1 171	2 811	4 729	1 339
Tobacco products	425	1 875	3 881	6 884	17 432	26 152	42 183	60 249	67 264	90 857
Liquid fuel and gas	1 073	3 478	7 466	15 269	44 490	56 478	75 664	102 846	116 409	161 666
Electricity	72	205	538	591	607	590	637	1 768	2 358	7 818
Motor vehicles	59	20	0	27	121	88	265	476	337	443
Other	189	96	724	2 485	4 189	4 503	6 229	9 942	8 311	14 275
5122 Profits of fiscal monopolies	0	0	0	0	0	0	0	0	0	0

Table 5.2. **Argentina** *(cont.)*

Details of tax revenue / Ingresos tributarios detallados

Million ARS

	1990	2000	2007	2010	2014	2015	2016	2017	2018	2019
5123 Customs and import duties	219	1 976	7 015	11 428	30 058	35 512	56 365	70 635	107 178	163 076
Import duties	166	1 938	6 859	11 183	29 482	34 822	55 305	69 259	104 991	132 405
Import fees	53	38	156	246	576	691	1 060	1 376	2 187	30 671
5124 Taxes on exports	724	32	20 450	45 547	84 088	75 939	71 509	66 121	114 160	398 312
5125 Taxes on investment goods	0	0	0	0	0	0	0	0	0	0
5126 Taxes on specific services	163	1 233	674	1 429	3 533	4 420	5 782	7 792	9 293	9 729
Insurance services	42	194	11	21	65	88	118	167	198	289
Financial services	32	855	1	0	0	0	0	0	0	0
Telephone services	82	33	417	936	1 983	2 301	2 911	4 061	4 626	3 350
Other specific services	7	151	246	472	1 486	2 031	2 753	3 564	4 469	6 090
5127 Other taxes on internat. trade and transactions	98	74	214	404	1 136	1 601	2 349	4 616	5 876	9 281
5128 Other taxes	8	0	0	0	0	0	0	0	0	0
5130 Unallocable between 5110 and 5120	0	0	0	0	0	0	0	0	0	0
5200 Taxes on use of goods and perform activities	177	833	1 921	3 598	12 006	17 035	23 941	35 873	41 642	57 483
5210 Recurrent taxes	177	833	1 921	3 598	12 006	17 035	23 941	35 873	41 642	57 483
5211 Paid by households: motor vehicles	177	833	1 921	3 598	12 006	17 035	23 941	35 873	41 642	57 483
5212 Paid by others: motor vehicles	0	0	0	0	0	0	0	0	0	0
5213 Paid in respect of other goods	0	0	0	0	0	0	0	0	0	0
5220 Non-recurrent taxes	0	0	0	0	0	0	0	0	0	0
5300 Unallocable between 5100 and 5200	-3	-583	-1 912	-3 056	-11 215	-8 831	-14 983	-24 953	-34 600	-29 270
6000 Other taxes	**292**	**1 704**	**3 371**	**5 497**	**13 281**	**17 463**	**129 330**	**74 878**	**33 497**	**45 049**
6100 Paid solely by business	0	354	1 063	2 093	4 259	5 624	6 873	10 544	16 052	20 635
Simplified system for small taxpayers	..	354	1 063	2 093	4 259	5 624	6 873	10 544	16 052	20 635
6200 Other	292	1 351	2 308	3 404	9 021	11 839	122 457	64 334	17 445	24 414
Tax debt payments	135	24	38	293	1 340	1 306	110 721	46 131	-8 646	-1 070
Special payments	79	6	0	0	0	0	0	0	0	0
Other national level	0	12	0	0	0	0	0	0	0	0
Other provincial level	78	1 309	2 269	3 110	7 681	10 533	11 736	18 203	26 092	25 485

.. Not available

Note: Year ending 31st December.

The data are on a cash basis.

The figures exclude local government tax revenues as the data are not available (but include provincial revenues).

Heading 2000: The figures may be under-estimated as they exclude certain types of social security contributions for which data are not readily available..

Heading 5212: In ECLAC data, property tax on motor vehicles is classified in category 4000.

Heading 5300: The figures are negative as they represent general reimbursements of exports and specific taxes on goods and services.

Heading 6200: The tax debt payments from 2016 include revenue following the implementation of a new voluntary disclosure regime in July 2016 (Law 27260).

Source: Subsecretaría de Ingresos Públicos, Dirección Nacional de Investigaciones y Análisis Fiscal, Ministerio de Hacienda (Undersecretary of Public Revenue, National Direction of Research and Fiscal Analysis, Ministry of Finance).

StatLink https://doi.org/10.1787/888934235506

Table 5.3. **Bahamas**

Details of tax revenue / Ingresos tributarios detallados

Million BSD

	1990	2000	2007	2010	2014	2015	2016	2017	2018	2019
Total tax revenue	**505**	**965**	**1 360**	**1 277**	**1 490**	**1 761**	**1 940**	**2 118**	**2 126**	**2 509**
1000 Taxes on income, profits and capital gains	**0**	**0**	**0**	**0**	**0**	**0**	**0**	**0**	**0**	**0**
1100 Of individuals	0	0	0	0	0	0	0	0	0	0
1110 On income and profits	..	..	..	..	..	..	..	..	..	..
1120 On capital gains	..	..	..	..	..	..	..	..	..	..
1200 Corporate	0	0	0	0	0	0	0	0	0	0
1210 On profits	..	..	..	..	..	..	..	..	..	..
1220 On capital gains of corporates	..	..	..	..	..	..	..	..	..	..
1300 Unallocable between 1100 and 1200	0	0	0	0	0	0	0	0	0	0
2000 Social security contributions	**66**	**115**	**155**	**167**	**245**	**260**	**261**	**277**	**290**	**310**
2100 Employees	..	..	..	60	91	98	102	110	..	..
2110 On a payroll basis	..	..	..	..	..	..	..	..	..	..
2120 On an income tax basis	..	..	..	..	..	..	..	..	..	..
2200 Employers	..	..	..	104	149	157	154	161	..	..
2210 On a payroll basis	..	..	..	..	..	..	..	..	..	..
2220 On an income tax basis	..	..	..	..	..	..	..	..	..	..
2300 Self-employed or non-employed	..	..	..	3	6	6	7	7	..	..
2310 On a payroll basis	..	..	..	..	..	..	..	..	..	..
2320 On an income tax basis	..	..	..	..	..	..	..	..	..	..
2400 Unallocable between 2100, 2200 and 2300	66	115	155	0	-1	-1	-1	-1	290	310
2410 On a payroll basis	..	..	..	..	..	..	..	..	..	..
2420 On an income tax basis	..	..	..	..	..	..	..	..	..	..
3000 Taxes on payroll and workforce	**0**	**0**	**0**	**0**	**0**	**0**	**0**	**0**	**0**	**0**
4000 Taxes on property	**56**	**208**	**450**	**269**	**268**	**298**	**204**	**233**	**237**	**345**
4100 Recurrent taxes on immovable property	19	32	79	92	104	107	104	121	124	109
4110 Households	0	0	0	0	0	0	0	0	0	0
4120 Others	19	32	79	92	104	107	104	121	124	109
4200 Recurrent taxes on net wealth	0	0	0	0	0	0	0	0	0	0
4210 Individual	..	..	..	..	..	..	..	..	..	..
4220 Corporate	..	..	..	..	..	..	..	..	..	..
4300 Estate, inheritance and gift taxes	0	0	0	0	0	0	0	0	0	0
4310 Estate and inheritance taxes	..	..	..	..	..	..	..	..	..	..
4320 Gift taxes	..	..	..	..	..	..	..	..	..	..
4400 Taxes on financial and capital transactions	37	176	371	177	164	191	100	112	114	235
Stamp Tax from Imports	0	102	143	15	0	0	0	0	0	0
Stamp Tax from Exports	0	0	0	0	0	0	0	0	0	0
All Other Stamp Tax	37	74	228	162	164	191	100	112	114	235
4500 Non-recurrent taxes	0	0	0	0	0	0	0	0	0	0
4510 On net wealth	..	..	..	..	..	..	..	..	..	..
4520 Other non-recurrent taxes	..	..	..	..	..	..	..	..	..	..
4600 Other recurrent taxes on property	0	0	0	0	0	0	0	0	0	0
5000 Taxes on goods and services	**386**	**620**	**737**	**780**	**986**	**1 203**	**1 475**	**1 608**	**1 598**	**1 854**
5100 Taxes on production, sale, transfer, etc	354	552	638	657	772	993	1 297	1 386	1 407	1 623
5110 General taxes	0	0	0	0	0	219	628	638	681	897
5111 Value added taxes	0	0	0	0	0	219	628	638	681	897
5112 Sales tax	..	..	..	..	..	0	0	0	0	0
5113 Other	..	..	..	..	..	0	0	0	0	0
5120 Taxes on specific goods and services	354	552	638	657	772	775	669	747	726	727
5121 Excises	0	0	0	188	249	262	231	289	257	242
Fuel surcharges	..	..	..	..	..	..	1	1	1	1
Other excises	..	..	..	..	..	..	230	287	255	241
5122 Profits of fiscal monopolies	0	0	0	0	0	0	0	0	0	0
5123 Customs and import duties	289	435	507	348	336	307	263	286	270	284
5124 Taxes on exports	6	13	14	14	10	9	13	9	18	13
5125 Taxes on investment goods	0	0	0	0	0	0	0	0	0	0
5126 Taxes on specific services	59	104	117	106	178	197	162	163	180	187
Departure tax	27	64	77	70	125	147	135	135	143	147
Gaming tax	27	20	14	10	8	25	26	27	37	40
Hotel occupancy tax	5	20	26	25	45	25	1	1	0	0
5127 Other taxes on internat. trade and transactions	0	0	0	0	0	0	0	0	0	0
5128 Other taxes	0	0	0	0	0	0	0	0	0	0
5130 Unallocable between 5110 and 5120	0	0	0	0	0	0	0	0	0	0
5200 Taxes on use of goods and perform activities	32	69	99	123	214	209	178	222	192	231
5210 Recurrent taxes	32	69	99	123	214	209	178	222	192	231
Motor vehicle tax	10	14	20	21	29	29	29	30	37	35
5211 Paid by households: motor vehicles	..	..	..	..	..	..	..	..	..	..
5212 Paid by others: motor vehicles	..	..	..	..	..	..	..	..	..	..

Table 5.3. **Bahamas** *(cont.)*

Details of tax revenue / Ingresos tributarios detallados

Million BSD

	1990	2000	2007	2010	2014	2015	2016	2017	2018	2019
5213 Paid in respect of other goods	22	55	78	102	185	180	149	193	155	195
Company fees and registration	0	5	5	5	5	5	0	0	0	0
International business companies	0	17	20	19	17	16	0	0	0	0
Others	22	33	54	78	163	159	149	193	155	195
5220 Non-recurrent taxes	0	0	0	0	0	0	0	0	0	0
5300 Unallocable between 5100 and 5200	0	0	0	0	0	0	0	0	0	0
6000 Other taxes	**-4**	**21**	**17**	**60**	**-8**	**0**	**0**	**0**	**0**	**0**
6100 Paid solely by business	0	0	0	0	0	0	0	..	..	..
6200 Other	-4	21	17	60	-8	0	0	..	..	..
Incentive acts and other refunds	-8	14	-5	11	-8	0	..	..	..	..
Other taxes	4	7	22	49	0	0	..	..	..	..

.. Not available

Note: Fiscal year ending on 30th June. For example, the data for 2019 represent July 2018 to June 2019.
The data are on a cash basis.
The data for 2018 and 2019 are preliminary and taken from the Central Bank of The Bahamas.
The figures exclude local government tax revenues as the data are not available.
Heading 2000: The data are estimated for 2018 and 2019.
Heading 2400: This heading includes refunds of social security contributions as reported by the National Insurance Board (NIB).
Heading 4400: This heading includes all stamp taxes.
Heading 5111: A value added tax was enforced on 1st January 2015.
Heading 5121: Fuel surcharges for different petroleum products are identified and separated from other excises between 2016 and 2019 in this edition.

Source: The Central Bank of The Bahamas; Ministry of Finance of The Bahamas; National Insurance Board of The Bahamas.

StatLink https://doi.org/10.1787/888934235525

Table 5.4. **Barbados**

Details of tax revenue / Ingresos tributarios detallados

Million BBD

	1990	2000	2007	2010	2014	2015	2016	2017	2018	2019
Total tax revenue	**1 026**	**1 892**	**2 824**	**2 736**	**2 715**	**2 813**	**3 041**	**3 218**	**3 385**	**3 358**
1000 Taxes on income, profits and capital gains	**250**	**599**	**947**	**766**	**678**	**714**	**802**	**783**	**921**	**823**
1100 Of individuals	140	293	335	395	441	433	492	463	482	455
1110 On income and profits	140	293	335	395	441	433	492	463	482	455
Personal income tax	140	293	335	395	413	397	488	463	482	455
Consolidation tax	0	0	0	0	28	36	3	0	0	0
1120 On capital gains	..	..	..	..	..	..	..	..	..	..
1200 Corporate	95	269	521	294	156	215	248	275	355	309
1210 On profits	95	269	521	294	156	215	248	275	355	309
1220 On capital gains of corporates	..	..	..	..	..	..	..	..	..	..
1300 Unallocable between 1100 and 1200	15	37	91	76	81	66	63	45	83	59
2000 Social security contributions	**134**	**295**	**487**	**565**	**532**	**546**	**547**	**562**	**572**	**586**
2100 Employees	..	..	..	..	..	..	..	..	..	..
2110 On a payroll basis	..	..	..	..	..	..	..	..	..	..
2120 On an income tax basis	..	..	..	..	..	..	..	..	..	..
2200 Employers	..	..	..	..	..	..	..	..	..	..
2210 On a payroll basis	..	..	..	..	..	..	..	..	..	..
2220 On an income tax basis	..	..	..	..	..	..	..	..	..	..
2300 Self-employed or non-employed	..	..	..	..	..	..	..	..	..	..
2310 On a payroll basis	..	..	..	..	..	..	..	..	..	..
2320 On an income tax basis	..	..	..	..	..	..	..	..	..	..
2400 Unallocable between 2100, 2200 and 2300	134	295	487	565	532	546	547	562	572	586
2410 On a payroll basis	..	..	..	..	..	..	..	..	..	..
2420 On an income tax basis	..	..	..	..	..	..	..	..	..	..
3000 Taxes on payroll and workforce	**0**	**0**	**0**	**0**	**0**	**0**	**0**	**0**	**0**	**0**
4000 Taxes on property	**147**	**108**	**125**	**130**	**207**	**143**	**145**	**148**	**172**	**226**
4100 Recurrent taxes on immovable property	46	95	103	118	196	133	135	138	161	215
Property tax	46	95	103	118	164	133	135	138	161	215
Municipal solid waste tax	0	0	0	0	32	0	0	0	0	0
4110 Households	..	..	..	..	..	..	..	..	..	..
4120 Others	..	..	..	..	..	..	..	..	..	..
4200 Recurrent taxes on net wealth	0	0	0	0	0	0	0	0	0	0
4210 Individual	..	..	..	..	..	..	..	..	..	..
4220 Corporate	..	..	..	..	..	..	..	..	..	..
4300 Estate, inheritance and gift taxes	0	0	0	0	0	0	0	0	0	0
4310 Estate and inheritance taxes	..	..	..	..	..	..	..	..	..	..
4320 Gift taxes	..	..	..	..	..	..	..	..	..	..
4400 Taxes on financial and capital transactions	101	13	22	12	11	10	9	11	11	11
Stamp duties	101	13	22	12	11	10	9	11	11	11
4500 Non-recurrent taxes	0	0	0	0	0	0	0	0	0	0
4510 On net wealth	..	..	..	..	..	..	..	..	..	..
4520 Other non-recurrent taxes	..	..	..	..	..	..	..	..	..	..
4600 Other recurrent taxes on property	0	0	0	0	0	0	0	0	0	0
5000 Taxes on goods and services	**495**	**889**	**1 265**	**1 276**	**1 298**	**1 410**	**1 547**	**1 726**	**1 719**	**1 723**
5100 Taxes on production, sale, transfer, etc	424	788	1 151	1 105	1 193	1 291	1 423	1 610	1 599	1 607
5110 General taxes	197	492	790	768	806	861	920	1 039	990	967
5111 Value added taxes	0	492	790	768	806	861	890	887	941	967
5112 Sales tax	197	0	0	0	0	0	29	152	49	0
Social responsibility levy	0	0	..	..	..	..	29	152	49	0
Consumption tax	197	0	..	..	..	..	0	0	0	0
5113 Other	0	0	0	0	0	0	0	0	0	0
5120 Taxes on specific goods and services	227	296	362	337	386	430	503	570	608	640
5121 Excises	91	175	164	146	136	169	226	303	271	251
Excises	0	160	164	146	136	169	226	303	271	251
Levies	91	15	0	0	0	0	0	0	0	0
5122 Profits of fiscal monopolies	0	0	0	0	0	0	0	0	0	0
5123 Customs and import duties	118	121	197	191	224	232	245	219	282	314
Import duties	118	121	197	191	224	232	245	219	214	232
Fuel tax	0	0	0	0	0	0	0	0	69	82
5124 Taxes on exports	0	0	0	0	0	0	0	0	0	0
5125 Taxes on investment goods	0	0	0	0	0	0	0	0	0	0
5126 Taxes on specific services	17	1	0	0	27	29	33	49	55	76
Hotel and restaurant tax	17	1	..	..	0	0	0	0	0	0
Banks and other asset tax	0	0	..	..	27	29	33	49	45	47
Room rate levy	0	0	..	..	0	0	0	0	10	28
5127 Other taxes on internat. trade and transactions	0	0	0	0	0	0	0	0	0	0
5128 Other taxes	0	0	0	0	0	0	0	0	0	0
5130 Unallocable between 5110 and 5120	0	0	0	0	0	0	0	0	0	0

Table 5.4. **Barbados** *(cont.)*

Details of tax revenue / Ingresos tributarios detallados

Million BBD

	1990	2000	2007	2010	2014	2015	2016	2017	2018	2019
5200 Taxes on use of goods and perform activities	71	101	114	171	105	119	124	116	121	115
5210 Recurrent taxes	71	101	114	171	105	119	124	116	121	115
5211 Paid by households: motor vehicles	0	0	0	0	0	0	0	0	0	0
5212 Paid by others: motor vehicles	0	0	0	0	0	0	0	0	0	0
5213 Paid in respect of other goods	71	101	114	171	105	119	124	116	121	115
5220 Non-recurrent taxes	0	0	0	0	0	0	0	0	0	0
5300 Unallocable between 5100 and 5200	0	0	0	0	0	0	0	0	0	0
6000 Other taxes	**0**	**0**	**0**	**0**	**0**	**0**	**0**	**0**	**0**	**0**
6100 Paid solely by business	..	..	..	..	..	..	..	..	..	..
6200 Other	..	..	..	..	..	..	..	..	..	..

.. Not available

Note: Year ending 31st March. For example, the data for 2019 represent April 2019 to March 2020.

The data are on a cash basis.

The figures exclude local government tax revenues as the data are not available.

Heading 1300: This heading includes withholding taxes levied on both individuals and corporate entities.

Heading 2000: Social security contributions refer to contribution income of National Insurance Scheme obtained from Actuarial Reviews of the National Insurance, Unemployment and Severance Funds. Data for 2015-19 are best-estimate projections in the 15th Actuarial Review.

Heading 5123: Fuel tax is classified under heading 5123 in this edition. It was previously under heading 5213.

Heading 5126: Room rate levy is classified under heading 5126 in this edition. It was previously under heading 5213.

Heading 5213: This heading includes miscellaneous indirect taxes levied on a recurrent basis such as revenues from various licenses.

Source: The Central Bank of Barbados; National Insurance Board of Barbados.

StatLink https://doi.org/10.1787/888934235544

Table 5.5. **Belize / Belice**

Details of tax revenue / Ingresos tributarios detallados

Million BZD

	1990	2000	2007	2010	2014	2015	2016	2017	2018	2019
Total tax revenue	**178**	**318**	**652**	**740**	**927**	**947**	**1 005**	**1 054**	**1 129**	**1 190**
1000 Taxes on income, profits and capital gains	**37**	**76**	**180**	**248**	**272**	**254**	**261**	**269**	**286**	**300**
1100 Of individuals	21	19	45	52	74	82	88	93	101	103
1110 On income and profits	21	19	45	52	74	82	88	93	101	103
Income tax (PAYE)	20	19	45	52	74	82	88	93	101	103
Income tax on individuals	1	0	0	0	0	0	0	0	0	0
1120 On capital gains	..	..	..	..	..	..	..	..	..	..
1200 Corporate	12	51	127	189	183	159	162	166	173	185
Income tax (companies)	12	1	11	51	16	1	0	0	3	3
Income tax (business tax)	0	51	115	138	167	158	162	166	170	181
Income tax (supplemental petroleum tax)	0	0	0	0	0	0	0	0	0	0
1210 On profits	..	..	..	..	..	..	..	..	..	..
1220 On capital gains of corporates	..	..	..	..	..	..	..	..	..	..
1300 Unallocable between 1100 and 1200	4	6	9	7	15	13	11	10	12	12
Income tax (arrears)	4	3	5	1	2	2	2	2	3	2
Income tax (withholding)	0	3	4	6	13	11	9	8	10	10
2000 Social security contributions	**10**	**18**	**53**	**60**	**72**	**77**	**80**	**83**	**87**	**100**
2100 Employees	..	..	..	..	..	..	..	..	..	..
2110 On a payroll basis	..	..	..	..	..	..	..	..	..	..
2120 On an income tax basis	..	..	..	..	..	..	..	..	..	..
2200 Employers	..	..	..	..	..	..	..	..	..	..
2210 On a payroll basis	..	..	..	..	..	..	..	..	..	..
2220 On an income tax basis	..	..	..	..	..	..	..	..	..	..
2300 Self-employed or non-employed	..	..	..	..	..	..	..	..	..	..
2310 On a payroll basis	..	..	..	..	..	..	..	..	..	..
2320 On an income tax basis	..	..	..	..	..	..	..	..	..	..
2400 Unallocable between 2100, 2200 and 2300	10	18	53	60	72	77	80	83	87	100
2410 On a payroll basis	..	..	..	..	..	..	..	..	..	..
2420 On an income tax basis	..	..	..	..	..	..	..	..	..	..
3000 Taxes on payroll and workforce	**0**	**0**	**0**	**0**	**0**	**0**	**0**	**0**	**0**	**0**
4000 Taxes on property	**34**	**13**	**31**	**23**	**35**	**35**	**31**	**32**	**49**	**41**
4100 Recurrent taxes on immovable property	1	2	7	7	6	5	7	6	6	6
4110 Households	1	2	7	7	6	5	7	6	6	6
4120 Others	0	0	0	0	0	0	0	0	0	0
4200 Recurrent taxes on net wealth	0	0	0	0	0	0	0	0	0	0
4210 Individual	..	..	..	..	..	..	..	..	..	..
4220 Corporate	..	..	..	..	..	..	..	..	..	..
4300 Estate, inheritance and gift taxes	0	0	0	0	0	0	0	0	0	0
4310 Estate and inheritance taxes	..	0	0	0	0	0	0	0	0	0
4320 Gift taxes	..	0	0	0	0	0	0	0	0	0
4400 Taxes on financial and capital transactions	33	11	24	16	29	29	25	26	44	35
Stamp duties on customs	28	0	0	0	0	0	0	0	0	0
Stamp duties (other departments)	5	11	24	16	29	29	25	26	44	24
Stamp duties (land transactions)	0	0	0	0	0	0	0	0	0	12
4500 Non-recurrent taxes	0	0	0	0	0	0	0	0	0	0
4510 On net wealth	..	..	..	..	..	..	..	..	..	..
4520 Other non-recurrent taxes	..	..	..	..	..	..	..	..	..	..
4600 Other recurrent taxes on property	0	0	0	0	0	0	0	0	0	0
5000 Taxes on goods and services	**97**	**211**	**389**	**409**	**548**	**580**	**633**	**670**	**707**	**749**
5100 Taxes on production, sale, transfer, etc.	94	207	380	400	540	571	630	662	696	737
5110 General taxes	0	82	175	199	270	275	292	292	317	348
5111 Value added taxes	0	0	174	199	270	275	292	292	317	348
5112 Sales tax	..	82	0	0	0	0	0	0	0	0
5113 Other	..	0	0	0	0	0	0	0	0	0
5120 Taxes on specific goods and services	94	125	205	200	269	296	338	369	379	389
5121 Excises	35	47	72	31	38	39	159	187	193	191
Revenue replacement duty	18	39	49	7	15	15	1	1	1	1
Excise duties	17	8	22	22	22	23	157	186	191	190
Excise on locally refined petroleum products	0	0	0	0	0	1	0	0	1	0
Excise on locally extracted crude oil	0	0	0	1	1	0	1	1	1	1
5122 Profits of fiscal monopolies	0	0	0	0	0	0	0	0	0	0
5123 Customs and import duties	50	64	113	144	196	221	154	139	139	140
Import duties	50	64	92	123	167	190	123	98	98	98
Environmental tax	0	0	21	21	29	31	31	40	41	43
Imports into EPZs	0	0	0	0	0	0	0	0	0	0
5124 Taxes on exports	0	0	0	0	0	0	0	0	0	0
5125 Taxes on investment goods	0	0	0	0	0	0	0	0	0	0
5126 Taxes on specific services	0	0	0	0	0	0	0	0	0	0

Table 5.5. **Belize / Belice** *(cont.)*

Details of tax revenue / Ingresos tributarios detallados

Million BZD

	1990	2000	2007	2010	2014	2015	2016	2017	2018	2019
5127 Other taxes on internat. trade and transactions	8	14	21	25	35	35	24	43	47	58
Goods in transit - administration charge	3	1	1	1	1	1	1	1	1	1
Goods in transit - social fee	0	5	6	8	12	11	10	17	23	23
Taxes on foreign currency transactions	6	8	14	16	22	23	13	25	23	34
5128 Other taxes	0	0	0	0	0	0	0	0	0	0
5130 Unallocable between 5110 and 5120	0	0	0	0	0	0	0	0	0	0
5200 Taxes on use of goods and perform activities	3	4	8	9	9	9	3	9	11	11
5210 Recurrent taxes	3	4	8	9	9	9	3	9	11	11
5211 Paid by households: motor vehicles	2	3	6	3	4	4	0	5	5	4
5212 Paid by others: motor vehicles	0	0	0	0	0	0	0	0	0	0
5213 Paid in respect of other goods	1	1	3	6	5	5	3	4	6	7
5220 Non-recurrent taxes	0	0	0	0	0	0	0	0	0	0
5300 Unallocable between 5100 and 5200	0	0	0	0	0	0	0	0	0	0
6000 Other taxes	**0**	**0**	**0**	**0**	**0**	**0**	**0**	**0**	**0**	**0**
6100 Paid solely by business	..	..	..	..	..	..	..	..	..	..
6200 Other	..	..	..	..	..	..	..	..	..	..

.. Not available

Note: Year ending 31st March. For example, the data for 2019 represent April 2019 to March 2020.

The data are on a cash basis.

The data for 2019 represent the revised estimates for the 2019/20 fiscal year reported in the *Approved Estimates of Revenue and Expenditure for Fiscal Year 2020/2021*.

Heading 2000: Social security contributions refer to total contributions to the Social Security Fund excluding government contributions to the National Health Insurance (NHI) fund. The government contributions are government subsidies to the social security system and hence are not considered as tax revenues according to the OECD classification described in the Interpretative Guide.

Heading 4400: This heading includes all stamp duties. Stamp duties for land transactions have been added in this edition.

Source: Ministry of Finance of Belize; Social Security Board Belize.

StatLink https://doi.org/10.1787/888934235563

Table 5.6. **Bolivia**

Details of tax revenue / Ingresos tributarios detallados

Million BOB

	1990	2000	2007	2010	2014	2015	2016	2017	2018	2019
Total tax revenue	**1 005**	**10 462**	**22 912**	**31 549**	**63 508**	**67 264**	**65 492**	**67 072**	**69 535**	**69 785**
1000 Taxes on income, profits and capital gains	**68**	**1 209**	**3 433**	**6 294**	**12 723**	**12 809**	**10 876**	**10 152**	**10 591**	**11 356**
1100 Of individuals	68	214	217	263	439	508	496	502	525	518
1110 On income and profits	68	214	217	263	439	508	496	502	525	518
Value added supplementary scheme	62	161	195	237	401	461	442	441	475	464
Fiscal notes on value added supplementary scheme	6	52	23	26	38	47	55	61	50	53
1120 On capital gains	..	..	..	..	..	..	..	..	..	..
1200 Corporate	0	995	3 215	6 031	12 284	12 302	10 379	9 650	10 066	10 838
1210 On profits	..	995	3 215	6 031	12 284	12 302	10 379	9 650	10 066	10 838
Corporate tax	..	804	2 922	5 089	9 062	10 260	8 638	8 655	9 165	9 724
Fiscal notes on corporate tax	..	191	293	942	3 222	2 041	1 742	995	901	1 115
1220 On capital gains of corporates	..	..	..	..	..	..	..	..	..	..
1300 Unallocable between 1100 and 1200	0	0	0	0	0	0	0	0	0	0
2000 Social security contributions	**..**	**1 977**	**3 598**	**5 265**	**12 513**	**14 235**	**14 828**	**15 915**	**16 767**	**17 500**
2100 Employees	..	..	..	..	..	..	..	..	..	..
2110 On a payroll basis	..	..	..	..	..	..	..	..	..	..
2120 On an income tax basis	..	..	..	..	..	..	..	..	..	..
2200 Employers	..	..	..	..	..	..	..	..	..	..
2210 On a payroll basis	..	..	..	..	..	..	..	..	..	..
2220 On an income tax basis	..	..	..	..	..	..	..	..	..	..
2300 Self-employed or non-employed	..	..	..	..	..	..	..	..	..	..
2310 On a payroll basis	..	..	..	..	..	..	..	..	..	..
2320 On an income tax basis	..	..	..	..	..	..	..	..	..	..
2400 Unallocable between 2100, 2200 and 2300	..	1 977	3 598	5 265	12 513	14 235	14 828	15 915	16 767	17 500
2410 On a payroll basis	..	1 977	3 598	5 265	12 513	14 235	14 828	15 915	16 767	17 500
2420 On an income tax basis	..	0	0	0	0	0	0	0	0	0
3000 Taxes on payroll and workforce	**0**	**0**	**0**	**0**	**0**	**0**	**0**	**0**	**0**	**0**
4000 Taxes on property	**1**	**3**	**334**	**367**	**433**	**424**	**455**	**492**	**543**	**522**
4100 Recurrent taxes on immovable property	0	0	0	0	0	0	0	0	0	0
4110 Households	..	..	..	..	..	..	..	..	..	..
4120 Others	..	..	..	..	..	..	..	..	..	..
4200 Recurrent taxes on net wealth	0	0	0	0	0	0	0	0	0	0
4210 Individual	..	..	..	..	..	..	..	..	..	..
4220 Corporate	..	..	..	..	..	..	..	..	..	..
4300 Estate, inheritance and gift taxes	1	3	11	20	32	36	15	1	0	0
4310 Estate and inheritance taxes	1	3	11	20	32	36	15	1	0	0
4320 Gift taxes	0	0	0	0	0	0	0	0	0	0
4400 Taxes on financial and capital transactions	0	0	324	347	401	388	439	491	543	522
4500 Non-recurrent taxes	0	0	0	0	0	0	0	0	0	0
4510 On net wealth	..	..	..	..	..	..	..	..	..	..
4520 Other non-recurrent taxes	..	..	..	..	..	..	..	..	..	..
4600 Other recurrent taxes on property	0	0	0	0	0	0	0	0	0	0
5000 Taxes on goods and services	**907**	**6 656**	**14 261**	**17 791**	**33 910**	**34 759**	**33 441**	**34 022**	**35 215**	**34 187**
5100 Taxes on production, sale, transfer, etc.	907	6 656	14 261	17 791	33 910	34 759	33 441	34 022	35 215	34 187
5110 General taxes	584	3 953	9 568	12 541	24 714	25 247	24 327	24 591	25 615	25 405
5111 Value added taxes	432	2 949	7 487	10 259	20 580	20 756	19 902	20 199	20 977	20 391
VAT (internal market)	178	1 204	3 001	4 100	9 273	9 914	10 318	9 910	10 155	10 000
VAT (imports)	178	1 445	3 734	5 193	9 389	9 738	8 458	9 154	9 387	8 594
VAT fiscal notes (internal market)	56	223	654	581	760	666	622	439	411	271
VAT fiscal notes (imports)	20	76	99	385	1 158	438	504	696	1 024	1 526
5112 Sales tax	0	0	0	0	0	0	0	0	0	0
5113 Other	151	1 005	2 081	2 282	4 134	4 491	4 425	4 392	4 638	5 014
Transactions tax	136	943	1 905	2 174	4 081	4 463	4 386	4 323	4 547	4 652
Fiscal note on transactions tax	15	62	176	107	53	28	39	69	92	362
5120 Taxes on specific goods and services	324	2 702	4 693	5 250	9 196	9 511	9 114	9 430	9 600	8 782
5121 Excises	118	2 047	3 546	3 658	5 663	5 853	6 040	6 032	6 191	5 187
Excises (internal market)	61	244	598	933	1 365	1 486	1 687	1 450	1 649	1 456
Excises (Imports)	22	298	485	379	1 051	1 109	917	953	1 091	785
Special tax on hydrocarbons and derivatives	0	1 348	2 073	1 070	1 998	2 581	2 695	3 105	3 076	1 911
Fiscal notes on excises	35	118	119	155	328	262	103	442	272	442
Fiscal notes on special tax on hydrocarb. and deriv.	0	40	271	1 121	921	415	638	82	103	594
5122 Profits of fiscal monopolies	0	0	0	0	0	0	0	0	0	0
5123 Customs and import duties	204	640	1 114	1 545	3 102	3 254	2 893	3 198	3 185	3 376
Customs and import duties	163	616	1 079	1 504	2 879	3 057	2 786	3 043	2 937	2 976
Fiscal notes on customs and import duties	41	24	34	41	223	197	107	155	248	399
5124 Taxes on exports	0	0	0	0	0	0	0	0	0	0
5125 Taxes on investment goods	0	0	0	0	0	0	0	0	0	0

Table 5.6. **Bolivia** *(cont.)*

Details of tax revenue / Ingresos tributarios detallados

Million BOB

	1990	2000	2007	2010	2014	2015	2016	2017	2018	2019
5126 Taxes on specific services	2	15	33	47	120	127	175	200	224	218
Air departure tax	2	15	33	47	90	102	116	122	128	130
Tax on gambling	0	0	0	0	30	25	59	78	96	88
5127 Other taxes on internat. trade and transactions	0	0	0	0	311	277	6	0	0	0
5128 Other taxes	0	0	0	0	0	0	0	0	0	0
5130 Unallocable between 5110 and 5120	0	0	0	0	0	0	0	0	0	0
5200 Taxes on use of goods and perform activities	0	0	0	0	0	0	0	0	0	0
5210 Recurrent taxes	..	..	..	..	..	..	..	..	..	..
5211 Paid by households: motor vehicles	..	..	..	..	..	..	..	..	..	..
5212 Paid by others: motor vehicles	..	..	..	..	..	..	..	..	..	..
5213 Paid in respect of other goods	..	..	..	..	..	..	..	..	..	..
5220 Non-recurrent taxes	..	..	..	..	..	..	..	..	..	..
5300 Unallocable between 5100 and 5200	0	0	0	0	0	0	0	0	0	0
6000 Other taxes	**30**	**617**	**1 286**	**1 832**	**3 929**	**5 037**	**5 893**	**6 491**	**6 419**	**6 220**
6100 Paid solely by business	4	6	8	12	20	25	35	30	33	36
Simplified tax regime	3	6	8	12	20	25	35	30	33	36
Integrated tax system	1	0	0	0	0	0	0	0	0	0
6200 Other	26	611	1 278	1 819	3 908	5 012	5 858	6 461	6 386	6 184
Municipal taxes	0	575	961	1 381	2 145	2 585	3 073	3 737	3 561	3 203
Other taxes	20	35	279	422	1 716	2 378	2 696	2 685	2 784	2 866
Fiscal notes on other taxes	3	0	31	3	25	23	63	8	9	88
Unified agricultural regime	2	1	7	14	23	26	27	31	32	28

.. Not available

Note: Year ending 31st December.

The data are on a cash basis.

Central tax revenues have been updated with new information from Servicio de Impuestos Nacionales (SIN) and Aduana Nacional de Bolivia (ANB). The figures exclude local government tax revenues for the period 1990-1993 as the data are not available.

Heading 1210: Corporate tax under heading 1210 includes revenues from IUE (corporate tax), IUE-RE (corporate tax remittances) and IUM (mining profits). Fiscal notes on corporate tax include fiscal notes on IUE and IUM.

Heading 2000: The figures in this edition include social security contributions to Bolivia's pension system and healthcare related funds.

Heading 5113: This heading includes both IT (transactions tax) and its fiscal notes.

Heading 5127: This heading includes IVME (tax on the sales of foreign currency).

Heading 6200: Other taxes include revenues from conceptos varios (miscellaneous concepts), programa transitorio (transitional programme) and otros ingresos en efectivo (other cash revenue). Fiscal notes on other taxes include fiscal notes on conceptos varios

Source: Ministerio de Economía y Finanzas Públicas de Bolivia (Ministry of Economy and Public Finance of Bolivia); Servicio de Impuestos Nacionales (National Tax Service); Aduana Nacional de Bolivia (National Customs of Bolivia).

StatLink https://doi.org/10.1787/888934235582

Table 5.7. **Brazil / Brasil**

Details of tax revenue / Ingresos tributarios detallados

Million BRL

	1990	2000	2007	2010	2014	2015	2016	2017	2018	2019
Total tax revenue	**3**	**352 456**	**913 145**	**1 259 118**	**1 835 289**	**1 919 188**	**2 017 949**	**2 123 999**	**2 286 010**	**2 401 994**
1000 Taxes on income, profits and capital gains	**1**	**68 667**	**193 054**	**258 738**	**381 844**	**400 993**	**453 127**	**458 312**	**490 793**	**537 937**
1100 Of individuals	0	3 406	60 336	87 828	140 420	148 739	161 833	177 377	196 314	220 195
1110 On income and profits	0	3 406	60 336	87 828	140 420	148 739	161 833	177 377	196 314	220 195
Withholding income tax (IRRF)	0	0	47 631	71 579	114 638	121 540	133 549	146 872	163 801	182 495
Other personal income taxes	0	3 406	12 706	16 248	25 782	27 199	28 284	30 504	32 513	37 700
1120 On capital gains	..	..	..	..	..	..	..	..	..	..
1200 Corporate	0	25 430	99 062	128 255	171 352	164 057	197 941	184 501	194 814	207 505
1210 On profits	0	25 430	99 062	128 255	171 352	164 057	197 941	184 501	194 814	207 505
Corporate income tax	0	16 680	65 767	82 474	109 020	104 910	131 181	113 815	119 063	127 130
Social contribution on net profits (CSLL)	0	8 750	33 295	45 780	62 332	59 147	66 760	70 686	75 751	80 374
1220 On capital gains of corporates	..	..	..	..	..	..	..	..	..	..
1300 Unallocable between 1100 and 1200	0	39 831	33 656	42 656	70 072	88 196	93 353	96 434	99 666	110 237
Withholding tax on non-resident income (remittances abroad)	..	..	7 868	11 537	19 703	24 669	24 892	27 270	35 331	39 307
Withholding tax on capital income	..	..	21 384	24 887	41 288	53 692	59 404	59 470	53 585	57 184
Withholding tax on other income	..	..	4 404	6 232	9 082	9 836	9 057	9 694	10 749	13 746
2000 Social security contributions	**1**	**83 469**	**214 508**	**316 530**	**482 515**	**503 222**	**528 423**	**556 408**	**585 684**	**617 445**
2100 Employees	..	..	51 984	75 509	111 311	114 653	121 969	128 517	139 970	..
2110 On a payroll basis	..	..	51 984	75 509	111 311	114 653	121 969	128 517	139 970	..
2120 On an income tax basis	..	..	0	0	0	0	0	0	0	..
2200 Employers	0	18 709	161 934	240 280	351 454	369 094	389 923	408 005	430 521	128 710
2210 On a payroll basis	0	18 709	161 934	240 280	351 454	369 094	389 923	408 005	430 521	128 710
2220 On an income tax basis	0	0	0	0	0	0	0	0	0	0
2300 Self-employed or non-employed	..	..	..	..	..	..	..	..	..	..
2310 On a payroll basis	..	..	..	..	..	..	..	..	..	..
2320 On an income tax basis	..	..	..	..	..	..	..	..	..	..
2400 Unallocable between 2100, 2200 and 2300	1	64 760	590	741	19 750	19 474	16 531	19 885	15 192	488 736
2410 On a payroll basis	1	64 760	590	741	19 750	19 474	16 531	19 885	15 192	488 736
2420 On an income tax basis	0	0	0	0	0	0	0	0	0	0
3000 Taxes on payroll and workforce	**0**	**5 437**	**13 985**	**21 348**	**35 953**	**37 891**	**38 629**	**39 824**	**42 223**	**42 527**
Payroll-based contribution to education	0	2 791	7 089	11 049	18 411	19 039	19 473	20 010	21 979	21 977
"S" System contributions	0	2 646	6 592	9 925	16 884	18 153	18 428	19 075	19 820	20 549
Other payroll taxes	0	0	304	374	658	699	728	739	423	0
4000 Taxes on property	**0**	**23 524**	**61 870**	**52 847**	**72 698**	**83 677**	**85 931**	**91 687**	**99 861**	**110 821**
4100 Recurrent taxes on immovable property	0	4 753	13 140	17 929	27 673	32 626	35 459	39 700	44 900	48 683
Tax on rural land property (ITR)	0	234	317	485	900	1 105	1 126	1 273	1 419	1 630
Tax on urban land property (IPTU)	0	4 519	12 822	17 444	26 773	31 521	34 333	38 427	43 481	47 053
4110 Households	..	..	..	..	..	..	..	..	..	..
4120 Others	..	..	..	..	..	..	..	..	..	..
4200 Recurrent taxes on net wealth	0	0	0	0	0	0	0	0	0	0
4210 Individual	..	..	..	..	..	..	..	..	..	..
4220 Corporate	..	..	..	..	..	..	..	..	..	..
4300 Estate, inheritance and gift taxes	0	329	1 207	2 518	4 698	6 461	7 345	7 242	7 330	8 625
4310 Estate and inheritance taxes	..	..	..	..	..	..	..	..	..	..
4320 Gift taxes	..	..	..	..	..	..	..	..	..	..
4400 Taxes on financial and capital transactions	0	18 442	47 523	32 400	40 327	44 591	43 126	44 745	47 630	53 513
Tax on financial operations (IOF)	0	3 096	7 818	26 571	29 756	34 681	33 645	34 660	36 615	40 945
Tax on real estate property transfers (ITBI)	0	950	3 383	5 840	10 507	9 904	9 482	10 062	11 013	12 568
Other	0	14 396	36 323	-12	63	5	0	23	3	0
4500 Non-recurrent taxes	0	0	0	0	0	0	0	0	0	0
4510 On net wealth	..	..	..	..	..	..	..	..	..	..
4520 Other non-recurrent taxes	..	..	..	..	..	..	..	..	..	..
4600 Other recurrent taxes on property	0	0	0	0	0	0	0	0	0	0
5000 Taxes on goods and services	**2**	**169 181**	**406 743**	**578 496**	**816 930**	**844 372**	**855 787**	**918 927**	**1 010 015**	**1 028 896**
5100 Taxes on production, sale, transfer, etc	2	163 887	388 675	551 730	775 518	799 376	808 229	870 841	957 625	981 655
5110 General taxes	1	136 743	335 395	483 061	685 125	704 240	724 180	780 810	853 288	878 380
5111 Value added taxes	1	82 279	187 190	268 117	384 287	396 428	413 175	441 039	479 310	508 832
Tax on the circulation of goods and services (ICMS)	1	82 279	187 190	268 117	384 287	396 428	413 175	441 039	479 310	508 832
5112 Sales tax	0	0	0	0	0	0	0	0	0	0
5113 Other	0	54 464	148 205	214 944	300 839	307 811	311 005	339 771	373 977	369 548
Contribution to COFINS	0	38 707	100 946	140 939	194 696	199 876	201 517	221 670	244 287	237 372
Contribution to PIS	0	8 339	21 813	30 714	41 950	42 632	44 797	49 380	54 461	51 390
Contribution to PASEP	0	1 312	4 049	9 880	9 491	9 958	10 026	11 395	12 066	12 626
Tax on general services (ISS)	0	6 106	20 673	32 756	53 888	54 455	53 838	56 403	62 126	68 160
Others	0	0	723	656	813	890	826	922	1 038	0
5120 Taxes on specific goods and services	0	27 144	53 280	68 669	90 392	95 136	84 049	90 031	104 338	103 276

Table 5.7. **Brazil / Brasil** *(cont.)*

Details of tax revenue / Ingresos tributarios detallados

Million BRL

	1990	2000	2007	2010	2014	2015	2016	2017	2018	2019
5121 Excises	0	18 699	39 241	45 053	49 227	51 320	47 853	52 863	57 913	55 233
Vehicles	..	..	5 238	5 787	4 940	4 367	3 299	4 467	5 713	5 639
Beverages	..	..	2 595	2 431	3 401	2 599	2 684	2 944	2 768	3 641
Tobacco	..	..	2 806	3 704	5 688	5 692	5 718	5 210	5 208	5 559
Fuels	..	..	7 943	7 759	26	3 271	6 001	5 821	3 928	2 793
Other excises	..	..	20 660	25 372	35 172	35 391	30 150	34 421	40 297	37 601
5122 Profits of fiscal monopolies	0	0	0	0	0	0	0	0	0	0
5123 Customs and import duties	0	8 445	12 157	21 072	36 612	38 870	31 308	32 284	40 575	42 842
5124 Taxes on exports	0	0	61	47	162	99	139	66	129	91
5125 Taxes on investment goods	0	0	0	0	0	0	0	0	0	0
5126 Taxes on specific services	0	0	1 017	1 286	1 892	1 863	1 809	1 807	1 623	0
Contribution on revenues of telecom companies	..	..	935	1 186	1 628	1 657	1 608	1 610	1 440	..
Contribution on billing of IT companies	..	..	80	100	262	206	200	196	182	..
Other taxes on specific services	..	..	1	1	3	1	0	1	1	..
5127 Other taxes on internat. trade and transactions	0	0	805	1 212	2 499	2 983	2 940	3 011	4 097	5 110
CIDE on remittances abroad	..	..	805	1 212	2 499	2 983	2 940	3 011	4 097	5 110
5128 Other taxes	0	0	0	0	0	0	0	0	0	0
5130 Unallocable between 5110 and 5120	0	0	0	0	0	0	0	0	0	0
5200 Taxes on use of goods and perform activities	0	5 294	18 068	26 765	41 412	44 997	47 559	48 087	52 389	47 241
5210 Recurrent taxes	0	5 294	16 687	24 417	38 209	41 992	44 817	45 225	48 668	47 241
5211 Paid by households: motor vehicles	0	5 294	16 523	24 197	36 422	40 460	43 336	43 810	45 432	47 241
Motor vehicle property tax (IPVA)	0	5 294	14 627	21 367	32 453	36 219	39 093	40 509	43 120	46 213
Contributions to DPVAT	0	0	1 896	2 830	3 969	4 242	4 243	3 302	2 312	1 027
5212 Paid by others: motor vehicles	0	0	0	0	0	0	0	0	0	0
5213 Paid in respect of other goods	0	0	164	220	1 787	1 531	1 481	1 415	3 235	0
CONDECINE	..	..	39	49	981	1 062	1 225	1 133	1 084	..
Others	..	..	125	170	806	469	256	281	2 151	..
5220 Non-recurrent taxes	0	0	1 381	2 349	3 204	3 005	2 741	2 862	3 722	0
AFRMM	..	..	1 381	2 349	3 204	3 005	2 741	2 862	3 722	..
5300 Unallocable between 5100 and 5200	0	0	0	0	0	0	0	0	0	0
6000 Other taxes	**0**	**2 178**	**22 986**	**31 159**	**45 349**	**49 033**	**56 053**	**58 840**	**57 434**	**64 368**
6100 Paid solely by business	0	0	0	0	0	0	0	0	0	0
6200 Other	0	2 178	22 986	31 159	45 349	49 033	56 053	58 840	57 434	64 368

.. Not available

Note: Year ending 31st December.

The data are on a cash basis.

Data between 2002 and 2018 have been updated with detailed information from Carga Tributária no Brasil by the Secretaria da Receita Federal do Brasil. Data for 2019 are sourced from latest reports of Secretaria do Tesouro Nacional.

Heading 2000: Contributions to the General Social Security Regime (RGPS) for private sectors and contributions to the Own Social Security Schemes (RPPS) for public servants have been divided into employer and employee contributions in this edition. Contributions to military pensions, a share of contributions to the RPPS, have been classified under heading 2110 in this edition. They were previously under heading 2410. Contributions to the health fund for military police and military fire department have been classified under heading 2410 in this edition. They were previously under heading 6200.

Heading 3000: This heading includes contributions to aviation education and contributions to professional maritime education in this edition. They were previously under heading 6200. The rural contribution has been added and classified under heading 3000 in this edition. It refers to a rural industrial contribution levied on the payroll of companies which is no longer mandatory following a union contribution reform in 2017.

Heading 5113: Contributions to PASEP are included in contributions to PIS before 2000 as they cannot be distinguished. The contribution on revenues of electricity permissionaires and concessionaires has been classified under heading 5113 in this edition. It was previously under heading 6200.

Heading 5123: This heading includes tax on exports before 2002.

Heading 5126: This heading includes contributions on revenues of telecommunications companies, contributions on the billing of IT companies, contributions to bingo games and contributions on betting in equestrian competitions in this edition. They were previously under heading 6200. The additional tax on domestic airline tickets has been added and classified under this heading in this edition.

Heading 5213: This heading includes contributions to the development of the national film industry (CONDECINE), contributions on Lojas Francas (duty free stores) and contributions to the promotion of public broadcasting in this edition. They were previously under heading 6200.

Heading 5220: This heading includes the additional tax on freight for renovation of the merchant navy in this edition. It was previously under heading 5126.

Heading 6100: "Contributions to FUNDAF" has been removed in this edition as the components of these contributions have been identified using a new data source, and these have been allocated to their respective categories.

Heading 6200: Federal fees (Taxas Federais) and share of union contributions (Cota-Parte Contrib. Sindical) have been added in this edition. Share of union contributions refers to the 20% of total compulsory union contributions which are directly managed by the government. Since union contributions are no longer mandatory after a reform in 2017, data will not be included after this year. Voluntary contributions to Montepio Civil, other economic contributions (fees and penalties), contributions to the National Integration Program (PIN) and contributions to PROTERRA have been removed in this edition as they are not considered as tax revenues according to the OECD classification described in the Interpretative Guide.

Source: Secretaria da Receita Federal do Brasil, Ministério da Economia (Special Department of Federal Revenue of Brazil under Ministry of Economy); Secretaria do Tesouro Nacional, Ministério da Economia (National Treasury Secretariat under Ministry of Economy).

StatLink https://doi.org/10.1787/888934235601

Table 5.8. **Chile**

Details of tax revenue / Ingresos tributarios detallados

Million CLP

	1990	2000	2007	2010	2014	2015	2016	2017	2018	2019
Total tax revenue	**1 777 218**	**7 901 998**	**20 598 963**	**21 845 693**	**29 145 219**	**32 532 354**	**34 129 982**	**36 238 558**	**40 314 703**	**40 991 994**
1000 Taxes on income, profits and capital gains	**412 974**	**1 841 630**	**9 412 056**	**8 329 060**	**9 628 037**	**11 840 521**	**11 445 244**	**12 516 154**	**14 418 859**	**14 283 183**
1100 Of individuals	99 154	604 100	989 348	1 492 837	2 114 296	3 199 876	2 990 653	3 500 023	2 701 416	2 937 532
Second category tax	65 552	490 980	993 129	1 449 099	2 140 345	2 350 120	2 458 249	2 585 694	2 848 205	3 015 794
Global complementary tax	33 603	113 120	-3 781	43 738	-26 050	-36 757	-213 365	50 495	-146 789	-78 261
Others	0	0	0	0	0	886 513	745 769	863 834	0	0
1110 On income and profits	..	..	..	..	..	..	..	..	..	..
1120 On capital gains	..	..	..	..	..	..	..	..	..	..
1200 Corporate	219 586	882 896	6 054 487	4 448 745	6 196 077	6 839 133	7 147 331	7 658 420	8 920 497	9 597 472
First category tax	200 891	815 747	5 084 996	3 913 870	5 182 214	6 183 830	6 688 868	7 049 471	7 836 379	8 880 080
Surtax on state owned enterprises	16 074	47 634	113 334	194 203	100 851	132 352	88 362	193 058	184 442	122 054
Mining tax	0	0	835 452	298 558	801 647	323 507	106 560	101 970	184 382	277 861
Other	2 621	19 516	20 705	42 114	111 365	199 444	263 541	313 921	715 293	317 477
1210 On profits	..	..	..	..	..	..	..	..	..	..
1220 On capital gains of corporates	..	..	..	..	..	..	..	..	..	..
1300 Unallocable between 1100 and 1200	94 233	354 634	2 368 221	2 387 478	1 317 664	1 801 512	1 307 260	1 357 711	2 796 947	1 748 179
Additional tax	59 082	350 301	1 462 715	1 414 057	1 454 847	1 429 758	1 331 564	1 453 577	2 127 948	1 902 585
Other	35 151	4 332	905 507	973 421	-137 183	371 755	-24 304	-95 865	668 998	-154 406
2000 Social security contributions	**159 559**	**576 758**	**1 148 647**	**1 493 987**	**2 110 087**	**2 252 489**	**2 441 419**	**2 627 558**	**2 786 173**	**2 994 906**
2100 Employees	154 021	553 937	1 098 620	1 433 159	2 044 356	2 188 575	2 373 777	2 553 916	2 703 261	2 894 725
2110 On a payroll basis	154 021	553 937	1 098 620	1 433 159	2 044 356	2 188 575	2 373 777	2 553 916	2 703 261	2 894 725
2120 On an income tax basis	0	0	0	0	0	0	0	0	0	0
2200 Employers	5 538	22 821	50 027	60 828	65 731	63 914	67 642	73 643	82 912	100 181
2210 On a payroll basis	5 538	22 821	50 027	60 828	65 731	63 914	67 642	73 643	82 912	100 181
2220 On an income tax basis	0	0	0	0	0	0	0	0	0	0
2300 Self-employed or non-employed	0	0	0	0	0	0	0	0	0	0
2310 On a payroll basis	..	..	..	..	..	..	..	..	..	..
2320 On an income tax basis	..	..	..	..	..	..	..	..	..	..
2400 Unallocable between 2100, 2200 and 2300	0	0	0	0	0	0	0	0	0	0
2410 On a payroll basis	..	..	..	..	..	..	..	..	..	..
2420 On an income tax basis	..	..	..	..	..	..	..	..	..	..
3000 Taxes on payroll and workforce	**0**	**0**	**0**	**0**	**0**	**0**	**0**	**0**	**0**	**0**
4000 Taxes on property	**109 319**	**554 037**	**1 013 571**	**898 607**	**1 228 961**	**1 421 274**	**1 731 723**	**1 950 217**	**2 086 866**	**2 217 646**
4100 Recurrent taxes on immovable property	59 968	302 244	496 311	662 368	924 062	1 056 920	1 171 399	1 229 195	1 373 495	1 482 267
4110 Households	..	..	..	..	..	..	..	..	..	..
4120 Others	..	..	..	..	..	..	..	..	..	..
4200 Recurrent taxes on net wealth	0	0	0	0	0	0	0	0	0	0
4210 Individual	..	..	..	..	..	..	..	..	..	..
4220 Corporate	..	..	..	..	..	..	..	..	..	..
4300 Estate, inheritance and gift taxes	3 444	10 906	28 501	39 338	31 340	92 236	100 490	202 376	125 649	62 824
4310 Estate and inheritance taxes	..	..	..	..	..	..	..	..	..	..
4320 Gift taxes	..	..	..	..	..	..	..	..	..	..
4400 Taxes on financial and capital transactions	45 907	240 886	488 759	196 901	273 559	272 118	459 834	518 645	587 721	672 555
4500 Non-recurrent taxes	0	0	0	0	0	0	0	0	0	0
4510 On net wealth	..	..	..	..	..	..	..	..	..	..
4520 Other non-recurrent taxes	..	..	..	..	..	..	..	..	..	..
4600 Other recurrent taxes on property	0	0	0	0	0	0	0	0	0	0
5000 Taxes on goods and services	**1 118 722**	**5 041 769**	**9 023 666**	**11 185 156**	**16 127 855**	**17 597 378**	**18 629 617**	**19 858 881**	**21 470 498**	**21 749 749**
5100 Taxes on production, sale, transfer, etc	1 074 009	4 789 827	8 578 636	10 532 904	15 131 675	16 515 485	17 449 222	18 597 180	19 953 036	20 162 591
5110 General taxes	664 421	3 306 350	6 781 501	8 399 926	12 133 710	13 273 958	14 073 050	15 069 540	16 211 646	16 348 944
5111 Value added taxes	664 421	3 306 350	6 781 501	8 399 926	12 133 710	13 273 958	14 073 050	15 069 540	16 211 646	16 348 944
5112 Sales tax	0	0	0	0	0	0	0	0	0	0
5113 Other	0	0	0	0	0	0	0	0	0	0
5120 Taxes on specific goods and services	409 588	1 483 477	1 797 135	2 132 978	2 997 965	3 241 527	3 376 172	3 527 640	3 741 389	3 813 647
5121 Excises	166 050	816 160	1 299 844	1 561 205	2 224 223	2 412 773	2 568 863	2 682 659	2 796 033	2 862 327
Cigarettes and tobacco	60 604	283 275	455 595	647 637	856 595	981 422	1 009 034	978 696	981 456	973 335
Gasoline and diesel	105 445	532 885	844 249	913 568	1 361 724	1 388 218	1 502 039	1 629 561	1 727 392	1 811 132
Oil stabilisation fund	0	0	0	0	0	0	0	0	0	0
Fisheries Law Extraction Rights	0	0	0	0	5 890	8 558	9 998	11 749	19 623	17 662
Additional tax on new motor vehicles	0	0	0	0	14	34 575	47 792	62 654	67 561	60 197
5122 Profits of fiscal monopolies	0	0	0	0	0	0	0	0	0	0
5123 Customs and import duties	222 486	548 571	300 416	267 331	337 839	343 491	308 871	321 156	347 555	331 846
5124 Taxes on exports	0	0	0	0	0	0	0	0	0	0
5125 Taxes on investment goods	0	0	0	0	0	0	0	0	0	0
5126 Taxes on specific services	21 052	118 746	196 875	304 442	435 903	485 263	498 438	523 824	597 802	619 474
5127 Other taxes on internat. trade and transactions	0	0	0	0	0	0	0	0	0	0
5128 Other taxes	0	0	0	0	0	0	0	0	0	0
5130 Unallocable between 5110 and 5120	0	0	0	0	0	0	0	0	0	0

Table 5.8. **Chile** *(cont.)*

Details of tax revenue / Ingresos tributarios detallados

Million CLP

	1990	2000	2007	2010	2014	2015	2016	2017	2018	2019
5200 Taxes on use of goods and perform activities	44 714	251 942	445 030	652 252	996 180	1 081 893	1 180 395	1 261 702	1 517 462	1 587 157
5210 Recurrent taxes	44 714	251 942	445 030	652 252	996 180	1 081 893	1 180 395	1 261 702	1 402 110	1 459 057
Motor vehicles	24 469	93 880	155 158	218 219	365 316	397 608	434 137	482 009	539 918	590 600
5211 Paid by households: motor vehicles	0	0	0	0	0	0	0	0	0	0
5212 Paid by others: motor vehicles	0	0	0	0	0	0	0	0	0	0
5213 Paid in respect of other goods	20 245	158 062	289 872	434 033	630 864	684 285	746 258	779 693	862 192	868 457
Municipal permits	18 401	136 138	263 996	396 944	578 671	630 943	692 974	725 954	806 734	812 276
Mining patents	3 374	34 730	25 184	36 213	50 448	51 767	51 641	52 254	53 854	54 696
Other	-1 530	-12 806	692	876	1 745	1 575	1 643	1 485	1 604	1 485
5220 Non-recurrent taxes	0	0	0	0	0	0	0	0	115 352	128 100
Tax on polluting fixed sources	..	..	..	..	..	..	..	..	115 352	128 100
5300 Unallocable between 5100 and 5200	0	0	0	0	0	0	0	0	0	0
6000 Other taxes	**-23 356**	**-112 195**	**1 023**	**-61 117**	**50 279**	**-579 308**	**-118 021**	**-714 253**	**-447 692**	**-253 490**
6100 Paid solely by business	0	0	0	0	0	0	0	0	0	0
6200 Other	-23 356	-112 195	1 023	-61 117	50 279	-579 308	-118 021	-714 253	-447 692	-253 490

.. Not available

Note: Year ending 31st December.

The data are on a cash basis.

Heading 5121: In ECLAC data, figures from the Oil Prices Stabilisation Fund (FEPP) are considered as non-tax revenues.

Source: Servicio de Impuestos Internos (Chile's Tax Service).

StatLink https://doi.org/10.1787/888934235620

Table 5.9. **Colombia**

Details of tax revenue / Ingresos tributarios detallados

Million COP

	1990	2000	2007	2010	2014	2015	2016	2017	2018	2019
Total tax revenue	**2 579 426**	**30 598 630**	**82 697 457**	**98 455 335**	**149 150 432**	**160 157 693**	**164 800 001**	**174 735 823**	**190 299 911**	**209 039 764**
1000 Taxes on income, profits and capital gains	**771 694**	**7 103 525**	**24 010 404**	**26 218 852**	**50 083 349**	**52 656 876**	**54 326 726**	**57 615 236**	**64 043 928**	**67 518 500**
1100 Of individuals	47 210	1 499 345	4 751 580	5 192 384	8 344 422	9 210 448	9 833 084	10 367 606	12 215 963	12 888 180
1110 On income and profits	47 210	1 499 345	4 751 580	5 192 384	8 344 422	9 210 448	9 833 084	10 367 606	12 215 963	12 888 180
Income tax	47 210	1 499 345	4 751 580	5 192 384	8 344 422	9 210 448	9 833 084	10 367 606	12 215 963	12 882 271
Simple tax regime	0	0	0	0	0	0	0	0	0	5 908
1120 On capital gains	..	..	..	..	..	..	..	..	..	..
1200 Corporate	359 758	5 119 828	18 427 899	20 405 209	40 435 726	41 398 731	42 351 554	44 970 528	48 529 320	51 151 754
1210 On profits	359 758	5 119 828	18 427 899	20 405 209	40 435 726	41 398 731	42 351 554	44 970 528	48 529 320	51 151 754
Income tax	359 758	5 119 828	18 427 899	20 405 209	27 974 251	27 472 562	28 240 820	40 124 337	48 396 597	51 036 347
Pro Equity Income Tax - CREE	0	0	0	0	12 461 475	13 926 169	14 110 734	4 846 190	132 723	99 798
Simple tax regime	0	0	0	0	0	0	0	0	0	15 609
1220 On capital gains of corporates	..	..	..	..	..	..	..	..	..	..
1300 Unallocable between 1100 and 1200	364 726	484 352	830 925	621 258	1 303 200	2 047 697	2 142 087	2 277 102	3 298 645	3 478 566
Income tax	364 726	484 352	830 925	621 258	1 303 200	2 047 697	2 142 087	2 277 102	3 298 645	3 478 566
Pro Equity Income Tax - CREE	0	0	0	0	0	0	0	0	0	0
2000 Social security contributions	**203 596**	**4 989 000**	**9 694 000**	**11 478 085**	**13 715 710**	**13 585 138**	**15 443 016**	**13 351 711**	**18 192 049**	**19 875 398**
2100 Employees	..	..	..	..	..	..	..	..	..	..
2110 On a payroll basis	..	..	..	..	..	..	..	..	..	..
2120 On an income tax basis	..	..	..	..	..	..	..	..	..	..
2200 Employers	..	..	..	..	..	..	..	..	..	..
2210 On a payroll basis	..	..	..	..	..	..	..	..	..	..
2220 On an income tax basis	..	..	..	..	..	..	..	..	..	..
2300 Self-employed or non-employed	..	..	..	..	..	..	..	..	..	..
2310 On a payroll basis	..	..	..	..	..	..	..	..	..	..
2320 On an income tax basis	..	..	..	..	..	..	..	..	..	..
2400 Unallocable between 2100, 2200 and 2300	203 596	4 989 000	9 694 000	11 478 085	13 715 710	13 585 138	15 443 016	13 351 711	18 192 049	19 875 398
2410 On a payroll basis	203 596	4 989 000	9 694 000	11 478 085	13 715 710	13 585 138	15 443 016	13 351 711	18 192 049	19 875 398
2420 On an income tax basis	0	0	0	0	0	0	0	0	0	0
3000 Taxes on payroll and workforce	**0**	**1 286 803**	**2 798 906**	**4 022 503**	**2 627 958**	**2 797 308**	**2 998 237**	**3 200 238**	**3 461 352**	**3 604 071**
4000 Taxes on property	**56 160**	**2 027 654**	**6 459 259**	**8 535 238**	**15 984 365**	**18 156 105**	**18 090 331**	**17 950 494**	**15 265 472**	**18 984 414**
4100 Recurrent taxes on immovable property	56 160	991 070	2 298 829	3 338 935	5 424 320	6 061 965	6 571 134	7 310 244	7 981 989	8 743 115
4110 Households	0	0	0	0	0	0	0	0	0	0
4120 Others	56 160	991 070	2 298 829	3 338 935	5 424 320	6 061 965	6 571 134	7 310 244	7 981 989	8 743 115
4200 Recurrent taxes on net wealth	0	0	1 170 908	1 970 530	4 118 075	5 352 940	4 440 142	3 868 595	467 925	923 255
4210 Individual	..	..	1 170 908	1 970 530	4 118 075	5 352 940	4 440 142	3 868 595	467 925	923 255
4220 Corporate	..	..	0	0	0	0	0	0	0	0
4300 Estate, inheritance and gift taxes	0	0	0	0	0	0	0	0	0	0
4310 Estate and inheritance taxes	..	..	..	..	..	..	..	..	..	..
4320 Gift taxes	..	..	..	..	..	..	..	..	..	..
4400 Taxes on financial and capital transactions	0	1 036 584	2 989 522	3 225 773	6 441 969	6 741 200	7 079 055	6 771 655	6 815 558	8 190 516
4500 Non-recurrent taxes	0	0	0	0	0	0	0	0	0	1 127 528
4510 On net wealth	..	..	..	..	..	..	..	..	..	0
4520 Other non-recurrent taxes	..	..	..	..	..	..	..	..	..	1 127 528
4600 Other recurrent taxes on property	0	0	0	0	0	0	0	0	0	0
5000 Taxes on goods and services	**1 388 653**	**14 180 450**	**36 766 741**	**44 411 642**	**60 969 982**	**65 716 566**	**66 962 420**	**75 381 123**	**81 408 789**	**89 767 476**
5100 Taxes on production, sale, transfer, etc	1 388 653	14 048 655	36 447 297	44 038 074	59 908 784	64 688 081	65 786 951	74 003 567	79 935 336	88 064 039
5110 General taxes	672 368	9 585 866	26 910 512	33 333 802	45 197 474	48 684 900	49 355 123	58 565 799	64 316 019	71 237 059
5111 Value added taxes	583 078	8 445 776	23 377 821	28 811 682	38 749 869	41 659 696	41 878 886	50 619 849	55 879 110	61 938 202
5112 Sales tax	89 290	1 140 090	3 532 691	4 522 121	6 447 605	7 025 204	7 476 238	7 945 950	8 436 909	9 298 856
Industry and commerce tax (State)	89 290	1 140 090	3 532 691	4 522 121	6 447 605	7 025 204	7 476 238	7 945 950	8 436 909	9 298 856
5113 Other	0	0	0	0	0	0	0	0	0	0
5120 Taxes on specific goods and services	716 285	4 462 789	9 536 785	10 704 271	14 711 310	16 003 181	16 431 827	15 437 768	15 619 317	16 826 980
5121 Excises	404 699	2 718 692	5 276 999	6 052 273	10 724 586	11 412 250	12 318 641	11 616 844	12 061 132	12 993 986
Oil	141 270	833 004	1 211 511	1 418 766	2 980 883	3 297 392	3 335 157	1 352 793	1 517 546	1 585 141
Tobacco (State)	52 898	213 412	330 016	390 472	481 589	524 357	595 476	887 534	1 145 879	1 278 561
Beer (State)	85 722	471 135	1 203 838	1 432 453	2 108 721	2 305 895	2 549 949	2 572 771	2 637 674	2 611 470
Liquors (State)	124 808	520 394	834 390	929 328	1 345 827	1 253 466	1 574 864	1 907 802	1 800 605	2 147 129
Restaurant, vehicles sale and mobile telephony	0	0	0	0	1 648 467	1 684 179	1 700 069	1 948 718	2 047 419	2 207 848
Carbon	0	0	0	0	0	0	0	474 596	288 373	436 914
Plastic bags	0	0	0	0	0	0	0	6 546	28 099	37 331
Medicinal cannabis	0	0	0	0	0	0	0	10	3	145
Diesel surcharge	0	85 716	388 091	500 405	579 952	598 993	590 233	546 243	579 613	599 600
Petrol surcharge	0	595 031	1 309 154	1 380 848	1 579 147	1 747 969	1 972 893	1 919 830	2 015 922	2 089 846
5122 Profits of fiscal monopolies	0	0	0	0	0	0	0	0	0	0
5123 Customs and import duties	311 586	1 744 097	4 259 786	4 651 999	3 986 724	4 590 931	4 113 187	3 820 924	3 558 185	3 832 994
Custom duties	180 989	1 744 097	4 259 786	4 651 999	3 986 724	4 590 931	4 113 187	3 820 924	3 558 185	3 832 994
Imports surcharge	130 597	0	0	0	0	0	0	0	0	0

Table 5.9. **Colombia** *(cont.)*

Details of tax revenue / Ingresos tributarios detallados

Million COP

	1990	2000	2007	2010	2014	2015	2016	2017	2018	2019
5124 Taxes on exports	0	0	0	0	0	0	0	0	0	0
5125 Taxes on investment goods	0	0	0	0	0	0	0	0	0	0
5126 Taxes on specific services	0	0	0	0	0	0	0	0	0	0
5127 Other taxes on internat. trade and transactions	0	0	0	0	0	0	0	0	0	0
5128 Other taxes	0	0	0	0	0	0	0	0	0	0
5130 Unallocable between 5110 and 5120	0	0	0	0	0	0	0	0	0	0
5200 Taxes on use of goods and perform activities	0	131 795	319 444	373 568	1 061 198	1 028 485	1 175 469	1 377 556	1 473 453	1 703 437
5210 Recurrent taxes	..	131 795	319 444	373 568	1 061 198	1 028 485	1 175 469	1 377 556	1 473 453	1 703 437
5211 Paid by households: motor vehicles	..	131 795	319 444	373 568	1 061 198	1 028 485	1 175 469	1 377 556	1 473 453	1 703 437
Tax on motor vehicle ownership	..	131 795	319 444	373 568	1 061 198	1 028 485	1 175 469	1 377 556	1 473 453	1 703 437
5212 Paid by others: motor vehicles	..	..	..	..	..	..	..	..	..	..
5213 Paid in respect of other goods	..	..	..	..	..	..	..	..	..	..
5220 Non-recurrent taxes	..	..	..	..	..	..	..	..	..	..
5300 Unallocable between 5100 and 5200	0	0	0	0	0	0	0	0	0	0
6000 Other taxes	**159 323**	**1 011 197**	**2 968 147**	**3 789 014**	**5 769 069**	**7 245 701**	**6 979 271**	**7 237 021**	**7 928 320**	**9 289 906**
6100 Paid solely by business	0	0	0	0	0	0	0	0	0	0
6200 Other	159 323	1 011 197	2 968 147	3 789 014	5 769 069	7 245 701	6 979 271	7 237 021	7 928 320	9 289 906
Stamp tax	0	401 497	759 787	357 160	72 425	101 668	97 492	75 493	79 868	85 799
Other	78 306	79 287	86 297	126 602	260 721	318 271	357 863	403 473	461 160	533 852
Other (sub-national)	81 017	530 413	2 122 062	3 305 252	5 435 923	6 825 762	6 523 916	6 758 055	7 387 293	8 670 255

.. Not available

Note: Year ending 31st December.

The data are on a cash basis.

Includes the reported consolidated revenues of the territorial entities (departments and municipalities).

Heading 1000: The income tax figures under headings 1100, 1200 and 1300 are estimated as 2019 data are only available for simple tax regime and Pro Equity Income Tax - CREE.

Heading 2000: Before 2013, social security contributions did not include all the contributions entering FOSYGA (Solidarity and Guarantee Fund). Only the portion of the contributions used to finance the subsidised regime (up to 1.5 pp of the 12.5% of the monthly wage paid by employers and employees as an obligatory health contribution) was included. The part of the contributions entering FOSYGA to finance the contributory regime was classified in the social security sector as "other incomes". From 2013 onwards, all of the health contributions entering FOSYGA are classified as social security contributions. The portion of the contributions not entering FOSYGA that is both collected and spent by the health insurers – EPS - is not part of the fiscal accounts.

Source: Dirección de Impuestos y Aduanas Nacionales de Colombia, Ministerio de Hacienda y Crédito Público y Banco Central de Colombia. (National Tax and Customs Administration, Ministry of Finance and Public Credit and Central Bank of Colombia).

StatLink https://doi.org/10.1787/888934235639

Table 5.10. **Costa Rica**

Details of tax revenue / Ingresos tributarios detallados

Million CRC

	1990	2000	2007	2010	2014	2015	2016	2017	2018	2019
Total tax revenue	**117 711**	**978 114**	**3 213 401**	**4 382 367**	**6 330 931**	**6 923 575**	**7 528 752**	**7 893 642**	**8 339 991**	**8 855 885**
1000 Taxes on income, profits and capital gains	**11 820**	**128 805**	**531 552**	**748 093**	**1 091 470**	**1 247 308**	**1 416 218**	**1 562 063**	**1 699 258**	**1 854 866**
1100 Of individuals	..	..	123 194	202 849	349 139	386 241	414 247	446 519	483 645	540 954
1110 On income and profits	..	..	123 194	202 849	349 139	386 241	414 247	446 519	483 645	535 412
1120 On capital gains	..	..	..	..	..	..	..	..	..	..
1200 Corporate	..	..	348 826	450 312	574 137	659 951	742 011	843 879	915 284	1 058 086
1210 On profits	..	..	348 826	450 312	574 137	659 951	742 011	843 879	915 284	955 908
1220 On capital gains of corporates	..	..	..	..	..	..	..	..	..	..
1300 Unallocable between 1100 and 1200	11 820	128 805	59 531	94 932	168 194	201 116	259 961	271 664	300 330	255 827
2000 Social security contributions	**33 990**	**297 069**	**885 053**	**1 450 531**	**2 114 124**	**2 305 133**	**2 539 755**	**2 640 785**	**2 859 467**	**3 026 691**
2100 Employees	..	..	..	..	..	..	..	..	..	..
2110 On a payroll basis	..	..	..	..	..	..	..	..	..	..
2120 On an income tax basis	..	..	..	..	..	..	..	..	..	..
2200 Employers	3 447	37 313	107 398	207 206	294 486	318 652	331 124	361 161	368 865	381 940
Government contributions	3 447	37 313	107 398	207 206	294 486	318 652	331 124	361 161	368 865	381 940
2210 On a payroll basis	..	..	..	..	..	..	..	..	..	..
2220 On an income tax basis	..	..	..	..	..	..	..	..	..	..
2300 Self-employed or non-employed	..	..	..	..	..	..	..	..	..	..
2310 On a payroll basis	..	..	..	..	..	..	..	..	..	..
2320 On an income tax basis	..	..	..	..	..	..	..	..	..	..
2400 Unallocable between 2100, 2200 and 2300	30 543	259 756	777 654	1 243 325	1 819 638	1 986 481	2 208 631	2 279 624	2 490 602	2 644 751
Contributions by employees and non-government employers	30 543	249 182	727 844	1 139 265	1 648 831	1 785 522	1 985 151	1 971 472	2 157 256	2 274 644
Contributions for the special regimes	0	10 574	49 811	104 060	170 806	200 959	223 480	237 004	247 939	292 634
2410 On a payroll basis	..	..	..	..	..	..	..	..	..	..
2420 On an income tax basis	..	..	..	..	..	..	..	..	..	..
3000 Taxes on payroll and workforce	**7 575**	**61 796**	**170 996**	**260 664**	**388 869**	**423 616**	**453 369**	**471 206**	**498 577**	**522 529**
Contributions by non-government employers	7 484	59 129	165 677	248 259	372 869	406 296	435 328	453 128	478 523	501 734
Contributions by government employers	91	2 666	5 320	12 405	16 000	17 321	18 041	18 078	20 054	20 795
4000 Taxes on property	**1 566**	**8 396**	**42 658**	**63 706**	**114 313**	**123 261**	**134 332**	**145 955**	**149 310**	**167 952**
4100 Recurrent taxes on immovable property	1 200	5 390	23 293	48 963	81 613	90 003	97 869	107 156	113 586	125 398
Land tax	0	0	0	0	0	0	0	0	0	0
Additional land tax	0	0	0	0	0	0	0	0	0	0
Tax on sumptuary constructions	0	0	0	0	0	0	0	0	0	0
Immovable property tax	0	0	0	3 527	4 013	4 076	4 098	4 255	4 468	4 699
Municipal immovable property tax	1 200	5 390	23 293	45 436	77 600	85 927	93 771	102 901	109 119	120 698
4110 Households	..	..	..	..	..	..	..	..	..	..
4120 Others	..	..	..	..	..	..	..	..	..	..
4200 Recurrent taxes on net wealth	0	0	0	0	0	0	0	0	0	0
4210 Individual	..	..	..	..	..	..	..	..	..	..
4220 Corporate	..	..	..	..	..	..	..	..	..	..
4300 Estate, inheritance and gift taxes	0	0	0	0	0	0	0	0	0	0
4310 Estate and inheritance taxes	..	..	..	..	..	..	..	..	..	..
4320 Gift taxes	..	..	..	..	..	..	..	..	..	..
4400 Taxes on financial and capital transactions	366	3 007	19 366	14 743	32 700	33 258	36 462	38 799	35 724	42 554
4500 Non-recurrent taxes	0	0	0	0	0	0	0	0	0	0
4510 On net wealth	..	..	..	..	..	..	..	..	..	..
4520 Other non-recurrent taxes	..	..	..	..	..	..	..	..	..	..
4600 Other recurrent taxes on property	0	0	0	0	0	0	0	0	0	0
5000 Taxes on goods and services	**53 509**	**456 851**	**1 505 510**	**1 766 914**	**2 468 087**	**2 661 902**	**2 794 229**	**2 875 333**	**2 918 471**	**3 081 941**
5100 Taxes on production, sale, transfer, etc	49 867	425 713	1 406 100	1 600 302	2 222 962	2 388 900	2 508 186	2 575 411	2 608 864	2 756 759
5110 General taxes	21 326	222 775	797 850	920 298	1 306 110	1 368 601	1 420 938	1 466 986	1 513 677	1 662 503
5111 Value added taxes	21 326	222 775	797 850	920 298	1 266 798	1 336 075	1 414 358	1 453 348	1 487 620	1 634 986
5112 Sales tax	0	0	0	0	0	0	0	0	0	0
5113 Other	0	0	0	0	39 313	32 526	6 580	13 638	26 057	27 517
5120 Taxes on specific goods and services	28 541	202 939	608 250	680 004	916 851	1 020 299	1 087 248	1 108 425	1 095 187	1 094 256
5121 Excises	11 096	157 204	447 168	523 617	706 016	798 412	846 864	870 225	858 424	864 985
Fuels and energy	0	0	250 577	320 638	404 901	457 827	472 644	510 260	517 666	552 017
Alcohol beverages	0	8 229	23 802	28 035	36 293	43 095	43 400	43 176	45 610	43 849
Non alcoholic beverages	0	0	18 263	26 566	34 874	36 353	39 764	39 781	40 182	41 247
Soaps	0	0	883	1 317	1 493	2 562	2 912	2 332	2 712	3 020
Cement	0	0	0	227	340	304	267	311	289	216
Tobacco	0	0	0	0	32 277	33 681	32 560	30 590	30 766	27 185
Abolished specific taxes on production and consumption	0	0	0	0	0	0	0	0	0	0
Other specific taxes on consumption	11 096	148 975	153 643	146 834	195 838	224 590	255 317	243 775	221 200	197 452
5122 Profits of fiscal monopolies	0	0	0	0	0	0	0	0	0	0

Table 5.10. **Costa Rica** *(cont.)*

Details of tax revenue / Ingresos tributarios detallados

Million CRC

	1990	2000	2007	2010	2014	2015	2016	2017	2018	2019
5123 Customs and import duties	15 052	40 485	134 576	126 134	169 120	174 568	185 544	179 188	175 368	164 224
Import duties	13 977	32 336	107 565	103 851	142 226	148 666	158 559	152 756	149 017	140 919
Custom duties	1 075	8 149	27 011	22 284	26 894	25 902	26 986	26 432	26 351	23 305
Import duties on animals	0	0	0	0	0	0	0	0	0	0
5124 Taxes on exports	2 113	2 238	2 432	3 973	4 853	4 468	5 073	5 638	5 468	5 412
Export duties	2 113	2 088	2 260	3 816	3 067	2 701	3 250	3 673	3 594	3 502
Export duties Law 133	0	0	0	0	0	0	0	0	0	0
Export duties Law 5519	0	0	0	0	0	0	0	0	0	0
Tax on banana exports	0	150	172	157	176	156	184	199	193	184
Export duties on ground transportation	0	0	0	0	1 610	1 611	1 638	1 766	1 682	1 726
5125 Taxes on investment goods	0	0	0	0	0	0	0	0	0	0
5126 Taxes on specific services	280	2 929	23 242	24 767	34 081	38 687	44 934	48 290	50 554	54 556
Casinos and gambling	0	225	442	445	940	1 455	1 609	891	1 060	1 241
Port cargo movements	0	6	0	0	0	0	0	0	0	0
Overseas departure tax	0	0	22 799	24 322	33 141	37 232	43 325	47 399	49 494	53 315
10% on public shows	0	0	0	0	0	0	0	0	0	0
Pro-national airport's stamp tax	0	0	0	0	0	0	0	0	0	0
Stamp tax on the use of borders and ports	280	2 697	0	0	0	0	0	0	0	0
5127 Other taxes on internat. trade and transactions	0	83	832	1 513	2 782	3 093	3 512	3 695	3 785	3 841
5128 Other taxes	0	0	0	0	0	1 071	1 320	1 389	1 589	1 238
5130 Unallocable between 5110 and 5120	0	0	0	0	0	0	0	0	0	0
5200 Taxes on use of goods and perform activities	3 642	31 138	99 410	166 612	245 125	273 003	286 044	299 922	309 607	325 182
5210 Recurrent taxes	3 642	31 138	99 410	166 612	245 125	273 003	286 044	299 922	309 607	325 182
5211 Paid by households: motor vehicles	0	0	0	0	0	0	0	0	0	0
5212 Paid by others: motor vehicles	1 425	15 374	52 511	94 102	130 000	145 894	156 517	164 034	171 523	181 198
Property tax on vehicles, aircraft and boats	1 425	15 374	52 511	94 102	130 000	145 894	156 517	164 034	171 523	181 198
5213 Paid in respect of other goods	2 217	15 763	46 899	72 510	115 125	127 109	129 527	135 888	138 084	143 984
Local taxes	1 262	11 898	43 874	68 808	110 120	122 248	124 862	130 639	132 514	137 979
Hunting and fishing licences	0	0	0	0	0	0	0	0	0	0
Spirits licence	0	0	0	0	0	0	0	0	0	0
Revenue stamps	955	3 866	3 025	3 702	5 005	4 861	4 664	5 249	5 571	6 004
Sport stamp tax	0	0	0	0	0	0	0	0	0	0
5220 Non-recurrent taxes	0	0	0	0	0	0	0	0	0	0
5300 Unallocable between 5100 and 5200	0	0	0	0	0	0	0	0	0	0
6000 Other taxes	**9 251**	**25 198**	**77 632**	**92 460**	**154 069**	**162 355**	**190 850**	**198 300**	**214 908**	**201 906**
6100 Paid solely by business	0	0	0	0	0	0	0	0	0	0
6200 Other	9 251	25 198	77 632	92 460	154 069	162 355	190 850	198 300	214 908	201 906
Transfers of vehicles, aircraft and boats	497	2 530	9 937	12 311	19 099	20 999	23 022	21 872	22 265	23 223
Tax revenue from decentralised units	2 764	15 048	22 257	29 969	46 591	49 334	67 584	68 127	63 329	67 968
Other taxes	5 990	7 620	45 438	50 180	88 379	92 022	100 243	108 181	129 268	110 654

.. Not available

Note: Year ending 31st December.

The data are on a cash basis.

Heading 2000: In ECLAC data, social security contributions also include INA (National Institute of Apprenticeship), IMAS (Joint Social Aid Institute), and FODESAF (Social Development and Family Allowances Fund).

Heading 3000: In Costa Rica and for ECLAC, social security contributions from decentralised institutions are classified under heading 2000.

Heading 5123: Revenues from import duties on animals have been added in this edition.

Heading 5212: In ECLAC data, tax on ownership of vehicles, aircraft and boats is classified in category 4000.

Heading 6200: The figures include the tax revenue of decentralised bodies (other than social security contributions). The tax revenue of decentralised bodies is classified under central government. In Costa Rica this revenue is classified under a separate unit (decentralised) considered to be separate from the central government.

In ECLAC data, the tax on the transfer of used vehicles Law No. 7088 of 30/11/87 is classified as a property tax.

Source: Secretaría Técnica de la Autoridad Presupuestaria, Ministerio de Finanzas y Contraloría General de la República (Technical Secretary of the Budgeting Authority, Ministry of Finance and National General Comptroller).

StatLink https://doi.org/10.1787/888934235658

Table 5.11. **Cuba**

Details of tax revenue / Ingresos tributarios detallados

Million CUP

	1990	2000	2007	2010	2014	2015	2016	2017	2018	2019
Total tax revenue	**6 265**	**11 367**	**25 787**	**23 949**	**29 940**	**33 182**	**37 597**	**41 021**	**42 307**	**43 504**
1000 Taxes on income, profits and capital gains	**14**	**1 826**	**3 403**	**3 603**	**5 995**	**6 676**	**8 018**	**9 931**	**11 094**	**12 257**
1100 Of individuals	14	291	404	554	1 308	1 848	2 343	3 279	4 002	4 762
1110 On income and profits	..	..	..	..	..	..	..	..	..	..
1120 On capital gains	..	..	..	..	..	..	..	..	..	..
1200 Corporate	0	1 535	2 999	3 049	4 687	4 828	5 675	6 651	7 092	7 495
1210 On profits	..	..	..	..	..	..	..	..	..	..
1220 On capital gains of corporates	..	..	..	..	..	..	..	..	..	..
1300 Unallocable between 1100 and 1200	0	0	0	0	0	0	0	0	0	0
2000 Social security contributions	**691**	**1 181**	**2 412**	**2 974**	**3 622**	**4 322**	**4 710**	**5 108**	**5 206**	**5 727**
2100 Employees	..	..	..	..	..	..	..	..	..	..
2110 On a payroll basis	..	..	..	..	..	..	..	..	..	..
2120 On an income tax basis	..	..	..	..	..	..	..	..	..	..
2200 Employers	..	..	..	..	..	..	..	..	..	..
2210 On a payroll basis	..	..	..	..	..	..	..	..	..	..
2220 On an income tax basis	..	..	..	..	..	..	..	..	..	..
2300 Self-employed or non-employed	..	..	..	..	..	..	..	..	..	..
2310 On a payroll basis	..	..	..	..	..	..	..	..	..	..
2320 On an income tax basis	..	..	..	..	..	..	..	..	..	..
2400 Unallocable between 2100, 2200 and 2300	691	1 181	2 412	2 974	3 622	4 322	4 710	5 108	5 206	5 727
2410 On a payroll basis	691	1 181	2 412	2 974	3 622	4 322	4 710	5 108	5 206	5 727
2420 On an income tax basis	0	0	0	0	0	0	0	0	0	0
3000 Taxes on payroll and workforce	**0**	**970**	**3 417**	**4 414**	**2 939**	**2 753**	**2 411**	**1 385**	**1 273**	**1 415**
4000 Taxes on property	**0**	**0**	**0**	**0**	**0**	**0**	**0**	**0**	**0**	**0**
4100 Recurrent taxes on immovable property	..	..	..	..	..	..	..	..	..	..
4110 Households	..	..	..	..	..	..	..	..	..	..
4120 Others	..	..	..	..	..	..	..	..	..	..
4200 Recurrent taxes on net wealth	..	..	..	..	..	..	..	..	..	..
4210 Individual	..	..	..	..	..	..	..	..	..	..
4220 Corporate	..	..	..	..	..	..	..	..	..	..
4300 Estate, inheritance and gift taxes	..	..	..	..	..	..	..	..	..	..
4310 Estate and inheritance taxes	..	..	..	..	..	..	..	..	..	..
4320 Gift taxes	..	..	..	..	..	..	..	..	..	..
4400 Taxes on financial and capital transactions	..	..	..	..	..	..	..	..	..	..
4500 Non-recurrent taxes	..	..	..	..	..	..	..	..	..	..
4510 On net wealth	..	..	..	..	..	..	..	..	..	..
4520 Other non-recurrent taxes	..	..	..	..	..	..	..	..	..	..
4600 Other recurrent taxes on property	..	..	..	..	..	..	..	..	..	..
5000 Taxes on goods and services	**5 443**	**6 732**	**15 875**	**12 283**	**15 912**	**17 742**	**20 309**	**22 055**	**21 969**	**20 995**
5100 Taxes on production, sale, transfer, etc	5 443	6 732	15 875	12 283	15 912	17 742	20 309	22 055	21 969	20 995
5110 General taxes	5 017	6 131	14 464	10 525	14 171	15 611	17 690	17 961	17 623	16 619
5111 Value added taxes	0	0	0	0	0	0	0	0	0	0
5112 Sales tax	5 017	6 131	14 464	10 525	14 171	15 611	17 690	17 961	17 623	16 619
5113 Other	0	0	0	0	0	0	0	0	0	0
5120 Taxes on specific goods and services	426	602	1 412	1 758	1 740	2 131	2 618	4 094	4 346	4 376
5121 Excises	..	..	..	..	..	..	..	..	..	..
5122 Profits of fiscal monopolies	..	..	..	..	..	..	..	..	..	..
5123 Customs and import duties	..	..	..	..	..	..	..	..	..	..
5124 Taxes on exports	..	..	..	..	..	..	..	..	..	..
5125 Taxes on investment goods	..	..	..	..	..	..	..	..	..	..
5126 Taxes on specific services	..	..	..	..	..	..	..	..	..	..
5127 Other taxes on internat. trade and transactions	..	..	..	..	..	..	..	..	..	..
5128 Other taxes	..	..	..	..	..	..	..	..	..	..
5130 Unallocable between 5110 and 5120	0	0	0	0	0	0	0	0	0	0
5200 Taxes on use of goods and perform activities	0	0	0	0	0	0	0	0	0	0
5210 Recurrent taxes	..	..	..	..	..	..	..	..	..	..
5211 Paid by households: motor vehicles	..	..	..	..	..	..	..	..	..	..
5212 Paid by others: motor vehicles	..	..	..	..	..	..	..	..	..	..
5213 Paid in respect of other goods	..	..	..	..	..	..	..	..	..	..
5220 Non-recurrent taxes	..	..	..	..	..	..	..	..	..	..
5300 Unallocable between 5100 and 5200	0	0	0	0	0	0	0	0	0	0
6000 Other taxes	**117**	**657**	**681**	**675**	**1 472**	**1 690**	**2 149**	**2 543**	**2 766**	**3 110**
6100 Paid solely by business	..	..	..	..	..	..	..	..	..	..
6200 Other	..	..	..	..	..	..	..	..	..	..

Table 5.11. **Cuba** *(cont.)*

Details of tax revenue / Ingresos tributarios detallados

.. Not available

Note: Year ending 31st December.

The data are on a cash basis.

The figures for the sub-categories under the heading 5120 are not available.

Central and local government tax revenues are only available between 2002 and 2012.

There are minor discrepancies between national tax revenue data and the sum of central and local tax revenues mainly due to rounding.

Heading 5112: Taxes on circulation and sales (Impuesto de circulación y sobre Ventas) are larger for national data than the combined central and local data by approximately CUP 538.8 million in 2012.

Source: Ministerio de Finanzas y Precios de la República de Cuba (Ministry of Finance and Prices of the Republic of Cuba); Oficina Nacional de Estadísticas de Cuba (National Statistics Office of Cuba).

StatLink https://doi.org/10.1787/888934235677

Table 5.12. **Dominican Republic / República Dominicana**

Details of tax revenue / Ingresos tributarios detallados

Million DOP

	1990	2000	2007	2010	2014	2015	2016	2017	2018	2019
Total tax revenue	**6 424**	**48 310**	**218 887**	**245 327**	**395 248**	**416 611**	**455 827**	**503 494**	**560 962**	**617 802**
1000 Taxes on income, profits and capital gains	**1 670**	**10 782**	**55 232**	**53 643**	**125 098**	**119 819**	**135 700**	**155 024**	**170 561**	**194 281**
1100 Of individuals	..	4 088	14 665	17 088	31 525	35 549	40 193	43 553	51 425	59 448
1110 On income and profits	..	4 070	14 577	16 901	31 119	35 187	39 775	43 097	51 031	58 842
1120 On capital gains	..	18	87	187	406	361	418	456	394	606
1200 Corporate	..	4 679	29 203	21 475	72 865	61 695	69 362	83 047	83 778	91 545
1210 On profits	..	4 605	29 063	21 325	72 628	61 455	69 079	82 785	83 521	91 291
1220 On capital gains of corporates	..	74	140	151	238	240	283	262	257	254
Casinos	..	59	140	151	173	184	228	237	228	225
Racetracks	..	15	0	0	0	0	0	0	0	0
Phone gaming	..	0	0	0	64	56	55	25	30	28
1300 Unallocable between 1100 and 1200	1 670	2 015	11 365	15 080	20 708	22 576	26 144	28 425	35 358	43 289
2000 Social security contributions	**53**	**490**	**860**	**1 845**	**1 515**	**1 483**	**1 550**	**2 635**	**2 514**	**2 553**
2100 Employees	..	..	775	1 720	1 355	1 321	1 392	1 535	..	..
2110 On a payroll basis	..	..	..	..	..	..	..	..	..	..
2120 On an income tax basis	..	..	..	..	..	..	..	..	..	..
2200 Employers	..	..	85	125	160	163	158	1 099	..	..
2210 On a payroll basis	..	..	..	..	..	..	..	..	..	..
2220 On an income tax basis	..	..	..	..	..	..	..	..	..	..
2300 Self-employed or non-employed	..	..	0	0	0	0	0	0	..	..
2310 On a payroll basis	..	..	..	..	..	..	..	..	..	..
2320 On an income tax basis	..	..	..	..	..	..	..	..	..	..
2400 Unallocable between 2100, 2200 and 2300	53	490	0	0	0	0	0	0	2 514	2 553
2410 On a payroll basis	53	490	..	..	..	..	..	..	2 514	2 553
2420 On an income tax basis	0	0	..	..	..	..	..	..	0	0
3000 Taxes on payroll and workforce	**0**	**0**	**927**	**1 385**	**2 091**	**2 366**	**2 636**	**2 912**	**3 282**	**3 502**
4000 Taxes on property	**74**	**689**	**9 996**	**13 315**	**18 183**	**19 044**	**20 717**	**22 942**	**25 716**	**29 564**
4100 Recurrent taxes on immovable property	9	115	594	555	1 579	1 755	1 871	2 166	2 527	2 904
4110 Households	9	115	594	555	1 579	1 755	1 871	2 166	2 527	2 904
4120 Others	0	0	0	0	0	0	0	0	0	0
4200 Recurrent taxes on net wealth	0	0	1 281	2 449	3 458	3 445	3 544	4 113	4 609	5 155
Tax on assets	..	..	1 281	2 449	3 454	3 445	3 544	4 113	4 609	5 155
4210 Individual	..	..	..	..	..	..	..	..	..	..
4220 Corporate	..	..	..	..	4	..	..	..	..	..
4300 Estate, inheritance and gift taxes	11	96	143	231	325	418	388	455	526	715
4310 Estate and inheritance taxes	..	..	..	..	..	..	..	..	..	..
4320 Gift taxes	..	..	..	..	..	..	..	..	..	..
4400 Taxes on financial and capital transactions	40	377	7 375	8 658	11 394	12 067	13 265	13 995	15 675	17 594
Tax on checks	0	0	3 833	4 262	5 620	5 951	6 591	7 117	8 139	8 646
Real estate operations	22	217	3 291	3 864	4 876	5 169	5 668	5 802	6 320	7 526
Tax on the transfer of immovable property	18	160	252	533	898	947	1 005	1 076	1 215	1 422
4500 Non-recurrent taxes	3	32	270	488	677	591	681	711	553	931
4510 On net wealth	3	32	270	488	677	591	681	711	553	931
4520 Other non-recurrent taxes	0	0	0	0	0	0	0	0	0	0
4600 Other recurrent taxes on property	11	70	333	934	751	769	969	1 503	1 827	2 266
5000 Taxes on goods and services	**4 467**	**35 853**	**150 325**	**175 139**	**248 361**	**273 898**	**295 223**	**319 980**	**358 888**	**387 900**
5100 Taxes on production, sale, transfer, etc	4 398	35 135	143 884	168 641	239 526	263 435	282 288	306 680	344 706	370 718
5110 General taxes	970	9 912	66 613	81 226	130 447	147 039	159 212	169 629	194 725	214 324
5111 Value added taxes	970	9 912	66 613	81 226	130 447	147 039	159 212	169 629	194 725	214 324
5112 Sales tax	0	0	0	0	0	0	0	0	0	0
5113 Other	0	0	0	0	0	0	0	0	0	0
5120 Taxes on specific goods and services	3 429	25 224	77 271	87 415	109 080	116 396	123 076	137 051	149 981	156 394
5121 Excises	495	6 614	47 888	56 024	72 399	74 586	78 105	89 681	97 278	102 087
Alcoholic beverages	251	2 451	13 101	15 054	19 779	22 371	23 617	25 694	28 882	30 610
Tobacco products	102	469	3 284	4 529	4 382	4 532	4 117	5 120	4 355	3 923
Petroleum products	89	3 143	29 985	34 598	44 335	43 315	45 698	53 075	57 053	60 828
Other excises	52	551	1 518	1 843	3 904	4 367	4 674	5 792	6 988	6 725
5122 Profits of fiscal monopolies	0	0	0	0	0	0	0	0	0	0
5123 Customs and import duties	1 548	13 459	19 337	19 455	21 315	25 212	27 286	28 703	32 096	32 478
Import duties	615	13 456	19 336	19 455	21 238	24 378	26 397	27 276	30 931	32 478
Others	933	3	1	0	76	834	889	1 426	1 165	0
5124 Taxes on exports	6	4	83	146	12	8	0	0	0	0
5125 Taxes on investment goods	0	0	0	0	0	0	0	0	0	0

Table 5.12. **Dominican Republic / República Dominicana** *(cont.)*

Details of tax revenue / Ingresos tributarios detallados

Million DOP

	1990	2000	2007	2010	2014	2015	2016	2017	2018	2019
5126 Taxes on specific services	344	1 590	9 211	11 411	14 956	16 245	17 361	18 287	20 173	21 318
Telecommunications	85	0	3 867	4 886	6 129	6 375	6 607	6 781	7 146	7 313
Insurance premiums	33	584	2 211	3 088	3 965	4 301	4 828	5 236	5 976	6 782
Departure tax	204	809	3 131	3 428	4 839	5 535	5 892	6 252	6 933	7 180
Hotels	22	191	0	0	0	0	0	0	0	0
Others	0	7	2	9	24	35	34	18	119	43
5127 Other taxes on internat. trade and transactions	1 037	3 556	753	379	397	346	323	380	435	511
Exchange commission	857	3 412	233	70	0	0	0	0	0	0
Consular fees	77	32	342	132	142	137	149	153	153	156
Others	103	112	178	176	256	209	174	227	281	355
5128 Other taxes	0	0	0	0	0	0	0	0	0	0
5130 Unallocable between 5110 and 5120	0	0	0	0	0	0	0	0	0	0
5200 Taxes on use of goods and perform activities	69	718	6 441	6 498	8 835	10 463	12 935	13 300	14 182	17 183
5210 Recurrent taxes	69	718	2 301	2 265	2 736	2 958	3 365	3 553	3 804	4 906
5211 Paid by households: motor vehicles	45	268	1 391	1 277	1 289	1 558	1 932	2 081	2 310	3 407
5212 Paid by others: motor vehicles	0	0	0	0	0	0	0	0	0	0
5213 Paid in respect of other goods	24	450	910	988	1 447	1 400	1 433	1 472	1 494	1 499
Licences to carry firearms	17	237	316	296	200	171	190	176	192	182
Licences to operate gambling houses	0	114	217	211	1 221	1 208	1 210	1 250	1 262	1 268
Licences to operate slot machines	4	60	371	458	0	0	0	0	0	0
Others	4	39	7	24	26	21	34	46	41	49
5220 Non-recurrent taxes	0	0	4 140	4 234	6 099	7 505	9 570	9 747	10 378	12 277
Vehicle property registration	..	..	4 140	4 234	5 683	6 990	8 903	9 072	9 667	11 442
Ecological taxes	..	..	0	0	416	515	667	675	711	835
5300 Unallocable between 5100 and 5200	0	0	0	0	0	0	0	0	0	0
6000 Other taxes	**159**	**495**	**1 546**	**0**	**1**	**1**	**1**	**1**	**1**	**2**
6100 Paid solely by business	0	0	0	..	0	0	0	0	0	0
6200 Other	159	495	1 546	..	1	1	1	1	1	2

.. Not available

Note: Year ending 31st December.

The data are on a cash basis.

The figures exclude local government tax revenues as the data are not available.

Heading 2000: The data exclude social security contributions to general government managed by the private sector. An additional breakdown has been available since 2015 to distinguish between social security contributions paid by employees and those paid by employers.

Heading 3000: This heading includes the mandatory non-pensions contributions to the Instituto de Formacion Tecnico Profesinal (INFOTEP). The tax revenue is classified under the central government. In Dominican Republic this revenue is classified under a separate unit (decentralised) considered to be different to the central government.

Heading 5211: In ECLAC data, the vehicle transfer tax is classified as a property tax (4000).

Source: Ministerio de Hacienda (Ministry of Finance); Instituto Nacional de Formación Técnico Profesional (National Institute for Technical and Vocational Training).

StatLink https://doi.org/10.1787/888934235696

Table 5.13. **Ecuador**

Details of tax revenue / Ingresos tributarios detallados

Million USD

	1990	2000	2007	2010	2014	2015	2016	2017	2018	2019
Total tax revenue	**1 078**	**2 125**	**7 698**	**11 133**	**19 577**	**21 146**	**19 883**	**20 745**	**22 238**	**21 608**
1000 Taxes on income, profits and capital gains	**139**	**268**	**1 743**	**2 363**	**4 219**	**4 780**	**4 386**	**4 134**	**5 238**	**4 670**
1100 Of individuals	..	10	39	80	177	192	224	180	193	197
1110 On income and profits	..	10	39	80	177	192	224	180	193	197
Personal income tax	..	10	39	80	177	192	164	176	193	197
Solidarity contribution on remuneration	..	0	0	0	0	0	60	5	0	0
1120 On capital gains	..	..	..	0	0	0	0	0	..	..
1200 Corporate	..	53	424	485	1 121	1 575	1 377	1 074	1 894	1 308
1210 On profits	..	53	424	485	1 121	1 575	1 377	1 074	1 894	1 308
Corporate income tax	..	53	424	474	1 045	1 507	943	991	1 808	1 232
Income tax on oil companies and others	..	0	0	11	77	68	79	63	81	75
Solidarity contribution on profits	..	0	0	0	0	0	355	19	4	0
1220 On capital gains of corporates	..	..	..	..	..	..	..	..	..	..
1300 Unallocable between 1100 and 1200	139	206	1 279	1 798	2 920	3 013	2 784	2 880	3 151	3 165
Withholding tax	0	190	1 047	1 560	2 584	2 702	2 411	2 578	2 858	2 847
Income tax advances	0	14	227	298	381	335	335	343	353	394
Income tax refunds	0	0	0	-75	-113	-99	-32	-112	-132	-151
Other income taxes (local)	1	2	5	15	69	75	71	71	73	75
2000 Social security contributions	**243**	**228**	**1 792**	**2 541**	**4 718**	**5 057**	**4 741**	**5 415**	**5 541**	**5 863**
2100 Employees	..	..	..	..	..	..	..	..	..	..
2110 On a payroll basis	..	..	..	..	..	..	..	..	..	..
2120 On an income tax basis	..	..	..	..	..	..	..	..	..	..
2200 Employers	..	..	..	..	..	..	..	..	..	..
2210 On a payroll basis	..	..	..	..	..	..	..	..	..	..
2220 On an income tax basis	..	..	..	..	..	..	..	..	..	..
2300 Self-employed or non-employed	..	..	..	..	..	..	..	..	..	..
2310 On a payroll basis	..	..	..	..	..	..	..	..	..	..
2320 On an income tax basis	..	..	..	..	..	..	..	..	..	..
2400 Unallocable between 2100, 2200 and 2300	243	228	1 792	2 541	4 718	5 057	4 741	5 415	5 541	5 863
2410 On a payroll basis	..	..	..	..	..	..	..	..	..	..
2420 On an income tax basis	..	..	..	..	..	..	..	..	..	..
3000 Taxes on payroll and workforce	**0**	**0**	**0**	**0**	**0**	**0**	**0**	**0**	**0**	**0**
4000 Taxes on property	**16**	**17**	**91**	**159**	**261**	**303**	**639**	**347**	**375**	**343**
4100 Recurrent taxes on immovable property	13	8	48	68	124	134	142	162	135	121
Rural land tax	0	0	0	3	10	9	8	7	2	0
4110 Households	0	0	0	0	0	0	0	0	0	0
4120 Others	13	8	48	66	113	125	134	155	133	121
Tax on urban properties	12	7	40	55	96	106	113	129	133	121
Tax on rural properties	1	1	8	10	17	19	21	26	0	0
4200 Recurrent taxes on net wealth	0	0	0	35	44	49	47	35	30	35
4210 Individual	..	..	..	0	0	0	0	0	0	0
4220 Corporate	..	..	..	35	44	49	47	35	30	35
Tax on foreign assets	..	..	..	35	44	49	47	35	30	35
4300 Estate, inheritance and gift taxes	0	0	3	5	11	29	15	26	27	24
4310 Estate and inheritance taxes	..	..	3	5	11	29	15	26	27	24
4320 Gift taxes	..	..	0	0	0	0	0	0	0	0
4400 Taxes on financial and capital transactions	0	0	0	0	0	0	0	0	0	0
4500 Non-recurrent taxes	0	0	0	0	0	0	343	19	7	0
4510 On net wealth	..	..	..	..	..	..	343	19	7	..
Solidarity contribution on equity	..	..	..	..	..	..	202	16	6	..
Solidarity contribution on foreign assets	..	..	..	..	..	..	141	3	1	..
4520 Other non-recurrent taxes	..	..	..	..	..	..	0	0	0	..
4600 Other recurrent taxes on property	3	9	40	50	83	91	92	106	176	164
5000 Taxes on goods and services	**679**	**1 609**	**4 072**	**6 066**	**10 378**	**10 996**	**10 098**	**10 830**	**11 061**	**10 710**
5100 Taxes on production, sale, transfer, etc	671	1 580	3 958	5 863	9 905	10 503	9 639	10 371	10 605	10 247
5110 General taxes	306	928	2 819	3 801	6 454	6 431	6 116	6 718	6 705	6 618
5111 Value added taxes	302	923	2 787	3 759	6 376	6 352	6 042	6 643	6 633	6 539
VAT (internal operations)	..	557	1 518	2 506	4 513	4 778	4 375	4 672	4 789	4 885
VAT (imports)	..	381	1 486	1 668	2 035	1 722	1 329	1 646	1 947	1 800
2% contribution on VAT	..	0	0	0	0	0	402	412	4	0
VAT refunds	..	-14	-218	-416	-172	-148	-65	-87	-107	-146
Other VATs (local)	..	0	0	0	0	0	0	0	0	0
5112 Sales tax	0	0	0	0	0	0	0	0	0	0
5113 Other	4	5	32	41	78	79	74	75	72	79
5120 Taxes on specific goods and services	365	652	1 139	2 062	3 451	4 072	3 524	3 653	3 900	3 629

Table 5.13. **Ecuador** *(cont.)*

Details of tax revenue / Ingresos tributarios detallados

Million USD

	1990	2000	2007	2010	2014	2015	2016	2017	2018	2019
5121 Excises	90	89	269	508	783	806	769	919	955	885
Beer	..	29	81	119	166	188	194	237	239	246
Cigarettes	..	30	74	117	178	195	158	126	112	103
Fizzy drinks	..	9	16	40	53	59	109	103	94	93
Vehicles	..	6	11	55	106	98	50	67	63	42
Alcohol and alcoholic products	..	4	11	23	45	44	35	38	43	40
Non-returnable plastic bottles	..	0	0	0	22	22	28	31	35	36
Telephone	..	0	0	0	0	0	24	37	32	29
Water heaters	..	0	0	0	0	3	14	32	26	2
Perfumes	..	0	0	17	19	44	23	24	25	21
Non-alcoholic drinks	..	0	0	0	0	0	8	11	11	11
Other excises (internal operations)	..	0	0	0	5	13	2	4	5	5
Excises on imports	..	10	76	138	188	142	124	209	271	257
5122 Profits of fiscal monopolies	0	0	0	0	0	0	0	0	0	0
5123 Customs and import duties	227	217	679	1 153	1 357	2 026	1 633	1 468	1 561	1 418
5124 Taxes on exports	0	0	0	0	0	0	0	0	0	0
5125 Taxes on investment goods	0	0	0	0	0	0	0	0	0	0
5126 Taxes on specific services	26	343	192	30	52	146	157	169	178	186
Contribution to comprehensive cancer care	0	0	0	0	0	81	90	97	104	116
Prepaid television services	0	0	0	14	40	54	56	60	64	60
Club membership fees	0	0	0	0	0	1	1	1	1	1
Casino services	0	0	0	8	0	0	0	0	0	0
Telecommunications	0	0	188	0	3	0	0	0	0	0
Capital circulation tax	0	322	0	0	0	0	0	0	0	0
Departure tax	7	16	0	0	0	0	0	0	0	0
Tax on credit operations	18	2	0	1	0	0	0	0	0	0
Other service taxes (local)	1	2	4	7	8	10	9	10	9	9
5127 Other taxes on internat. trade and transactions	22	4	0	371	1 260	1 094	965	1 098	1 206	1 140
Foreign Currency Exit Tax (ISD)	0	0	..	371	1 260	1 094	965	1 098	1 206	1 140
Tax on purchase of foreign currency	22	4	..	0	0	0	0	0	0	0
5128 Other taxes	0	0	0	0	0	0	0	0	0	0
5130 Unallocable between 5110 and 5120	0	0	0	0	0	0	0	0	0	0
5200 Taxes on use of goods and perform activities	8	29	114	203	472	493	459	460	456	464
5210 Recurrent taxes	5	28	114	203	460	473	441	441	456	464
5211 Paid by households: motor vehicles	5	23	85	168	363	358	328	323	334	345
Motor vehicle tax	5	23	85	168	248	245	216	212	215	223
Environmental tax on vehicle pollution	0	0	0	0	115	113	112	111	119	122
5212 Paid by others: motor vehicles	0	0	0	0	0	0	0	0	0	0
5213 Paid in respect of other goods	1	5	29	35	97	115	113	118	122	118
5220 Non-recurrent taxes	2	1	0	0	12	20	18	18	0	0
5300 Unallocable between 5100 and 5200	0	0	0	0	0	0	0	0	0	0
6000 Other taxes	**2**	**2**	**1**	**4**	**1**	**10**	**18**	**19**	**23**	**22**
6100 Paid solely by business	0	0	0	0	0	0	0	0	0	0
6200 Other	2	2	1	4	1	10	18	19	23	22
Simplified taxation system of Ecuador (RISE)	0	0	0	6	20	20	19	22	23	22
Other tax refunds	0	0	0	-2	-18	-10	-1	-3	-2	-2
Other taxes (local)	2	2	1	1	0	0	0	0	2	2

.. Not available

Note: Year ending 31st December.

The data are on a cash basis.

Central tax revenues mainly come from Servicio de Rentas Internas while some are from the Central Bank.

Local tax revenues in 2018 have been updated with data from the Inter-American Centre of Tax Administrations (CIAT). Local tax revenues in 2019 are estimated as data are not available.

Heading 2000: The data are collected from non-financial public sector operations published by the Central Bank of Ecuador.

Heading 5123: The data are collected from general budget of the consolidated state government published by the Central Bank of Ecuador.

Heading 5126: This heading includes the tax on credit operations from the general budget of the consolidated state government published by the Central Bank of Ecuador.

Heading 5127: This heading includes the tax on purchase of foreign currency from the general budget of the consolidated state government published by the Central Bank of Ecuador.

Source: Servicio de Rentas Internas (Internal Revenue Service); Banco Central del Ecuador (Central Bank of Ecuador), Centro Interamericano de Administraciones Tributarias (Inter-American Centre of Tax Administrations).

StatLink https://doi.org/10.1787/888934235715

Table 5.14. **El Salvador**

Details of tax revenue / Ingresos tributarios detallados

Million USD

	1990	2000	2007	2010	2014	2015	2016	2017	2018	2019
Total tax revenue	**543**	**1 669**	**3 192**	**3 447**	**4 478**	**4 659**	**4 963**	**5 230**	**5 539**	**5 629**
1000 Taxes on income, profits and capital gains	**95**	**429**	**933**	**996**	**1 521**	**1 545**	**1 659**	**1 733**	**1 819**	**1 885**
1100 Of individuals	..	..	395	590	686	774	732	759	795	836
1110 On income and profits	..	..	395	590	686	774	732	759	795	836
1120 On capital gains	..	..	..	..	..	..	..	..	..	..
1200 Corporate	..	..	573	420	693	622	763	804	845	848
1210 On profits	..	..	573	420	693	622	763	804	845	848
1220 On capital gains of corporates	..	..	..	..	..	..	..	..	..	..
1300 Unallocable between 1100 and 1200	95	429	-35	-14	142	148	164	170	180	201
Withholding income tax	..	..	0	41	170	178	195	209	220	249
Income tax refunds	..	..	-35	-55	-28	-30	-31	-39	-40	-48
2000 Social security contributions	**104**	**325**	**391**	**470**	**571**	**608**	**655**	**684**	**705**	**722**
2100 Employees	..	75	137	165	200	214	228	239	246	251
2110 On a payroll basis	..	75	137	165	200	214	228	239	246	251
2120 On an income tax basis	..	0	0	0	0	0	0	0	0	0
2200 Employers	..	176	254	306	370	393	427	444	459	471
2210 On a payroll basis	..	176	254	306	370	393	427	444	459	471
2220 On an income tax basis	..	0	0	0	0	0	0	0	0	0
2300 Self-employed or non-employed	..	13	0	0	0	0	0	0	0	0
2310 On a payroll basis	..	13	..	..	..	..	..	..	..	..
2320 On an income tax basis	..	0	..	..	..	..	..	..	..	..
2400 Unallocable between 2100, 2200 and 2300	104	62	0	0	0	0	0	0	0	0
2410 On a payroll basis	104	62	..	..	..	..	..	..	..	..
2420 On an income tax basis	0	0	..	..	..	..	..	..	..	..
3000 Taxes on payroll and workforce	**0**	**0**	**19**	**21**	**27**	**30**	**33**	**36**	**37**	**38**
4000 Taxes on property	**26**	**12**	**24**	**19**	**51**	**112**	**112**	**112**	**119**	**44**
4100 Recurrent taxes on immovable property	0	0	3	3	5	5	5	5	6	7
4110 Households	..	..	..	..	..	..	..	..	..	..
4120 Others	..	..	..	..	..	..	..	..	..	..
4200 Recurrent taxes on net wealth	16	0	0	0	0	0	0	0	0	0
4210 Individual	..	..	..	..	..	..	..	..	..	..
4220 Corporate	..	..	..	..	..	..	..	..	..	..
4300 Estate, inheritance and gift taxes	0	0	0	0	0	0	0	0	0	0
4310 Estate and inheritance taxes	..	..	..	..	..	..	..	..	..	..
4320 Gift taxes	..	..	..	..	..	..	..	..	..	..
4400 Taxes on financial and capital transactions	10	12	21	16	46	107	107	107	113	37
Property transfers	10	12	21	16	24	20	23	23	24	29
Checks and electronic transfers of funds	0	0	0	0	15	55	54	53	56	5
Withholding for liquidity control	0	0	0	0	7	31	31	32	34	3
4500 Non-recurrent taxes	0	0	0	0	0	0	0	0	0	0
4510 On net wealth	..	..	..	..	..	..	..	..	..	..
4520 Other non-recurrent taxes	..	..	..	..	..	..	..	..	..	..
4600 Other recurrent taxes on property	0	0	0	0	0	0	0	0	0	0
5000 Taxes on goods and services	**259**	**903**	**1 775**	**1 878**	**2 217**	**2 278**	**2 413**	**2 578**	**2 763**	**2 850**
5100 Taxes on production, sale, transfer, etc	259	903	1 770	1 863	2 193	2 254	2 386	2 550	2 732	2 821
5110 General taxes	133	714	1 389	1 433	1 720	1 764	1 813	1 903	2 054	2 109
5111 Value added taxes	0	714	1 389	1 433	1 720	1 764	1 813	1 903	2 054	2 109
5112 Sales tax	0	0	0	0	0	0	0	0	0	0
5113 Other	133	0	0	0	0	0	0	0	0	0
5120 Taxes on specific goods and services	127	189	381	431	473	490	573	647	678	712
5121 Excises	65	49	169	224	261	285	355	423	437	466
Alcoholic beverages	..	..	15	22	22	22	23	24	24	25
Cigarettes	..	..	27	38	34	29	28	27	24	24
Soft drinks	..	..	25	31	43	48	49	49	49	52
Beer	..	..	30	29	49	55	61	65	73	82
Weapons, ammunition and explosives	..	..	1	1	1	1	1	1	1	1
Ad-valorem on fuels	..	..	0	0	0	7	9	8	7	8
Special contribution- Sugar	..	..	1	1	1	1	1	1	1	1
Special contribution- Public transportation	..	..	0	35	37	40	43	45	47	48
Special contribution- FOVIAL	..	..	70	69	74	80	86	89	93	96
Special contribution- Public security	..	..	0	0	0	2	56	116	118	129
5122 Profits of fiscal monopolies	0	0	0	0	0	0	0	0	0	0
5123 Customs and import duties	61	141	204	151	181	194	206	211	227	232
5124 Taxes on exports	0	0	0	0	0	0	0	0	0	0
5125 Taxes on investment goods	0	0	0	0	0	0	0	0	0	0
5126 Taxes on specific services	0	0	8	56	31	11	12	13	14	13
5127 Other taxes on internat. trade and transactions	0	0	0	0	0	0	0	0	0	0
5128 Other taxes	0	0	0	0	0	0	0	0	0	0

Table 5.14. **El Salvador** *(cont.)*

Details of tax revenue / Ingresos tributarios detallados

Million USD

	1990	2000	2007	2010	2014	2015	2016	2017	2018	2019
5130 Unallocable between 5110 and 5120	0	0	0	0	0	0	0	0	0	0
5200 Taxes on use of goods and perform activities	0	0	5	15	24	24	26	27	31	29
5210 Recurrent taxes	..	..	5	7	13	12	12	14	16	13
5211 Paid by households: motor vehicles	..	..	0	0	0	0	0	0	0	0
5212 Paid by others: motor vehicles	..	..	0	0	0	0	0	0	0	0
5213 Paid in respect of other goods	..	..	5	7	13	12	12	14	16	13
5220 Non-recurrent taxes	..	..	0	7	11	12	14	14	15	16
5300 Unallocable between 5100 and 5200	0	0	0	0	0	0	0	0	0	0
6000 Other taxes	**58**	**0**	**49**	**63**	**91**	**86**	**91**	**88**	**96**	**89**
6100 Paid solely by business	0	0	0	0	0	0	0	0	0	0
6200 Other	58	0	49	63	91	86	91	88	96	89

.. Not available

Note: Year ending 31st December.

The data are on a cash basis.

Heading 1000: Disaggregated individual and corporate income taxes are not available before 2002.

Heading 2000: The figures include social security contributions paid to the Salvadoran Institute of Social Security (ISSS), National Public Employees Pension Institute (INPEP), Social Security Institute of the Armed Forces (IPSFA) and Salvadoran Institute of Teacher Welfare (ISBM). The figures exclude payments to privately managed pension funds (AFPs) and may include small amount of voluntary contributions which are undistinguishable from the public social security contribution data. Data since 2004 have been updated with more detailed information from the Department of Financial Analysis and Statistics in this edition.

Heading 3000: Vocational training contributions to the Instituto Salvadoreño de Formación Profesional (INSAFORP) have been added in this edition. The tax revenue is classified under the central government. In El Salvador this revenue is classified under a separate unit considered to be different to the central government.

Source: Dirección General de Tesorería en Ministerio de Hacienda (General Treasury Directorate in Ministry of Finance); Dirección General de Contabilidad Gubernamental en Ministerio de Hacienda (General Directorate of Government Accounting in Ministry of Finance); Departamento de Análisis Financiero y Estadística en Ministerio de Hacienda (Department of Financial Analysis and Statistics in Ministry of Finance); Instituto Salvadoreño del Seguro Social (Salvadoran Social Security Institute); Centro Interamericano de Administraciones Tributarias (Inter-American Center of Tax Administrations)

StatLink https://doi.org/10.1787/888934235734

Table 5.15. **Guatemala**

Details of tax revenue / Ingresos tributarios detallados

Million GTQ

	1990	2000	2007	2010	2014	2015	2016	2017	2018	2019
Total tax revenue	**2 569**	**16 531**	**36 702**	**41 537**	**59 170**	**60 817**	**66 401**	**69 691**	**72 505**	**77 121**
1000 Taxes on income, profits and capital gains	**507**	**3 295**	**8 654**	**10 319**	**17 752**	**17 534**	**20 572**	**20 693**	**20 893**	**21 930**
1100 Of individuals	25	143	877	1 225	1 784	1 826	2 082	2 468	2 603	2 813
1110 On income and profits	25	143	877	1 225	1 784	1 826	2 082	2 468	2 603	2 813
1120 On capital gains	..	..	..	..	..	..	..	..	..	..
1200 Corporate	482	3 149	5 729	6 520	12 426	11 801	14 418	13 846	13 633	14 287
1210 On profits	482	3 149	5 729	6 520	12 426	11 801	14 418	13 846	13 633	14 287
Corporate income tax	482	1 858	5 720	6 518	12 423	11 801	14 417	13 839	13 633	14 285
Commercial and agricultural enterprises	0	1 291	9	2	3	0	1	6	0	2
1220 On capital gains of corporates	..	..	..	..	..	..	..	..	..	..
1300 Unallocable between 1100 and 1200	0	2	2 048	2 574	3 543	3 907	4 072	4 380	4 656	4 829
Extraordinary and temporary solidarity tax in support of peace agreements	..	0	2 047	44	9	1	1	28	10	63
Solidarity tax	..	0	0	2 530	3 533	3 906	4 070	4 352	4 646	4 766
Extraordinary and temporary solidarity tax	..	2	1	0	0	0	0	0	0	0
2000 Social security contributions	**436**	**2 569**	**5 069**	**6 312**	**9 263**	**9 778**	**10 974**	**11 523**	**12 102**	**12 957**
2100 Employees	..	..	..	..	..	..	..	..	..	..
2110 On a payroll basis	..	..	..	..	..	..	..	..	..	..
2120 On an income tax basis	..	..	..	..	..	..	..	..	..	..
2200 Employers	..	..	..	..	..	..	..	..	..	..
2210 On a payroll basis	..	..	..	..	..	..	..	..	..	..
2220 On an income tax basis	..	..	..	..	..	..	..	..	..	..
2300 Self-employed or non-employed	..	..	..	..	..	..	..	..	..	..
2310 On a payroll basis	..	..	..	..	..	..	..	..	..	..
2320 On an income tax basis	..	..	..	..	..	..	..	..	..	..
2400 Unallocable between 2100, 2200 and 2300	436	2 569	5 069	6 312	9 263	9 778	10 974	11 523	12 102	12 957
2410 On a payroll basis	436	2 569	5 069	6 312	9 263	9 778	10 974	11 523	12 102	12 957
2420 On an income tax basis	0	0	0	0	0	0	0	0	0	0
3000 Taxes on payroll and workforce	**0**	**0**	**381**	**447**	**673**	**736**	**792**	**862**	**903**	**933**
Contributions to INTECAP	..	..	199	233	351	384	414	449	469	484
Contributions to IRTRA	..	..	183	214	322	352	379	413	434	449
4000 Taxes on property	**149**	**347**	**832**	**1 202**	**1 035**	**1 050**	**957**	**1 247**	**1 354**	**1 177**
4100 Recurrent taxes on immovable property	0	153	426	621	661	693	565	710	865	685
4110 Households	..	0	0	0	0	0	0	0	0	0
4120 Others	..	153	426	621	661	693	565	710	865	685
Property tax	..	6	1	1	1	1	1	1	2	2
Property tax (municipal)	..	147	426	620	660	692	564	709	863	683
4200 Recurrent taxes on net wealth	0	0	0	0	0	0	0	0	0	0
4210 Individual	..	..	..	..	..	..	..	..	..	..
4220 Corporate	..	..	..	..	..	..	..	..	..	..
4300 Estate, inheritance and gift taxes	0	0	0	0	0	0	0	0	0	0
4310 Estate and inheritance taxes	..	..	..	..	..	..	..	..	..	..
4320 Gift taxes	..	..	..	..	..	..	..	..	..	..
4400 Taxes on financial and capital transactions	149	194	406	581	373	357	393	537	489	492
Stamp duty	104	182	392	572	359	336	370	508	463	451
Tax on property transfer	45	12	14	10	14	20	23	29	26	40
4500 Non-recurrent taxes	0	0	0	0	0	0	0	0	0	0
4510 On net wealth	..	..	..	..	..	..	..	..	..	..
4520 Other non-recurrent taxes	..	..	..	..	..	..	..	..	..	..
4600 Other recurrent taxes on property	0	0	0	0	0	0	0	0	0	0
5000 Taxes on goods and services	**1 477**	**10 317**	**21 764**	**23 255**	**30 447**	**31 719**	**33 105**	**35 365**	**37 253**	**40 124**
5100 Taxes on production, sale, transfer, etc	1 449	10 131	21 411	22 750	29 128	30 088	31 356	33 586	35 420	38 216
5110 General taxes	762	6 259	15 382	16 980	23 153	23 271	24 215	26 187	27 733	29 920
5111 Value added taxes	762	6 259	15 382	16 980	23 153	23 271	24 215	26 187	27 733	29 920
VAT domestic	361	2 903	6 647	7 995	11 325	12 023	13 308	14 380	14 573	15 897
VAT imports	401	4 189	10 532	11 127	14 094	13 630	13 361	14 148	15 560	16 331
Tax credit refunds	0	-834	-1 797	-2 142	-2 267	-2 381	-2 455	-2 342	-2 401	-2 307
5112 Sales tax	0	0	0	0	0	0	0	0	0	0
5113 Other	0	0	0	0	0	0	0	0	0	0
5120 Taxes on specific goods and services	687	3 872	6 029	5 770	5 975	6 816	7 140	7 400	7 687	8 296
5121 Excises	181	1 797	2 946	3 101	3 579	4 289	4 422	4 518	4 668	5 107
Tobacco and derivatives	76	205	355	347	404	369	365	348	337	363
Beer	0	97	144	159	243	293	306	314	322	365
Alcoholic beverages	0	77	87	97	86	88	90	96	103	109
Soft drinks	0	15	195	220	300	328	348	348	365	396
Other beverages	0	12	1	2	0	0	1	0	0	0
Cement	0	0	117	99	100	312	117	114	123	131
Oil and derivatives	105	1 389	2 047	2 179	2 445	2 899	3 195	3 296	3 417	3 743

Table 5.15. **Guatemala** *(cont.)*

Details of tax revenue / Ingresos tributarios detallados

Million GTQ

	1990	2000	2007	2010	2014	2015	2016	2017	2018	2019
5122 Profits of fiscal monopolies	0	0	0	0	0	0	0	0	0	0
5123 Customs and import duties	506	1 806	2 654	2 368	2 044	2 157	2 323	2 455	2 576	2 712
5124 Taxes on exports	0	0	0	0	0	0	0	0	0	0
5125 Taxes on investment goods	0	0	0	0	0	0	0	0	0	0
5126 Taxes on specific services	0	269	429	301	352	370	396	427	443	477
Departure tax	..	135	229	224	252	263	280	300	312	338
INGUATE	..	40	78	73	96	104	110	120	125	132
Transportation and communications	..	94	122	3	4	4	5	7	6	7
5127 Other taxes on internat. trade and transactions	0	0	0	0	0	0	0	0	0	0
5128 Other taxes	0	0	0	0	0	0	0	0	0	0
5130 Unallocable between 5110 and 5120	0	0	0	0	0	0	0	0	0	0
5200 Taxes on use of goods and perform activities	28	186	353	505	1 320	1 631	1 750	1 779	1 834	1 908
5210 Recurrent taxes	28	186	353	505	1 320	1 631	1 750	1 779	1 834	1 908
5211 Paid by households: motor vehicles	0	0	0	0	747	914	967	953	953	999
5212 Paid by others: motor vehicles	28	186	353	505	572	717	782	826	881	909
5213 Paid in respect of other goods	0	0	0	0	0	0	0	0	0	0
5220 Non-recurrent taxes	0	0	0	0	0	0	0	0	0	0
5300 Unallocable between 5100 and 5200	0	0	0	0	0	0	0	0	0	0
6000 Other taxes	**0**	**4**	**1**	**1**	**0**	**0**	**0**	**0**	**0**	**0**
6100 Paid solely by business	..	0	0	0	0	0	0	0	0	0
6200 Other	..	4	1	1	0	0	0	0	0	0

.. Not available

Note: Year ending 31st December.

The data are on a cash basis.

Local government tax revenues include revenues from the municipal property tax (IUSI).

Heading 1000: Personal and corporate income taxes also include taxes on income from financial products.

Heading 2000: Figures include contributions to the Guatemalan Social Security Institute (IGSS) and payments by public employees to the government's pension fund.

Heading 3000: Contributions to INTECAP and contributions to IRTRA have been added and classified as payroll taxes in this edition. The tax revenues are classified under the central government. In Guatemala these revenues are classified under a separate unit considered to be different to the central government.

Heading 4400: Before 2000, tax on property transfer under heading 4400 also includes other central government property tax under heading 4120 as they cannot be distinguished.

Heading 5121: Other beverages contain all alcoholic and non-alcoholic beverages before 2000.

Source: Superintendencia de Administración Tributaria (Superintendency of Tax Administration); Ministerio de Finanzas Públicas (Ministry of Public Finance); Contraloría General de Cuentas (General Comptroller's Office).

StatLink https://doi.org/10.1787/888934235753

Table 5.16. **Guyana**

Details of tax revenue / Ingresos tributarios detallados

Million GYD

	1990	2000	2007	2010	2014	2015	2016	2017	2018	2019
Total tax revenue	**5 232**	**42 750**	**85 991**	**111 906**	**151 382**	**159 895**	**170 305**	**191 513**	**220 421**	**250 240**
1000 Taxes on income, profits and capital gains	**1 752**	**16 179**	**29 520**	**39 561**	**51 611**	**55 011**	**61 127**	**68 088**	**78 956**	**94 504**
1100 Of individuals	333	7 734	12 832	17 816	21 389	23 300	26 773	26 564	32 037	35 249
1110 On income and profits	333	7 734	12 832	17 816	21 389	23 300	26 773	26 564	32 037	35 249
Personal	306	7 157	12 832	15 419	17 900	19 894	22 727	21 669	25 808	29 213
Self-employed	27	577	0	2 397	3 490	3 407	4 045	4 895	6 229	6 036
1120 On capital gains	..	..	..	..	..	..	..	..	..	..
1200 Corporate	1 375	8 266	16 460	21 427	29 794	31 200	33 852	41 183	46 198	58 346
1210 On profits	1 375	8 266	16 460	21 427	29 794	31 200	33 852	41 183	46 198	58 346
1220 On capital gains of corporates	..	..	..	..	..	..	..	..	..	..
1300 Unallocable between 1100 and 1200	43	179	229	317	428	511	502	341	721	908
2000 Social security contributions	**191**	**4 868**	**8 061**	**10 047**	**14 985**	**16 644**	**18 211**	**19 911**	**21 178**	**23 728**
2100 Employees	..	..	..	..	..	..	..	..	..	..
2110 On a payroll basis	..	..	..	..	..	..	..	..	..	..
2120 On an income tax basis	..	..	..	..	..	..	..	..	..	..
2200 Employers	..	..	..	..	..	..	..	..	..	..
2210 On a payroll basis	..	..	..	..	..	..	..	..	..	..
2220 On an income tax basis	..	..	..	..	..	..	..	..	..	..
2300 Self-employed or non-employed	..	..	..	..	..	..	..	..	..	..
2310 On a payroll basis	..	..	..	..	..	..	..	..	..	..
2320 On an income tax basis	..	..	..	..	..	..	..	..	..	..
2400 Unallocable between 2100, 2200 and 2300	191	4 868	8 061	10 047	14 985	16 644	18 211	19 911	21 178	23 728
2410 On a payroll basis	..	..	..	..	..	..	..	..	..	..
2420 On an income tax basis	..	..	..	..	..	..	..	..	..	..
3000 Taxes on payroll and workforce	**0**	**0**	**0**	**0**	**0**	**0**	**0**	**0**	**0**	**0**
4000 Taxes on property	**53**	**701**	**962**	**2 068**	**3 062**	**3 676**	**3 572**	**4 027**	**4 875**	**4 917**
4100 Recurrent taxes on immovable property	40	681	943	1 562	2 381	3 201	3 172	3 579	4 377	4 312
4110 Households	0	0	0	0	0	588	659	781	1 016	933
4120 Others	40	681	943	1 562	2 381	2 613	2 513	2 798	3 361	3 379
4200 Recurrent taxes on net wealth	0	0	0	0	0	0	0	0	0	0
4210 Individual	..	..	..	..	..	..	..	..	..	..
4220 Corporate	..	..	..	..	..	..	..	..	..	..
4300 Estate, inheritance and gift taxes	13	20	19	31	42	37	37	39	44	41
4310 Estate and inheritance taxes	13	20	19	31	42	37	37	39	44	41
4320 Gift taxes	0	0	0	0	0	0	0	0	0	0
4400 Taxes on financial and capital transactions	0	0	0	476	640	438	363	409	454	565
Stamp duties	..	..	..	476	640	438	363	409	454	565
4500 Non-recurrent taxes	0	0	0	0	0	0	0	0	0	0
4510 On net wealth	..	..	..	..	..	..	..	..	..	..
4520 Other non-recurrent taxes	..	..	..	..	..	..	..	..	..	..
4600 Other recurrent taxes on property	0	0	0	0	0	0	0	0	0	0
5000 Taxes on goods and services	**2 200**	**20 798**	**46 544**	**59 360**	**81 104**	**83 924**	**86 445**	**97 502**	**113 216**	**124 952**
5100 Taxes on production, sale, transfer, etc	2 162	20 530	45 937	58 846	80 431	83 227	85 499	96 386	111 770	123 710
5110 General taxes	1 399	14 861	22 755	27 044	37 307	35 374	37 468	42 728	48 155	52 735
5111 Value added taxes	0	0	21 329	27 044	37 307	35 374	36 268	42 423	48 036	52 676
Imports	..	..	..	14 877	20 370	19 366	18 477	23 261	27 819	29 302
Domestic supply	..	..	..	12 168	16 937	16 008	17 791	19 162	20 216	23 374
5112 Sales tax	0	0	0	0	0	0	0	0	0	0
5113 Other	1 399	14 861	1 426	0	0	0	1 200	305	119	60
5120 Taxes on specific goods and services	763	5 669	23 182	31 802	43 124	47 853	48 031	53 659	63 615	70 975
5121 Excises	32	609	16 057	22 070	29 267	33 827	31 083	35 162	41 659	45 979
Motor vehicle (imports)	..	..	..	7 702	8 800	8 499	7 088	5 443	6 781	7 977
Petroleum products (imports)	..	..	..	9 437	13 759	19 355	18 007	21 745	26 359	29 124
Tobacco (imports)	..	..	..	1 077	1 317	1 224	1 063	1 078	1 204	1 427
Alcoholic beverages (imports)	..	..	..	719	1 169	875	884	844	867	785
Alcoholic beverages (domestic)	..	..	..	2 358	3 190	3 377	4 040	4 348	4 468	4 486
Purchase tax - motor cars	..	..	..	0	0	0	0	0	0	0
Environmental tax	..	..	..	777	1 033	496	0	1 703	1 979	2 179
5122 Profits of fiscal monopolies	0	0	0	0	0	0	0	0	0	0
5123 Customs and import duties	544	3 943	6 005	8 302	12 167	12 357	14 887	16 273	19 321	22 140
5124 Taxes on exports	94	7	9	7	14	12	13	23	33	29
5125 Taxes on investment goods	0	0	0	0	0	0	0	0	0	0
5126 Taxes on specific services	92	1 110	1 112	1 423	1 676	1 658	2 048	2 201	2 603	2 827
Entertainment tax	12	27	1	0	0	0	0	0	0	0
Travel tax	80	1 084	1 112	1 423	1 676	1 658	2 048	2 201	2 603	2 827
5127 Other taxes on internat. trade and transactions	0	0	0	0	0	0	0	0	0	0
5128 Other taxes	0	0	0	0	0	0	0	0	0	0
5130 Unallocable between 5110 and 5120	0	0	0	0	0	0	0	0	0	0

Table 5.16. **Guyana** *(cont.)*

Details of tax revenue / Ingresos tributarios detallados

Million GYD

	1990	2000	2007	2010	2014	2015	2016	2017	2018	2019
5200 Taxes on use of goods and perform activities	38	268	607	514	673	697	945	1 116	1 446	1 242
5210 Recurrent taxes	38	268	607	514	673	697	945	1 116	1 446	1 242
5211 Paid by households: motor vehicles	27	239	306	475	637	653	868	1 039	1 095	1 150
5212 Paid by others: motor vehicles	0	0	0	0	0	0	0	0	0	0
5213 Paid in respect of other goods	12	29	301	39	35	44	78	77	352	92
Other licences	12	29	301	39	35	44	78	77	352	92
5220 Non-recurrent taxes	0	0	0	0	0	0	0	0	0	0
5300 Unallocable between 5100 and 5200	0	0	0	0	0	0	0	0	0	0
6000 Other taxes	**1 037**	**204**	**904**	**870**	**620**	**640**	**950**	**1 985**	**2 196**	**2 139**
6100 Paid solely by business	0	0	0	0	0	0	0	0	0	0
6200 Other	1 037	204	904	870	620	640	950	1 985	2 196	2 139

.. Not available

Note: Year ending 31st December.

The data are on a cash basis.

Central government tax revenues are based on Budget Estimates by the Ministry of Finance. Data on local government tax revenues include payments of local taxes by public corporations and come from Bank of Guyana.

Heading 1210: Corporate income tax is classified under heading 1210 instead of its parent heading 1200 in this edition.

Heading 2000: The figures include contributions to National Insurance Scheme.

Heading 4100: Disaggregated property tax data on companies and individuals have become available since 2008 in this edition based on new data from the Ministry of Finance.

Heading 4400: Stamp duties are classified under heading 4400 in this edition. They were previously under heading 6200.

Heading 5121: Components of excises have been identified and added in this edition based on more detailed data from the Ministry of Finance.

Source: Ministry of Finance; Bank of Guyana; National Insurance Scheme.

StatLink https://doi.org/10.1787/888934235772

Table 5.17. **Honduras**

Details of tax revenue / Ingresos tributarios detallados

Million HNL

	1990	2000	2007	2010	2014	2015	2016	2017	2018	2019
Total tax revenue	**2 118**	**18 299**	**46 161**	**54 544**	**84 448**	**96 889**	**112 502**	**120 190**	**128 781**	**134 720**
1000 Taxes on income, profits and capital gains	**431**	**2 907**	**11 833**	**13 232**	**21 347**	**25 003**	**29 584**	**33 055**	**36 071**	**34 533**
1100 Of individuals	157	992	3 919	4 528	7 312	8 147	9 566	10 533	11 368	11 365
1110 On income and profits	157	992	3 919	4 528	7 312	8 147	9 566	10 533	11 368	11 365
1120 On capital gains	..	..	..	..	..	..	..	..	..	..
1200 Corporate	274	1 916	7 915	8 705	14 034	16 856	20 018	22 522	24 702	23 167
1210 On profits	274	1 916	7 915	8 705	14 034	16 856	20 018	22 522	24 702	23 167
Corporate income tax	274	1 916	6 877	7 400	12 756	15 206	18 020	20 668	22 083	20 538
Income tax surcharge	0	0	1 038	1 305	1 265	1 637	1 985	1 841	2 601	2 612
Special contribution of the cooperative sector	0	0	0	0	13	13	13	14	19	17
1220 On capital gains of corporates	..	..	..	..	..	..	..	..	..	..
1300 Unallocable between 1100 and 1200	0	0	0	0	0	0	0	0	0	0
2000 Social security contributions	**179**	**1 727**	**6 037**	**8 671**	**12 467**	**13 524**	**15 550**	**17 911**	**19 302**	**21 068**
2100 Employees	..	..	..	..	..	..	..	..	..	..
2110 On a payroll basis	..	..	..	..	..	..	..	..	..	..
2120 On an income tax basis	..	..	..	..	..	..	..	..	..	..
2200 Employers	..	..	..	..	..	..	..	..	..	..
2210 On a payroll basis	..	..	..	..	..	..	..	..	..	..
2220 On an income tax basis	..	..	..	..	..	..	..	..	..	..
2300 Self-employed or non-employed	..	..	..	..	..	..	..	..	..	..
2310 On a payroll basis	..	..	..	..	..	..	..	..	..	..
2320 On an income tax basis	..	..	..	..	..	..	..	..	..	..
2400 Unallocable between 2100, 2200 and 2300	179	1 727	6 037	8 671	12 467	13 524	15 550	17 911	19 302	21 068
2410 On a payroll basis	179	1 727	6 037	8 671	12 467	13 524	15 550	17 911	19 302	21 068
2420 On an income tax basis	0	0	0	0	0	0	0	0	0	0
3000 Taxes on payroll and workforce	**0**	**0**	**398**	**485**	**746**	**1 007**	**869**	**925**	**1 025**	**1 005**
4000 Taxes on property	**16**	**266**	**439**	**994**	**2 300**	**2 635**	**2 726**	**3 046**	**3 243**	**3 428**
4100 Recurrent taxes on immovable property	16	189	291	254	275	298	330	344	435	446
4110 Households	..	..	..	..	..	..	..	..	..	..
4120 Others	..	..	..	..	..	..	..	..	..	..
4200 Recurrent taxes on net wealth	0	78	148	359	389	334	294	349	278	341
4210 Individual	..	..	..	..	..	..	..	..	..	..
4220 Corporate	..	..	..	..	..	..	..	..	..	..
4300 Estate, inheritance and gift taxes	0	0	0	0	0	0	0	0	0	0
4310 Estate and inheritance taxes	..	..	..	..	..	..	..	..	..	..
4320 Gift taxes	..	..	..	..	..	..	..	..	..	..
4400 Taxes on financial and capital transactions	0	0	0	0	1 636	2 003	2 102	2 353	2 531	2 641
4500 Non-recurrent taxes	0	0	0	380	0	0	0	0	0	0
4510 On net wealth	..	..	0	0	..	..	..	..	..	..
4520 Other non-recurrent taxes	..	..	0	380	..	..	..	..	..	..
4600 Other recurrent taxes on property	0	0	0	0	0	0	0	0	0	0
5000 Taxes on goods and services	**1 401**	**12 436**	**25 985**	**28 937**	**44 945**	**52 217**	**58 638**	**63 111**	**66 735**	**69 468**
5100 Taxes on production, sale, transfer, etc	1 401	12 436	25 985	28 937	44 945	52 217	58 638	63 111	66 735	69 468
5110 General taxes	344	5 146	14 170	16 050	27 734	32 273	36 521	39 228	41 562	42 891
5111 Value added taxes	344	5 146	14 170	16 050	27 734	32 273	36 521	39 228	41 562	42 891
5112 Sales tax	0	0	0	0	0	0	0	0	0	0
5113 Other	0	0	0	0	0	0	0	0	0	0
5120 Taxes on specific goods and services	1 057	7 290	11 815	12 887	17 211	19 944	22 117	23 883	25 173	26 577
5121 Excises	256	4 592	7 606	8 458	11 588	13 349	14 953	16 405	17 011	18 285
Beer	70	376	358	376	525	668	824	974	1 150	1 339
Soft drinks	25	240	419	514	754	838	890	938	979	1 075
Liquors	32	48	80	121	188	194	190	192	227	217
Petroleum products	43	347	0	0	0	0	0	0	0	0
Cigarettes	57	369	582	607	610	598	564	563	565	514
Fuel tax	0	2 954	5 578	6 288	8 874	10 317	11 594	12 773	13 061	14 131
Other	28	258	589	551	638	735	890	965	1 028	1 010
5122 Profits of fiscal monopolies	0	0	0	0	0	0	0	0	0	0
5123 Customs and import duties	498	2 083	2 869	2 505	2 974	3 541	3 998	4 244	4 485	4 474
Petroleum	0	297	0	0	0	0	0	0	0	0
Other	498	1 786	2 869	2 505	2 974	3 541	3 998	4 244	4 485	4 474
5124 Taxes on exports	217	6	0	0	107	84	72	79	90	18
Bananas	39	5	..	..	0	0	0	0	0	0
Coffee	1	0	..	..	0	0	0	0	0	0
Temporary export tax	163	0	..	..	0	0	0	0	0	0
Special contribution of the mining sector	0	0	..	..	107	84	72	79	90	18
Other	15	1	..	..	0	0	0	0	0	0
5125 Taxes on investment goods	0	0	0	0	0	0	0	0	0	0

Table 5.17. **Honduras** *(cont.)*

Details of tax revenue / Ingresos tributarios detallados

Million HNL

	1990	2000	2007	2010	2014	2015	2016	2017	2018	2019
5126 Taxes on specific services	0	0	0	0	90	91	86	84	80	49
Special contribution of mobile services	..	..	..	..	67	67	60	55	49	35
Special contribution of the food and services sector	..	..	..	..	20	21	23	25	26	9
Special contribution of casino games and slot machines	..	..	..	..	3	3	3	4	4	5
5127 Other taxes on internat. trade and transactions	0	0	0	0	0	0	0	0	0	0
5128 Other taxes	87	610	1 340	1 924	2 451	2 880	3 007	3 070	3 508	3 750
5130 Unallocable between 5110 and 5120	0	0	0	0	0	0	0	0	0	0
5200 Taxes on use of goods and perform activities	0	0	0	0	0	0	0	0	0	0
5210 Recurrent taxes	..	..	..	..	..	..	..	..	..	..
5211 Paid by households: motor vehicles	..	..	..	..	..	..	..	..	..	..
5212 Paid by others: motor vehicles	..	..	..	..	..	..	..	..	..	..
5213 Paid in respect of other goods	..	..	..	..	..	..	..	..	..	..
5220 Non-recurrent taxes	..	..	..	..	..	..	..	..	..	..
5300 Unallocable between 5100 and 5200	0	0	0	0	0	0	0	0	0	0
6000 Other taxes	**91**	**962**	**1 469**	**2 225**	**2 644**	**2 503**	**5 136**	**2 142**	**2 404**	**5 220**
6100 Paid solely by business	0	0	0	0	0	0	0	0	0	0
6200 Other	91	962	1 469	2 225	2 644	2 503	5 136	2 142	2 404	5 220

.. Not available

Note: Year ending 31st December.

The data are on a cash basis.

Figures for local tax revenues may include non-tax revenues and central government transfers which are are not considered as tax revenues according to the OECD classification described in the Interpretative Guide but it has not been possible to distinguish the different components within the aggregate data.

Heading 3000: The employer contributions to National Institute of Vocational Training (INFOP) have been added and classified as payroll tax in this edition. The tax revenue is classified under the central government. In Honduras this revenue is classified under a separate unit considered to be different to the central government.

Source: Servicio de Administración de Rentas (Revenue Administration Service); Secretaría de Finanzas (Ministry of Finance).

StatLink https://doi.org/10.1787/888934235791

Table 5.18. **Jamaica**

Details of tax revenue / Ingresos tributarios detallados

Million JMD

	1990	2000	2007	2010	2014	2015	2016	2017	2018	2019
Total tax revenue	**7 748**	**87 713**	**219 435**	**287 139**	**381 799**	**427 640**	**467 350**	**517 091**	**562 009**	**602 592**
1000 Taxes on income, profits and capital gains	**3 944**	**39 277**	**97 924**	**118 708**	**134 698**	**149 990**	**158 409**	**155 790**	**173 122**	**186 434**
1100 Of individuals	1 687	17 441	48 220	54 798	70 868	74 538	72 175	60 306	62 644	69 323
1110 On income and profits	1 687	17 441	48 220	54 798	70 868	74 538	72 175	60 306	62 644	69 323
PAYE	1 489	16 515	45 533	50 828	66 645	70 075	67 591	54 879	57 472	63 716
Other individuals	198	926	2 687	3 969	4 223	4 463	4 584	5 427	5 173	5 607
1120 On capital gains	..	..	..	..	..	..	..	..	..	..
1200 Corporate	1 280	7 627	19 758	33 091	32 606	40 198	47 530	61 401	62 504	67 623
1210 On profits	1 280	7 627	19 758	33 091	32 606	40 198	47 530	61 401	62 504	67 623
Bauxite/alumina	134	430	1 626	866	0	0	0	0	0	0
Other companies	1 146	7 197	18 132	32 224	31 991	39 668	46 823	60 431	61 427	67 251
Minimum business tax	0	0	0	0	615	529	707	970	1 077	372
1220 On capital gains of corporates	..	..	..	..	..	..	..	..	..	..
1300 Unallocable between 1100 and 1200	977	14 209	29 946	30 820	31 224	35 255	38 704	34 083	47 974	49 488
Tax on dividends	68	854	1 928	1 059	1 904	979	1 408	1 801	1 987	2 368
Tax on interests	605	9 535	18 120	16 970	10 103	13 519	14 451	6 417	17 446	15 827
Education tax	305	3 821	9 898	12 792	19 217	20 757	22 845	25 865	28 541	31 294
2000 Social security contributions	**..**	**..**	**6 349**	**8 199**	**15 865**	**16 449**	**17 978**	**19 249**	**21 033**	**24 569**
2100 Employees	..	..	..	..	..	..	..	..	..	..
2110 On a payroll basis	..	..	..	..	..	..	..	..	..	..
2120 On an income tax basis	..	..	..	..	..	..	..	..	..	..
2200 Employers	..	..	..	..	..	..	..	..	..	..
2210 On a payroll basis	..	..	..	..	..	..	..	..	..	..
2220 On an income tax basis	..	..	..	..	..	..	..	..	..	..
2300 Self-employed or non-employed	..	..	..	..	..	..	..	..	..	..
2310 On a payroll basis	..	..	..	..	..	..	..	..	..	..
2320 On an income tax basis	..	..	..	..	..	..	..	..	..	..
2400 Unallocable between 2100, 2200 and 2300	..	..	6 349	8 199	15 865	16 449	17 978	19 249	21 033	24 569
2410 On a payroll basis	..	..	..	..	..	..	..	..	..	..
2420 On an income tax basis	..	..	..	..	..	..	..	..	..	..
3000 Taxes on payroll and workforce	**0**	**0**	**0**	**0**	**0**	**0**	**0**	**0**	**0**	**0**
4000 Taxes on property	**965**	**4 262**	**12 617**	**9 939**	**18 009**	**19 411**	**21 149**	**23 583**	**24 793**	**19 117**
4100 Recurrent taxes on immovable property	67	639	1 788	2 600	6 138	7 271	7 101	8 523	8 478	9 020
4110 Households	67	639	1 788	2 600	6 138	7 271	7 101	8 523	8 478	9 020
Municipal property tax	0	639	1 788	2 600	6 138	7 271	7 101	8 523	8 478	9 020
Other property taxes	67	0	0	0	0	0	0	0	0	0
4120 Others	0	0	0	0	0	0	0	0	0	0
4200 Recurrent taxes on net wealth	0	0	0	0	0	0	0	0	0	0
4210 Individual	..	..	..	..	..	..	..	..	..	..
4220 Corporate	..	..	..	..	..	..	..	..	..	..
4300 Estate, inheritance and gift taxes	0	0	0	0	0	0	0	0	0	0
4310 Estate and inheritance taxes	..	..	..	..	..	..	..	..	..	..
4320 Gift taxes	..	..	..	..	..	..	..	..	..	..
4400 Taxes on financial and capital transactions	898	3 623	10 829	7 339	11 870	12 140	14 048	15 060	16 315	10 097
Stamp duty	898	3 623	10 829	7 339	11 870	12 140	14 048	15 060	16 315	10 097
4500 Non-recurrent taxes	0	0	0	0	0	0	0	0	0	0
4510 On net wealth	..	..	..	..	..	..	..	..	..	..
4520 Other non-recurrent taxes	..	..	..	..	..	..	..	..	..	..
4600 Other recurrent taxes on property	0	0	0	0	0	0	0	0	0	0
5000 Taxes on goods and services	**2 824**	**43 907**	**101 639**	**149 544**	**212 319**	**240 795**	**268 569**	**316 601**	**340 651**	**370 321**
5100 Taxes on production, sale, transfer, etc	2 760	43 107	100 317	147 500	209 302	237 456	265 064	311 911	335 189	363 429
5110 General taxes	297	22 356	65 030	84 409	121 073	138 501	149 111	171 584	187 576	203 297
5111 Value added taxes	293	22 356	63 948	82 407	118 756	135 827	146 030	168 112	183 646	199 150
General consumption tax	293	22 356	63 948	82 407	118 756	135 827	146 030	168 112	183 646	199 150
5112 Sales tax	4	0	0	0	0	0	0	0	0	0
Sales tax on used cars	4	..	..	..	..	..	..	..	..	..
5113 Other	0	0	1 082	2 002	2 318	2 674	3 081	3 472	3 930	4 147
Environmental levy	..	..	1 082	2 002	2 318	2 674	3 081	3 472	3 930	4 147
5120 Taxes on specific goods and services	2 463	20 752	35 287	63 091	88 228	98 955	115 953	140 327	147 613	160 133
5121 Excises	1 158	9 751	13 289	38 112	41 347	49 202	59 327	75 152	75 169	80 773
Special consumption tax	1 115	9 751	13 289	38 112	41 347	49 202	59 327	75 112	75 103	80 693
Quarry tax	0	0	0	0	0	0	0	39	66	80
Other excises	44	0	0	0	0	0	0	0	0	0
5122 Profits of fiscal monopolies	0	0	0	0	0	0	0	0	0	0
5123 Customs and import duties	782	8 498	18 640	19 959	26 289	28 771	34 033	37 737	41 243	44 809
5124 Taxes on exports	0	0	0	0	0	0	0	0	0	0
5125 Taxes on investment goods	0	0	0	0	0	0	0	0	0	0

Table 5.18. **Jamaica** *(cont.)*

Details of tax revenue / Ingresos tributarios detallados

Million JMD

	1990	2000	2007	2010	2014	2015	2016	2017	2018	2019
5126 Taxes on specific services	523	2 503	3 359	5 020	20 592	20 982	22 593	27 438	31 202	34 550
Travel tax	86	1 999	2 144	3 512	9 344	9 979	12 726	18 659	20 114	21 954
Telephone call tax	86	0	0	0	6 687	6 157	4 810	3 543	3 247	3 568
Betting, gaming and lottery	50	504	1 215	1 508	2 661	2 797	2 802	2 639	5 205	6 152
Accommodation tax	87	0	0	0	1 901	2 050	2 254	2 598	2 636	2 877
Bank and trust	204	0	0	0	0	0	0	0	0	0
Entertainment tax	11	0	0	0	0	0	0	0	0	0
5127 Other taxes on internat. trade and transactions	0	0	0	0	0	0	0	0	0	0
5128 Other taxes	0	0	0	0	0	0	0	0	0	0
5130 Unallocable between 5110 and 5120	0	0	0	0	0	0	0	0	0	0
5200 Taxes on use of goods and perform activities	64	800	1 322	2 045	3 017	3 339	3 505	4 690	5 463	6 892
5210 Recurrent taxes	64	800	1 322	2 045	3 017	3 339	3 505	4 690	5 463	6 892
5211 Paid by households: motor vehicles	47	751	1 012	1 775	2 666	2 901	3 032	3 768	4 334	4 863
5212 Paid by others: motor vehicles	0	0	0	0	0	0	0	0	0	0
5213 Paid in respect of other goods	17	49	310	270	351	438	473	922	1 129	2 029
5220 Non-recurrent taxes	0	0	0	0	0	0	0	0	0	0
5300 Unallocable between 5100 and 5200	0	0	0	0	0	0	0	0	0	0
6000 Other taxes	**16**	**266**	**907**	**748**	**909**	**994**	**1 245**	**1 868**	**2 410**	**2 151**
6100 Paid solely by business	0	0	0	0	0	0	0	0	0	0
6200 Other	16	266	907	748	909	994	1 245	1 868	2 410	2 151
Contractors levy	16	266	907	748	909	994	1 245	1 868	2 410	2 151

.. Not available

Note: Year ending 31st December, except for 1990-2003 which refer to fiscal year ending 31st March due to data availability.
The data are on a cash basis.
Heading 2000: The figures include contributions to National Insurance Scheme (NIS).

Source: Ministry of Finance and the Public Service; Tax Administration Jamaica.

StatLink https://doi.org/10.1787/888934235810

Table 5.19. **Mexico / México**

Details of tax revenue / Ingresos tributarios detallados

Million MXN

	1990	2000	2007	2010	2014	2015	2016	2017	2018	2019
Total tax revenue	**102 005**	**767 216**	**1 382 103**	**1 716 243**	**2 394 279**	**2 953 480**	**3 343 314**	**3 527 032**	**3 797 888**	**3 765 880**
1000 Taxes on income, profits and capital gains	**34 673**	**276 548**	**554 099**	**683 604**	**979 251**	**1 230 555**	**1 427 114**	**1 571 954**	**1 671 513**	**1 694 804**
1100 Of individuals	..	..	238 938	313 473	514 208	609 384	681 784	754 109	804 236	829 501
Tax on income of individuals	..	..	238 938	313 473	514 208	609 384	681 784	754 109	804 236	829 501
1110 On income and profits	..	..	..	..	..	..	..	..	..	..
1120 On capital gains	..	..	..	..	..	..	..	..	..	..
1200 Corporate	..	..	217 790	246 745	441 317	592 443	700 925	769 193	809 834	803 643
Tax on income of corporations	..	..	217 790	246 745	441 317	592 443	700 925	769 193	809 834	803 643
1210 On profits	..	..	..	..	..	..	..	..	..	..
1220 On capital gains of corporates	..	..	..	..	..	..	..	..	..	..
1300 Unallocable between 1100 and 1200	34 673	276 548	97 370	123 386	23 726	28 728	44 405	48 652	57 443	61 660
Tax on income of other individuals and corporations	..	244 841	54 785	66 937	31 076	36 268	44 225	46 004	50 878	54 686
Tax on asset	..	13 913	15 670	-624	-735	-502	-918	-1 069	-396	-585
Credit on salary	..	17 794	23 177	9 708	2 423	993	1 144	1 036	1 172	1 951
Oil yields tax	..	0	3 738	2 296	4 669	0	0	0	0	0
IETU	..	0	0	45 069	-13 707	-11 777	-4 039	-1 648	319	-195
Imposed by Activity Exploration and extraction of hydrocarbon	..	0	0	0	0	3 746	3 994	4 330	5 470	5 803
2000 Social security contributions	**17 165**	**138 223**	**236 727**	**277 459**	**378 373**	**409 249**	**434 998**	**467 619**	**509 087**	**552 058**
2100 Employees	..	..	..	..	..	..	..	..	..	..
2110 On a payroll basis	..	..	..	..	..	..	..	..	..	..
2120 On an income tax basis	..	..	..	..	..	..	..	..	..	..
2200 Employers	..	..	..	..	..	..	..	..	..	..
2210 On a payroll basis	..	..	..	..	..	..	..	..	..	..
2220 On an income tax basis	..	..	..	..	..	..	..	..	..	..
2300 Self-employed or non-employed	..	..	..	..	..	..	..	..	..	..
2310 On a payroll basis	..	..	..	..	..	..	..	..	..	..
2320 On an income tax basis	..	..	..	..	..	..	..	..	..	..
2400 Unallocable between 2100, 2200 and 2300	17 165	138 223	236 727	277 459	378 373	409 249	434 998	467 619	509 087	552 058
2410 On a payroll basis	..	138 223	236 727	277 459	378 373	409 249	434 998	467 619	509 087	552 058
2420 On an income tax basis	..	0	0	0	0	0	0	0	0	0
3000 Taxes on payroll and workforce	**1 797**	**11 217**	**28 071**	**36 911**	**64 713**	**70 221**	**76 762**	**84 099**	**93 303**	**0**
Substitute tax on salary	..	0	0	0	0	0	0	0	0	0
Payroll tax	..	11 101	20 277	27 813	64 581	69 866	76 304	83 608	92 833	0
Tax on remuneration to the personal work	..	65	7 578	8 841	0	152	225	246	270	0
Tax on professions and fees	..	36	68	71	51	106	99	103	111	0
Tax on operations by contract	..	15	148	186	81	96	134	141	90	0
4000 Taxes on property	**1 914**	**13 964**	**33 161**	**38 955**	**54 978**	**57 673**	**63 273**	**67 836**	**77 110**	**0**
4100 Recurrent taxes on immovable property	1 036	9 948	19 425	25 724	37 751	37 961	40 357	44 680	49 445	0
4110 Households	0	0	0	0	0	0	0	0	0	0
4120 Others	1 036	9 948	19 425	25 724	37 751	37 961	40 357	44 680	49 445	0
Property tax	..	9 948	19 425	25 724	37 751	37 961	40 357	44 680	49 445	0
4200 Recurrent taxes on net wealth	0	0	0	0	0	0	0	0	0	0
4210 Individual	..	..	..	..	..	..	..	..	..	..
4220 Corporate	..	..	..	..	..	..	..	..	..	..
4300 Estate, inheritance and gift taxes	8	0	0	0	0	0	0	0	0	0
4310 Estate and inheritance taxes	8	..	..	..	..	..	..	..	..	..
4320 Gift taxes	0	..	..	..	..	..	..	..	..	..
4400 Taxes on financial and capital transactions	870	4 017	13 736	13 231	17 227	19 712	22 917	23 156	27 665	0
Alienation of immovable property	..	1 763	1 076	1 122	1 308	1 595	1 723	1 623	1 823	0
Transfer of ownership of real estate	..	2 236	8 147	5 027	5 008	6 671	9 593	7 016	8 658	0
Purchasing property	..	18	4 513	7 082	10 911	11 447	11 600	14 516	17 184	0
4500 Non-recurrent taxes	0	0	0	0	0	0	0	0	0	0
4510 On net wealth	..	..	..	..	..	..	..	..	..	..
4520 Other non-recurrent taxes	..	..	..	..	..	..	..	..	..	..
4600 Other recurrent taxes on property	0	0	0	0	0	0	0	0	0	0
5000 Taxes on goods and services	**44 837**	**319 612**	**513 140**	**651 915**	**880 153**	**1 141 170**	**1 295 653**	**1 283 049**	**1 381 659**	**1 477 876**
5100 Taxes on production, sale, transfer, etc	44 171	310 325	491 928	630 123	859 302	1 120 610	1 274 738	1 262 770	1 364 208	1 477 157
5110 General taxes	26 635	189 606	409 013	504 509	667 085	707 213	791 700	816 048	922 238	933 327
5111 Value added taxes	26 635	189 606	409 013	504 509	667 085	707 213	791 700	816 048	922 238	933 327
5112 Sales tax	0	0	0	0	0	0	0	0	0	0
5113 Other	0	0	0	0	0	0	0	0	0	0
5120 Taxes on specific goods and services	17 519	120 720	82 915	125 614	192 217	413 397	483 038	446 722	441 970	543 831
5121 Excises	10 072	86 163	47 008	86 098	160 754	361 538	420 448	378 537	358 577	470 993
Special tax on production and services	..	81 544	41 532	81 427	154 327	354 294	411 390	367 834	347 436	460 496
Tax on new automobiles	..	4 619	5 476	4 671	6 427	7 244	9 058	10 703	11 142	10 497
Tax on luxury goods and services	..	0	0	0	0	0	0	0	0	0
5122 Profits of fiscal monopolies	0	0	0	0	0	0	0	0	0	0

Table 5.19. **Mexico / México** *(cont.)*

Details of tax revenue / Ingresos tributarios detallados

Million MXN

	1990	2000	2007	2010	2014	2015	2016	2017	2018	2019
5123 Customs and import duties	6 998	33 285	33 344	26 602	36 841	45 366	51 889	53 793	67 232	66 295
Step customs officer	..	423	1 156	2 071	2 913	1 270	1 336	1 463	1 690	1 554
Import taxes	..	32 861	32 188	24 531	33 928	44 096	50 553	52 330	65 543	64 741
5124 Taxes on exports	75	4	3	0	1	1	0	0	0	0
Tax on exports	..	4	3	0	1	1	0	0	0	0
5125 Taxes on investment goods	0	0	0	0	0	0	0	0	0	0
5126 Taxes on specific services	132	1 042	2 146	10 958	-7 417	1 763	5 630	7 778	8 692	-405
IDE	..	0	0	8 022	-12 322	-3 323	-1 262	-739	-629	-405
Tax on lodging	..	504	1 059	1 384	2 067	2 561	3 009	3 598	3 945	0
Public entertainment tax	..	240	365	462	543	689	858	839	909	0
Tax on lotteries, raffles and gambling	..	267	705	923	1 218	1 416	1 828	2 717	2 947	0
Tax on commercials	..	4	17	166	216	210	906	1 082	1 231	0
Various indirect taxes	..	28	0	1	861	209	291	282	288	0
5127 Other taxes on internat. trade and transactions	0	0	0	0	0	0	0	0	0	0
5128 Other taxes	242	226	414	1 956	2 040	4 730	5 070	6 613	7 468	6 947
Mining fees	..	226	414	1 956	2 040	4 730	5 070	6 613	7 468	6 947
5130 Unallocable between 5110 and 5120	17	0	0	0	0	0	0	0	0	0
5200 Taxes on use of goods and perform activities	666	9 287	21 212	21 793	20 851	20 560	20 915	20 279	17 451	719
5210 Recurrent taxes	666	9 287	21 212	21 793	20 851	20 560	20 915	20 279	17 451	719
5211 Paid by households: motor vehicles	567	8 878	20 692	21 319	20 370	19 880	20 192	19 530	16 533	0
Tax on motor vehicules	..	8 878	20 692	21 319	20 370	19 880	20 192	19 530	16 533	0
5212 Paid by others: motor vehicles	0	301	275	281	367	439	503	554	640	645
Tax on federal auto transport	..	301	275	281	367	439	503	554	640	645
5213 Paid in respect of other goods	99	108	246	193	114	240	220	194	278	74
Sport fishing	..	40	98	59	65	62	68	71	73	73
Sport hunting	..	3	0	0	0	0	0	0	0	0
Tax on commercial activities	..	63	147	50	33	64	46	28	115	0
Trade in books and magazines	..	0	0	0	1	1	1	0	0	0
Tax on industrial activities	..	2	0	82	13	93	78	77	73	0
Mining	..	0	0	1	2	21	28	18	17	0
5220 Non-recurrent taxes	0	0	0	0	0	0	0	0	0	0
5300 Unallocable between 5100 and 5200	0	0	0	0	0	0	0	0	0	0
6000 Other taxes	**1 619**	**7 651**	**16 905**	**27 398**	**36 810**	**44 612**	**45 514**	**52 475**	**65 217**	**41 142**
6100 Paid solely by business	0	0	0	0	0	0	0	0	0	0
6200 Other	1 619	7 651	16 905	27 398	36 810	44 612	45 514	52 475	65 217	41 142
Accessories	..	5 504	12 403	22 206	23 717	23 211	28 480	32 153	45 864	41 063
Unallocable between 1000 and 5000 caused in exercices fiscal previous liquidation slopes or of payment	..	374	222	30	504	4 168	329	281	400	79
Additional state and local taxes	..	1 773	4 280	5 162	12 590	17 232	16 705	20 042	18 952	0

.. Not available

Note: Year ending 31st December.

The data are on a cash basis.

The 2019 data for tax revenues at the state and local levels of government are not available. They comprise revenues in categories 3000, 4000, 5000 and 6000.

Heading 1000: In ECLAC data, income taxes are presented net of credit on salary figures.

Heading 2000: In ECLAC data, social security contributions are presented net of transfers from the Federal government for the payment of IMSS (Mexican Social Security Institute) pensions.

Some amounts of social security contributions are treated as non-tax revenue to align with the reporting to other international organisations.

Source: Ministry of Finance, Economic Department.

StatLink https://doi.org/10.1787/888934235829

Table 5.20. **Nicaragua**

Details of tax revenue / Ingresos tributarios detallados

Million NIO

	1990	2000	2007	2010	2014	2015	2016	2017	2018	2019
Total tax revenue	..	**9 300**	**25 811**	**36 162**	**67 119**	**77 567**	**88 483**	**98 803**	**95 457**	**107 333**
1000 Taxes on income, profits and capital gains	..	**1 144**	**5 746**	**8 351**	**18 033**	**21 313**	**24 911**	**28 557**	**29 258**	**33 036**
1100 Of individuals	..	299	1 488	1 857	3 768	4 432	5 396	6 468	6 780	6 561
1110 On income and profits	..	299	1 488	1 857	3 768	4 432	5 396	6 468	6 780	6 561
1120 On capital gains	..	..	..	..	..	..	..	..	..	..
1200 Corporate	..	845	4 258	6 494	14 265	16 881	19 515	22 089	22 478	26 475
1210 On profits	..	845	4 258	6 494	14 265	16 881	19 515	22 089	22 478	26 475
1220 On capital gains of corporates	..	..	..	..	..	..	..	..	..	..
1300 Unallocable between 1100 and 1200	..	0	0	0	0	0	0	0	0	0
2000 Social security contributions	..	**1 678**	**4 921**	**8 090**	**15 161**	**18 194**	**21 296**	**23 868**	**24 624**	**27 586**
2100 Employees	..	..	..	..	..	..	..	..	..	..
2110 On a payroll basis	..	..	..	..	..	..	..	..	..	..
2120 On an income tax basis	..	..	..	..	..	..	..	..	..	..
2200 Employers	..	..	..	..	..	..	..	..	..	..
2210 On a payroll basis	..	..	..	..	..	..	..	..	..	..
2220 On an income tax basis	..	..	..	..	..	..	..	..	..	..
2300 Self-employed or non-employed	..	..	..	..	..	..	..	..	..	..
2310 On a payroll basis	..	..	..	..	..	..	..	..	..	..
2320 On an income tax basis	..	..	..	..	..	..	..	..	..	..
2400 Unallocable between 2100, 2200 and 2300	..	1 678	4 921	8 090	15 161	18 194	21 296	23 868	24 624	27 586
2410 On a payroll basis	..	1 678	4 921	8 090	15 161	18 194	21 296	23 868	24 624	27 586
2420 On an income tax basis	..	0	0	0	0	0	0	0	0	0
3000 Taxes on payroll and workforce	..	**0**	**0**	**0**	**0**	**0**	**0**	**0**	**0**	**0**
4000 Taxes on property	..	**11**	**338**	**423**	**714**	**771**	**834**	**896**	**961**	**1 196**
4100 Recurrent taxes on immovable property	..	0	318	403	627	682	744	808	881	1 129
4110 Households	..	..	..	..	..	..	..	..	..	..
4120 Others	..	..	..	..	..	..	..	..	..	..
4200 Recurrent taxes on net wealth	..	0	0	0	0	0	0	0	0	0
4210 Individual	..	..	..	..	..	..	..	..	..	..
4220 Corporate	..	..	..	..	..	..	..	..	..	..
4300 Estate, inheritance and gift taxes	..	0	0	0	0	0	0	0	0	0
4310 Estate and inheritance taxes	..	..	..	..	..	..	..	..	..	..
4320 Gift taxes	..	..	..	..	..	..	..	..	..	..
4400 Taxes on financial and capital transactions	..	11	20	20	87	90	90	88	80	67
Stamp duties	..	11	20	20	87	90	90	88	80	67
4500 Non-recurrent taxes	..	0	0	0	0	0	0	0	0	0
4510 On net wealth	..	..	..	..	..	..	..	..	..	..
4520 Other non-recurrent taxes	..	..	..	..	..	..	..	..	..	..
4600 Other recurrent taxes on property	..	0	0	0	0	0	0	0	0	0
5000 Taxes on goods and services	..	**5 584**	**14 522**	**18 951**	**32 597**	**36 599**	**40 697**	**44 563**	**39 815**	**44 608**
5100 Taxes on production, sale, transfer, etc	..	5 584	14 283	18 608	31 923	35 798	39 855	43 619	38 780	43 674
5110 General taxes	..	2 931	9 155	11 932	22 265	23 787	26 273	29 201	25 791	27 933
5111 Value added taxes	..	2 931	8 025	10 353	19 385	20 714	22 822	25 551	21 905	24 116
5112 Sales tax	..	0	0	0	0	0	0	0	0	0
5113 Other	..	0	1 129	1 579	2 880	3 073	3 452	3 650	3 886	3 817
5120 Taxes on specific goods and services	..	2 653	5 128	6 676	9 659	12 011	13 581	14 419	12 990	15 741
5121 Excises	..	2 034	4 099	5 541	7 755	9 773	10 950	11 764	10 931	13 616
Alcoholic beverages	..	84	144	198	230	264	305	355	353	583
Beer	..	203	480	645	1 184	1 370	1 476	1 649	1 663	1 857
Cigarettes	..	70	158	45	0	0	0	0	0	0
Soft drinks	..	123	146	248	423	501	525	545	523	470
Petroleum products	..	1 359	2 108	2 699	3 938	4 396	5 021	5 534	5 395	5 589
Gaming machines	..	0	0	0	0	0	0	0	90	120
Excises on imports	..	196	1 025	1 559	1 902	3 105	3 505	3 541	2 763	4 805
Other excises	..	-1	37	148	78	136	117	140	145	193
5122 Profits of fiscal monopolies	..	0	0	0	0	0	0	0	0	0
5123 Customs and import duties	..	619	1 030	1 135	1 904	2 238	2 631	2 654	2 058	2 125
Custom duties	..	452	1 004	1 094	1 828	2 155	2 509	2 623	2 058	2 125
Temporary protection duty	..	96	0	0	0	0	0	0	0	0
On products originating in Colombia or Honduras	..	72	26	41	76	83	123	31	0	0
5124 Taxes on exports	..	0	0	0	0	0	0	0	0	0
5125 Taxes on investment goods	..	0	0	0	0	0	0	0	0	0
5126 Taxes on specific services	..	0	0	0	0	0	0	0	0	0
5127 Other taxes on internat. trade and transactions	..	0	0	0	0	0	0	0	0	0
5128 Other taxes	..	0	0	0	0	0	0	0	0	0
5130 Unallocable between 5110 and 5120	..	0	0	0	0	0	0	0	0	0
5200 Taxes on use of goods and perform activities	..	0	239	343	674	801	842	943	1 035	934
5210 Recurrent taxes	..	..	18	20	41	60	59	59	59	61

Table 5.20. **Nicaragua** *(cont.)*

Details of tax revenue / Ingresos tributarios detallados

Million NIO

	1990	2000	2007	2010	2014	2015	2016	2017	2018	2019
5211 Paid by households: motor vehicles	..	..	18	20	41	60	59	59	59	61
5212 Paid by others: motor vehicles	..	..	0	0	0	0	0	0	0	0
5213 Paid in respect of other goods	..	..	0	0	0	0	0	0	0	0
5220 Non-recurrent taxes	..	..	221	323	633	741	783	884	976	874
5300 Unallocable between 5100 and 5200	..	0	0	0	0	0	0	0	0	0
6000 Other taxes	**..**	**0**	**284**	**347**	**614**	**690**	**745**	**919**	**798**	**907**
6100 Paid solely by business	..	..	0	0	0	0	0	0	0	0
6200 Other	..	..	284	347	614	690	745	919	798	907

.. Not available

Note: Year ending 31st December.

The data are on a cash basis.

Comparable statistics for 1990 cannot be shown due to the devaluation of the Nicaraguan cordoba.

Heading 1000: Personal income tax and corporate income tax are separated between 2000 and 2019 in this edition.

Heading 5113: The fixed quota tax has been added in this edition. It has revenues in 2018 and 2019.

Source: Ministerio de Hacienda y Crédito Público (Ministry of Finance and Public Credit); Centro Interamericano de Administraciones Tributarias (Inter-American Centre of Tax Administrations).

StatLink https://doi.org/10.1787/888934235848

Table 5.21. **Panama / Panamá**

Details of tax revenue / Ingresos tributarios detallados

Million PAB

	1990	2000	2007	2010	2014	2015	2016	2017	2018	2019
Total tax revenue	**948**	**1 942**	**3 298**	**4 815**	**7 832**	**8 193**	**9 004**	**9 366**	**9 631**	**9 394**
1000 Taxes on income, profits and capital gains	**217**	**485**	**940**	**1 317**	**1 998**	**2 066**	**2 400**	**2 451**	**2 672**	**2 445**
1100 Of individuals	140	295	393	440	722	799	870	1 088	1 193	1 135
1110 On income and profits	140	295	393	440	722	799	870	1 088	1 193	1 135
Payroll	115	222	303	353	602	689	733	931	1 049	992
Personal income tax	14	20	28	35	58	45	54	68	54	49
Panama Canal Authority withholding	10	53	62	52	62	65	83	89	90	94
1120 On capital gains	..	..	..	..	..	..	..	..	..	..
1200 Corporate	66	159	382	603	896	851	1 036	943	955	903
1210 On profits	66	159	382	603	896	851	1 036	943	955	903
Colón Free Zone	5	3	12	20	43	36	36	41	53	45
Corporate income tax	61	155	370	584	853	815	1 000	902	901	858
1220 On capital gains of corporates	..	..	..	..	..	..	..	..	..	..
1300 Unallocable between 1100 and 1200	11	31	164	273	380	416	494	420	524	407
Dividends and complimentary tax	11	31	89	166	243	265	282	253	307	266
Capital gains	0	0	75	107	137	151	212	167	217	142
2000 Social security contributions	**325**	**742**	**1 104**	**1 637**	**2 886**	**3 152**	**3 426**	**3 654**	**3 797**	**3 894**
2100 Employees	..	..	..	..	..	..	..	..	..	..
2110 On a payroll basis	..	..	..	..	..	..	..	..	..	..
2120 On an income tax basis	..	..	..	..	..	..	..	..	..	..
2200 Employers	..	..	..	..	..	..	..	..	..	..
2210 On a payroll basis	..	..	..	..	..	..	..	..	..	..
2220 On an income tax basis	..	..	..	..	..	..	..	..	..	..
2300 Self-employed or non-employed	..	..	..	..	..	..	..	..	..	..
2310 On a payroll basis	..	..	..	..	..	..	..	..	..	..
2320 On an income tax basis	..	..	..	..	..	..	..	..	..	..
2400 Unallocable between 2100, 2200 and 2300	325	742	1 104	1 637	2 886	3 152	3 426	3 654	3 797	3 894
2410 On a payroll basis	..	..	..	..	..	..	..	..	..	..
2420 On an income tax basis	..	..	..	..	..	..	..	..	..	..
3000 Taxes on payroll and workforce	**0**	**36**	**40**	**59**	**134**	**111**	**111**	**127**	**130**	**140**
Education insurance	..	36	40	59	134	111	111	127	130	140
4000 Taxes on property	**32**	**43**	**119**	**138**	**220**	**199**	**209**	**251**	**244**	**169**
4100 Recurrent taxes on immovable property	28	34	74	108	176	151	168	207	209	134
4110 Households	28	34	74	108	176	151	168	207	209	134
4120 Others	0	0	0	0	0	0	0	0	0	0
4200 Recurrent taxes on net wealth	0	0	0	0	0	0	0	0	0	0
4210 Individual	..	..	..	..	..	..	..	..	..	..
4220 Corporate	..	..	..	..	..	..	..	..	..	..
4300 Estate, inheritance and gift taxes	0	0	0	0	0	0	0	0	0	0
4310 Estate and inheritance taxes	..	..	..	..	..	..	..	..	..	..
4320 Gift taxes	..	..	..	..	..	..	..	..	..	..
4400 Taxes on financial and capital transactions	3	9	45	30	45	48	41	44	36	35
4500 Non-recurrent taxes	0	0	0	0	0	0	0	0	0	0
4510 On net wealth	..	..	..	..	..	..	..	..	..	..
4520 Other non-recurrent taxes	..	..	..	..	..	..	..	..	..	..
4600 Other recurrent taxes on property	0	0	0	0	0	0	0	0	0	0
5000 Taxes on goods and services	**349**	**608**	**1 057**	**1 623**	**2 553**	**2 627**	**2 823**	**2 849**	**2 754**	**2 716**
5100 Taxes on production, sale, transfer, etc	332	546	961	1 473	2 319	2 376	2 555	2 570	2 474	2 435
5110 General taxes	80	69	205	766	1 351	1 357	1 510	1 529	1 477	1 453
5111 Value added taxes	80	69	205	766	1 351	1 357	1 510	1 529	1 477	1 453
ITBMS on sales	31	69	205	399	794	798	974	983	957	980
ITBMS on imports	49	0	0	367	558	559	536	546	519	473
5112 Sales tax	0	0	0	0	0	0	0	0	0	0
5113 Other	0	0	0	0	0	0	0	0	0	0
5120 Taxes on specific goods and services	251	477	756	707	967	1 019	1 045	1 041	997	982
5121 Excises	0	141	140	239	452	496	519	480	449	466
Petroleum products	..	109	90	97	133	157	214	190	168	195
Beer	..	18	25	31	42	48	49	49	53	54
Cigarette	..	0	0	0	24	32	23	21	24	24
Wine and liquor	..	12	11	11	23	15	10	6	18	16
Soft drinks	..	2	4	6	7	7	6	7	11	10
Automobiles	..	0	0	0	176	182	172	182	149	139
Other excises	..	0	11	95	48	53	46	25	27	27
5122 Profits of fiscal monopolies	0	0	0	0	0	0	0	0	0	0
5123 Customs and import duties	125	298	574	390	381	391	355	358	338	313
5124 Taxes on exports	13	0	0	0	0	0	0	0	0	0
5125 Taxes on investment goods	0	0	0	0	0	0	0	0	0	0

Table 5.21. **Panama / Panamá** *(cont.)*

Details of tax revenue / Ingresos tributarios detallados

Million PAB

	1990	2000	2007	2010	2014	2015	2016	2017	2018	2019
5126 Taxes on specific services	1	37	41	78	134	133	171	203	211	203
Insurance premiums	0	17	24	47	63	46	52	86	90	86
Cable and telecommunications	0	16	8	17	45	39	41	40	42	41
Gambling	0	0	1	1	2	23	53	52	53	50
Banks, financial institutions and exchange houses	0	2	9	12	24	24	25	25	26	26
Commercial activities and services	1	3	0	0	0	0	0	0	0	0
5127 Other taxes on internat. trade and transactions	0	0	0	0	0	0	0	0	0	0
5128 Other taxes	0	0	0	0	0	0	0	0	0	0
5130 Unallocable between 5110 and 5120	0	0	0	0	0	0	0	0	0	0
5200 Taxes on use of goods and perform activities	15	62	97	151	234	251	268	279	280	280
Other indirect taxes	0	0	0	36	52	59	65	69	66	61
5210 Recurrent taxes	12	58	83	115	182	192	204	210	214	219
5211 Paid by households: motor vehicles	0	7	10	0	0	0	0	0	0	0
5212 Paid by others: motor vehicles	0	5	5	0	0	0	0	0	0	0
5213 Paid in respect of other goods	12	46	68	115	182	192	204	210	214	219
Commercial licences	12	19	35	75	116	120	123	121	124	126
Permission to conduct commercial and service activities	0	25	31	38	62	69	77	84	86	89
Permission to conduct industrial activities	0	2	2	2	3	3	4	4	4	4
Others	0	0	0	0	0	0	0	0	0	0
5220 Non-recurrent taxes	4	4	13	0	0	0	0	0	0	0
Building and construction	0	4	13	..	..	..	..	..	..	..
Ship registration	4	0	0	..	..	..	..	..	..	..
5300 Unallocable between 5100 and 5200	2	0	0	0	0	0	0	0	0	0
6000 Other taxes	**26**	**27**	**38**	**41**	**41**	**37**	**35**	**34**	**34**	**30**
6100 Paid solely by business	0	0	0	0	0	0	0	0	0	0
6200 Other	26	27	38	41	41	37	35	34	34	30
Stamp duties	17	27	38	41	41	37	35	34	34	30
Others	9	0	0	0	0	0	0	0	0	0

.. Not available

Note: Year ending 31st December.

The data are on a cash basis.

Tax revenue data are exclusive of documentos fiscales which are considered as wastable tax credits according to the OECD classification described in the Interpretative Guide.

Heading 2000: Social security contributions include regular and special contributions and professional risks premium collected by the Caja de Seguro Social (CSS). Data between 2014 and 2018 were previously collected from Contraloria General and have been replaced with data directly from CSS in this edition. Data before 2010 have been updated with information from CIAT.

Heading 3000: In ECLAC data, education insurance is classified as "Other taxes" (6000).

Heading 5126: In CIAT and ECLAC data, tax on banks, financial institutions and exchange houses is classified as a property tax (4000).

Heading 6200: Stamp duties before 2000 include tax on telephone calls and cables which cannot be distinguished due to data availability.

Source: Contraloría General de la República de Panamá (Comptroller General of the Republic of Panama); Ministerio de Economía y Finanzas de Panamá (Ministry of Economy and Finance of Panama); Caja de Seguro Social (Social Security Fund); Centro Interamericano de Administraciones Tributarias (Inter-American Centre of Tax Administrations).

StatLink https://doi.org/10.1787/888934235867

Table 5.22. **Paraguay**

Details of tax revenue / Ingresos tributarios detallados

Million PYG

	1990	2000	2007	2010	2014	2015	2016	2017	2018	2019
Total tax revenue	**608 021**	**3 587 445**	**9 669 201**	**15 638 531**	**24 895 179**	**25 855 185**	**27 466 261**	**30 731 221**	**31 954 693**	**33 008 733**
1000 Taxes on income, profits and capital gains	**73 726**	**470 388**	**1 228 684**	**2 096 498**	**3 678 392**	**3 922 384**	**4 429 169**	**5 086 803**	**5 265 609**	**6 022 875**
1100 Of individuals	..	15 042	11 966	31 263	361 079	409 238	396 573	526 704	626 525	620 038
1110 On income and profits	..	15 042	11 966	31 263	361 079	409 238	396 573	526 704	626 525	620 038
IRAGRO-IMAGRO	..	15 042	11 200	30 113	277 157	283 401	256 019	326 555	360 003	327 328
Personal income tax	..	0	766	1 150	83 921	125 837	140 554	200 150	266 523	292 710
1120 On capital gains	..	..	..	..	..	..	..	..	..	..
1200 Corporate	..	455 346	1 216 718	2 065 235	3 317 314	3 513 146	4 032 596	4 560 099	4 639 084	5 402 837
1210 On profits	..	455 346	1 216 718	2 065 235	3 317 314	3 513 146	4 032 596	4 560 099	4 639 084	5 402 837
Income tax on small businesses	..	0	4 620	9 380	9 063	14 563	18 567	22 848	25 540	26 824
Single tax	..	4 238	8 411	715	72	5	3	2	1	0
Single tax on maquiladoras companies	..	0	1 401	3 310	9 783	10 892	12 087	20 194	27 070	31 201
IRACIS	..	451 108	1 202 286	2 051 830	3 298 396	3 487 686	4 001 939	4 517 056	4 586 475	5 344 811
1220 On capital gains of corporates	..	..	..	..	..	..	..	..	..	..
1300 Unallocable between 1100 and 1200	73 726	0	0	0	0	0	0	0	0	0
Others	73 726	..	..	..	..	..	..	..	..	..
2000 Social security contributions	**28 882**	**919 527**	**2 265 097**	**3 552 640**	**6 705 101**	**7 044 316**	**7 048 846**	**8 052 403**	**8 209 087**	**8 729 492**
2100 Employees	..	..	..	..	..	..	..	..	..	..
2110 On a payroll basis	..	..	..	..	..	..	..	..	..	..
2120 On an income tax basis	..	..	..	..	..	..	..	..	..	..
2200 Employers	..	..	..	..	..	..	..	..	..	..
2210 On a payroll basis	..	..	..	..	..	..	..	..	..	..
2220 On an income tax basis	..	..	..	..	..	..	..	..	..	..
2300 Self-employed or non-employed	..	..	..	..	..	..	..	..	..	..
2310 On a payroll basis	..	..	..	..	..	..	..	..	..	..
2320 On an income tax basis	..	..	..	..	..	..	..	..	..	..
2400 Unallocable between 2100, 2200 and 2300	28 882	919 527	2 265 097	3 552 640	6 705 101	7 044 316	7 048 846	8 052 403	8 209 087	8 729 492
2410 On a payroll basis	28 882	919 527	2 265 097	3 552 640	6 705 101	7 044 316	7 048 846	8 052 403	8 209 087	8 729 492
2420 On an income tax basis	0	0	0	0	0	0	0	0	0	0
3000 Taxes on payroll and workforce	**0**	**0**	**0**	**0**	**0**	**0**	**0**	**0**	**0**	**0**
4000 Taxes on property	**17 162**	**71 777**	**276 985**	**276 119**	**375 780**	**435 473**	**571 590**	**565 323**	**415 570**	**443 521**
4100 Recurrent taxes on immovable property	17 162	0	196 504	258 423	351 463	405 806	540 423	529 986	389 962	417 177
4110 Households	17 162	..	196 504	258 423	351 463	405 806	540 423	529 986	389 962	417 177
Real estate tax	17 162	..	190 924	249 697	340 479	390 772	514 404	501 873	359 235	378 712
Tax on vacant lots	0	..	2 046	2 925	4 147	4 818	10 284	13 600	17 411	20 985
Large estate and land tax	0	..	3 533	5 801	6 837	10 216	15 736	14 513	13 315	17 480
4120 Others	0	..	0	0	0	0	0	0	0	0
4200 Recurrent taxes on net wealth	0	0	0	0	0	0	0	0	0	0
4210 Individual	..	..	..	..	..	..	..	..	..	..
4220 Corporate	..	..	..	..	..	..	..	..	..	..
4300 Estate, inheritance and gift taxes	0	0	0	0	0	0	0	0	0	0
4310 Estate and inheritance taxes	..	..	..	..	..	..	..	..	..	..
4320 Gift taxes	..	..	..	..	..	..	..	..	..	..
4400 Taxes on financial and capital transactions	0	71 777	80 466	15 955	23 482	29 601	29 897	33 872	24 583	24 912
Real estate transfer tax	..	0	6 412	11 766	17 565	22 406	22 978	26 263	17 228	17 216
Municipal Seal and Stamp Paper Tax	..	0	2 923	3 857	5 812	6 912	6 515	7 464	7 326	7 346
Registration and stamp duties	..	71 777	71 130	332	106	282	403	144	30	350
4500 Non-recurrent taxes	0	0	0	0	0	0	0	0	0	0
4510 On net wealth	..	..	..	..	..	..	..	..	..	..
4520 Other non-recurrent taxes	..	..	..	..	..	..	..	..	..	..
4600 Other recurrent taxes on property	0	0	16	1 742	835	66	1 269	1 466	1 025	1 432
5000 Taxes on goods and services	**438 444**	**2 080 878**	**5 813 827**	**9 462 461**	**13 898 774**	**14 279 329**	**15 225 947**	**16 813 348**	**17 901 774**	**17 610 929**
5100 Taxes on production, sale, transfer, etc	438 444	2 080 878	5 685 560	9 245 877	13 617 105	13 860 634	14 746 697	16 356 200	17 550 296	17 230 758
5110 General taxes	0	1 150 496	3 496 977	5 991 694	9 363 648	9 768 800	10 482 238	11 221 710	11 851 395	11 794 402
5111 Value added taxes	0	1 150 496	3 496 977	5 991 694	9 363 648	9 768 800	10 482 238	11 221 710	11 851 395	11 794 402
5112 Sales tax	..	0	0	0	0	0	0	0	0	0
5113 Other	..	0	0	0	0	0	0	0	0	0
5120 Taxes on specific goods and services	438 444	930 382	2 188 583	3 254 183	4 253 457	4 091 834	4 264 459	5 134 490	5 698 901	5 436 356
5121 Excises	300 219	456 561	1 335 412	1 710 531	2 455 139	2 404 222	2 589 108	2 890 013	3 156 091	2 992 813
Fuels	41 087	316 694	1 000 894	1 126 143	1 787 112	1 775 479	1 830 782	2 032 235	2 300 311	2 084 712
Other excises	259 132	136 194	309 463	537 887	655 783	616 342	745 189	843 123	841 900	886 475
Animal health and quality service	0	3 673	24 923	46 501	12 244	12 401	13 137	14 656	13 881	13 875
Livestock trade	0	0	132	0	0	0	0	0	0	7 751
5122 Profits of fiscal monopolies	0	0	0	0	0	0	0	0	0	0
5123 Customs and import duties	138 225	473 821	838 494	1 524 252	1 776 724	1 659 535	1 642 818	2 206 934	2 512 883	2 420 302
5124 Taxes on exports	0	0	0	0	0	0	0	0	0	0
5125 Taxes on investment goods	0	0	0	0	0	0	0	0	0	0

Table 5.22. **Paraguay** *(cont.)*

Details of tax revenue / Ingresos tributarios detallados

Million PYG

	1990	2000	2007	2010	2014	2015	2016	2017	2018	2019
5126 Taxes on specific services	0	0	14 677	19 401	21 594	28 076	32 533	37 542	29 927	23 241
Advertising	..	..	3 613	5 249	7 836	7 428	8 424	9 489	7 387	6 741
Public transport	..	..	4 173	4 363	4 923	4 297	4 316	4 080	4 196	3 420
Gambling	..	..	162	16	911	4 654	3 683	7 131	6 448	6 617
Advertising and gambling	..	..	5 361	8 884	7 924	9 357	12 715	14 821	9 796	4 447
Other taxes on specific services	..	..	1 368	888	0	2 341	3 395	2 021	2 099	2 017
5127 Other taxes on internat. trade and transactions	0	0	0	0	0	0	0	0	0	0
5128 Other taxes	0	0	0	0	0	0	0	0	0	0
5130 Unallocable between 5110 and 5120	0	0	0	0	0	0	0	0	0	0
5200 Taxes on use of goods and perform activities	0	0	126 958	216 347	280 834	395 856	451 842	426 115	350 893	379 208
5210 Recurrent taxes	..	..	107 077	183 622	220 649	329 518	386 360	365 303	315 178	329 087
5211 Paid by households: motor vehicles	..	..	0	0	0	0	0	0	0	0
5212 Paid by others: motor vehicles	..	..	28 343	52 365	80 509	94 393	106 200	109 084	106 872	109 402
Motor vehicle licences	..	..	28 343	52 365	80 509	94 393	106 200	109 084	106 872	109 402
5213 Paid in respect of other goods	..	..	78 735	131 257	140 140	235 125	280 161	256 219	208 305	219 685
Licencing fees	..	..	75 323	126 965	135 164	229 686	274 468	250 528	203 605	214 555
slaughter tax	..	..	3 363	4 271	4 976	5 074	5 584	5 395	4 635	4 991
Tax to the owners of animals	..	..	48	21	0	365	109	296	65	140
5220 Non-recurrent taxes	..	..	19 881	32 725	60 186	66 338	65 482	60 812	35 715	50 121
Tax on construction	..	..	16 168	31 696	60 129	65 403	64 284	60 092	34 999	49 375
Luxury automobile tax	..	..	2 750	91	57	54	152	7	0	0
Trademarks registration	..	..	962	938	0	881	1 045	713	716	746
5300 Unallocable between 5100 and 5200	0	0	1 309	237	835	22 838	27 409	31 034	585	962
6000 Other taxes	**49 807**	**44 875**	**84 608**	**250 812**	**237 132**	**173 684**	**190 709**	**213 344**	**162 652**	**201 917**
6100 Paid solely by business	0	0	0	0	0	0	0	0	0	0
6200 Other	49 807	44 875	84 608	250 812	237 132	173 684	190 709	213 344	162 652	201 917
Taxes replaced	0	0	0	0	0	0	0	0	0	0
Other	49 807	44 875	84 608	250 812	237 132	173 684	190 709	213 344	162 652	201 917

.. Not available

Note: Year ending 31st December.

The data are on a cash basis.

The figures for years before 2006 exclude local government tax revenues as the data are not available. This affects data in categories 4000, 5000 and 6000.

Heading 2000: Social security contributions before 1999 have been added in this edition and they do not include social security contributions collected by decentralised institutions as the data are not available.

Source: Subsecretaría de Estado de Tributación, Ministerio de Hacienda del Paraguay (Tax Undersecretary, Ministry of Finance of Paraguay); Centro Interamericano de Administraciones Tributarias (Inter-American Centre of Tax Administrations).

StatLink https://doi.org/10.1787/888934235886

Table 5.23. **Peru / Perú**

Details of tax revenue / Ingresos tributarios detallados

Million PEN

	1990	2000	2007	2010	2014	2015	2016	2017	2018	2019
Total tax revenue	**637**	**26 771**	**59 187**	**74 803**	**110 144**	**106 183**	**106 042**	**107 028**	**121 844**	**127 950**
1000 Taxes on income, profits and capital gains	**37**	**5 078**	**24 139**	**27 317**	**43 577**	**37 772**	**40 360**	**39 846**	**43 979**	**46 753**
1100 Of individuals	3	2 117	4 645	6 518	11 423	11 137	11 760	13 008	13 598	14 744
First category	..	167	217	160	374	443	504	532	580	624
Second category	..	7	611	869	1 214	1 287	1 536	1 581	1 772	2 412
Fourth category	..	234	408	521	834	783	871	894	960	1 023
Fifth category	..	1 641	3 241	4 735	8 473	8 044	8 248	8 444	9 162	9 760
Tax debt payments	..	68	168	233	529	581	601	1 558	1 125	926
1110 On income and profits	..	..	..	..	..	..	..	..	..	..
1120 On capital gains	..	..	..	..	..	..	..	..	..	..
1200 Corporate	32	2 526	18 724	19 561	26 593	24 266	24 786	24 604	28 830	29 449
1210 On profits	32	2 526	18 724	19 561	26 593	24 266	24 786	24 604	28 830	29 449
Third category	..	2 023	13 258	14 652	18 536	16 817	16 496	15 499	17 268	17 679
Income tax on mining	..	0	0	0	372	208	236	638	770	545
Income tax special regime	..	47	60	118	275	310	335	323	344	354
Other incomes corporate	..	18	95	148	193	167	215	233	251	257
Tax debt payments	..	438	3 829	2 856	3 703	3 066	3 204	3 327	5 244	5 438
Temporary tax on net assets	..	0	1 483	1 788	3 513	3 697	4 300	4 585	4 953	5 176
1220 On capital gains of corporates	..	..	..	..	..	..	..	..	..	..
1300 Unallocable between 1100 and 1200	1	436	770	1 239	5 561	2 369	3 814	2 233	1 550	2 560
Income tax on non-residents	1	487	961	1 511	6 027	3 248	5 205	3 462	3 560	4 135
Income tax refunds	0	-51	-191	-272	-466	-879	-1 391	-1 228	-2 009	-1 575
2000 Social security contributions	**50**	**3 185**	**5 244**	**7 929**	**11 847**	**12 681**	**13 186**	**13 676**	**14 873**	**15 453**
2100 Employees	..	566	1 005	2 468	3 211	3 508	3 646	3 796	4 216	4 202
2110 On a payroll basis	..	566	978	1 700	3 100	3 371	3 550	3 662	3 940	4 023
2120 On an income tax basis	..	0	26	767	112	137	97	134	275	179
Solidarity contribution for pension plan	..	..	26	767	112	137	97	134	275	179
2200 Employers	..	2 515	4 221	5 454	8 631	9 170	9 536	9 878	10 653	11 245
2210 On a payroll basis	..	2 432	4 039	5 216	8 413	8 926	9 282	9 591	10 299	10 883
2220 On an income tax basis	..	83	182	238	218	244	255	287	354	362
2300 Self-employed or non-employed	..	95	8	7	4	2	3	2	4	6
2310 On a payroll basis	..	0	0	0	0	0	0	0	0	0
2320 On an income tax basis	..	95	8	7	4	2	3	2	4	6
2400 Unallocable between 2100, 2200 and 2300	50	9	11	0	1	0	0	1	1	0
2410 On a payroll basis	50	9	11	0	1	0	0	1	1	..
2420 On an income tax basis	0	0	0	0	0	0	0	0	0	..
3000 Taxes on payroll and workforce	**0**	**1 176**	**-40**	**57**	**0**	**92**	**91**	**91**	**99**	**99**
Extraordinary solidarity tax (IES)	..	1 151	9	3	3	5	1	0	1	0
IES refunds	..	-2	-48	-2	-86	-1	0	-2	0	-3
National Housing Fund (FONAVI)	..	27	0	0	0	0	0	0	0	0
Contributions to SENATI	..	0	0	56	82	88	90	93	98	102
4000 Taxes on property	**87**	**323**	**1 931**	**2 231**	**2 154**	**2 429**	**2 637**	**2 573**	**2 680**	**3 063**
4100 Recurrent taxes on immovable property	0	298	554	727	1 230	1 463	1 629	1 718	1 748	2 026
4110 Households	..	..	..	..	..	..	..	..	..	..
4120 Others	..	..	..	..	..	..	..	..	..	..
4200 Recurrent taxes on net wealth	49	0	0	0	0	0	0	0	0	0
4210 Individual	..	..	..	..	..	..	..	..	..	..
4220 Corporate	..	..	..	..	..	..	..	..	..	..
4300 Estate, inheritance and gift taxes	0	0	0	0	0	0	0	0	0	0
4310 Estate and inheritance taxes	..	..	..	..	..	..	..	..	..	..
4320 Gift taxes	..	..	..	..	..	..	..	..	..	..
4400 Taxes on financial and capital transactions	38	25	1 377	1 504	925	966	1 008	855	932	1 037
Financial transactions tax	0	0	1 031	944	153	161	168	175	200	224
Real estate transfer tax	0	25	347	560	772	805	840	680	732	813
Tax Law Decree 519	38	0	0	0	0	0	0	0	0	0
4500 Non-recurrent taxes	0	0	0	0	0	0	0	0	0	0
4510 On net wealth	..	..	..	..	..	..	..	..	..	..
4520 Other non-recurrent taxes	..	..	..	..	..	..	..	..	..	..
4600 Other recurrent taxes on property	0	0	0	0	0	0	0	0	0	0
5000 Taxes on goods and services	**454**	**16 263**	**27 142**	**36 353**	**49 933**	**51 102**	**48 247**	**50 061**	**58 551**	**60 366**
5100 Taxes on production, sale, transfer, etc	454	16 239	27 075	36 199	49 668	50 820	47 943	49 774	58 257	60 064
5110 General taxes	109	9 646	20 151	29 094	41 779	42 612	39 462	41 036	49 038	49 197
5111 Value added taxes	109	9 646	20 151	29 094	41 779	42 612	39 462	41 036	49 038	49 197
VAT (internal)	69	6 992	13 586	19 629	28 732	30 410	31 040	32 114	35 125	37 892
VAT (imports)	41	4 961	11 673	15 908	21 620	21 259	21 652	22 529	25 541	25 613
VAT refunds	0	-2 307	-5 107	-6 442	-8 573	-9 056	-13 231	-13 606	-11 628	-14 307
5112 Sales tax	0	0	0	0	0	0	0	0	0	0
5113 Other	0	0	0	0	0	0	0	0	0	0

Table 5.23. **Peru / Perú** *(cont.)*

Details of tax revenue / Ingresos tributarios detallados

Million PEN

	1990	2000	2007	2010	2014	2015	2016	2017	2018	2019
5120 Taxes on specific goods and services	345	6 593	6 924	7 105	7 889	8 208	8 482	8 737	9 219	10 867
5121 Excises	232	3 518	4 445	4 875	5 488	5 796	6 175	6 588	7 011	8 668
Fuels	151	2 145	2 419	2 410	2 041	2 211	2 423	2 604	2 565	3 212
Gasoline sales tax	3	97	174	210	380	332	312	363	437	456
Other excises	78	1 304	1 872	2 258	3 094	3 284	3 479	3 711	4 295	5 005
Excise tax refunds	0	-28	-20	-4	-27	-31	-39	-91	-286	-4
5122 Profits of fiscal monopolies	0	0	0	0	0	0	0	0	0	0
5123 Customs and import duties	64	2 960	2 198	1 803	1 790	1 775	1 606	1 448	1 455	1 424
5124 Taxes on exports	2	0	0	0	0	0	0	0	0	0
5125 Taxes on investment goods	0	0	0	0	0	0	0	0	0	0
5126 Taxes on specific services	0	115	281	427	612	637	701	702	754	774
Casinos and slot machines	..	81	109	187	279	279	298	297	318	310
Tourism tax	..	0	87	105	127	144	173	174	193	215
Municipal taxes on services	..	34	85	135	206	214	230	230	243	250
5127 Other taxes on internat. trade and transactions	48	0	0	0	0	0	0	0	0	0
5128 Other taxes	0	0	0	0	0	0	0	0	0	0
5130 Unallocable between 5110 and 5120	0	0	0	0	0	0	0	0	0	0
5200 Taxes on use of goods and perform activities	0	25	67	154	264	282	303	288	294	302
5210 Recurrent taxes	..	25	67	154	264	282	303	288	294	302
5211 Paid by households: motor vehicles	..	..	..	..	..	..	..	..	..	..
5212 Paid by others: motor vehicles	..	..	..	..	..	..	..	..	..	..
5213 Paid in respect of other goods	..	..	..	..	..	..	..	..	..	..
5220 Non-recurrent taxes	..	0	0	0	0	0	0	0	0	0
5300 Unallocable between 5100 and 5200	0	0	0	0	0	0	0	0	0	0
6000 Other taxes	**9**	**745**	**770**	**914**	**2 633**	**2 108**	**1 522**	**780**	**1 662**	**2 215**
6100 Paid solely by business	0	84	82	108	158	179	185	140	133	135
Single simplified regime	..	84	82	108	158	179	185	140	133	135
University Development Fund	..	0	0	0	0	0	0	0	0	0
6200 Other	9	662	688	806	2 475	1 929	1 337	639	1 529	2 080
Tax debt payments	9	542	510	714	814	922	1 068	1 109	1 320	1 843
Other taxes	0	133	253	280	2 060	1 790	1 114	785	1 225	1 349
Other tax refunds	0	-14	-74	-188	-399	-783	-845	-1 255	-1 016	-1 112

.. Not available

Note: Year ending 31st December.

The data are on a cash basis.

The figures for years up to 2000 exclude local government tax revenues as the data are not available.

Heading 2000: All contributions pertaining to pensions are only made by employees and contributions to healthcare are made by employers. The exceptions are special regimes which apply to self-employed and are levied on an income basis. Social security contributions at local level have been added in this edition.

Heading 3000: Contributions to SENATI have been added in this edition. The tax revenue is classified under the central government. In Peru this revenue is classified under a separate unit considered to be different to the central government.

Heading 5123: Import tax refunds are classified under 6200 because they cannot be distinguished from other tax refunds.

Source: Superintendencia Nacional de Aduanas y de Administración Tributaria (National Superintendence of Customs and Tax Administration - SUNAT); Banco de la Nación (Bank of the Nation); Ministerio de Economía y Finanzas (Ministry of Economy and Finance); Servicio Nacional de Adiestramiento en Trabajo Industrial (National Industrial Work Training Service).

StatLink https://doi.org/10.1787/888934235905

Table 5.24. **Saint Lucia / Santa Lucía**

Details of tax revenue / Ingresos tributarios detallados

Million XCD

	1990	2000	2007	2010	2014	2015	2016	2017	2018	2019
Total tax revenue	..	**480**	**765**	**828**	**981**	**1 045**	**1 090**	**1 100**	**1 163**	**1 179**
1000 Taxes on income, profits and capital gains	..	**137**	**196**	**224**	**224**	**242**	**259**	**247**	**268**	**256**
1100 Of individuals	..	49	71	83	101	105	106	124	131	134
1110 On income and profits	..	49	71	83	101	105	106	124	131	134
Personal income tax	..	49	71	83	101	105	106	104	113	116
Arrears on personal income tax	..	0	0	0	0	0	0	21	18	18
1120 On capital gains	..	..	..	..	..	..	..	..	..	..
1200 Corporate	..	63	92	95	71	78	99	102	115	111
1210 On profits	..	63	92	95	71	78	99	102	115	111
Corporate income tax	..	63	92	95	71	78	99	89	92	93
Arrears on corporate income tax	..	0	0	0	0	0	0	13	23	18
1220 On capital gains of corporates	..	..	..	..	..	..	..	..	..	..
1300 Unallocable between 1100 and 1200	..	26	33	46	53	58	53	21	23	11
Withholdings	..	7	5	14	27	25	24	24	28	16
Arrears	..	25	35	42	33	44	39	7	5	7
Tax Refunds	..	-6	-8	-10	-7	-10	-10	-10	-11	-11
2000 Social security contributions	..	**48**	**77**	**92**	**108**	**111**	**113**	**114**	**124**	**124**
2100 Employees	..	..	..	..	..	..	..	..	..	..
2110 On a payroll basis	..	..	..	..	..	..	..	..	..	..
2120 On an income tax basis	..	..	..	..	..	..	..	..	..	..
2200 Employers	..	..	..	..	..	..	..	..	..	..
2210 On a payroll basis	..	..	..	..	..	..	..	..	..	..
2220 On an income tax basis	..	..	..	..	..	..	..	..	..	..
2300 Self-employed or non-employed	..	..	..	..	..	..	..	..	..	..
2310 On a payroll basis	..	..	..	..	..	..	..	..	..	..
2320 On an income tax basis	..	..	..	..	..	..	..	..	..	..
2400 Unallocable between 2100, 2200 and 2300	..	48	77	92	108	111	113	114	124	124
2410 On a payroll basis	..	48	77	92	108	111	113	114	124	124
2420 On an income tax basis	..	0	0	0	0	0	0	0	0	0
3000 Taxes on payroll and workforce	..	**0**	**0**	**0**	**0**	**0**	**0**	**0**	**0**	**0**
4000 Taxes on property	..	**11**	**37**	**19**	**24**	**23**	**26**	**26**	**26**	**25**
4100 Recurrent taxes on immovable property	..	2	5	3	9	11	12	12	10	8
4110 Households	..	..	..	..	..	..	..	..	..	..
4120 Others	..	..	..	..	..	..	..	..	..	..
4200 Recurrent taxes on net wealth	..	0	0	0	0	0	0	0	0	0
4210 Individual	..	..	..	..	..	..	..	..	..	..
4220 Corporate	..	..	..	..	..	..	..	..	..	..
4300 Estate, inheritance and gift taxes	..	0	0	0	0	0	0	0	0	0
4310 Estate and inheritance taxes	..	..	..	..	..	..	..	..	..	..
4320 Gift taxes	..	..	..	..	..	..	..	..	..	..
4400 Taxes on financial and capital transactions	..	9	32	16	14	12	14	14	17	18
4500 Non-reccurrent taxes	..	0	0	0	0	0	0	0	0	0
4510 On net wealth	..	..	..	..	..	..	..	..	..	..
4520 Other non-recurrent taxes	..	..	..	..	..	..	..	..	..	..
4600 Other recurrent taxes on property	..	0	0	0	0	0	0	0	0	0
5000 Taxes on goods and services	..	**284**	**456**	**493**	**625**	**670**	**694**	**712**	**744**	**774**
5100 Taxes on production, sale, transfer, etc	..	277	430	467	603	642	663	685	717	745
5110 General taxes	..	101	122	119	334	347	335	309	331	342
5111 Value added taxes	..	0	0	0	334	346	335	309	331	342
VAT (domestic)	..	..	..	..	183	184	177	170	181	..
VAT (imports)	..	..	..	..	151	163	159	139	149	..
5112 Sales tax	..	101	122	119	0	0	0	0	0	0
Consumption tax (domestic)	..	11	10	6	0	0	..	..	..	..
Consumption tax (Imports)	..	90	112	114	0	0	..	..	..	..
5113 Other	..	0	0	0	0	0	0	0	0	0
5120 Taxes on specific goods and services	..	176	308	348	268	295	328	376	386	402
5121 Excises	..	34	49	85	78	92	112	128	134	140
Excise tax (domestic)	..	28	3	14	4	4	4	5	5	5
Excise tax (imports)	..	0	43	68	67	74	87	103	109	114
Fuel Surcharge	..	3	4	4	8	15	21	21	20	21
Surcharge on international calls	..	4	0	0	0	0	0	0	0	0
5122 Profits of fiscal monopolies	..	0	0	0	0	0	0	0	0	0
5123 Customs and import duties	..	108	194	187	164	179	189	202	207	205
Import Duty	..	64	107	101	101	106	114	121	123	122
Thruput Charge	..	1	3	6	2	3	4	5	4	4
Service Charge (imports) and security charges	..	33	66	64	61	70	72	76	80	80
Environmental Levy	..	9	18	16	0	0	0	0	0	0
5124 Taxes on exports	..	0	0	0	0	0	0	0	0	0

Table 5.24. **Saint Lucia / Santa Lucía** *(cont.)*

Details of tax revenue / Ingresos tributarios detallados

Million XCD

	1990	2000	2007	2010	2014	2015	2016	2017	2018	2019
5125 Taxes on investment goods	..	0	0	0	0	0	0	0	0	0
5126 Taxes on specific services	..	34	65	76	27	24	26	46	45	57
Hotel occupancy tax	..	23	34	34	3	1	0	0	0	1
Insurance premium tax	..	4	7	7	8	8	8	9	9	10
Cellular tax	..	0	12	18	0	0	0	0	0	0
Passenger facility fee	..	0	3	5	4	4	3	4	3	3
Travel tax	..	3	3	4	4	4	4	5	5	4
Airport tax	..	5	6	9	8	7	11	29	28	39
5127 Other taxes on internat. trade and transactions	..	0	0	0	0	0	0	0	0	0
5128 Other taxes	..	0	0	0	0	0	0	0	0	0
5130 Unallocable between 5110 and 5120	..	0	0	0	0	0	0	0	0	0
5200 Taxes on use of goods and to perform activities	..	7	25	26	22	29	31	27	28	29
5210 Recurrent taxes	..	7	25	26	22	29	31	27	28	29
5211 Paid by households: motor vehicles	..	0	0	0	0	0	0	0	0	0
5212 Paid by others: motor vehicles	..	0	0	0	0	0	0	0	0	0
5213 Paid in respect of other goods	..	7	25	26	22	29	31	27	28	29
5220 Non-recurrent taxes	..	0	0	0	0	0	0	0	0	0
5300 Unallocable between 5100 and 5200	..	0	0	0	0	0	0	0	0	0
6000 Other taxes	**..**	**0**	**0**	**0**	**0**	**0**	**0**	**0**	**0**	**0**
6100 Paid solely by business	..	..	..	..	..	..	..	..	..	..
6200 Other	..	..	..	..	..	..	..	..	..	..

.. Not available

Note: Year ending 31st March. For example, the data for 2019 represent April 2019 to March 2020.

The data are on a cash basis.

The figures do not include local tax revenues because data are not available.

Heading 1000: Arrears on PIT and CIT have been added as country specific taxes under headings 1100 and 1200 in this edition. They were previously grouped together under heading 1300.

Heading 2000: Social security contribution data have been added in this edition based on annual reports of National Insurance Corporation. Social security contributions follow financial year from July to June, instead of April to March. For example, social security contributions in 2019 are between 1st July 2018 and 30th June 2019. The figures for 2018 and 2019 are estimated.

Heading 4000: Property tax is classified under heading 4100 in this edition. It was previously under heading 4500.

Heading 5123: Data for security charge in 2019 is estimated.

Heading 5213: The figure in 2019 is estimated.

Source: The Central Statistical Office of Saint Lucia; Department of Finance of Saint Lucia; National Insurance Corporation of Saint Lucia.

StatLink https://doi.org/10.1787/888934235924

Table 5.25. **Trinidad and Tobago / Trinidad y Tobago**

Details of tax revenue / Ingresos tributarios detallados

Million TTD

	1990	2000	2007	2010	2014	2015	2016	2017	2018	2019
Total tax revenue	**4 923**	**10 953**	**37 099**	**39 720**	**50 911**	**46 559**	**33 984**	**31 164**	**36 813**	**38 468**
1000 Taxes on income, profits and capital gains	**2 595**	**6 224**	**26 853**	**27 213**	**36 371**	**29 628**	**17 057**	**16 133**	**19 411**	**22 346**
1100 Of individuals	669	2 325	3 426	4 674	6 859	7 752	7 458	6 570	6 840	7 170
1110 On income and profits	669	2 325	3 426	4 674	6 859	7 752	7 458	6 570	6 840	7 170
Health surcharge	92	149	170	185	210	264	226	218	184	191
Insurance surrender tax	6	7	16	22	29	42	46	48	57	65
Individuals (Ch. 75:01)	571	2 169	3 239	4 467	6 620	7 445	7 187	6 303	6 599	6 915
1120 On capital gains	..	..	..	..	..	..	..	..	..	..
1200 Corporate	1 856	3 704	22 252	21 659	28 570	20 810	8 608	8 736	11 713	13 816
1210 On profits	1 856	3 704	22 252	21 659	28 570	20 810	8 608	8 736	11 713	13 816
Oil companies	1 439	2 441	16 206	13 834	16 970	10 513	1 036	1 116	2 093	3 755
Other companies	383	1 041	4 797	6 630	10 151	9 481	7 003	6 919	8 858	8 694
Business levy	0	65	138	206	210	215	438	603	608	649
National recovery impost	34	0	0	0	0	0	0	0	0	0
Unemployment Fund	0	157	1 111	989	1 240	601	131	99	153	718
1220 On capital gains of corporates	..	..	..	..	..	..	..	..	..	..
1300 Unallocable between 1100 and 1200	70	195	1 175	881	942	1 067	990	827	858	1 360
2000 Social security contributions	**183**	**702**	**1 502**	**2 645**	**3 624**	**4 261**	**4 252**	**4 608**	**4 670**	**4 757**
2100 Employees	..	..	..	..	..	..	..	..	..	..
2110 On a payroll basis	..	..	..	..	..	..	..	..	..	..
2120 On an income tax basis	..	..	..	..	..	..	..	..	..	..
2200 Employers	..	..	..	..	..	..	..	..	..	..
2210 On a payroll basis	..	..	..	..	..	..	..	..	..	..
2220 On an income tax basis	..	..	..	..	..	..	..	..	..	..
2300 Self-employed or non-employed	..	..	..	..	..	..	..	..	..	..
2310 On a payroll basis	..	..	..	..	..	..	..	..	..	..
2320 On an income tax basis	..	..	..	..	..	..	..	..	..	..
2400 Unallocable between 2100, 2200 and 2300	183	702	1 502	2 645	3 624	4 261	4 252	4 608	4 670	4 757
2410 On a payroll basis	..	..	..	..	..	..	..	..	..	..
2420 On an income tax basis	..	..	..	..	..	..	..	..	..	..
3000 Taxes on payroll and workforce	**0**	**0**	**0**	**0**	**0**	**0**	**0**	**0**	**0**	**0**
4000 Taxes on property	**90**	**175**	**385**	**194**	**289**	**406**	**332**	**322**	**362**	**405**
4100 Recurrent taxes on immovable property	39	64	84	22	3	3	3	3	4	50
4110 Households	..	..	..	..	..	..	..	..	..	..
4120 Others	..	..	..	..	..	..	..	..	..	..
4200 Recurrent taxes on net wealth	0	0	0	0	0	0	0	0	0	0
4210 Individual	..	..	..	..	..	..	..	..	..	..
4220 Corporate	..	..	..	..	..	..	..	..	..	..
4300 Estate, inheritance and gift taxes	1	0	0	0	0	0	0	0	0	0
4310 Estate and inheritance taxes	1	..	..	..	..	..	..	..	..	..
4320 Gift taxes	0	..	..	..	..	..	..	..	..	..
4400 Taxes on financial and capital transactions	49	111	301	172	285	403	329	319	359	356
Stamp duties	49	111	301	172	285	403	329	319	359	356
4500 Non-recurrent taxes	0	0	0	0	0	0	0	0	0	0
4510 On net wealth	..	..	..	..	..	..	..	..	..	..
4520 Other non-recurrent taxes	..	..	..	..	..	..	..	..	..	..
4600 Other recurrent taxes on property	0	0	0	0	0	0	0	0	0	0
5000 Taxes on goods and services	**2 055**	**3 852**	**8 358**	**9 667**	**10 627**	**12 264**	**12 344**	**10 101**	**12 370**	**10 960**
5100 Taxes on production, sale, transfer, etc	1 973	3 603	8 010	9 282	10 047	11 678	11 765	9 675	12 026	10 657
5110 General taxes	980	1 890	5 105	6 358	6 126	7 569	7 617	5 876	8 087	6 836
5111 Value added taxes	927	1 890	4 829	6 032	5 745	7 223	7 005	5 050	7 245	5 848
5112 Sales tax	54	0	0	0	0	0	0	1	0	0
5113 Other	0	0	276	325	381	346	612	825	842	988
Green Fund	..	..	276	325	381	346	612	803	813	957
Tax on online purchases	..	..	..	0	0	0	0	22	29	31
5120 Taxes on specific goods and services	993	1 713	2 904	2 924	3 921	4 108	4 148	3 798	3 939	3 822
5121 Excises	481	801	614	708	680	703	735	739	793	680
Alcohol products	..	..	..	156	157	154	168	150	183	187
Beer	..	..	..	202	172	189	181	202	202	173
Petroleum products	..	..	..	105	94	88	132	102	98	23
Cigarette products	..	..	..	243	235	243	226	253	269	262
Malt beverages	..	..	..	2	23	29	28	33	41	35
5122 Profits of fiscal monopolies	0	0	0	0	0	0	0	0	0	0
5123 Customs and import duties	260	748	2 004	1 905	2 861	3 014	3 016	2 684	2 732	2 672
5124 Taxes on exports	0	0	0	0	0	0	0	0	0	0
5125 Taxes on investment goods	0	0	0	0	0	0	0	0	0	0

Table 5.25. **Trinidad and Tobago / Trinidad y Tobago** *(cont.)*

Details of tax revenue / Ingresos tributarios detallados

Million TTD

	1990	2000	2007	2010	2014	2015	2016	2017	2018	2019
5126 Taxes on specific services	49	163	284	311	380	391	397	375	414	470
Insurance premium tax	0	56	130	167	197	191	181	163	170	180
Transaction tax on financial services	0	23	42	53	75	75	87	93	97	103
Hotel room tax	0	23	48	46	56	64	54	52	52	55
Betting and entertainment taxes	4	17	0	12	0	0	0	0	0	0
Other taxes on goods and services	45	44	63	33	52	61	75	67	95	132
5127 Other taxes on internat. trade and transactions	202	0	2	1	0	0	0	1	0	0
5128 Other taxes	0	0	0	0	0	0	0	0	0	0
5130 Unallocable between 5110 and 5120	0	0	0	0	0	0	0	0	0	0
5200 Taxes on use of goods and perform activities	81	249	348	386	580	586	580	426	344	303
5210 Recurrent taxes	81	249	348	386	580	586	580	426	344	303
Motor vehicle taxes and duties	76	239	338	375	569	575	569	415	334	291
5211 Paid by households: motor vehicles	..	..	..	..	..	..	..	..	..	..
5212 Paid by others: motor vehicles	..	..	..	..	..	..	..	..	..	..
5213 Paid in respect of other goods	5	10	10	10	11	11	11	11	11	12
Liquor and miscellaneous business licence fees	5	10	10	10	11	11	11	11	11	12
5220 Non-recurrent taxes	0	0	0	0	0	0	0	0	0	0
5300 Unallocable between 5100 and 5200	0	0	0	0	0	0	0	0	0	0
6000 Other taxes	**0**	**0**	**0**	**0**	**0**	**0**	**0**	**0**	**0**	**0**
6100 Paid solely by business	..	..	..	..	..	..	..	..	..	..
6200 Other	..	..	..	..	..	..	..	..	..	..

.. Not available

Note: Fiscal year ending on 30th September. For example, the data for 2019 represent October 2018 to September 2019.

The data are on a cash basis.

The figures exclude local government tax revenues as the data are not available.

Heading 2000: Social security contributions follow financial year from July to June, instead of October to September. For example, social security contributions in 2019 are between 1st July 2018 and 30th June 2019. The figures include total contribution income of National Insurance Board minus refunds. A small amount of voluntary contributions have been identified and removed from the figures since 2013. Data for 2019 is estimated.

Source: Ministry of Finance; The National Insurance Board.

StatLink https://doi.org/10.1787/888934235943

Table 5.26. **Uruguay**

Details of tax revenue / Ingresos tributarios detallados

Million UYU

	1990	2000	2007	2010	2014	2015	2016	2017	2018	2019
Total tax revenue	**2 399**	**64 183**	**141 132**	**212 907**	**365 043**	**398 274**	**441 875**	**494 901**	**534 519**	**573 642**
1000 Taxes on income, profits and capital gains	**114**	**8 698**	**20 540**	**42 583**	**73 120**	**84 141**	**101 738**	**125 295**	**140 527**	**149 920**
1100 Of individuals	0	3 597	8 362	19 148	40 334	45 451	51 679	68 948	78 571	85 847
Personal income tax (IRP)	..	3 597	3 519	0	0	0	0	0	0	0
1110 On income and profits	..	..	4 262	16 790	35 367	39 613	44 817	60 570	69 083	75 944
IRPF second category	..	..	4 262	14 643	31 365	34 881	39 883	54 327	61 077	67 254
Social security assistance	..	..	0	2 651	5 518	6 576	7 480	9 448	11 091	12 336
Personal income tax refunds	..	..	0	-504	-1 517	-1 844	-2 545	-3 204	-3 085	-3 646
1120 On capital gains	..	..	581	2 358	4 967	5 838	6 862	8 377	9 488	9 903
IRPF first category	..	..	581	2 358	4 967	5 838	6 862	8 377	9 488	9 903
1200 Corporate	114	5 102	11 829	21 772	29 549	34 814	45 535	51 169	56 316	58 071
1210 On profits	114	5 102	11 829	21 772	29 549	34 814	45 535	51 169	56 316	58 071
Income tax for economic activities (IRAE)	0	0	709	21 437	29 407	34 720	45 461	51 081	56 316	58 071
Industry and commerce income tax (IRIC)	97	5 096	11 055	333	142	94	73	88	0	0
Agricultural income tax (IRA)	10	3	65	2	0	0	1	0	0	0
Tax on agricultural activities (IMAGRO)	7	3	0	0	0	0	0	0	0	0
1220 On capital gains of corporates	..	..	..	..	..	..	..	..	..	..
1300 Unallocable between 1100 and 1200	0	0	349	1 662	3 237	3 875	4 523	5 179	5 639	6 002
Non-resident income tax (IRNR)	..	..	349	1 662	3 237	3 875	4 523	5 179	5 639	6 002
2000 Social security contributions	**717**	**17 679**	**28 485**	**49 742**	**100 993**	**109 282**	**119 101**	**131 545**	**139 561**	**151 589**
2100 Employees	..	..	..	..	..	..	..	..	..	..
2110 On a payroll basis	..	..	..	..	..	..	..	..	..	..
2120 On an income tax basis	..	..	..	..	..	..	..	..	..	..
2200 Employers	..	..	..	..	..	..	..	..	..	..
2210 On a payroll basis	..	..	..	..	..	..	..	..	..	..
2220 On an income tax basis	..	..	..	..	..	..	..	..	..	..
2300 Self-employed or non-employed	..	..	..	..	..	..	..	..	..	..
2310 On a payroll basis	..	..	..	..	..	..	..	..	..	..
2320 On an income tax basis	..	..	..	..	..	..	..	..	..	..
2400 Unallocable between 2100, 2200 and 2300	717	17 679	28 485	49 742	100 993	109 282	119 101	131 545	139 561	151 589
2410 On a payroll basis	717	17 679	28 485	49 742	100 993	109 282	119 101	131 545	139 561	151 589
2420 On an income tax basis	0	0	0	0	0	0	0	0	0	0
3000 Taxes on payroll and workforce	**0**	**0**	**0**	**0**	**0**	**0**	**0**	**0**	**0**	**0**
4000 Taxes on property	**213**	**5 508**	**13 243**	**18 965**	**29 226**	**32 422**	**36 441**	**38 460**	**40 508**	**44 178**
4100 Recurrent taxes on immovable property	87	3 248	5 686	8 140	13 016	14 884	16 812	18 180	19 648	21 056
Primary education tax	0	378	691	1 064	1 612	2 386	2 474	2 781	2 961	3 271
Farm property tax	0	155	0	189	921	886	852	764	728	750
Property tax surcharge	0	0	0	0	541	503	511	543	476	471
Primary education tax refunds	0	0	0	0	0	0	0	0	-3	-2
Other property taxes	87	2 715	4 995	6 887	9 942	11 109	12 975	14 092	15 485	16 567
4110 Households	..	..	..	..	..	..	..	..	..	..
4120 Others	..	..	..	..	..	..	..	..	..	..
4200 Recurrent taxes on net wealth	94	1 769	5 392	8 760	13 714	14 776	16 652	17 057	17 473	19 717
4210 Individual	64	108	340	382	629	606	684	711	760	707
4220 Corporate	30	1 661	5 052	8 378	13 085	14 170	15 968	16 346	16 713	19 010
Corporate wealth tax	28	1 507	4 805	8 165	13 079	14 167	15 967	16 345	16 713	19 010
Tax on financial investment companies (ISAFI)	1	154	247	213	6	3	1	1	1	0
4300 Estate, inheritance and gift taxes	0	0	0	0	0	0	0	0	0	0
4310 Estate and inheritance taxes	..	..	..	..	..	..	..	..	..	..
4320 Gift taxes	..	..	..	..	..	..	..	..	..	..
4400 Taxes on financial and capital transactions	31	476	1 831	1 740	1 994	2 241	2 439	2 662	2 819	2 841
Property transfer tax (ITP)	11	372	1 405	1 347	1 442	1 601	1 724	1 927	1 984	1 859
Tax on transfer of rights over athletes	0	0	50	3	0	0	0	0	0	0
Auction tax	20	104	376	390	553	639	714	735	835	982
4500 Non-recurrent taxes	0	0	0	0	0	0	0	0	0	0
4510 On net wealth	..	..	..	..	..	..	..	..	..	..
4520 Other non-recurrent taxes	..	..	..	..	..	..	..	..	..	..
4600 Other recurrent taxes on property	1	15	335	326	502	522	538	560	567	564
Corporation control tax (ICOSA)	1	15	236	325	502	522	538	560	567	564
Financial system control tax (ICOSIFI)	0	0	99	0	0	0	0	0	0	0
5000 Taxes on goods and services	**1 358**	**32 139**	**77 673**	**100 282**	**159 646**	**170 279**	**182 082**	**196 669**	**210 711**	**224 394**
5100 Taxes on production, sale, transfer, etc	1 301	29 562	74 369	96 494	153 184	162 739	172 823	186 355	199 329	212 218
5110 General taxes	660	18 009	50 943	69 951	108 918	114 627	123 262	129 663	137 400	145 846
5111 Value added taxes	660	17 995	49 064	69 921	108 918	114 627	123 262	129 663	137 400	145 846
5112 Sales tax	1	14	1 879	30	0	0	0	0	0	0
Social security financing tax (COFIS)	0	0	1 859	30	..	..	..	..	..	..
Other sales taxes	1	14	20	0	..	..	..	..	..	..
5113 Other	0	0	0	0	0	0	0	0	0	0

Table 5.26. **Uruguay** *(cont.)*

Details of tax revenue / Ingresos tributarios detallados

Million UYU

	1990	2000	2007	2010	2014	2015	2016	2017	2018	2019
5120 Taxes on specific goods and services	641	11 553	23 426	26 543	44 266	48 111	49 561	56 692	61 928	66 372
5121 Excises	393	7 896	13 409	17 300	27 770	31 197	32 528	37 779	39 214	42 183
Fuels	203	4 067	5 694	6 551	11 816	14 096	15 222	17 129	18 662	20 094
Tobacco products	80	1 741	3 085	4 236	4 913	5 778	6 144	6 995	7 518	7 703
Motor vehicles	20	656	1 333	2 289	3 924	4 017	3 960	4 313	3 789	3 799
Non-alcoholic beverages	19	464	804	1 172	1 926	2 131	2 330	2 547	2 687	2 754
Agricultural products	4	299	1 396	1 349	2 144	2 223	2 227	2 369	2 636	2 998
Beer	8	205	372	602	1 035	1 102	1 109	1 357	1 526	1 494
Advances of import excises	0	27	-250	-136	398	312	-62	1 372	704	1 591
Greases and lubricants	5	119	306	390	519	525	559	623	652	677
Alcoholic beverages	22	212	415	562	883	789	774	766	617	677
Other excises	32	106	254	283	213	224	265	309	423	397
5122 Profits of fiscal monopolies	0	0	0	0	0	0	0	0	0	0
5123 Customs and import duties	214	1 967	7 077	8 478	15 167	15 440	15 384	17 198	20 878	22 124
5124 Taxes on exports	1	32	274	325	520	582	658	664	770	858
5125 Taxes on investment goods	0	0	0	0	0	0	0	0	0	0
5126 Taxes on specific services	34	1 392	2 145	440	809	892	991	1 052	1 067	1 207
Bank asset tax (IMABA)	31	1 092	686	2	1	0	0	0	0	0
Income tax for insurance companies	3	76	336	366	691	763	845	902	916	1 004
Other services taxes	0	224	1 123	72	117	129	146	150	152	202
5127 Other taxes on internat. trade and transactions	0	265	520	0	0	0	0	0	0	0
5128 Other taxes	0	0	0	0	0	0	0	0	0	0
5130 Unallocable between 5110 and 5120	0	0	0	0	0	0	0	0	0	0
5200 Taxes on use of goods and perform activities	57	2 576	3 303	3 788	6 463	7 540	9 259	10 313	11 382	12 176
5210 Recurrent taxes	57	2 576	3 303	3 788	6 463	7 540	9 259	10 313	11 382	12 176
5211 Paid by households: motor vehicles	0	0	0	0	0	0	0	0	0	0
5212 Paid by others: motor vehicles	57	2 576	3 303	3 788	6 463	7 540	9 259	10 313	11 382	12 176
5213 Paid in respect of other goods	0	0	0	0	0	0	0	0	0	0
5220 Non-recurrent taxes	0	0	0	0	0	0	0	0	0	0
5300 Unallocable between 5100 and 5200	0	0	0	0	0	0	0	0	0	0
6000 Other taxes	**-3**	**159**	**1 191**	**1 335**	**2 057**	**2 151**	**2 513**	**2 933**	**3 212**	**3 560**
6100 Paid solely by business	-10	-145	626	586	741	796	850	925	980	1 039
Small business tax (minimum VAT)	0	296	563	586	741	796	850	925	980	1 039
Credit card tax	0	0	63	0	0	0	0	0	0	0
Other tax refunds	-10	-440	0	0	0	0	0	0	0	0
6200 Other	7	303	565	748	1 316	1 355	1 663	2 008	2 232	2 521

.. Not available

Note: Year ending 31st December.

The data are on a cash basis.

Heading 2000: Figures for 1990-98 are estimated by the General Tax Directorate (DGI). The figures have included income from Social Security Bank (BPS) published by the Ministry of Economy and Finance since 1999.

Heading 5112: The tax on the sale of goods by public auctions recorded under other sales taxes is classified in category 4000 in ECLAC data.

Source: Dirección General Impositiva (General Tax Directorate); Ministerio de Economía y Finanzas (Ministry of Economy and Finance).

StatLink https://doi.org/10.1787/888934235962

Table 5.27. **Venezuela**

Details of tax revenue / Ingresos tributarios detallados

VES

	1990	2000	2007	2010	2014	2015	2016	2017	2018	2019
Total tax revenue	**4 115**	**108 486**	**838 614**	**1 200 840**	..	..	..	..	..	..
1000 Taxes on income, profits and capital gains	**3 444**	**46 856**	**375 642**	**368 365**	**1 878 840**	**2 847 864**	..	..	..	..
1100 Of individuals	..	..	..	..	..	..	..	..	..	..
1110 On income and profits	..	..	..	..	..	..	..	..	..	..
1120 On capital gains	..	..	..	..	..	..	..	..	..	..
1200 Corporate	3 148	33 683	199 585	86 998	676 007	473 879	..	..	..	..
1210 On profits	3 148	33 683	199 585	86 998	676 007	473 879	..	..	..	..
Oil	3 148	33 683	199 585	86 998	676 007	473 879	..	..	..	..
1220 On capital gains of corporates	..	..	..	..	..	..	..	..	..	..
1300 Unallocable between 1100 and 1200	297	13 173	176 057	281 367	1 202 834	2 373 986	7 331 699	31 378 510	..	..
2000 Social security contributions	**202**	**5 905**	**42 176**	**96 896**	..	..	..	..	..	..
2100 Employees	..	..	..	..	..	..	..	..	..	..
2110 On a payroll basis	..	..	..	..	..	..	..	..	..	..
2120 On an income tax basis	..	..	..	..	..	..	..	..	..	..
2200 Employers	..	..	..	..	..	..	..	..	..	..
2210 On a payroll basis	..	..	..	..	..	..	..	..	..	..
2220 On an income tax basis	..	..	..	..	..	..	..	..	..	..
2300 Self-employed or non-employed	..	..	..	..	..	..	..	..	..	..
2310 On a payroll basis	..	..	..	..	..	..	..	..	..	..
2320 On an income tax basis	..	..	..	..	..	..	..	..	..	..
2400 Unallocable between 2100, 2200 and 2300	202	5 905	42 176	96 896	..	..	..	..	..	..
2410 On a payroll basis	..	..	..	..	..	..	..	..	..	..
2420 On an income tax basis	..	..	..	..	..	..	..	..	..	..
3000 Taxes on payroll and workforce	**0**	**0**	**0**	**0**	**0**	**0**	**0**	**0**	..	..
4000 Taxes on property	**11**	**3 999**	**27 147**	**2 217**	**10 463**	**29 459**	**90 877**	**24 353 035**	..	..
4100 Recurrent taxes on immovable property	0	0	0	0	0	0	0	0	..	..
4110 Households	..	..	..	..	..	..	..	..	..	..
4120 Others	..	..	..	..	..	..	..	..	..	..
4200 Recurrent taxes on net wealth	0	0	0	0	0	0	0	0	..	..
4210 Individual	..	..	..	..	..	..	..	..	..	..
4220 Corporate	..	..	..	..	..	..	..	..	..	..
4300 Estate, inheritance and gift taxes	11	191	1 050	2 217	10 463	29 459	90 877	361 298	..	..
4310 Estate and inheritance taxes	11	191	1 050	2 217	10 463	29 459	90 877	361 298	..	..
4320 Gift taxes	0	0	0	0	0	0	0	0	..	..
4400 Taxes on financial and capital transactions	0	3 808	26 097	0	0	0	0	23 991 737	..	..
Bank debits	..	2 918	26 097	..	..	..	..	0	..	..
Registration of immovable property rights	..	890	0	..	..	..	..	0	..	..
Tax on Large Financial Transactions (IGTF)	..	0	0	..	..	..	..	23 991 737	..	..
4500 Non-recurrent taxes	0	0	0	0	0	0	0	0	..	..
4510 On net wealth	..	..	..	..	..	..	..	..	..	..
4520 Other non-recurrent taxes	..	..	..	..	..	..	..	..	..	..
4600 Other recurrent taxes on property	0	0	0	0	0	0	0	0	..	..
5000 Taxes on goods and services	**457**	**51 726**	**393 649**	**733 363**	**3 462 719**	**9 128 199**	**25 580 149**	**148 669 517**	..	..
5100 Taxes on production, sale, transfer, etc	457	51 726	393 649	733 363	3 462 719	9 128 199	25 580 149	148 669 517	..	..
5110 General taxes	0	32 716	278 954	561 005	2 721 869	7 027 427	19 070 779	112 990 174	..	..
5111 Value added taxes	0	32 716	278 954	561 005	2 721 869	7 027 427	19 070 779	112 990 174	..	..
5112 Sales tax	..	0	0	0	0	0	0	0	..	..
5113 Other	..	0	0	0	0	0	0	0	..	..
5120 Taxes on specific goods and services	457	19 011	114 695	172 357	740 850	2 100 772	6 509 370	35 679 343	..	..
5121 Excises	157	7 742	29 778	88 722	305 249	1 165 755	4 399 252	29 679 186	..	..
Oil	57	4 679	7 039	12 798	0	0	0	0	..	..
Alcoholic beverages	58	852	9 081	21 915	108 885	444 982	1 568 778	14 113 397	..	..
Tobacco	42	2 201	13 641	54 009	196 364	720 772	2 830 474	15 565 789	..	..
Matches	0	9	17	0	0	0	0	0	..	..
5122 Profits of fiscal monopolies	0	0	0	0	0	0	0	0	..	..
5123 Customs and import duties	300	9 716	82 713	81 333	433 979	932 598	2 103 519	5 986 482	..	..
5124 Taxes on exports	0	0	0	0	0	0	0	0	..	..
5125 Taxes on investment goods	0	0	0	0	0	0	0	0	..	..
5126 Taxes on specific services	0	1 552	2 204	2 302	1 621	2 419	6 600	13 675	..	..
Telecommunications	0	1 505	1 658	0	0	0	0	0	..	..
Casinos, bingo and slot machines	0	47	546	2 302	1 621	2 419	6 600	13 675	..	..
5127 Other taxes on internat. trade and transactions	0	0	0	0	0	0	0	0	..	..
5128 Other taxes	0	0	0	0	0	0	0	0	..	..
5130 Unallocable between 5110 and 5120	0	0	0	0	0	0	0	0	..	..
5200 Taxes on use of goods and perform activities	0	0	0	0	0	0	0	0	..	..
5210 Recurrent taxes	..	..	..	..	..	..	..	..	..	..
5211 Paid by households: motor vehicles	..	..	..	..	..	..	..	..	..	..
5212 Paid by others: motor vehicles	..	..	..	..	..	..	..	..	..	..

Table 5.27. **Venezuela** *(cont.)*

Details of tax revenue / Ingresos tributarios detallados

VES

	1990	2000	2007	2010	2014	2015	2016	2017	2018	2019
5213 Paid in respect of other goods	..	..	..	..	..	..	..	..	..	..
5220 Non-recurrent taxes	..	..	..	..	..	..	..	..	..	..
5300 Unallocable between 5100 and 5200	0	0	0	0	0	0	0	0	..	..
6000 Other taxes	**0**	**0**	**0**	**0**	**80 237**	**158 333**	**263 062**	**1 225 170**	**..**	**..**
6100 Paid solely by business	..	..	..	..	0	0	0	0	..	..
6200 Other	..	..	..	..	80 237	158 333	263 062	1 225 170	..	..

.. Not available

Note: Year ending 31st December.

The data are on a cash basis.

Data are not available for 2018 and 2019.

The figures exclude state and local government tax revenues as the data are not available.

The figures since 2015 should be interpreted with caution as they have been affected by the high rate of inflation over this period.

Total tax revenue data have not been available since 2014 due to missing data for social security contributions since 2014 and oil revenues since 2016 (classified in heading 1210 taxes on corporate profits).

Source: Servicio Nacional Integrado de Administración Aduanera (National Integrated Service of Customs); Ministerio de Finanzas (Ministry of Finance).

StatLink https://doi.org/10.1787/888934235981

Chapter 6

Tax revenues by sub-sectors of general government

Capítulo 6

Ingresos tributarios por subsectores de gobierno general

Chapter 6 / Capítulo 6

Tax revenues by sub-sectors of general government

Revenues of Latin American, Caribbean and OECD countries have been attributed to the different levels of government according to the revised guidelines set out in the final version of the 2008 System of National Accounts (SNA). Under this, revenues are generally attributed to the level of government that exercises the authority to impose the tax or has the final discretion to set and vary the tax rate.

Ingresos tributarios por subsectores de gobierno general

Los ingresos de los países latinoamericanos, del Caribe y de los países de la OCDE se han atribuido a los diferentes niveles de gobierno de acuerdo con lo recogido en la versión final 2008 del Sistema de Cuentas Nacionales (SCN). Según este los ingresos se atribuyen por lo general al nivel de gobierno que ejerce la facultad de aplicar el impuesto o que puede a su discreción establecer y modificar la tasa del impuesto.

Table 6.1. **Antigua and Barbuda, tax revenues by subsectores of government**

Million XCD

	Federal government					State/Regional				
	1990	2000	2010	2015	2019	1990	2000	2010	2015	2019
1000 Taxes on income, profits and capital gains	**..**	**38**	**92**	**89**	**79**	**..**	**..**	**..**	**..**	**..**
1100 Of individuals	..	0	33	37	1	..	..	..	..	..
1200 Corporate	..	37	59	52	79	..	..	..	..	..
1300 Unallocable between 1100 and 1200	..	0	0	0	0	..	..	..	..	..
2000 Social security contributions	**..**	**0**	**0**	**0**	**0**	**..**	**..**	**..**	**..**	**..**
2100 Employees	..	..	..	..	..	..	..	..	..	..
2200 Employers	..	..	..	..	..	..	..	..	..	..
2300 Self-employed or non-employed	..	..	..	..	..	..	..	..	..	..
2400 Unallocable between 2100, 2200 and 2300	..	..	..	..	..	..	..	..	..	..
3000 Taxes on payroll and workforce	**..**	**0**	**0**	**0**	**0**	**..**	**..**	**..**	**..**	**..**
4000 Taxes on property	**..**	**13**	**49**	**52**	**72**	**..**	**..**	**..**	**..**	**..**
4100 Recurrent taxes on immovable property	..	0	18	18	29	..	..	..	..	..
4200 Recurrent taxes on net wealth	..	0	0	0	0	..	..	..	..	..
4300 Estate, inheritance and gift taxes	..	0	0	0	0	..	..	..	..	..
4400 Taxes on financial and capital transactions	..	13	32	34	43	..	..	..	..	..
4500 Non-recurrent taxes	..	0	0	0	0	..	..	..	..	..
4600 Other recurrent taxes on property	..	0	0	0	0	..	..	..	..	..
5000 Taxes on goods and services	**..**	**217**	**435**	**481**	**521**	**..**	**..**	**..**	**..**	**..**
5100 Taxes on production, sale, transfer, etc	..	217	429	478	517	..	..	..	..	..
5110 General taxes	..	0	179	307	333	..	..	..	..	..
5120 Taxes on specific goods and services	..	217	250	171	185	..	..	..	..	..
5130 Unallocable between 5110 and 5120	..	0	0	0	0	..	..	..	..	..
5200 Taxes on use of goods and perform activities	..	0	6	3	4	..	..	..	..	..
5300 Unallocable between 5100 and 5200	..	0	0	0	0	..	..	..	..	..
6000 Other taxes	**..**	**0**	**0**	**0**	**0**	**..**	**..**	**..**	**..**	**..**
6100 Paid solely by business	..	..	..	..	..	..	..	..	..	..
6200 Other	..	..	..	..	..	..	..	..	..	..
Total tax revenue	**..**	**268**	**577**	**623**	**672**	**..**	**..**	**..**	**..**	**..**

Million XCD

	Local government[1]					Social Security Funds[2]				
	1990	2000	2010	2015	2019	1990	2000	2010	2015	2019
1000 Taxes on income, profits and capital gains	**..**	**..**	**..**	**..**	**..**	**..**	**..**	**0**	**0**	**0**
1100 Of individuals	..	..	..	..	..	..	..	..	..	..
1200 Corporate	..	..	..	..	..	..	..	..	..	..
1300 Unallocable between 1100 and 1200	..	..	..	..	..	..	..	..	..	..
2000 Social security contributions	**..**	**..**	**..**	**..**	**..**	**..**	**..**	**83**	**113**	**143**
2100 Employees	..	..	..	..	..	..	..	..	..	..
2200 Employers	..	..	..	..	..	..	..	..	..	..
2300 Self-employed or non-employed	..	..	..	..	..	..	..	..	..	..
2400 Unallocable between 2100, 2200 and 2300	..	..	..	..	..	..	..	83	113	143
3000 Taxes on payroll and workforce	**..**	**..**	**..**	**..**	**..**	**..**	**..**	**0**	**0**	**0**
4000 Taxes on property	**..**	**..**	**..**	**..**	**..**	**..**	**..**	**0**	**0**	**0**
4100 Recurrent taxes on immovable property	..	..	..	..	..	..	..	..	..	..
4200 Recurrent taxes on net wealth	..	..	..	..	..	..	..	..	..	..
4300 Estate, inheritance and gift taxes	..	..	..	..	..	..	..	..	..	..
4400 Taxes on financial and capital transactions	..	..	..	..	..	..	..	..	..	..
4500 Non-recurrent taxes	..	..	..	..	..	..	..	..	..	..
4600 Other recurrent taxes on property	..	..	..	..	..	..	..	..	..	..
5000 Taxes on goods and services	**..**	**..**	**..**	**..**	**..**	**..**	**..**	**0**	**0**	**0**
5100 Taxes on production, sale, transfer, etc	..	..	..	..	..	..	..	..	..	..
5110 General taxes	..	..	..	..	..	..	..	..	..	..
5120 Taxes on specific goods and services	..	..	..	..	..	..	..	..	..	..
5130 Unallocable between 5110 and 5120	..	..	..	..	..	..	..	..	..	..
5200 Taxes on use of goods and perform activities	..	..	..	..	..	..	..	..	..	..
5300 Unallocable between 5100 and 5200	..	..	..	..	..	..	..	..	..	..
6000 Other taxes	**..**	**..**	**..**	**..**	**..**	**..**	**..**	**0**	**0**	**0**
6100 Paid solely by business	..	..	..	..	..	..	..	..	..	..
6200 Other	..	..	..	..	..	..	..	..	..	..
Total tax revenue	**..**	**..**	**..**	**..**	**..**	**..**	**..**	**83**	**113**	**143**

.. Not available

1. Local government tax revenues are not available.
2. Figures for 2019 are estimated.

StatLink https://doi.org/10.1787/888934236000

Table 6.2. **Argentina, tax revenues by subsectores of government**

Million ARS

	Federal government					State/Regional				
	1990	2000	2010	2015	2019	1990	2000	2010	2015	2019
1000 Taxes on income, profits and capital gains	**542**	**11 303**	**78 427**	**384 536**	**1 102 982**	**0**	**0**	**0**	**0**	**0**
1100 Of individuals	141	3 937	23 980	188 218	434 464	..	..	..	..	..
1200 Corporate	357	6 575	50 664	185 725	591 961	..	..	..	..	..
1300 Unallocable between 1100 and 1200	43	792	3 783	10 593	76 556	..	..	..	..	..
2000 Social security contributions[1]	**0**	**0**	**0**	**0**	**0**	**0**	**0**	**0**	**0**	**0**
2100 Employees	..	..	..	..	..	..	..	..	..	..
2200 Employers	..	..	..	..	..	..	..	..	..	..
2300 Self-employed or non-employed	..	..	..	..	..	..	..	..	..	..
2400 Unallocable between 2100, 2200 and 2300	..	..	..	..	..	..	..	..	..	..
3000 Taxes on payroll and workforce	**0**	**0**	**0**	**0**	**0**	**0**	**0**	**0**	**0**	**0**
4000 Taxes on property	**616**	**1 254**	**32 674**	**117 274**	**387 518**	**549**	**2 614**	**10 864**	**48 908**	**174 217**
4100 Recurrent taxes on immovable property	0	0	0	0	0	419	1 809	5 035	21 738	88 405
4200 Recurrent taxes on net wealth	246	1 084	5 248	18 538	32 383	0	0	0	0	0
4300 Estate, inheritance and gift taxes	0	0	0	0	0	0	0	0	0	0
4400 Taxes on financial and capital transactions	330	100	27 423	98 736	355 135	130	804	5 829	27 170	85 812
4500 Non-recurrent taxes	40	70	3	0	0	0	0	0	0	0
4600 Other recurrent taxes on property	0	0	0	0	0	0	0	0	0	0
5000 Taxes on goods and services	**4 669**	**27 592**	**198 346**	**634 068**	**2 366 688**	**967**	**6 947**	**54 746**	**255 256**	**841 605**
5100 Taxes on production, sale, transfer, etc	4 671	28 174	201 402	642 899	2 395 958	791	6 114	51 148	238 221	784 122
5110 General taxes	1 594	19 009	116 386	433 076	1 532 597	791	6 114	51 148	238 221	784 122
5120 Taxes on specific goods and services	3 077	9 166	85 016	209 822	863 362	0	0	0	0	0
5130 Unallocable between 5110 and 5120	0	0	0	0	0	0	0	0	0	0
5200 Taxes on use of goods and perform activities[2]	..	..	..	..	..	177	833	3 598	17 035	57 483
5300 Unallocable between 5100 and 5200	-3	-583	-3 056	-8 831	-29 270	0	0	0	0	0
6000 Other taxes	**214**	**395**	**2 386**	**6 931**	**19 565**	**78**	**1 309**	**3 110**	**10 533**	**25 484**
6100 Paid solely by business	0	354	2 093	5 624	20 635	0	0	0	0	0
6200 Other[3]	214	41	294	1 306	-1 070	78	1 309	3 110	10 533	25 484
Total tax revenue	**6 040**	**40 544**	**311 834**	**1 142 808**	**3 876 753**	**1 594**	**10 870**	**68 720**	**314 697**	**1 041 306**

Million ARS

	Local government[4]					Social Security Funds				
	1990	2000	2010	2015	2019	1990	2000	2010	2015	2019
1000 Taxes on income, profits and capital gains	..	..	..	..	..	**0**	**0**	**0**	**0**	**0**
1100 Of individuals	..	..	..	..	..	..	..	..	..	..
1200 Corporate	..	..	..	..	..	..	..	..	..	..
1300 Unallocable between 1100 and 1200	..	..	..	..	..	..	..	..	..	..
2000 Social security contributions[1]	..	..	..	..	..	**2 583**	**9 670**	**102 460**	**415 410**	**1 225 673**
2100 Employees	..	..	..	..	..	..	2 486	37 990	163 590	475 772
2200 Employers	..	..	..	..	..	..	6 069	54 713	235 610	704 555
2300 Self-employed or non-employed	..	..	..	..	..	98	1 115	9 757	16 210	45 346
2400 Unallocable between 2100, 2200 and 2300	..	..	..	..	..	2 485	0	0	0	0
3000 Taxes on payroll and workforce	..	..	..	..	..	**0**	**0**	**0**	**0**	**0**
4000 Taxes on property	..	..	..	..	..	**0**	**0**	**0**	**0**	**0**
4100 Recurrent taxes on immovable property	..	..	..	..	..	..	..	..	..	..
4200 Recurrent taxes on net wealth	..	..	..	..	..	..	..	..	..	..
4300 Estate, inheritance and gift taxes	..	..	..	..	..	..	..	..	..	..
4400 Taxes on financial and capital transactions	..	..	..	..	..	..	..	..	..	..
4500 Non-recurrent taxes	..	..	..	..	..	..	..	..	..	..
4600 Other recurrent taxes on property	..	..	..	..	..	..	..	..	..	..
5000 Taxes on goods and services	..	..	..	..	..	**0**	**0**	**0**	**0**	**0**
5100 Taxes on production, sale, transfer, etc	..	..	..	..	..	..	..	..	..	..
5110 General taxes	..	..	..	..	..	..	..	..	..	..
5120 Taxes on specific goods and services	..	..	..	..	..	..	..	..	..	..
5130 Unallocable between 5110 and 5120	..	..	..	..	..	..	..	..	..	..
5200 Taxes on use of goods and perform activities[2]	..	..	..	..	..	..	..	..	..	..
5300 Unallocable between 5100 and 5200	..	..	..	..	..	..	..	..	..	..
6000 Other taxes	..	..	..	..	..	**0**	**0**	**0**	**0**	**0**
6100 Paid solely by business	..	..	..	..	..	..	..	..	..	..
6200 Other[3]	..	..	..	..	..	..	..	..	..	..
Total tax revenue	..	..	..	..	..	**2 583**	**9 670**	**102 460**	**415 410**	**1 225 673**

.. Not available

1. The figures may be under-estimated as they exclude certain types of social security contributions for which data are not readily available.
2. In ECLAC data, tax on ownership of motor vehicles is classified in category 4000.
3. The tax debt payments in 2016 include revenue following the implementation of a new voluntary disclosure regime in July 2016 (Law 27260).
4. The figures exclude local government tax revenues as the data are not available.

StatLink https://doi.org/10.1787/888934236019

Table 6.3. **Bahamas, tax revenues by subsectores of government**

Million BSD

	Federal government[1]					State/Regional				
	1990	2000	2010	2015	2019	1990	2000	2010	2015	2019
1000 Taxes on income, profits and capital gains	**0**	**0**	**0**	**0**	**0**	..	..	..	..	..
1100 Of individuals	0	0	0	0	0	..	..	..	..	..
1200 Corporate	0	0	0	0	0	..	..	..	..	..
1300 Unallocable between 1100 and 1200	0	0	0	0	0	..	..	..	..	..
2000 Social security contributions	**0**	**0**	**0**	**0**	**0**	..	..	..	..	..
2100 Employees	..	..	..	..	..	..	..	..	..	..
2200 Employers	..	..	..	..	..	..	..	..	..	..
2300 Self-employed or non-employed	..	..	..	..	..	..	..	..	..	..
2400 Unallocable between 2100, 2200 and 2300	..	..	..	..	..	..	..	..	..	..
3000 Taxes on payroll and workforce	**0**	**0**	**0**	**0**	**0**	..	..	..	..	..
4000 Taxes on property	**56**	**208**	**269**	**298**	**345**	..	..	..	..	..
4100 Recurrent taxes on immovable property	19	32	92	107	109	..	..	..	..	..
4200 Recurrent taxes on net wealth	0	0	0	0	0	..	..	..	..	..
4300 Estate, inheritance and gift taxes	0	0	0	0	0	..	..	..	..	..
4400 Taxes on financial and capital transactions	37	176	177	191	235	..	..	..	..	..
4500 Non-recurrent taxes	0	0	0	0	0	..	..	..	..	..
4600 Other recurrent taxes on property	0	0	0	0	0	..	..	..	..	..
5000 Taxes on goods and services	**386**	**620**	**780**	**1 203**	**1 854**	..	..	..	..	..
5100 Taxes on production, sale, transfer, etc	354	552	657	993	1 623	..	..	..	..	..
5110 General taxes	0	0	0	219	897	..	..	..	..	..
5120 Taxes on specific goods and services	354	552	657	775	727	..	..	..	..	..
5130 Unallocable between 5110 and 5120	0	0	0	0	0	..	..	..	..	..
5200 Taxes on use of goods and perform activities	32	69	123	209	231	..	..	..	..	..
5300 Unallocable between 5100 and 5200	0	0	0	0	0	..	..	..	..	..
6000 Other taxes	**-4**	**21**	**60**	**0**	**0**	..	..	..	..	..
6100 Paid solely by business	0	0	0	0	..	..	..	..	..	..
6200 Other	-4	21	60	0	..	..	..	..	..	..
Total tax revenue	**438**	**849**	**1 109**	**1 500**	**2 199**	..	..	..	..	..

Million BSD

	Local government[2]					Social Security Funds[3]				
	1990	2000	2010	2015	2019	1990	2000	2010	2015	2019
1000 Taxes on income, profits and capital gains	..	..	..	..	..	**0**	**0**	**0**	**0**	**0**
1100 Of individuals	..	..	..	..	..	..	..	..	..	..
1200 Corporate	..	..	..	..	..	..	..	..	..	..
1300 Unallocable between 1100 and 1200	..	..	..	..	..	..	..	..	..	..
2000 Social security contributions	..	..	..	..	..	**66**	**115**	**167**	**260**	**310**
2100 Employees	..	..	..	..	..	..	..	60	98	..
2200 Employers	..	..	..	..	..	..	..	104	157	..
2300 Self-employed or non-employed	..	..	..	..	..	..	..	3	6	..
2400 Unallocable between 2100, 2200 and 2300	..	..	..	..	..	66	115	0	-1	310
3000 Taxes on payroll and workforce	..	..	..	..	..	**0**	**0**	**0**	**0**	**0**
4000 Taxes on property	..	..	..	..	..	**0**	**0**	**0**	**0**	**0**
4100 Recurrent taxes on immovable property	..	..	..	..	..	..	..	..	..	..
4200 Recurrent taxes on net wealth	..	..	..	..	..	..	..	..	..	..
4300 Estate, inheritance and gift taxes	..	..	..	..	..	..	..	..	..	..
4400 Taxes on financial and capital transactions	..	..	..	..	..	..	..	..	..	..
4500 Non-recurrent taxes	..	..	..	..	..	..	..	..	..	..
4600 Other recurrent taxes on property	..	..	..	..	..	..	..	..	..	..
5000 Taxes on goods and services	..	..	..	..	..	**0**	**0**	**0**	**0**	**0**
5100 Taxes on production, sale, transfer, etc	..	..	..	..	..	..	..	..	..	..
5110 General taxes	..	..	..	..	..	..	..	..	..	..
5120 Taxes on specific goods and services	..	..	..	..	..	..	..	..	..	..
5130 Unallocable between 5110 and 5120	..	..	..	..	..	..	..	..	..	..
5200 Taxes on use of goods and perform activities	..	..	..	..	..	..	..	..	..	..
5300 Unallocable between 5100 and 5200	..	..	..	..	..	..	..	..	..	..
6000 Other taxes	..	..	..	..	..	**0**	**0**	**0**	**0**	..
6100 Paid solely by business	..	..	..	..	..	..	..	..	..	..
6200 Other	..	..	..	..	..	..	..	..	..	..
Total tax revenue	..	..	..	..	..	**66**	**115**	**167**	**260**	**310**

.. Not available

1. The data for 2018 and 2019 are preliminary as published by the Central Bank of The Bahamas.
2. Local government tax revenues are not available.
3. The data for social security contributions are estimated for 2018 and 2019.

StatLink https://doi.org/10.1787/888934236038

Table 6.4. **Barbados, tax revenues by subsectores of government**

Million BBD

	Federal government					State/Regional				
	1990	2000	2010	2015	2019	1990	2000	2010	2015	2019
1000 Taxes on income, profits and capital gains	**250**	**599**	**766**	**714**	**823**	**..**	**..**	**..**	**..**	**..**
1100 Of individuals	140	293	395	433	455	..	..	..	..	..
1200 Corporate	95	269	294	215	309	..	..	..	..	..
1300 Unallocable between 1100 and 1200	15	37	76	66	59	..	..	..	..	..
2000 Social security contributions	**0**	**0**	**0**	**0**	**0**	**..**	**..**	**..**	**..**	**..**
2100 Employees	..	..	..	..	..	..	..	..	..	..
2200 Employers	..	..	..	..	..	..	..	..	..	..
2300 Self-employed or non-employed	..	..	..	..	..	..	..	..	..	..
2400 Unallocable between 2100, 2200 and 2300	..	..	..	..	..	..	..	..	..	..
3000 Taxes on payroll and workforce	**0**	**0**	**0**	**0**	**0**	**..**	**..**	**..**	**..**	**..**
4000 Taxes on property	**147**	**108**	**130**	**143**	**226**	**..**	**..**	**..**	**..**	**..**
4100 Recurrent taxes on immovable property	46	95	118	133	215	..	..	..	..	..
4200 Recurrent taxes on net wealth	0	0	0	0	0	..	..	..	..	..
4300 Estate, inheritance and gift taxes	0	0	0	0	0	..	..	..	..	..
4400 Taxes on financial and capital transactions	101	13	12	10	11	..	..	..	..	..
4500 Non-recurrent taxes	0	0	0	0	0	..	..	..	..	..
4600 Other recurrent taxes on property	0	0	0	0	0	..	..	..	..	..
5000 Taxes on goods and services	**495**	**889**	**1 276**	**1 410**	**1 723**	**..**	**..**	**..**	**..**	**..**
5100 Taxes on production, sale, transfer, etc	424	788	1 105	1 291	1 607	..	..	..	..	..
5110 General taxes	197	492	768	861	967	..	..	..	..	..
5120 Taxes on specific goods and services	227	296	337	430	640	..	..	..	..	..
5130 Unallocable between 5110 and 5120	0	0	0	0	0	..	..	..	..	..
5200 Taxes on use of goods and perform activities	71	101	171	119	115	..	..	..	..	..
5300 Unallocable between 5100 and 5200	0	0	0	0	0	..	..	..	..	..
6000 Other taxes	**0**	**0**	**0**	**0**	**0**	**..**	**..**	**..**	**..**	**..**
6100 Paid solely by business	..	..	..	..	..	..	..	..	..	..
6200 Other	..	..	..	..	..	..	..	..	..	..
Total tax revenue	**892**	**1 596**	**2 171**	**2 266**	**2 771**	**..**	**..**	**..**	**..**	**..**

Million BBD

	Local government[1]					Social Security Funds[2]				
	1990	2000	2010	2015	2019	1990	2000	2010	2015	2019
1000 Taxes on income, profits and capital gains	**..**	**..**	**..**	**..**	**..**	**0**	**0**	**0**	**0**	**0**
1100 Of individuals	..	..	..	..	..	..	..	..	..	..
1200 Corporate	..	..	..	..	..	..	..	..	..	..
1300 Unallocable between 1100 and 1200	..	..	..	..	..	..	..	..	..	..
2000 Social security contributions	**..**	**..**	**..**	**..**	**..**	**134**	**295**	**565**	**546**	**586**
2100 Employees	..	..	..	..	..	..	..	..	..	..
2200 Employers	..	..	..	..	..	..	..	..	..	..
2300 Self-employed or non-employed	..	..	..	..	..	..	..	..	..	..
2400 Unallocable between 2100, 2200 and 2300	..	..	..	..	..	134	295	565	546	586
3000 Taxes on payroll and workforce	**..**	**..**	**..**	**..**	**..**	**0**	**0**	**0**	**0**	**0**
4000 Taxes on property	**..**	**..**	**..**	**..**	**..**	**0**	**0**	**0**	**0**	**0**
4100 Recurrent taxes on immovable property	..	..	..	..	..	..	..	..	..	..
4200 Recurrent taxes on net wealth	..	..	..	..	..	..	..	..	..	..
4300 Estate, inheritance and gift taxes	..	..	..	..	..	..	..	..	..	..
4400 Taxes on financial and capital transactions	..	..	..	..	..	..	..	..	..	..
4500 Non-recurrent taxes	..	..	..	..	..	..	..	..	..	..
4600 Other recurrent taxes on property	..	..	..	..	..	..	..	..	..	..
5000 Taxes on goods and services	**..**	**..**	**..**	**..**	**..**	**0**	**0**	**0**	**0**	**0**
5100 Taxes on production, sale, transfer, etc	..	..	..	..	..	..	..	..	..	..
5110 General taxes	..	..	..	..	..	..	..	..	..	..
5120 Taxes on specific goods and services	..	..	..	..	..	..	..	..	..	..
5130 Unallocable between 5110 and 5120	..	..	..	..	..	..	..	..	..	..
5200 Taxes on use of goods and perform activities	..	..	..	..	..	..	..	..	..	..
5300 Unallocable between 5100 and 5200	..	..	..	..	..	..	..	..	..	..
6000 Other taxes	**..**	**..**	**..**	**..**	**..**	**0**	**0**	**0**	**0**	**0**
6100 Paid solely by business	..	..	..	..	..	..	..	..	..	..
6200 Other	..	..	..	..	..	..	..	..	..	..
Total tax revenue	**..**	**..**	**..**	**..**	**..**	**134**	**295**	**565**	**546**	**586**

.. Not available

1. Local government tax revenues are not available.
2. The data for social security contributions are government projections for 2015-19.

StatLink https://doi.org/10.1787/888934236057

Table 6.5. **Belize, tax revenues by subsectores of government**

Million BZD

	Federal government[1]					State/Regional				
	1990	2000	2010	2015	2019	1990	2000	2010	2015	2019
1000 Taxes on income, profits and capital gains	**37**	**76**	**248**	**254**	**300**	..	..	..	..	..
1100 Of individuals	21	19	52	82	103	..	..	..	..	..
1200 Corporate	12	51	189	159	185	..	..	..	..	..
1300 Unallocable between 1100 and 1200	4	6	7	13	12	..	..	..	..	..
2000 Social security contributions	**0**	**0**	**0**	**0**	**0**	..	..	..	..	..
2100 Employees	..	..	..	..	..	..	..	..	..	..
2200 Employers	..	..	..	..	..	..	..	..	..	..
2300 Self-employed or non-employed	..	..	..	..	..	..	..	..	..	..
2400 Unallocable between 2100, 2200 and 2300	..	..	..	..	..	..	..	..	..	..
3000 Taxes on payroll and workforce	**0**	**0**	**0**	**0**	**0**	..	..	..	..	..
4000 Taxes on property	**33**	**11**	**16**	**29**	**35**	..	..	..	..	..
4100 Recurrent taxes on immovable property	0	0	0	0	0	..	..	..	..	..
4200 Recurrent taxes on net wealth	0	0	0	0	0	..	..	..	..	..
4300 Estate, inheritance and gift taxes	0	0	0	0	0	..	..	..	..	..
4400 Taxes on financial and capital transactions	33	11	16	29	35	..	..	..	..	..
4500 Non-recurrent taxes	0	0	0	0	0	..	..	..	..	..
4600 Other recurrent taxes on property	0	0	0	0	0	..	..	..	..	..
5000 Taxes on goods and services	**97**	**211**	**409**	**580**	**749**	..	..	..	..	..
5100 Taxes on production, sale, transfer, etc	94	207	400	571	737	..	..	..	..	..
5110 General taxes	0	82	199	275	348	..	..	..	..	..
5120 Taxes on specific goods and services	94	125	200	296	389	..	..	..	..	..
5130 Unallocable between 5110 and 5120	0	0	0	0	0	..	..	..	..	..
5200 Taxes on use of goods and perform activities	3	4	9	9	11	..	..	..	..	..
5300 Unallocable between 5100 and 5200	0	0	0	0	0	..	..	..	..	..
6000 Other taxes	**0**	**0**	**0**	**0**	**0**	..	..	..	..	..
6100 Paid solely by business	..	..	..	..	..	..	..	..	..	..
6200 Other	..	..	..	..	..	..	..	..	..	..
Total tax revenue	**167**	**298**	**673**	**864**	**1 083**	..	..	..	..	..

Million BZD

	Local government[1]					Social Security Funds				
	1990	2000	2010	2015	2019	1990	2000	2010	2015	2019
1000 Taxes on income, profits and capital gains	**0**	**0**	**0**	**0**	**0**	**0**	**0**	**0**	**0**	**0**
1100 Of individuals	..	..	..	..	..	..	..	..	..	..
1200 Corporate	..	..	..	..	..	..	..	..	..	..
1300 Unallocable between 1100 and 1200	..	..	..	..	..	..	..	..	..	..
2000 Social security contributions	**0**	**0**	**0**	**0**	**0**	**10**	**18**	**60**	**77**	**100**
2100 Employees	..	..	..	..	..	..	..	..	..	..
2200 Employers	..	..	..	..	..	..	..	..	..	..
2300 Self-employed or non-employed	..	..	..	..	..	..	..	..	..	..
2400 Unallocable between 2100, 2200 and 2300	..	..	..	..	..	10	18	60	77	100
3000 Taxes on payroll and workforce	**0**	**0**	**0**	**0**	**0**	**0**	**0**	**0**	**0**	**0**
4000 Taxes on property	**1**	**2**	**7**	**5**	**6**	**0**	**0**	**0**	**0**	**0**
4100 Recurrent taxes on immovable property	1	2	7	5	6	..	..	..	..	..
4200 Recurrent taxes on net wealth	0	0	0	0	0	..	..	..	..	..
4300 Estate, inheritance and gift taxes	0	0	0	0	0	..	..	..	..	..
4400 Taxes on financial and capital transactions	0	0	0	0	0	..	..	..	..	..
4500 Non-recurrent taxes	0	0	0	0	0	..	..	..	..	..
4600 Other recurrent taxes on property	0	0	0	0	0	..	..	..	..	..
5000 Taxes on goods and services	**0**	**0**	**0**	**0**	**0**	**0**	**0**	**0**	**0**	**0**
5100 Taxes on production, sale, transfer, etc	..	..	..	..	..	..	..	..	..	..
5110 General taxes	..	..	..	..	..	..	..	..	..	..
5120 Taxes on specific goods and services	..	..	..	..	..	..	..	..	..	..
5130 Unallocable between 5110 and 5120	..	..	..	..	..	..	..	..	..	..
5200 Taxes on use of goods and perform activities	..	..	..	..	..	..	..	..	..	..
5300 Unallocable between 5100 and 5200	..	..	..	..	..	..	..	..	..	..
6000 Other taxes	**0**	**0**	**0**	**0**	**0**	**0**	**0**	**0**	**0**	**0**
6100 Paid solely by business	..	..	..	..	..	..	..	..	..	..
6200 Other	..	..	..	..	..	..	..	..	..	..
Total tax revenue	**1**	**2**	**7**	**5**	**6**	**10**	**18**	**60**	**77**	**100**

.. Not available

1. The data for 2019 are revised estimates as presented by the *Approved Estimates of Revenue and Expenditure for Fiscal Year 2020/2021.*

StatLink https://doi.org/10.1787/888934236076

Table 6.6. **Bolivia, tax revenues by subsectores of government**

Million BOB

	Federal government					State/Regional				
	1990	2000	2010	2015	2019	1990	2000	2010	2015	2019
1000 Taxes on income, profits and capital gains	**68**	**1 209**	**6 294**	**12 809**	**11 356**	**..**	**..**	**..**	**..**	**..**
1100 Of individuals	68	214	263	508	518	..	..	..	..	..
1200 Corporate	0	995	6 031	12 302	10 838	..	..	..	..	..
1300 Unallocable between 1100 and 1200	0	0	0	0	0	..	..	..	..	..
2000 Social security contributions	**0**	**0**	**0**	**0**	**0**	**..**	**..**	**..**	**..**	**..**
2100 Employees	..	..	..	..	..	..	..	..	..	..
2200 Employers	..	..	..	..	..	..	..	..	..	..
2300 Self-employed or non-employed	..	..	..	..	..	..	..	..	..	..
2400 Unallocable between 2100, 2200 and 2300	..	..	..	..	..	..	..	..	..	..
3000 Taxes on payroll and workforce	**0**	**0**	**0**	**0**	**0**	**..**	**..**	**..**	**..**	**..**
4000 Taxes on property	**1**	**3**	**367**	**424**	**522**	**..**	**..**	**..**	**..**	**..**
4100 Recurrent taxes on immovable property	0	0	0	0	0	..	..	..	..	..
4200 Recurrent taxes on net wealth	0	0	0	0	0	..	..	..	..	..
4300 Estate, inheritance and gift taxes	1	3	20	36	0	..	..	..	..	..
4400 Taxes on financial and capital transactions	0	0	347	388	522	..	..	..	..	..
4500 Non-recurrent taxes	0	0	0	0	0	..	..	..	..	..
4600 Other recurrent taxes on property	0	0	0	0	0	..	..	..	..	..
5000 Taxes on goods and services	**907**	**6 656**	**17 791**	**34 759**	**34 187**	**..**	**..**	**..**	**..**	**..**
5100 Taxes on production, sale, transfer, etc	907	6 656	17 791	34 759	34 187	..	..	..	..	..
5110 General taxes	584	3 953	12 541	25 247	25 405	..	..	..	..	..
5120 Taxes on specific goods and services	324	2 702	5 250	9 511	8 782	..	..	..	..	..
5130 Unallocable between 5110 and 5120	0	0	0	0	0	..	..	..	..	..
5200 Taxes on use of goods and perform activities	0	0	0	0	0	..	..	..	..	..
5300 Unallocable between 5100 and 5200	0	0	0	0	0	..	..	..	..	..
6000 Other taxes	**30**	**42**	**451**	**2 452**	**3 017**	**..**	**..**	**..**	**..**	**..**
6100 Paid solely by business	4	6	12	25	36	..	..	..	..	..
6200 Other	26	36	439	2 427	2 981	..	..	..	..	..
Total tax revenue	**1 005**	**7 910**	**24 903**	**50 444**	**49 082**	**..**	**..**	**..**	**..**	**..**

Million BOB

	Local government[1]					Social Security Funds[2]				
	1990	2000	2010	2015	2019	1990	2000	2010	2015	2019
1000 Taxes on income, profits and capital gains	**..**	**0**	**0**	**0**	**0**	**..**	**0**	**0**	**0**	**0**
1100 Of individuals	..	..	..	..	..	..	..	..	..	..
1200 Corporate	..	..	..	..	..	..	..	..	..	..
1300 Unallocable between 1100 and 1200	..	..	..	..	..	..	..	..	..	..
2000 Social security contributions	**..**	**0**	**0**	**0**	**0**	**..**	**1 977**	**5 265**	**14 235**	**17 500**
2100 Employees	..	..	..	..	..	..	..	..	..	..
2200 Employers	..	..	..	..	..	..	..	..	..	..
2300 Self-employed or non-employed	..	..	..	..	..	..	..	..	..	..
2400 Unallocable between 2100, 2200 and 2300	..	..	..	..	..	..	1 977	5 265	14 235	17 500
3000 Taxes on payroll and workforce	**..**	**0**	**0**	**0**	**0**	**..**	**0**	**0**	**0**	**0**
4000 Taxes on property	**..**	**0**	**0**	**0**	**0**	**..**	**0**	**0**	**0**	**0**
4100 Recurrent taxes on immovable property	..	..	..	..	..	..	..	..	..	..
4200 Recurrent taxes on net wealth	..	..	..	..	..	..	..	..	..	..
4300 Estate, inheritance and gift taxes	..	..	..	..	..	..	..	..	..	..
4400 Taxes on financial and capital transactions	..	..	..	..	..	..	..	..	..	..
4500 Non-recurrent taxes	..	..	..	..	..	..	..	..	..	..
4600 Other recurrent taxes on property	..	..	..	..	..	..	..	..	..	..
5000 Taxes on goods and services	**..**	**0**	**0**	**0**	**0**	**..**	**0**	**0**	**0**	**0**
5100 Taxes on production, sale, transfer, etc	..	..	..	..	..	..	..	..	..	..
5110 General taxes	..	..	..	..	..	..	..	..	..	..
5120 Taxes on specific goods and services	..	..	..	..	..	..	..	..	..	..
5130 Unallocable between 5110 and 5120	..	..	..	..	..	..	..	..	..	..
5200 Taxes on use of goods and perform activities	..	..	..	..	..	..	..	..	..	..
5300 Unallocable between 5100 and 5200	..	..	..	..	..	..	..	..	..	..
6000 Other taxes	**..**	**575**	**1 381**	**2 585**	**3 203**	**..**	**0**	**0**	**0**	**0**
6100 Paid solely by business	..	0	0	0	0	..	..	..	..	..
6200 Other	..	575	1 381	2 585	3 203	..	..	..	..	..
Total tax revenue	**..**	**575**	**1 381**	**2 585**	**3 203**	**..**	**1 977**	**5 265**	**14 235**	**17 500**

.. Not available

1. The figures exclude local government tax revenues for the period 1990-1993 as the data are not available.
2. The data for social security contributions include contributions to Bolivia's pension system and healthcare related funds.

StatLink https://doi.org/10.1787/888934236095

Table 6.7. **Brazil, tax revenues by subsectores of government**

Million BRL

	Federal government					State/Regional				
	1990	2000	2010	2015	2019	1990	2000	2010	2015	2019
1000 Taxes on income, profits and capital gains	**1**	**68 667**	**258 738**	**400 993**	**537 937**	**0**	**0**	**0**	**0**	**0**
1100 Of individuals	0	3 406	87 828	148 739	220 195	..	..	..	..	..
1200 Corporate	0	25 430	128 255	164 057	207 505	..	..	..	..	..
1300 Unallocable between 1100 and 1200	0	39 831	42 656	88 196	110 237	..	..	..	..	..
2000 Social security contributions	**0**	**0**	**0**	**0**	**0**	**0**	**0**	**0**	**0**	**0**
2100 Employees	..	..	..	..	..	..	..	..	..	..
2200 Employers	..	..	..	..	..	..	..	..	..	..
2300 Self-employed or non-employed	..	..	..	..	..	..	..	..	..	..
2400 Unallocable between 2100, 2200 and 2300	..	..	..	..	..	..	..	..	..	..
3000 Taxes on payroll and workforce	**0**	**5 437**	**21 348**	**37 891**	**42 527**	**0**	**0**	**0**	**0**	**0**
4000 Taxes on property	**0**	**17 726**	**27 044**	**35 791**	**42 575**	**0**	**329**	**2 518**	**6 461**	**8 625**
4100 Recurrent taxes on immovable property	0	234	485	1 105	1 630	0	0	0	0	0
4200 Recurrent taxes on net wealth	0	0	0	0	0	0	0	0	0	0
4300 Estate, inheritance and gift taxes	0	0	0	0	0	0	329	2 518	6 461	8 625
4400 Taxes on financial and capital transactions	0	17 492	26 559	34 686	40 945	0	0	0	0	0
4500 Non-recurrent taxes	0	0	0	0	0	0	0	0	0	0
4600 Other recurrent taxes on property	0	0	0	0	0	0	0	0	0	0
5000 Taxes on goods and services	**1**	**75 502**	**256 256**	**357 270**	**405 691**	**1**	**87 573**	**289 483**	**432 647**	**555 045**
5100 Taxes on production, sale, transfer, etc	1	75 502	250 857	348 492	404 664	1	82 279	268 117	396 428	508 832
5110 General taxes[1]	0	48 358	182 188	253 356	301 388	1	82 279	268 117	396 428	508 832
5120 Taxes on specific goods and services	0	27 144	68 669	95 136	103 276	0	0	0	0	0
5130 Unallocable between 5110 and 5120	0	0	0	0	0	0	0	0	0	0
5200 Taxes on use of goods and perform activities	0	0	5 399	8 778	1 027	0	5 294	21 367	36 219	46 213
5300 Unallocable between 5100 and 5200	0	0	0	0	0	0	0	0	0	0
6000 Other taxes[2]	**0**	**1 479**	**5 548**	**5 423**	**16 516**	**0**	**322**	**17 038**	**28 983**	**26 145**
6100 Paid solely by business	0	0	0	0	0	0	0	0	0	0
6200 Other	0	1 479	5 548	5 423	16 516	0	322	17 038	28 983	26 145
Total tax revenue	**1**	**168 811**	**568 934**	**837 368**	**1 045 245**	**1**	**88 224**	**309 040**	**468 091**	**589 815**

Million BRL

	Local government					Social Security Funds				
	1990	2000	2010	2015	2019	1990	2000	2010	2015	2019
1000 Taxes on income, profits and capital gains	**0**	**0**	**0**	**0**	**0**	**0**	**0**	**0**	**0**	**0**
1100 Of individuals	..	..	..	..	..	..	..	..	..	..
1200 Corporate	..	..	..	..	..	..	..	..	..	..
1300 Unallocable between 1100 and 1200	..	..	..	..	..	..	..	..	..	..
2000 Social security contributions	**0**	**0**	**0**	**0**	**0**	**1**	**83 469**	**316 530**	**503 222**	**617 445**
2100 Employees	..	..	..	..	..	..	..	75 509	114 653	..
2200 Employers	..	..	..	..	..	0	18 709	240 280	369 094	128 710
2300 Self-employed or non-employed	..	..	..	..	..	..	..	..	..	..
2400 Unallocable between 2100, 2200 and 2300	..	..	..	..	..	1	64 760	741	19 474	488 736
3000 Taxes on payroll and workforce	**0**	**0**	**0**	**0**	**0**	**0**	**0**	**0**	**0**	**0**
4000 Taxes on property	**0**	**5 469**	**23 285**	**41 426**	**59 621**	**0**	**0**	**0**	**0**	**0**
4100 Recurrent taxes on immovable property	0	4 519	17 444	31 521	47 053	..	..	..	..	..
4200 Recurrent taxes on net wealth	0	0	0	0	0	..	..	..	..	..
4300 Estate, inheritance and gift taxes	0	0	0	0	0	..	..	..	..	..
4400 Taxes on financial and capital transactions	0	950	5 840	9 904	12 568	..	..	..	..	..
4500 Non-recurrent taxes	0	0	0	0	0	..	..	..	..	..
4600 Other recurrent taxes on property	0	0	0	0	0	..	..	..	..	..
5000 Taxes on goods and services	**0**	**6 106**	**32 756**	**54 455**	**68 160**	**0**	**0**	**0**	**0**	**0**
5100 Taxes on production, sale, transfer, etc	0	6 106	32 756	54 455	68 160	..	..	..	..	..
5110 General taxes[1]	0	6 106	32 756	54 455	68 160	..	..	..	..	..
5120 Taxes on specific goods and services	0	0	0	0	0	..	..	..	..	..
5130 Unallocable between 5110 and 5120	0	0	0	0	0	..	..	..	..	..
5200 Taxes on use of goods and perform activities	0	0	0	0	0	..	..	..	..	..
5300 Unallocable between 5100 and 5200	0	0	0	0	0	..	..	..	..	..
6000 Other taxes[2]	**0**	**377**	**8 572**	**14 627**	**21 707**	**0**	**0**	**0**	**0**	**0**
6100 Paid solely by business	0	0	0	0	0	..	..	..	..	..
6200 Other	0	377	8 572	14 627	21 707	..	..	..	..	..
Total tax revenue	**0**	**11 952**	**64 613**	**110 507**	**149 488**	**1**	**83 469**	**316 530**	**503 222**	**617 445**

.. Not available

1. The PASEP (Program of Formation of the Patrimony of the Public Servants) contributions are added to the PIS (Social Integration Program) contributions in heading 5110 for the years prior to 2000.
2. The FUNDAF (Special Fund for Development and Improvement of Auditing Activities) contributions are included in heading 6200 after 2008.

StatLink https://doi.org/10.1787/888934236114

Table 6.8. **Chile, tax revenues by subsectors of government**

Million CLP

	Federal government					State/Regional				
	1990	2000	2010	2015	2019	1990	2000	2010	2015	2019
1000 Taxes on income, profits and capital gains	**412 974**	**1 841 630**	**8 329 060**	**11 840 521**	**14 283 183**	**..**	**..**	**..**	**..**	**..**
1100 Of individuals	99 154	604 100	1 492 837	3 199 876	2 937 532	..	..	..	..	..
1200 Corporate	219 586	882 896	4 448 745	6 839 133	9 597 472	..	..	..	..	..
1300 Unallocable between 1100 and 1200	94 233	354 634	2 387 478	1 801 512	1 748 179	..	..	..	..	..
2000 Social security contributions	**66 738**	**232 728**	**371 386**	**434 658**	**495 073**	**..**	**..**	**..**	**..**	**..**
2100 Employees	61 200	209 907	310 558	370 744	394 892	..	..	..	..	..
2200 Employers	5 538	22 821	60 828	63 914	100 181	..	..	..	..	..
2300 Self-employed or non-employed	0	0	0	0	0	..	..	..	..	..
2400 Unallocable between 2100, 2200 and 2300	0	0	0	0	0	..	..	..	..	..
3000 Taxes on payroll and workforce	**0**	**0**	**0**	**0**	**0**	**..**	**..**	**..**	**..**	**..**
4000 Taxes on property	**59 682**	**255 371**	**245 044**	**379 603**	**759 291**	**..**	**..**	**..**	**..**	**..**
4100 Recurrent taxes on immovable property	10 331	3 578	8 805	15 249	23 912	..	..	..	..	..
4200 Recurrent taxes on net wealth	0	0	0	0	0	..	..	..	..	..
4300 Estate, inheritance and gift taxes	3 444	10 906	39 338	92 236	62 824	..	..	..	..	..
4400 Taxes on financial and capital transactions	45 907	240 886	196 901	272 118	672 555	..	..	..	..	..
4500 Non-recurrent taxes	0	0	0	0	0	..	..	..	..	..
4600 Other recurrent taxes on property	0	0	0	0	0	..	..	..	..	..
5000 Taxes on goods and services	**1 063 677**	**4 719 255**	**10 330 378**	**16 181 720**	**19 839 047**	**..**	**..**	**..**	**..**	**..**
5100 Taxes on production, sale, transfer, etc	1 060 304	4 684 525	10 294 165	16 129 953	19 656 251	..	..	..	..	..
5110 General taxes	664 421	3 306 350	8 399 926	13 273 958	16 348 944	..	..	..	..	..
5120 Taxes on specific goods and services[1]	395 883	1 378 175	1 894 239	2 855 995	3 307 307	..	..	..	..	..
5130 Unallocable between 5110 and 5120	0	0	0	0	0	..	..	..	..	..
5200 Taxes on use of goods and perform activities	3 374	34 730	36 213	51 767	182 796	..	..	..	..	..
5300 Unallocable between 5100 and 5200	0	0	0	0	0	..	..	..	..	..
6000 Other taxes	**-23 356**	**-112 195**	**-61 117**	**-579 308**	**-253 490**	**..**	**..**	**..**	**..**	**..**
6100 Paid solely by business	0	0	0	0	0	..	..	..	..	..
6200 Other	-23 356	-112 195	-61 117	-579 308	-253 490	..	..	..	..	..
Total tax revenue	**1 579 715**	**6 936 788**	**19 214 751**	**28 257 194**	**35 123 104**	**..**	**..**	**..**	**..**	**..**

Million CLP

	Local government					Social Security Funds				
	1990	2000	2010	2015	2019	1990	2000	2010	2015	2019
1000 Taxes on income, profits and capital gains	**0**	**0**	**0**	**0**	**0**	**0**	**0**	**0**	**0**	**0**
1100 Of individuals	..	..	..	..	..	..	..	..	..	..
1200 Corporate	..	..	..	..	..	..	..	..	..	..
1300 Unallocable between 1100 and 1200	..	..	..	..	..	..	..	..	..	..
2000 Social security contributions	**0**	**0**	**0**	**0**	**0**	**92 821**	**344 030**	**1 122 601**	**1 817 831**	**2 499 833**
2100 Employees	..	..	..	..	..	92 821	344 030	1 122 601	1 817 831	2 499 833
2200 Employers	..	..	..	..	..	0	0	0	0	0
2300 Self-employed or non-employed	..	..	..	..	..	0	0	0	0	0
2400 Unallocable between 2100, 2200 and 2300	..	..	..	..	..	0	0	0	0	0
3000 Taxes on payroll and workforce	**0**	**0**	**0**	**0**	**0**	**0**	**0**	**0**	**0**	**0**
4000 Taxes on property	**49 637**	**298 666**	**653 563**	**1 041 671**	**1 458 355**	**0**	**0**	**0**	**0**	**0**
4100 Recurrent taxes on immovable property	49 637	298 666	653 563	1 041 671	1 458 355	..	..	..	..	..
4200 Recurrent taxes on net wealth	0	0	0	0	0	..	..	..	..	..
4300 Estate, inheritance and gift taxes	0	0	0	0	0	..	..	..	..	..
4400 Taxes on financial and capital transactions	0	0	0	0	0	..	..	..	..	..
4500 Non-recurrent taxes	0	0	0	0	0	..	..	..	..	..
4600 Other recurrent taxes on property	0	0	0	0	0	..	..	..	..	..
5000 Taxes on goods and services	**55 045**	**322 514**	**854 778**	**1 415 658**	**1 910 702**	**0**	**0**	**0**	**0**	**0**
5100 Taxes on production, sale, transfer, etc	13 705	105 302	238 739	385 532	506 341	..	..	..	..	..
5110 General taxes	0	0	0	0	0	..	..	..	..	..
5120 Taxes on specific goods and services[1]	13 705	105 302	238 739	385 532	506 341	..	..	..	..	..
5130 Unallocable between 5110 and 5120	0	0	0	0	0	..	..	..	..	..
5200 Taxes on use of goods and perform activities	41 340	217 212	616 039	1 030 126	1 404 361	..	..	..	..	..
5300 Unallocable between 5100 and 5200	0	0	0	0	0	..	..	..	..	..
6000 Other taxes	**0**	**0**	**0**	**0**	**0**	**0**	**0**	**0**	**0**	**0**
6100 Paid solely by business	..	..	..	..	..	..	..	..	..	..
6200 Other	..	..	..	..	..	..	..	..	..	..
Total tax revenue	**104 682**	**621 180**	**1 508 341**	**2 457 329**	**3 369 057**	**92 821**	**344 030**	**1 122 601**	**1 817 831**	**2 499 833**

.. Not available

1. ECLAC classifies Oil Prices Stabilisation Fund (FEPP) revenues as non-tax revenues.

StatLink https://doi.org/10.1787/888934236133

Table 6.9. **Colombia, tax revenues by subsectores of government**

Million COP

	Federal government					State/Regional[1]				
	1990	2000	2010	2015	2019	1990	2000	2010	2015	2019
1000 Taxes on income, profits and capital gains	**771 694**	**7 103 525**	**26 218 852**	**52 656 876**	**67 518 500**	**0**	**0**	**0**	**0**	**0**
1100 Of individuals	47 210	1 499 345	5 192 384	9 210 448	12 888 180	..	..	..	..	..
1200 Corporate	359 758	5 119 828	20 405 209	41 398 731	51 151 754	..	..	..	..	..
1300 Unallocable between 1100 and 1200	364 726	484 352	621 258	2 047 697	3 478 566	..	..	..	..	..
2000 Social security contributions	**0**	**0**	**0**	**0**	**0**	**0**	**0**	**0**	**0**	**0**
2100 Employees	..	..	..	..	..	..	..	..	..	..
2200 Employers	..	..	..	..	..	..	..	..	..	..
2300 Self-employed or non-employed	..	..	..	..	..	..	..	..	..	..
2400 Unallocable between 2100, 2200 and 2300	..	..	..	..	..	..	..	..	..	..
3000 Taxes on payroll and workforce	**0**	**1 286 803**	**4 022 503**	**2 797 308**	**3 604 071**	**0**	**0**	**0**	**0**	**0**
4000 Taxes on property	**0**	**1 036 584**	**5 196 303**	**12 094 140**	**10 241 299**	**0**	**0**	**0**	**0**	**0**
4100 Recurrent taxes on immovable property	..	0	0	0	0	..	..	..	..	..
4200 Recurrent taxes on net wealth	..	0	1 970 530	5 352 940	923 255	..	..	..	..	..
4300 Estate, inheritance and gift taxes	..	0	0	0	0	..	..	..	..	..
4400 Taxes on financial and capital transactions	..	1 036 584	3 225 773	6 741 200	8 190 516	..	..	..	..	..
4500 Non-recurrent taxes	..	0	0	0	1 127 528	..	..	..	..	..
4600 Other recurrent taxes on property	..	0	0	0	0	..	..	..	..	..
5000 Taxes on goods and services	**1 035 934**	**11 108 594**	**35 382 852**	**51 831 190**	**70 638 176**	**263 429**	**1 481 725**	**3 406 301**	**4 986 314**	**7 465 044**
5100 Taxes on production, sale, transfer, etc	1 035 934	11 108 594	35 382 852	51 831 190	70 638 176	263 429	1 349 930	3 032 733	4 456 650	6 493 375
5110 General taxes	583 078	8 445 776	28 811 682	41 659 696	61 938 202	0	0	0	0	0
5120 Taxes on specific goods and services	452 856	2 662 818	6 571 170	10 171 494	8 699 973	263 429	1 349 930	3 032 733	4 456 650	6 493 375
5130 Unallocable between 5110 and 5120	0	0	0	0	0	0	0	0	0	0
5200 Taxes on use of goods and perform activities	0	0	0	0	0	0	131 795	373 568	529 665	971 670
5300 Unallocable between 5100 and 5200	0	0	0	0	0	0	0	0	0	0
6000 Other taxes	**78 306**	**480 784**	**483 762**	**419 939**	**619 651**	**0**	**241 471**	**1 374 970**	**2 624 769**	**2 975 868**
6100 Paid solely by business	0	0	0	0	0	..	0	0	0	0
6200 Other	78 306	480 784	483 762	419 939	619 651	..	241 471	1 374 970	2 624 769	2 975 868
Total tax revenue	**1 885 934**	**21 016 290**	**71 304 272**	**119 799 453**	**152 621 696**	**263 429**	**1 723 196**	**4 781 271**	**7 611 084**	**10 440 912**

Million COP

	Local government[1]					Social Security Funds[2]				
	1990	2000	2010	2015	2019	1990	2000	2010	2015	2019
1000 Taxes on income, profits and capital gains	**0**	**0**	**0**	**0**	**0**	**0**	**0**	**0**	**0**	**0**
1100 Of individuals	..	..	..	..	..	..	..	..	..	..
1200 Corporate	..	..	..	..	..	..	..	..	..	..
1300 Unallocable between 1100 and 1200	..	..	..	..	..	..	..	..	..	..
2000 Social security contributions	**0**	**0**	**0**	**0**	**0**	**203 596**	**4 989 000**	**11 478 085**	**13 585 138**	**19 875 398**
2100 Employees	..	..	..	..	..	..	..	..	..	..
2200 Employers	..	..	..	..	..	..	..	..	..	..
2300 Self-employed or non-employed	..	..	..	..	..	..	..	..	..	..
2400 Unallocable between 2100, 2200 and 2300	..	..	..	..	..	203 596	4 989 000	11 478 085	13 585 138	19 875 398
3000 Taxes on payroll and workforce	**0**	**0**	**0**	**0**	**0**	**0**	**0**	**0**	**0**	**0**
4000 Taxes on property	**56 160**	**991 070**	**3 338 935**	**6 061 965**	**8 743 115**	**0**	**0**	**0**	**0**	**0**
4100 Recurrent taxes on immovable property	56 160	991 070	3 338 935	6 061 965	8 743 115	..	..	..	..	..
4200 Recurrent taxes on net wealth	0	0	0	0	0	..	..	..	..	..
4300 Estate, inheritance and gift taxes	0	0	0	0	0	..	..	..	..	..
4400 Taxes on financial and capital transactions	0	0	0	0	0	..	..	..	..	..
4500 Non-recurrent taxes	0	0	0	0	0	..	..	..	..	..
4600 Other recurrent taxes on property	0	0	0	0	0	..	..	..	..	..
5000 Taxes on goods and services	**89 290**	**1 590 132**	**5 622 489**	**8 899 062**	**11 664 256**	**0**	**0**	**0**	**0**	**0**
5100 Taxes on production, sale, transfer, etc	89 290	1 590 132	5 622 489	8 400 241	10 932 488	..	..	..	..	..
5110 General taxes	89 290	1 140 090	4 522 121	7 025 204	9 298 856	..	..	..	..	..
5120 Taxes on specific goods and services	0	450 042	1 100 368	1 375 037	1 633 632	..	..	..	..	..
5130 Unallocable between 5110 and 5120	0	0	0	0	0	..	..	..	..	..
5200 Taxes on use of goods and perform activities	0	0	0	498 821	731 768	..	..	..	..	..
5300 Unallocable between 5100 and 5200	0	0	0	0	0	..	..	..	..	..
6000 Other taxes	**81 017**	**288 942**	**1 930 282**	**4 200 992**	**5 694 388**	**0**	**0**	**0**	**0**	**0**
6100 Paid solely by business	0	0	0	0	0	..	..	..	..	..
6200 Other	81 017	288 942	1 930 282	4 200 992	5 694 388	..	..	..	..	..
Total tax revenue	**226 467**	**2 870 144**	**10 891 707**	**19 162 019**	**26 101 758**	**203 596**	**4 989 000**	**11 478 085**	**13 585 138**	**19 875 398**

.. Not available

1. The data correspond to the reported consolidated revenues of the territorial entities (departments and municipalities).
2. All of the health contributions pertaining to FOSYGA (Solidarity and Guarantee Fund) are classified as social security contributions from 2013. Prior to 2013, only the portion of the contributions used to finance the subsidised regime was included and the part to finance the contributory regime was classified in the social security sector as "other incomes".

StatLink https://doi.org/10.1787/888934236152

Table 6.10. **Costa Rica, tax revenues by subsectores of government**

Million CRC

	Federal government					State/Regional				
	1990	2000	2010	2015	2019	1990	2000	2010	2015	2019
1000 Taxes on income, profits and capital gains	**11 820**	**128 805**	**748 093**	**1 247 308**	**1 854 866**	..	..	..	..	..
1100 Of individuals	..	..	202 849	386 241	540 954	..	..	..	..	..
1200 Corporate	..	..	450 312	659 951	1 058 086	..	..	..	..	..
1300 Unallocable between 1100 and 1200	11 820	128 805	94 932	201 116	255 827	..	..	..	..	..
2000 Social security contributions[1]	**1 345**	**18 677**	**61 193**	**63 458**	**77 472**	..	..	..	..	..
2100 Employees	..	..	..	..	..	..	..	..	..	..
2200 Employers	..	..	..	..	..	..	..	..	..	..
2300 Self-employed or non-employed	..	..	..	..	..	..	..	..	..	..
2400 Unallocable between 2100, 2200 and 2300	1 345	18 677	61 193	63 458	77 472	..	..	..	..	..
3000 Taxes on payroll and workforce	**0**	**0**	**0**	**0**	**0**	..	..	..	..	..
4000 Taxes on property	**366**	**3 007**	**18 270**	**37 334**	**47 254**	..	..	..	..	..
4100 Recurrent taxes on immovable property	0	0	3 527	4 076	4 699	..	..	..	..	..
4200 Recurrent taxes on net wealth	0	0	0	0	0	..	..	..	..	..
4300 Estate, inheritance and gift taxes	0	0	0	0	0	..	..	..	..	..
4400 Taxes on financial and capital transactions	366	3 007	14 743	33 258	42 554	..	..	..	..	..
4500 Non-recurrent taxes	0	0	0	0	0	..	..	..	..	..
4600 Other recurrent taxes on property	0	0	0	0	0	..	..	..	..	..
5000 Taxes on goods and services	**52 248**	**444 870**	**1 696 593**	**2 536 562**	**2 940 121**	..	..	..	..	..
5100 Taxes on production, sale, transfer, etc	49 867	425 630	1 598 789	2 385 807	2 752 919	..	..	..	..	..
5110 General taxes	21 326	222 775	920 298	1 368 601	1 662 503	..	..	..	..	..
5120 Taxes on specific goods and services[2]	28 541	202 856	678 491	1 017 206	1 090 415	..	..	..	..	..
5130 Unallocable between 5110 and 5120	0	0	0	0	0	..	..	..	..	..
5200 Taxes on use of goods and perform activities	2 380	19 240	97 804	150 755	187 202	..	..	..	..	..
5300 Unallocable between 5100 and 5200	0	0	0	0	0	..	..	..	..	..
6000 Other taxes[3]	**9 251**	**23 956**	**92 452**	**162 200**	**201 844**	..	..	..	..	..
6100 Paid solely by business	0	0	0	0	0	..	..	..	..	..
6200 Other	9 251	23 956	92 452	162 200	201 844	..	..	..	..	..
Total tax revenue	**75 030**	**619 314**	**2 616 600**	**4 046 862**	**5 121 557**	..	..	..	..	..

Million CRC

	Local government					Social Security Funds				
	1990	2000	2010	2015	2019	1990	2000	2010	2015	2019
1000 Taxes on income, profits and capital gains	**0**	**0**	**0**	**0**	**0**	**0**	**0**	**0**	**0**	**0**
1100 Of individuals	..	..	..	..	..	..	..	..	..	..
1200 Corporate	..	..	..	..	..	..	..	..	..	..
1300 Unallocable between 1100 and 1200	..	..	..	..	..	..	..	..	..	..
2000 Social security contributions[1]	**0**	**0**	**0**	**0**	**0**	**32 645**	**278 392**	**1 389 338**	**2 241 674**	**2 949 219**
2100 Employees	..	..	..	..	..	..	..	..	..	..
2200 Employers	..	..	..	..	..	3 447	37 313	207 206	318 652	381 940
2300 Self-employed or non-employed	..	..	..	..	..	..	..	..	..	..
2400 Unallocable between 2100, 2200 and 2300	..	..	..	..	..	29 198	241 079	1 182 132	1 923 022	2 567 279
3000 Taxes on payroll and workforce	**0**	**0**	**0**	**0**	**0**	**7 575**	**61 796**	**260 664**	**423 616**	**522 529**
4000 Taxes on property	**1 200**	**5 390**	**45 436**	**85 927**	**120 698**	**0**	**0**	**0**	**0**	**0**
4100 Recurrent taxes on immovable property	1 200	5 390	45 436	85 927	120 698	..	..	..	..	..
4200 Recurrent taxes on net wealth	0	0	0	0	0	..	..	..	..	..
4300 Estate, inheritance and gift taxes	0	0	0	0	0	..	..	..	..	..
4400 Taxes on financial and capital transactions	0	0	0	0	0	..	..	..	..	..
4500 Non-recurrent taxes	0	0	0	0	0	..	..	..	..	..
4600 Other recurrent taxes on property	0	0	0	0	0	..	..	..	..	..
5000 Taxes on goods and services	**1 262**	**11 981**	**70 321**	**125 341**	**141 820**	**0**	**0**	**0**	**0**	**0**
5100 Taxes on production, sale, transfer, etc	0	83	1 513	3 093	3 841	..	..	..	..	..
5110 General taxes	..	0	0	0	0	..	..	..	..	..
5120 Taxes on specific goods and services[2]	..	83	1 513	3 093	3 841	..	..	..	..	..
5130 Unallocable between 5110 and 5120	..	0	0	0	0	..	..	..	..	..
5200 Taxes on use of goods and perform activities	1 262	11 898	68 808	122 248	137 979	..	..	..	..	..
5300 Unallocable between 5100 and 5200	0	0	0	0	0	..	..	..	..	..
6000 Other taxes[3]	**0**	**1 242**	**8**	**155**	**62**	**0**	**0**	**0**	**0**	**0**
6100 Paid solely by business	..	0	0	0	0	..	..	..	..	..
6200 Other	..	1 242	8	155	62	..	..	..	..	..
Total tax revenue	**2 461**	**18 613**	**115 765**	**211 422**	**262 580**	**40 220**	**340 187**	**1 650 002**	**2 665 291**	**3 471 748**

.. Not available

1. The data include social security contributions paid by the governments for their employees as well as the contributions for special regimes (teachers and magistrates). In ECLAC data, social security contributions also include INA (National Institute of Apprenticeship), IMAS (Joint Social Aid Institute) and FODESAF (Social Development and Family Allowances Fund).
2. In ECLAC data, the tax on ownership of vehicles, aircraft and boats is classified in category 4000.
3. The tax revenue of decentralised bodies is classified under the central government. In Costa Rica this revenue is classified under a separate unit (decentralised) considered to be different to the central government.

StatLink https://doi.org/10.1787/888934236171

Table 6.11. **Cuba, tax revenues by subsectores of government**

Million CUP

	Federal government[1]					State/Regional				
	1990	2000	2010	2015	2019	1990	2000	2010	2015	2019
1000 Taxes on income, profits and capital gains	..	..	**1 857**	..	..	..	..	..	..	..
1100 Of individuals	..	..	0	..	..	..	..	..	..	..
1200 Corporate	..	..	1 857	..	..	..	..	..	..	..
1300 Unallocable between 1100 and 1200	..	..	0	..	..	..	..	..	..	..
2000 Social security contributions	..	..	**0**	..	..	..	..	..	..	..
2100 Employees	..	..	..	..	..	..	..	..	..	..
2200 Employers	..	..	..	..	..	..	..	..	..	..
2300 Self-employed or non-employed	..	..	..	..	..	..	..	..	..	..
2400 Unallocable between 2100, 2200 and 2300	..	..	..	..	..	..	..	..	..	..
3000 Taxes on payroll and workforce	..	..	**289**	..	..	..	..	..	..	..
4000 Taxes on property	..	..	**0**	..	..	..	..	..	..	..
4100 Recurrent taxes on immovable property	..	..	..	..	..	..	..	..	..	..
4200 Recurrent taxes on net wealth	..	..	..	..	..	..	..	..	..	..
4300 Estate, inheritance and gift taxes	..	..	..	..	..	..	..	..	..	..
4400 Taxes on financial and capital transactions	..	..	..	..	..	..	..	..	..	..
4500 Non-recurrent taxes	..	..	..	..	..	..	..	..	..	..
4600 Other recurrent taxes on property	..	..	..	..	..	..	..	..	..	..
5000 Taxes on goods and services	..	..	**5 757**	..	..	..	..	..	..	..
5100 Taxes on production, sale, transfer, etc	..	..	5 757	..	..	..	..	..	..	..
5110 General taxes	..	..	4 924	..	..	..	..	..	..	..
5120 Taxes on specific goods and services	..	..	833	..	..	..	..	..	..	..
5130 Unallocable between 5110 and 5120	..	..	0	..	..	..	..	..	..	..
5200 Taxes on use of goods and perform activities	..	..	0	..	..	..	..	..	..	..
5300 Unallocable between 5100 and 5200	..	..	0	..	..	..	..	..	..	..
6000 Other taxes	..	..	**569**	..	..	..	..	..	..	..
6100 Paid solely by business	..	..	..	..	..	..	..	..	..	..
6200 Other	..	..	..	..	..	..	..	..	..	..
Total tax revenue	..	..	**8 472**	..	..	..	..	..	..	..

Million CUP

	Local government[2]					Social Security Funds				
	1990	2000	2010	2015	2019	1990	2000	2010	2015	2019
1000 Taxes on income, profits and capital gains	..	..	**1 746**	..	..	**0**	**0**	**0**	**0**	**0**
1100 Of individuals	..	..	554	..	..	..	..	..	..	..
1200 Corporate	..	..	1 193	..	..	..	..	..	..	..
1300 Unallocable between 1100 and 1200	..	..	0	..	..	..	..	..	..	..
2000 Social security contributions	..	..	**0**	..	..	**691**	**1 181**	**2 974**	**4 322**	**5 727**
2100 Employees	..	..	..	..	..	..	..	..	..	..
2200 Employers	..	..	..	..	..	..	..	..	..	..
2300 Self-employed or non-employed	..	..	..	..	..	..	..	..	..	..
2400 Unallocable between 2100, 2200 and 2300	..	..	..	..	..	691	1 181	2 974	4 322	5 727
3000 Taxes on payroll and workforce	..	..	**4 125**	..	..	**0**	**0**	**0**	**0**	**0**
4000 Taxes on property	..	..	**0**	..	..	**0**	**0**	**0**	**0**	**0**
4100 Recurrent taxes on immovable property	..	..	..	..	..	..	..	..	..	..
4200 Recurrent taxes on net wealth	..	..	..	..	..	..	..	..	..	..
4300 Estate, inheritance and gift taxes	..	..	..	..	..	..	..	..	..	..
4400 Taxes on financial and capital transactions	..	..	..	..	..	..	..	..	..	..
4500 Non-recurrent taxes	..	..	..	..	..	..	..	..	..	..
4600 Other recurrent taxes on property	..	..	..	..	..	..	..	..	..	..
5000 Taxes on goods and services	..	..	**6 526**	..	..	**0**	**0**	**0**	**0**	**0**
5100 Taxes on production, sale, transfer, etc	..	..	6 526	..	..	..	..	..	..	..
5110 General taxes	..	..	5 601	..	..	..	..	..	..	..
5120 Taxes on specific goods and services	..	..	925	..	..	..	..	..	..	..
5130 Unallocable between 5110 and 5120	..	..	0	..	..	..	..	..	..	..
5200 Taxes on use of goods and perform activities	..	..	0	..	..	..	..	..	..	..
5300 Unallocable between 5100 and 5200	..	..	0	..	..	..	..	..	..	..
6000 Other taxes	..	..	**106**	..	..	**0**	**0**	**0**	**0**	**0**
6100 Paid solely by business	..	..	..	..	..	..	..	..	..	..
6200 Other	..	..	..	..	..	..	..	..	..	..
Total tax revenue	..	..	**12 503**	..	..	**691**	**1 181**	**2 974**	**4 322**	**5 727**

.. Not available

1. The figures include central government tax revenues between 2002 and 2012. Central tax revenues are not available for other years.
2. The figures include local government tax revenues between 2002 and 2012. Local tax revenues are not available for other years.

StatLink https://doi.org/10.1787/888934236190

Table 6.12. **Dominican Republic, tax revenues by subsectores of government**

Million DOP

	Federal government					State/Regional				
	1990	2000	2010	2015	2019	1990	2000	2010	2015	2019
1000 Taxes on income, profits and capital gains	**1 670**	**10 782**	**53 643**	**119 819**	**194 281**	..	..	..	..	..
1100 Of individuals	..	4 088	17 088	35 549	59 448	..	..	..	..	..
1200 Corporate	..	4 679	21 475	61 695	91 545	..	..	..	..	..
1300 Unallocable between 1100 and 1200	1 670	2 015	15 080	22 576	43 289	..	..	..	..	..
2000 Social security contributions	**0**	**0**	**0**	**0**	**0**	..	..	..	..	..
2100 Employees	..	..	..	..	..	..	..	..	..	..
2200 Employers	..	..	..	..	..	..	..	..	..	..
2300 Self-employed or non-employed	..	..	..	..	..	..	..	..	..	..
2400 Unallocable between 2100, 2200 and 2300	..	..	..	..	..	..	..	..	..	..
3000 Taxes on payroll and workforce[1]	**0**	**0**	**1 385**	**2 366**	**3 502**	..	..	..	..	..
4000 Taxes on property	**74**	**689**	**13 315**	**19 044**	**29 564**	..	..	..	..	..
4100 Recurrent taxes on immovable property	9	115	555	1 755	2 904	..	..	..	..	..
4200 Recurrent taxes on net wealth	0	0	2 449	3 445	5 155	..	..	0	0	0
4300 Estate, inheritance and gift taxes	11	96	231	418	715	..	..	..	..	..
4400 Taxes on financial and capital transactions	40	377	8 658	12 067	17 594	..	..	..	..	..
4500 Non-recurrent taxes	3	32	488	591	931	..	..	..	..	..
4600 Other recurrent taxes on property	11	70	934	769	2 266	..	..	..	..	..
5000 Taxes on goods and services	**4 467**	**35 853**	**175 139**	**273 898**	**387 900**	..	..	..	..	..
5100 Taxes on production, sale, transfer, etc	4 398	35 135	168 641	263 435	370 718	..	..	..	..	..
5110 General taxes	970	9 912	81 226	147 039	214 324	..	..	..	..	..
5120 Taxes on specific goods and services	3 429	25 224	87 415	116 396	156 394	..	..	..	..	..
5130 Unallocable between 5110 and 5120	0	0	0	0	0	..	..	..	..	..
5200 Taxes on use of goods and perform activities	69	718	6 498	10 463	17 183	..	..	..	..	..
5300 Unallocable between 5100 and 5200	0	0	0	0	0	..	..	..	..	..
6000 Other taxes	**159**	**495**	**0**	**1**	**2**	..	..	..	..	..
6100 Paid solely by business	0	0	..	0	0	..	..	..	..	..
6200 Other	159	495	..	1	2	..	..	..	..	..
Total tax revenue	**6 371**	**47 820**	**243 482**	**415 128**	**615 249**	..	..	..	..	..

Million DOP

	Local government[2]					Social Security Funds[3]				
	1990	2000	2010	2015	2019	1990	2000	2010	2015	2019
1000 Taxes on income, profits and capital gains	..	..	..	..	..	**0**	**0**	**0**	**0**	**0**
1100 Of individuals	..	..	..	..	..	..	..	..	..	..
1200 Corporate	..	..	..	..	..	..	..	..	..	..
1300 Unallocable between 1100 and 1200	..	..	..	..	..	..	..	..	..	..
2000 Social security contributions	..	..	..	..	..	**53**	**490**	**1 845**	**1 483**	**2 553**
2100 Employees	..	..	..	..	..	..	..	1 720	1 321	..
2200 Employers	..	..	..	..	..	..	..	125	163	..
2300 Self-employed or non-employed	..	..	..	..	..	..	..	0	0	..
2400 Unallocable between 2100, 2200 and 2300	..	..	..	..	..	53	490	0	0	2 553
3000 Taxes on payroll and workforce[1]	..	..	..	..	..	**0**	**0**	**0**	**0**	**0**
4000 Taxes on property	..	..	..	..	..	**0**	**0**	**0**	**0**	**0**
4100 Recurrent taxes on immovable property	..	..	..	..	..	..	..	..	..	..
4200 Recurrent taxes on net wealth	..	..	..	..	..	..	..	..	..	..
4300 Estate, inheritance and gift taxes	..	..	..	..	..	..	..	..	..	..
4400 Taxes on financial and capital transactions	..	..	..	..	..	..	..	..	..	..
4500 Non-recurrent taxes	..	..	..	..	..	..	..	..	..	..
4600 Other recurrent taxes on property	..	..	..	..	..	..	..	..	..	..
5000 Taxes on goods and services	..	..	..	..	..	**0**	**0**	**0**	**0**	**0**
5100 Taxes on production, sale, transfer, etc	..	..	..	..	..	..	..	..	..	..
5110 General taxes	..	..	..	..	..	..	..	..	..	..
5120 Taxes on specific goods and services	..	..	..	..	..	..	..	..	..	..
5130 Unallocable between 5110 and 5120	..	..	..	..	..	..	..	..	..	..
5200 Taxes on use of goods and perform activities	..	..	..	..	..	..	..	..	..	..
5300 Unallocable between 5100 and 5200	..	..	..	..	..	..	..	..	..	..
6000 Other taxes	..	..	..	..	..	**0**	**0**	**0**	**0**	**0**
6100 Paid solely by business	..	..	..	..	..	..	..	..	..	..
6200 Other	..	..	..	..	..	..	..	..	..	..
Total tax revenue	..	..	..	..	..	**53**	**490**	**1 845**	**1 483**	**2 553**

.. Not available

1. This heading includes the mandatory non-pensions contributions to the Instituto de Formacion Tecnico Profesinal (INFOTEP). The tax revenue is classified under the central government. In Dominican Republic this revenue is classified under a separate unit (decentralised) considered to be different to the central government.
2. The figures exclude local government tax revenues as the data are not available.
3. The figures exclude social security contributions to general government managed by the private sector.

StatLink https://doi.org/10.1787/888934236209

Table 6.13. **Ecuador, tax revenues by subsectores of government**

Million USD

	Federal government					State/Regional				
	1990	2000	2010	2015	2019	1990	2000	2010	2015	2019
1000 Taxes on income, profits and capital gains	**138**	**267**	**2 348**	**4 705**	**4 595**	**..**	**..**	**..**	**..**	**..**
1100 Of individuals	..	10	80	192	197	..	..	..	..	..
1200 Corporate	..	53	485	1 575	1 308	..	..	..	..	..
1300 Unallocable between 1100 and 1200	138	204	1 783	2 938	3 090	..	..	..	..	..
2000 Social security contributions	**0**	**0**	**0**	**0**	**0**	**..**	**..**	**..**	**..**	**..**
2100 Employees	..	..	..	..	..	..	..	..	..	..
2200 Employers	..	..	..	..	..	..	..	..	..	..
2300 Self-employed or non-employed	..	..	..	..	..	..	..	..	..	..
2400 Unallocable between 2100, 2200 and 2300	..	..	..	..	..	..	..	..	..	..
3000 Taxes on payroll and workforce	**0**	**0**	**0**	**0**	**0**	**..**	**..**	**..**	**..**	**..**
4000 Taxes on property	**0**	**0**	**43**	**87**	**59**	**..**	**..**	**..**	**..**	**..**
4100 Recurrent taxes on immovable property	..	..	3	9	0	..	..	..	..	..
4200 Recurrent taxes on net wealth	..	..	35	49	35	..	..	..	..	..
4300 Estate, inheritance and gift taxes	..	..	5	29	24	..	..	..	..	..
4400 Taxes on financial and capital transactions	..	..	0	0	0	..	..	..	..	..
4500 Non-recurrent taxes	..	..	0	0	0	..	..	..	..	..
4600 Other recurrent taxes on property	..	..	0	0	0	..	..	..	..	..
5000 Taxes on goods and services	**668**	**1 596**	**5 969**	**10 751**	**10 504**	**..**	**..**	**..**	**..**	**..**
5100 Taxes on production, sale, transfer, etc	665	1 574	5 814	10 414	10 159	..	..	..	..	..
5110 General taxes	302	923	3 759	6 352	6 539	..	..	..	..	..
5120 Taxes on specific goods and services	363	651	2 054	4 062	3 620	..	..	..	..	..
5130 Unallocable between 5110 and 5120	0	0	0	0	0	..	..	..	..	..
5200 Taxes on use of goods and perform activities	3	22	156	336	345	..	..	..	..	..
5300 Unallocable between 5100 and 5200	0	0	0	0	0	..	..	..	..	..
6000 Other taxes	**0**	**0**	**4**	**10**	**20**	**..**	**..**	**..**	**..**	**..**
6100 Paid solely by business	..	..	0	0	0	..	..	..	..	..
6200 Other	..	..	4	10	20	..	..	..	..	..
Total tax revenue	**806**	**1 863**	**8 364**	**15 553**	**15 178**	**..**	**..**	**..**	**..**	**..**

Million USD

	Local government[1]					Social Security Funds[2]				
	1990	2000	2010	2015	2019	1990	2000	2010	2015	2019
1000 Taxes on income, profits and capital gains	**1**	**2**	**15**	**75**	**75**	**0**	**0**	**0**	**0**	**0**
1100 Of individuals	..	..	0	0	..	..	..	..	..	..
1200 Corporate	..	..	..	..	..	..	..	..	..	..
1300 Unallocable between 1100 and 1200	1	2	15	75	75	..	..	..	..	..
2000 Social security contributions	**0**	**0**	**0**	**0**	**0**	**243**	**228**	**2 541**	**5 057**	**5 863**
2100 Employees	..	..	..	..	..	..	..	..	..	..
2200 Employers	..	..	..	..	..	..	..	..	..	..
2300 Self-employed or non-employed	..	..	..	..	..	..	..	..	..	..
2400 Unallocable between 2100, 2200 and 2300	..	..	..	..	..	243	228	2 541	5 057	5 863
3000 Taxes on payroll and workforce	**0**	**0**	**0**	**0**	**0**	**0**	**0**	**0**	**0**	**0**
4000 Taxes on property	**16**	**17**	**116**	**216**	**285**	**0**	**0**	**0**	**0**	**0**
4100 Recurrent taxes on immovable property	13	8	66	125	121	..	..	..	..	..
4200 Recurrent taxes on net wealth	0	0	0	0	0	..	..	..	..	..
4300 Estate, inheritance and gift taxes	0	0	0	0	0	..	..	..	..	..
4400 Taxes on financial and capital transactions	0	0	0	0	0	..	..	..	..	..
4500 Non-recurrent taxes	0	0	0	0	0	..	..	..	..	..
4600 Other recurrent taxes on property	3	9	50	91	164	..	..	..	..	..
5000 Taxes on goods and services	**10**	**13**	**97**	**246**	**206**	**0**	**0**	**0**	**0**	**0**
5100 Taxes on production, sale, transfer, etc	6	6	49	89	88	..	..	..	..	..
5110 General taxes	4	5	41	79	79	..	..	..	..	..
5120 Taxes on specific goods and services	1	2	8	10	9	..	..	..	..	..
5130 Unallocable between 5110 and 5120	0	0	0	0	0	..	..	..	..	..
5200 Taxes on use of goods and perform activities	5	7	48	157	118	..	..	..	..	..
5300 Unallocable between 5100 and 5200	0	0	0	0	0	..	..	..	..	..
6000 Other taxes	**2**	**2**	**1**	**0**	**2**	**0**	**0**	**0**	**0**	**0**
6100 Paid solely by business	0	0	0	0	0	..	..	..	..	..
6200 Other	2	2	1	0	2	..	..	..	..	..
Total tax revenue	**29**	**34**	**228**	**537**	**568**	**243**	**228**	**2 541**	**5 057**	**5 863**

.. Not available

1. Local tax revenues in 2018 have been updated with data from the Inter-American Centre of Tax Administrations (CIAT). The figures in 2019 are estimated.
2. Social security contributions are collected from non-financial public sector operations published by the Central Bank of Ecuador.

StatLink https://doi.org/10.1787/888934236228

Table 6.14. **El Salvador, tax revenues by subsectores of government**

Million USD

	Federal government					State/Regional				
	1990	2000	2010	2015	2019	1990	2000	2010	2015	2019
1000 Taxes on income, profits and capital gains	**95**	**429**	**996**	**1 545**	**1 885**	..	..	..	..	..
1100 Of individuals	..	..	590	774	836	..	..	..	..	..
1200 Corporate	..	..	420	622	848	..	..	..	..	..
1300 Unallocable between 1100 and 1200	95	429	-14	148	201	..	..	..	..	..
2000 Social security contributions	**0**	**0**	**0**	**0**	**0**	..	..	..	..	..
2100 Employees	..	..	..	..	..	..	..	..	..	..
2200 Employers	..	..	..	..	..	..	..	..	..	..
2300 Self-employed or non-employed	..	..	..	..	..	..	..	..	..	..
2400 Unallocable between 2100, 2200 and 2300	..	..	..	..	..	..	..	..	..	..
3000 Taxes on payroll and workforce[1]	**0**	**0**	**21**	**30**	**38**	..	..	..	..	..
4000 Taxes on property	**26**	**12**	**16**	**107**	**37**	..	..	..	..	..
4100 Recurrent taxes on immovable property	0	0	0	0	0	..	..	..	..	..
4200 Recurrent taxes on net wealth	16	0	0	0	0	..	..	..	..	..
4300 Estate, inheritance and gift taxes	0	0	0	0	0	..	..	..	..	..
4400 Taxes on financial and capital transactions	10	12	16	107	37	..	..	..	..	..
4500 Non-recurrent taxes	0	0	0	0	0	..	..	..	..	..
4600 Other recurrent taxes on property	0	0	0	0	0	..	..	..	..	..
5000 Taxes on goods and services	**259**	**903**	**1 871**	**2 266**	**2 837**	..	..	..	..	..
5100 Taxes on production, sale, transfer, etc	259	903	1 863	2 254	2 821	..	..	..	..	..
5110 General taxes	133	714	1 433	1 764	2 109	..	..	..	..	..
5120 Taxes on specific goods and services	127	189	431	490	712	..	..	..	..	..
5130 Unallocable between 5110 and 5120	0	0	0	0	0	..	..	..	..	..
5200 Taxes on use of goods and perform activities	0	0	7	12	16	..	..	..	..	..
5300 Unallocable between 5100 and 5200	0	0	0	0	0	..	..	..	..	..
6000 Other taxes	**58**	**0**	**0**	**0**	**0**	..	..	..	..	..
6100 Paid solely by business	0	0	..	..	..	..	..	..	..	..
6200 Other	58	0	..	..	..	..	..	..	..	..
Total tax revenue	**438**	**1 344**	**2 903**	**3 947**	**4 798**	..	..	..	..	..

Million USD

	Local government					Social Security Funds[2]				
	1990	2000	2010	2015	2019	1990	2000	2010	2015	2019
1000 Taxes on income, profits and capital gains	..	..	**0**	**0**	**0**	**0**	**0**	**0**	**0**	**0**
1100 Of individuals	..	..	..	..	..	..	..	..	..	..
1200 Corporate	..	..	..	..	..	..	..	..	..	..
1300 Unallocable between 1100 and 1200	..	..	..	..	..	..	..	..	..	..
2000 Social security contributions	..	..	**0**	**0**	**0**	**104**	**325**	**470**	**608**	**722**
2100 Employees	..	..	..	..	..	..	75	165	214	251
2200 Employers	..	..	..	..	..	..	176	306	393	471
2300 Self-employed or non-employed	..	..	..	..	..	..	13	0	0	0
2400 Unallocable between 2100, 2200 and 2300	..	..	..	..	..	104	62	0	0	0
3000 Taxes on payroll and workforce[1]	..	..	**0**	**0**	**0**	**0**	**0**	**0**	**0**	**0**
4000 Taxes on property	..	..	**3**	**5**	**7**	**0**	**0**	**0**	**0**	**0**
4100 Recurrent taxes on immovable property	..	..	3	5	7	..	..	..	..	..
4200 Recurrent taxes on net wealth	..	..	0	0	0	..	..	..	..	..
4300 Estate, inheritance and gift taxes	..	..	0	0	0	..	..	..	..	..
4400 Taxes on financial and capital transactions	..	..	0	0	0	..	..	..	..	..
4500 Non-recurrent taxes	..	..	0	0	0	..	..	..	..	..
4600 Other recurrent taxes on property	..	..	0	0	0	..	..	..	..	..
5000 Taxes on goods and services	..	..	**7**	**12**	**13**	**0**	**0**	**0**	**0**	**0**
5100 Taxes on production, sale, transfer, etc	..	..	0	0	0	..	..	..	..	..
5110 General taxes	..	..	..	..	..	..	..	..	..	..
5120 Taxes on specific goods and services	..	..	..	..	..	..	..	..	..	..
5130 Unallocable between 5110 and 5120	..	..	..	..	..	..	..	..	..	..
5200 Taxes on use of goods and perform activities	..	..	7	12	13	..	..	..	..	..
5300 Unallocable between 5100 and 5200	..	..	0	0	0	..	..	..	..	..
6000 Other taxes	..	..	**63**	**86**	**89**	**0**	**0**	**0**	**0**	**0**
6100 Paid solely by business	..	..	0	0	0	..	..	..	..	..
6200 Other	..	..	63	86	89	..	..	..	..	..
Total tax revenue	..	..	**74**	**104**	**109**	**104**	**325**	**470**	**608**	**722**

.. Not available

1. Vocational training contributions to the Instituto Salvadoreño de Formación Profesional (INSAFORP) have been added in this edition. The tax revenue is classified under the central government. In El Salvador this revenue is classified under a separate unit considered to be different to the central government.
2. Social security contributions are those paid to the Salvadoran Institute of Social Security (ISSS), National Public Employees Pension Institute (INPEP), Social Security Institute of the Armed Forces (IPSFA) and Salvadoran Institute of Teacher Welfare (ISBM). The figures exclude contributions to the privately managed regime and may include small amount of voluntary contributions which are undistinguishable from the public social security contribution data.

StatLink https://doi.org/10.1787/888934236247

Table 6.15. **Guatemala, tax revenues by subsectores of government**

Million GTQ

	Federal government					State/Regional				
	1990	2000	2010	2015	2019	1990	2000	2010	2015	2019
1000 Taxes on income, profits and capital gains	**507**	**3 295**	**10 319**	**17 534**	**21 930**	..	..	..	..	..
1100 Of individuals	25	143	1 225	1 826	2 813	..	..	..	..	..
1200 Corporate	482	3 149	6 520	11 801	14 287	..	..	..	..	..
1300 Unallocable between 1100 and 1200	0	2	2 574	3 907	4 829	..	..	..	..	..
2000 Social security contributions	**0**	**0**	**0**	**0**	**0**	..	..	..	..	..
2100 Employees	..	..	..	..	..	..	..	..	..	..
2200 Employers	..	..	..	..	..	..	..	..	..	..
2300 Self-employed or non-employed	..	..	..	..	..	..	..	..	..	..
2400 Unallocable between 2100, 2200 and 2300	..	..	..	..	..	..	..	..	..	..
3000 Taxes on payroll and workforce[1]	**0**	**0**	**447**	**736**	**933**	..	..	..	..	..
4000 Taxes on property	**149**	**199**	**582**	**358**	**494**	..	..	..	..	..
4100 Recurrent taxes on immovable property	0	6	1	1	2	..	..	..	..	..
4200 Recurrent taxes on net wealth	0	0	0	0	0	..	..	..	..	..
4300 Estate, inheritance and gift taxes	0	0	0	0	0	..	..	..	..	..
4400 Taxes on financial and capital transactions	149	194	581	357	492	..	..	..	..	..
4500 Non-recurrent taxes	0	0	0	0	0	..	..	..	..	..
4600 Other recurrent taxes on property	0	0	0	0	0	..	..	..	..	..
5000 Taxes on goods and services	**1 477**	**10 317**	**23 255**	**31 719**	**40 124**	..	..	..	..	..
5100 Taxes on production, sale, transfer, etc	1 449	10 131	22 750	30 088	38 216	..	..	..	..	..
5110 General taxes	762	6 259	16 980	23 271	29 920	..	..	..	..	..
5120 Taxes on specific goods and services	687	3 872	5 770	6 816	8 296	..	..	..	..	..
5130 Unallocable between 5110 and 5120	0	0	0	0	0	..	..	..	..	..
5200 Taxes on use of goods and perform activities	28	186	505	1 631	1 908	..	..	..	..	..
5300 Unallocable between 5100 and 5200	0	0	0	0	0	..	..	..	..	..
6000 Other taxes	**0**	**4**	**1**	**0**	**0**	..	..	..	..	..
6100 Paid solely by business	..	0	0	0	0	..	..	..	..	..
6200 Other	..	4	1	0	0	..	..	..	..	..
Total tax revenue	**2 133**	**13 815**	**34 605**	**50 347**	**63 481**	..	..	..	..	..

Million GTQ

	Local government					Social Security Funds[2]				
	1990	2000	2010	2015	2019	1990	2000	2010	2015	2019
1000 Taxes on income, profits and capital gains	..	**0**	**0**	**0**	**0**	**0**	**0**	**0**	**0**	**0**
1100 Of individuals	..	..	..	..	..	..	..	..	..	..
1200 Corporate	..	..	..	..	..	..	..	..	..	..
1300 Unallocable between 1100 and 1200	..	..	..	..	..	..	..	..	..	..
2000 Social security contributions	..	**0**	**0**	**0**	**0**	**436**	**2 569**	**6 312**	**9 778**	**12 957**
2100 Employees	..	..	..	..	..	..	..	..	..	..
2200 Employers	..	..	..	..	..	..	..	..	..	..
2300 Self-employed or non-employed	..	..	..	..	..	..	..	..	..	..
2400 Unallocable between 2100, 2200 and 2300	..	..	..	..	..	436	2 569	6 312	9 778	12 957
3000 Taxes on payroll and workforce[1]	..	**0**	**0**	**0**	**0**	**0**	**0**	**0**	**0**	**0**
4000 Taxes on property	..	**147**	**620**	**692**	**683**	**0**	**0**	**0**	**0**	**0**
4100 Recurrent taxes on immovable property	..	147	620	692	683	..	..	..	..	..
4200 Recurrent taxes on net wealth	..	0	0	0	0	..	..	..	..	..
4300 Estate, inheritance and gift taxes	..	0	0	0	0	..	..	..	..	..
4400 Taxes on financial and capital transactions	..	0	0	0	0	..	..	..	..	..
4500 Non-recurrent taxes	..	0	0	0	0	..	..	..	..	..
4600 Other recurrent taxes on property	..	0	0	0	0	..	..	..	..	..
5000 Taxes on goods and services	..	**0**	**0**	**0**	**0**	**0**	**0**	**0**	**0**	**0**
5100 Taxes on production, sale, transfer, etc	..	..	..	..	..	..	..	..	..	..
5110 General taxes	..	..	..	..	..	..	..	..	..	..
5120 Taxes on specific goods and services	..	..	..	..	..	..	..	..	..	..
5130 Unallocable between 5110 and 5120	..	..	..	..	..	..	..	..	..	..
5200 Taxes on use of goods and perform activities	..	..	..	..	..	..	..	..	..	..
5300 Unallocable between 5100 and 5200	..	..	..	..	..	..	..	..	..	..
6000 Other taxes	..	**0**	**0**	**0**	**0**	**0**	**0**	**0**	**0**	**0**
6100 Paid solely by business	..	..	..	..	..	..	..	..	..	..
6200 Other	..	..	..	..	..	..	..	..	..	..
Total tax revenue	..	**147**	**620**	**692**	**683**	**436**	**2 569**	**6 312**	**9 778**	**12 957**

.. Not available

1. Contributions to INTECAP and contributions to IRTRA have been added and classified as payroll taxes in this edition. The tax revenues are classified under the central government. In Guatemala these revenues are classified under a separate unit considered to be different to the central government.
2. Corresponds to social security contributions to the Guatemalan Social Security Institute (IGSS) and payments by public employees to the government's pension fund.

StatLink https://doi.org/10.1787/888934236266

Table 6.16. **Guyana, tax revenues by subsectores of government**

Million GYD

	Federal government[1]					State/Regional				
	1990	2000	2010	2015	2019	1990	2000	2010	2015	2019
1000 Taxes on income, profits and capital gains	**1 752**	**16 179**	**39 561**	**55 011**	**94 504**	**..**	**..**	**..**	**..**	**..**
1100 Of individuals	333	7 734	17 816	23 300	35 249	..	..	..	..	..
1200 Corporate	1 375	8 266	21 427	31 200	58 346	..	..	..	..	..
1300 Unallocable between 1100 and 1200	43	179	317	511	908	..	..	..	..	..
2000 Social security contributions	**0**	**0**	**0**	**0**	**0**	**..**	**..**	**..**	**..**	**..**
2100 Employees	..	..	..	..	..	..	..	..	..	..
2200 Employers	..	..	..	..	..	..	..	..	..	..
2300 Self-employed or non-employed	..	..	..	..	..	..	..	..	..	..
2400 Unallocable between 2100, 2200 and 2300	..	..	..	..	..	..	..	..	..	..
3000 Taxes on payroll and workforce	**0**	**0**	**0**	**0**	**0**	**..**	**..**	**..**	**..**	**..**
4000 Taxes on property	**53**	**701**	**2 068**	**3 676**	**4 917**	**..**	**..**	**..**	**..**	**..**
4100 Recurrent taxes on immovable property	40	681	1 562	3 201	4 312	..	..	..	..	..
4200 Recurrent taxes on net wealth	0	0	0	0	0	..	..	..	..	..
4300 Estate, inheritance and gift taxes	13	20	31	37	41	..	..	..	..	..
4400 Taxes on financial and capital transactions	0	0	476	438	565	..	..	..	..	..
4500 Non-recurrent taxes	0	0	0	0	0	..	..	..	..	..
4600 Other recurrent taxes on property	0	0	0	0	0	..	..	..	..	..
5000 Taxes on goods and services	**2 200**	**20 798**	**59 360**	**83 924**	**124 952**	**..**	**..**	**..**	**..**	**..**
5100 Taxes on production, sale, transfer, etc	2 162	20 530	58 846	83 227	123 710	..	..	..	..	..
5110 General taxes	1 399	14 861	27 044	35 374	52 735	..	..	..	..	..
5120 Taxes on specific goods and services	763	5 669	31 802	47 853	70 975	..	..	..	..	..
5130 Unallocable between 5110 and 5120	0	0	0	0	0	..	..	..	..	..
5200 Taxes on use of goods and perform activities	38	268	514	697	1 242	..	..	..	..	..
5300 Unallocable between 5100 and 5200	0	0	0	0	0	..	..	..	..	..
6000 Other taxes	**1 037**	**204**	**757**	**599**	**2 072**	**..**	**..**	**..**	**..**	**..**
6100 Paid solely by business	0	0	0	0	0	..	..	..	..	..
6200 Other	1 037	204	757	599	2 072	..	..	..	..	..
Total tax revenue	**5 041**	**37 882**	**101 746**	**143 210**	**226 445**	**..**	**..**	**..**	**..**	**..**

Million GYD

	Local government[2]					Social Security Funds[3]				
	1990	2000	2010	2015	2019	1990	2000	2010	2015	2019
1000 Taxes on income, profits and capital gains	**..**	**..**	**0**	**0**	**0**	**0**	**0**	**0**	**0**	**0**
1100 Of individuals	..	..	..	..	..	..	..	..	..	..
1200 Corporate	..	..	..	..	..	..	..	..	..	..
1300 Unallocable between 1100 and 1200	..	..	..	..	..	..	..	..	..	..
2000 Social security contributions	**..**	**..**	**0**	**0**	**0**	**191**	**4 868**	**10 047**	**16 644**	**23 728**
2100 Employees	..	..	..	..	..	..	..	..	..	..
2200 Employers	..	..	..	..	..	..	..	..	..	..
2300 Self-employed or non-employed	..	..	..	..	..	..	..	..	..	..
2400 Unallocable between 2100, 2200 and 2300	..	..	..	..	..	191	4 868	10 047	16 644	23 728
3000 Taxes on payroll and workforce	**..**	**..**	**0**	**0**	**0**	**0**	**0**	**0**	**0**	**0**
4000 Taxes on property	**..**	**..**	**0**	**0**	**0**	**0**	**0**	**0**	**0**	**0**
4100 Recurrent taxes on immovable property	..	..	..	..	..	..	..	..	..	..
4200 Recurrent taxes on net wealth	..	..	..	..	..	..	..	..	..	..
4300 Estate, inheritance and gift taxes	..	..	..	..	..	..	..	..	..	..
4400 Taxes on financial and capital transactions	..	..	..	..	..	..	..	..	..	..
4500 Non-recurrent taxes	..	..	..	..	..	..	..	..	..	..
4600 Other recurrent taxes on property	..	..	..	..	..	..	..	..	..	..
5000 Taxes on goods and services	**..**	**..**	**0**	**0**	**0**	**0**	**0**	**0**	**0**	**0**
5100 Taxes on production, sale, transfer, etc	..	..	..	..	..	..	..	..	..	..
5110 General taxes	..	..	..	..	..	..	..	..	..	..
5120 Taxes on specific goods and services	..	..	..	..	..	..	..	..	..	..
5130 Unallocable between 5110 and 5120	..	..	..	..	..	..	..	..	..	..
5200 Taxes on use of goods and perform activities	..	..	..	..	..	..	..	..	..	..
5300 Unallocable between 5100 and 5200	..	..	..	..	..	..	..	..	..	..
6000 Other taxes	**..**	**..**	**113**	**41**	**68**	**0**	**0**	**0**	**0**	**0**
6100 Paid solely by business	..	..	0	0	0	..	..	..	..	..
6200 Other	..	..	113	41	68	..	..	..	..	..
Total tax revenue	**..**	**..**	**113**	**41**	**68**	**191**	**4 868**	**10 047**	**16 644**	**23 728**

.. Not available

1. Central government tax revenues are based on Budget Estimates by the Ministry of Finance.
2. Local government tax revenues include payments of local taxes by public corporations and come from Bank of Guyana.
3. Social security figures include contributions to National Insurance Scheme.

StatLink https://doi.org/10.1787/888934236285

Table 6.17. **Honduras, tax revenues by subsectores of government**

Million HNL

	Federal government					State/Regional				
	1990	2000	2010	2015	2019	1990	2000	2010	2015	2019
1000 Taxes on income, profits and capital gains	**431**	**2 907**	**13 232**	**25 003**	**34 533**	**..**	**..**	**..**	**..**	**..**
1100 Of individuals	157	992	4 528	8 147	11 365	..	..	..	..	..
1200 Corporate	274	1 916	8 705	16 856	23 167	..	..	..	..	..
1300 Unallocable between 1100 and 1200	0	0	0	0	0	..	..	..	..	..
2000 Social security contributions	**0**	**0**	**0**	**0**	**0**	**..**	**..**	**..**	**..**	**..**
2100 Employees	..	..	..	..	..	..	..	..	..	..
2200 Employers	..	..	..	..	..	..	..	..	..	..
2300 Self-employed or non-employed	..	..	..	..	..	..	..	..	..	..
2400 Unallocable between 2100, 2200 and 2300	..	..	..	..	..	..	..	..	..	..
3000 Taxes on payroll and workforce[1]	**0**	**0**	**485**	**1 007**	**1 005**	**..**	**..**	**..**	**..**	**..**
4000 Taxes on property	**16**	**266**	**994**	**2 635**	**3 428**	**..**	**..**	**..**	**..**	**..**
4100 Recurrent taxes on immovable property	16	189	254	298	446	..	..	..	..	..
4200 Recurrent taxes on net wealth	0	78	359	334	341	..	..	..	..	..
4300 Estate, inheritance and gift taxes	0	0	0	0	0	..	..	..	..	..
4400 Taxes on financial and capital transactions	0	0	0	2 003	2 641	..	..	..	..	..
4500 Non-recurrent taxes	0	0	380	0	0	..	..	..	..	..
4600 Other recurrent taxes on property	0	0	0	0	0	..	..	..	..	..
5000 Taxes on goods and services	**1 401**	**12 436**	**28 937**	**52 217**	**69 468**	**..**	**..**	**..**	**..**	**..**
5100 Taxes on production, sale, transfer, etc	1 401	12 436	28 937	52 217	69 468	..	..	..	..	..
5110 General taxes	344	5 146	16 050	32 273	42 891	..	..	..	..	..
5120 Taxes on specific goods and services	1 057	7 290	12 887	19 944	26 577	..	..	..	..	..
5130 Unallocable between 5110 and 5120	0	0	0	0	0	..	..	..	..	..
5200 Taxes on use of goods and perform activities	0	0	0	0	0	..	..	..	..	..
5300 Unallocable between 5100 and 5200	0	0	0	0	0	..	..	..	..	..
6000 Other taxes	**1**	**2**	**9**	**8**	**18**	**..**	**..**	**..**	**..**	**..**
6100 Paid solely by business	0	0	0	0	0	..	..	..	..	..
6200 Other	1	2	9	8	18	..	..	..	..	..
Total tax revenue	**1 849**	**15 612**	**43 657**	**80 870**	**108 450**	**..**	**..**	**..**	**..**	**..**

Million HNL

	Local government[2]					Social Security Funds				
	1990	2000	2010	2015	2019	1990	2000	2010	2015	2019
1000 Taxes on income, profits and capital gains	**0**	**0**	**0**	**0**	**0**	**0**	**0**	**0**	**0**	**0**
1100 Of individuals	..	..	..	..	..	..	..	..	..	..
1200 Corporate	..	..	..	..	..	..	..	..	..	..
1300 Unallocable between 1100 and 1200	..	..	..	..	..	..	..	..	..	..
2000 Social security contributions	**0**	**0**	**0**	**0**	**0**	**179**	**1 727**	**8 671**	**13 524**	**21 068**
2100 Employees	..	..	..	..	..	..	..	..	..	..
2200 Employers	..	..	..	..	..	..	..	..	..	..
2300 Self-employed or non-employed	..	..	..	..	..	..	..	..	..	..
2400 Unallocable between 2100, 2200 and 2300	..	..	..	..	..	179	1 727	8 671	13 524	21 068
3000 Taxes on payroll and workforce[1]	**0**	**0**	**0**	**0**	**0**	**0**	**0**	**0**	**0**	**0**
4000 Taxes on property	**0**	**0**	**0**	**0**	**0**	**0**	**0**	**0**	**0**	**0**
4100 Recurrent taxes on immovable property	..	..	..	..	..	..	..	..	..	..
4200 Recurrent taxes on net wealth	..	..	..	..	..	..	..	..	..	..
4300 Estate, inheritance and gift taxes	..	..	..	..	..	..	..	..	..	..
4400 Taxes on financial and capital transactions	..	..	..	..	..	..	..	..	..	..
4500 Non-recurrent taxes	..	..	..	..	..	..	..	..	..	..
4600 Other recurrent taxes on property	..	..	..	..	..	..	..	..	..	..
5000 Taxes on goods and services	**0**	**0**	**0**	**0**	**0**	**0**	**0**	**0**	**0**	**0**
5100 Taxes on production, sale, transfer, etc	..	..	..	..	..	..	..	..	..	..
5110 General taxes	..	..	..	..	..	..	..	..	..	..
5120 Taxes on specific goods and services	..	..	..	..	..	..	..	..	..	..
5130 Unallocable between 5110 and 5120	..	..	..	..	..	..	..	..	..	..
5200 Taxes on use of goods and perform activities	..	..	..	..	..	..	..	..	..	..
5300 Unallocable between 5100 and 5200	..	..	..	..	..	..	..	..	..	..
6000 Other taxes	**90**	**960**	**2 216**	**2 495**	**5 202**	**0**	**0**	**0**	**0**	**0**
6100 Paid solely by business	0	0	0	0	0	..	..	..	..	..
6200 Other	90	960	2 216	2 495	5 202	..	..	..	..	..
Total tax revenue	**90**	**960**	**2 216**	**2 495**	**5 202**	**179**	**1 727**	**8 671**	**13 524**	**21 068**

.. Not available

1. The employer contributions to National Institute of Vocational Training (INFOP) have been added and classified as payroll tax in this edition. The tax revenue is classified under the central government. In Honduras this revenue is classified under a separate unit considered to be different to the central government.
2. The figures may include non-tax revenues and central government transfers but it has not been possible to distinguish the different components of local government tax revenues.

StatLink https://doi.org/10.1787/888934236304

Table 6.18. **Jamaica, tax revenues by subsectores of government**

Million JMD

	Federal government[1]					State/Regional				
	1990	2000	2010	2015	2019	1990	2000	2010	2015	2019
1000 Taxes on income, profits and capital gains	**3 944**	**39 277**	**118 708**	**149 990**	**186 434**	..	..	..	..	..
1100 Of individuals	1 687	17 441	54 798	74 538	69 323	..	..	..	..	..
1200 Corporate	1 280	7 627	33 091	40 198	67 623	..	..	..	..	..
1300 Unallocable between 1100 and 1200	977	14 209	30 820	35 255	49 488	..	..	..	..	..
2000 Social security contributions	**0**	**0**	**0**	**0**	**0**	..	..	..	..	..
2100 Employees	..	..	..	..	..	..	..	..	..	..
2200 Employers	..	..	..	..	..	..	..	..	..	..
2300 Self-employed or non-employed	..	..	..	..	..	..	..	..	..	..
2400 Unallocable between 2100, 2200 and 2300	..	..	..	..	..	..	..	..	..	..
3000 Taxes on payroll and workforce	**0**	**0**	**0**	**0**	**0**	..	..	..	..	..
4000 Taxes on property	**965**	**3 623**	**7 339**	**12 140**	**10 097**	..	..	..	..	..
4100 Recurrent taxes on immovable property	67	0	0	0	0	..	..	..	..	..
4200 Recurrent taxes on net wealth	0	0	0	0	0	..	..	..	..	..
4300 Estate, inheritance and gift taxes	0	0	0	0	0	..	..	..	..	..
4400 Taxes on financial and capital transactions	898	3 623	7 339	12 140	10 097	..	..	..	..	..
4500 Non-recurrent taxes	0	0	0	0	0	..	..	..	..	..
4600 Other recurrent taxes on property	0	0	0	0	0	..	..	..	..	..
5000 Taxes on goods and services	**2 824**	**43 907**	**149 544**	**240 795**	**370 321**	..	..	..	..	..
5100 Taxes on production, sale, transfer, etc	2 760	43 107	147 500	237 456	363 429	..	..	..	..	..
5110 General taxes	297	22 356	84 409	138 501	203 297	..	..	..	..	..
5120 Taxes on specific goods and services	2 463	20 752	63 091	98 955	160 133	..	..	..	..	..
5130 Unallocable between 5110 and 5120	0	0	0	0	0	..	..	..	..	..
5200 Taxes on use of goods and perform activities	64	800	2 045	3 339	6 892	..	..	..	..	..
5300 Unallocable between 5100 and 5200	0	0	0	0	0	..	..	..	..	..
6000 Other taxes	**16**	**266**	**748**	**994**	**2 151**	..	..	..	..	..
6100 Paid solely by business	0	0	0	0	0	..	..	..	..	..
6200 Other	16	266	748	994	2 151	..	..	..	..	..
Total tax revenue	**7 748**	**87 074**	**276 340**	**403 919**	**569 003**	..	..	..	..	..

Million JMD

	Local government[1]					Social Security Funds[1]				
	1990	2000	2010	2015	2019	1990	2000	2010	2015	2019
1000 Taxes on income, profits and capital gains	..	**0**	**0**	**0**	**0**	..	..	**0**	**0**	**0**
1100 Of individuals	..	..	..	..	..	..	..	..	..	..
1200 Corporate	..	..	..	..	..	..	..	..	..	..
1300 Unallocable between 1100 and 1200	..	..	..	..	..	..	..	..	..	..
2000 Social security contributions	..	**0**	**0**	**0**	**0**	..	..	**8 199**	**16 449**	**24 569**
2100 Employees	..	..	..	..	..	..	..	..	..	..
2200 Employers	..	..	..	..	..	..	..	..	..	..
2300 Self-employed or non-employed	..	..	..	..	..	..	..	..	..	..
2400 Unallocable between 2100, 2200 and 2300	..	..	..	..	..	..	..	8 199	16 449	24 569
3000 Taxes on payroll and workforce	..	**0**	**0**	**0**	**0**	..	..	**0**	**0**	**0**
4000 Taxes on property	..	**639**	**2 600**	**7 271**	**9 020**	..	..	**0**	**0**	**0**
4100 Recurrent taxes on immovable property	..	639	2 600	7 271	9 020	..	..	..	..	..
4200 Recurrent taxes on net wealth	..	0	0	0	0	..	..	..	..	..
4300 Estate, inheritance and gift taxes	..	0	0	0	0	..	..	..	..	..
4400 Taxes on financial and capital transactions	..	0	0	0	0	..	..	..	..	..
4500 Non-recurrent taxes	..	0	0	0	0	..	..	..	..	..
4600 Other recurrent taxes on property	..	0	0	0	0	..	..	..	..	..
5000 Taxes on goods and services	..	**0**	**0**	**0**	**0**	..	..	**0**	**0**	**0**
5100 Taxes on production, sale, transfer, etc	..	..	..	..	..	..	..	..	..	..
5110 General taxes	..	..	..	..	..	..	..	..	..	..
5120 Taxes on specific goods and services	..	..	..	..	..	..	..	..	..	..
5130 Unallocable between 5110 and 5120	..	..	..	..	..	..	..	..	..	..
5200 Taxes on use of goods and perform activities	..	..	..	..	..	..	..	..	..	..
5300 Unallocable between 5100 and 5200	..	..	..	..	..	..	..	..	..	..
6000 Other taxes	..	**0**	**0**	**0**	**0**	..	..	**0**	**0**	**0**
6100 Paid solely by business	..	..	..	..	..	..	..	..	..	..
6200 Other	..	..	..	..	..	..	..	..	..	..
Total tax revenue	..	**639**	**2 600**	**7 271**	**9 020**	..	..	**8 199**	**16 449**	**24 569**

.. Not available

1. The figures refer to fiscal year ending 31st March for 1990-2003 and then calendar year ending 31st December.

StatLink https://doi.org/10.1787/888934236323

Table 6.19. **Mexico, tax revenues by subsectores of government**

Million MXN

	Federal government					State/Regional				
	1990	2000	2010	2015	2019	1990	2000	2010	2015	2019
1000 Taxes on income, profits and capital gains[1]	**34 668**	**276 548**	**683 604**	**1 230 555**	**1 694 804**	**3**	**0**	**0**	**0**	..
1100 Of individuals	..	..	313 473	609 384	829 501	..	..	..	..	..
1200 Corporate	..	..	246 745	592 443	803 643	..	..	..	..	..
1300 Unallocable between 1100 and 1200	34 668	276 548	123 386	28 728	61 660	3	..	..	..	..
2000 Social security contributions	**0**	**0**	**0**	**0**	**0**	**0**	**0**	**0**	**0**	..
2100 Employees	..	..	..	..	..	..	..	..	..	..
2200 Employers	..	..	..	..	..	..	..	..	..	..
2300 Self-employed or non-employed	..	..	..	..	..	..	..	..	..	..
2400 Unallocable between 2100, 2200 and 2300	..	..	..	..	..	..	..	..	..	..
3000 Taxes on payroll and workforce	**818**	**0**	**0**	**0**	**0**	**972**	**11 215**	**36 818**	**70 221**	..
4000 Taxes on property	**3**	**0**	**0**	**0**	**0**	**894**	**7 018**	**13 137**	**22 481**	..
4100 Recurrent taxes on immovable property	0	..	..	..	..	482	5 238	8 522	14 245	..
4200 Recurrent taxes on net wealth	0	..	..	..	..	0	0	0	0	..
4300 Estate, inheritance and gift taxes	0	..	..	..	..	7	0	0	0	..
4400 Taxes on financial and capital transactions	3	..	..	..	..	405	1 781	4 615	8 235	..
4500 Non-recurrent taxes	0	..	..	..	..	0	0	0	0	..
4600 Other recurrent taxes on property	0	..	..	..	..	0	0	0	0	..
5000 Taxes on goods and services	**44 605**	**318 065**	**645 623**	**1 116 026**	**1 477 876**	**118**	**1 346**	**5 805**	**24 355**	..
5100 Taxes on production, sale, transfer, etc	44 029	309 283	627 187	1 115 525	1 477 157	45	910	2 470	4 357	..
5110 General taxes	26 635	189 606	504 509	707 213	933 327	..	0	0	0	..
5120 Taxes on specific goods and services	17 394	119 677	122 678	408 312	543 831	30	910	2 470	4 357	..
5130 Unallocable between 5110 and 5120	0	0	0	0	0	15	0	0	0	..
5200 Taxes on use of goods and perform activities	576	8 782	18 436	501	719	73	436	3 335	19 998	..
5300 Unallocable between 5100 and 5200	0	0	0	0	0	0	0	0	0	..
6000 Other taxes	**1 340**	**5 878**	**22 236**	**27 379**	**41 142**	**165**	**907**	**2 546**	**6 489**	..
6100 Paid solely by business	0	0	0	0	0	0	0	0	0	..
6200 Other	1 340	5 878	22 236	27 379	41 142	165	907	2 546	6 489	..
Total tax revenue	**81 434**	**600 491**	**1 351 463**	**2 373 960**	**3 213 821**	**2 152**	**20 485**	**58 307**	**123 545**	..

Million MXN

	Local government					Social Security Funds[2]				
	1990	2000	2010	2015	2019	1990	2000	2010	2015	2019
1000 Taxes on income, profits and capital gains[1]	**2**	**0**	**0**	**0**	..	**0**	**0**	**0**	**0**	**0**
1100 Of individuals	..	..	..	..	..	..	..	..	..	..
1200 Corporate	..	..	..	..	..	..	..	..	..	..
1300 Unallocable between 1100 and 1200	2	..	..	..	..	..	..	..	..	..
2000 Social security contributions	**0**	**0**	**0**	**0**	..	**17 165**	**138 223**	**277 459**	**409 249**	**552 058**
2100 Employees	..	..	..	..	..	..	..	..	..	..
2200 Employers	..	..	..	..	..	..	..	..	..	..
2300 Self-employed or non-employed	..	..	..	..	..	..	..	..	..	..
2400 Unallocable between 2100, 2200 and 2300	..	..	..	..	..	17 165	138 223	277 459	409 249	552 058
3000 Taxes on payroll and workforce	**7**	**2**	**93**	**1**	..	**0**	**0**	**0**	**0**	**0**
4000 Taxes on property	**1 017**	**6 946**	**25 818**	**35 193**	..	**0**	**0**	**0**	**0**	**0**
4100 Recurrent taxes on immovable property	554	4 710	17 202	23 715	..	..	..	..	..	..
4200 Recurrent taxes on net wealth	0	0	0	0	..	..	..	..	..	..
4300 Estate, inheritance and gift taxes	1	0	0	0	..	..	..	..	..	..
4400 Taxes on financial and capital transactions	462	2 236	8 616	11 477	..	..	..	..	..	..
4500 Non-recurrent taxes	0	0	0	0	..	..	..	..	..	..
4600 Other recurrent taxes on property	0	0	0	0	..	..	..	..	..	..
5000 Taxes on goods and services	**114**	**202**	**487**	**789**	..	**0**	**0**	**0**	**0**	**0**
5100 Taxes on production, sale, transfer, etc	97	133	466	728	..	..	..	..	..	..
5110 General taxes	..	0	0	0	..	..	..	..	..	..
5120 Taxes on specific goods and services	95	133	466	728	..	..	..	..	..	..
5130 Unallocable between 5110 and 5120	2	0	0	0	..	..	..	..	..	..
5200 Taxes on use of goods and perform activities	17	69	21	61	..	..	..	..	..	..
5300 Unallocable between 5100 and 5200	0	0	0	0	..	..	..	..	..	..
6000 Other taxes	**114**	**866**	**2 616**	**10 743**	..	**0**	**0**	**0**	**0**	**0**
6100 Paid solely by business	0	0	0	0	..	..	..	..	..	..
6200 Other	114	866	2 616	10 743	..	..	..	..	..	..
Total tax revenue	**1 254**	**8 016**	**29 014**	**46 726**	..	**17 165**	**138 223**	**277 459**	**409 249**	**552 058**

.. Not available

Note: The 2019 data for tax revenues at the state and local levels of government are not available. They comprise revenues in categories 3000, 4000, 5000 and 6000.

1. In ECLAC data, income taxes are presented net of credit on salary figures.
2. Some amounts of social security contributions are now treated as non-tax revenue to align with reporting to other international organisations. In ECLAC data, social security contributions are presented net of transfers from the Federal government for the payment of IMSS (Mexican Social Security Institute) pensions.

StatLink https://doi.org/10.1787/888934236342

Table 6.20. Nicaragua, tax revenues by subsectores of government

Million NIO

	Federal government					State/Regional				
	1990	2000	2010	2015	2019	1990	2000	2010	2015	2019
1000 Taxes on income, profits and capital gains	..	**1 144**	**8 351**	**21 313**	**33 036**	..	..	..	..	..
1100 Of individuals	..	299	1 857	4 432	6 561	..	..	..	..	..
1200 Corporate	..	845	6 494	16 881	26 475	..	..	..	..	..
1300 Unallocable between 1100 and 1200	..	0	0	0	0	..	..	..	..	..
2000 Social security contributions	..	**0**	**0**	**0**	**0**	..	..	..	..	..
2100 Employees	..	..	..	..	..	..	..	..	..	..
2200 Employers	..	..	..	..	..	..	..	..	..	..
2300 Self-employed or non-employed	..	..	..	..	..	..	..	..	..	..
2400 Unallocable between 2100, 2200 and 2300	..	..	..	..	..	..	..	..	..	..
3000 Taxes on payroll and workforce	..	**0**	**0**	**0**	**0**	..	..	..	..	..
4000 Taxes on property	..	**11**	**20**	**90**	**67**	..	..	..	..	..
4100 Recurrent taxes on immovable property	..	0	0	0	0	..	..	..	..	..
4200 Recurrent taxes on net wealth	..	0	0	0	0	..	..	..	..	..
4300 Estate, inheritance and gift taxes	..	0	0	0	0	..	..	..	..	..
4400 Taxes on financial and capital transactions	..	11	20	90	67	..	..	..	..	..
4500 Non-recurrent taxes	..	0	0	0	0	..	..	..	..	..
4600 Other recurrent taxes on property	..	0	0	0	0	..	..	..	..	..
5000 Taxes on goods and services	..	**5 584**	**17 029**	**32 725**	**40 176**	..	..	..	..	..
5100 Taxes on production, sale, transfer, etc	..	5 584	17 029	32 725	40 176	..	..	..	..	..
5110 General taxes	..	2 931	10 353	20 714	24 435	..	..	..	..	..
5120 Taxes on specific goods and services	..	2 653	6 676	12 011	15 741	..	..	..	..	..
5130 Unallocable between 5110 and 5120	..	0	0	0	0	..	..	..	..	..
5200 Taxes on use of goods and perform activities	..	0	0	0	0	..	..	..	..	..
5300 Unallocable between 5100 and 5200	..	0	0	0	0	..	..	..	..	..
6000 Other taxes	..	**0**	**0**	**0**	**0**	..	..	..	..	..
6100 Paid solely by business	..	..	..	..	..	..	..	..	..	..
6200 Other	..	..	..	..	..	..	..	..	..	..
Total tax revenue	..	**6 739**	**25 400**	**54 128**	**73 278**	..	..	..	..	..

Million NIO

	Local government					Social Security Funds				
	1990	2000	2010	2015	2019	1990	2000	2010	2015	2019
1000 Taxes on income, profits and capital gains	..	**0**	**0**	**0**	**0**	..	**0**	**0**	**0**	**0**
1100 Of individuals	..	..	..	..	..	..	..	..	..	..
1200 Corporate	..	..	..	..	..	..	..	..	..	..
1300 Unallocable between 1100 and 1200	..	..	..	..	..	..	..	..	..	..
2000 Social security contributions	..	**0**	**0**	**0**	**0**	..	**1 678**	**8 090**	**18 194**	**27 586**
2100 Employees	..	..	..	..	..	..	..	..	..	..
2200 Employers	..	..	..	..	..	..	..	..	..	..
2300 Self-employed or non-employed	..	..	..	..	..	..	..	..	..	..
2400 Unallocable between 2100, 2200 and 2300	..	..	..	..	..	..	1 678	8 090	18 194	27 586
3000 Taxes on payroll and workforce	..	**0**	**0**	**0**	**0**	..	**0**	**0**	**0**	**0**
4000 Taxes on property	..	**0**	**403**	**682**	**1 129**	..	**0**	**0**	**0**	**0**
4100 Recurrent taxes on immovable property	..	..	403	682	1 129	..	..	..	..	..
4200 Recurrent taxes on net wealth	..	..	0	0	0	..	..	..	..	..
4300 Estate, inheritance and gift taxes	..	..	0	0	0	..	..	..	..	..
4400 Taxes on financial and capital transactions	..	..	0	0	0	..	..	..	..	..
4500 Non-recurrent taxes	..	..	0	0	0	..	..	..	..	..
4600 Other recurrent taxes on property	..	..	0	0	0	..	..	..	..	..
5000 Taxes on goods and services	..	**0**	**1 922**	**3 874**	**4 432**	..	**0**	**0**	**0**	**0**
5100 Taxes on production, sale, transfer, etc	..	..	1 579	3 073	3 498	..	..	..	..	..
5110 General taxes	..	..	1 579	3 073	3 498	..	..	..	..	..
5120 Taxes on specific goods and services	..	..	0	0	0	..	..	..	..	..
5130 Unallocable between 5110 and 5120	..	..	0	0	0	..	..	..	..	..
5200 Taxes on use of goods and perform activities	..	..	343	801	934	..	..	..	..	..
5300 Unallocable between 5100 and 5200	..	..	0	0	0	..	..	..	..	..
6000 Other taxes	..	**0**	**347**	**690**	**907**	..	**0**	**0**	**0**	**0**
6100 Paid solely by business	..	..	0	0	0	..	..	..	..	..
6200 Other	..	..	347	690	907	..	..	..	..	..
Total tax revenue	..	**882**	**2 672**	**5 246**	**6 468**	..	**1 678**	**8 090**	**18 194**	**27 586**

.. Not available

Note: Comparable statistics for 1990 cannot be shown due to the devaluation of the Nicaraguan cordoba.

StatLink https://doi.org/10.1787/888934236361

Table 6.21. **Panama, tax revenues by subsectores of government**

Million PAB

	Federal government[3]					State/Regional				
	1990	2000	2010	2015	2019	1990	2000	2010	2015	2019
1000 Taxes on income, profits and capital gains	**217**	**485**	**1 317**	**2 066**	**2 445**	**..**	**..**	**..**	**..**	**..**
1100 Of individuals	140	295	440	799	1 135	..	..	..	..	..
1200 Corporate	66	159	603	851	903	..	..	..	..	..
1300 Unallocable between 1100 and 1200	11	31	273	416	407	..	..	..	..	..
2000 Social security contributions	**0**	**0**	**0**	**0**	**0**	**..**	**..**	**..**	**..**	**..**
2100 Employees	..	..	..	..	..	..	..	..	..	..
2200 Employers	..	..	..	..	..	..	..	..	..	..
2300 Self-employed or non-employed	..	..	..	..	..	..	..	..	..	..
2400 Unallocable between 2100, 2200 and 2300	..	..	..	..	..	..	..	..	..	..
3000 Taxes on payroll and workforce[1]	**0**	**36**	**59**	**111**	**140**	**..**	**..**	**..**	**..**	**..**
4000 Taxes on property	**32**	**43**	**138**	**199**	**169**	**..**	**..**	**..**	**..**	**..**
4100 Recurrent taxes on immovable property	28	34	108	151	134	..	..	..	..	..
4200 Recurrent taxes on net wealth	0	0	0	0	0	..	..	..	..	..
4300 Estate, inheritance and gift taxes	0	0	0	0	0	..	..	..	..	..
4400 Taxes on financial and capital transactions	3	9	30	48	35	..	..	..	..	..
4500 Non-recurrent taxes	0	0	0	0	0	..	..	..	..	..
4600 Other recurrent taxes on property	0	0	0	0	0	..	..	..	..	..
5000 Taxes on goods and services	**349**	**565**	**1 547**	**2 496**	**2 562**	**..**	**..**	**..**	**..**	**..**
5100 Taxes on production, sale, transfer, etc	332	546	1 473	2 376	2 435	..	..	..	..	..
5110 General taxes	80	69	766	1 357	1 453	..	..	..	..	..
5120 Taxes on specific goods and services[2]	251	477	707	1 019	982	..	..	..	..	..
5130 Unallocable between 5110 and 5120	0	0	0	0	0	..	..	..	..	..
5200 Taxes on use of goods and perform activities	15	19	75	120	126	..	..	..	..	..
5300 Unallocable between 5100 and 5200	2	0	0	0	0	..	..	..	..	..
6000 Other taxes	**26**	**27**	**41**	**37**	**30**	**..**	**..**	**..**	**..**	**..**
6100 Paid solely by business	0	0	0	0	0	..	..	..	..	..
6200 Other	26	27	41	37	30	..	..	..	..	..
Total tax revenue	**624**	**1 157**	**3 102**	**4 910**	**5 346**	**..**	**..**	**..**	**..**	**..**

Million PAB

	Local government					Social Security Funds[4]				
	1990	2000	2010	2015	2019	1990	2000	2010	2015	2019
1000 Taxes on income, profits and capital gains	**..**	**0**	**0**	**0**	**0**	**0**	**0**	**0**	**0**	**0**
1100 Of individuals	..	..	..	..	..	..	..	..	..	..
1200 Corporate	..	..	..	..	..	..	..	..	..	..
1300 Unallocable between 1100 and 1200	..	..	..	..	..	..	..	..	..	..
2000 Social security contributions	**..**	**0**	**0**	**0**	**0**	**325**	**742**	**1 637**	**3 152**	**3 894**
2100 Employees	..	..	..	..	..	..	..	..	..	..
2200 Employers	..	..	..	..	..	..	..	..	..	..
2300 Self-employed or non-employed	..	..	..	..	..	..	..	..	..	..
2400 Unallocable between 2100, 2200 and 2300	..	..	..	..	..	325	742	1 637	3 152	3 894
3000 Taxes on payroll and workforce[1]	**..**	**0**	**0**	**0**	**0**	**0**	**0**	**0**	**0**	**0**
4000 Taxes on property	**..**	**0**	**0**	**0**	**0**	**0**	**0**	**0**	**0**	**0**
4100 Recurrent taxes on immovable property	..	0	..	..	..	..	..	..	..	..
4200 Recurrent taxes on net wealth	..	0	..	..	..	..	..	..	..	..
4300 Estate, inheritance and gift taxes	..	0	..	..	..	..	..	..	..	..
4400 Taxes on financial and capital transactions	..	0	..	..	..	..	..	..	..	..
4500 Non-recurrent taxes	..	0	..	..	..	..	..	..	..	..
4600 Other recurrent taxes on property	..	0	..	..	..	..	..	..	..	..
5000 Taxes on goods and services	**..**	**43**	**76**	**131**	**154**	**0**	**0**	**0**	**0**	**0**
5100 Taxes on production, sale, transfer, etc	..	0	0	0	0	..	..	..	..	..
5110 General taxes	..	0	..	..	..	..	..	..	..	..
5120 Taxes on specific goods and services[2]	..	0	..	..	..	..	..	..	..	..
5130 Unallocable between 5110 and 5120	..	0	..	..	..	..	..	..	..	..
5200 Taxes on use of goods and perform activities	..	43	76	131	154	..	..	..	..	..
5300 Unallocable between 5100 and 5200	..	0	0	0	0	..	..	..	..	..
6000 Other taxes	**..**	**0**	**0**	**0**	**0**	**0**	**0**	**0**	**0**	**0**
6100 Paid solely by business	..	0	..	..	..	..	..	..	..	..
6200 Other	..	0	..	..	..	..	..	..	..	..
Total tax revenue	**..**	**43**	**76**	**131**	**154**	**325**	**742**	**1 637**	**3 152**	**3 894**

.. Not available

1. In ECLAC data, education insurance is classified as "Other taxes" (6000).
2. In CIAT and ECLAC data, the tax on banks, financial institutions and currency exchange is classified as a property tax (4000).
3. The figures exclude documentos fiscales as they are not considered as tax revenues according to the OECD classification, described in the interpretative guide.
4. Social security contributions have been updated with data from Caja de Seguro Social and CIAT in this edition.

StatLink https://doi.org/10.1787/888934236380

Table 6.22. **Paraguay, tax revenues by subsectores of government**

Million PYG

	Federal government					State/Regional				
	1990	2000	2010	2015	2019	1990	2000	2010	2015	2019
1000 Taxes on income, profits and capital gains	**73 726**	**470 388**	**2 096 498**	**3 922 384**	**6 022 875**	**..**	**..**	**..**	**..**	**..**
1100 Of individuals	..	15 042	31 263	409 238	620 038	..	..	..	..	..
1200 Corporate	..	455 346	2 065 235	3 513 146	5 402 837	..	..	..	..	..
1300 Unallocable between 1100 and 1200	73 726	0	0	0	0	..	..	..	..	..
2000 Social security contributions	**0**	**0**	**0**	**0**	**0**	**..**	**..**	**..**	**..**	**..**
2100 Employees	..	..	..	..	..	..	..	..	..	..
2200 Employers	..	..	..	..	..	..	..	..	..	..
2300 Self-employed or non-employed	..	..	..	..	..	..	..	..	..	..
2400 Unallocable between 2100, 2200 and 2300	..	..	..	..	..	..	..	..	..	..
3000 Taxes on payroll and workforce	**0**	**0**	**0**	**0**	**0**	**..**	**..**	**..**	**..**	**..**
4000 Taxes on property	**17 162**	**71 777**	**332**	**91**	**76**	**..**	**..**	**..**	**..**	**..**
4100 Recurrent taxes on immovable property	17 162	0	0	0	0	..	..	..	..	..
4200 Recurrent taxes on net wealth	0	0	0	0	0	..	..	..	..	..
4300 Estate, inheritance and gift taxes	0	0	0	0	0	..	..	..	..	..
4400 Taxes on financial and capital transactions	0	71 777	332	91	76	..	..	..	..	..
4500 Non-recurrent taxes	0	0	0	0	0	..	..	..	..	..
4600 Other recurrent taxes on property	0	0	0	0	0	..	..	..	..	..
5000 Taxes on goods and services	**438 444**	**2 080 878**	**9 226 584**	**13 837 266**	**17 214 152**	**..**	**..**	**..**	**..**	**..**
5100 Taxes on production, sale, transfer, etc	438 444	2 080 878	9 226 493	13 837 212	17 214 152	..	..	..	..	..
5110 General taxes	0	1 150 496	5 991 694	9 768 800	11 794 402	..	..	..	..	..
5120 Taxes on specific goods and services	438 444	930 382	3 234 799	4 068 411	5 419 750	..	..	..	..	..
5130 Unallocable between 5110 and 5120	0	0	0	0	0	..	..	..	..	..
5200 Taxes on use of goods and perform activities	0	0	91	54	0	..	..	..	..	..
5300 Unallocable between 5100 and 5200	0	0	0	0	0	..	..	..	..	..
6000 Other taxes	**49 807**	**44 875**	**109 001**	**128 632**	**150 081**	**..**	**..**	**..**	**..**	**..**
6100 Paid solely by business	0	0	0	0	0	..	..	..	..	..
6200 Other	49 807	44 875	109 001	128 632	150 081	..	..	..	..	..
Total tax revenue	**579 139**	**2 667 918**	**11 432 415**	**17 888 373**	**23 387 184**	**..**	**..**	**..**	**..**	**..**

Million PYG

	Local government[1]					Social Security Funds[2]				
	1990	2000	2010	2015	2019	1990	2000	2010	2015	2019
1000 Taxes on income, profits and capital gains	**..**	**..**	**0**	**0**	**0**	**0**	**0**	**0**	**0**	**0**
1100 Of individuals	..	..	..	..	..	..	..	..	..	..
1200 Corporate	..	..	..	..	..	..	..	..	..	..
1300 Unallocable between 1100 and 1200	..	..	..	..	..	..	..	..	..	..
2000 Social security contributions	**..**	**..**	**0**	**0**	**0**	**28 882**	**919 527**	**3 552 640**	**7 044 316**	**8 729 492**
2100 Employees	..	..	..	..	..	..	..	..	..	..
2200 Employers	..	..	..	..	..	..	..	..	..	..
2300 Self-employed or non-employed	..	..	..	..	..	..	..	..	..	..
2400 Unallocable between 2100, 2200 and 2300	..	..	..	..	..	28 882	919 527	3 552 640	7 044 316	8 729 492
3000 Taxes on payroll and workforce	**..**	**..**	**0**	**0**	**0**	**0**	**0**	**0**	**0**	**0**
4000 Taxes on property	**..**	**..**	**275 787**	**435 382**	**443 444**	**0**	**0**	**0**	**0**	**0**
4100 Recurrent taxes on immovable property	..	..	258 423	405 806	417 177	..	..	..	..	..
4200 Recurrent taxes on net wealth	..	..	0	0	0	..	..	..	..	..
4300 Estate, inheritance and gift taxes	..	..	0	0	0	..	..	..	..	..
4400 Taxes on financial and capital transactions	..	..	15 623	29 510	24 836	..	..	..	..	..
4500 Non-recurrent taxes	..	..	0	0	0	..	..	..	..	..
4600 Other recurrent taxes on property	..	..	1 742	66	1 432	..	..	..	..	..
5000 Taxes on goods and services	**..**	**..**	**235 877**	**442 063**	**396 776**	**0**	**0**	**0**	**0**	**0**
5100 Taxes on production, sale, transfer, etc	..	..	19 384	23 423	16 606	..	..	..	..	..
5110 General taxes	..	..	0	0	0	..	..	..	..	..
5120 Taxes on specific goods and services	..	..	19 384	23 423	16 606	..	..	..	..	..
5130 Unallocable between 5110 and 5120	..	..	0	0	0	..	..	..	..	..
5200 Taxes on use of goods and perform activities	..	..	216 256	395 802	379 208	..	..	..	..	..
5300 Unallocable between 5100 and 5200	..	..	237	22 838	962	..	..	..	..	..
6000 Other taxes	**..**	**..**	**141 811**	**45 052**	**51 836**	**0**	**0**	**0**	**0**	**0**
6100 Paid solely by business	..	..	0	0	0	..	..	..	..	..
6200 Other	..	..	141 811	45 052	51 836	..	..	..	..	..
Total tax revenue	**..**	**..**	**653 476**	**922 496**	**892 057**	**28 882**	**919 527**	**3 552 640**	**7 044 316**	**8 729 492**

.. Not available

1. The figures for years before 2006 exclude local government tax revenues as the data are not available.
2. Social security contributions before 1999 do not include contributions collected by decentralised institutions as the data are not available.

StatLink https://doi.org/10.1787/888934236399

Table 6.23. **Peru, tax revenues by subsectores of government**

Million PEN

	Federal government					State/Regional				
	1990	2000	2010	2015	2019	1990	2000	2010	2015	2019
1000 Taxes on income, profits and capital gains	**37**	**5 078**	**27 317**	**37 772**	**46 753**	..	..	..	..	..
1100 Of individuals	3	2 117	6 518	11 137	14 744	..	..	..	..	..
1200 Corporate	32	2 526	19 561	24 266	29 449	..	..	..	..	..
1300 Unallocable between 1100 and 1200	1	436	1 239	2 369	2 560	..	..	..	..	..
2000 Social security contributions	**0**	**0**	**0**	**0**	**0**	..	..	..	..	..
2100 Employees	..	..	..	..	..	..	..	..	..	..
2200 Employers	..	..	..	..	..	..	..	..	..	..
2300 Self-employed or non-employed	..	..	..	..	..	..	..	..	..	..
2400 Unallocable between 2100, 2200 and 2300	..	..	..	..	..	..	..	..	..	..
3000 Taxes on payroll and workforce[1]	**0**	**1 176**	**57**	**92**	**99**	..	..	..	..	..
4000 Taxes on property	**87**	**0**	**944**	**161**	**224**	..	..	..	..	..
4100 Recurrent taxes on immovable property	0	0	0	0	0	..	..	..	..	..
4200 Recurrent taxes on net wealth	49	0	0	0	0	..	..	..	..	..
4300 Estate, inheritance and gift taxes	0	0	0	0	0	..	..	..	..	..
4400 Taxes on financial and capital transactions	38	0	944	161	224	..	..	..	..	..
4500 Non-recurrent taxes	0	0	0	0	0	..	..	..	..	..
4600 Other recurrent taxes on property	0	0	0	0	0	..	..	..	..	..
5000 Taxes on goods and services	**454**	**16 205**	**36 064**	**50 606**	**59 814**	..	..	..	..	..
5100 Taxes on production, sale, transfer, etc	454	16 205	36 064	50 606	59 814	..	..	..	..	..
5110 General taxes	109	9 646	29 094	42 612	49 197	..	..	..	..	..
5120 Taxes on specific goods and services	345	6 558	6 970	7 994	10 617	..	..	..	..	..
5130 Unallocable between 5110 and 5120	0	0	0	0	0	..	..	..	..	..
5200 Taxes on use of goods and perform activities	0	0	0	0	0	..	..	..	..	..
5300 Unallocable between 5100 and 5200	0	0	0	0	0	..	..	..	..	..
6000 Other taxes	**9**	**697**	**888**	**2 088**	**2 202**	..	..	..	..	..
6100 Paid solely by business	0	84	108	179	135	..	..	..	..	..
6200 Other	9	614	780	1 909	2 067	..	..	..	..	..
Total tax revenue	**587**	**23 156**	**65 270**	**90 719**	**109 092**	..	..	..	..	..

Million PEN

	Local government[2]					Social Security Funds				
	1990	2000	2010	2015	2019	1990	2000	2010	2015	2019
1000 Taxes on income, profits and capital gains	..	**0**	**0**	**0**	**0**	**0**	**0**	**0**	**0**	**0**
1100 Of individuals	..	..	..	..	..	..	..	..	..	..
1200 Corporate	..	..	..	..	..	..	..	..	..	..
1300 Unallocable between 1100 and 1200	..	..	..	..	..	..	..	..	..	..
2000 Social security contributions	..	**0**	**0**	**0**	**0**	**50**	**3 185**	**7 929**	**12 681**	**15 453**
2100 Employees	..	..	..	..	..	..	566	2 468	3 508	4 202
2200 Employers	..	..	..	..	..	..	2 515	5 454	9 170	11 245
2300 Self-employed or non-employed	..	..	..	..	..	..	95	7	2	6
2400 Unallocable between 2100, 2200 and 2300	..	..	..	..	..	50	9	0	0	0
3000 Taxes on payroll and workforce[1]	..	**0**	**0**	**0**	**0**	**0**	**0**	**0**	**0**	**0**
4000 Taxes on property	..	**323**	**1 287**	**2 268**	**2 839**	**0**	**0**	**0**	**0**	**0**
4100 Recurrent taxes on immovable property	..	298	727	1 463	2 026	..	..	..	..	..
4200 Recurrent taxes on net wealth	..	0	0	0	0	..	..	..	..	..
4300 Estate, inheritance and gift taxes	..	0	0	0	0	..	..	..	..	..
4400 Taxes on financial and capital transactions	..	25	560	805	813	..	..	..	..	..
4500 Non-recurrent taxes	..	0	0	0	0	..	..	..	..	..
4600 Other recurrent taxes on property	..	0	0	0	0	..	..	..	..	..
5000 Taxes on goods and services	..	**59**	**290**	**496**	**552**	**0**	**0**	**0**	**0**	**0**
5100 Taxes on production, sale, transfer, etc	..	34	135	214	250	..	..	..	..	..
5110 General taxes	..	0	0	0	0	..	..	..	..	..
5120 Taxes on specific goods and services	..	34	135	214	250	..	..	..	..	..
5130 Unallocable between 5110 and 5120	..	0	0	0	0	..	..	..	..	..
5200 Taxes on use of goods and perform activities	..	25	154	282	302	..	..	..	..	..
5300 Unallocable between 5100 and 5200	..	0	0	0	0	..	..	..	..	..
6000 Other taxes	..	**48**	**26**	**19**	**13**	**0**	**0**	**0**	**0**	**0**
6100 Paid solely by business	..	0	0	0	0	..	..	..	..	..
6200 Other	..	48	26	19	13	..	..	..	..	..
Total tax revenue	..	**430**	**1 603**	**2 784**	**3 404**	**50**	**3 185**	**7 929**	**12 681**	**15 453**

.. Not available

1. Contributions to SENATI have been added in this edition. The tax revenue is classified under the central government. In Peru this revenue is classified under a separate unit considered to be different to the central government.
2. The figures for years up to 2000 exclude local government tax revenues as the data are not available.

StatLink https://doi.org/10.1787/888934236418

Table 6.24. **Saint Lucia, tax revenues by subsectores of government**

Million XCD

	Federal government					State/Regional				
	1990	2000	2010	2015	2019	1990	2000	2010	2015	2019
1000 Taxes on income, profits and capital gains	..	**137**	**224**	**242**	**256**	..	..	..	..	..
1100 Of individuals	..	49	83	105	134	..	..	..	..	..
1200 Corporate	..	63	95	78	111	..	..	..	..	..
1300 Unallocable between 1100 and 1200	..	26	46	58	11	..	..	..	..	..
2000 Social security contributions	..	**0**	..	**0**	**0**	..	..	..	..	..
2100 Employees	..	..	..	..	..	..	..	..	..	..
2200 Employers	..	..	..	..	..	..	..	..	..	..
2300 Self-employed or non-employed	..	..	..	..	..	..	..	..	..	..
2400 Unallocable between 2100, 2200 and 2300	..	..	..	..	..	..	..	..	..	..
3000 Taxes on payroll and workforce	..	**0**	**0**	**0**	**0**	..	..	..	..	..
4000 Taxes on property	..	**11**	**19**	**23**	**25**	..	..	..	..	..
4100 Recurrent taxes on immovable property	..	2	3	11	8	..	..	..	..	..
4200 Recurrent taxes on net wealth	..	0	..	0	0	..	..	..	..	..
4300 Estate, inheritance and gift taxes	..	0	0	0	0	..	..	..	..	..
4400 Taxes on financial and capital transactions	..	9	16	12	18	..	..	..	..	..
4500 Non-recurrent taxes	..	0	0	0	0	..	..	..	..	..
4600 Other recurrent taxes on property	..	0	0	0	0	..	..	..	..	..
5000 Taxes on goods and services	..	**284**	**493**	**670**	**774**	..	..	..	..	..
5100 Taxes on production, sale, transfer, etc	..	277	467	642	745	..	..	..	..	..
5110 General taxes	..	101	119	347	342	..	..	..	..	..
5120 Taxes on specific goods and services	..	176	348	295	402	..	..	..	..	..
5130 Unallocable between 5110 and 5120	..	0	0	0	0	..	..	..	..	..
5200 Taxes on use of goods and perform activities	..	7	26	29	29	..	..	..	..	..
5300 Unallocable between 5100 and 5200	..	0	0	0	0	..	..	..	..	..
6000 Other taxes	..	**0**	**0**	**0**	**0**	..	..	..	..	..
6100 Paid solely by business	..	..	..	..	..	..	..	..	..	..
6200 Other	..	..	..	..	..	..	..	..	..	..
Total tax revenue	..	**432**	**737**	**935**	**1 055**	..	..	..	..	..

Million XCD

	Local government[1]					Social Security Funds				
	1990	2000	2010	2015	2019	1990	2000	2010	2015	2019
1000 Taxes on income, profits and capital gains	..	..	..	..	..	..	**0**	**0**	**0**	**0**
1100 Of individuals	..	..	..	..	..	..	..	..	..	..
1200 Corporate	..	..	..	..	..	..	..	..	..	..
1300 Unallocable between 1100 and 1200	..	..	..	..	..	..	..	..	..	..
2000 Social security contributions	..	..	..	..	..	..	**48**	**92**	**111**	**124**
2100 Employees	..	..	..	..	..	..	..	..	..	..
2200 Employers	..	..	..	..	..	..	..	..	..	..
2300 Self-employed or non-employed	..	..	..	..	..	..	..	..	..	..
2400 Unallocable between 2100, 2200 and 2300	..	..	..	..	..	..	48	92	111	124
3000 Taxes on payroll and workforce	..	..	..	..	..	..	**0**	**0**	**0**	**0**
4000 Taxes on property	..	..	..	..	..	..	**0**	**0**	**0**	**0**
4100 Recurrent taxes on immovable property	..	..	..	..	..	..	..	..	..	..
4200 Recurrent taxes on net wealth	..	..	..	..	..	..	..	..	..	..
4300 Estate, inheritance and gift taxes	..	..	..	..	..	..	..	..	..	..
4400 Taxes on financial and capital transactions	..	..	..	..	..	..	..	..	..	..
4500 Non-recurrent taxes	..	..	..	..	..	..	..	..	..	..
4600 Other recurrent taxes on property	..	..	..	..	..	..	..	..	..	..
5000 Taxes on goods and services	..	..	..	..	..	..	**0**	**0**	**0**	**0**
5100 Taxes on production, sale, transfer, etc	..	..	..	..	..	..	..	..	..	..
5110 General taxes	..	..	..	..	..	..	..	..	..	..
5120 Taxes on specific goods and services	..	..	..	..	..	..	..	..	..	..
5130 Unallocable between 5110 and 5120	..	..	..	..	..	..	..	..	..	..
5200 Taxes on use of goods and perform activities	..	..	..	..	..	..	..	..	..	..
5300 Unallocable between 5100 and 5200	..	..	..	..	..	..	..	..	..	..
6000 Other taxes	..	..	..	..	..	..	**0**	**0**	**0**	**0**
6100 Paid solely by business	..	..	..	..	..	..	..	..	..	..
6200 Other	..	..	..	..	..	..	..	..	..	..
Total tax revenue	..	..	..	..	..	..	**48**	**92**	**111**	**124**

.. Not available

1. Local government tax revenues are not available.

StatLink https://doi.org/10.1787/888934236437

Table 6.25. **Trinidad and Tobago, tax revenues by subsectores of government**

Million TTD

	Federal government					State/Regional				
	1990	2000	2010	2015	2019	1990	2000	2010	2015	2019
1000 Taxes on income, profits and capital gains	**2 595**	**6 224**	**27 213**	**29 628**	**22 346**	..	..	..	..	..
1100 Of individuals	669	2 325	4 674	7 752	7 170	..	..	..	..	..
1200 Corporate	1 856	3 704	21 659	20 810	13 816	..	..	..	..	..
1300 Unallocable between 1100 and 1200	70	195	881	1 067	1 360	..	..	..	..	..
2000 Social security contributions	**0**	**0**	**0**	**0**	**0**	..	..	..	..	..
2100 Employees	..	..	..	..	..	..	..	..	..	..
2200 Employers	..	..	..	..	..	..	..	..	..	..
2300 Self-employed or non-employed	..	..	..	..	..	..	..	..	..	..
2400 Unallocable between 2100, 2200 and 2300	..	..	..	..	..	..	..	..	..	..
3000 Taxes on payroll and workforce	**0**	**0**	**0**	**0**	**0**	..	..	..	..	..
4000 Taxes on property	**90**	**175**	**194**	**406**	**405**	..	..	..	..	..
4100 Recurrent taxes on immovable property	39	64	22	3	50	..	..	..	..	..
4200 Recurrent taxes on net wealth	0	0	0	0	0	..	..	..	..	..
4300 Estate, inheritance and gift taxes	1	0	0	0	0	..	..	..	..	..
4400 Taxes on financial and capital transactions	49	111	172	403	356	..	..	..	..	..
4500 Non-recurrent taxes	0	0	0	0	0	..	..	..	..	..
4600 Other recurrent taxes on property	0	0	0	0	0	..	..	..	..	..
5000 Taxes on goods and services	**2 055**	**3 852**	**9 667**	**12 264**	**10 960**	..	..	..	..	..
5100 Taxes on production, sale, transfer, etc	1 973	3 603	9 282	11 678	10 657	..	..	..	..	..
5110 General taxes	980	1 890	6 358	7 569	6 836	..	..	..	..	..
5120 Taxes on specific goods and services	993	1 713	2 924	4 108	3 822	..	..	..	..	..
5130 Unallocable between 5110 and 5120	0	0	0	0	0	..	..	..	..	..
5200 Taxes on use of goods and perform activities	81	249	386	586	303	..	..	..	..	..
5300 Unallocable between 5100 and 5200	0	0	0	0	0	..	..	..	..	..
6000 Other taxes	**0**	**0**	**0**	**0**	**0**	..	..	..	..	..
6100 Paid solely by business	..	..	..	..	..	..	..	..	..	..
6200 Other	..	..	..	..	..	..	..	..	..	..
Total tax revenue	**4 740**	**10 251**	**37 074**	**42 298**	**33 711**	..	..	..	..	..

Million TTD

	Local government[1]					Social Security Funds[2]				
	1990	2000	2010	2015	2019	1990	2000	2010	2015	2019
1000 Taxes on income, profits and capital gains	..	..	..	..	..	**0**	**0**	**0**	**0**	**0**
1100 Of individuals	..	..	..	..	..	..	..	..	..	..
1200 Corporate	..	..	..	..	..	..	..	..	..	..
1300 Unallocable between 1100 and 1200	..	..	..	..	..	..	..	..	..	..
2000 Social security contributions	..	..	..	..	..	**183**	**702**	**2 645**	**4 261**	**4 757**
2100 Employees	..	..	..	..	..	..	..	..	..	..
2200 Employers	..	..	..	..	..	..	..	..	..	..
2300 Self-employed or non-employed	..	..	..	..	..	..	..	..	..	..
2400 Unallocable between 2100, 2200 and 2300	..	..	..	..	..	183	702	2 645	4 261	4 757
3000 Taxes on payroll and workforce	..	..	..	..	..	**0**	**0**	**0**	**0**	**0**
4000 Taxes on property	..	..	..	..	..	**0**	**0**	**0**	**0**	**0**
4100 Recurrent taxes on immovable property	..	..	..	..	..	..	..	..	..	..
4200 Recurrent taxes on net wealth	..	..	..	..	..	..	..	..	..	..
4300 Estate, inheritance and gift taxes	..	..	..	..	..	..	..	..	..	..
4400 Taxes on financial and capital transactions	..	..	..	..	..	..	..	..	..	..
4500 Non-recurrent taxes	..	..	..	..	..	..	..	..	..	..
4600 Other recurrent taxes on property	..	..	..	..	..	..	..	..	..	..
5000 Taxes on goods and services	..	..	..	..	..	**0**	**0**	**0**	**0**	**0**
5100 Taxes on production, sale, transfer, etc	..	..	..	..	..	..	..	..	..	..
5110 General taxes	..	..	..	..	..	..	..	..	..	..
5120 Taxes on specific goods and services	..	..	..	..	..	..	..	..	..	..
5130 Unallocable between 5110 and 5120	..	..	..	..	..	..	..	..	..	..
5200 Taxes on use of goods and perform activities	..	..	..	..	..	..	..	..	..	..
5300 Unallocable between 5100 and 5200	..	..	..	..	..	..	..	..	..	..
6000 Other taxes	..	..	..	..	..	**0**	**0**	**0**	**0**	**0**
6100 Paid solely by business	..	..	..	..	..	..	..	..	..	..
6200 Other	..	..	..	..	..	..	..	..	..	..
Total tax revenue	..	..	..	..	..	**183**	**702**	**2 645**	**4 261**	**4 757**

.. Not available

1. Data are not available for local government tax revenues.
2. The figures follow financial year from July to June.

StatLink https://doi.org/10.1787/888934236456

Table 6.26. **Uruguay, tax revenues by subsectores of government**

Million UYU

	Federal government					State/Regional				
	1990	2000	2010	2015	2019	1990	2000	2010	2015	2019
1000 Taxes on income, profits and capital gains	**114**	**8 698**	**42 583**	**84 141**	**149 920**	..	..	..	..	..
1100 Of individuals	0	3 597	19 148	45 451	85 847	..	..	..	..	..
1200 Corporate	114	5 102	21 772	34 814	58 071	..	..	..	..	..
1300 Unallocable between 1100 and 1200	0	0	1 662	3 875	6 002	..	..	..	..	..
2000 Social security contributions	**0**	**0**	**0**	**0**	**0**	..	..	..	..	..
2100 Employees	..	..	..	..	..	..	..	..	..	..
2200 Employers	..	..	..	..	..	..	..	..	..	..
2300 Self-employed or non-employed	..	..	..	..	..	..	..	..	..	..
2400 Unallocable between 2100, 2200 and 2300	..	..	..	..	..	..	..	..	..	..
3000 Taxes on payroll and workforce	**0**	**0**	**0**	**0**	**0**	..	..	..	..	..
4000 Taxes on property	**105**	**2 690**	**11 688**	**20 673**	**26 629**	..	..	..	..	..
4100 Recurrent taxes on immovable property	0	533	1 252	3 775	4 490	..	..	..	..	..
4200 Recurrent taxes on net wealth	94	1 769	8 760	14 776	19 717	..	..	..	..	..
4300 Estate, inheritance and gift taxes	0	0	0	0	0	..	..	..	..	..
4400 Taxes on financial and capital transactions	11	372	1 350	1 601	1 859	..	..	..	..	..
4500 Non-recurrent taxes	0	0	0	0	0	..	..	..	..	..
4600 Other recurrent taxes on property	1	15	326	522	564	..	..	..	..	..
5000 Taxes on goods and services	**1 301**	**29 556**	**96 432**	**162 611**	**212 015**	..	..	..	..	..
5100 Taxes on production, sale, transfer, etc	1 301	29 556	96 432	162 611	212 015	..	..	..	..	..
5110 General taxes[1]	660	18 009	69 951	114 627	145 846	..	..	..	..	..
5120 Taxes on specific goods and services	641	11 546	26 480	47 983	66 170	..	..	..	..	..
5130 Unallocable between 5110 and 5120	0	0	0	0	0	..	..	..	..	..
5200 Taxes on use of goods and perform activities	0	0	0	0	0	..	..	..	..	..
5300 Unallocable between 5100 and 5200	0	0	0	0	0	..	..	..	..	..
6000 Other taxes	**-10**	**-145**	**586**	**796**	**1 039**	..	..	..	..	..
6100 Paid solely by business	-10	-145	586	796	1 039	..	..	..	..	..
6200 Other	0	0	0	0	0	..	..	..	..	..
Total tax revenue	**1 510**	**40 799**	**151 289**	**268 221**	**389 604**	..	..	..	..	..

Million UYU

	Local government					Social Security Funds[2]				
	1990	2000	2010	2015	2019	1990	2000	2010	2015	2019
1000 Taxes on income, profits and capital gains	**0**	**0**	**0**	**0**	**0**	**0**	**0**	**0**	**0**	**0**
1100 Of individuals	..	..	..	..	..	..	..	..	..	..
1200 Corporate	..	..	..	..	..	..	..	..	..	..
1300 Unallocable between 1100 and 1200	..	..	..	..	..	..	..	..	..	..
2000 Social security contributions	**0**	**0**	**0**	**0**	**0**	**717**	**17 679**	**49 742**	**109 282**	**151 589**
2100 Employees	..	..	..	..	..	..	..	..	..	..
2200 Employers	..	..	..	..	..	..	..	..	..	..
2300 Self-employed or non-employed	..	..	..	..	..	..	..	..	..	..
2400 Unallocable between 2100, 2200 and 2300	..	..	..	..	..	717	17 679	49 742	109 282	151 589
3000 Taxes on payroll and workforce	**0**	**0**	**0**	**0**	**0**	**0**	**0**	**0**	**0**	**0**
4000 Taxes on property	**107**	**2 819**	**7 277**	**11 749**	**17 549**	**0**	**0**	**0**	**0**	**0**
4100 Recurrent taxes on immovable property	87	2 715	6 887	11 109	16 567	..	..	..	..	..
4200 Recurrent taxes on net wealth	0	0	0	0	0	..	..	..	..	..
4300 Estate, inheritance and gift taxes	0	0	0	0	0	..	..	..	..	..
4400 Taxes on financial and capital transactions	20	104	390	639	982	..	..	..	..	..
4500 Non-recurrent taxes	0	0	0	0	0	..	..	..	..	..
4600 Other recurrent taxes on property	0	0	0	0	0	..	..	..	..	..
5000 Taxes on goods and services	**57**	**2 583**	**3 851**	**7 668**	**12 379**	**0**	**0**	**0**	**0**	**0**
5100 Taxes on production, sale, transfer, etc	0	7	63	128	202	..	..	..	..	..
5110 General taxes[1]	0	0	0	0	0	..	..	..	..	..
5120 Taxes on specific goods and services	0	7	63	128	202	..	..	..	..	..
5130 Unallocable between 5110 and 5120	0	0	0	0	0	..	..	..	..	..
5200 Taxes on use of goods and perform activities	57	2 576	3 788	7 540	12 176	..	..	..	..	..
5300 Unallocable between 5100 and 5200	0	0	0	0	0	..	..	..	..	..
6000 Other taxes	**7**	**303**	**748**	**1 355**	**2 521**	**0**	**0**	**0**	**0**	..
6100 Paid solely by business	0	0	0	0	0	..	..	..	..	..
6200 Other	7	303	748	1 355	2 521	..	..	..	..	..
Total tax revenue	**171**	**5 705**	**11 876**	**20 772**	**32 449**	**717**	**17 679**	**49 742**	**109 282**	**151 589**

.. Not available

1. The tax on the sale of goods by public auctions under this heading is classified in category 4000 in ECLAC data.
2. Figures for 1990-98 are estimated by the General Tax Directorate (DGI). Since 1999 the figures include income from Social Security Bank (BPS) published by the Ministry of Economy and Finance.

StatLink https://doi.org/10.1787/888934236475

Table 6.27. **Venezuela, tax revenues by subsectores of government**

VES

	Federal government[2]					State/Regional[3]				
	1990	2000	2010	2015	2019	1990	2000	2010	2015	2019
1000 Taxes on income, profits and capital gains	**3 444**	**46 856**	**368 365**	**2 847 864**	..	..	..	..	..	..
1100 Of individuals	..	..	..	..	..	..	..	..	..	..
1200 Corporate[1]	3 148	33 683	86 998	473 879	..	..	..	..	..	..
1300 Unallocable between 1100 and 1200	297	13 173	281 367	2 373 986	..	..	..	..	..	..
2000 Social security contributions	**0**	**0**	**0**	..	..	..	..	..	..	..
2100 Employees	..	..	..	..	..	..	..	..	..	..
2200 Employers	..	..	..	..	..	..	..	..	..	..
2300 Self-employed or non-employed	..	..	..	..	..	..	..	..	..	..
2400 Unallocable between 2100, 2200 and 2300	..	..	..	..	..	..	..	..	..	..
3000 Taxes on payroll and workforce	**0**	**0**	**0**	**0**	..	..	..	..	..	..
4000 Taxes on property	**11**	**3 999**	**2 217**	**29 459**	..	..	..	..	..	..
4100 Recurrent taxes on immovable property	0	0	0	0	..	..	..	..	..	..
4200 Recurrent taxes on net wealth	0	0	0	0	..	..	..	..	..	..
4300 Estate, inheritance and gift taxes	11	191	2 217	29 459	..	..	..	..	..	..
4400 Taxes on financial and capital transactions	0	3 808	0	0	..	..	..	..	..	..
4500 Non-recurrent taxes	0	0	0	0	..	..	..	..	..	..
4600 Other recurrent taxes on property	0	0	0	0	..	..	..	..	..	..
5000 Taxes on goods and services	**457**	**51 726**	**733 363**	**9 128 199**	..	..	..	..	..	..
5100 Taxes on production, sale, transfer, etc	457	51 726	733 363	9 128 199	..	..	..	..	..	..
5110 General taxes	0	32 716	561 005	7 027 427	..	..	..	..	..	..
5120 Taxes on specific goods and services	457	19 011	172 357	2 100 772	..	..	..	..	..	..
5130 Unallocable between 5110 and 5120	0	0	0	0	..	..	..	..	..	..
5200 Taxes on use of goods and perform activities	0	0	0	0	..	..	..	..	..	..
5300 Unallocable between 5100 and 5200	0	0	0	0	..	..	..	..	..	..
6000 Other taxes	**0**	**0**	**0**	**158 333**	..	..	..	..	..	..
6100 Paid solely by business	..	..	..	0	..	..	..	..	..	..
6200 Other	..	..	..	158 333	..	..	..	..	..	..
Total tax revenue	**3 913**	**102 581**	**1 103 944**	**12 163 855**	..	..	..	..	..	..

VES

	Local government[3]					Social Security Funds[2,4]				
	1990	2000	2010	2015	2019	1990	2000	2010	2015	2019
1000 Taxes on income, profits and capital gains	..	..	..	..	..	**0**	**0**	**0**	..	..
1100 Of individuals	..	..	..	..	..	..	..	..	..	..
1200 Corporate[1]	..	..	..	..	..	..	..	..	..	..
1300 Unallocable between 1100 and 1200	..	..	..	..	..	..	..	..	..	..
2000 Social security contributions	..	..	..	..	..	**202**	**5 905**	**96 896**	..	..
2100 Employees	..	..	..	..	..	..	..	..	..	..
2200 Employers	..	..	..	..	..	..	..	..	..	..
2300 Self-employed or non-employed	..	..	..	..	..	..	..	..	..	..
2400 Unallocable between 2100, 2200 and 2300	..	..	..	..	..	202	5 905	96 896	..	..
3000 Taxes on payroll and workforce	..	..	..	..	..	**0**	**0**	**0**	..	..
4000 Taxes on property	..	..	..	..	..	**0**	**0**	**0**	..	..
4100 Recurrent taxes on immovable property	..	..	..	..	..	..	..	..	..	..
4200 Recurrent taxes on net wealth	..	..	..	..	..	..	..	..	..	..
4300 Estate, inheritance and gift taxes	..	..	..	..	..	..	..	..	..	..
4400 Taxes on financial and capital transactions	..	..	..	..	..	..	..	..	..	..
4500 Non-recurrent taxes	..	..	..	..	..	..	..	..	..	..
4600 Other recurrent taxes on property	..	..	..	..	..	..	..	..	..	..
5000 Taxes on goods and services	..	..	..	..	..	**0**	**0**	**0**	..	..
5100 Taxes on production, sale, transfer, etc	..	..	..	..	..	..	..	..	..	..
5110 General taxes	..	..	..	..	..	..	..	..	..	..
5120 Taxes on specific goods and services	..	..	..	..	..	..	..	..	..	..
5130 Unallocable between 5110 and 5120	..	..	..	..	..	..	..	..	..	..
5200 Taxes on use of goods and perform activities	..	..	..	..	..	..	..	..	..	..
5300 Unallocable between 5100 and 5200	..	..	..	..	..	..	..	..	..	..
6000 Other taxes	..	..	..	..	..	**0**	**0**	**0**	..	..
6100 Paid solely by business	..	..	..	..	..	..	..	..	..	..
6200 Other	..	..	..	..	..	..	..	..	..	..
Total tax revenue	..	..	..	..	..	**202**	**5 905**	**96 896**	..	..

.. Not available

1. Data for revenues from taxes on oil profits (classified in heading 1200) are not available from 2016.
2. Data are not available for 2018 and 2019. The figures for 2015-17 should be interpreted with caution as they have been affected by the high rate of inflation over this period.
3. The figures exclude state and local government tax revenues as the data are not available.
4. Data on social security contributions are not available from 2014.

StatLink https://doi.org/10.1787/888934236494

ANNEX A

The OECD classification of taxes and interpretative guide[1]

Table of contents

A.1. The OECD classification of taxes

1. **1000 Taxes on income, profits and capital gains**
   - 1100 Taxes on income, profits and capital gains of individuals
     - 1110 On income and profits
     - 1120 On capital gains
   - 1200 Corporate taxes on income, profits and capital gains
     - 1210 On income and profits
     - 1220 On capital gains
   - 1300 Unallocable as between 1100 and 1200
2. **2000 Social security contributions**
   - 2100 Employees
     - 2110 On a payroll basis
     - 2120 On an income tax basis
   - 2200 Employers
     - 2210 On a payroll basis
     - 2220 On an income tax basis
   - 2300 Self-employed or non-employed
     - 2310 On a payroll basis
     - 2320 On an income tax basis
   - 2400 Unallocable as between 2100, 2200 and 2300
     - 2410 On a payroll basis
     - 2420 On an income tax basis
3. **3000 Taxes on payroll and workforce**
4. **4000 Taxes on property**
   - 4100 Recurrent taxes on immovable property
     - 4110 Households
     - 4120 Other
   - 4200 Recurrent taxes on net wealth
     - 4210 Individual
     - 4220 Corporate
   - 4300 Estate, inheritance and gift taxes
     - 4310 Estate and inheritance taxes
     - 4320 Gift taxes
   - 4400 Taxes on financial and capital transactions
   - 4500 Other non-recurrent taxes on property
     - 4510 On net wealth
     - 4520 Other non-recurrent taxes
   - 4600 Other recurrent taxes on property

5. **5000** **Taxes on goods and services**

5100 Taxes on production, sale, transfer, leasing and delivery of goods and rendering of services

5110 General taxes

5111 Value added taxes

5112 Sales taxes

5113 Turnover and other general taxes on goods and services

5120 Taxes on specific goods and services

5121 Excises

5122 Profits of fiscal monopolies

5123 Customs and import duties

5124 Taxes on exports

5125 Taxes on investment goods

5126 Taxes on specific services

5127 Other taxes on international trade and transactions

5128 Other taxes on specific goods and services

5130 Unallocable as between 5110 and 5120

5200 Taxes on use of goods, or on permission to use goods or perform activities

5210 Recurrent taxes

5211 Paid by households in respect of motor vehicles

5212 Paid by others in respect of motor vehicles

5213 Other recurrent taxes

5220 Non-recurrent taxes

5300 Unallocable as between 5100 and 5200

6. **6000** **Other taxes**

6100 Paid solely by business

6200 Paid by other than business or unidentifiable

A.2. Coverage

General criteria

1. In the OECD classification the term "taxes" is confined to compulsory unrequited payments to the general government or to a supranational authority. Taxes are unrequited in the sense that benefits provided by government to taxpayers are not normally in proportion to their payments.

2. The term "tax" does not include fines, penalties and compulsory loans paid to government. Borderline cases between tax and non-tax revenues in relation to certain fees and charges are discussed in §12-15.

3. General government consists of the central administration, agencies whose operations are under its effective control, state and local governments and their administrations, certain social security schemes and autonomous governmental entities, excluding public enterprises. This definition of government follows that of the 2008 *System of National Accounts* (SNA).[2] In that publication, the general government sector and its sub-sectors are defined in Chapter 4, paragraphs 4.117 to 4.165.

4. Extra-budgetary units are part of the general government system. These are general government entities with individual budgets that are not fully covered by the main or general budget. These entities operate under the authority or control of a central, state, or local government. Extra-budgetary entities may have their own revenue sources, which may be supplemented by grants (transfers) from the general budget or from other sources. Even though their budgets may be subject to approval by the legislature, similar to that of budgetary accounts, they have discretion over the volume and composition of their spending. Such entities may be established to carry out specific government functions, such as road construction, or the nonmarket production of health or education services. Budgetary arrangements vary widely across countries, and various terms are used to describe these entities, but they are often referred to as "extra-budgetary funds" or "decentralised agencies."

5. Compulsory, unrequited payments collected by national governments and paid to supranational authorities are also included as taxes under the definition in paragraph 1. Taxes that are collected by national governments and paid to a supranational authority are included as tax revenues at the level of the supranational authority in the SNA2008 (paragraphs 22.60-61, 22.88 and 22.99 refer) and the ESA2010 (paragraph 20.165 refers). In Revenue Statistics, these taxes include customs duties, contributions to the EU Single Resolution Fund, and any other taxes collected by EU member states on behalf of the European Union. They are included in the tax revenue amounts in the country tables (Chapter 5) of the country in which they are collected and are attributed to the supranational level of government (see §101).

6. In countries where the church forms part of general government, church taxes are included, provided they meet the criteria set out in §1 above. As the data refer to receipts of general government and to supranational authorities, levies paid to non-government bodies, welfare agencies or social insurance schemes outside general government, trade unions or trade associations, even where such levies are compulsory, are excluded. Compulsory payments to general government earmarked for such bodies are, however, included, provided that the government is not simply acting in an agency capacity.[3] Profits from fiscal monopolies are distinguished from those of other public enterprises and are treated as taxes because they reflect the exercise of the taxing power of the state by the use of monopoly

powers (see §66-68), as are profits received by the government from the purchase and sale of foreign exchange at different rates (see §76).

7. Taxes paid by governments (e.g., social security contributions and payroll taxes paid by governments in their capacity as an employer, consumption taxes on their purchases or taxes on their property) are not excluded from the data provided. However, where it is possible to identify the amounts of revenue involved,[4] they are shown in Table 5.39 of this Report.

8. The relationship between this classification and that of the System of National Accounts (SNA) is set out in Sections A.9 and A.11 below. Because of the differences between the two classifications, the data shown in national accounts are sometimes calculated or classified differently from the practice set out in this guide. These and other differences are mentioned where appropriate (e.g., in §31 below) but it is not possible to refer to all of them. There may also be some differences between this classification and that employed domestically by certain national administrations (e.g., see §13 below), so that OECD and national statistics data may not always be consistent: any such differences, however, are likely to be very slight in terms of amounts of revenues involved.

Social security contributions

9. Compulsory social security contributions, as defined in §40, and paid to general government, are treated here as tax revenues. They may, however, differ from other taxes in that the receipt of social security benefits depends, in most countries, upon appropriate contributions having been made, although the size of the benefits is not necessarily related to the amount of the contributions. Better comparability between countries is obtained by treating social security contributions as taxes, but they are listed under a separate heading so that they can be distinguished in any analysis.

10. The strict dividing line between tax revenues (compulsory unrequited payments to general government or a supranational authority) and non-tax compulsory payments (NTCPs) (payments that are either requited or made to other institutions) is clearly defined. However, within the range of different compulsory payments to governments existing across countries, it is not always straightforward in practice to decide whether specific payments are either taxes or NTCPs. For example, compulsory pension savings that are controlled by general government and that accumulate on an individual account earning a market return or a rate that compensates for inflation would at first sight be categorised as NTCPs as opposed to taxes. However, even these payments might still be 'unrequited' and therefore classify as taxes instead of NTCPs (for example if these pension savings are not paid out when the taxpayer dies before reaching the pension age and the funds are then used to provide a minimum pension to all taxpayers that are insured). These issues result in the social security revenue figures reported for most countries being based on the premise that all types of compulsory payments to general government are judged to some extent to have a re-distributional element. It should be noted that this conclusion is based on a typically broad interpretation of the term 'unrequited' in the tax definition.

11. Social security contributions which are either voluntary or not payable to general government (see §1) are not treated as taxes, though in some countries, as indicated in the country footnotes, there are difficulties in completely eliminating voluntary contributions and certain compulsory payments to the private sector from the revenue figures. Imputed social security contributions are also not treated as taxes.

Fees, user charges and licence fees

12. Apart from vehicle licence fees, which are universally regarded as taxes, it is not easy to distinguish between those fees and user charges which are to be treated as taxes and those which are not, since, whilst a fee or charge is levied in connection with a specific service or activity, the strength of the link between the fee and the service provided may vary considerably, as may the relation between the amount of the fee and the cost of providing the service. Where the recipient of a service pays a fee clearly related to the cost of providing the service, the levy may be regarded as requited and under the definition of §1 would not be considered as a tax. In the following cases, however, a levy could be considered as 'unrequited':

a) where the charge greatly exceeds the cost of providing the service;

b) where the payer of the levy is not the receiver of the benefit (e.g., a fee collected from slaughterhouses to finance a service which is provided to farmers);

c) where government is not providing a specific service in return for the levy which it receives even though a licence may be issued to the payer (e.g., where the government grants a hunting, fishing or shooting licence which is not accompanied by the right to use a specific area of government land);

d) where benefits are received only by those paying the levy but the benefits received by each individual are not necessarily in proportion to his payments (e.g., a milk marketing levy paid by dairy farmers and used to promote the consumption of milk).

13. In marginal cases, however, the application of the criteria set out in §1 can be particularly difficult. The solution adopted — given the desirability of international uniformity and the relatively small amounts of revenue usually involved — is to follow the predominant practice among tax administrations rather than to allow each country to adopt its own view as to whether such levies are regarded as taxes or as non-tax revenue.[5]

14. A list of the main fees and charges in question and their normal[6] treatment in this publication is as follows:

Non-tax revenues:	court fees; driving licence fees; harbour fees; passport fees; radio and television licence fees where public authorities provide the service.
Taxes within heading 5200:	permission to perform such activities as distributing films; hunting, fishing and shooting; providing entertainment or gambling facilities; selling alcohol or tobacco; permission to own dogs or to use or own motor vehicles or guns; severance taxes.

15. In practice it may not always be possible to isolate tax receipts from non-tax revenue receipts when they are recorded together. If it is estimated that the bulk of the receipts derive from non-tax revenues, the whole amount involved is treated as a non-tax revenue; otherwise, such government receipts are included and classified according to the rules provided in §33 below.

Royalties

16. The ownership of subsoil assets in the form of deposits of minerals or fossil fuels (coal, oil, or natural gas) depends upon the way in which property rights are defined by law and also on international agreements in the case of deposits below international waters. In

some cases, either the ground below which the mineral deposits are located, the deposits themselves or both may belong to a local or central government unit.

17. In such cases, these general government units may grant leases to other institutional units that permit them to extract these deposits over a specified period of time in return for a payment or series of payments. These payments are often described as 'royalties' but they are essentially rent that accrues to owners of natural resources in return for putting these assets at the disposal of other units for specified periods of time. The rent may take the form of periodic payments of fixed amounts, irrespective of the rate of extraction, or, more commonly, they may be a function of the quantity, volume, or value of the asset extracted. Enterprises engaged in exploration on government land may make payments to general government units in exchange for the right to undertake test drilling or otherwise investigate the existence and location of subsoil assets. Such payments are also recorded as rents even though no extraction may take place. These payments are therefore classified as non-tax revenues.

18. The same principles apply when other institutional units are granted leases that permit them to fell timber in natural forests on land owned by general government units. These payments are also classified as non-tax revenues.

19. These rents or royalties paid to general government should not be confused with taxes on income and profits, severance taxes, business licenses, or other taxes. If the payments are levied on the profits from the extraction activity, then they should be classified as taxes on incomes, profits and gains (1000). In addition, any severance payments that are imposed on the extraction of minerals and fossil fuels from reserves owned privately or by another government should be classified as taxes. Payments related to the gross value of production should be classified as other taxes on goods and services (5128). Payments for a license or permit to conduct extraction operations should be classified as taxes on use of goods and on permission to use goods or perform activities (5213).

Fines and penalties

20. In principle, fines and penalties charged on overdue taxes or penalties imposed for the attempted evasion of taxes should not be recorded as tax revenues. However, it may not be possible to separate payments of fines or other penalties from the revenues from the taxes to which they relate. In this case the fines and penalties relating to a particular tax are recorded together with the revenues from that tax and fines and penalties paid with revenue from unidentifiable taxes are classified as other taxes in Category 6000. Fines not relating to tax offences (e.g., for parking offences), or not identifiable as relating to tax offences, are also not treated as tax revenues.

A.3. Basis of reporting

Accrual reporting

21. The data reported in this publication for recent years are predominantly recorded on an accrual basis, i.e. recorded at the time that the tax liability was created. Further information is provided in the footnotes to the country table in Chapter 5 of the Report.

22. However, data for earlier years are still predominantly recorded on a cash basis, i.e. at the time at which the payment was received by government. Thus, for example, taxes withheld by employers in one year but paid to the government in the following year and taxes due in one year but actually paid in the following year are both included in the receipts of the

second year. Corrective transactions, such as refunds, repayments and drawbacks, are deducted from gross revenues of the period in which they are made.

23. Data on tax revenues are recorded without offsets for the administrative expenses connected with tax collection. Similarly, where the proceeds of tax are used to subsidise particular members of the community, the subsidy is not deducted from the yield of the tax, though the tax may be shown net of subsidies in the national records of some countries.

24. As regards fiscal monopolies (heading 5122), only the amount actually transferred to the government is included in government revenues. However, if any expenditures of fiscal monopolies are considered to be government expenditures (e.g., social expenditures undertaken by fiscal monopolies at the direction of the government) they are added back for the purpose of arriving at tax revenue figures (see §66 below).

The distinction between tax and expenditure provisions[7]

25. Because this publication is concerned only with the revenue side of government operations, no account being taken of the expenditure side, a distinction has to be made between tax and expenditure provisions. Normally there is no difficulty in making this distinction as expenditures are made outside the tax system and the tax accounts and under legislation separate from the tax legislation. In borderline cases, cash flow is used to distinguish between tax provisions and expenditure provisions. Insofar as a provision affects the flow of tax payments from the taxpayer to the government, it is regarded as a tax provision and is taken into account in the data shown in this publication. A provision, which does not affect this flow, is seen as an expenditure provision and is disregarded in the data recorded in this publication.

26. Tax allowances, exemptions and deductions against the tax base clearly affect the amount of tax paid to the government and are therefore considered as tax provisions. At the other extreme, those subsidies which cannot be offset against tax liability and which are clearly not connected with the assessment process, do not reduce tax revenues as recorded in this publication. Tax credits are amounts deductible from tax payable (as distinct from deductions from the tax base). Two types of tax credits are distinguished, those (referred to here as wastable tax credits) which are limited to the amount of the tax liability and therefore cannot give rise to a payment by the authorities to the taxpayer, and those (referred to as non-wastable tax credits) which are not so limited, so that the excess of the credit over the tax liability can be paid to the taxpayer.[8] A wastable tax credit, like a tax allowance, clearly affects the amount of tax paid to the government, and is therefore considered as a tax provision. The practice followed for non-wastable tax credits[9] is to distinguish between the 'tax expenditure component',[10] which is that portion of the credit that is used to reduce or eliminate a taxpayer's liability, and the 'transfer component', which is the portion that exceeds the taxpayer's liability and is paid to that taxpayer. Reported tax revenues should be reduced by the amount of the tax expenditure component but not by the amount of the transfer component. In addition, the amounts of the tax expenditure and transfer components should be reported as memorandum items in the country tables. Countries that are unable to distinguish between the tax expenditure and transfer components should indicate whether or not the tax revenues have been reduced by the total of these components, and provide any available estimates of the amounts of the two components. Further information is given in Chapter 1 of the Report, which illustrates the effect of alternative treatments of non-wastable tax credits on tax to GDP.

Calendar and fiscal years

27. National authorities whose fiscal years do not correspond to the calendar year show data, where possible, on a calendar year basis to permit maximum comparability with the data of other countries. There remain a few countries where data refer to fiscal years. For these the GDP data used in the comparative tables also correspond to the fiscal years.

A.4. General classification criteria

The main classification criteria

28. The classification of receipts among the main headings (1000, 2000, 3000, 4000, 5000 and 6000) is generally governed by the base on which the tax is levied: 1000 income, profits and capital gains; 2000 and 3000 earnings, payroll or number of employees; 4000 property; 5000 goods and services; 6000 multiple bases, other bases or unidentifiable bases. Where a tax is calculated on more than one base, the receipts are, where possible, split among the various headings (see §33 and §83). The headings 4000 and 5000 cover not only taxes where the tax base is the property, goods or services themselves but also certain related taxes. Thus, taxes on the transfer of property are included in 4400[11] and taxes on the use of goods or on permission to perform activities in 5200. In headings 4000 and 5000 a distinction is made in certain sub-headings between recurrent and non-recurrent taxes: recurrent taxes are defined as those levied at regular intervals (usually annually) and non-recurrent taxes are levied once and for all (see also §48 to §51, §54, §55 and §81 for particular applications of this distinction).

29. Earmarking of a tax for specific purposes does not affect the classification of tax receipts. However, as explained in §40 on the classification of social security contributions, the conferment of an entitlement to social benefits is crucial to the definition of the 2000 main heading.

30. The way that a tax is levied or collected (e.g., by use of stamps) does not affect classification.

Classification of taxpayers

31. In certain sub-headings, distinctions are made between different categories of taxpayers. These distinctions vary from tax to tax:

a) Between individuals and corporations in relation to income and net wealth taxes

The basic distinction is that corporation income taxes, as distinct from individual income taxes, are levied on the corporation as an entity, not on the individuals who own it, and without regard to the personal circumstances of these individuals. The same distinction applies to net wealth taxes on corporations and those on individuals. Taxes paid on the profits of partnerships and the income of institutions, such as life insurance or pension funds, are classified according to the same rule. They are classified as corporate taxes (1200) if they are charged on the partnership or institution as an entity without regard to the personal circumstances of the owners. Otherwise, they are treated as individual taxes (1100). Usually, there is different legislation for the corporation taxes and for the individual taxes.[12] The distinction made here between individuals and corporations does not follow the sector classification between households, enterprises, and so on of the System of National Accounts for income and outlay accounts. The SNA classification requires certain unincorporated businesses[13] to be excluded from the household sector and included with non-financial enterprises and financial institutions. The tax on the profits of these businesses, however, cannot always be separated from the tax on the other income of their owners, or can be separated only on an arbitrary basis. No attempt at this separation is made here and the whole of the individual income tax is shown together without regard to the nature of the income chargeable.

b) Between households and others in relation to taxes on immovable property

Here the distinction is that adopted by the SNA for the production and consumption expenditure accounts. The distinction is between households as consumers (i.e. excluding non-incorporated business) on the one hand and producers on the other hand. However, taxes on dwellings occupied by households, whether paid by owner-occupiers, tenants or landlords, are classified under households. This follows the common distinction made between taxes on domestic property versus taxes on business property. Some countries are not, however, in a position to make this distinction.

c) Between households and others in relation to motor vehicle licences

Here the distinction is between households as consumers on the one hand and producers on the other, as in the production and consumption expenditure accounts of the SNA.

d) Between business and others in relation to the residual taxes (6000)

The distinction is the same as in c) above between producers on the one hand and households as consumers on the other hand. Taxes which are included under the heading 6000 because they involve more than one tax base or because the tax base does not fall within any of the previous categories but which are identifiable as levyable only on producers and not on households are included under 'business'. The rest of the taxes which are included under the heading 6000 are shown as 'other' or non-identified.

Surcharges

32. Receipts from surcharges in respect of particular taxes are usually classified with the receipts from the relevant tax whether or not the surcharge is temporary. If, however, the surcharge has a characteristic which would render it classifiable in a different heading of the OECD list, receipts from the surcharge are classified under that heading separately from the relevant tax.

Unidentifiable tax receipts and residual sub-headings

33. A number of cases arise where taxes cannot be identified as belonging entirely to a heading or sub-heading of the OECD classification and the following practices are applied in such cases:

a) The heading is known, but it is not known how receipts should be allocated between sub-headings: receipts are classified in the appropriate residual sub-heading (1300, 2400, 4520, 4600, 5130, 5300 or 6200).

b) It is known that the bulk of receipts from a group of taxes (usually local taxes) is derived from taxes within a particular heading or sub-heading, but some of the taxes in the group whose amount cannot be precisely ascertained may be classifiable in other headings or sub-headings: receipts are shown in the heading or sub-heading under which most of the receipts fall.

c) Neither the heading nor sub-heading of a tax (usually local) can be identified: the tax is classified in 6200 unless it is known that it is a tax on business in which case it is classified in 6100.

A.5. Commentaries on items of the list

1000 — *Taxes on income, profits and capital gains*

34. This heading covers taxes levied on the net income or profits (i.e. gross income minus allowable tax reliefs) of individuals and enterprises. Also covered are taxes levied on the capital gains of individuals and enterprises, and gains from gambling.

35. Included in the heading are:

a) taxes levied predominantly on income or profits, though partially on other bases. Taxes on various bases which are not predominantly income or profits are classified according to the principles laid down in §33 and §83;

b) taxes on property, which are levied on a presumed or estimated income as part of an income tax (see also §48(a), (c) and (d));

c) compulsory payments to social security fund contributions that are levied on income but do not confer an entitlement to social benefits. When such contributions do confer an entitlement to social benefits, they are included in heading 2000 (see §40);

d) receipts from integrated scheduler income tax systems are classified as a whole in this heading, even though certain of the scheduler taxes may be based upon gross income and may not take into account the personal circumstances of the taxpayer.

36. The main subdivision of this heading is between levies on individuals (1100) and those on corporate enterprises (1200). Under each subdivision a distinction is made between taxes on income and profits (1110 and 1210), and taxes on capital gains (1120 and 1220). If certain receipts cannot be identified as appropriate to either 1100 or 1200, or if in practice this distinction cannot be made (e.g., because there are no reliable data on the recipients of payments from which withholding taxes are deducted) they are classified in 1300 as not-allocable.

Treatment of credits under imputation systems

37. Under imputation systems of corporate income tax, a company's shareholders are wholly or partly relieved of their liability to income tax on dividends paid by the company out of income or profits liable to corporate income tax. In countries with such systems,[14] part of the tax on the company's profits is available to provide relief against the shareholders' own tax liability. The relief to the shareholder takes the form of a tax credit, the amount of which may be less than, equal to, or more than the shareholder's overall tax liability. If the tax credit exceeds this tax liability the excess may be payable to the shareholder. As this type of tax credit is an integral part of the imputation system of corporate income tax, any payment to the shareholders is treated as a repayment of tax and not as expenditure (compare the treatment of other tax credits described in §26).

38. As the tax credit under imputation systems (even when exceeding tax liability) is to be regarded as a tax provision, the question arises whether it should be deducted from individual income tax receipts (1110) or corporate income tax receipts (1210). In this Report, the full amount of corporate income tax paid is shown under 1210 and no imputed tax is included under 1110. Thus, the full amount of the credit reduces the amount of 1110 whether the credit results in a reduction of personal income tax liability or whether an actual refund is made because the credit exceeds the income tax liability. (Where, however, such tax credits are deducted from corporation tax in respect of dividends paid to corporations the amounts are deducted from the receipts of 1210).

1120 and 1220 — Taxes on capital gains

39. These sub-headings comprise taxes imposed on capital gains, 1120 covering those levied on the gains of individuals and 1220 those levied on the gains of corporate enterprises, where receipts from such taxes can be separately identified. In many countries this is not the case and the receipts from such taxes are then classified with those from the income tax. Heading 1120 also includes taxes on gains from gambling.

2000 — Social security contributions

40. Classified here are all compulsory payments to general government that confer an entitlement to receive a (contingent) future social benefit. Such payments are usually earmarked to finance social benefits and are often paid to institutions of general government that provide such benefits. However, such earmarking is not part of the definition of social security contributions and is not required for a tax to be classified here. However, conferment of an entitlement is required for a tax to be classified under this heading. So, levies on income or payroll that are earmarked for social security funds but do not confer an entitlement to benefit are excluded from this heading and shown under personal income taxes (1100) or taxes on payroll and workforce (3000). Taxes on other bases, such as goods and services, which are earmarked for social security benefits are not shown here but are classified according to their respective bases because they generally confer no entitlement to social security benefits.

41. Contributions for the following types of social security benefits would, *inter alia*, be included: unemployment insurance benefits and supplements, accident, injury and sickness benefits, old-age, disability and survivors' pensions, family allowances, reimbursements for medical and hospital expenses or provision of hospital or medical services. Contributions may be levied on both employees and employers.

42. Contributions may be based on earnings or payroll ('on a payroll basis') or on net income after deductions and exemptions for personal circumstances ('on an income tax basis'), and the revenues from the two bases should be separately identified if possible. However, where contributions to a general social security scheme are on a payroll basis, but the contributions of particular groups (such as the self-employed) cannot be assessed on this basis and net income is used as a proxy for gross earnings, the receipts may still be classified as being on a payroll basis. In principle, this heading excludes voluntary contributions paid to social security schemes. When separately identifiable these are shown in the memorandum item on the financing of social security benefits. In practice, however, they cannot always be separately identified from compulsory contributions, in which case they are included in this heading.

43. Contributions to social insurance schemes, which are not institutions of general government and, to other types of insurance schemes, provident funds, pension funds, friendly societies or other saving schemes are not considered as social security contributions. Provident funds are arrangements under which the contributions of each employee and of the corresponding employer on his/her behalf are kept in a separate account earning interest and withdrawable under specific circumstances. Pension funds are separately organised schemes negotiated between employees and employers and carry provisions for different contributions and benefits, sometimes more directly tied to salary levels and length of service than under social security schemes. When contributions to these schemes are compulsory or quasi-compulsory (e.g., by virtue of agreement with professional and union organisations) they are shown in the memorandum item (refer to Table 5.38 of the Report).

44. Contributions by government employees and by governments in respect of their employees, to social security schemes classified within general government are included in this heading. Contributions to separate schemes for government employees, which can be regarded as replacing general social security schemes, are also regarded as taxes.[15] Where, however, a separate scheme is not seen as replacing a general scheme and has been negotiated between the government, in its role as an employer, and its employees, it is not regarded as social security and contributions to it are not regarded as taxes, even though the scheme may have been established by legislation.

45. This heading excludes 'imputed' contributions, which correspond to social benefits paid directly by employers to their employees or former employees or to their representatives (e.g., when employers are legally obliged to pay sickness benefits for a certain period).

46. Contributions are divided into those of employees (2100), employers (2200), and self-employed or non-employed (2300), and then further sub-divided according to the basis on which they are levied. Employees are defined for this purpose as all persons engaged in activities of business units, government bodies, private non-profit institutions, or other paid employment, except the proprietors and their unpaid family members in the case of unincorporated businesses. Members of the armed forces are included, irrespective of the duration and type of their service, if they contribute to social security schemes. The contributions of employers are defined as their payments on account of their employees to social security schemes. Where employees or employers are required to continue the payment of social security contributions when the employee becomes unemployed these contributions, data permitting, are shown in 2100 and 2200 respectively. Accordingly, the sub-heading 2300 is confined to contributions paid by the self-employed and by those outside of the labour force (e.g., disabled or retired individuals).

3000 — Taxes on payroll and workforce

47. These consist of taxes payable by enterprises assessed either as a proportion of the wages or salaries paid or as a fixed amount per person employed. They do not include compulsory social security contributions paid by employers or any taxes paid by employees themselves out of their wages or salaries.

4000 — Taxes on property

48. This heading covers recurrent and non-recurrent taxes on the use, ownership or transfer of property. These include taxes on immovable property or net wealth, taxes on the change of ownership of property through inheritance or gift and taxes on financial and capital transactions. The following kinds of tax are excluded from this heading:

- *a)* taxes on capital gains resulting from the sale of a property (1120 or 1220);
- *b)* taxes on the use of goods or on permission to use goods or perform activities (5200); see §78;
- *c)* taxes on immovable property levied on the basis of a presumed net income which take into account the personal circumstances of the taxpayer. They are classified as income taxes along with taxes on income and capital gains derived from property (1100);
- *d)* taxes on the use of property for residence, where the tax is payable by either proprietor or tenant and the amount payable is a function of the user's personal circumstances (pay, dependants, and so on). They are classified as taxes on income (1100);

e) taxes on building in excess of permitted maximum density, taxes on the enlargement, construction or alteration of certain buildings beyond a permitted value and taxes on building construction. They are classified as taxes on permission to perform activities (5200);

f) taxes on the use of one's own property for special trading purposes like selling alcohol, tobacco, meat or for exploitation of land resources (e.g., United States severance taxes). They are classified as taxes on permission to perform activities (5200).

4100 — *Recurrent taxes on immovable property*

49. This sub-heading covers taxes levied regularly in respect of the use or ownership of immovable property.

- These taxes are levied on land and buildings.
- They can be in the form of a percentage of an assessed property value based on a national rental income, sales price, or capitalised yield; or in terms of other characteristics of real property, (for example size or location) from which a presumed rent or capital value can be derived.
- Such taxes can be levied on proprietors, tenants, or both. They can also be paid by one level of government to another level of government in respect of property under the jurisdiction of the latter.
- Debts are not taken into account in the assessment of these taxes, and they differ from taxes on net wealth in this respect.

50. Taxes on immovable property are further sub-divided into those paid by households (4110) and those paid by other entities (4120), according to the criteria set out in §31(*b*) above.

4200 — *Recurrent taxes on net wealth*

51. This sub-heading covers taxes levied regularly (in most cases annually) on net wealth, i.e. taxes on a wide range of movable and immovable property, net of debt. It is sub-divided into taxes paid by individuals (4210) and taxes paid by corporate enterprises (4220) according to the criteria set out in §31(*a*) above. If separate figures exist for receipts paid by institutions, the tax payments involved are added to those paid by corporations.

4300 — *Estate, inheritance and gift taxes*

52. This sub-heading is divided into taxes on estates and inheritances (4310) and taxes on gifts (4320).[16] Estate taxes are charged on the amount of the total estate whereas inheritance taxes are charged on the shares of the individual recipients; in addition, the latter may take into account the relationship of the individual recipients to the deceased.

4400 — *Taxes on financial and capital transactions*

53. This sub-heading comprises, *inter alia*, taxes on the issue, transfer, purchase and sale of securities, taxes on cheques, and taxes levied on specific legal transactions such as validation of contracts and the sale of immovable property. The heading does not include:

a) taxes on the use of goods or property or permission to perform certain activities (5200);

b) fees paid to cover court charges, charges for birth, marriage or death certificates, which are normally regarded as non-tax revenues (see §12);

c) taxes on capital gains (1000);

d) recurrent taxes on immovable property (4100);

e) recurrent taxes on net wealth (4200);

f) once-and-for-all levies on property or wealth (4500).

4500 — *Other non-recurrent taxes on property*

54. This sub-heading covers once-and-for-all, as distinct from recurrent, levies on property. It is divided into taxes on net wealth (4510) and other non-recurrent taxes on property (4520). Heading 4510 would include taxes levied to meet emergency expenditures, or for redistribution purposes. Heading 4520 would cover taxes levied to take account of increases in land value due to permission given to develop or provision of additional local facilities by general government, any taxes on the revaluation of capital and once-and-for-all taxes on particular items of property.

4600 — *Other recurrent taxes on property*

55. These rarely exist in OECD member countries, but the heading would include taxes on goods such as cattle, jewellery, windows, and other external signs of wealth.

5000 — *Taxes on goods and services*

56. All taxes and duties levied on the production, extraction, sale, transfer, leasing or delivery of goods, and the rendering of services (5100), or in respect of the use of goods or permission to use goods or to perform activities (5200) are included here. The heading thus covers:

a) multi-stage cumulative taxes;

b) general sales taxes — whether levied at manufacture/production, wholesale or retail level;

c) value-added taxes;

d) excises;

e) taxes levied on the import and export of goods;

f) taxes levied in respect of the use of goods and taxes on permission to use goods, or perform certain activities;

g) taxes on the extraction, processing or production of minerals and other products.

57. Borderline cases between this heading and heading 4000 (taxes on property) and 6100 (other taxes on business) are referred to in §48, §53 and §80. Residual sub-headings (5300) and (5130) cover tax receipts which cannot be allocated between 5100 and 5200 and between 5110 and 5120, respectively; see §33.

5100 — *Taxes on the production, sale, transfer, leasing and delivery of goods and rendering of services*

58. This sub-heading consists of all taxes, levied on transactions in goods and services on the basis of their intrinsic characteristics (e.g., value, weight of tobacco, strength of alcohol, and so on) as distinct from taxes imposed on the use of goods, or permission to use goods or perform activities, which fall under 5200.

5110 — *General taxes on goods and services*

59. This sub-heading includes all taxes, other than import and export duties (5123 and 5124), levied on the production, leasing, transfer, delivery or sales of a wide range of goods and/or the rendering of a wide range of services, irrespective of whether they are domestically

produced or imported and irrespective of the stage of production or distribution at which they are levied. It thus covers value-added taxes, sales taxes and multi-stage cumulative taxes. Receipts from border adjustments in respect of such taxes when goods are imported are added to gross receipts for this category, and repayments of such taxes when goods are exported are deducted. These taxes are subdivided into 5111 value-added taxes, 5112 sales taxes, 5113 turnover and other general taxes on goods and services.

60. Borderline cases arise between this heading and taxes on specific goods (5120) when taxes are levied on a large number of goods, for example, the United Kingdom purchase tax (repealed in 1973) and the Japanese commodity tax (repealed in 1988). In conformity with national views, the former United Kingdom purchase tax is classified as a general tax (5112) and the former Japanese commodity tax as excises (5121).

5111 — *Value-added taxes*

61. All general consumption taxes charged on value-added are classified in this sub-heading, irrespective of the method of deduction and the stages at which the taxes are levied. In practice, all OECD countries with value-added taxes normally allow immediate deduction of taxes on purchases by all but the final consumer and impose tax at all stages. In some countries the heading may include certain taxes, such as those on financial and insurance activities, either because receipts from them cannot be identified separately from those from the value-added tax, or because they are regarded as an integral part of the value-added tax, even though similar taxes in other countries might be classified elsewhere (e.g., 5126 as taxes on services or 4400 as taxes on financial and capital transactions).

5112 — *Sales taxes*

62. All general taxes levied at one stage only, whether at manufacturing or production, wholesale or retail stage are classified here.

5113 — *Turnover and other general taxes on goods and services*

63. These are multi-stage cumulative taxes and taxes where elements of consumption taxes are combined with multistage taxes. These taxes are levied each time a transaction takes place without deduction for taxes paid on inputs. Multi-stage taxes can be combined with elements of value-added or sales taxes.

5120 — *Taxes on specific goods and services*

64. Excises, profits generated and transferred from fiscal monopolies, and customs and imports duties as well as taxes on exports, foreign exchange transactions, investment goods and betting stakes and special taxes on services, which do not form part of a general tax of 5110, are included in this category.

5121 — Excises

65. Excises are taxes levied as a product specific unit tax on a predefined limited range of goods. Excises are usually levied at differentiated rates on nonessential or luxury goods, alcoholic beverages, tobacco, and energy. Excises may be imposed at any stage of production or distribution and are usually assessed as a specific charge per unit based on characteristics by reference to the value, weight, strength, or quantity of the product. Included are special taxes on individual products such as sugar, sugar beets, matches, and chocolates; taxes levied at varying rates on a certain range of goods; and taxes levied on tobacco goods, alcoholic drinks, motor fuels, and hydrocarbon oils. If a tax collected principally on imported goods

also applies, or would apply, under the same law to comparable domestically produced goods, then the revenue from this tax is classified as arising from excises rather than from import duties. This principle applies even if there is no comparable domestic production or no possibility of such production. Taxes on the use of utilities such as water, electricity, gas, and energy are regarded as excises rather than taxes on specific services (5126). Excises exclude those taxes that are levied as general taxes on goods and services (5110); profits of fiscal monopolies (5122); customs and other import duties (5123); or taxes on exports (5124).

5122 — *Profits of fiscal monopolies*

66. This sub-heading covers that part of the profits of fiscal monopolies which is transferred to general government or which is used to finance any expenditures considered to be government expenditures (see §24). Amounts are shown when they are transferred to general government or used to make expenditures considered to be government expenditures.

67. Fiscal monopolies reflect the exercise of the taxing power of government by the use of monopoly powers. Fiscal monopolies are non-financial public enterprises exercising a monopoly in most cases over the production or distribution of tobacco, alcoholic beverages, salt, matches, playing cards and petroleum or agricultural products (i.e. on the kind of products which are likely to be, alternatively or additionally, subject to the excises of 5121), to raise the government revenues which in other countries are gathered through taxes on dealings in such commodities by private business units. The government monopoly may be at the production stage or, as in the case of government-owned and controlled liquor stores, at the distribution stage.

68. Fiscal monopolies are distinguished from public utilities such as rail transport, electricity, post offices, and other communications, which may enjoy a monopoly or quasi-monopoly position but where the primary purpose is normally to provide basic services rather than to raise revenue for government. Transfers from such other public enterprises to the government are considered as non-tax revenues. The traditional concept of fiscal monopoly is not generally extended to include state lotteries, the profits of which are usually accordingly regarded as non-tax revenues. However, they can be included as tax revenues if the prime reason for their operation is to raise revenues to finance government expenditure. Fiscal monopoly profits are distinguished from export and import monopoly profits (5127) transferred from marketing boards or other enterprises dealing with international trade.

5123 — *Customs and other import duties*

69. Taxes, stamp duties and surcharges restricted by law to imported products are included here. Also included are levies on imported agricultural products, which are imposed in member countries of the European Union and amounts, paid by certain of these countries under the Monetary Compensation Accounts (MCA) system.[17] Customs duties collected by European Union member states on behalf of the European Union are reported under this heading at the supranational level of government in the country tables (in Chapter 5 of the Report). Excluded here are taxes collected on imports as part of a general tax on goods and services, or an excise applicable to both imported and domestically produced goods.

5124 — *Taxes on exports*

70. In the 1970s, export duties were levied in Australia, Canada and Portugal as a regular measure and they have been used in Finland for counter-cyclical purposes. Some member countries of the European Union pay, as part of the MCA system, a levy on exports (see

note 16 to §69). Where these amounts are identifiable, they are shown in this heading. This heading does not include repayments of general consumption taxes or excises or customs duties on exported goods, which should be deducted from the gross receipts under 5110, 5121 or 5123, as appropriate.

5125 — *Taxes on investment goods*

71. This sub-heading covers taxes on investment goods, such as machinery. These taxes may be imposed for a number of years or temporarily for counter-cyclical purposes. Taxes on industrial inputs which are also levied on consumers [e.g., the Swedish energy tax which is classified under (5121)] are not included here.

5126 — *Taxes on specific services*

72. All taxes assessed on the payment for specific services, such as taxes on insurance premiums, banking services, gambling and betting stakes (e.g., from horse races, football pools, lottery tickets), transport, entertainment, restaurant and advertising charges, fall into this category. Taxes levied on the gross income of companies providing the service (e.g., gross insurance premiums or gambling stakes received by the company) are also classified under this heading.

73. Tax revenues from bank levies and payments to deposit insurance and financial stability schemes are also included here:

- Compulsory payments of stability fees, bank levies and deposit insurance should generally be treated as tax revenues where the payments are made to general government or supranational authorities and are allocated to the governments' consolidated or general funds so that the government is free to make immediate use of the money for the purposes that it chooses. This principle would apply regardless of whether the government is promising to make payments to guarantee the banks' customer deposits in some future contingency.
- If the compulsory payments are made to general government and placed in funds that are earmarked to be entirely channelled back to the sector of the economy that comprises the companies that are subject to the payment, they would still generally be treated as tax revenues on the grounds that the funds would be available for the government and would reduce its budget deficit, the fee is unrequited for an individual entity and the amounts raised could be unrelated to any eventual pay out to depositors or expenditure on wider support for the financial sector.
- Payments to made to the smaller long-standing schemes for insuring 'retail' deposits, where the payment levels are consistent with the costs of insurance should be classified as fee for service.
- Any payments which involve governments realising the assets of a failed institution or receiving a priority claim on its assets in liquidation in order to fund payments of compensation to customers for their lost deposits would be treated as a fee for a service as opposed to tax revenues.
- Compulsory payments that are made to funds operated outside the government sector and non-state institutions backed by the deposit takers and all payments to voluntary schemes should not be treated as tax revenues.
- Contributions made to the EU Single Resolution Fund are also included here and recorded under the supranational level of government in the country tables.

74. Excluded from this sub-heading are:

a) taxes on services forming part of a general tax on goods and services (5110);

b) taxes on electricity, gas and energy (5121 as excises);

c) taxes on individual gains from gambling (1120 as taxes on capital gains of individuals and non-corporate enterprises) and lump-sum taxes on the transfer of private lotteries or on the permission to set up lotteries (5200);[18]

d) taxes on cheques and on the issue, transfer or redemption of securities (4400 as taxes on financial and capital transactions).

5127 — *Other taxes on international trade and transactions*

75. This sub-heading covers revenue received by the government from the purchase and sale of foreign exchange at different rates. When the government exercises monopoly powers to extract a margin between the purchase and sales price of foreign exchange, other than to cover administrative costs, the revenue derived constitutes a compulsory levy exacted in indeterminate proportions from both purchaser and seller of foreign exchange. It is the common equivalent of an import duty and export duty levied in a single exchange rate system or of a tax on the sale or purchase of foreign exchange. Like the profits of fiscal monopolies and import or export monopolies transferred to government, it represents the exercise of monopoly powers for tax purposes and is included in tax revenues.

76. The sub-heading covers also the profits of export or import monopolies, which do not however exist in OECD countries, taxes on purchase or sale of foreign exchange, and any other taxes levied specifically on international trade or transactions.

5128 — *Other taxes on specific goods and services*

77. This item includes taxes on the extraction of minerals, fossil fuels and other exhaustible resources from deposits owned privately or by another government together with any other unidentifiable receipts from taxes on specific goods and services. Taxes on the extraction of exhaustible resources are usually a fixed amount per unit of quality or weight, but can be a percentage of value. The taxes are recorded when the resources are extracted. Payments from the extraction of exhaustible resources from deposits owned by the government unit receiving the payment are classified as rent.

5200 — *Taxes on use of goods or on permission to use goods or perform activities*

78. This sub-heading covers taxes which are levied in respect of the use of goods as distinct from taxes on the goods themselves. Unlike the latter taxes – reported under 5100 –, they are not assessed on the value of the goods but usually as fixed amounts. Taxes on permission to use goods or to perform activities are also included here, as are pollution taxes not based upon the value of particular goods. It is sometimes difficult to distinguish between compulsory user charges and licence fees which are regarded as taxes and those which are excluded as non-tax revenues. The criteria which are employed are noted in §12-13.

79. Although the sub-heading refers to the 'use' of goods, registration of ownership rather than use may be what generates liability to tax, so that the taxes of this heading may apply to the ownership of animals or goods rather than their use (e.g., race horses, dogs and motor vehicles) and may apply even to unusable goods (e.g., unusable motor vehicles or guns).

80. Borderline cases arise with:

a) taxes on the permission to perform business activities which are levied on a combined income, payroll or turnover base and, accordingly, are classified following the rules in §83;

b) taxes on the ownership or use of property of headings 4100, 4200 and 4600. The heading 4100 is confined to taxes on the ownership or tenancy of immovable property and – unlike the taxes of 5200 – they are related to the value of the property. The net wealth taxes and taxes on chattels of 4200 and 4600 respectively are confined to the ownership rather than the use of assets, apply to groups of assets rather than particular goods and again are related to the value of the assets,

5210 — *Recurrent taxes on use of goods and on permission to use goods or perform activities*

81. The principal characteristic of taxes classified here is that they are levied at regular intervals and that they are usually fixed amounts. The most important item in terms of revenue receipts is vehicle licence taxes. This sub-heading also covers taxes on permission to hunt, shoot, fish or to sell certain products and taxes on the ownership of dogs and on the performance of certain services, provided that they meet the criteria set out in §12-13. The sub-divisions of 5210 are user taxes on motor vehicles paid by households (5211) and those paid by others (5212). Sub-heading 5213 covers dog licences and user charges for permission to perform activities such as selling meat or liquor when the levies are on a recurring basis. It also covers recurrent general licences for hunting, shooting and fishing where the right to carry out these activities is not granted as part of a normal commercial transaction (e.g., the granting of the licence is not accompanied by the right to use a specific area which is owned by government).

5220 — *Non-recurrent taxes on use of goods and on permission to use goods or perform activities*

82. This section covers non-recurrent taxes levied on the use of goods or on permission to use goods or perform activities and taxes levied each time goods are used. It includes taxes levied on the emission or discharge into the environment of noxious gases, liquids or other harmful substances.

- Payments for tradable emission permits issued by governments under cap and trade schemes should be recorded here at the time the emissions occur. No revenue should be recorded for permits that governments issue free of charge. The accrual basis of recording means that there can be a timing difference between the cash being received by government for the permits and the time the emission occurs. In the national accounts, this timing gives rise to a financial liability for government during the period.
- Payments made for the collection and disposal of waste or noxious substances by public authorities should be excluded as they constitute a sale of services to enterprises.

83. Other taxes falling under heading 5200 that are not levied recurrently are also included here. Thus, once-and-for-all payments for permission to sell liquor or tobacco or to set up betting shops are included provided they meet the criteria set out in §12-13.

6000 — Other taxes

84. Taxes levied on a base, or bases, other than those described under headings 1000, 3000, 4000 and 5000, or on bases of which cannot be considered to be related to any one of these headings, are included here. Where taxes are levied on a multiple base and it is possible to estimate the receipts related to each base the separate amounts are included under the appropriate headings. If separate amounts cannot be estimated and it is known that most of the receipts are derived from one base, the whole of the receipts are classified according to that base. Otherwise, they are classified here. Other revenues included here are presumptive taxes not included elsewhere in the classification system, taxes on individuals in the form of a poll tax or capitation tax, stamp taxes not related to financial and capital transactions nor falling exclusively on a single category of transaction, expenditure taxes where personal deductions or exemptions are applied and unidentifiable tax receipts. A subdivision is made between taxes levied wholly or predominantly on business (6100) and those levied on others (6200).

A.6. Conciliation with National Accounts

85. This section of the tables provides a re-conciliation between the OECD calculation of total tax revenues and the total of all taxes and social contributions paid to general government as recorded in the country's National Accounts. Where the country is a member of the European Union (EU), the comparison is between the OECD calculation of total tax revenues and the sum of tax revenues and social contributions recorded in the combination of the general government and the institutions of the EU sectors of the National Accounts.

A.7. Memorandum item on the financing of social security benefits

86. In view of the varying relationship between taxation and social security contributions and the cases referred to in §40 to §46, a memorandum item collects together all payments earmarked for social security-type benefits, other than voluntary payments to the private sector. Data are presented as follows (refer Table 5.38 of the Report):

- *a)* Taxes of 2000 series.
- *b)* Taxes earmarked for social security benefits.
- *c)* Voluntary contributions to the government.
- *d)* Compulsory contributions to the private sector.

Guidance on the breakdown of (a) to (d) above is provided in §40 to §46.

A.8. Memorandum item on identifiable taxes paid by government

87. Identifiable taxes actually paid by government are presented in a memorandum item classified by the main headings of the OECD classification of taxes. In the vast majority of countries, only social security contributions and payroll taxes paid by government can be identified. These are, however, usually the most important taxes paid by governments (refer to Table 5.39 of the Report).

A.9. Relation of OECD classification of taxes to national accounting systems

88. A system of national accounts (SNA) seeks to provide a coherent framework for recording and presenting the main flows relating respectively to production, consumption, accumulation and external transactions of a given economic area, usually a country or a major region within a country. Government revenues are an important part of the transactions

recorded in SNA. The final version of the 2008 SNA was jointly published by five international organisations: the United Nations, the International Monetary Fund, the European Union, the Organisation for Economic Co-operation and Development, and the World Bank in August 2009. The *System* is a comprehensive, consistent and flexible set of macroeconomic accounts. It is designed for use in countries with market economies, whatever their stage of economic development, and also in countries in transition to market economies. The important parts of the SNA's conceptual framework and its definitions of the various sectors of the economy have been reflected in the OECD's classification of taxes.

89. There are, however, some differences between the OECD classification of taxes and SNA concepts that are listed below. They arise because the aim of the former is to provide the maximum disaggregation of statistical data on what are generally regarded as taxes by tax administrations.

a) OECD includes compulsory social security contributions paid to general government in total tax revenues. Imputed and voluntary contributions plus those paid to private funds are not treated as taxes (§9 and §11 above);

b) there are different points of view on whether or not some levies and fees are classified as taxes (§12 and §13 above);

c) OECD excludes imputed taxes or subsidies resulting from the operation of official multiple exchange rates or from the central bank paying a rate of interest on required reserves that is different from other market rates;

d) there are differences in the treatment of non-wastable tax credits

90. As noted in §1 and §2, headings 1000 to 6000 of the OECD list of taxes cover all unrequited payments to general government or to a supranational authority, other than compulsory loans and fines. Such unrequited payments including fines, but excluding compulsory loans can be obtained from adding together the following figures in the 2008 SNA

- value-added type taxes (D.211);
- taxes and duties on imports, excluding VAT (D.212);
- export taxes (D.213);
- taxes on products, excluding VAT, import and export taxes (D.214);
- other taxes on production (D.29);
- taxes on income (D.51);
- other current taxes (D.59);
- actual social contributions (D.611 and D613), excluding voluntary contributions and payments to employment-related schemes that are not social security schemes;
- capital taxes (D.91).

A.10. The OECD classification of taxes and the International Monetary Fund (GFS) system

91. The coverage and valuation of tax revenues in the GFS system and the 2008 SNA are very similar. Therefore, the differences between the OECD classification and that of the 2008 SNA (see §89 above) also apply to the GFS. In addition, the International Monetary Fund subdivides the OECD 5000 heading into section IV (Domestic Taxes on Goods and Services) and section V (Taxes on International Trade and Transactions). This reflects the fact that

while the latter usually yield insignificant amounts of revenue in OECD countries, this is not the case in many non-OECD countries.

A.11. Comparison of the OECD classification of taxes with other international classifications

92. The table below describes an item by item comparison of the OECD classification of taxes and the classifications used in the following:

a) System of National Accounts (2008 SNA);

b) European System of Accounts (2010 ESA);

c) IMF Government Finance Statistics Manual (GFSM2014).

93. These comparisons represent those that would be expected to apply in the majority of cases. However, in practice some flexibility should be used in their application. This is because in particular cases, countries can adopt varying approaches to the classification of revenues in National Accounts.

OECD Classification	2008 SNA	2010 ESA	GFSM2014
1000 Taxes on income, profits and capital gains			
1100 Individuals			
1110 Income and profits	D51-8.61a	D51A	1111
1120 Capital gains	D51-8.61c, d	D51C, D	1111
1200 Corporations			
1210 Income and profits	D51-8.61b	D51B	1112
1220 Capital gains	D51-8.61c	D51C	1112
1300 Unallocable as between 1100 and 1200			1113
2000 Social security contributions			
2100 Employees	D613-8.85	D613	1211
2200 Employers	D611-8.83	D611	1212
2300 Self-employed, non-employed	D613-8.85	D613	1213
2400 Unallocable as between 2100, 2200 and 2300			1214
3000 Taxes on payroll and workforce	D29-7.97a	D29C	112
4000 Taxes on property			
4100 Recurrent taxes on immovable property			
4110 Households	D59-8.63a	D59A	1131
4120 Other	D29-7.97b	D29A	1131
4200 Recurrent net wealth taxes			
4210 Individual	D59-8.63b	D59A	1132
4220 Corporations	D59-8.63b	D59A	1132
4300 Estate, inheritance and gift taxes			
4310 Estate and inheritance taxes	D91-10.207b	D91A	1133
4320 Gift taxes	D91-10.207b	D91A	1133
4400 Taxes on financial and capital transactions	D59-7.96d; D29-7.97e	D214B, C	114114; 1161
4500 Other non-recurrent taxes on property	D91-10.207a	D91B	1135
4600 Other recurrent taxes on property	D59-8.63c	D59A	1136
5000 Taxes on goods and services			
5100 Taxes on production, sale and transfer of goods and services			
5110 General taxes on goods and services			
5111 Value-added taxes	D211-7.89	D211; D29G	11411
5112 Sales taxes	D2122-7.94a; D214-7.96a	D21224; D214I	11412
5113 Other general taxes on goods and services	D214-7.96a	D214I	11413

OECD Classification				2008 SNA	2010 ESA	GFSM2014
	5120	Taxes on specific goods and services				
		5121	Excises	D2122-7.94b; D214-7.96b	D21223; D214A, B, D	1142
		5122	Profits of fiscal monopolies	D214-7.96e	D214J	1143
		5123	Customs and other import duties	D2121-7.93	D2121; D21221, 2	1151
		5124	On exports	D213-7.95a	D214K	1152-4
		5125	On investment goods			
		5126	On specific services	D2122-7.94c; D214-7.96c	D21225; D214E, F, G, H; D29F	1144; 1156
		5127	Other taxes on international trade and transactions	D2122-7.94d D29-7.95b D29-7.97g D59-8.64d	D21226; D29D; D59E	1153; 1155-6
		5128	Other taxes on specific goods and services			1146
	5130	Unallocable between 5110 and 5120				
5200	Taxes on use of goods and on permission to use goods or perform activities					
	5210	Recurrent taxes on use of goods and on permission to use goods or perform activities				
		5211	Motor vehicle taxes households	D59-8.64c	D59D	11451
		5212	Motor vehicles taxes others	D29-7.97d	D214D; D29B	11451
		5213	Other recurrent taxes on use of goods and on permission to use goods or perform activities	D29-7.97c, d, f D59-8.64c	D29B, E, F; D59D	11452
	5220	Non-recurrent taxes on permission to use goods or perform activities				11452
5300	Unallocable as between 5100 and 5200					
6000	Other taxes					
6100	Payable solely by business					1161
6200	Payable by other than business, or unidentifiable			D59-8.64a, b	D59B, C	1162

A.12. Attribution of tax revenues by sub-sectors of general government

94. The OECD classification requires a breakdown of tax revenues by sub-sectors of government. The definition of each sub-sector and the criteria to be used to attribute tax revenues between these sub-sectors are set out below. They follow the guidance of the 2008 SNA and GFSM 2014.

Sub-sectors of general government to be identified

a) Central government

95. The central government sub-sector includes all governmental departments, offices, establishments and other bodies which are agencies or instruments of the central authority whose competence extends over the whole territory, with the exception of the administration of social security funds. Central government therefore has the authority to impose taxes on all resident and non-resident units engaged in economic activities within the country.

b) State, provincial or regional government

96. This sub-sector consists of intermediate units of government exercising a competence at a level below that of central government. It includes all such units operating independently of central government in a part of a country's territory encompassing a number of smaller localities, with the exception of the administration of social security funds. In unitary countries, regional governments may be considered to have a separate existence where they have substantial autonomy to raise a significant proportion of their revenues from sources within their control and their officers are independent of external administrative control in the actual operation of the unit's activities.

97. At present, federal countries comprise the majority of cases where revenues attributed to intermediate units of government are identified separately. Colombia and Spain are the only two unitary countries in this position. In the remaining unitary countries, regional revenues are included with those of local governments.

c) Local government

98. This sub-sector includes all other units of government exercising an independent competence in part of the territory of a country, with the exception of the administration of social security funds. It encompasses various urban and/or rural jurisdictions (e.g., local authorities, municipalities, cities, boroughs, districts).

d) Social security funds

99. Social security funds form a separate sub-sector of general government. The social security sub-sector is defined in the 2008 SNA by the following extracts from paragraphs 4.124 to 4.126 and 4.147:

> *"Social security schemes are social insurance schemes covering the community as a whole or large section of the community that are imposed and controlled by government units. The schemes cover a wide variety of programmes, providing benefits in cash or in kind for old age, invalidity or death, survivors, sickness and maternity, work injury, unemployment, family allowance, health care, etc. There is not necessarily a direct link between the amount of the contribution paid by an individual and the benefits he or she may receive." (Paragraph 4.124).*
>
> *"When social security schemes are separately organised from the other activities of government units and hold their assets and liabilities separately from the latter and engage in financial transactions on their own account they qualify as institutional units that are described as social security funds." (Paragraph 4.125).*
>
> *"The amounts raised, and paid out, in social security contributions and benefits may be deliberately varied in order to achieve objectives of government policy that have no direct connection with the concept of social security as a scheme to provide social benefits to members of the community. They may be raised or lowered in order to influence the level of aggregate demand in the economy, for example. Nevertheless, so long as they remain separately constituted funds, they must be treated as separate institutional units in the SNA. (Paragraph 4.126).*
>
> *"The social security funds sub-sector (of general government) consists of the social security funds operating at all levels of government. Such funds are social insurance schemes covering the community as a whole or large section of the community that are imposed by government units." (Paragraph 4.147).*

100. This definition of social security funds is followed in the OECD classification with the two following exceptions which are excluded

- Schemes imposed by government and operated by bodies outside the general government sector, as defined in §3 of this manual; and
- Schemes to which all contributions are voluntary.

Supra-national authorities

101. This sub-sector covers the revenue-raising operations of supra-national authorities within a country. In practice, the only relevant supranational authority in the OECD area is that of the institutions of the European Union (EU). Tax revenues collected by member countries and paid to the EU are included in the *Revenue Statistics* at the supranational

level of government. Income taxes and social security contributions collected by European Institutions and paid by European civil servants who are resident of EU member countries should not be included.

Criteria to be used for the attribution of tax revenues

102. When a government collects taxes and pays them over in whole or in part to other governments, it is necessary to determine whether the revenues should be considered to be those of the collecting government which it distributes to others as grants, or those of the beneficiary governments which the collecting government receives and passes on only as their agent. The criteria to be used in the attribution of revenues are set out in §103 to §106 which replicate paragraphs 3.70 to 3.73 from the 2008 SNA.

103. In general, a tax is attributed to the government unit that

a) exercises the authority to impose the tax (either as a principal or through the delegated authority of the principal),

b) has final discretion to set and vary the rate of the tax

104. Where an amount is collected by one government for and on behalf of another government, and the latter government has the authority to impose the tax, and set and vary its rate, then the former is acting as an agent for the latter and the tax is reassigned. Any amount retained by the collecting government as a collection charge should be treated as a payment for a service. Any other amount retained by the collecting government, such as under a tax-sharing arrangement, should be treated as a current grant. If the collecting government was delegated the authority to set and vary the rate, then the amount collected should be treated as tax revenue of this government.

105. Where different governments jointly and equally set the rate of a tax and jointly and equally decide on the distribution of the proceeds, with no individual government having ultimate overriding authority, then the tax revenues are attributed to each government according to its respective share of the proceeds. If an arrangement allows one government unit to exercise ultimate overriding authority, then all of the tax revenue is attributed to that unit.

106. There may also be the circumstance where a tax is imposed under the constitutional or other authority of one government, but other governments individually set the tax rate in their jurisdictions. The proceeds of the tax generated in each respective government's jurisdiction are attributed as tax revenues of that government.

107. The levies paid by the member states of the EU take the form specific levies which include

a) custom duties and levies on agricultural goods (5123);

b) gross monetary compensation accounts (5123 if relating to imports and 5124 if relating to exports);

c) contributions to the Single Resolution Fund (5126); and

d) Steel, coal, sugar and milk levies (5128).

108. The custom duties collected by member states on behalf of the EU are recorded

- on a gross of collection fee basis;
- using figures adjusted so that duties are shown on a 'final destination' as opposed to a 'country of first entry' basis where such adjustments can be made. These adjustments concern in particular duties collected at important (sea) ports. Although the EU duties are collected by the authorities of the country of first entry, when possible these duties

should be excluded from the revenue of the collecting country and be included in the revenue of the country of final destination.

109. These are the specific EU levies that most clearly conform to the attribution criterion described in §101 above. Consequently, these amounts are footnoted as a memorandum item to the EU member state country tables (in Chapter 5) and are shown as supranational revenues against each of the tax headings identified in §107.

Notes

1. References in this OECD Interpretative Guide to Sections or Parts of "this Report" refer to OECD (2020), Revenue Statistics 2020, OECD Publishing, Paris.
2. All references to SNA are to the 2008 edition.
3. See section A.12 of this guide for a discussion of the concept of agency capacity.
4. It is usually possible to identify amounts of social security contributions and payroll taxes, but not other taxes paid by government.
5. If, however, a levy which is considered as non-tax revenue by most countries is regarded as a tax — or raises substantial revenue — in one or more countries, the amounts collected are footnoted at the end of the relevant country tables, even though the amounts are not included in total tax revenues.
6. Names, however, can frequently be misleading. For example, though a passport fee would normally be considered a non-tax revenue, if a supplementary levy on passports (as is the case in Portugal) were imposed in order to raise substantial amounts of revenue relative to the cost of providing the passport, the levy would be regarded as a tax under 5200.
7. A more detailed explanation of this distinction can be found in the special feature, 'Current issues in reporting tax revenues', in the 2001 edition of the *Revenue Statistics*.
8. Sometimes the terms 'non-refundable' and 'refundable' are used, but it may be considered illogical to talk of 'refundable' when nothing has been paid.
9. A different treatment, however, is accorded to non-wastable tax credits under imputation systems of corporate income tax (§37-39).
10. This is not strictly a true tax expenditure in the formal sense. Such tax expenditures require identification of a benchmark tax system for each country or, preferably, a common international benchmark. In practice, it has not been possible to reach agreement on a common international benchmark.
11. Unless based on the profit made on a sale, in which case they would be classified as capital gains taxes under 1120 or 1220.
12. In some countries, the same legislation applies to both individual and corporate enterprises for particular taxes on income. However, the receipts from such taxes are usually allocable between individuals and enterprises and can therefore be shown in the appropriate sub-heading.
13. For example, "... sufficiently self-contained and independent that they behave in the same way as corporations... (including) keeping a complete set of accounts" (2008 SNA, section 4.44).
14. In Canada — a country also referred to as having an imputation system — the (wastable) tax credit for the shareholder is in respect of domestic corporation tax deemed to have been paid whether or not a corporation tax liability has arisen. As there is no integral connection between the corporation tax liability and the credit given against income tax under such systems, these credits for dividends are treated, along with other tax credits, on the lines described in §26.
15. This may also apply where a scheme for government employees existed prior to the introduction of a general social security scheme.
16. In the 2008 SNA these are regarded as capital transfers and not as taxes (see section A.8).
17. This is the system by which the European Union adjusts for differences between the exchange rates used to determine prices under the Common Market Agricultural Policy and actual exchange rates. Payments under the system may relate to imports or exports and where these amounts are separately identifiable, they are shown under the appropriate heading (5123 or 5124). In this Report, these amounts are shown gross (i.e. without deducting any subsidies paid out under the MCA system).
18. Transfers of profits of State lotteries are regarded as non-tax revenues (see also §68).

Anexo A

Guía de interpretación de la OCDE[1]

Índice

Página

A.1. Clasificación de impuestos de la OCDE

1. 1000 **Impuestos sobre la renta, las utilidades y las ganancias de capital**

    1100 Impuestos sobre la renta, utilidades y ganancias de capital de personas físicas

        1110 Renta y utilidades

        1120 Ganancias de capital

    1200 Impuesto sobre la renta, utilidades y ganancias de capital de sociedades.

        1210 Renta y utilidades

        1220 Ganancias de capital

    1300 No clasificables entre 1100 y 1200

2. 2000 **Contribuciones a la seguridad social**

    2100 Empleados

        2110 Sobre la base de la nómina

        2120 Sobre la base del impuesto sobre la renta

    2200 Empleadores

        2210 Sobre la base de la nómina

        2220 Sobre la base del impuesto sobre la renta

    2300 Trabajadores por cuenta propia o no empleados

        2310 Sobre la base de la nómina

        2320 Sobre la base del impuesto sobre la renta

    2400 No clasificables entre 2100, 2200 y 2300

        2410 Sobre la base de la nómina

        2420 Sobre la base del impuesto sobre la renta

3. 3000 **Impuestos sobre la nómina y la fuerza de trabajo**

4. 4000 **Impuestos sobre la propiedad**

    4100 Impuestos recurrentes sobre la propiedad inmueble

        4110 Hogares

        4120 Otros

    4200 Impuestos recurrentes sobre la riqueza neta

        4210 Personas físicas

        4220 Sociedades

    4300 Impuestos sobre sucesiones, herencias y donaciones

        4310 Impuestos sobre sucesiones y herencias

        4320 Impuestos sobre donaciones

    4400 Impuestos sobre transacciones financieras y de capital

    4500 Otros impuestos no recurrentes sobre la propiedad

        4510 Otros impuestos sobre la riqueza neta

        4520 Otros impuestos no recurrentes

    4600 Otros impuestos recurrentes sobre la propiedad

5. 5000 Impuestos sobre los bienes y servicios

5100 Impuestos sobre la producción, venta, transferencia , arrendamiento y entrega de bienes y prestación de servicios

5110 Impuestos generales

5111 Impuestos sobre el valor agregado

5112 Impuestos sobre las ventas

5113 Otros impuestos generales sobre ingresos brutos y sobre bienes y servicios

5120 Impuestos sobre bienes y servicios específicos

5121 Impuestos selectivos

5122 Utilidades de los monopolios fiscales

5123 Derechos de aduanas y otros derechos de importación

5124 Impuestos sobre las exportaciones

5125 Impuestos sobre los bienes de inversión

5126 Impuestos sobre servicios específicos

5127 Otros impuestos sobre el comercio y las transacciones internacionales

5128 Otros impuestos sobre bienes y servicios específicos

5130 No clasificables entre 5110 y 5120

5200 Impuestos sobre el uso de bienes y sobre el permiso para usar bienes y realizar actividades

5210 Impuestos recurrentes

5211 Pagados por los hogares sobre vehículos automotores.

5212 Pagados por otros sobre vehículos automotores

5213 Otros impuestos recurrentes

5220 Impuestos no recurrentes

5300 No clasificables entre 5100 y 5200

6. 6000 Otros impuestos

6100 Pagados únicamente por empresas

6200 Pagados por otros distintos de las empresas o no identificables

A.2. Cobertura

Criterios generales

1. En la clasificación de la OCDE, el término “impuestos” se circunscribe exclusivamente a los pagos sin contraprestación efectuados al gobierno general o una autoridad supranacional. Los impuestos carecen de contraprestación en el sentido en que, normalmente, las prestaciones proporcionadas por el gobierno a los contribuyentes no guardan relación directa con los pagos realizados por estos.

2. El término “impuestos” no incluye las multas, sanciones pecuniarias, ni préstamos obligatorios pagados al gobierno. La delimitación entre ingresos tributarios y no tributarios en relación con ciertas tasas y cargos se abordan en los § 12-15.

3. El gobierno general comprende la Administración central y los organismos que se hallan bajo su control efectivo, los gobiernos estatales y locales y sus respectivas administraciones, y ciertos regímenes de seguridad social y entidades gubernamentales autónomas, excluidas las empresas públicas. Esta definición del gobierno proviene del *Sistema de Cuentas Nacionales* (SCN) 2008;[2] en esa publicación, el sector del gobierno general y sus subsectores se hallan definidos en el capítulo 4, párrafos 4.117 a 4.165 de la versión en inglés.

4. Las unidades extrapresupuestarias son parte del sistema de gobierno general. Estas son entidades del gobierno general con presupuestos individuales que no están completamente cubiertos por el presupuesto principal o general. Estas entidades operan bajo la autoridad o el control de un gobierno central, estatal o local. Las entidades extrapresupuestarias pueden tener sus propias fuentes de ingresos, que pueden complementarse con subvenciones (transferencias) del presupuesto general o de otras fuentes. A pesar de que sus presupuestos pueden estar sujetos a la aprobación de la legislatura, similar a la de las cuentas presupuestarias, tienen discreción sobre el volumen y la composición de sus gastos. Dichas entidades pueden establecerse para llevar a cabo funciones gubernamentales específicas, como la construcción de carreteras o la producción de servicios de salud o educación pública. Los arreglos presupuestarios varían ampliamente entre países, y se utilizan diversos términos para describir estas entidades, pero a menudo se los denomina “fondos extrapresupuestarios” o “agencias descentralizadas”.

5. Los pagos obligatorios y sin contraprestación recaudados por los gobiernos nacionales y abonados a las autoridades supranacionales se considerarán también como impuestos, según la definición del párrafo 1. Los ingresos tributarios que recaudan los gobiernos nacionales y que se pagan a una autoridad supranacional se asignan como ingresos fiscales a la autoridad supranacional en el SCN 2008 (véanse los párrafos 22.60-61, 22.88 y 22.99) y en el SEC 2010 (véase el párrafo 20.165). En las estadísticas tributarias, estos ingresos tributarios incluyen los derechos de aduana, las contribuciones al Fondo de Resolución Única de la UE y cualquier otro impuesto recaudado por los Estados miembros de la UE en nombre de la Unión Europea. Se incluyen en los importes de los ingresos tributarios en los cuadros de países (capítulo 5) del país en el que se recaudan y se atribuyen a la autoridad supranacional (véase el § 101).

6. En los países en los que la Iglesia forma parte del gobierno general y las autoridades supranacionales, se computan los impuestos eclesiásticos, siempre que reúnan los criterios establecidos en el § 1. Además, habida cuenta de que los datos hacen referencia a las entradas que recibe el gobierno general, quedan excluidos los gravámenes abonados a órganos no gubernamentales, organismos de bienestar o regímenes de seguro social externos al gobierno

general, y sindicatos u organizaciones profesionales, aun cuando dichos gravámenes sean obligatorios; sin embargo, los pagos obligatorios al gobierno general asignados a esos entes sí están incluidos aquí siempre que el gobierno no actúe como mero agente de estos[3]. Las utilidades de los monopolios fiscales se diferencian de las de otras empresas públicas, y se tratan como impuestos porque reflejan el ejercicio del poder tributario del Estado mediante el uso de prerrogativas monopolísticas (véanse los § 66-68), al igual que las utilidades percibidas por el gobierno por la compra y la venta de divisas a diferentes tipos de cambio (véase el § 76).

7. Los impuestos pagados por el gobierno (p. ej., contribuciones a la seguridad social e impuestos sobre la nómina pagados por el gobierno en su calidad de empleador, impuestos sobre el consumo en sus compras o impuestos sobre sus propiedades) no se han excluido de los datos presentados. Sin embargo, cuando ha sido posible identificar las cantidades de ingreso implicadas[4], se han mostrado en el Cuadro 5.39 de la publicación *Estadísticas Tributarias en países de la OCDE*.

8. La relación entre esta clasificación y la del Sistema de Cuentas Nacionales (SCN) se aclara en los apartados A.9 y A.11 infra.; dado que estas dos clasificaciones no coinciden en todos sus aspectos, en ocasiones, los datos presentados en las cuentas nacionales se calculan o clasifican de forma diferente a lo establecido en la presente guía y, aunque esas y otras diferencias se han mencionado en determinados casos (p. ej., en el § 31 infra.), no ha sido posible hacer referencia a todas ellas. Por otra parte, pueden darse asimismo ciertas disparidades entre la presente clasificación y la empleada internamente por algunas administraciones nacionales (véase el § 13), por lo que quizá las estadísticas de la OCDE y las nacionales no siempre concuerden; sin embargo, es más que probable que esas diferencias sean mínimas en lo que a la cuantía de ingresos se refiere.

Contribuciones a la seguridad social

9. Las contribuciones obligatorias a la seguridad social, tal y como se definen en el § 40, abonadas al gobierno general, se tratan aquí como ingresos tributarios. No obstante, pueden diferir de otros impuestos por el hecho de que la recepción de prestaciones de la seguridad social depende, en numerosos países, de que se hayan aportado las debidas contribuciones, aunque la magnitud de dichas prestaciones no tiene por qué estar supeditada obligatoriamente al importe de las contribuciones. Al tratar las contribuciones sociales como impuestos, se obtiene un mayor grado de comparabilidad entre países, aunque se han consignado en una categoría separada para poder distinguirlas en cualquier análisis.

10. La estricta distinción entre los ingresos tributarios (pagos obligatorios sin contraprestaciones directas a los gobiernos generales o una autoridad supranacional) y los pagos obligatorios no tributarios (NTCPs por sus siglas en inglés) (pagos que con derechos a contraprestaciones o que se realizan a otras instituciones) está claramente definida. Sin embargo, dentro del rango de diferentes pagos obligatorios realizados a los gobiernos en todos los países, no siempre es sencillo en la práctica decidir si los pagos específicos son impuestos o NTCPs. Por ejemplo, los ahorros de pensión obligatorios que son controlados por el gobierno general y que se acumulan en una cuenta individual obteniendo una rentabilidad del mercado o una tasa que compensa la inflación se clasificarían a primera vista como NTCPs en lugar de impuestos. Sin embargo, incluso estos pagos podrían no dar origen a "reembolsos" y clasificarse como impuestos en lugar de NTCPs (por ejemplo, si estos ahorros no se pagan cuando el contribuyente muere antes de alcanzar la edad de jubilación y los fondos se utilizan para proporcionar una pensión mínima a todos los contribuyentes que están asegurados). Estos problemas hacen que

las cifras de ingresos de la seguridad social reportadas para la mayoría de los países se basen en la premisa de que todos los tipos de pagos obligatorios a las administraciones públicas se consideran en cierta medida como elementos de redistribución. Cabe señalar que esta conclusión se basa en una interpretación generalmente amplia del término "no correspondido" en la definición del impuesto.

11. Por el contrario, las contribuciones a la seguridad social voluntarias o no pagaderas al gobierno general (véase el § 1) no se tratan como impuestos, aunque en ciertos países, tal y como se indica debidamente en cada caso en las notas que figuran al pie de los cuadros, plantea dificultades el eliminar tanto las contribuciones voluntarias como algunos pagos obligatorios al sector privado de las cifras de recaudo tributario. Las contribuciones a la seguridad social imputadas tampoco son considerados impuestos.

Tasas, cargos a usuarios y licencias

12. Aparte de las tasas por licencia de vehículos, universalmente consideradas como impuestos, no resulta fácil distinguir entre las tasas y cargos a usuarios que deben tratarse como impuestos y las que no, ya que, aunque toda tasa o cargo se impone en conexión con un servicio o una actividad específicos, la intensidad del vínculo entre el derecho cobrado y el servicio prestado puede variar considerablemente, al igual que puede hacerlo la relación entre la cuantía de la tasa y el costo que supone proporcionar el servicio en cuestión. En todo caso, cuando el beneficiario del servicio pague una tasa claramente relacionada con el costo que supone prestar un servicio, puede inferirse que el gravamen tiene contraprestación y, de acuerdo con la definición reseñada en el § 1, no se considerará como impuesto. En sentido contrario, puede estimarse que el gravamen "carece de contraprestación" cuando:

- *a)* el cargo exceda con creces el costo que supone prestar el servicio;
- *b)* el pagador o sujeto pasivo del gravamen no sea el beneficiario del servicio (p. ej., tasas recaudadas de los mataderos para financiar un servicio proporcionado a los titulares de explotaciones agropecuarias);
- *c)* el gobierno no proporcione un servicio específico a cambio del pago del gravamen, aun y cuando se emita un permiso en beneficio del sujeto pasivo (p. ej., cuando el gobierno concede licencias de caza, pesca o tiro que no otorgan el derecho a usar una zona específica propiedad del gobierno);
- *d)* los servicios beneficien únicamente a los pagadores del gravamen, pero las utilidades recibidas por cada persona no guarden necesariamente proporción con sus pagos (p. ej., el gravamen sobre la comercialización de la leche que recae en los criadores de ganado lechero y que se utiliza para fomentar el consumo de la leche).

13. Pese a las anteriores consideraciones, en ciertos casos excepcionales la aplicación de los criterios plasmados en el § 1 puede resultar particularmente compleja. La solución adoptada – dada la conveniencia de uniformidad internacional y las cantidades de ingreso relativamente bajas implicadas por lo general – ha consistido en seguir la práctica dominante en la mayoría de las administraciones, en lugar de permitir que cada país aplique su propia visión sobre si estos gravámenes deben considerarse ingresos tributarios o no tributarios.[5]

14. Seguidamente, se ofrece una lista de las principales tasas y cargos en cuestión, y su tratamiento normal[6] en esta publicación:

Ingresos no tributarios:	tasas procesales, permisos de conducir, tasas portuarias, tasas por expedición de pasaportes, licencias de radio y televisión cuando las autoridades públicas proporcionan el servicio de difusión.
Impuestos de la partida 5200:	permiso para realizar actividades tales como distribución cinematográfica; caza, pesca o tiro; suministro de instalaciones para actividades recreativas o de ocio o juegos de azar; venta de bebidas alcohólicas o tabaco; posesión de animales domésticos o uso de vehículos automotores; derechos sobre la extracción.

15. En la práctica, puede que no siempre resulte posible aislar las entradas tributarias de las no tributarias cuando estas se registran conjuntamente. En ese caso, si se considera que la mayoría de las entradas proviene de ingresos no tributarios, se tratará el importe total como tal; de lo contrario, esas entradas del gobierno se incluirán y clasificarán según las normas recogidas en el § 33.

Regalías

16. La propiedad de los activos del subsuelo en forma de depósitos de minerales o combustibles fósiles (carbón, petróleo o gas natural) depende de la forma en que los derechos de propiedad están definidos por la ley y también de los acuerdos internacionales en el caso de depósitos bajo aguas internacionales. En algunos casos, ya sea en el terreno por debajo del cual se encuentran los depósitos minerales, los depósitos en sí o ambos pueden pertenecer a una unidad del gobierno local o central.

17. En tales casos, estas unidades del gobierno general pueden otorgar arrendamientos a otras unidades institucionales que les permitan extraer estos depósitos durante un período de tiempo específico a cambio de un pago o una serie de pagos. Estos pagos a menudo se describen como “regalías”, pero son esencialmente rentas que se acumulan a los propietarios de los recursos naturales a cambio de poner estos activos a disposición de otros agentes durante períodos de tiempo específicos. El alquiler puede tomar la forma de pagos periódicos de cantidades fijas, independientemente de la tasa de extracción, o, más comúnmente, pueden ser una función de la cantidad, el volumen o el valor del activo extraído. Las empresas dedicadas a la exploración en tierras del gobierno pueden hacer pagos a las unidades del gobierno general a cambio del derecho a realizar perforaciones de prueba o investigar de otro modo la existencia y ubicación de los activos del subsuelo. Dichos pagos también se registran como rentas aunque no se realice ninguna extracción. Por lo tanto, estos pagos se clasifican como ingresos no tributarios.

18. Los mismos principios se aplican cuando a otras unidades institucionales se les conceden arrendamientos que les permiten talar madera en bosques naturales en tierras que son propiedad de unidades del gobierno general. Estos pagos también se clasifican como ingresos no tributarios.

19. Estas rentas o regalías pagadas al gobierno general no deben confundirse con los impuestos sobre los ingresos y las ganancias, los impuestos sobre la extracción de recursos naturales, las licencias comerciales u otros impuestos. Si los pagos se aplican a las ganancias de la actividad de extracción, entonces deben clasificarse como impuestos sobre ingresos,

utilidades y ganancias (1000). Además, cualquier pago que se imponga a la extracción de minerales y combustibles fósiles de las reservas de propiedad privada o de otro gobierno se debe clasificar como impuestos. Los pagos relacionados con el valor bruto de la producción deben clasificarse como otros impuestos sobre bienes y servicios (5128). Los pagos de una licencia o permiso para realizar operaciones de extracción se deben clasificar como impuestos sobre el uso de bienes y sobre el permiso para usar bienes o realizar actividades (5213).

Multas y sanciones pecuniarias

20. En principio, las multas y sanciones pecuniarias impuestas por el pago tardío de los impuestos o por el intento de evasión de los impuestos no deben registrarse como ingresos tributarios. Sin embargo, en ocasiones no es posible distinguir y separar los pagos por multas y penalidades del recaudo del impuesto a los que estos están relacionados. En este caso, las multas y sanciones pecuniarias vinculadas a un determinado impuesto se registran con los ingresos de ese impuesto. Las multas y penalidades pagadas sobre el recaudo de impuestos no identificados se clasifican como otros impuestos en la partida 6000. Las multas que no están relacionadas con delitos tributarios (por ejemplo, las infracciones por estacionamiento indebido), o que no puedan ser identificadas como ofensas tributarias, no serán tratadas como ingresos tributarios.

A.3. Principios de registro

Criterio de devengo

21. Los datos recogidos en esta publicación relativos a los últimos años se han registrado predominantemente según el criterio de devengo, esto es, se han computado en el momento en que nace la obligación. Se ofrece más información al respecto en las notas que figuran al pie de los cuadros de países en el Capítulo 5 del informe.

22. Sin embargo, los datos relativos a años anteriores han seguido registrándose principalmente según el criterio de caja, es decir, en el momento en que el gobierno recibió el pago. Por lo tanto, por ejemplo, los impuestos descontados por los empleadores en un año pero pagados al gobierno al año siguiente y los impuestos debidos un año pero liquidados el año después constan ambos en las entradas del segundo año. Las transacciones correctoras, tales como devoluciones, reembolsos y reintegros, se deducen de los ingresos brutos del periodo en que se realizan.

23. Los datos sobre ingresos tributarios se registran sin deducción de los gastos administrativos propios de la recaudación impositiva. De igual modo, cuando los recursos generados por un impuesto se emplean para subvencionar a miembros particulares de la comunidad, el subsidio no se descuenta del producto impositivo, aunque puede que el impuesto aparezca sin los subsidios en los registros nacionales de algunos países.

24. En lo que a los monopolios fiscales se refiere (5122), únicamente se incluye en los ingresos del gobierno el importe realmente transferido a este. Sin embargo, si cualquier gasto de los monopolios fiscales se considera gasto del gobierno (p. ej., gastos sociales emprendidos por los monopolios fiscales en beneficio del gobierno), se añadirán posteriormente con el fin de llegar a cifras de ingreso tributario (véase el § 66 infra.).

Distinción entre disposiciones tributarias y disposiciones relativas al gasto[7]

25. Dado que la presente publicación aborda únicamente la actividad del gobierno desde el punto de vista del ingreso, sin tener en cuenta los aspectos relacionados con el gasto, resulta preciso realizar una distinción entre las disposiciones que rigen estos dos elementos. Por lo

general, no existe dificultad alguna en diferenciar ambos aspectos, ya que los gastos operan en un ámbito externo al sistema tributario y sus cuentas, y se rigen por una legislación separada de la impositiva. En los casos de difícil delimitación, se emplea el flujo de caja para distinguir entre disposiciones tributarias y disposiciones relativas al gasto. En la medida en que una disposición incida en el flujo de pagos tributarios del contribuyente al gobierno, se entenderá que reviste un carácter tributario y se tendrá en cuenta en los datos recogidos en esta publicación. Cualquier disposición que no afecte a ese flujo se reputará como relativa al gasto y no se tendrá en consideración en la información plasmada en la publicación.

26. Las desgravaciones, exenciones y deducciones tributarias sobre la base imponible afectan claramente a la cantidad transferida al gobierno y, por ende, se consideran disposiciones de naturaleza tributaria. En el extremo opuesto, los subsidios o exoneraciones que no compensen la obligación tributaria y que estén claramente desvinculados del proceso de evaluación, no reducen los ingresos tributarios consignados en esta publicación. De particular interés en este ámbito resultan los créditos fiscales, que son cantidades deducibles del impuesto liquidable (lo que los diferencia de las deducciones sobre la base imponible). Cabe distinguir dos tipos de créditos fiscales: los créditos fiscales no exigibles (a veces denominados desaprovechables), limitados al importe de la obligación tributaria y que, por ende, no pueden generar un pago de las autoridades al contribuyente; y los créditos fiscales exigibles (o no desaprovechables), que no están sometidos a dicho límite, de forma que toda cantidad que exceda la obligación tributaria puede abonarse al contribuyente[8]. Al igual que las desgravaciones, un crédito fiscal no exigible afecta claramente a la cantidad transferida al gobierno y, por ende, se considerará como tributario. La práctica seguida para los créditos fiscales exigibles[9] consiste en distinguir entre "el componente de gasto tributario"[10] que es la porción del crédito empleada en reducir o eliminar la obligación del contribuyente" y el "componente de transferencia", constituido por la parte que excede la obligación del contribuyente y que se paga a este. Al registrar los ingresos tributarios deberá restarse la parte equivalente al componente de gasto tributario, pero no la correspondiente al componente de transferencia. Además, las cantidades de ambos componentes deberán figurar como partidas informativas en los cuadros de países. Los países que no puedan diferenciar entre estos dos componentes deberán indicar si se ha restado de los ingresos tributarios el total de ellos y presentar las evaluaciones disponibles del valor que ambos representan. Para mayor información, consúltese el Capítulo 1 de la publicación Revenue Statistics de la OCDE, que examina el efecto de los diversos tratamientos de los créditos fiscales exigibles en la relación impuestos sobre PIB.

Calendario y ejercicio fiscal

27. Las autoridades nacionales cuyos ejercicios fiscales no coinciden con el año calendario deben presentar los datos, siempre que sea posible, sobre la base del año calendario, a fin de permitir el mayor grado posible de comparación con la información de otros países. Subsisten algunos países en los que los datos hacen referencia a los ejercicios fiscales; para ellos, los datos relativos al PIB utilizados en los cuadros comparativos corresponden igualmente a los ejercicios fiscales.

A.4. Criterios generales de clasificación

Principales criterios de clasificación

28. El desglose de las entradas fiscales en las diversas categorías (1000, 2000, 3000, 4000, 5000 y 6000) se rige en general por la base sobre la cual recae el impuesto: 1000, renta, utilidades y ganancias de capital; 2000 y 3000, remuneraciones, nómina o número de empleados (fuerza

de trabajo); 4000, propiedad; 5000, bienes y servicios; 6000, bases múltiples, otras bases o bases no identificables. Cuando un impuesto se calcula sobre más de una base, las entradas que genera se distribuyen, en la medida de lo posible, entre las diversas categorías (véanse los § 33 y 83). Las categorías 4000 y 5000 no sólo cubren aquellos impuestos en los que la base tributaria está constituida por la propiedad, los bienes o los servicios en sí mismos, sino también ciertos impuestos afines; y así, por ejemplo, los impuestos sobre transmisiones patrimoniales se incluyen en la partida 4400,[11] y los impuestos sobre el uso de bienes y sobre el permiso para realizar actividades, en la 5200. En las categorías 4000 y 5000, se distingue en ocasiones entre impuestos recurrentes y no recurrentes: son impuestos recurrentes los que se recaudan a intervalos regulares (por lo general, anualmente), y no recurrentes, los que se imponen una sola vez (véanse los § 48 al § 51, § 54, § 55 y § 81 para profundizar en las aplicaciones particulares de esta distinción).

29. La asignación de un impuesto a fines específicos no afecta a la clasificación de las entradas fiscales que genera. Sin embargo, tal y como se explica en el § 40 en relación con la clasificación de las contribuciones a la seguridad social, el hecho de que estas confieran un derecho a recibir prestaciones sociales es decisivo para la definición de la categoría 2000.

30. La forma en que se establece o recauda un impuesto (p.ej., mediante el uso de timbres) no afecta a su clasificación.

Clasificación de los contribuyentes

31. En ocasiones, se distingue entre diversas clases de contribuyentes. Esas distinciones dependen de cada impuesto.

a) Entre personas físicas y sociedades en relación con los impuestos sobre la renta y sobre la riqueza neta

La distinción básica aquí es que los impuestos sobre la renta de las sociedades (impuesto de sociedades), a diferencia de los impuestos sobre la renta de las personas físicas, gravan a la sociedad como entidad y no a sus propietarios, independientemente de las circunstancias personales de estos; la misma distinción se aplica a los impuestos sobre la riqueza neta de las sociedades y de las personas físicas. Los impuestos liquidados sobre las utilidades de las asociaciones y sobre la renta de las instituciones, tales como seguros de vida o fondos de pensiones, se clasifican siguiendo la misma regla, y así, se considerarán impuestos sobre las sociedades (1200) si se cargan a la asociación o institución como persona jurídica sin tener en cuenta las circunstancias personales de sus propietarios, o impuestos sobre las personas físicas en el caso contrario (1100). Por lo general, los impuestos aplicados a las sociedades y a las personas físicas se rigen por legislaciones diferentes.[12] La distinción realizada aquí entre personas físicas y sociedades no sigue la categorización por sectores entre hogares, empresas, etcétera, del Sistema de Cuentas Nacionales para las cuentas de ingresos y desembolsos. La clasificación del SCN requiere que ciertas empresas no constituidas en sociedad[13] se excluyan del sector de los hogares y vengan a sumarse a las empresas no financieras y las instituciones financieras. Sin embargo, el impuesto sobre las utilidades de esos negocios no siempre puede separarse del impuesto sobre la renta de sus propietarios o, como mucho, puede deslindarse sólo arbitrariamente. Por ello, no se ha intentado reproducir aquí esa separación, y la totalidad del impuesto sobre la renta de las personas físicas se ha recogido en un solo bloque, independientemente de la naturaleza del ingreso imponible.

b) Entre hogares y otros en relación con los impuestos sobre la propiedad inmueble

Esta distinción es la misma que la adoptada por el SCN para las cuentas de gasto del consumo final de los hogares y de producción. Se trata pues de diferenciar a los hogares como consumidores (esto es, excluidas las empresas no constituidas en sociedad), por una parte, y a los productores, por otra. Los impuestos sobre las viviendas ocupadas por los hogares, tanto a cargo de los propietarios-ocupantes como de los arrendatarios o de los arrendadores, se incluyen en los hogares, lo que coincide con la diferenciación que suele hacerse comúnmente entre los impuestos sobre la propiedad doméstica y los impuestos sobre la propiedad empresarial. No obstante, algunos países no se hallan en situación de operar esta distinción.

c) Entre hogares y otros en relación con las licencias de vehículos automotores

Se distingue aquí entre los hogares como consumidores, por una parte, y los productores, por otra, al igual que en las cuentas de gasto del consumo final de los hogares y de producción del SCN.

d) Entre empresas y otros en relación con los impuestos residuales (6000)

La distinción es la misma que en c), esta vez, entre los productores, por una parte, y los hogares como consumidores, por otra. Los impuestos recogidos en la categoría 6000 bien porque gravan más de una base tributaria, o bien porque su base no entra dentro del ámbito de ninguna de las categorías anteriores pero es identificable como imponible sobre los productores, y no sobre los hogares, se incluyen en 'empresas'. El resto de los impuestos de la categoría 6000 se imputan a 'otros' o no identificables.

Recargos

32. Las entradas procedentes de recargos relacionados con impuestos particulares se clasifican por lo general en base al impuesto correspondiente, ya sea el recargo temporal o no. Pero si el recargo posee una característica que lo califica para ser clasificada en una categoría diferente de la lista de la OCDE, las entradas generadas por el recargo se recogen en dicha categoría, separadas de las del correspondiente impuesto.

Entradas tributarias no identificables y partidas residuales

33. En un cierto número de casos, no logra determinarse que los impuestos pertenezcan enteramente a una categoría o partida de la clasificación de la OCDE y, en esos casos, se aplican las siguientes pautas:

a) Se conoce la categoría, pero no la forma de distribuir las entradas entre las diversas subdivisiones: las entradas se clasifican en la correspondiente partida o subpartida residual (1300, 2400, 4520, 4600, 5130, 5300 o 6200).

b) Se sabe que la mayor parte de las entradas procedentes de un grupo de impuestos (normalmente, impuestos locales) proviene de impuestos de una categoría o una partida particulares, pero algunos de los impuestos del grupo cuya cuantía no puede determinarse con exactitud pueden clasificarse en otras categorías o partidas: las entradas se consignan en la categoría o partida a la que pertenezca la mayoría de ellas.

c) No puede identificarse ni la categoría ni la partida correspondiente al impuesto (normalmente, local): el impuesto se incorpora a la partida 6200, a menos que se conozca que se trata de un impuesto sobre las empresas, en cuyo caso se incluye en la partida 6100.

A.5. Comentarios sobre ítems de la lista

1000 – Impuestos sobre la renta, las utilidades y las ganancias de capital

34. Esta categoría cubre los impuestos aplicados a la renta o a las utilidades netas (esto es, la renta bruta menos las deducciones permitidas) de las personas físicas y las sociedades, así como los impuestos a los que se someten las ganancias de capital de esos mismos sujetos pasivos, y las ganancias obtenidas en juegos de azar.

35. Se incluyen en esta categoría:

a) los impuestos que gravan predominantemente la renta o las utilidades, aunque recaigan parcialmente sobre otras bases; los impuestos aplicados a varias bases que no sean mayoritariamente la renta o las utilidades se clasifican de acuerdo con los principios establecidos en los § 33 y 83;

b) los impuestos sobre la propiedad aplicados a un ingreso presunto o estimado como parte de un impuesto sobre la renta (véase el § 48(a), (c) y (d));

c) los pagos obligatorios al fondo de contribuciones de la seguridad social impuestos sobre la renta que no confieran un derecho a prestaciones sociales; si esas contribuciones otorgan derecho a prestaciones sociales, se incluyen en la categoría 2000 (véase el § 40);

d) el producto de los sistemas integrados de impuestos sobre la renta de régimen cedular se clasifican como un todo en esta categoría, aunque algunos de los impuestos cedulares puedan basarse en la renta bruta y no tener en cuenta las circunstancias personales del contribuyente.

36. La principal división de esta categoría se efectúa entre los gravámenes a personas físicas (1100) y aquellos a sociedades (1200). A su vez, en cada partida, se separa entre impuestos sobre la renta y las utilidades (1110 y 1210) e impuestos sobre las ganancias de capital (1120 y 1220). Si algunas entradas no pueden atribuirse pertinentemente a la partida 1100 o a la 1200, o si no puede realizarse esta distinción en la práctica (p. ej., por falta de datos fiables sobre los receptores de los pagos de los que se deducen los impuestos con retención en la fuente), las entradas se incorporan a la partida 1300 como "no clasificables".

Tratamiento de los créditos fiscales en los sistemas de imputación

37. En los sistemas de imputación del impuesto de sociedades, los accionistas están exentos, total o parcialmente, de responder en concepto del impuesto sobre la renta por los dividendos abonados por la compañía a partir de la renta o de las utilidades sometidas al impuesto de sociedades. En los países con este sistema,[14] una parte del impuesto sobre las utilidades de la sociedad está disponible para exonerar a los accionistas de su propia obligación tributaria. La exoneración del accionista reviste la forma de un crédito fiscal, cuyo importe puede ser inferior, igual o superior al pasivo tributario total del accionista. Si el crédito fiscal excede al pasivo tributario, puede que ese exceso sea pagadero al accionista. Dado que este tipo de crédito fiscal es parte integrante del sistema de imputación del impuesto sobre la renta de las sociedades, cualquier pago a los accionistas se trata como devolución tributaria, y no como gasto (compárese con el tratamiento de otros créditos fiscales descrito en el § 26).

38. Puesto que en los sistemas de imputación el crédito fiscal (incluso cuando excede la obligación tributaria) debe considerarse como disposición tributaria, se plantea la cuestión de determinar si deberá deducirse de las entradas en concepto de impuesto sobre la renta de las personas físicas (1110) o de las entradas atribuibles al impuesto sobre la renta de las

sociedades (1210). En este informe, la cantidad total pagada a título del impuesto sobre la renta de las sociedades se recoge en la subpartida 1210, y el impuesto no imputado en la subpartida 1110. Por lo tanto, la cuantía total del crédito se resta de esta última subpartida, tanto si el crédito da lugar a una reducción de la obligación tributaria por renta personal, como si se realiza un reembolso porque el crédito fiscal excede el pasivo tributario por este concepto. (No obstante, si los créditos fiscales se deducen del impuesto de sociedades por dividendos repartidos a otras sociedades, las correspondientes cantidades se descuentan de las entradas registradas en la subpartida 1210.)

1120 y 1220 – Impuestos sobre las ganancias de capital

39. Como su nombre indica, estas subpartidas engloban los impuestos sobre las ganancias de capital, ya de las personas físicas (1120), ya de las sociedades (1220), siempre que las entradas procedentes de estos impuestos puedan identificarse por separado. Ese no es el caso en numerosos países, y las entradas de estos impuestos se clasifican junto con las del impuesto sobre la renta. La subpartida 1120 contiene asimismo los impuestos sobre las ganancias obtenidas en juegos de azar.

2000 – Contribuciones a la seguridad social

40. Entran en esta categoría todos los pagos obligatorios a las administraciones públicas que confieran un derecho a recibir una prestación social futura (contingente). Esos pagos suelen estar asignados al financiamiento de prestaciones sociales y, a menudo, se pagan a las instituciones del gobierno general que proporcionan dichas prestaciones. Sin embargo, esa asignación no forma parte de la definición de las contribuciones a la seguridad social y no es necesaria para que un impuesto sea clasificado en esta categoría, pero, para que un impuesto se incluya aquí, sí será preciso que confiera un derecho. Y así, los gravámenes sobre la renta o la nómina asignados a los fondos de seguridad social pero que no confieran el derecho a recibir prestaciones sociales quedan excluidos de la presente categoría y se registran bien entre los impuestos sobre la renta de las personas físicas (1100), bien junto con los impuestos sobre la nómina y la fuerza de trabajo (3000). Los impuestos aplicados sobre otras bases, como los bienes y servicios, no se consignarán aquí aunque estén asignados a prestaciones de la seguridad social, sino que se catalogarán según sus respectivas bases, ya que por lo general no otorgarán derecho alguno a prestaciones sociales.

41. Entre otras, se incluirán aquí las contribuciones a los siguientes tipos de prestaciones de la seguridad social: prestaciones y suplementos por seguro de desempleo; prestaciones por accidente, lesión o enfermedad; pensiones por jubilación, invalidez y supervivencia; ayudas familiares; reembolsos de gastos médicos u hospitalarios o prestación de servicios médicos u hospitalarios. Las contribuciones pueden recaudarse tanto de los empleados como de los empleadores.

42. Las contribuciones pueden tener como base bien las remuneraciones o la nómina ('sobre la base de la nómina'), bien la renta neta tras deducciones y exenciones por circunstancias personales ('sobre la base del impuesto sobre la renta'), y el producto de ambas bases deberá identificarse separadamente en la medida de lo posible. Cuando las contribuciones al régimen general de la seguridad social se basen en la nómina, pero las de grupos particulares (tales como los trabajadores por cuenta propia) no puedan evaluarse en función de esta base y se emplee en ese caso la renta neta como una aproximación de las remuneraciones brutas, las entradas seguirán clasificándose sobre la base de la nómina. En principio, esta categoría excluye las contribuciones voluntarias aportadas a los regímenes de seguridad social, que,

cuando sea posible identificarlas de forma separada, se recogerán en la partida informativa sobre el financiamiento de las prestaciones sociales; sin embargo, en la práctica, estas aportaciones no siempre pueden desvincularse de las contribuciones obligatorias, en cuyo caso se incluirán igualmente en esta categoría.

43. Las contribuciones a los regímenes de seguro social no vinculados a instituciones del gobierno general, así como las aportaciones a otros tipos de sistemas de seguro, tales como planes de previsión o planes de pensiones, mutualidades u otros planes de ahorro, no se consideran contribuciones a la seguridad social. Los planes de previsión son acuerdos por los que las contribuciones de cada empleado y la parte correspondiente del empleador en nombre de aquél se conservan en una cuenta separada que genera interés, de la que pueden retirarse en circunstancias específicas. Por su parte, los planes de pensiones son regímenes organizados separadamente, negociados entres empleados y empleadores, que conllevan disposiciones sobre diversas contribuciones y prestaciones, a veces más directamente vinculadas a los niveles salariales y a la duración del servicio que en otros esquemas sociales. Cuando las contribuciones a esos regímenes son obligatorias o cuasiobligatorias (p. ej., en virtud de un acuerdo con sindicatos u organizaciones profesionales), se hacen constar en la partida informativa (véase el Cuadro 5.38 de este Reporte).

44. Las contribuciones de los empleados del gobierno y de este con respecto a sus empleados a los regímenes de seguridad social incluidos en el gobierno general se clasifican en esta categoría. También se consideran impuestos las contribuciones de los empleados del gobierno a regímenes diferentes que puedan reputarse sustitutivos de los regímenes generales de seguridad social.[15] Por el contrario, cuando un régimen diferente no pueda considerarse sustitutivo de uno general y haya sido negociado entre el gobierno, en su papel de empleador, y sus empleados, no se estimará como régimen de seguridad social y, por lo tanto, las contribuciones a él no se tendrán como impuestos, aunque el régimen haya sido instaurado por la legislación.

45. Esta categoría excluye las contribuciones 'imputadas', que corresponden a las prestaciones sociales pagadas directamente por los empleadores a sus empleados, antiguos empleados o personas a cargo de estos (p. ej., cuando los empleadores están legalmente obligados a correr con las prestaciones por enfermedad durante cierto tiempo).

46. Las contribuciones se dividen en tres partidas principales – empleados (2100), empleadores (2200) y trabajadores por cuenta propia o no empleados (2300) – y se subdividen posteriormente en función de la base que gravan. A efectos de la presente publicación, se entiende por empleados todas las personas contratadas en actividades de unidades empresariales, órganos gubernamentales, instituciones privadas sin ánimo de lucro u otro tipo de empleo remunerado, con excepción de los dueños de empresas no constituidas en sociedad y de los miembros no remunerados de sus familias. También se consideran empleados los miembros de las Fuerzas Armadas, independientemente de la duración y del tipo de su servicio, siempre que coticen a regímenes de la seguridad social. Por su parte, las contribuciones de los empleadores se definen como las aportaciones que estos realizan por cuenta de sus empleados a los sistemas de seguridad social. Si los empleados o los empleadores tienen la obligación de continuar cotizando a la seguridad social en el caso de desempleo de un empleado, esas contribuciones se muestran en las partidas 2100 y 2200, respectivamente, siempre que los datos lo permitan. En consecuencia, la partida 2300 queda reservada a las contribuciones abonadas por los trabajadores por cuenta propia y por quienes no se hallan incluidos en la población activa (p. ej., incapacitados o jubilados).

3000 – *Impuestos sobre la nómina y la fuerza de trabajo*

47. Consiste en los impuestos pagados por las firmas o empresas, ya sea como una proporción de los salarios o la nómina, ya como una cantidad fija por persona empleada. No incluyen pagos a la seguridad social obligatorios pagados por empleadores u otros impuestos pagados por los empleados mismos de sus salarios o remuneraciones.

4000 – *Impuestos sobre la propiedad*

48. Esta categoría engloba los impuestos, recurrentes y no recurrentes, sobre el uso, la titularidad o la transmisión de la propiedad, lo que incluye impuestos sobre la propiedad inmueble y la riqueza neta, sobre el cambio de titularidad en la propiedad por herencia o donación, y sobre transacciones financieras y de capital. Quedan excluidas de esta categoría los siguientes tipos de impuestos:

a) los impuestos sobre las ganancias de capital procedentes de la venta de propiedad (1120 o 1220);

b) los impuestos sobre el uso de bienes y sobre el permiso para usar bienes o realizar actividades (5200): véase el § 78;

c) los impuestos sobre los bienes inmuebles gravados sobre la base de un ingreso neto presunto que tiene en cuenta las circunstancias personales del contribuyente: se clasifican como impuestos sobre la renta junto con los impuestos sobre la renta y sobre las ganancias de capital derivadas de la propiedad (1100);

d) los impuestos sobre el uso de la propiedad con fines residenciales, tanto si debe responder del impuesto el propietario como el arrendatario, siempre que la cantidad debida tenga en cuenta las circunstancias personales del usuario (ingresos, personas a cargo, etcétera): se integran en los impuestos sobre la renta (1100);

e) los impuestos sobre los edificios con una densidad máxima superior a la permitida; sobre la ampliación, construcción o modificación de ciertos edificios más allá de un valor umbral; y sobre la construcción de edificios: todos ellos se integran en los impuestos sobre el permiso para realizar actividades (5200);

f) los impuestos sobre el uso de la propiedad propia para fines comerciales especiales, tales como la venta de bebidas alcohólicas, tabaco o carne, o para la explotación de tierras (p. ej., impuestos sobre la extracción en Estados Unidos): se integran en los impuestos sobre el permiso para realizar actividades (5200).

4100 – *Impuestos recurrentes sobre la propiedad inmueble*

49. Esta partida comprende los impuestos con que se grava de forma regular el uso o la titularidad de bienes inmuebles.

- Estos impuestos gravan las tierras y los edificios.
- Pueden consistir en un porcentaje del valor tasado de una propiedad, basado a su vez en un ingreso por alquiler hipotético, en el precio de venta, en un rendimiento capitalizado o en otras características de la propiedad inmueble (por ejemplo, el tamaño o la ubicación) de las que quepa inferir un alquiler o un valor de capital hipotéticos.
- Estos impuestos pueden aplicarse a los propietarios, a los arrendatarios o a ambos. También pueden pagarse de un nivel de gobierno a otro en relación con los bienes bajo jurisdicción de este último.
- Para la evaluación de estos impuestos, no se tienen en cuenta las deudas y, en ese sentido, difieren de los impuestos sobre la riqueza neta.

50. Los impuestos recurrentes sobre la propiedad inmueble se subdividen a su vez en los pagados por los hogares (4110) y los abonados por otros sujetos pasivos (4120), de acuerdo con los criterios establecidos en el § 31(b) supra.

4200 – Impuestos recurrentes sobre la riqueza neta

51. Esta partida abarca los impuestos con que se grava periódicamente (por lo general, anualmente) la riqueza neta, esto es, los impuestos sobre un amplio abanico de bienes muebles e inmuebles, descontadas sus deudas. Esta partida se subdivide a su vez en los impuestos pagados por las personas físicas (4210) y los abonados por las sociedades (4220), de acuerdo con los criterios establecidos en el § 31(a) supra. Si existen cifras separadas para las entradas correspondientes a pagos realizados por instituciones, se añaden a la subpartida de las sociedades.

4300 – Impuestos sobre sucesiones, herencias y donaciones

52. Esta partida se divide entre impuestos sobre sucesiones o herencias (4310) e impuestos sobre donaciones (4320).[16] Los impuestos sobre sucesiones gravan el valor total de la sucesión o del caudal hereditario, mientras los impuestos sobre herencias se aplican a las cuotas recibidas por los causahabientes individualmente considerados o en función de la relación de estos con el difunto.

4400 – Impuestos sobre transacciones financieras y de capital

53. Esta partida incluye, entre otros, los impuestos sobre la emisión, transmisión, compra y venta de valores, sobre los cheques, y sobre transacciones legales específicas, tales como la validación de contratos o la venta de bienes inmuebles. La partida no incluye:

a) los impuestos sobre el uso de bienes y sobre el permiso para realizar ciertas actividades (5200);

b) las tasas abonadas en concepto de costos procesales o expedición de actas de nacimiento, matrimonio o defunción, que suelen considerarse como ingresos no tributarios (véase el § 12);

c) los impuestos sobre ganancias de capital (1000);

d) los impuestos recurrentes sobre la propiedad inmueble (4100);

e) los impuestos recurrentes sobre la riqueza neta (4200);

f) otros impuestos no recurrentes sobre la propiedad o la riqueza (4500).

4500 – Otros impuestos no recurrentes sobre la propiedad16

54. Esta partida cubre los gravámenes sobre la propiedad que, a diferencia de los impuestos recurrentes, se recaudan una sola vez. Se divide en impuestos no recurrentes sobre la riqueza neta (4510) y otros impuestos no recurrentes sobre la propiedad (4520). La subpartida 4510 contiene los impuestos que se recaudan a fin de hacer frente a gastos excepcionales o de redistribuir la riqueza. Por su parte, la subpartida 4520 comprende los impuestos que gravan los incrementos de valor de la tierra, debido, por ejemplo, a permisos para su desarrollo concedidos por el gobierno general o a la provisión por parte de este de instalaciones locales adicionales; cualesquiera impuestos sobre la reevaluación del capital; y aquellos impuestos gravados una sola vez sobre determinados tipos de propiedad.

4600 – Otros impuestos recurrentes sobre la propiedad

55. Aunque este tipo de impuestos rara vez se dan en los países miembros de la OCDE, esta partida incluye los impuestos sobre bienes tales como ganado bovino, joyas, ventanas y otros signos externos de riqueza.

5000 – Impuestos sobre los bienes y servicios

56. Se incluyen en esta categoría todos los impuestos y derechos sobre la producción, extracción, venta, transmisión, arrendamiento y entrega de bienes, así como sobre la prestación de servicios (5100), y también los impuestos aplicados al uso de bienes y al permiso para usar bienes o realizar actividades (5200). Por lo tanto, esta categoría comprende:

- *a)* los impuestos acumulativos de etapas múltiples;
- *b)* los impuestos generales sobre las ventas aplicados, ya sea en la fabricación/producción, ya sea en la venta al por mayor o al por menor;
- *c)* los impuestos sobre el valor agregado;
- *d)* los impuestos selectivos;
- *e)* los impuestos sobre las importaciones y exportaciones de bienes;
- *f)* los impuestos sobre el uso de bienes y sobre el permiso para usar bienes o realizar ciertas actividades;
- *g)* los impuestos sobre la extracción, el procesamiento o la producción de minerales y otros productos.

57. Los casos de difícil delimitación entre esta categoría y la categoría 4000 (impuestos sobre la propiedad) o la partida 6100 (otros impuestos pagados únicamente por empresas) se tratan en los § 48, § 53 y § 80. La partida 5300 y la subpartida 5130, ambas residuales, incluyen, respectivamente, las entradas tributarias que no hayan podido clasificarse entre las partidas 5100 y 5200 o entre las subpartidas 5110 y 5120, respectivamente, veáse § 33.

5100 – Impuestos sobre la producción, venta, transmisión, arrendamiento y entrega de bienes, y la prestación de servicios

58. Esta partida comprende todos los impuestos aplicados a transacciones de bienes y servicios por las características intrínsecas de estos (p. ej., valor, peso del tabaco, graduación de las bebidas alcohólicas, etcétera) a diferencia de los impuestos determinados por el uso de bienes o por el permiso para usar bienes o realizar actividades, que entran dentro del ámbito de la partida 5200.

5110 – Impuestos generales

59. En esta subpartida, se incluyen todos los impuestos, aparte de los derechos de importación y exportación (5123 y 5124, respectivamente), que gravan la producción, el arrendamiento, la transmisión, la entrega o la venta de un amplio abanico de bienes o la prestación de una gran variedad de servicios, independientemente de que sean de producción nacional o importados, o de la etapa de producción o de distribución en la que recaigan. Por ende, comprende los impuestos sobre el valor agregado, los impuestos sobre las ventas y los impuestos acumulativos de etapas múltiples. A las entradas brutas generadas, se añaden las entradas por ajustes fronterizos en concepto de esos impuestos cuando se importan bienes, y se restan las devoluciones de dichos impuestos cuando se exportan bienes. Esta subpartida se divide a su vez en los epígrafes 5111, impuestos sobre

el valor agregado; 5112, impuestos sobre las ventas; y 5113, otros impuestos generales sobre los ingresos brutos y sobre bienes y servicios.

60. Suelen plantearse dificultades de delimitación entre esta subpartida y la dedicada a los impuestos sobre bienes y servicios específicos (5120) cuando los impuestos se aplican a un gran número de bienes, como, por ejemplo, en el caso del impuesto sobre las compras del Reino Unido (abolido en 1973) o el impuesto sobre mercancías de Japón (abolido en 1988). De acuerdo con las respectivas perspectivas nacionales, el antiguo impuesto sobre las compras británico se ha clasificado como impuesto general (5112), mientras el desaparecido impuesto sobre mercancías japonés se ha incluido entre los impuestos selectivos (5121).

5111 – Impuestos sobre el valor agregado

61. Todos los impuestos generales al consumo cargados sobre el valor agregado entran dentro de este epígrafe, independientemente del método de deducción y de las etapas en las que recaiga el impuesto. En la práctica, todos los países de la OCDE con este tipo de impuestos permiten que todos los intermediarios, excepto el consumidor final, se deduzcan inmediatamente los impuestos sobre las compras e imponen tributación en todas las etapas. Para algunos países, puede que se incluyan en este epígrafe otros impuestos, tales como los aplicados sobre actividades financieras y de seguros, o bien porque las entradas que generan no pueden identificarse separadamente de las procedentes del impuesto sobre el valor agregado, o bien porque se considera que forman parte de este último, aunque esos mismos impuestos puedan clasificarse diferentemente en terceros países (p. ej., como impuestos sobre servicios específicos (5126) o impuestos sobre transacciones financieras y de capital (4400).

5112 – Impuestos sobre las ventas

62. Se clasifican aquí todos los impuestos generales aplicados a una sola etapa, ya sea en la fabricación/producción, o en la venta al por mayor o al por menor.

5113 – Otros impuestos generales sobre los ingresos brutos y sobre bienes y servicios

63. Estos son impuestos acumulativos de etapas múltiplese impuestos en los que el impuesto al consumo se combina con otros impuestos multifásicos. Estos impuestos se aplican cada vez que se realiza una transacción sin deducción del valor de los impuestos pagados sobre los insumos. Los impuestos multifásicos pueden combinarse con elementos de los impuestos sobre el valor agregado o sobre las ventas.

5120 – Impuestos sobre bienes y servicios específicos

64. Se incluyen en esta subpartida los impuestos selectivos, las utilidades generadas y transferidas por los monopolios fiscales, y los derechos de aduana y otros derechos de importación, así como los impuestos sobre las exportaciones, las transacciones de divisas, los bienes de inversión y las apuestas, y los impuestos especiales sobre los servicios que no formen parte de uno de los impuestos generales de la subpartida 5110.

5121 – Impuestos selectivos

65. Los impuestos selectivos gravan la unidad de un producto específico de una gama predefinida y limitada de bienes. Los impuestos generalmente se aplican a tasas diferenciadas sobre bienes no esenciales o de lujo, bebidas alcohólicas, tabaco y la energía. Los selectivos pueden imponerse en cualquier etapa de la producción o distribución y generalmente se

aplican como un cargo específico por unidad en función de las características del bien con referencia al valor, peso, intensidad o cantidad del producto. Se incluyen impuestos especiales sobre productos como el azúcar, la remolacha azucarera, fósforos y chocolates; e impuestos que gravan a tasas variables una cierta gama de bienes; e impuestos aplicados a los productos de tabaco, bebidas alcohólicas, combustibles para motores e hidrocarburos. Si un impuesto recaudado principalmente sobre bienes importados también se aplica, o se aplicaría, bajo la misma ley a bienes comparables de producción nacional, entonces los ingresos de este impuesto se clasifican como impuestos selectivos más que de derechos de importación. Este principio se aplica incluso si no hay producción nacional comparable o no hay posibilidad de tal producción. Los impuestos sobre el uso de servicios como agua, electricidad, gas y energía se consideran como impuestos selectivos más que impuestos sobre servicios específicos (5126). Los selectivos no incluyen los gravámenes que se aplican como impuestos generales sobre bienes y servicios (5110); beneficios de los monopolios fiscales (5122); derechos de aduana y otros derechos de importación (5123); o impuestos a las exportaciones (5124).

5122 – *Utilidades de los monopolios fiscales*

66. Este epígrafe comprende la parte de las utilidades de los monopolios fiscales transferida al gobierno general o usada para financiar gastos considerados como gastos del gobierno (véase el § 24). Las cantidades implicadas se registran cuando se transfieren al gobierno general o cuando se usan para gastos considerados como gastos del gobierno.

67. Los monopolios fiscales reflejan el ejercicio del poder tributario del gobierno mediante el uso de prerrogativas monopolísticas. Se trata de empresas públicas no financieras que ejercen un monopolio, en la mayoría de los casos sobre la producción o la distribución de tabaco, bebidas alcohólicas, sal, fósforos, cartas de juego, productos derivados del petróleo y productos agrícolas (es decir, sobre el tipo de productos susceptibles de estar sometidos, alternativa o adicionalmente, a los impuestos selectivos del epígrafe 5121), con el fin de recaudar ingresos para el gobierno que en otros países se obtienen gravando las operaciones que sobre dichos bienes efectúan las unidades empresariales privadas. El monopolio del gobierno puede intervenir en la etapa de producción o, en el caso de los establecimientos de licores propiedad del gobierno o bajo control de éste, en la etapa de distribución.

68. Cabe distinguir los monopolios fiscales de los servicios públicos, tales como el transporte ferroviario, la electricidad, los servicios de correos y otras comunicaciones, que pueden gozar también de una posición monopolística o cuasi-monopolística, pero cuyo fin primero suele ser la prestación de servicios básicos y no la obtención de ingresos para el gobierno; las transferencias de esas otras empresas públicas al gobierno se consideran ingresos no tributarios. Generalmente, el concepto tradicional de monopolio fiscal no abarca a las loterías estatales, cuyas utilidades usualmente se consideran, en consecuencia, ingresos no tributarios. No obstante, se pueden considerar como ingresos tributarios si su función principal es la de recaudar para financiar gasto gubernamental. Las utilidades de los monopolios fiscales se han separado de las de los monopolios de importación y exportación (5127) transferidas de juntas de comercialización u otras empresas dedicadas al comercio internacional.

5123 – *Derechos de aduana y otros derechos de importación*

69. Se incluyen aquí los impuestos, derechos de timbre y sobrecargas limitados por ley a los productos importados, así como los gravámenes sobre los productos agrícolas importados impuestos en los países miembros de la Unión Europea y las cantidades satisfechas por

algunos de esos países a tenor del sistema de montantes compensatorios monetarios (MCM).[17] Los derechos de aduana recaudados por los Estados miembros de la Unión Europea en nombre de ésta ya se registran en este epígrafe a nivel de autoridad supranacional en los cuadros de países (Capítulo 4 de la publicación Revenue Statistics de la OCDE). Quedan excluidos aquí los impuestos recaudados de las importaciones como parte de un impuesto general sobre los bienes y servicios, así como los impuestos selectivos aplicables tanto a bienes importados como a bienes de producción nacional.

5124 – *Impuestos sobre las exportaciones*

70. En los años 1970, los derechos de exportación se aplicaban en Australia, Canadá y Portugal como una medida de carácter regular, y en Finlandia se han utilizado con fines contracíclicos. Algunos países miembros de la Unión Europea pagan un gravamen sobre las exportaciones, en el marco del sistema MCM (véase la nota a pie de página § 16 en el § 69). Cuando las cantidades recaudadas son identificables, se integran en este epígrafe, que no incluye, sin embargo, las devoluciones de impuestos generales al consumo, de impuestos selectivos o de derechos de aduana sobre los bienes exportados, que se deducirán de las entradas brutas de 5110, 5121 o 5123, según corresponda.

5125 – *Impuestos sobre los bienes de inversión*

71. Este epígrafe cubre los impuestos sobre los bienes de inversión, tales como la maquinaria. Estos impuestos pueden cargarse por un cierto número de años o temporalmente con fines contracíclicos. No se incluyen aquí aquellos impuestos sobre los insumos industriales que recaen también en los consumidores (p. ej., el impuesto sobre la energía en Suecia, que se clasifica en 5121).

5126 – *Impuestos sobre servicios específicos*

72. Todos los impuestos sobre el pago por servicios específicos, tales como los impuestos sobre las primas de seguro, los servicios bancarios, los juegos de azar y las apuestas (p. ej., carreras de caballos, quinielas de fútbol, lotería), el transporte, las actividades recreativas o de ocio, los restaurantes y la publicidad, entran dentro de este epígrafe. También se clasifican aquí los impuestos sobre el ingreso bruto de las empresas que prestan el servicio (p. ej., primas de seguro o apuestas brutas recibidas por una empresa).

73. Los ingresos tributarios procedentes de gravámenes bancarios y pagos a sistemas de seguro de depósitos y de estabilidad financiera se han incluido también en este epígrafe

- Los pagos obligatorios de tasas de estabilidad, gravámenes bancarios y primas de seguro de depósitos se tratarán por lo general como ingresos tributarios cuando se abonen al gobierno general o una autoridad supranacional y se asignen a los fondos consolidados o generales de este, de forma que el gobierno pueda utilizar libre e inmediatamente el dinero para los fines que elija. Este principio se aplicará independientemente de que el gobierno prometa revertir esos pagos para garantizar los depósitos de los clientes de los bancos en caso de necesidad futura.
- Si los pagos obligatorios se abonan al gobierno general y se destinan a fondos afectados exclusivamente a volver al sector de la economía que engloba a las sociedades sujetas a dichos pagos, éstos seguirán considerándose ingresos tributarios dado que los fondos estarán disponibles para el gobierno y podrán reducir su déficit presupuestario, que la tasa no conlleva contraprestación para una entidad individual y que las cantidades recaudadas no tienen relación con cualquier pago posterior a

los depositantes o cualquier gasto realizado como medio de respaldo más amplio al sector financiero.

- Se clasificarán como tasa por servicio los pagos que deban aportarse a sistemas permanentes más reducidos para garantizar los depósitos de "particulares" cuando los niveles de pago concuerden con el costo del seguro.
- También se clasificarán como tasa por servicio, y no como ingreso tributario, los pagos que impliquen que el gobierno ejecute los activos de una institución en quiebra o tenga un derecho prioritario sobre la liquidación de activos de esta con objeto de financiar los pagos de compensación a los clientes por la pérdida de sus depósitos.

a) Los pagos obligatorios a fondos gestionados fuera del sector público y a instituciones no estatales apoyadas por depositantes, así como todos los pagos a planes voluntarios, no deben tratarse como ingresos tributarios.

b) También se incluyen aquí las contribuciones al Fondo de Resolución Única de la UE, que se atribuyen a la autoridad supranacional en los cuadros de los países.

74. Se excluyen de este epígrafe:

a) los impuestos sobre servicios que formen parte de un impuesto general sobre los bienes y servicios (5110);

b) los impuestos sobre la electricidad, el gas y la energía (5121, impuestos selectivos);

c) los impuestos sobre las ganancias de las personas físicas en los juegos de azar (1120, impuestos sobre las ganancias de capital de las personas físicas o de las empresas no constituidas en sociedad) y los impuestos fijos sobre la transferencia de loterías privadas o sobre el permiso para crear loterías (5200);[18]

d) los impuestos sobre los cheques y sobre la emisión, transmisión o compra y venta de valores (4400, impuestos sobre transacciones financieras y de capital).

5127 – *Otros impuestos sobre el comercio y las transacciones internacionales*

75. Este epígrafe abarca los ingresos percibidos por el gobierno por la compra y la venta de divisas a diferentes tipos de cambio. Cuando el gobierno ejerce poderes monopolísticos para obtener un margen entre los precios de compra y de venta de divisas superior al que sería necesario para cubrir los costos administrativos, el ingreso generado constituye un gravamen obligatorio impuesto en proporciones indeterminadas tanto sobre el comprador como sobre el vendedor de divisas. Es un equivalente común de los derechos de importación y exportación cargados en un sistema con tipo de cambio único o de un impuesto sobre la compraventa de divisas. Al igual que las utilidades de los monopolios fiscales o de los monopolios de importación y exportación transferidas al gobierno, representa el ejercicio de las prerrogativas monopolísticas con fines fiscales y, por lo tanto, se incluye en los ingresos tributarios.

76. El epígrafe engloba asimismo las utilidades de los monopolios de importación y exportación, que, sin embargo, son inexistentes en los países de la OCDE; los impuestos sobre la compraventa de divisas; y cualesquiera otros impuestos que recaigan sobre el comercio o las transacciones internacionales.

5128 – *Otros impuestos sobre bienes y servicios específicos*

77. Este epígrafe incluye los impuestos sobre la extracción de minerales, combustibles fósiles y otros recursos agotables de yacimientos de propieddad privada o de otro nivel de gobierno, así como cualesquiera otras entradas no identificables procedentes de impuestos

sobre bienes y servicios específicos. Los impuestos sobre la extracción de recursos agotables suelen traducirse en un importe fijo por cantidad o peso, pero también pueden adoptar un valor porcentual. Los impuestos se registran en el momento de extracción de los recursos. Los pagos por extracción de recursos agotables de yacimientos propiedad de la unidad de gobierno que recibe el pago se clasifican como alquiler.

5200 – Impuestos sobre el uso de bienes y sobre el permiso para usar bienes o realizar actividades

78. Esta partida incluye los impuestos aplicados al uso de bienes a diferencia de los impuestos sobre los propios bienes. Al contrario que los impuestos de este último tipo (registrados en la partida 5100), los impuestos considerados aquí no se basan en el valor de los bienes, sino que suelen revestir la forma de importes fijos. Los impuestos sobre el permiso para usar bienes o realizar actividades entran asimismo en esta partida, como, por ejemplo, los impuestos sobre la contaminación que no se basan en el valor de bienes particulares. En ocasiones, resulta complejo distinguir entre cargos obligatorios a los usuarios y tasas de licencia que se consideran como impuestos y aquellos que quedan excluidos por reputarse como ingresos no tributarios; los criterios de deslinde empleados se explican en los § 12 y § 13.

79. Aunque el título de esta partida menciona el "uso" de bienes, es posible que sea el registro de la propiedad, y no el uso, lo que dé lugar a la obligación tributaria, y que los impuestos contenidos aquí se apliquen más al hecho de ser titular de ciertos animales o bienes (p. ej., caballos de carreras, perros y vehículos automotores) que al uso que se hace de ellos, o que recaigan incluso en bienes inutilizables (p. ej., vehículos automotores o armas inservibles).

80. Se plantean casos de difícil delimitación con respecto a:

a) los impuestos sobre el permiso para realizar actividades empresariales que parten de una base combinada de renta, nómina o volumen de ventas, que se clasifican de acuerdo con las normas del § 83;

b) los impuestos sobre la propiedad o el uso de la propiedad de las partidas 4100, 4200 y 4600; la partida 4100 se dedica exclusivamente a los impuestos sobre la titularidad o la posesión de bienes inmuebles y, a diferencia de los impuestos de la partida 5200, recaen siempre sobre el valor de la propiedad; los impuestos sobre la riqueza neta (4200) y otros impuestos recurrentes sobre la propiedad (4600) se circunscriben al hecho de ser titular de propiedades, y no al uso de activos; se aplican a grupos de activos, y no a bienes particulares; y están en todo caso relacionados con el valor de los activos en cuestión.

5210 – Impuestos recurrentes sobre el uso de bienes y sobre el permiso para usar bienes o realizar actividades

81. La principal característica de los impuestos consignados aquí es que se recaudan a intervalos regulares y se cobran por lo general según una cantidad fija. En términos de ingresos, el elemento más importante está constituido por los impuestos por licencia de vehículos, aunque también integran esta subpartida los impuestos sobre los permisos de caza, pesca o tiro o sobre la venta de ciertos productos, así como los impuestos sobre la propiedad de animales domésticos y sobre la prestación de ciertos servicios siempre que estos reúnan los criterios establecidos en los § 12 y § 13. Los epígrafes en que se divide la partida 5210 son: los impuestos sobre vehículos automotores pagados por los hogares (5211) y los satisfechos por otros sujetos pasivos (5212); por su parte, el epígrafe 5213 abarca

las licencias a propietarios de animales domésticos y los cargos a usuarios por el permiso de realizar actividades, tales como la venta de carne o de bebidas alcohólica cuando los gravámenes se imponen de forma recurrente, así como las licencias generales periódicas de caza, pesca y tiro cuando el derecho a emprender esas actividades no se otorga como parte de una transacción comercial normal (p. ej., la concesión de la licencia no implica el derecho a usar una zona específica propiedad del gobierno).

5220 – Impuestos no recurrentes sobre el uso de bienes y sobre el permiso para usar bienes o realizar actividades

82. Se incluyen aquí los impuestos no recurrentes aplicados sobre el uso de bienes y sobre el permiso para utilizar bienes o realizar actividades, así como los impuestos aplicados cada vez que se utilizan los bienes.

- Entran en esta subpartida los impuestos sobre la emisión o liberación en el medio ambiente de gases y líquidos nocivos y otras sustancias peligrosas. Los pagos por permisos negociables de emisión expedidos por los gobiernos en el marco de programas de límites máximos y comercio de emisiones deberán registrarse aquí en la fecha en que se produzcan las emisiones. No se computarán ingresos por los permisos que los gobiernos expidan a título gratuito. El registro según el criterio de devengo implica que habrá una diferencia temporal entre el momento en que el gobierno reciba el pago por los permisos y el momento en que se produzca la emisión. En las cuentas nacionales, esta diferencia genera un pasivo para el gobierno durante ese periodo.
- Se excluirán los pagos efectuados por la recogida y eliminación de desechos o sustancias nocivas por parte de los poderes públicos, ya que constituyen una venta de servicios a las empresas.

83. También se incluyen aquí otros impuestos que entren dentro del ámbito de aplicación de la partida 5200 y que no se recauden recurrentemente. Por lo tanto, quedarán comprendidos los pagos únicos por permisos para la venta de alcohol o tabaco o para la creación de centros de apuestas, siempre que cumplan los criterios de los § 12-13.

6000 – Otros impuestos

84. Esta categoría recoge los impuestos que reposan en una o varias bases diferentes de las descritas en las categorías 1000, 3000, 4000 y 5000, o en bases que no puedan considerarse relacionadas a ninguna de estas categorías, se incluyen aquí. Los impuestos de base múltiple, y si es posible estimar las entradas relacionadas con cada base las cantidades desglosadas se repartirán en las correspondientes categorías de acuerdo a su base. Si no pueden calcularse los valores por separado y se sabe que la mayoría de las entradas proceden de una base determinada, el total de estas se atribuirán de acuerdo con dicha base. En caso contrario, las entradas se clasificarán aquí. Otros ingresos incluidos aquí son los impuestos presuntos no incluidos en el sistema de clasificación, los impuestos a las personas en forma de impuesto de capitación, impuestos de sellos no relacionados con las transacciones financieras y de capital que no pertenecen exclusivamente a una sola categoría de transacción, impuestos a los gastos donde se aplican deducciones o exenciones personales y recibos de impuestos no identificables. Esta categoría se subdivide entre los impuestos pagados completa o principalmente por las empresas (6100) y los abonados por otros sujetos pasivos (6200).

A.6. Conciliación con las cuentas nacionales

85. Esta sección de los cuadros reconcilia el cálculo de la recaudación tributaria total realizado por la OCDE y el total de todos los impuestos y contribuciones sociales pagados al gobierno general tal y como figuran en el registro de las cuentas nacionales de cada país. Cuando el país es miembro de la Unión Europea (UE), la comparación se establece entre el cálculo de la recaudación tributaria total realizado por la OCDE y la suma de los ingresos tributarios y contribuciones sociales registrado en la combinación del gobierno general y de las instituciones de los sectores de la UE de las cuentas nacionales.

A.7. Partida informativa sobre el financiamiento de las prestaciones sociales

86. A la vista de la variedad de relaciones entre la tributación y las contribuciones a la seguridad social y de los casos mencionados en los § 40 al § 46, se ha previsto una partida informativa que recopile todos los pagos asignados a las prestaciones tipo de la seguridad social, aparte de los pagos voluntarios al sector privado. Los datos se presentan de la forma siguiente (véase el Cuadro 5.38 de este Reporte):

a) Impuestos de la categoría 2000.

b) Impuestos asignados a las prestaciones de la seguridad social.

c) Contribuciones voluntarias al gobierno.

d) Contribuciones obligatorias al sector privado.

Los § 40 al § 46 ofrecen las debidas orientaciones para efectuar el desglose entre las rúbricas (a) a (d).

A.8. Partida informativa sobre impuestos identificables pagados por el gobierno

87. Los impuestos identificables realmente pagados por el gobierno se presentan en una partida informativa, desglosados según las principales categorías de la clasificación de impuestos de la OCDE. En la vasta mayoría de los países, sólo pueden identificarse las contribuciones a la seguridad social y los impuestos sobre la nómina satisfechos por el gobierno, que, sin embargo, suelen ser los gravámenes más importantes liquidados por los gobiernos (véase el Cuadro 5.39 de este Reporte).

A.9. Relación de la clasificación de impuestos de la OCDE con el Sistema de Cuentas Nacionales

88. El Sistema de Cuentas Nacionales (SCN) pretende proporcionar un marco coherente para registrar y presentar los principales flujos relacionados con la producción, el consumo, la acumulación y las transacciones con el exterior de una determinada zona económica, por lo general, un país o una región destacada de un país, y, en este sentido, los ingresos del gobierno constituyen una importante parte de las transacciones registradas en todo sistema de cuentas nacionales. En agosto de 2009, la versión final del SCN 2008 se publicó conjuntamente por cinco organizaciones internacionales: la Organización de las Naciones Unidas, el Fondo Monetario Internacional, la Unión Europea, la Organización para la Cooperación y el Desarrollo Económicos, y el Banco Mundial. La publicación está diseñada para ser empleada en países con economías de mercado, sea cual sea su estadio de desarrollo económico, así como en países en transición hacia economías de mercado. Las principales partes del marco conceptual y las definiciones de los diversos sectores económicos del SCN se han plasmado en la clasificación de impuestos de la OCDE.

89. Sin embargo, existen ciertas diferencias, reseñadas seguidamente, entre la clasificación de impuestos de la OCDE y los conceptos del SCN, debidas a que la finalidad de la clasificación de la OCDE consiste en lograr la máxima desagregación posible de los datos estadísticos en relación con lo que, por lo general, las Administraciones tributarias consideran como impuestos. Y así:

a) la OCDE incluye las contribuciones a la seguridad social obligatorias, pagadas al gobierno general en la recaudación tributaria total. No se consideran como impuestos las contribuciones imputadas y voluntarias, además de aquellas pagadas a fondos privados (véanse los § 9 y § 11 supra.);

b) los puntos de vista sobre la calificación de algunos gravámenes y tasas como impuestos son diferentes (§ 12 y § 13 supra.);

c) la OCDE excluye los impuestos imputados o los subsidios procedentes de la aplicación de múltiples tipos de cambio oficiales, o del pago de una tasa diferente a otras del mercado sobre reservas requeridas que pueda hacer el banco central;

d) los créditos fiscales exigibles se tratan de forma diferente.

90. Tal y como se ha apuntado en los § 1 y § 2, las categorías 1000 a 6000 de la lista de impuestos de la OCDE cubren todos los pagos sin contraprestación al gobierno general o una autoridad supranacional, aparte de las multas y los préstamos obligatorios. Esos pagos sin contraprestación, incluidas las multas pero excluidos los préstamos obligatorios, pueden obtenerse añadiendo los siguientes valores del SCN 2008:

- impuestos sobre el valor agregado (D211);
- impuestos y derechos sobre las importaciones, IVA no incluido (D212);
- impuestos sobre las exportaciones (D213);
- impuestos sobre los productos, IVA e impuestos sobre las importaciones y exportaciones no incluidos (D214);
- otros impuestos sobre la producción (D29);
- impuestos sobre la renta (D51);
- otros impuestos corrientes (D59);
- las contribuciones efectivas a la seguridad social (D.611 y D1613), con exclusión de las contribuciones voluntarias y los pagos a planes de seguro social relacionados con el empleo que no sean planes de seguridad social;
- impuestos sobre el capital (D91).

A.10. Relación de la clasificación de impuestos de la OCDE con el sistema de estadísticas de finanzas públicas del Fondo Monetario Internacional

91. La cobertura y la valoración de los ingresos tributarios en el sistema de estadísticas de finanzas públicas (EFP) y en el SCN 2008 son muy similares. Por lo tanto, a excepción del tratamiento dado a los créditos fiscales exigibles, las diferencias entre la clasificación de la OCDE y la del SCN 2008 (véase el § 89 supra.) son de aplicación igualmente al sistema de EFP. Además, el Fondo Monetario Internacional (FMI) escinde la categoría única 5000 de la OCDE en dos categorías distintas dedicadas a los impuestos nacionales sobre bienes y servicios (114) y a los impuestos sobre el comercio y las transacciones internacionales (115). Esto refleja el hecho de que, mientras estos últimos impuestos suelen generar insignificantes cantidades de ingresos en la zona de la OCDE, ese no es el caso en la mayoría de los países no pertenecientes a la Organización.

A.11. Comparación de la clasificación de impuestos de la OCDE con otras clasificaciones internacionales

92. El cuadro siguiente recoge una comparación ítem por ítem entre la clasificación de impuestos de la OCDE y las clasificaciones empleadas en:

a) el Sistema de Cuentas Nacionales (SCN 2008);

b) el Sistema Europeo de Cuentas (SEC 2010);

d) el Manual de estadísticas de finanzas públicas del FMI (MEFP 2014).

93. Estas comparaciones representan equivalencias que podrán aplicarse en la mayoría de los casos. Con todo, deberán emplearse con cierta flexibilidad, ya que, en casos particulares, los países pueden adoptar enfoques diferentes para la clasificación de los ingresos en las cuentas nacionales.

Clasificación de la OCDE	SCN 2008	SEC 2010	MEFP 2014
1000 Impuestos sobre los ingresos, utilidades y ganancias de capital			
1100 Personas			
1110 Ingresos y utilidades	D51-8.61a	D51A	1111
1120 Ganancias de capital	D51-8.61c, d	D51C, D	1111
1200 Corporaciones			
1210 Ingresos y ganancias	D51-8.61b	D51B	1112
1220 Ganancias de capital	D51-8.61c	D51C	1112
1300 No clasificables entre 1100 y 1200			1113
2000 Contribuciones a la seguridad social			
2100 Empleados	D613-8.85	D613	1211
2200 Empleadores	D611-8.83	D611	1212
2300 Auto-empleados y no empleados	D613-8.85	D613	1213
2400 No asignables entre 2100, 2200 y 2300			1214
3000 Impuestos sobre la nómina y fuerza de trabajo	D29-7.97a	D29C	112
4000 Impuesos sobre la propiedad			
4100 Impuestos recurrentes sobre la propiedad inmueble			
4110 Hogares	D59-8.63a	D59A	1131
4120 Other	D29-7.97b	D29A	1131
4200 Impuestos recurrentes sobre la riqueza neta			
4210 Hogares	D59-8.63b	D59A	1132
4220 Corporaciones	D59-8.63b	D59A	1132
4300 Impuestos sobre sucesiones, herencias y donaciones			
4310 Impuestos sobre sucesiones y herencias	D91-10.207b	D91A	1133
4320 Impuestos sobre donaciones	D91-10.207b	D91A	1133
4400 Impuestos sobre transacciones financieras y de capital	D59-7.96d; D29-7.97e	D214B, C	114114; 1161
4500 Otros impuestos no recurrentes sobre la propiedad	D91-10.207a	D91B	1135
4600 Otros impuestos recurrentes sobre la propiedad	D59-8.63c	D59A	1136
5000 Impuestos sobre los bienes y servicios			
5100 Impuestos sobre la producción, venta y transmisión de bienes y prestación de servicios			
5110 Impuestos generales sobre bienes y servicios			
5111 Impuestos sobre el valor agregado	D211-7.89	D211; D29G	11411
5112 Impuestos sobre las ventas	D2122-7.94a; D214-7.96a	D21224; D214I	11412
5113 Otros impuestos generales sobre los ingresos brutos y sobre bienes y servicios	D214-7.96a	D214I	11413

Clasificación de la OCDE				SCN 2008	SEC 2010	MEFP 2014
		5120	Impuestos sobre bienes y servicios específicos			
			5121 Impuestos selectivos	D2122-7.94b; D214-7.96b	D21223; D214A, B, D	1142
			5122 Utilidades de los monopolios fiscales	D214-7.96e	D214J	1143
			5123 Derechos de aduanas y otros derechos de importación	D2121-7.93	D2121; D21221, 2	1151
			5124 Sobre las exportaciones	D213-7.95a	D214K	1152-4
			5125 Sobre los bienes de inversión			
			5126 Sobre servicios específicos	D2122-7.94c; D214-7.96c	D21225; D214E, F, G, H; D29F	1144; 1156
			5127 Otros impuestos sobre el comercio y las transacciones internacionales	D2122-7.94d D29-7.95b D29-7.97g D59-8.64d	D21226; D29D; D59E	1153; 1155-6
			5128 Otros impuestos sobre bienes y servicios específicos			1146
		5130	No clasificables entre 5110 y 5120			
	5200	Impuestos sobre el uso de bienes y sobre el permiso para usar bienes y realizar actividades				
		5210	Impuestos recurrentes			
			5211 Sobre vehículos automotores: hogares	D59-8.64c	D59D	11451
			5212 Sobre vehículos automotores: otros	D29-7.97d	D214D; D29B	11451
			5213 Otros impuestos recurrentes en el uso de bienes y en el permiso para el uso de bienes y la realización de actividades	D29-7.97c, d, f D59-8.64c	D29B, E, F; D59D	11452
		5220	Impuestos no recurrentes sobre el permiso para el uso de bienes o la realización de actividades			11452
	5300	No clasificables entre 5100 y 5200				
6000	Otros impuestos					
	6100	Pagados únicamente por empresas				1161
	6200	Pagados por otros distintos de las empresas o no identificables		D59-8.64a, b	D59B, C	1162

A.12. Atribución de ingresos tributarios por subsectores del gobierno general

94. La clasificación de la OCDE requiere un desglose de los ingresos tributarios por subsectores del gobierno general. Seguidamente, se establecen la definición de cada subsector y los criterios que deben emplearse para atribuir los ingresos tributarios entre ellos, que siguen las orientaciones del SCN 2008 y del MEFP 2014.

Identificación de los subsectores del gobierno general

a) Gobierno central

95. El subsector del gobierno central incluye todos los departamentos, oficinas y establecimientos del gobierno, así como otros órganos que constituyen organismos o instrumentos de la autoridad central, cuya competencia se extiende a todo el territorio, con excepción de la administración de los fondos de seguridad social. En consecuencia, el gobierno central tiene la facultad de someter a tributación a todas las unidades residentes y no residentes que emprendan actividades económicas en el país.

b) Gobierno estatal, provincial o regional

96. Este subsector está compuesto por unidades intermedias del gobierno que ejercen su competencia a un nivel inferior al del gobierno central. Incluye a todas las unidades que operan independientemente del gobierno central en una parte del territorio de un país que engloba numerosas pequeñas localidades, con la excepción de la administración de los fondos de seguridad social. En los países unitarios, puede considerarse que los gobiernos regionales tienen una existencia separada, en la que cuentan con la suficiente autonomía como para recaudar sus ingresos de fuentes bajo su control, y sus funcionarios son independientes del control administrativo externo en el ejercicio de las actividades de la unidad.

97. En la actualidad, los países federales representan la mayoría de los casos en los que los ingresos atribuidos a unidades intermedias del gobierno se identifican de forma separada. España es el único país unitario en ese caso; en el resto de los países unitarios, los ingresos regionales se computan junto con los de los gobiernos locales.

c) Gobierno local

98. Este subsector incluye todas las demás unidades del gobierno que ejercen una competencia independiente en parte del territorio de un país, con excepción de la administración de los fondos de seguridad social. Engloba varios entes urbanos o rurales (p. ej., autoridades locales, municipios, ciudades, delegaciones, distritos).

d) Fondos de seguridad social

99. Los fondos de seguridad social forman un subsector separado del gobierno general. El SCN 2008 define el subsector de la seguridad social según lo expuesto en sus párrafos 4.124 a 4.126 y 4.147, citados seguidamente:

> *"Los regímenes de seguridad social son sistemas de seguros sociales que cubren a la comunidad en su conjunto o a amplios sectores de la misma, y que son impuestos y controlados por unidades del gobierno. Los sistemas abarcan una gran variedad de programas, y ofrecen prestaciones en dinero o en especie por vejez, invalidez o muerte, supervivencia, enfermedad y maternidad, accidentes de trabajo, desempleo, ayudas familiares, asistencia sanitaria, etc. No existe necesariamente una relación directa entre la cuantía de la contribución pagada por un individuo y las prestaciones que este pueda recibir." (Párrafo 4.124)*
>
> *"Cuando los sistemas de seguridad social se organizan por separado de las demás actividades de las unidades del gobierno, mantienen sus activos y pasivos separados de estas últimas, y realizan operaciones financieras por cuenta propia, se califican de unidades institucionales, que reciben el nombre de fondos de seguridad social." (Párrafo 4.125)*
>
> *"Las cantidades recaudadas y pagadas por contribuciones y prestaciones de la seguridad social pueden modificarse deliberadamente con el fin de alcanzar determinados objetivos de la política del gobierno que no tengan relación directa con el concepto de la seguridad social como sistema destinado a ofrecer prestaciones sociales a los miembros de la comunidad. Pueden aumentarse o disminuirse, por ejemplo, con el fin de influir en el nivel de la demanda agregada de la economía. No obstante, mientras se mantengan como fondos constituidos por separado, han de ser tratados, en el SCN, como unidades institucionales diferentes." (Párrafo 4.126)*
>
> *"El subsector de los fondos de seguridad social [del gobierno general] está conformado por los fondos de seguridad social que operan en todos los niveles del gobierno. Dichos fondos son sistemas de seguros sociales que cubren a la comunidad en su conjunto o a amplios sectores de la misma, y que son impuestos por unidades del gobierno." (Párrafo 4.147)*

100. La clasificación de la OCDE sigue esta definición de los fondos de seguridad social con las dos siguientes excepciones, por las se excluyen:

- los sistemas impuestos por el gobierno pero administrados por órganos externos al sector del gobierno general, tal y como se ha definido en el § 3 de este manual; y
- los sistemas en los que todas las contribuciones son voluntarias.

Autoridades supranacionales

101. Este subsector engloba las operaciones de recaudación fiscal de autoridades supranacionales dentro de un país. En la práctica, la única autoridad supranacional que cabe tener en cuenta en la zona de la OCDE es la que conforman las instituciones de la Unión Europea (UE). Los ingresos tributarios recaudados por los países miembros y remitidos a la UE se incluyen en las estadísticas tributarias a nivel de autoridad supranacional. No se deben incluir los impuestos sobre la renta y las contribuciones a la seguridad social recaudados por las instituciones de la Unión Europea y pagados por funcionarios de la Unión Europea residentes en países miembros de la Unión Europea.

Criterios de atribución de los ingresos tributarios

102. Cuando un gobierno recauda impuestos y los transfiere, en todo o en parte, a otros gobiernos, es necesario determinar si esos ingresos se imputarán al gobierno recaudador que los distribuye a otros en forma de donaciones, o si se atribuirán a los gobiernos beneficiarios para los que el gobierno recaudador actúa como mero agente, recibiendo el producto de los impuestos y transfiriéndolos posteriormente. Los criterios de atribución de los ingresos se establecen en los § 103-106 siguientes, y siguen lo dispuesto en los puntos 3.70 a 3.73 del SCN 2008.

103. Por regla general, un impuesto se atribuye a la unidad de gobierno que:

a) ejerce la facultad de aplicar el impuesto (como entidad principal o a través de la autoridad delegada por la entidad principal); y

b) puede a su discreción establecer y modificar la tasa del impuesto.

104. Cuando un gobierno recauda impuestos para y en nombre de otro, y este último tiene la facultad de aplicar el impuesto y establecer y modificar su tasa impositiva, entonces el gobierno recaudador actúa como agente de este, y el impuesto se reasigna. Cualquier cantidad retenida por el gobierno recaudador como cargo por la recaudación deberá tratarse como pago por un servicio. Cualquier otra cantidad retenida por el gobierno recaudador, por ejemplo, en el marco de un arreglo de coparticipación de impuestos, deberá tratarse como una donación corriente. Si se delegó al gobierno recaudador la autoridad para establecer y modificar la tasa impositiva entonces las cantidades recaudadas deberán tratarse como ingresos tributarios de este gobierno.

105. Cuando diferentes gobiernos establecen conjuntamente y por igual la tasa de un impuesto y el uso de los recursos, sin que ninguno de ellos tengan la autoridad final y exclusiva, entonces los ingresos tributarios se atribuyen a cada gobierno según la proporción de recursos que le corresponda; si el acuerdo permite a una unidad del gobierno ejercer el control final y exclusivo, entonces todos los ingresos tributarios se atribuirán a dicha unidad.

106. También puede ocurrir que un gobierno tenga la autoridad constitucional o de otra índole de aplicar un impuesto, pero que otros gobiernos establezcan individualmente la tasa de ese impuesto en sus jurisdicciones; los recursos generados por el impuesto en

cuestión en la jurisdicción de cada gobierno se atribuirán como ingresos tributarios a los respectivos gobiernos.

107. Los gravámenes satisfechos por los Estados miembros de la Unión Europea (UE) revisten la forma de:

a) derechos de aduana y gravámenes sobre los bienes agrícolas (5123);

b) cuentas de compensación monetaria brutas (5123 en relación con las importaciones y 5124 en relación con las exportaciones);

c) contribuciones al Fondo de la Resolución Única (5126); y

d) gravámenes sobre el acero, el carbón, el azúcar y la leche (5128).

108. Los derechos de aduana recaudados por los Estados miembros de la UE en nombre de esta se registran de la siguiente forma:

- sobre la base de un coeficiente de recaudación bruta;
- ajustando los resultados, siempre que sea posible, de forma que esos derechos se muestren en relación con una base de "destino final", por oposición a la base de "país de primera entrada"; estos ajustes atañen particularmente a los derechos colectados en importantes puertos (marítimos); aunque los derechos de la UE se perciben por las autoridades del país de primera entrada, siempre que sea posible cabrá excluir esos derechos del ingreso del país recaudador e incluirlos en el ingreso del país de destino final.

109. Son los gravámenes específicos de la UE los que cumplen más claramente con el criterio de asignación descrito en el § 101 anterior. Por consiguiente, estas cantidades se indican en notas a pie de página en los cuadros por país de los Estados miembros de la UE (en el capítulo 5) y aparecen como ingresos supranacionales en cada uno de los epígrafes fiscales identificados en el § 107.

Notas

1. Las referencias a la publicación *Revenue Statistics* de la OCDE en esta Guía Interpretativa, aluden a OECD (2020), *Revenue Statistics 2020*, OECD Publishing, Paris.
2. Todas las referencias al SCN deberán entenderse hechas a la edición de 2008.
3. Véase el apartado A.12 de la presente guía para el análisis del concepto de agente.
4. Por lo general, es posible identificar la cuantía de las contribuciones a la seguridad social y de los impuestos sobre la nómina, pero no otros impuestos asumidos por el gobierno.
5. Sin embargo, si un gravamen considerado como ingreso no tributario en la mayoría de los países se califica de tributario – o permite recaudar sustanciales ingresos – en uno o más países, las entradas en concepto de dicho gravamen se indican en las notas que figuran al pie de los cuadros de países, pero no se incluyen en la recaudación tributaria total.
6. Obsérvese, no obstante, que los nombres pueden dar lugar a confusión. Por ejemplo, aunque una tasa sobre los pasaportes se trataría normalmente como ingreso no tributario, si se impone un gravamen suplementario sobre los pasaportes (como en el caso de Portugal) con el fin de conseguir un ingreso sustancialmente mayor que el costo que supone proporcionar el pasaporte, dicho gravamen deberá considerarse como un impuesto sobre el uso de bienes (5200).
7. Para una explicación más detallada de esta distinción, consúltese el estudio especial sobre cuestiones de actualidad en relación con el registro de los ingresos tributarios Current issues in reporting tax revenues, en la edición 2001 de Revenue Statistics.
8. En ocasiones, se emplean asimismo los términos "no reembolsable" y "reembolsable", pero puede parecer ilógico hablar de "reembolsable" cuando no se ha pagado nada.
9. Con la excepción del diferente tratamiento dado a los créditos fiscales exigibles en los sistemas de imputación del impuesto sobre sociedades (§ 37-39)

10. No se trata aquí de verdaderos gastos tributarios en sentido formal, ya que tales gastos requieren que se identifique un sistema tributario de referencia para cada país o, mejor si cabe, una referencia internacional común y, en la práctica, no se ha logrado acuerdo sobre esta última.
11. A menos que se basen en la plusvalía obtenida con la venta, en cuyo caso se clasificarían como impuestos sobre las ganancias de capital, en las subpartidas 1120 o 1220.
12. Con todo, algunos países aplican la misma legislación a ambos en impuestos particulares sobre la renta, aunque las entradas procedentes de dichos impuestos suelen ser fácilmente atribuibles a uno u otro caso y pueden, por lo tanto, consignarse en la debida partida.
13. Por ejemplo, "[...] que son suficientemente autónomas e independientes y se comportan como si fueran sociedades [...] (incluido en el hecho de llevar) conjuntos completos de cuentas" (SCN 2008, 4.44).
14. En Canadá, país en el que se considera que rige un sistema de imputación, el crédito fiscal (no exigible) para el accionista nace en relación con el impuesto nacional sobre sociedades que se reputa haber pagado, tanto si ha surgido una obligación tributaria para la sociedad como si no. Habida cuenta de que no existe una conexión íntegra entre la obligación tributaria de la sociedad y el crédito concedido en relación con el impuesto sobre la renta en esos sistemas, los créditos por dividendos se tratan, junto con otros créditos fiscales, según lo descrito en el § 26.
15. Esto puede darse, por ejemplo, cuando ya existía un régimen para los empleados del gobierno previo a la introducción de un régimen general de seguridad social.
16. En el SCN 2008, se consideran transferencias de capital y no impuestos (véase la sección A.8.).
17. Mediante este sistema, la Unión Europea ajusta las diferencias entre los tipos de cambio empleados para determinar los precios de la política agrícola común (PAC) y los tipos de cambio reales. Los pagos realizados en este sistema pueden estar relacionados con importaciones o exportaciones y, cuando ha sido posible identificar por separado las respectivas cantidades, se han mostrado en el correspondiente epígrafe (5123 o 5124). En el presente informe, esas cantidades se han consignado en valores brutos (esto es, sin deducir ningún subsidio otorgado en el marco del sistema MCM).
18. Las transferencias de las utilidades de las loterías del Estado se consideran ingresos no tributarios (véase el § 68).

www.ingramcontent.com/pod-product-compliance
Lightning Source LLC
Chambersburg PA
CBHW061159240926
51846CB00006B/1063